A GUIDE TO
OLD ENGLISH

A GUIDE TO OLD ENGLISH

EIGHTH EDITION

**Bruce Mitchell and
Fred C. Robinson**

WILEY-BLACKWELL

A John Wiley & Sons, Ltd., Publication

This eighth edition first published 2012
© 2012 John Wiley & Sons Ltd

Edition History:
Bruce Mitchell (1e, 1964 and 2e, 1968); Bruce Mitchell and Fred C. Robinson (3e, 1982;
4e, 1986; 5e, 1992; 6e, 2001; and 7e, 2007)

Wiley-Blackwell is an imprint of John Wiley & Sons, formed by the merger of
Wiley's global Scientific, Technical and Medical business with Blackwell Publishing.

Registered Office
John Wiley & Sons Ltd, The Atrium, Southern Gate, Chichester, West Sussex, PO19 8SQ, UK

Editorial Offices
350 Main Street, Malden, MA 02148-5020, USA
9600 Garsington Road, Oxford, OX4 2DQ, UK
The Atrium, Southern Gate, Chichester, West Sussex, PO19 8SQ, UK

For details of our global editorial offices, for customer services, and for information about how to
apply for permission to reuse the copyright material in this book please see our website at
www.wiley.com/wiley-blackwell.

The right of Bruce Mitchell and Fred C. Robinson to be identified as the authors has been
asserted in accordance with the UK Copyright, Designs and Patents Act 1988.

Library of Congress Cataloging-in-Publication Data
Mitchell, Bruce, 1920–2010.
A guide to old English / Bruce Mitchell and Fred C. Robinson. — 8th ed.
    p. cm.
    Includes bibliographical references and index.
    ISBN 978-0-470-67107-8 (pbk.)
    1. English language—Old English, ca. 450-1100—Grammar.   2. English language—
Old English, ca. 450-1100—Readers.   3. English philology—Old English, ca. 450-1100—
Handbooks, manuals, etc.   I. Robinson, Fred C.   II. Title.
PE131.M5 2011
429'.82421—dc23

                                                                          2011026041

A catalogue record for this book is available from the British Library.

This book is published in the following electronic formats: ePDFs 9781119950264;
ePub 9781119950271; Mobi 9781119950288

Set in 10.5/12pt Ehrhardt by Graphicraft Limited, Hong Kong
Printed in Singapore by Ho Printing Singapore Pte Ltd

1 2012

In Memoriam
DONOVAN F. MITCHELL
AND
IRENE K. MITCHELL

Foreword to the Eighth Edition

Sadly, this is the first edition of *The Guide* in which Bruce Mitchell, who died in January 2010, has had no part. After Mitchell's death Fred Robinson was invited by the editors of Blackwell Publishing to prepare an eighth revised edition.

In preparing this edition I have made a complete review of all parts of the book with an eye to clarifying and sharpening our phrasing and updating the contents in all discussions of both grammar and texts. In addition, two new features have been added: the first twenty-five lines of *Beowulf* have been introduced to the selections from that poem (text number 18), and these lines have been provided with an exceptionally detailed commentary dealing with the language, style, and content of the poem. This addition has been made in response to readers' request that *The Guide* provide students with a full and detailed introduction to the poem that in most colleges and universities is taken up in a course following the introductory course in Old English. A second addition is Appendix F, which provides a brief but fairly comprehensive account of the First Consonant Shift ('Grimm's and Verner's Laws') to which we make allusion in §§105–109 but without spelling out just what these consonant shifts were.

A special feature of *The Guide* ever since the First Edition has been the detailed explanation of OE syntax (§§139–214). Occasional reference is made elsewhere in *The Guide* to specific passages in the discussion of syntax, and these passages should be helpful to students. But most teachers do not assign the entire fifty-odd pages on syntax to beginning students, these pages being directed to the more advanced student of OE. To the more advanced student and to Old English scholars in general the discussion of syntax can be quite useful, and so I am retaining it in this edition.

In preparing this Eighth Edition I have received valuable advice and assistance from several colleagues, including Traugott Lawler, Roberta Frank, J. R. Hall, and Theodore Leinbaugh. I am most grateful for their help. Eight anonymous readers enlisted by the publisher have also provided very helpful insights and suggestions. And, as always, I am indebted to Alfred Bammesberger for his brilliant textual studies.

Danish settlement
in the ninth century

Lindisfarne
Yeavering • Bamburgh
BERNICIA

This map, which does not represent
any particular moment in time,
contains some basic details with the
addition of the more important sites
mentioned in this book. Further
information can be sought from the
map and the accompanying material
on pp. 729–34 of F. M. Stenton's
Anglo-Saxon England (§188).

Ruthwell •
• Carlisle

Jarrow
• Monkwearmouth
• Durham
• Escomb

Isle of
Man

N
O
R
T
H
U
M
B
R
I
A

• Whitby

DEIRA

Stamford Bridge
• York
R. Humber

Anglesey

Leeds •

Flixborough •

Gwynedd

• Chester

Powys

R. Trent

• Lincoln

NORTH
WALES

Ofa's Dyke

R. Severn

Derby •
• Nottingham
Repton •
Lichfield
Leicester

Stamford
• Peterborough

Norwich •

MERCIA
MIDDLE
ANGLES

Ely •
Cambridge

E∧ST
ANGLIA
Dunwich •

Hereford •
Worcester
• Earl's
Barton

Sutton Hoo •

• Deerhurst

St
Albans

EAST

SAXONS

• Maldon

Dyfed

R. Wye

Langford •
Oxford
Dorchester •
Malmesbury

MIDDLE
SAXONS
R. Thames

• London

• Cheddar
Bath
WESSEX

Athelney •

Exeter •

Selwood
(Sealwudu)

Guildford •

Surrey

Winchester •
Romsey •

The Weald
(Andredesweald)
SOUTH SAXONS

KENT
Canterbury

Rochester •

Hastings

WEST
WALES

Isle of
Wight

0   50 miles
0   80 km

Anglo-Saxon England

Contents

PART TWO: PROSE AND VERSE TEXTS

Abbreviations and Symbols

LANGUAGES AND DIALECTS

Gmc.	Germanic	nWS	non-West-Saxon
IE	Indo-European	OE	Old English
Lat.	Latin	OHG	Old High German
ME	Middle English	WS	West-Saxon
MnE	Modern English		

Before the name of a language or dialect

e = Early   l = Late   Pr = Primitive

GRAMMATICAL TERMS

acc.	accusative	pass.	passive
adj.	adjective	p.d.	see §100
adv.	adverb	pers.	person
compar.	comparative	pl.	plural
conj.	conjunction	poss.	possessive
cons.	consonant	prep.	preposition
dat.	dative	pres.	present
dem.	demonstrative	pret.	preterite
fem.	feminine	pret.-pres.	preterite-present
gen.	genitive	pron.	pronoun
imp.	imperative	ptc.	participle
ind.	indicative	s.	subject
inf.	infinitive	sg.	singular
infl.	inflected	st.	strong
inst.	instrumental	subj.	subjunctive
masc.	masculine	superl.	superlative
neut.	neuter	v.	verb
nom.	nominative	wk.	weak
o.	object		

's' may be added where appropriate to form a plural.

SYMBOLS

>	became
<	came from
*	this precedes a form which is not recorded. Usually it is a form which probably once existed and which scholars reconstruct to explain the stages in sound-changes; see §103.3. Sometimes it is a form which certainly never existed but which is invented to show that one sound-change preceded another. An example is *ċierfan* in §100, note.
¯	over a letter denotes a long vowel or diphthong.
˘	over a letter denotes a short vowel or diphthong.
⏓	means ‘short and long’, e.g. *ē̆* in §100.
– ⏑	in §41 denote a long and short syllable respectively.
´ ` ×	denote respectively a syllable carrying full, secondary, or no, stress.
[ ]	enclose phonetic symbols.

How to Use this Guide

This section is particularly addressed to those of you who are working without a teacher.

THE IMPORTANCE OF READING AND PARSING

The ability to recognize forms in the texts you are reading and an awareness of the basic structure of Old English are far more important than a parrot knowledge of the paradigms. Hence, from the beginning, you must get into the habit of analysing and thoroughly understanding each form you meet in your texts.

Important in the reading of OE is 'parsing'—that is, identifying what part of speech each word in a sentence is (noun, pronoun, adjective, verb, and so on) and what particular form the word has in the sentence (accusative case, present tense, subjunctive mood, and so on). If you are uncertain about the meaning of the parts of speech listed below or of other terms such as 'article', 'infinitive', or 'participle', you are advised to consult Appendix D. For further details see A. J. Thomson and A. V. Martinet *A Practical English Grammar* (4th ed., Oxford, 1986) or David Crystal *A Dictionary of Linguistics and Phonetics* (2nd ed., Basil Blackwell, 1985).

The information needed when parsing Old English words is:

Noun: Meaning, gender, number, case, and the reason for the case, e.g. accusative because it is object, genitive denoting possession, or dative of the indirect object.

Pronoun: Same as for noun. Here you need to know the noun to which the pronoun refers. (If it is a relative pronoun, see §162.)

Adjective: Same as for noun. Sometimes, of course, an adjective is used with a noun, sometimes it is used alone, either as a complement or where a noun is more usual, e.g. 'The good die young'.

Verb: If you have the infinitive, you merely need the meaning. Otherwise you need to work out the person, number, tense, and mood, and then deduce the infinitive. Unless you are familiar with the verb, you will have to do all this before you can find its meaning. For hints on how to do it, see §134.

A Guide to Old English, Eighth Edition. Bruce Mitchell and Fred C. Robinson.

Adverbs and interjections (a name given to words like 'Oh!', 'Alas!', and 'Lo!') will give little trouble. It is important to notice the case of a word governed by a preposition, for a difference in case sometimes indicates a difference in meaning; see §§213–214. Conjunctions are a greater source of difficulty. Lists of them are given in §§168, 171, and 184, and references to discussions on them are set out in 'Understanding the Syntax' below.

Note

The importance of gender varies. Sometimes it is obvious, sometimes it is of no real importance. But at times it provides a vital clue. Thus in *Hē ġehīerþ þās word and þā myrcð, þās* and *þā* could be acc. sg. fem. or acc. pl. Only the fact that *word* is neuter will tell us that we must translate 'He hears these words and carries them out'.

LENGTH MARKS

Long vowels have been marked (ˉ) throughout, with the exception noted below. A knowledge of the length of vowels (or 'quantity', as it is called) is essential for proficiency in reading, for accuracy in translation (compare *god* 'god' with *gōd* 'good'), for the understanding of OE metre, and for the serious study of phonology. Hence, when you learn the inflexions, you will need to remember both the form of the word and the length of its vowels. Long vowels are marked in the Texts and you should take advantage of this by noting carefully those which occur in both familiar and unfamiliar words.

But since the length-marks are not shown in the Old English manuscripts, many editions of prose and verse texts do not show them. Examples are the standard editions of the Anglo-Saxon Chronicle and of the Homilies of Ælfric and Wulfstan, the texts published by Methuen (in their Old English Library) and by the Early English Text Society, and *The Anglo-Saxon Poetic Records* (published by Columbia University Press), which contain virtually all the extant poetry. You will have to use one or more of these works fairly early in your career. In the hope that you will find the transition to such texts easier if you have already seen short passages in the form in which they appear in these works, we have not regularized the spelling (see §3) or marked vowel-length in the illustrative quotations in chapters 5 and 6. Most of the passages quoted are taken from texts which appear in Part Two. You can use these passages by writing them out, marking in the length-marks yourself, and then comparing them with the correct version. You can check individual words in the Glossary. But you will find it more interesting if you track down the context of the longer prose passages and those in verse with the help of the references in the Glossary. By so doing, you will improve your knowledge of vowel quantity and widen your acquaintance with OE literature.

LEARNING THE INFLEXIONS

Those who want to test their knowledge of the paradigms and to try their hand at translating into Old English (a very useful way of learning the language, especially important since no one speaks it today) will find A. S. Cook *Exercises in Old English* (Ginn, 1895) a useful book. There are second-hand copies about. Stephen Pollington's *Wordcraft, Wordhoard and Wordlists: Concise New English to Old English Dictionary and Thesaurus* (Anglo-Saxon Books, 1996) will give easy access to the Old English vocabulary.

We suggest that those coming to this book without any knowledge of Old English learn the inflexions in the order set out below. But remember that texts must be read and an understanding of the syntax acquired at the same time. Hints on how to do this are given later in this section.

1 Read §§1–4.

2 Now work through §§5–9. Make sure that you can recognize the new letters æ, þ, and ð, and practise reading aloud the Practice Sentences (Text 1), following generally the natural stress of MnE.

3 Now read §§10–12.

4 The next step is to learn the paradigms in A below, in the order in which they are set out there.

5 (*a*) When you have learnt the pronouns, nouns, and adjectives, in A, you can see whether §§77–81 help or hinder you. Experience on this point differs.

(*b*) When you have learnt the verbs in A, you should read §§131–134.

6 You can now turn to the paradigms referred to in B below. B contains what may be called the 'derived paradigms', i.e. those which can be derived from the paradigms set out in A when certain sound-changes are understood. The sound-changes are presented in the hope that they will make your work easier, not as an end in themselves. Thus, if you meet a word *hwatum* in your reading, you will not be able to find out its meaning unless you know that it comes from an adjective *hwæt* 'active, bold'. You will know this only if you have read §70.

7 The paradigms in C are important ones of fairly frequent occurrence which need not be learnt all at once. When you come across one of them in your reading, you can consult the relevant section. In this way, you will absorb them as need arises.

8 Because of the dialectal variations and inconsistencies in spelling noted in §§2–3, there are many ways of spelling even some of the most common words in the language; for examples, see the word *se* in the Glossary. If all the possible forms of this and other words were given in the paradigms in chapter 3, you would not see the wood for the trees. So

those less common variants which occur in the texts will be found as cross-references in the Glossary.

A Key Paradigms

These paradigms must be known thoroughly. At this stage, concentrate on them alone; disregard anything else in these sections.

1 The pronouns set out in §§15–21. Note particularly §19. (The dual forms in §21 may be passed over at first.)
2 *Nama* (§22) and, after reading §§63–64, *tila* (§65).
3 Now read §§26–32.
4 *Stān* (§33), *scip/word* (§34), and *ġiefu/lār* (§§47–48).
5 The strong declension of the adjectives (§§66–67).
6 Now read §§14, 87–89, and 115.
7 *Fremman* (§§116–117) and *lufian* (§§124–125).
8 *Habban* (§126), *bēon* (§127), and *weorþan* (Appendix A.3 (*b*)).
9 The principal parts of the strong verbs (§§90–95).
10 The conjugation of strong verbs (§§110–113).

B Derived Paradigms

The paradigms in this group may be derived from those in A as follows:

1 From *nama*, those in §§23–25.
2 From *stān*, *scip*, or *ġiefu*, those in §§35–44, 48–51, and 52–60. See now §13.
3 From *tila* and *til*, those in §§68–73.
4 From *fremman*, those in §§116–123.
5 From *lufian*, those in §§124–125.
6 From §§90–95, those in §§96–109.
7 From §§110–113, those in §114.

Note
Some nouns which often go like *stān*, *scip*, or *ġiefu*, once belonged to other declensions. As a result, they sometimes have unusual forms which may cause you difficulty in your reading. It might be just as well if you learnt to recognize these fairly early in your career. They include: *ċild* (§34), *hæleþ* and *mōnaþ* (§44), some nouns in *-e* (§§45–46), the feminine nouns discussed in §§49 and 51, the relationship nouns (§60), and the *u*-nouns (§§61–62).

C Other Paradigms

1 Other Strong Nouns (§§45–46 and 61–62).
2 Comparison of Adjectives (§§74–76).
3 Numerals (§§82–86).
4 Verbs
    (*a*) Class 3 weak verbs (§126).
    (*b*) *Dōn* and *gān* (§128).
    (*c*) *Willan* (§§129 and 211).
    (*d*) Preterite-present verbs (§§130 and 206–210).
5 Adverbs (§135).

LEARNING THE VOCABULARY

Many OE words are easily recognizable from their MnE counterparts, though sometimes the meaning may be different; see §4 and Part 2.1 below (i.e. the first OE text for practice reading) and look up the word 'lewd' in the Oxford English Dictionary.

Other words differ in spelling and pronunciation as a result of changes in ME and MnE. The short vowels *e*, *i*, *o*, *u*, have remained relatively constant (see §7). But the long vowels and the diphthongs have sometimes changed considerably. Words with a long vowel in OE sometimes appear in MnE with the vowel doubled, e.g. *fēt* (masc. pl.) 'feet' and *dōm* (masc.) 'doom'. Sometimes, they have *-e* at the end, e.g. *līf* (neut.) 'life' and (with, in addition, one of the differences discussed below) *hām* (masc.) 'home' and *hūs* (neut.) 'house'.

Correspondences like the last two are more difficult to spot. Yet a knowledge of them is easily acquired and will save you much hard work. Thus, if you know that OE *ā* often appears in MnE as *oa*, you will not need to use the Glossary to discover that *bār* (masc.) means 'boar', *bāt* (fem. or masc.) 'boat', *brād* 'broad', and *hār* 'hoar(y)'. Words like *āc* (fem.) 'oak', *hlaf* (masc.) 'loaf', and *hlāfas* (masc. pl.) 'loaves', will not present much more difficulty.

The table which follows will help you to recognize more of these correspondences. But it is not complete and the correspondences do not always apply. Thus OE *hāt* is MnE 'hot' and you may find it interesting to look up in a glossary or dictionary the four OE words spelt *ār* and see what has happened to them.

OE spelling	MnE spelling	Vowels	Consonants
fæt (neut.)	vat	æ = a	f = v
rǣdan	read	ǣ = ea	
dǣd (fem.)	deed	ǣ = ee	
lang	long	an = on	
hāliġ	holy	ā = o	
hām (masc.)	home	ā = o.e	
āc (fem.)	oak	ā = oa	c = k
hlāf (masc.)	loaf		hl = l
ecg (fem.)	edge		cg = dge
dēman	deem	ē = ee	
frēosan	freeze	ēo = ee	s = z
ċild (neut.)	child		ċ = ch
miht (fem.)	might		h = gh
scip (neut.)	ship		sc = sh
līf (neut.)	life	ī = i.e	
ġiellan	yell	ie = e	ġ = y
ġiefan	give	ie = i	ġ = g
dōm (masc.)	doom	ō = oo	
mūs (fem.)	mouse	ū = ou.e	
nū	now	ū = ow	
synn (fem.)	sin	y = i	
mȳs (fem.)	mice	ȳ = i.e	

See §253 (Barney) for a book which may help you to learn the vocabulary.

The principles on which words were formed in OE are set out in §§136–138. Once you understand these, you will be able to deduce the meaning of some new words by their similarity to words you already know; see §136. For correspondences in endings, see §138.

UNDERSTANDING THE SYNTAX

The fundamental differences between the syntax of Old English and that of Modern English are set out in §§139–153. These, and §§182–183, should be studied as soon as you can read simple sentences with some degree of fluency and before you pass on to the connected passages of Old English recommended below. Other sections which should be read fairly soon are §§154–155, 157–158, and 160 (noun clauses and their conjunctions), §162 (relative pronouns), §§166–167 and §§169–170 (conjunctions introducing adverb clauses), §189 note, and §§195–199 (the uses of the tenses and the syntax of the resolved verb forms).

The remaining parts of the syntax should be used for reference when the need arises; note especially the topics mentioned in §§141–142 and the lists of conjunctions in §§168, 171, and 184. When you begin to feel some confidence, you can try the exercise in §172.

If at first you find these sections too long and complicated, you are advised to use one of the books cited in §256.

TEXTS TO READ

Part Two of this book starts with a selection of prose texts for beginners, the texts being carefully coordinated with the explanations in the grammar sections. After you have worked your way through these, you will be ready for the poems, which are similarly annotated. This combination of texts should provide a foundation from which you can advance to *Beowulf* and to the prose and verse texts available in Methuen's Old English Library and the Manchester Series.

READING THE TEXTS

Before beginning to read the texts you should do two things: first, study carefully the introduction to the Glossary, and second, familiarize yourself with the function words and word-patterns listed in §§168 and 171. While reading the texts, you should make careful use not only of the Glossary, but also of the Index of Words and Appendix D.

WES ÞU HAL

It now remains for us to wish you success – and pleasure – in your studies. In 991, before the battle of Maldon, Byrhtnoth called across the cold waters of the river to his Danish foes:

> Nū ēow is gerȳmed;   gāð ricene tō ūs,
> Guman tō gūþe;   god āna wāt
> hwā þǣre wælstōwe   wealdan nōte.
> (*The Battle of Maldon*, ll. 93–95)

This can be paraphrased

> 'Now the way is clear for you; O warriors,
> hasten to the battle; God alone knows
> how things will turn out'.

It is our hope and wish that *your* efforts will prosper – *Wel þe þæs geweorces!*

Part One

Preliminary Remarks on the Language

§1   Old English (OE) is the vernacular Germanic language of Great Britain as it is recorded in manuscripts and inscriptions dating from before about 1100. It is one of the Germanic group of the Indo-European family of languages. Those who are unfamiliar with this concept should read about it in one of the histories of the English language cited in the Bibliography.

§2   There are four dialects distinguishable in the extant monuments – Northumbrian, Mercian, Kentish, West-Saxon. The differences are apparent in the spelling and vocabulary. After 900 West-Saxon was increasingly used as a standard written language. It is for this reason that, initially at any rate, you learn West-Saxon. But even here the spelling conventions were never as rigidly observed as they are in Great Britain or America today, where compositors, typists, and writers, in different parts of the country use the same spelling, no matter how different their pronunciations may be.

§3   Most OE primers therefore attempt to make things easier for the beginner by 'normalizing', i.e. regularizing, the spelling by eliminating all forms not belonging to the West-Saxon dialect. But difficulty arises because two stages can be distinguished – early West-Saxon (eWS), which is the language of the time of King Alfred (*c*. 900), and late West-Saxon (lWS), which is seen in the works of Ælfric (*c*. 1000). Norman Davis, in revising Sweet's *Anglo-Saxon Primer*, followed Sweet and used eWS as his basis. Quirk and Wrenn's *Old English Grammar*, however, normalizes on the basis of Ælfric's lWS. For the beginner, the most important difference is that eWS *ie* and *īe* appear in lWS texts as *y* and *ȳ*; this accounts for such differences as Sweet *ieldra*, *hīeran*, but Q. & W. *yldra*, *hȳran*. Another is that *ea* and *ēa* may be spelt *e* and *ē* in lWS (and sometimes in eWS) texts, e.g. *seah* and *scēap*, but *seh* and *scēp*. Since the other differences will scarcely trouble you and since there are some disadvantages in the use of lWS, the paradigms are given here in their eWS forms and the sound laws are discussed with eWS as the basis. Any important variations likely to cause difficulty – apart from those mentioned here – will be noted. Full lists of all dialectal variants will be found in the appropriate section of Alistair Campbell's *Old English Grammar*.

In the sections on syntax, the spelling of a standard edition has generally been followed, though occasionally an unusual form has been silently

A Guide to Old English, Eighth Edition. Bruce Mitchell and Fred C. Robinson.
© 2012 Bruce Mitchell and Fred C. Robinson. Published 2012 by Blackwell Publishing Ltd.

regularized. This should ease the transition to non-normalized texts. Similarly, in the prose texts provided for reading, we have moved from totally normalized to non-normalized texts. We have not normalized the poems.

§4   As has been explained in the Foreword, this book, after a brief discussion of orthography and pronunciation, deals with accidence, word formation, and syntax (including word-order), and attempts simple explanations of those sound-changes which will help you to learn the inflexions. Other sound-changes and semantics are not discussed. On the metre of poetry see Appendix C. It is important, however, to remember that many common words have changed their meaning. *Sellan* means 'to give', not just 'to give in exchange for money, to sell'. *Eorl* cannot always be translated 'earl' and *dēor* and *fugol* mean, not 'deer' and 'fowl', but 'any (wild) animal' and 'any bird' respectively. It is also important to note that, while Old English literature was written and/or transmitted by Christians, the Christian poetry was largely written in an originally pagan vocabulary which embodied the values of the heroic code. However, it does not follow that the poetry is rich in pagan elements. You will find that words like *lof* in *The Seafarer* and *wyrd* in *The Wanderer* have acquired Christian connotations. On this point, see further §§218 and 236–246. The Bibliography contains references to useful introductory discussions on all the topics not discussed in this book.

2

Orthography and Pronunciation

I ORTHOGRAPHY

§5 As a glance at the facsimile of the OE manuscript on page 278 will show, the letters used by Anglo-Saxon scribes were sometimes very like and sometimes very unlike those used today, both in shape and function. Printers of Anglo-Saxon texts generally use the equivalent modern letter form. Hence the sounds [f] and [v] are both represented by *f*, and the sounds ⌊s⌋ and [z] by *s* because the distinctions were less significant in OE; on these and other differences in representing the consonants, see §9.

The following symbols are not in use today: *æ* (ash), which represents the vowel in MnE 'hat', *þ* (thorn) and *ð* (eth or, as the Anglo-Saxons appear to have called it, *ðæt*), both of which represent MnE *th* as in 'cloth' and in 'clothe'. Capital *ð* is written *Ð*. To make the learning of paradigms as simple as possible, *þ* has been used throughout chapter 3.

The early texts of the Methuen Old English Library used the runic 'wynn' *ƿ* instead of *w* and the OE letter *ȝ* for *g*. In the latest volumes, these have been discarded.

As is customary, the punctuation in quotations and selections from OE is modern. See the facsimiles on pages 278 and 293 and note the absence of modern punctuation.

II STRESS

§6 The stress usually falls on the first syllable, as in MnE, e.g. mórgen 'morning'. The prefix *ge-* is always unaccented; hence *gebídan* 'await, abide'. Two main difficulties occur:

1 Prepositional prefixes, e.g. *for-*, *ofer-*, can be either accented (usually in nouns or adjectives, e.g. *fórwyrd* 'ruin') or unaccented (usually in verbs, e.g. *forwíernan* 'refúse').

2 Compound words in which both elements retain their full meaning, e.g. *sǽ-weall* 'sea-wall', have a secondary stress on the root syllable of the

A Guide to Old English, Eighth Edition. Bruce Mitchell and Fred C. Robinson.
© 2012 Bruce Mitchell and Fred C. Robinson. Published 2012 by Blackwell Publishing Ltd.

second element. There is some dispute about three-syllabled words with a long first syllable (see §26). Some say that *bindende* 'binding' and *timbrode* 'built' have a pattern like MnE 'manhandle', not like 'hástǐly'. But not everyone agrees.

III VOWELS

§7 Short vowels must be distinguished from long vowels, which are marked (ˉ) in this book (except as noted on pp. 2–3). Approximate pronunciations of OE vowels for those working without a teacher are given as far as possible in terms of Received Standard English.

a	as the first vowel in 'aha'
ā	as the second vowel in 'aha'
æ	as in 'mat'
ǣ	as in 'bad'[1]
e	as in 'bet'
ē	approx. as in 'hate', but a pure vowel [cf. German *See*]
i	as in 'tin'
ī	as in 'seen'
o	as in 'cough'
ō	approx. as in 'so', but a pure vowel [cf. German *so*]
u	as in 'pull' [NOT 'hut']
ū	as in 'cool'
y	as *i*, with lips in a whistling position [French *tu*]
ȳ	as *ī*, with lips in a whistling position [French *ruse*]

Vowels in unstressed syllables should be pronounced clearly. Failure to distinguish gen. sg. *eorles* from nom. acc. pl. *eorlas* is characteristic of ME, not of OE.

IV DIPHTHONGS

§8 If you are not sure of the distinction between vowels and diphthongs, see the definition and examples under 'diphthong' in Appendix D below. It is important to realize that OE words such as *heall*, *hēold*, *hielt*, which contain diphthongs, are just as much monosyllables as MnE 'meat' and 'field' (in which two letters represent one vowel) or MnE 'fine' and 'base', which contain diphthongs. The OE diphthongs, with approximate pronunciations, are

---

[1] If you experiment, you will notice that the vowel in 'bad' is longer than that in 'mat', though MnE [æ] is frequently described as a 'short vowel'.

$$ea = æ + a$$
$$ēa = ǣ + a$$
$$eo = e + o$$
$$ēo = ē + o$$
$$ie = i + e^1$$
$$īe = ī + e$$

A short diphthong is equal in length to a short vowel, a long diphthong to a long vowel. But remember that, like the MnE word 'cow', they are diphthongs, not two distinct vowels such as we get in the *ea* of 'Leander'.

V CONSONANTS

§9 All consonants must be pronounced, e.g. *c* in *cnapa*, *g* in *gnæt*, *h* in *hlāf*, *r* in *þǣr*, and *w* in *wrītan*.

Double consonants must be pronounced double or long. Thus, when you see *-dd-*, as in *biddan*, pronounce it as you do when you say 'red *D*', not as you do when you say 'ready'.

Most of the consonants are pronounced in the same way as in MnE. The main exceptions are set out below.

The letters *s*, *f*, *þ*, and *ð*, are pronounced voiced, i.e. like MnE *z*, *v*, and *th* in 'clothe', between vowels or other voiced sounds, e.g. *rīsan*, *hlāfas*, *paþas*, and *hēafdes*. In other positions, including the beginning and end of words, they are voiceless, i.e. like MnE *s*, *f*, and *th* in 'cloth', e.g. *sittan*, *hlāf*, *þæþ*, and *oft*. This accounts for the different sounds in MnE 'path' but 'paths', 'loaf' but 'loaves', and the like. Initial *ġe-* does not cause voicing; *findan* and its past ptc. *ġe-funden* both have the sound *f*.

The differences described in the preceding paragraph are due to the fact that the pairs *f* and *v*, *s* and *z*, and voiceless and voiced *þ* 'th', were merely variants ('allophones') in OE and not sounds of different significance ('phonemes'). This means that, whereas in MnE speech the distinctions between 'fat' and 'vat', 'sink' and 'zinc', and 'loath' and 'loathe', depend on whether we use a voiceless or voiced sound, both OE *fæt* 'fat' and OE *fæt* 'vat' could be pronounced with initial *f* or *v*, according to dialect.

At the beginning of a word ('initially') before a vowel, *h* is pronounced as in MnE 'hound'. Otherwise it is like German *ch* in *ich* [ç] or *ach* [x], according to the front or back quality of the neighbouring vowel. It can be pronounced like *ch* in Scots *loch*.

---

[1] The original pronunciation of *ie* and *īe* is not known with any certainty. It is simplest and most convenient for our purposes to assume that they represented diphthongs as explained above. But by King Alfred's time *ie* was pronounced as a simple vowel (monophthong), probably a vowel somewhere between *i* and *e*; *ie* is often replaced by *i* or *y*, and unstressed *i* is often replaced by *ie*, as in *hiene* for *hine*. Probably *īe* had a similar sound.

Before *a*, *o*, *u*, and *y*, *c* is pronounced *k* and *g* is pronounced as in MnE 'good'. Before *e* and *i*, *c* is usually pronounced like *ch* in MnE 'child' and *g* like *y* in MnE 'yet'. In Part One and in reading selections 1 through 3, the latter are printed *ċ* and *ġ* respectively, except in the examples quoted in chapters 5 and 6. *ċċ* in words like *wiċċecræft* is pronounced like modern *ch*.

After or between back vowels, *g* is pronounced [ɣ], like the *g* sometimes heard in dialectal German *sagen*. Those without a teacher can pronounce it as *w* in words like *dragan* and *boga*.

The combinations *sc* and *cg* are usually pronounced like MnE *sh* and *dge* respectively. Thus *scip* 'ship' and *ecg* 'edge' are pronounced the same in both OE and MnE. But in *ascian* 'ask', *-sc-* is pronounced *-sk-*.

Note

A detailed account of the pronunciation of Old English will be found in chapters VI–IX of Alistair Campbell's *Old English Grammar*.

3

Inflexions

INTRODUCTION

§10 Following (as most primers do) the conventional terminology, we distinguish in Old English the following parts of speech: nouns, adjectives, pronouns (including articles), verbs, adverbs, prepositions, conjunctions, and interjections. These terms are all explained in Appendix D.

§11 Like most inflected languages, OE distinguishes numbers, case, and gender, in nouns, pronouns, and adjectives. The numbers are singular and plural; a dual is found in the 1st and 2nd pers. pron. where, e.g. *wit* means 'we two', *ġit* 'you (ye) two'. The main cases are nominative, accusative, genitive, and dative, but in certain parts of the adjective and pronoun declensions an instrumental occurs; where it does not, the dative does its work. If you are unfamiliar with the concept of 'case', see Appendix D and the sections listed under that word in the Index of Subjects.

§12 There are three genders – masculine, feminine, and neuter. Gender sometimes agrees with sex, e.g. *se mann* (masc.) 'the man', *sēo sweostor* (fem.) 'the sister', or with lack of it, e.g. *þæt scip* (neut.) 'the ship'. This is often called 'natural gender'. But grammatical gender is often opposed to sex, e.g. (with persons) *se wīfmann* (masc.) 'the woman', *þæt wīf* (neut.) 'the woman', and (with inanimate objects) *se stān* (masc.) 'the stone', *sēo ġiefu* (fem.) 'the gift'. These opposing tendencies, which contribute to the later disappearance of grammatical gender in English, sometimes produce 'lack of concord'; see §187.2. Compounds follow the gender of the second element; hence *þæt wīf* (neut.) + *se mann* (masc.) = *se wīfmann* (masc.).

§13 OE nouns are traditionally divided into two groups – weak and strong. Generally, the gender of nouns must be learnt. The form of the demonstrative is the main clue (see §§16–17). The following nom. sg. endings, however, are significant:

Weak Masc.:   *-a*
Strong Masc.:   *-dōm, -els*, agent nouns in *-end* and *-ere, -hād*, concrete nouns in *-ing* and *-ling, -scipe*
Strong Fem.:   *-nes(s)*, abstract nouns in *-ing/ung, -ræden, -þo/þu*
Strong Neut.:   *-lāc*

A Guide to Old English, Eighth Edition. Bruce Mitchell and Fred C. Robinson.
© 2012 Bruce Mitchell and Fred C. Robinson. Published 2012 by Blackwell Publishing Ltd.

Notoriously ambiguous is the ending *-e*; see §77. On these endings, see further §138.

§14   Verbs. The differences between strong and weak verbs and the system of conjugating the OE verb are described in §§87–89. New developments, many of them important for MnE, are outlined in §§199–203.

I   PRONOUNS

§15   You are now ready to learn your first paradigms. The demonstrative *se* serves as a definite article. Both *se* 'that' and *þes* 'this' can be used with nouns, e.g. *se mann* 'the man', or as pronouns, e.g. *sē sorgaþ ymb þā* 'he is concerned about those (them)'.

§16   *se* 'the, that'

	Singular			Plural
	Masc.	Neut.	Fem.	All genders
Nom.	se	þæt	sēo, sīo	þā
Acc.	þone	þæt	þā	þā
Gen.	þæs	þæs	þære	þāra, þæra
Dat.	þæm, þām	þæm, þām	þære	þæm, þām
Inst.	þȳ, þon	þȳ, þon		

§17   *þes* 'this'

	Singular			Plural
	Masc.	Neut.	Fem.	All genders
Nom.	þes	þis	þēos	þās
Acc.	þisne	þis	þās	þās
Gen.	þisses	þisses	þisse, þisre	þissa, þisra
Dat.	þissum	þissum	þisse	þissum
Inst.	þȳs	þȳs		

§18   3rd Pers. Pron.

	Singular			Plural
	Masc.	Neut.	Fem.	All genders
Nom.	hē 'he'	hit 'it'	hēo, hīo 'she'	hīe, hī 'they'
Acc.	hine	hit	hīe, hī	hīe, hī
Gen.	his	his	hire	hira, hiera, heora, hiora
Dat.	him	him	hire	him, heom

§19   The following similarities in these declensions may be noted:

1   neut. sg. gen. dat. inst. are the same as the corresponding masc. forms;
2   nom. and acc. neut. sg. are the same;
3   gen. and dat. fem. sg. are the same;

4   pl. is the same for all genders;
5   acc. fem. sg. is the same as nom. and acc. pl.;
6   masc. and neut. dat. sg. is the same as dat. pl.

Note too the way in which the masc. and neut. sg., while agreeing with one another except in the nom. and acc., differ markedly in inflexion from the fem.

It should be mentioned that the personal pronouns (especially in the accusative case) are often used reflexively. (See 'reflexive' in Appendix D.) For example 'swa wæs hine getrymmende' ('thus he was strengthening himself'). OE verbs take reflexive objects much more frequently than do MnE verbs. For example 'se cyning hine . . . wende' ('the king went' – lit., 'the king betook himself').

§20   *Hwā* is interrogative 'who?' or indefinite 'anyone, someone'. It is not a relative pronoun in OE; see §159.

	Masc. and Fem.	*Neut.*
Nom.	hwā	hwæt
Acc.	hwone	hwæt
Gen.	hwæs	hwæs
Dat.	hwæm, hwām	hwæm, hwām
Inst.	hwȳ	hwȳ, hwon

Compare *hwā/hwæt* and *se/þæt*. The main difference is that the masc. and fem. of *hwā* are the same. This is understandable if we think of what *hwā* means.

§21   1st and 2nd Pers. Prons.

	Singular	*Dual*	*Plural*
Nom.	iċ 'I'	wit 'we two'	wē 'we'
Acc.	mē, meċ	unc	ūs, ūsic
Gen.	mīn	uncer	ūre
Dat.	mē	unc	ūs

	Singular	*Dual*	*Plural*
Nom.	þū 'thou'	git 'you two'	ġē 'ye, you'
Acc.	þē, þeċ	inc	ēow, ēowic
Gen.	þīn	incer	ēower
Dat.	þē	inc	ēow

The easiest way to learn these is to compare them with their MnE equivalents (the main differences are in pronunciation) and with one another.

Note
Unlike the indeclinable gen. forms *his, hire, hira* (§18), the six gen. forms given here can also be declined strong like adjs. (§63) to agree with nouns, e.g. 3/70 *minne cræft*. *Mīn* usually means 'my' but can mean 'of me' as in text 2/73.

II NOUNS AND SOUND-CHANGES RELEVANT TO THEM

Weak Nouns

§22   The basic paradigm of the weak or *-an* nouns is *nama* 'name' (masc.):

	Singular	*Plural*
Nom.	nama	naman
Acc.	naman	naman
Gen.	naman	namena
Dat.	naman	namum

Notes

1   Any noun with the nom. sg. ending *-a* is weak masc.
2   All other cases have the ending *-an* except gen. pl. *-ena* and dat. pl. *-um*.

Once *nama* is known, the rest follows quite simply without learning further paradigms.

§23   The weak fem. noun *sunne* 'sun' is declined exactly as *nama* apart from the nom. sg.

§24   The weak neut. noun *ēage* 'eye' is declined exactly as *nama* except that, as in all neut. nouns, the nom. and acc. sg. are the same.

§25   Nouns with a nom. sg. ending in a long vowel or diphthong form their oblique cases (i.e. any case other than the nom.) by adding the consonant of the inflexional ending. So *ġefēa* (masc.) 'joy' has oblique cases *ġefēa/n* except for gen. pl. *ġefēa/na* and dat. pl. *ġefēa/m*.

Some Technical Terms

§26   You now need to know some phonological terms. 'Short vowel' as in MnE 'hit' and 'long vowel' as in the second syllable in MnE 'machine' will present no difficulty. The word *wer* 'man' has a short vowel and is a short syllable. The word *stān* 'stone' has a long vowel and is a long syllable. Such words as *cniht* 'young man' and *cræft* 'strength' have a short vowel. But, since the short vowel is followed by *two* consonants, the syllable is long; cf. the rules of Latin prosody. To summarize, we have

short-stemmed monosyllables[1]	*wer, bæc, feoh*
long-stemmed monosyllables	*stān, cniht, crēap*
short-stemmed dissyllables	*miċel, yfel*
long-stemmed dissyllables	*ēþel, engel*

---

[1] The 'stem' of a word may be defined as that portion to which the inflexional ending is added, e.g. *scip* + *-es* = gen. sg. *scipes*. The stem of words ending in a vowel can usually be found by dropping the final vowel. So *ende* has stem *end-* + *-es* = gen. sg. *endes*.

Forms like *metodes* and *bysiğe* are called 'trisyllabic' and the *o* or *i* is sometimes called the 'medial vowel'.

§27   It is also important to distinguish open and closed syllables. An open syllable ends in a vowel, e.g. *hē* 'he'; a closed syllable ends in a consonant, e.g. *stān* 'stone'. This is clear enough. But difficulty arises with dissyllables. You must take on trust that the gen. sg. *stānes* is divided *stā/nes* (cf. MnE 'stone' but 'sto/ning'), while the infinitive *limpan* divides *lim/pan* (cf. MnE 'limb pad'). So we have

open syllables	*hē*	*stā/nes*
closed syllables	*stān*	*lim/pan*

§28   'Sometimes', it has been observed, 'things may be made darker by definition.' This must not deter us from attempting to define high and low vowels and back and front vowels. The adjectives 'high, low, back, front' all refer to the position in the mouth occupied by some part of the tongue. The tip of the tongue is not usually important; here it is assumed to be near or touching the lower front teeth. We are concerned with the movement of that part of the tongue which is highest when we pronounce a particular vowel.

§29   What follows is a conventionalized diagram showing the parts of the mouth in which the vowels are pronounced.

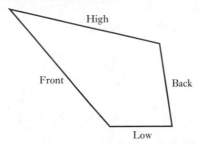

In front vowels the 'front' of the tongue is thrust forward in the mouth. It is also raised toward the hard palate and the upper front teeth to pronounce high front vowels (*i, y*). It is held midway between the upper and lower teeth to pronounce the mid front vowel *e*. Still in the front of the mouth, it is lowered to the back of the lower front teeth to pronounce the low front vowel *æ*. As the tongue moves from high front to low front position, the jaw drops. To pronounce the back vowels *u, o, a* the tongue is drawn to the back of the mouth toward the soft palate, and the jaw drops as one goes from *u* to *a*. You can try the following experiment, observing with the aid of a mirror the movements of jaw, lips, and tongue:

1   Practise individually the sounds you have learnt for the OE vowels, *i, e, æ, a, o, u.*

2   Sing them in a rough scale in the order given in 1, with the tip of the tongue near or touching the lower front teeth.

§30   Observe:

1   with *i, e, æ,*
   (*a*) a gradual lowering of the jaw;
   (*b*) a gradual lowering of the (front of the) tongue;
   (*c*) the roughly natural position of the lips, i.e. neither unduly spread out nor rounded;
   (*d*) a general feeling that the sounds are being made in the front of the mouth.

2   With the transition from *æ* to *a* a backward and slightly downward movement of the tongue.

3   with *a, o, u,*
   (*a*) progressive raising of the jaw and of the (back of the) tongue;
   (*b*) the way in which the lips become more rounded, i.e. form a progressively smaller circle;
   (*c*) the general feeling of 'backness'.

§31   From this, it should be clear why *i, e, æ,* are called front vowels and *a, o, u,* back vowels. The following diagram shows approximately where in the mouth the tongue is located when these vowels are pronounced.

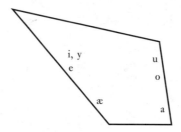

Since we can distinguish *i, u,* as high vowels and *æ, a,* as low vowels, we can now describe *i* as a high front vowel, *a* as a low back vowel, and so on.

§32   Of course, this is far from being a scientific description of the vowel sounds and you will need to consult a book on phonetics if you wish to learn more.

Strong Nouns like *stān* (masc.) and *scip* (neut.)

§33   Here we can take the masc. and neut. nouns together and deal with the fem. separately; cf. §19. The basic paradigm is the masc. *stān*:

	Singular	*Plural*
Nom.	stān	stānas
Acc.	stān	stānas
Gen.	stānes	stāna
Dat.	stāne	stānum

Notes

1   nom. and acc. sg. the same;

2   nom. and acc. pl. the same – the characteristic strong masc. *-as* which gives the MnE 's' plural;

3   gen. pl. in *-a*;

4   dat. pl. in *-um*. This is spelt *-an* or *-on* in some late texts.

§34   In the neut. we find

	Singular	Plural	Singular	Plural
Nom.	scip	scipu	word	word
Acc.	scip	scipu	word	word
Gen.	scipes	scipa	wordes	worda
Dat.	scipe	scipum	worde	wordum

These differ from *stān* and from one another only in the nom. and acc. pl. where the short-stemmed *scip* has *scipu* while the original *-u* is lost following a long-stemmed syllable, hence *word* is the same in nom. and acc. pl.; for this absence of *-u*, cf. *giefu/lār* (§48) and *sunu/hand* (§61).

Ċild 'child' may follow *word* or may add *r* before the pl. endings – *ċildru, ċildra, ċildrum*; hence MnE 'children', with final *n* from the weak declension. *Ǣġ* 'egg' has nom. acc. pl. *ǣġru*.

§35   Many nouns are exactly like *stān* (e.g. *āþ* 'oath', *dōm* 'judgement', *wer* 'man'), like *scip* (e.g. *god* 'god', *hof* 'dwelling'), or like *word* (e.g. *hūs* 'house', *wīf* 'woman'). But some differ in that, while THEY HAVE PERFECTLY NORMAL ENDINGS like those of *stān, scip,* or *word*, THEY SHOW SOME ABNORMALITY IN THE STEM (see §26, note) as the result of certain 'sound-changes' or 'sound-laws'. In 'sound law' 'laws' has the same meaning that it has in 'laws of nature', not the sense of man-made legal statute. Each language undergoes different sound changes at different periods. And the 'sound-laws' in which these changes are summed up are the result of observation by later scholars. Sometimes one of these 'laws' appears not to operate. This, however, is usually because something in a particular word or form prevented it. In such cases, another 'sound-law' was deduced to explain the exception. Thus the sound which was Gmc. *a* usually turns up in OE as *æ*. But in the nouns discussed in §36 we sometimes find *æ*, sometimes *a*. It was as a result of observing such differences that scholars first deduced the sound-changes. We can follow in their steps by examining the full paradigms of two nouns, noting the similarities and dissimilarities between them and regular nouns of the same declension, and so deducing the sound-changes necessary to explain the forms we have.

§36   These nouns are *dæġ* (masc.) 'day' and *fæt* (neut.) 'vessel':

	Singular	Plural	Singular	Plural
Nom.	dæġ	dagas	fæt	fatu
Acc.	dæġ	dagas	fæt	fatu
Gen.	dæġes	daga	fætes	fata
Dat.	dæġe	dagum	fæte	fatum

Observe:

1   that their endings are the same as in *stān* and *scip* respectively;
2   that they are short-stemmed monosyllables;
3   that the stem vowel of the nom. sg. is *æ*;
4   that both have *æ* throughout sg., *a* throughout pl.;
5   that where they have *a*, the ending is, or begins with, a back vowel;
6   that where they have *æ*, there is either no ending or an ending which is, or begins with, a front vowel.

Hence we can deduce that *æ* is found in a closed syllable (*dæġ*) or in an open syllable + a front vowel (*dæġes*), but appears as *a* in an open syllable + a back vowel (*dagas*). A simple rule is that these monosyllabic nouns have *æ* in the sg. stem, *a* in the pl. stem.

§37   Long-stemmed monosyllables ending in a vowel or diphthong + *h* take the endings of *stān* or *scip* but show syncopation (see Appendix D) of *h* when it occurs between two vowels. Subsequently the unaccented vowel is also absorbed. Thus the gen. sg. of *scōh* (masc.) 'shoe' is *scōhes > *scōes > scōs. The paradigm is

> *Singular*: *nom.* scōh, *acc.* scōh, *gen.* scōs, *dat.* scō
> *Plural*: *nom.* scōs, *acc.* scōs, *gen.* scōna (§38), *dat.* scōm

§38   The same thing happens in short-stemmed monosyllables ending in a vowel or diphthong + *h*. But when the *h* is dropped, the preceding short vowel or short diphthong is lengthened. So we get these recorded forms

> *eoh* (masc.) 'horse', but gen. sg. *ēos*
> *feoh* (neut.) 'money', but gen. sg. *f ēos*, dat. sg. *f ēo*

Theoretically, the gen. pl. of *feoh* should be *f ēo < *feoha, but *f ēona*, with the weak ending -*ena*, occurs – doubtless because *f ēo* was ambiguous. So also *scōna* (§37).

§39   Loss of *h* with lengthening of the preceding stem vowel or diphthong occurs between *r* or *l* and a vowel in monosyllabic nouns like *mearh* (masc.) 'horse' and *wealh* (masc.) 'foreigner'. The endings are those of *stān*.

	Singular	*Plural*	*Singular*	*Plural*
Nom.	mearh	mēaras	wealh	wēalas
Acc.	mearh	mēaras	wealh	wēalas
Gen.	mēares	mēara	wēales	wēala
Dat.	mēare	mēarum	wēale	wēalum

Note

Here the diphthong of the first syllable has been shown lengthened (as in *f ēos*), so that the first syllable of *mēares* is the same length as *mearh*. But metrical and placename evidence shows that forms with a short diphthong, e.g. *meares*, also occurred

under the influence of the short sound in *mearh*; in these, the whole word is the
metrical equivalent of *mearh*.

§40   The forms of *bearu, -o* (masc.) 'grove' and *searu, -o* (neut.) 'device' are

	Singular	Plural	Singular	Plural
Nom.	bearu	bearwas	searu	searu
Acc.	bearu	bearwas	searu	searu
Gen.	bearwes	bearwa	searwes	searwa
Dat.	bearwe	bearwum	searwe	searwum

Thus they add the endings of *stān* and *word* respectively to the stems which
before vowels become *bearw-* and *searw-* respectively; cf. §71.

§41   We turn now to dissyllabic nouns which take the endings of *stān*,
scip, or *word*.

Words with prefixes like *ġewrit* 'writing' and *ġebed* 'prayer' (both neut.),
where the stress falls on the second syllable, follow *scip*.

Dissyllabic nouns which are compounds of two nouns, or of an adjective
or adverb and a noun, have the second element declined, but not the first,
e.g. *hron-fisc* (masc.) 'whale', *hēah-clif* (neut.) 'high cliff', and *in-gang* (masc.)
'entrance'.

Other dissyllables with their stress on the first syllable may follow one of
four patterns:

		Masc.	*Neut.*
(a)	ˊ –	*cyning* 'king'	*fǣreld* (also masc.) 'journey'
(b)	ˊ –	*Hengest* 'Hengest'	*īsern* 'iron'
(c)	ˊ ˘	*engel* 'angel'	*hēafod* 'head'
(d)	ˊ ˘	*metod* 'creator'	*werod* 'troop'

Types *(a)* and *(b)* are quite regular and follow *stān* or *word* without any
variations of stem or ending.

§42   Type *(c)* – long-stemmed dissyllables – add the endings of *stān* or
scip. But they lose the medial vowel when an ending is added:

	Singular	Plural	Singular	Plural
Nom.	engel	englas	hēafod	hēafdu
Acc.	engel	englas	hēafod	hēafdu
Gen.	engles	engla	hēafdes	hēafda
Dat.	engle	englum	hēafde	hēafdum

Note

This loss of the medial vowel occurs only when an inflexional ending beginning
with a vowel is added or (to put it another way) when this medial vowel is in an open
syllable. Thus *engel* and *hēafod* have dat. pl. *englum* (NOT **enge/lum* – medial *e* is in
an open syllable) and *hēafdum* (NOT **hēafo/dum* – *o* is in an open syllable). Since all

the endings of *stān* and *scip* begin with a vowel, the simple statement made above suffices here. But the qualification is important for adjectives; see §68.

§43 Nouns of type (*d*) – short-stemmed dissyllables – are

	Singular	Plural	Singular	Plural
Nom.	metod	metodas	werod	werod
Acc.	metod	metodas	werod	werod
Gen.	metodes	metoda	werodes	weroda
Dat.	metode	metodum	werode	werodum

The masc. nouns therefore follow *stān* exactly. The neut. nouns remain unchanged in the nom. and acc. pl.; in other words, they are like *word*, not *scip*.

§44 But, as Dr. Johnson wisely observed, 'it may be reasonably imagined that what is so much in the power of men as language will very often be capriciously conducted'. For analogy often interferes with the historically correct forms given in §§42–43. A child learning to speak English today hears those around him forming past tenses of verbs by adding the sound *t*, e.g. 'baked', or *d*, e.g. 'sighed'. So quite naturally he says 'I maked a mud-pie today' or 'I buyed a hat in the shop today'. Thus the process of analogy can produce forms not accepted by most speakers of English today. But since we now have pretty strict notions of 'correctness', we tend to say to children 'No dear, I made a mud-pie' or 'I bought a hat', thereby helping to preserve the now-accepted form.

But many such variant forms are recorded in Old English texts. Alongside the regular nom. and acc. pls. *hēafdu* and *werod*, we find *hēafod*, *hēafodu*, and *weredu*.

Similarly, the process of analogy and earlier differences in some of the words themselves cause type (*d*) nouns ending in *l*, *r*, *m*, or *n*, to appear sometimes with no medial vowel in oblique cases. Thus *fugol* (masc.) 'bird' appears, like *engel*, without the medial vowel, and *wæter* may have gen. sg. *wæteres* or *wætres*, and nom. and acc. pl. *wæter*, *wætru*, or *wæteru*.

Hæleþ (masc.) 'man' and *mōnaþ* (masc.) 'month' may have nom. and acc. pl. the same or may add *-as*.

Masculine and Neuter Nouns in -*e*

§45 Masc. nouns with nom. sg. in -*e* are always strong, for weak masc. nouns have nom. sg. in -*a*. Neut. nouns in -*e* can be strong or weak (see §24). Historically speaking, strong nouns in -*e* belong either to a sub-class of the *stān*/*scip* declension or to another declension. As a general rule, it is safe to say that they drop the -*e* of the nom. sg. and add the endings of *stān* or *scip* as appropriate. Examples are

1 masc.: *ende* 'end', *here* 'army', *wine* 'friend', *stede* 'place';
2 neut.: *wīte* 'punishment', *rīce* 'kingdom', *spere* 'spear'.

The long-stemmed neuters, being dissyllabic in nom. sg., remain dissyllabic in the nom. acc. pl. *wītu*, *rīċu*.

§46　Words like *wine* and *stede* may have nom. and acc. pl. *wine* and *stede*.

A few masc. nouns have only the *-e* form in the nom. and acc. pl.; they include names of people, e.g. *Seaxe* 'Saxons' and *Dene* 'Danes', and the common nouns *ælde* 'men' and *lēode* 'people'.

Other forms you need to be able to recognize in your reading are

1　nom. acc. pl. *rīċiu* alongside *rīċu* 'kingdoms';
2　forms with *-(i)ġ(e)-*, e.g. nom. acc. pl. *her(i)ġ(e)as* alongside *heras* 'armies'.

Strong Feminine Nouns

§47　The basic paradigm is *ġiefu* 'gift':

	Singular	Plural
Nom.	ġiefu	ġiefa, -e
Acc.	ġiefe	ġiefa, -e
Gen.	ġiefe	ġiefa, -ena
Dat.	ġiefe	ġiefum

Note the following endings:

1　*-e* in acc. gen. and dat. sg.;
2　alternative nom. acc. pls. *-a*, *-e*;
3　weak *-ena* in gen. pl. alongside *-a*;
4　dat. pl. in *-um*.

§48　The long-stemmed monosyllable *lār* 'teaching' is identical except for nom. sg.; for absence of *-u* cf. *scipu/ word* (§34) and *sunu/ hand* (§61).

	Singular	Plural
Nom.	lār	lāra, -e
Acc.	lāre	lāra, -e
Gen.	lāre	lāra, -ena
Dat.	lāre	lārum

§49　Some fem. monosyllables with long front vowels, e.g. *cwēn* 'queen', originally had nom. and acc. sg. the same and *-e* in nom. acc. pl. Later most of them (by a perfectly natural confusion) sometimes followed *lār*. But it is important to note that *brȳd* 'bride', *cwēn* 'queen', *dǣd* 'deed', etc. may be acc. as well as nom. sg., and that all the long-stemmed fem. monosyllables may have *-a* or *-e* in nom. acc. pl.

§50　Long-stemmed dissyllables, e.g. *sāwol* 'soul' and *ċeaster* 'city', take the endings of *lār*, but (like *engel* and *hēafod* in §42) lose the medial vowel in trisyllabic forms.

§51 Some abstract nouns ending in *-þu* and *-u(-o)* can remain unchanged in the oblique cases (i.e. any case other than the nom.), e.g. *iermþu* 'poverty' and *ieldu* 'age'.

i-Mutation

§52 A sound-change which affects certain nouns and verbs must now be explained. The vowel *i* and the related consonant written in phonetic script [j] and pronounced as the first consonant in MnE 'yes' are high front sounds. When in OE one of these followed a stressed syllable, the vowel of that stressed syllable was subject to what is called '*i*-mutation'.[1] In simple terms, the organs of speech and the mind of the speaker got ready for the high front sound too soon and in the process.

the low front vowels were dragged up or 'raised'

and the back vowels were pulled forward or 'fronted'.

The *i* or [j] is usually lost but may appear in OE as *e* or *i*.

§53 This change can be explained (unscientifically) in terms of the diagram in §31 (p. 22) as follows:

1 The low front vowels *æ* and *e* move up one place.

2 The back vowels *a* and *o* are pushed straight forward to the corresponding front position.

3 *u* keeps its lip-rounding and goes forward to the rounded *y* described in §7.

The sections which follow give a Table of Correspondences in which the unmutated vowel (as it appears in OE) is shown on the left, and the OE mutated equivalent on the right.

Table of Correspondences

§54 Again in terms of the diagram on p. 22, the low front vowels are raised; only the short ones are affected.

ǣ	:	ĕ
ĕ	:	ĭ

Note

i is not affected because it cannot go any higher.

§55 The back vowels are fronted; both short and long are affected here.

ā̆	:	ā̆
ō̆	:	ē̆
ū̆	:	ȳ̆[2]
But ă + m, n	:	ĕ + m, n

---

[1] Unstressed vowels are sometimes affected. But this need not concern us here.

[2] Both *ō̆* and *ū̆* were fully rounded – *ō̆* to *ǣ* and *ū̆* to *ȳ*. But *ǣ* was usually unrounded to *ĕ*.

§56 The diphthongs *ea* and *eo* (short and long) are affected.

$$\breve{e}a \quad : \quad \breve{\imath}e$$
$$\breve{e}o \quad : \quad \breve{\imath}e$$

§57 Thirteen sounds are therefore affected – 2 front vowels, 7 back vowels (including *ă* in two ways), and 4 diphthongs. You should cull your own examples. A very good way to find some is to look at the strong verbs and to compare the stem vowel of the infinitive with the stem vowel of the 2nd and 3rd pers. sg. pres. ind.; see §112.1 and Appendix A. In most of them you will find the non-mutated vowel in the infinitive and its mutated equivalent in the 2nd and 3rd pers. sg. pres. ind. (both endings of which originally started with *i*). The *i* which caused *i*-mutation in these two forms has either disappeared or become *e*. For further effects of *i*-mutation, see Appendix B, pp. 154–55 below.

Nouns Affected by *i*-Mutation

§58 Typical paradigms for those masc. and fem. nouns affected by *i*-mutation are *mann* (masc.) 'man' and *bōc* (fem.) 'book':

	Singular	Plural	Singular	Plural
Nom.	mann	menn	bōc	bēc
Acc.	mann	menn	bōc	bēċ
Gen.	mannes	manna	bēċ, bōce	bōca
Dat.	menn	mannum	bēċ	bōcum

Notes

1 nom. and acc. sg. the same;

2 gen. sg. masc. like *stān*;

3 gen. and dat. pl. regular;

4 the mutated equivalent of the vowel of the nom. sg. appears in the dat. sg. and nom. and acc. pl. (with no inflexional ending);

5 the gen. sg. with the mutated vowel in the fem. nouns. This should not cause difficulty because the gen. and dat. sg. fem. are usually the same. *Bōce* arises by analogy with *lāre*.

Most of the masc. examples can be recognized by thinking of the MnE plural of the corresponding word, e.g. 'foot' (*fōt*), 'man' (*mann*), 'tooth' (*tōþ*). Most of the fem. nouns have become regular in MnE, e.g. 'book' (*bōc*), 'oak' (*āc*), 'goat' (*gāt*), but a few survive, e.g. 'goose' (*gōs*), 'louse' (*lūs*), 'mouse' (*mūs*).

§59 The nouns *frēond* 'friend' and *fēond* 'enemy', which are formed from pres. ptcs. of verbs, can follow *stān* or can have *īe* in dat. sg. and nom. and acc. pl.; cf. *mann*.

§60 Nouns ending in -*r* which denote relationship are: *fæder* 'father' and *brōþor* 'brother' (both masc.), *mōdor* 'mother', *dohtor* 'daughter', and *sweostor* 'sister' (all fem.). It is difficult to systematize these nouns, for many analogical variations exist, but the following observations may help:

1   All are regular in the gen. and dat. pl., ending in *-a* and *-um* respectively and losing the medial vowel if long-stemmed (§42).

2   All can have the nominative singular form in all remaining cases except for

> (*a*) *fæder* which takes *-as* in nom. acc. pl.;
>
> (*b*) *brōþor, mōdor, dohtor*, which may show *i*-mutation in dat. sg., viz. *brēþer, mēder, dehter*. These forms may also occur in gen. sg., by analogy with fem. nouns such as *lār* (§48), in which gen. and dat. sg. are the same. The paradigms of two nouns of relationship (*brōþor*) (masc.) and *dohtor* (fem.) will illustrate this declension.

	Singular	*Plural*	*Singular*	*Plural*
Nom.	brōþor	brōþor	dohtor	dohtor
Acc.	brōþor	brōþor	dohtor	dohtor
Gen.	brōþor	brōþra	dohtor	dohtra
Dat.	brōþor	brōþrum	dohtor	dohtrum

u-Nouns

§61   A few masc. and fem. nouns belong to the *u*-declension. They may be short-stemmed dissyllables with final *-u*, e.g. *sunu* (masc.) 'son' and *duru* (fem.) 'door', or long-stemmed monosyllables, e.g. *feld* (masc.) 'field' and *hand* (fem.) 'hand'; for the absence of *-u* in the latter cf. *scipu/word* and *ġiefu/lār*. Typical paradigms are *sunu* (masc.) and *hand* (fem.):

	Singular	*Plural*	*Singular*	*Plural*
Nom.	sunu	suna	hand	handa
Acc.	sunu	suna	hand	handa
Gen.	suna	suna	handa	handa
Dat.	suna	sunum	handa	handum

Notes

1   Nom. and acc. sg. are the same.

2   All other cases end in *-a* except of course the dat. pl. *-um*.

Other nouns which belong here are *wudu* 'wood', *ford* 'ford', and *weald* 'forest' – all masc.

§62   Masc. nouns like *feld* and fem. nouns like *duru/hand* are all to some extent influenced by *stān* and *ġiefu/lār* respectively and so hover uneasily between two declensions; hence gen. sg. *feldes* and the like. But the most important point to note here is that the ending *-a* is sometimes a dat. sg. in the texts, e.g. *felda* (selection 12, l. 241), *forda* (selection 12, l. 81), *wealda*.

III ADJECTIVES

Introduction

§63 Most adjectives can be declined strong or weak. Important exceptions are *ōþer* and the poss. adjs. *mīn*, *þīn*, etc. (see §21), which are declined strong, and comparatives, which end in *-a* in nom. sg. masc., e.g. *blindra* 'blinder', and are declined weak.

On participles, see §111.

§64 Which form of the adjective is used depends, not on the type of noun with which it is used, but on how it is used. The strong form is used when the adj. stands alone, e.g. 'The man is old' *se mann is eald*, or just with a noun, e.g. 'old men' *ealde menn*. The weak form appears when the adj. follows a dem., e.g. 'that old man' *se ealda mann*, or a poss. adj., e.g. 'my old friend' *mīn ealda frēond*. You can remember that the strong forms stand alone, while the weak forms need the support of a dem. or poss. pron.

Weak Declension

§65 The paradigm is *tila* 'good':

	Singular			Plural
	Masc.	*Neut.*	*Fem.*	*All genders*
Nom.	tila	tile	tile	tilan
Acc.	tilan	tile	tilan	tilan
Gen.	tilan	tilan	tilan	tilra, -ena
Dat.	tilan	tilan	tilan	tilum

The long-stemmed *gōda* 'good' is declined exactly the same. Here the endings are identical with those of the weak noun of the same gender with one addition – the strong form of gen. pl. *tilra* is generally preferred to *-ena*, except in eWS. The dat. pl. *-um* is frequently replaced by *-an* in WS texts and in lWS *-an* is found in the gen. pl. too. Stem changes in the weak declension of the adjectives follow the rules set out in §§68–73.

Strong Declension

§66 The paradigm is *til* 'good', which has a separate inst. form in the masc. and neut. sg.:

	Singular		
	Masc.	*Neut.*	*Fem.*
Nom.	til	til	tilu
Acc.	tilne	til	tile
Gen.	tiles	tiles	tilre
Dat.	tilum	tilum	tilre
Inst.	tile	tile	

	Plural		
	Masc.	*Neut.*	*Fem.*
Nom.	tile	tilu	tile, -a
Acc.	tile	tilu	tile, -a
Gen.	til*ra*	til*ra*	til*ra*
Dat.	tilum	tilum	tilum

Notes

1　Nom. and acc. pl. masc. end in *-e* (or occasionally *-a*), e.g. *cwice eorlas* 'living noblemen'; the ending *-as* belongs to the nouns only. This *-e* is sometimes found in fem. and neut. pl.; see §81.

2　All the other endings are familiar. Those italicized have already been met in the pronouns (§§16–18). The remainder are endings found in *stān*, *scip*, and *ġiefu*, respectively.

§67　The long-stemmed monosyllable *gōd* 'good' varies only in the nom. sg. fem. *gōd* as against *tilu* (cf. *lār/ġiefu*) and in the nom. and acc. neut. pl. *gōd* as against *tilu* (cf. *word/scipu*).

Stem Changes in Adjectives

§68　Long-stemmed dissyllables such as *hāliġ* add the weak or strong endings given above as appropriate. The medial vowel is not lost before endings beginning with a consonant, i.e. in closed syllables – hence *hāliġ/ne*, *hāliġ/re*, *hāliġ/ra*.

When the ending begins with a vowel, the medial vowel sometimes disappears; cf. the nouns *engel* and *hēafod* (§42) and *sāwol* (§50). Thus *hāliġ* has gen. sg. masc. strong *hālġes*. But analogical variations are common, and we find *hāliġan* alongside *hālġan*, *hāliġes* alongside *hālġes*, and so on.

In the nom. sg. fem. and nom./acc. pl. neut. *hāliġ* (cf. *lār/word*), *hāliġu* (cf. *ġiefu/scipu*), and *hālġu* (with loss of vowel) are all found.

§69　Short-stemmed dissyllabic adjectives show forms with no medial vowel more frequently than the corresponding nouns (§§43–44). Thus *miċel* 'great' may have acc. sg. fem. *miċele* or *miċle*, while *moniġ* 'many' and *yfel* 'evil' have dat. pl. *monigum* or *mongum* and gen. sg. masc. *yfeles* or *yfles*, respectively.

§70　Short-stemmed monosyllabic adjectives with the stem-vowel *æ* follow *glæd* 'glad', here declined strong:

	Singular		
	Masc.	*Neut.*	*Fem.*
Nom.	glæd	glæd	gladu
Acc.	glædne	glæd	glade
Gen.	glades	glades	glædre
Dat.	gladum	gladum	glædre
Inst.	glade	glade	

	Plural		
	Masc.	*Neut.*	*Fem.*
Nom.	glade	gladu	glade
Acc.	glade	gladu	glade
Gen.	glædra	glædra	glædra
Dat.	gladum	gladum	gladum

Here *æ/a* fluctuation occurs. As in the nouns (§36), we find *æ* in a closed syllable, i.e. in the simple form *glæd* and when an ending beginning with a consonant is added, e.g. *glæd/ne*. In open syllables, however, the adjectives have *a* irrespective of whether a front or back vowel follows, e.g. *gla/des*, *gla/dum*. This is the result of analogy.

§71 Adjectives like *ġearo, -u* 'ready' take the endings of *gōd*. Hence in the strong declension, they remain unchanged in the nom. sg. all genders, acc. sg. neut., and nom. and acc. pl. neut. Before consonants, the stem is *ġearo- –* hence *ġearone, ġearore, ġearora*, but before vowels it is *ġearw- –* hence *ġearwes, ġearwum*; cf. §40. Write out the paradigm. Then see A. Campbell *O.E. Grammar*, §649.

§72 Adjectives such as *hēah* 'high' and *fāh* 'hostile' usually lose their final *h* and contract where possible; cf. §§37 and 38. *Hēah* may have acc. sg. masc. strong *hēanne* or *hēane*.

§73 Adjectives in *-e*, e.g. *blīþe*, behave like the corresponding nouns (§45). Hence they drop the *-e* and add the endings of *til*.

Comparison of Adjectives

§74 Most adjectives add the endings *-ra, -ost* to the stem. Thus we find *lēof* 'dear', *lēofra* 'dearer', *lēofost* 'dearest'. Similarly *glæd* 'glad', *glædra* 'gladder', but *gladost* 'gladdest' (see §70). The comparative is declined weak, the superlative strong or weak (see §64).

§75 Some adjectives, however, add the endings *-ra, -est* (which were originally **-ira, *-ist*), and show an *i*-mutated vowel in the stem, e.g.

eald 'old'	ieldra	ieldest
ġeong 'young'	ġingra	ġingest
lang 'long'	lengra	lengest
strang 'strong'	strengra	strengest
hēah 'high'	hīerra	hīehst

§76 Irregular are:

lȳtel 'little'	læssa	læst
miċel 'great'	māra, mā	mæst
yfel 'bad'	wiersa	wierst
gōd 'good'	betera, sēlra	betst, sēlest

These, of course, can be compared with their MnE equivalents.

IV OBSERVATIONS ON NOUN, ADJECTIVE, AND PRONOUN DECLENSIONS

§77 The weak declension of nouns and adjectives, with *-an* throughout except in a few easily remembered places (see §§22–25), presents little difficulty. The weak masc. noun can always be recognized by *-a* in nom. sg. However, *-e* of the weak fem. and neut. is also found in strong masc. and neut. nouns. But a noun with final *-e* in nom. sg. cannot be strong fem.

§78 Nouns with their nom. sg. ending in a consonant are strong, but can be any gender. See again §13.

§79 In the strong nouns and the strong declension of the adj., the characteristic endings should be noted. The gen. pl. of the noun is *-a*, of the adj. *-ra*. But the weak ending *-ena* is found in nouns like *feoh/fēona* and *ġiefu/ġiefa* or *ġiefena*, and in the adj. The endings *-ne* (acc. sg. masc.) and *-re* (gen. and dat. sg. fem.) are found in adjs. (strong forms) and prons.

§80 Certain similarities may be noted in the declension of strong nouns, the strong form of the adj., and the dem. and pers. prons. (less 1st and 2nd pers.; on these, see §21). These are

1   neut. sg. nom. and acc. are always the same;
2   nom. and acc. sg. of masc. NOUNS are always the same;
3   nom. and acc. pl. are always the same;
4   gen. and dat. fem. sg. are always the same (with the reservations made in §§58 and 60);
5   within the same declension
    (*a*) masc. and neut. gen. sg. are the same;
    (*b*) masc. and neut. dat. sg. are the same;
    (*c*) masc. and neut. inst. sg. are the same.

§81 A possible source of confusion is the fact that in prons. and adjs., the acc. fem. sg. is the same as nom. and acc. pl., e.g. *þā/þā*, *þās/þās*, *hīe/hīe*, *cwice/cwice*. This last form *cwice* is properly the masc. pl. But in later texts especially, the ending *-e* is often used for all genders in the strong form of the adj., rather than *-u* or *-a* (§66).

V NUMERALS

§82 The numerals from 1 to 10 are

	Cardinal	*Ordinal*
1	ān	forma
2	twēġen	ōþer
3	þrīe	þridda
4	fēower	fēorþa
5	fīf	fifta

6	siex	siexta
7	seofon	seofoþa
8	eahta	eahtoþa
9	nigon	nigoþa
10	tīen	tēoþa

§83   When declined strong, *ān* means 'one'; when declined weak *āna*, it usually means 'alone'. Only the first three cardinal numbers are regularly declined.

Ordinals are declined weak, except *ōþer* which is always strong.

§84   *Twēġen* 'two' and *bēġen* 'both' are declined alike. In the nom. and acc. they have

Masc.	twēġen	*Neut.*	twā, tū	*Fem.*	twā
	bēġen		ba, bū		hā

The gen. and dat. are the same for all genders:

twēġra, twēġ(e)a;   bēġra, bēġ(e)a
twǣm;   bǣm

§85   In the nom. and acc. of *þrīe* 'three' we find

Masc.	þrīe	*Neut.*	þrēo	*Fem.*	þrēo

The gen. and dat. are *þrēora, þrim*.

§86   A knowledge of the remaining numerals is not essential at first. The meaning of many is obvious, e.g. *twēntiġ, þrītiġ, fēowertiġ, fīftiġ*, and those which occur in your texts will be glossed. Full lists will be found in any of the standard grammars. In OE manuscripts Roman numerals are often used.

VI   STRONG VERBS AND SOUND-CHANGES RELEVANT TO THEM

Introduction

§87   Like MnE, OE has two types of verbs – weak and strong. The weak verb forms its preterite and past participle by adding a dental suffix (-*ed*), the strong verb by changing its stem vowel; cf. MnE 'laugh, laughed' and 'judge, judged' with MnE 'sing, sang, sung'. The strong verbs are nearly all survivals from OE; new verbs when made up or borrowed today join the weak conjugation. Thus the strong verb 'drive, drove, driven' survives from OE. When in the thirteenth century 'strive' was borrowed from the French, it followed the pattern of 'drive' because the two infinitives rhymed; hence we get MnE 'strive, strove, striven'. But we conjugate the comparatively new verb 'contrive', not 'contrive, controve, contriven', but 'contrive, contrived', i.e. as a weak verb.

§88   Such patterns as 'drive, drove, driven' and 'contrive, contrived' are called the 'principal parts' of the verbs. This is important because, if you do not know the patterns which the various verbs display in their principal parts, you will be unable to find out their meaning. You will be in the same position as a foreign student of English looking up 'drove (verb)' in his dictionary. For he can find out what it means only by knowing that it is the preterite of 'drive'.

§89   Both weak and strong verbs in OE distinguish

1   two tenses – present and preterite;

2   indicative, subjunctive, and imperative moods, in addition to two infinitives – one without *to*, and one (the inflected infinitive) with *to* – and two participles, the present and the past (or second);

3   two numbers – singular and plural. The dual is found only in the 1st and 2nd person pronouns and is used with plural verb forms;

4   three persons, but only in the singular of the present and preterite indicative. All plurals and the singular of the subjunctives are the same throughout;

5   one voice only – the active. One true passive form survives from an earlier stage of the language, viz. *hātte* 'is called, was called'.

On the syntax of these forms and on the beginnings of new methods of expressing verbal relationships, see §§195 ff.

Principal Parts of the Strong Verbs

§90   These verbs show a change of vowel in the stressed syllable in the principal parts. This is known as 'gradation' and the vowels which change – e.g. *ī, ō, i* in 'drive, drove, driven' – are known as the 'gradation' series. The origin of these is to be found in the shifting stress of the original IE language (which later became fixed, usually on the first syllable, in OE). We can see how the pronunciation of a vowel can change according to the amount of stress the syllable carries if we compare the pronunciation of the following three versions of the same MnE sentence:

Cán he do it?

Can hé do it?

Can he dó it?

In the first, the vowel of 'can' has its full value; in the second, a reduced value; and in the third, it has almost disappeared and has what is sometimes called 'zero' value. Such variations in IE may well have been perpetuated when the stress became fixed.

§91   No MnE strong verb has more than three vowels in its gradation series; some, e.g. 'bind, bound, bound', have only two. But in OE, four parts of the verb may be distinguished by different vowels – the infinitive, two preterites, and the past participle, e.g. *crēopan* 'creep', *crēap*, *crupon*, *cropen*. But (for various reasons) the same vowel may occur more than once in the same verb. So we find, with three different vowels, *bindan* 'bind', *band*, *bundon*, *bunden*, and, with two only, *faran* 'go', *fōr*, *fōron*, *faren*.

§92 Many primers show five vowels for the strong verbs, viz. inf. (*crēopan*), 3rd sg. pres. ind. (*crīepþ*), pret. sg. or 1st pret. (*crēap*), pret. pl. or 2nd pret. (*crupon*), past ptc. (*cropen*). See §113.1 & 2. The 3rd sg. pres. ind. is not part of the gradation series; its stem vowel is the *i*-mutated equivalent of the vowel of the inf. and can be deduced from that vowel; see §57. So, when learning a strong verb, you will need to remember four vowels – those of the inf., two preterites, and the past ptc. There are in OE seven different 'classes' of strong verbs, each with a different gradation series. As we shall see (§94), there is also in some classes something distinctive about the consonant or consonants following the gradation vowel. (See footnotes 1 and 2 below.)

§93 Verbs characteristic of these classes are

Class	Inf.	1st Pret.	2nd Pret.	Past Ptc.
I	scīnan 'shine'	scān	scinon	scinen
II	crēopan 'creep'	crēap	crupon	cropen
	brūcan 'enjoy'	brēac	brucon	brocen
III	breġdan 'pull'	bræġd	brugdon	brogden
IV	beran 'bear'	bær	bǣron	boren
V	tredan 'tread'	træd	trǣdon	treden
VI	faran 'go'	fōr	fōron	faren
VII	(*a*) healdan 'hold'	hēold	hēoldon	healden
	(*b*) hātan 'command'	hēt	hēton	hāten

Roman numerals are here used for the classes of strong verbs, arabic numerals for those of the weak verbs. Thus *scīnan* I 'shine' and *lufian* 2 'love' tell us both the type and class of verb. Class VII verbs are sometimes called 'reduplicating' (abbreviation 'rd.').

Note The past ptc. frequently has the prefix *ġe-* (§6).

§94 From a study of these and the lists of strong verbs set out in Appendix A, the following gradation series will emerge:

Class	Consonant Structure	Inf.	1st Pret.	2nd Pret.	Past Ptc.
I	*ī* + one cons.	ī	ā	i	i
II	*ēo* + one cons.	ēo	ēa	u	o
	ū + one cons.	ū			
III	See §102				
IV	*e* + one cons.[1]	e	æ	ǣ	o
V	*e* + one cons.[2]	e	æ	ǣ	e
VI	*a* + one cons.[3]	a	ō	ō	a
VII	See §104				

[1] Usually a liquid (*l*, *r*). But note *brecan* 'break'. On the verbs with nasals, see §103.2.
[2] Usually a stop (*p*, *t*, *c*, *d*, *g*) or spirant (*f*, *þ*, *s*).
[3] *Standan* 'stand', with *-n-* in inf. and past ptc., belongs here.

§95   The gradation series of verbs in classes I and II are quite regular. Class III presents special difficulties because the stem vowels of most verbs are affected by one of several sound laws. For purposes of explanation, we can take the verb *breġdan* 'pull' as the basic paradigm in terms of which all the other verbs can be explained. *Breġdan* shows the following pattern:

III   *e* + TWO cons.   e   æ   u   o

A few other verbs, e.g. *streġdan* 'strew', *berstan* 'burst', *þerscan* 'thresh',[1] show the same vowel pattern. But the remainder fall into four groups which are represented by the verbs *weorpan* 'throw'/*feohtan* 'fight', *helpan* 'help', *ġieldan* 'pay', and *drincan* 'drink'. To understand the variations in these verbs, we have to know something about certain sound-changes.

Breaking

§96   The first of these is the diphthongization of a front vowel when it is followed by a consonant or group of consonants produced in the back of the mouth. When moving from a front vowel to a back consonant, the organs of speech do NOT move swiftly and cleanly from front vowel position to back consonant position; rather they glide more or less gradually from one position to the other. You can see the result of this process in an exaggerated form if you imagine that you have fallen overboard from a ship and are calling out 'Help'. If you call out loudly and long (you had better do this in a desert place!), you will find that the vowel of the word 'Help' is 'broken' as you glide from the front position of *e* to the back position of *lp*. If you spell it as you are pronouncing it, you will write something like 'Heulp'. Try the same experiment with words like 'bell', 'fell', 'tell'. You will probably find that a 'glide' develops between the short front vowel *e* and the following *l*. A similar process took place in OE. It is called 'breaking'.

§97   For our purposes, its most important effects are

1   before *h*, *h* + cons., *r* + cons.[2]

   ǽ > ĕa
   ĕ > ĕo

In terms of the diagram in §31, the organs of speech glide back to the back vowel nearest in height to the front vowel from which they started. (See §8, where we assume that the symbol *ea* is pronounced *æa*.)

2   before *l* (here made in the back of the throat) + cons.

   ǽ > ĕa

---

[1]   *Berstan* and *þerscan* were originally **brestan* and **þrescan*, with two medial consonants. But the *r* 'changed places'. This change, known as 'metathesis', is not uncommon; cf. OE *brid* with MnE 'bird'.
[2]   Here *r* was probably made with the tip of the tongue curved back.

But ĕ is not usually affected before *l*. We can call this 'limited breaking'; it occurs before *l*, with which the word 'limited' begins!

Note
ĕ does break before *lh*. See §133.2 for an example.

3   before *h* and *h* + cons.

   ī > īo > very often ēo

§98   We can now return to the verbs of class III where the basic gradation series is *e, æ, u, o* (§95). If we examine *weorpan* and *feohtan*, we find

weorpan	wearp	wurpon	worpen
feohtan	feaht	fuhton	fohten

Here the medial cons. groups *-rp-* and *-ht-* cause *e* and *æ* to break but do not affect the back vowels *u* and *o*. Hence we get as the gradation series, NOT *e, æ, u, o*, but *eo, ea, u, o*.

§99   In *helpan*, however, the medial group *-lp-* produces only limited breaking and so we get

   helpan   healp   hulpon   holpen

where only the 1st pret. *ea* differs from the basic series of *breġdan*, the *e* of the infinitive remaining unchanged.

Influence of Initial ġ, sc, ċ

§100   The results of the next sound-change to affect the verbs of class III are seen most commonly in the WS dialect, with which we are mainly concerned. Here the initial palatal consonants *ġ, sc,* and *ċ,* caused the following front vowels *ē* and *ǣ* to become *īe* and *ēa* respectively. The effect may be produced by an emphatic pronunciation of these consonants, which will produce a glide between the consonant and vowel. A modern parallel may be found in the prolonged 'Yes' in the sentence 'Well, yes, I suppose so' used when one gives hesitating assent or grudging permission; we might spell our pronunciation something like 'Yies'. This change is sometimes called 'palatal diphthongization' (p.d. for short). It is because of it that we find the inf. *ġieldan*. For further examples, see §103.1.

Note
The pret. *ġeald* could be the result of breaking or of p.d. But such forms as *ċeorfan*, which show *eo < e* as the result of breaking, suggest that breaking took place before p.d.; if it had not, we should have had **ċierfan* by p.d. P.d. can take place in such forms as *ġieldan* because *e* did not break before *-ld-* and hence remained until p.d. took place.

Influence of Nasals

§101 The last sound-change which affects verbs of class III is found in verbs in which the first of the two medial consonants is a nasal *m* or *n*. In these circumstances, *i* appears instead of *e*, *a* instead of *æ*, and *u* instead of *o*. So we get

drincan   dranc   druncon   druncen

with *i*, *a* (sometimes *o*; see §103.2), *u*, *u* instead of *e*, *æ*, *u*, *o*.

Summary of the Strong Verbs of Class III

§102 The following table summarizes class III verbs. Each of series (*b*)–(*e*) is to be explained by the appropriate sound-change operating on series (*a*). See also §§116 and 133.5.

Sound-Change	*Symbol*	*Example*	*Gradation Series*			
(*a*)						
Basic Series	*e* + 2 cons.	*breġdan*	e	æ	u	o
(*b*)						
Breaking before							
r + cons.	*eo* + *r* + cons.	*weorpan*				
h + cons.	*eo* + *h* + cons.	*feohtan*	eo	ea	u	o
(*c*)						
Limited break-							
ing before							
l + cons.	*e* + *l* + cons.	*helpan*	e	ea	u	o
(*d*)						
Palatal diph-	palatal + *ie* + 2	*ġieldan*	ie	ea	u	o
thongization	cons.					
(*e*)						
Nasal	*i* + nasal + cons.	*drincan*	i	a	u	u

The Effects of Sound-Changes on Other Strong Verbs

§103 Some of these sound-changes affect verbs of other classes.

1   Palatal diphthongization is seen in:

Class IV *scieran* 'cut', which has *ie*, *ea*, *ēa*, *o* instead of *e*, *æ*, *ǣ*, *o*;

Class V *ġiefan* 'give' with *ie*, *ea*, *ēa*, *ie*, instead of *e*, *æ*, *ǣ*, *e*, and in the class VI infinitive *scieppan* 'create'.

2   Nasals influence class IV *niman* 'take' with *i*, *a*/*o*, *ā*/*ō* (fluctuation between *a* and *o* is not uncommon before nasals) and *u* instead of *e*, *æ*, *ǣ*, *o*. On *niman* and *cuman* 'come' see also §109. Note that following contraction a short vowel is lengthened (e.g. *sēon*).

3   Breaking before *h* with subsequent loss of *h* between a diphthong and a vowel (see §§37–38) affects the infinitives of the contracted verbs of classes I, V, and VI. The stages can be set out thus:

I   *wrīhan > *wrēohan > wrēon 'cover'
V   *sehan > *seohan > sēon 'see'
VI   *slahan > *slæhan[1] > *sleahan > slēan 'strike'

4   The infinitives of contracted verbs of class II are affected by loss of *h* only, e.g.

*tēohan > tēon 'draw'

5   The contracted verbs of class VII – *fōn* 'take' and *hōn* 'hang' – have a complicated phonology; detailed explanation would be out of place here. But see §108.

6   On the principal parts of contracted verbs, see §§107–108. On 3rd sg. pres. ind. of contracted verbs, see §114. On the 'weak presents' of classes V–VII, see §116.

Strong Verbs of Class VII

§104   Strong verbs of class VII show the following characteristics:

1   the same stem vowel in inf. and past ptc. (except *wēpan*);
2   the same stem vowel in 1st and 2nd pret. – either *ēo* or *ē*. On this basis the two sub-classes (*a*) and (*b*) are distinguished. See Appendix A.7.

Important verbs here are: *cnāwan* 'know', *feallan* 'fall', *weaxan* 'grow' (all VII(*a*)), and *drǣdan* 'fear' and *lǣtan* 'let' (both VII(*b*)). It is worth noting that none of them can be mistaken for strong verbs of any other class, for the stem vowels of the inf. are different. But see further §§131–134.

Grimm's Law and Verner's Law

§105   Certain consonant changes that distinguish the Gmc. languages from the other IE languages were first formulated by the German philologist Grimm (of the Fairy Tales) and hence are known as Grimm's Law. But the fact that the expected consonant did not always appear in the Gmc. languages puzzled philologists until the Danish grammarian Karl Verner explained that the differences depended on the position of the stress in the original IE form of the word. See Appendix F.

§106   Grimm's Law accounts (*inter alia*) for the variations between Latin (which in the examples cited keeps the IE consonant) and OE seen in such pairs as

---

[1] This *a* – *æ* variation must be taken on trust. (Those interested can compare §§35–36.)

Lat.	*piscis*	OE	*fisc*	(*p/f*)
Lat.	*frater*	OE	*brōþor*	(*t/þ*)
Lat.	*genus*	OE	*cynn*	(*g/c*)
Lat.	*dentem*	OE	*tōþ*	(*d/t*)

But, if *fisc* corresponds to *piscis* and *brōþor* to *frāter*, we should expect **fæþer* alongside *păter*. But we have *fæder*. Verner explained exceptions like this.

We can see the sort of thing that happened if we compare MnE 'éxcellent' and 'ábsolute' on the one hand with MnE 'exám.' and 'absólve' on the other. In the first pair, the stress falls on the first syllable and the consonants which follow are voiceless; we could spell the words 'eks-' and 'abs-'. In the second pair, the stress is on the second syllable in IE. So the consonants are voiced, and the words could be spelt 'egz-' and 'abz-'. Similar variations, said Verner, arose in Pr. Gmc. because of similar differences. Greek φράτηρ = Latin *frāter* was stressed on the first syllable. Hence in its Pr. Gmc. equivalent the medial *t* developed regularly by Grimm's Law to voiceless *þ* (cf. MnE 'cloth') in Pr. OE.[1] But Greek πατήρ = Latin *păter* was stressed on the second syllable. So in Pr. Gmc. the voiceless *þ* which arose from the *t* by Grimm's Law was voiced to the sound in MnE 'clothe'. This voiced sound subsequently became *d*. (See Appendix F p. 175.)

§107 Many standard histories of the English language explain these two Laws in detail; for us their most important effect is seen in the OE strong verbs, where Verner's Law accounts for certain variations in the medial consonant. Thus in class I we find

snīþan   snāþ   snidon   sniden

Here the *þ* of the inf. and 1st pret. is the consonant we should expect by Grimm's Law. The *d* of the 2nd pret. and past ptc. (which originally had the accent on the second syllable) is the Verner's Law form. Similarly we find

II   ċēosan   ˙ċēas   curon   coren

and in contracted verbs (which originally had *h* in the inf.; see §§103.3 and 103.4)

I   wrēon   wrāh   wrigon   wrigen
V   sēon   seah   sāwon   sewen

In these strong verbs, the Verner's Law forms occur in the 2nd pret. and the past ptc., while the inf. and 1st pret. are regular. This is historically 'correct'; we see from the verbs marked † in Appendix A that by Verner's Law TH in the inf. and 1st pret. is LIKELY to be replaced by D in the 2nd pret. and past ptc., s by R, and (mostly in contracted verbs) H by G, W, or (in *hōn* and *fōn*: see below) by NG.[2]

---

[1] Its voicing (§9) comes later; see A. Campbell *Old English Grammar*, §444.

[2] Verner's Law forms are also seen in such related pairs as *ċēosan* 'choose'/*cyre* 'choice' and *rīsan* 'rise'/*ræran* 'raise'. See §136.

§108   The word 'LIKELY' is emphasized because the Verner's Law forms sometimes occur where historically they should not. Thus the principal parts of the contracted verbs of class VII are

hōn	hēng	hēngon	hangen
fōn	fēng	fēngon	fangen

Here the Verner's Law *ng* is extended by analogy into the 1st pret.; the same may be true of the *g* in

VI	slēan	slōg	slōgon	slæ̇gen[1]

Sometimes, on the other hand, the Verner's Law forms are completely eliminated, as in *mīþan* I 'conceal' and *rīsan* I 'rise'; this has happened to all Verner's Law forms in MnE except 'was/were'. This process of analogy or regularizing by the elimination of odd forms is sometimes called 'levelling'. But, as we see from verbs like *scrīþan*, with past ptc. *scriden* or *scriþen*, its results are often capricious because it is not conducted consciously and logically.

§109   These and other levellings which occur in OE can be seen as the first signs of two great changes which overtook the strong verbs as English developed through the centuries. First, we today distinguish fewer classes of strong verbs. For example, the verbs of class V have gone over to class IV. Thus, while OE *specan*, *tredan*, *wefan*, have *e* in their past ptcs., MnE 'speak', 'tread', 'weave', have *o*; cf. *beran* IV. Second, while in OE the stem vowels of the 1st and 2nd prets. are different except in classes VI and VII, they are today the same (again except in 'was/were'). The beginnings of this process are seen in *cuman* IV 'come' and *etan* V 'eat', where the vowel of the 2nd pret. is found in the 1st pret. too. The marked confusion of forms in *niman* IV 'take' also results from this levelling. Perhaps you can work out for yourself why *findan* sometimes has a 1st pret. *funde* instead of the normal *fand*.

Conjugation of the Strong Verb

§110   Our wanderings through what have been called 'the dusty deserts of barren philology' lead us now to the conjugation of the strong verb, here exemplified by *singan* III. Points which must be carefully noted when conjugating these and all strong verbs are set out below; on the uses of the tenses and moods, see §§195–198 and page 174.

§111   *Singan* 'sing' *sang sungon sungen* is conjugated

		Present Indicative	*Preterite Indicative*
Sg.	1	singe	sang
	2	singest	sunge
	3	singeþ	sang
Pl.		singaþ	sungon

---

[1] But *slōh* does occur, and ME forms suggest that the *g* in *slōg* may be merely a spelling variant of *h*.

	Present Subjunctive	Preterite Subjunctive
Sg.	singe	sunge
Pl.	singen	sungen

Before a 1st or 2nd pers. pron., the plural endings can be reduced to *-e*, e.g. *wē singaþ* but *singe wē*.

Imp. Sg.	sing	*Pl.*	singaþ
Inf.	singan	*Infl. Inf.*	tō singenne
Pres. Ptc.	singende	*Past Ptc.*	(ġe-)sungen

Participles may be declined like adjectives. Strong and weak forms occur, as appropriate.

§112   In the present tense, note:

1   The stem vowel of the inf. appears throughout except in 2nd and 3rd pers. sg. pres. ind., where its *i*-mutated equivalent is found if there is one. Hence *sing(e)st*, *sing(e)þ* but (< *bēodan*) *bīetst*, *bīett*.

2   The common WS reduction in these forms whereby the *e* of the endings *-est* and *-eþ* disappears – i.e. syncopation (see Appendix D for a definition of syncopation). If this leaves a combination which is difficult to pronounce, it is simplified. So from *bīdan* 'wait for', we get *bīdeþ* > *bīdþ > *bītþ > *bītt*. (Following the loss of *e* in *bīdeþ*, the voiceless *þ* adjacent to the voiced consonant *d* causes *d* to become unvoiced, which produces *t*. Then the voiceless *t* adjacent to *þ* causes the *þ* to become *t*. This process of adjacent sounds undergoing changes in order to become more similar or identical to each other is called *assimilation*. For a definition of *assimilation* see Appendix D.) Similarly, *bīteþ* from *bītan* 'bite' is also reduced to *bītt*. Hence theoretically *se mann bītt þæt wīf* could mean 'the man is waiting for the woman' or 'the man is biting the woman'.[1] But, when proper attention is paid to context, this ambiguity does not cause practical difficulty. The most important consequences for you are that 2nd pers. sg. pres. ind. ending in *-tst* and 3rd pers. sg. pres. ind. ending in *-tt* may be from verbs with *-tan* (e.g. *bītan*), *-dan* (e.g. *bīdan*), or *-ddan* (e.g. *biddan*). Since *-sest* and *-seþ* both become *-st*, *cīest* may be either 2nd or 3rd pers.[2]

3   The endings of the imp. – sg. NIL, pl. *-aþ*.

4   The imp. pl. is the same as the pres. ind. pl.

5   The subj. endings are sg. *-e* and pl. *-en*, which also occur in the pret.

6   The pres. subj. sg. is the same as the 1st pers. sg. pres. ind.

§113   In the preterite tense, note:

1   The so-called pret. sg. occurs in TWO PLACES ONLY – 1st and 3rd sg. pret. ind. Hence it is better called the 1st pret.

---

[1] *Bīdan* 'wait for' can take gen. or acc.   [2] See further, Appendix A.

2   The vowel of pret. pl. (better called the 2nd pret.) is found in all other places in the pret. Hence *þu sunge* may be either pret. ind. or pret. subj.

3   In actual practice, a similar ambiguity exists throughout the pret. pl. Many primers and grammars show *-on* as the ind. ending and *-en* as the subj. ending. But this distinction does not always hold in the manuscripts. This is because the process which led to the reduction of all the inflexional endings to *-e*, *-es*, *-en*, and so on, in ME had already begun in OE. MnE, with its fixed spelling system, still spells differently the second syllables of 'sofa', 'beggar', 'baker', 'actor', and (in some places) 'honour', all of which are pronounced the same by many speakers in Great Britain, and by many in other countries. But in OE the spelling system tended to be more phonetic and we often find scribes writing down in the manuscripts forms which represent the pronunciation they actually used and not the forms which are shown in the grammars. As a result, you may find in your reading pret. pl. forms ending, not only in *-on* and *-en*, but also in *-æn*, *-an*, and *-un*. Any of these may be ind. or subj. Hence the only places in the pret. of the strong verbs where ind. and subj. are clearly distinguished are the two places where the ind. has the 1st pret. form; see 1 above.

4   The variations in the medial cons. caused by Verner's Law; see §§107–108.

§114   Two groups of strong verbs present special difficulties in the present tense. The first – those in classes V and VI with weak presents – are discussed in §116. The others are the contracted verbs, exemplified here by *sēon* V 'see'. Only the present tense is given, for in the pret. it follows the rules given above.

		Present Indicative			*Present Subjunctive*
Sg. 1		sēo			sēo
	2	si(e)hst			sēo
	3	si(e)hþ			sēo
Pl.		sēoþ			sēon
Imp. Sg.		seoh		*Pl.*	sēoþ
Inf.		sēon		*Infl. Inf.*	tō sēonne
Pres. Ptc.		sēonde			

Note

We have already seen in §103.3 that *sēon* is a form produced by breaking and loss of *h*. The whole of the pres. tense except 2nd and 3rd sg. pres. ind. (forms which always require special attention in both strong and weak verbs) is affected by these two sound-changes, e.g.

1st sg. pres. ind. *iċ sehe > *iċ seohe > *iċ sēoe > iċ sēo

and so on for the other forms. But the 2nd and 3rd sg. pres. ind. are different. The vowel changes are the result of *i*-mutation; see §112.1. But *h* occurs in these forms because the *e* of the ending disappeared (see §112.2) before the *h* could be lost between vowels. Because the *h* did not disappear, the vowels remained short; cf. the imp. sg. *seoh*.

You may care to note that the pres. subj. sg. is the same as the 1st per. sg. pres. ind. (*sēo*) and that the subj. pl. and the inf. are the same (*sēon*). This is true of all contracted verbs.

VII WEAK VERBS AND SOUND-CHANGES RELEVANT TO THEM

Introduction

§115   There are three classes of weak verbs in OE. As in MnE, these verbs form their pret. and their past ptc. by the addition of a dental suffix. Normally the stem vowel is the same throughout; for exceptions, see §§122–123 and 126. As will become apparent, the inflexional endings of the strong and weak verbs have much in common.

Class I

§116   Class I of the weak verbs is divided into two sub-classes:

(*a*) exemplified by *fremman* 'do' and *nerian* 'save';
(*b*) exemplified by *hīeran* 'hear'.

Present Indicative

		(*a*)	(*a*)	(*b*)
Sg.	1	fremme	nerie	hīere
	2	fremest	nerest	hīerst
	3	fremeþ	nereþ	hīerþ
Pl.		fremmaþ	neriaþ	hīeraþ

Imperative

	(*a*)	(*a*)	(*b*)
Sg.	freme	nere	hīer
Pl.	fremmaþ	neriaþ	hīeraþ

Present Subjunctive

	(*a*)	(*a*)	(*b*)
Sg.	fremme	nerie	hīere
Pl.	fremmen	nerien	hīeren

Preterite Indicative

		(*a*)	(*a*)	(*b*)
Sg.	1	fremede	nerede	hīerde
	2	fremedest	neredest	hīerdest
	3	fremede	nerede	hīerde
Pl.		fremedon	neredon	hīerdon

Preterite Subjunctive

Sg.	fremede	nerede	hīerde
Pl.	fremeden	nereden	hīerden
Inf.	fremman	nerian	hīeran
Infl. Inf.	tō fremmenne	tō nerienne	tō hīerenne
Pres. Ptc.	fremmende	neriende	hīerende
Past Ptc.	(ġe-)fremed	(ġe-)nered	(ġe-)hīered

Participles may be declined like adjectives; cf. §111.

Like *fremman* are most verbs with short vowel + a double consonant, e.g. *cnyssan* 'knock'. The strong verbs of classes V and VI such as *biddan* 'pray' and *hebban* 'lift' are like *fremman* THROUGHOUT THE PRESENT.[1]

Like *nerian* are nearly all verbs ending in *-rian* (for exceptions, see §132.1). The class VI strong verb *swerian* is like *nerian* THROUGHOUT THE PRESENT.

Like *hīeran* are verbs with a long vowel + a single consonant, e.g. *dēman* 'judge', and verbs with a short vowel + two consonants not the same, e.g. *sendan* 'send'. A few verbs of the same pattern as *fremman*, but with a different history, also belong here; they include *fyllan* 'fill'. The strong verb *wēpan* (class VII(*a*)) is like *hīeran* THROUGHOUT THE PRESENT. Its past ptc. is *wōpen*.

As is shown in §117, all the verbs of this class have an *i*-mutated vowel throughout the stem except those discussed in §§122–123.

§117   A glance at the conjugation of these three verbs will show that *fremman* sometimes loses an *m*, *nerian* its *i*, and that (compared with *fremman* and *nerian*) *hīeran* sometimes loses an *e* in the inflexional endings. These 'losses' (an unhistorical name, as we shall see below) occur in the following places:

1   2nd and 3rd sg. pres. ind.;
2   imp. sg.;
3   throughout the pret. The pret. stems of these three verbs are respectively *fremed-* (with one *m*), *nered-* (with no *i*), and *hīerd-* (with no *e*);
4   in the past ptc., except that *hieran* usually has *hīered*.

Note

These variations can be explained briefly as follows. The infinitive of *fremman* was once **framjan*.[2] The *j* – a high front sound – operated like *i* and caused *i*-mutation of *a*, which before *m* became *e*. But *j* had another property denied to *i*; in short-stemmed words it caused lengthening or doubling of any cons. (except *r*) which preceded it, and then disappeared. So **framjan* > *fremman*. In **nærjan* the *j* merely caused *i*-mutation and remained as *i*; hence *nerian*.

---

[1] The only verbs with double medial cons. which are strong throughout belong to class III (e.g. *swimman*, *winnan*) and to class VII (e.g. *bannan*, *feallan*). Verbs whose infinitives rhyme with any of these four are always strong. See further §133.5.
[2] *j* here and elsewhere is the sound written [j] in phonetic script and pronounced something like MnE *y* in 'year'. It is a high front sound which can be made by saying *i* and then closing the gap between the tongue and the hard palate.

But in the places where *fremman* 'loses' an *m*, the inflexional ending originally began with *i*. So e.g., the 3rd sg. pres. ind. of **framjan* was **framjiþ*. Here the *j* was absorbed into the *i* before it could cause doubling; so we get **framiþ*. The *i* caused *i*-mutation and then became *e*, giving *fremeþ*. Similarly **nærjiþ > *næriþ > nereþ*. Similarly, absence of *j* in the pret. gave *fremede* and *nerede*. In *hīeran* and the other verbs of sub-class (*b*), the details and the results are different, and can be taken on trust for the time being.

§118   Once these variations are understood, we can observe certain similarities in the inflexional endings of the weak verbs of class 1 and those of the strong verbs. These are

1   The pres. ind. endings of the weak verbs are the same as the endings of the strong verbs. The *-est* and *-eþ* of the 2nd and 3rd sg. pres. ind. are subject to the same reductions as occurred in these forms in the strong verbs (§112.2). However, the weak verbs generally show more unreduced forms than the strong verbs.

2   The pres. and pret. subj. endings are the same in both weak and strong verbs.

3   The pres. subj. sg. is the same as the 1st pers. sg. pres. ind.

4   The endings of the pret. pl. ind. are the same.

5   The endings of the imp. pl., the pres. ptc., and the infs. respectively are the same.

6   The imp. pl. is the same as the pres. ind. pl.

§119   Important differences are seen in

1   the imp. sgs. *freme* and *nere*, where the strong verbs have no final *-e*; cf. the weak verb *hīer* (see §117.2);

2   the pret. ind. sg., where the endings are *-e*, *-est*, *-e*.

§120   As in the strong verbs, the pret. pl. endings *-on* and *-en* can be ambiguous in some manuscripts; see §113.3. In lWS the 2nd sg. ending *-est* is often extended to the subj. Hence the pret. ind. and subj. can no longer be distinguished in the weak verbs.

§121   Certain simplifications occur in the pret. and the past ptc.:

1   If in forming the pret. a double consonant followed another consonant, it was simplified. Hence *sendan* has pret. *sende*, not **sendde*.

2   A ptc. such as *sended* may be simplified to *send*.

3   After voiceless sounds (e.g. *p*, *s*, *t*) the dental suffix becomes *t*, e.g. *mētan* 'meet' has *mētte*; cf. MnE 'judged' with 'crept'.

4   **-cd-* becomes *-ht-*. Hence *tǣċan* 'teach' has pret. *tǣhte*, past ptc. (*ġe-*)*tǣht*.

§122   In MnE we have some weak verbs which change their stem vowel in the pret. and the past ptc. as well as adding the dental suffix. They include 'sell/sold', 'tell/told', 'seek/sought', 'buy/bought', 'bring/brought', and 'think/thought', which were weak verbs of class 1 in OE and had the same irregularity even then. There were more of them in OE, for some have disappeared, e.g. *reċċan* 'tell', and some have become regular weak verbs, e.g. *streċċan* 'stretch'.[1] It is simplest just to recognize these in the first instance. The most important ones are

Inf.	*Pret. Sg.*	*Past Ptc.*
sēċan 'seek'	sōhte	sōht
sellan 'give'	sealde	seald
cwellan 'kill'	cwealde	cweald
þenċan 'think'	þōhte	þōht
brenġan 'bring'	brōhte	brōht
þynċan 'seem'	þūhte	þūht
bycgan 'buy'	bohte	boht
wyrċan 'work'	worhte	worht

§123　The irregularity of these verbs is due to the fact that there was no *i* in the pret. or the past ptc. to cause *i*-mutation. Hence, while their present tenses have an *i*-mutated vowel like all the other verbs of this class, the vowel of the pret. and past ptc. is unmutated. This can be seen clearly by comparing *sēċan* (< *sōkjan) with *sōhte/sōht*. However, the parallels in most verbs are obscured by other sound-changes which affected the vowel of the pret. and past ptc. They are

1　Breaking, e.g. *cwellan/cwealde*. Here the original *æ* has been *i*-mutated to *e* in the pres. and broken to *ea* by the *ld* in the pret.

2　Loss of *n* before *h* with lengthening of the preceding vowel so that the word takes the same time to pronounce. Hence *þenċan/þōhte*, *þynċan/þūhte*, and *brenġan/brōhte*. The strong inf. *bringan* usually replaces *brenġan*.

3　A change by which Gmc. *u* under certain conditions became OE *o*. This accounts for the variations in *bycgan/bohte* and *wyrċan/worhte*, where an original *u* has been *i*-mutated to *y* in the pres. and has changed to *o* in the pret.

4　On the derivation of weak verbs of class 1, see Appendix B.

Class 2

§124　The weak verbs of class 2 present few problems. The traditional paradigm is *lufian* 'love'. The long-stemmed *lōcian* 'look' has exactly the same endings.

---

[1] As you will see from §121.4, the verb *tǣċan* 'teach' usually has the same vowel throughout in WS, but *tāhte*, *tāht*, do occur.

		Present Indicative		Preterite Indicative
Sg.	1	lufie		lufode
	2	lufast		lufodest
	3	lufaþ		lufode
Pl.		lufiaþ		lufodon

		Present Subjunctive		Preterite Subjunctive
Sg.		lufie		lufode
Pl.		lufien		lufoden
Imp. Sg.		lufa	*Pl.*	lufiaþ
Inf.		lufian	*Infl. Inf.*	tō lufienne
Pres. Ptc.		lufiende	*Past Ptc.*	(ġe-)lufod

All weak verbs of class 2 have an infinitive ending in *-ian*. However, most verbs ending in *-rian* belong, not to class 2, but to class 1(*a*) following *nerian* (see §116). But *andswarian* 'answer', *gadrian* 'gather', *timbrian* 'build', and one or two other verbs in *-rian*, usually follow *lufian*.

§125 Points to note in the conjugation of *lufian* are

1 The *i* disappears in the 2nd and 3rd sg. pres. ind., the imp. sg., all forms of the pret., and the past ptc. These are exactly the same places where *fremman* 'loses' its *m*, *nerian* its *i*, and *hīeran* its *e*.

2 The *-a* in 2nd and 3rd sg. pres. ind. *lufast*, *lufaþ*, and in imp. sg. *lufa*. So far the verb ending *-aþ* has always signified imp. or pres. ind. pl. In these verbs, *-aþ* is sg., *-iaþ* pl. Take note of this when reading your texts.

3 The *-od* in the pret. stem *lufod-* and in the past ptc. *lufod* where *fremman* has *-ed*.

Otherwise, the weak verbs of classes 1 and 2 are conjugated the same.

Class 3

§126 Class 3 contains four weak verbs – *habban* 'have', *libban* 'live', *secgan* 'say', and *hycgan* 'think'. These are conjugated:

Present Indicative

Sg.	1	hæbbe	libbe	secge	hycge
	2	hæfst	leofast	sæġst	hyġst
		hafast	lifast	seġ(e)st	hogast
	3	hæfþ	leofaþ	sæġþ	hyġþ
		hafaþ	lifaþ	seġ(e)þ	hogaþ
Pl.		habbaþ	libbaþ, leofaþ	secgaþ	hycgaþ

Present Subjunctive

Sg.	hæbbe	libbe	secge	hycge
Pl.	hæbben	libben	secgen	hycgen

Imperative

Sg.	hafa	leofa	saga, seġe	hoga, hyġe
Pl.	habbaþ	libbaþ, leofaþ	secgaþ	hycgaþ

Preterite Indicative

Sg. 1, 3	hæfde	lifde, leofode	sæġde, sæde	hog(o)de
Sg. 2	hæfdest	lifdest, leofodest	sæġdest, sædest	hog(o)dest
Pl.	hæfdon	lifdon, leofodon	sæġdon, sædon	hog(o)don

Preterite Subjunctive

Sg.	hæfde	lifde, leofode	sæġde, sæde	hog(o)de
Pl.	hæfden	lifden, leofoden	sæġden, sæden	hog(o)den
Inf.	habban	libban	secġan	hyċgan
Pres. Ptc.	hæbbende	libbende	secġende	hyċġende
Pass. Ptc.	hæfd	lifd	sæġd	hogod

VIII ANOMALOUS VERBS

Bēon

§127 *Bēon*, *wesan* 'be' has forms from different stems.

Indicative	Pres.	Pres.	Pret.
Sg. 1	eom	beo	wæs
2	eart	bist	wære
3	is	biþ	wæs
Pl.	sind(on), sint	bēoþ	wæron

Subjunctive			
Sg.	sīe	bēo	wære
Pl.	sīen	bēon	wæren

Imperative			
Sg.	wes	bēo	
Pl.	wesaþ	bēoþ	

On the distinction in meaning between *eom* and *bēo*, see §196.

Dōn and *gān*

§128 *Dōn* 'do' and *gān* 'go' have

Present Indicative		
Sg. 1	dō	gā
2	dēst	gǣst
3	dēþ	gǣþ
Pl.	dōþ	gāþ
Imp. Sg.	dō	gā
Pret. Ind. Sg., pl.	dyde, dydon	ēode, ēodon
Past Ptc.	ġedōn	ġegān

Note

i-mutation in 2nd and 3rd pers. sg. pres. ind.

The remaining forms can be constructed with the help of §118.

Willan

§129   *Willan* 'wish, will' has

	Present Indicative	*Present Subjunctive*
Sg. 1	wille	wille
2	wilt	wille
3	wile	wille
Pl.	willaþ	willen
Pret.	wolde	

Preterite-Present Verbs

§130   Preterite-Present verbs are the OE antecedents of what in MnE are called 'modal auxilliaries' (see §§206–207 and *Modal Auxilliaries* in Appendix D). The two groups function in identical ways. Some MnE modal auxiliaries are *can*, *may*, *shall*, and *must* (the OE forms being *cann*, *mæg*, *sceal*, and *mōste*.) The first thing to notice about these verbs is that they do not take the ending *-s* in the third person singular present indicative. The non-preterite-present verbs *I plan*, *he plans* and *I fan*, *he fans* follow the normal pattern of adding *-s* to the third person form (*he plans*). But in the modal auxiliaries we have *I can*, *he can*. Similarly, *I play*, *he plays* contrasts with the preterite-present *I may*, *he may*. Also, the modal auxiliaries (and the OE preterite-presents) when they combine with an infinitive do not take the infinitive sign *to*. Whereas we normally say 'I intend to do it' and 'I want to go', the modal auxiliaries say 'I can go' and 'I shall speak'. Similarly, in OE 'ic cann gān', 'ic sceal sprecan'. Although the MnE modal auxiliaries are often the same words as the OE preterite-presents (MnE *can*, OE *cann*; MnE *may*, OE *mæg*, MnE *dare*, OE *dearr*, MnE *shall*, OE *sceal*; etc.) there are some differences between the two groups. OE **dugan* 'avail', *gemunan* 'remember', OE *unnan* 'grant', OE *þurfan* 'need', OE *witan* 'know', have all died out, and other, non-preterite-present verbs have replaced them. OE *āgan* 'possess', and *mōtan* 'may' survive only in their preterite forms *ought* and *must* (with change of meaning). For changes of meaning in the other preterite-present verbs see §§206–211).

An examination of the origin of preterite-present verbs will explain why they are called 'preterite-present'. All of these verbs were originally strong verbs whose preterite forms acquired present-tense meanings, after which the original present-tense forms disappeared and new preterite forms were constructed by the addition of the weak-verb preterite suffix *-(e)d*. Thus **witan* 'know' was originally a strong Class I verb meaning 'see': **wītan*, *wāt*, *witon, witen*. But if one has seen something in the past, then one knows it in the present, and so the preterite forms *wāt, witon* 'saw' came to have the present meaning 'know'. Once this happened, new preterite forms were made by adding to the (originally preterite) root *wit-* the weak preterite endings *-de* and *-don*. Through normal sound changes *witede* and *witedon* then became *wiste* and *wiston* with the meaning 'knew'. The original strong present form *wītan* and its derivatives were then lost.

IX IS A VERB STRONG OR WEAK? TO WHICH CLASS DOES IT BELONG?

§131   If we assume that you can recognize on sight the strong contracted verbs, the four weak verbs of class 3 (§126), and the verbs discussed in §§127–130, the system set out below will enable you to answer the questions at the head of this section.

Verbs in *-ian*

§132   1   Verbs in *-rian* can be class 1 weak.
But note:

(*a*) *swerian* 'swear' (class VI strong with a weak present);
(*b*) *andswarian* 'answer' and a few other verbs which can follow *lufian* 'love'; see §124.

2   All other verbs in *-ian* are class 2 weak.

Verbs in *-an*

§133   These are either strong or class 1 weak. You will find that the recognition symbols for the strong verbs set out in §94 are almost always reliable. Thus if a verb ending in *-an* has *ī* + one cons. in the infinitive, it is probably class I strong. If it has *ū* + one cons., it is probably class II strong. And so on. Exceptions include

1   The strong verbs of classes V, VI, and VII (*wēpan* 'weep'), with weak presents. These too should be recognized on sight.
2   *Fēolan* 'press on' looks like class II strong, but belongs to class III, as the 1st pret. *fealh* shows. (*Felhan* > *feolhan* by breaking (§97.2) > *fēolan* by loss of *h* + lengthening; see §38.)
3   A verb with *ǣ* + one cons. may be either strong or weak; *lǣtan* 'let' is class VII strong, *lǣdan* 'lead' is class 1 weak.
4   For weak verbs with *ī* and *ēo*, see Appendix A.1 and 2.
5   Verbs with a short vowel + a double cons. are mostly weak class 1, e.g. *fremman*. The recognition symbols of the strong verbs of class III will enable

us to distinguish *swimman* 'swim' and *winnan* 'fight' as class III strong; note *i* before the nasals compared with the *e* of *fremman*. *Bannan* 'summon', *spannan* 'span', *feallan* 'fall', and *weallan* 'boil', are class VII strong. On *bringan*, see §123.2. On *hringan* and *ġeþingan*, see Appendix A.3.

§134   When you are reading Old English, your problem will often be to find the infinitive from which a certain verb form is derived. Let us take *bītt*, *stæl*, and *budon*, as examples.

For *bītt*, we note -*ī*- and -*tt*. Together these suggest the syncopated 3rd sg. pres. ind. of a strong verb of class I. The ending -*tt* we know to be a reduction of -*teþ* or -*deþ*. This gives us two possibilities – *bītan* 'bite' or *bīdan* 'await'. The context should determine which we have. In a text which does not mark long vowels, *bitt* could also be from *biddan* V 'ask'.

For *stæl* we note -*æ*-. This suggests the 1st pret. of class IV or V. Hence the inf. is *stelan* 'steal'. The medial *l* decides for class IV.

Budon is perhaps more difficult. Is it strong or (since it ends in -*don*) weak? If it is strong, the medial *u* and the single cons. suggest class II. Therefore the inf. could be *bēodan* or **būdan*. The glossary decides for *bēodan* 'command'. If it were a weak pret., the inf. would be *buan*. This would not fit *būan* 'dwell' with pret. pl. *būdon* unless the text did not mark long vowels. If this were the case, the context would again decide.

The verbs discussed in §122 present a problem, but you will soon become familiar with their preterites.

X   ADVERBS

Formation

§135   Characteristic endings of adverbs are -*e* (e.g. *hraþe* 'quickly'), -*līċe* (e.g. *hrædlīċe* 'quickly'), and -*unga* (e.g. *eallunga* 'entirely'). The ending -*an* usually means 'from', e.g. *norþ* 'north, northwards' but *norþan* 'from the north'.

The gen. and dat. can be used adverbially; see §§190 and 191.

The negative adverb is *ne*. For its use, see §184.4.

Comparison

Adverbs are normally compared by adding -*or*, -*ost*, e.g. *oft* 'often' *oftor oftost*, and (dropping the -*e* of the positive) *swīþe* 'greatly' *swīþor swīþost*.

Some have an *i*-mutated vowel in the comparative and superlative, e.g. *lange* 'long' *leng lengest* and *feorr* 'far' *fierr fierrest*.

A knowledge of the equivalent OE adjectives and MnE adverbs will enable you to recognize in reading the irregular comparatives and superlatives of the adverbs *wel* 'well', *yfle* 'evilly', *miċle* 'much', and *lȳt* 'little'.

4

Word Formation

INTRODUCTION

§136   Old English acquired new words in three ways – by borrowing from other languages (see §234), by making compounds of two words already existing in the language, e.g. *sǣ-weall* 'sea-wall', and by adding affixes to existing words to change their function or meaning, e.g. *blōd* (neut.) 'blood' but *blōd-iġ* 'bloody, blood-stained', and *bēodan* 'command' but *for-bēodan* 'forbid'. A knowledge of these last two methods and of the formative elements used will help you to deduce the meaning of many words which may at first sight seem unfamiliar.

In MnE we are able to use the same word as more than one part of speech without changing its form: *wound* can function as a noun ('the wound is painful', 'he gave him that wound', 'he was healed from the wound') or as a verb ('they wound the man', 'you wound the man', 'I wound him'). But in OE the noun form of a word like *wund* 'wound' is clearly differentiated from the verb *wundian* because of the distinctive grammatical endings which the two parts of speech take. The noun has forms like 'sīo *wund* is sāre,' 'hē forgeaf him þā *wunde*, 'hē wæs fram ðære *wunde* gehǣled,' while the verb has forms like hīe *wundiaþ* þone mann', 'þū *wundast* þone mann', 'ic *wundie* hine'. Similarly MnE *open* can serve as both adjective and verb without change of form, whereas the OE adj. *open* takes entirely different forms from the verb *openian*. Sometimes the noun form of an OE word (e.g. *weorc* 'work') is further distinguished from the verb form by i-umlaut (*wyrċan* 'to work'). See the examples of Class 1 weak verbs in Appendix B. The expansion of the OE vocabulary by making two different parts of speech out of one word (through the addition of appropriate endings, i-umlaut, etc.) is a major means of word-formation in OE.

Notes

1   On the gender and declension of nouns formed by compounding or by the addition of suffixes or endings, see §§12, 13, and 41.

2   The work by Stephen A. Barney mentioned in §253 lists the most frequently used OE words, calls attention to related MnE words, and cites OE derivatives. This makes for ease of learning, and is one of the reasons why the book is so useful.

A Guide to Old English, Eighth Edition. Bruce Mitchell and Fred C. Robinson.
© 2012 Bruce Mitchell and Fred C. Robinson. Published 2012 by Blackwell Publishing Ltd.

I COMPOUNDING

§137 The process of forming new words or compounds by joining together two separate words which already exist was common in OE. Some of the possible arrangements are exemplified below.

Nouns can be formed by combining

1 Noun and noun, e.g. *hell-waran* (masc. pl.) 'inhabitants of hell', *niht-waco* (fem.) 'night-watch', *scip-rāp* (masc.) 'ship-rope', *storm-sǣ* (masc. or fem.) 'stormy sea';

2 Adjective and noun, e.g. *eall-wealda* (masc.) 'ruler of all', *hēah-clif* (neut.) 'high cliff', *hēah-ġerēfa* (masc.) 'high reeve, chief officer', *wīd-sǣ* (masc. or fem.) '(open) sea';

3 Adverb and noun, e.g. *ǣr-dæġ* (masc.) 'early day, first dawn', *eft-sīþ* (masc.) 'return', *inn-faru* (fem.) 'expedition', *inn-gang* (masc.) 'entrance'.

Adjectives are found consisting of

1 Noun and adjective, e.g. *ælmes-ġeorn* 'alms-eager, generous, charitable', *ār-weorþ* 'honour-worthy, venerable', *dōm-ġeorn* 'eager for glory', *mere-wēriġ* 'sea-weary';

2 Adjective and adjective, e.g. *hēah-þungen* 'of high rank', *hrēow-ċeariġ* 'sad' (lit. 'sad-anxious'), *wīd-cūþ* 'widely known', *wīs-hycgende* 'wise-thinking';

3 Adverb and adjective, e.g. *ǣr-gōd* 'very good', *forþ-ġeorn* 'forth-eager, eager to advance', *wel-þungen* 'well-thriven, excellent', *wel-willende* 'well-wishing, benevolent';

4 Adjective and noun, e.g. *blanden-feax* 'having mixed hair, gray-haired', *blīþe-mōd* 'of kindly mind, friendly', *hrēowiġ-mōd* 'gloomy-minded, sad', *salu-pād* 'dark-coated'.

In all these words the first element is uninflected; cf. *folc-lagu* (fem.) 'law of the people, public law' with *Godes* (gen.) *lagu* 'God's law' and *wīn-druncen* 'wine-drunk' with *bēore* (dat.) *druncen* 'drunk with beer'. But occasionally compounds do occur with an inflected first element, e.g. *Engla-lond* 'land of the Angles, England' (but cf. *Frēs-lond* 'Frisian land, Frisia') and *eges-full* 'full of terror, terrible, wonderful' (but cf. *synn-full* 'sinful').

Note
Compounds of three elements are sometimes found, e.g. *wulf-hēafod-trēo* (neut.) 'wolf-head-tree, gallows, cross'.

Today, when we are faced with a new object or idea, we often express it by a compound made up of foreign or of native elements, e.g. 'tele-gram' and 'astro-naut', but 'one-up-man-ship' and 'fall-out'. But OE more often 'translated' foreign words. Sometimes the elements of a foreign word were represented by OE equivalents, e.g. *god-spel* (neut.) 'good news', based on *evangelium*, for 'gospel',[1] *þrī-nes* (fem.) representing *Trini-tas* 'The Trinity', and Ælfric's grammatical terms *fore-set-nes* (fem.) for Lat. *prae-positio* 'preposition' and *betwux-āleġed-nes* (fem.) 'between-laid-ness' for Lat. *inter-jectio* 'interjection'. Sometimes the word was analysed into its concepts and these were rendered into English, e.g. two words for 'Pharisees' – *sundor-halgan* (masc. pl.) 'apart-holies' and *ǣ-lārēowas* (masc. pl.) 'law-teachers'. That these processes are now less natural for speakers of English can be seen in two ways. First, many native compounds such as *tungol-cræft* (masc.) 'star-craft' for 'astronomy' and *lār-hūs* (neut.) 'lore-house' for 'school' have disappeared from the language. Secondly, proposed replacements like the sixteenth-century 'hundreder' for 'centurion' or the nineteenth-century 'folk-wain' for 'bus' seem to us ridiculous, whereas the Germans use *Sauerstoff*, not 'Oxygen', and *Wasserstoff*, not 'Hydrogen'.

To help provide the many synonyms beginning with different letters which were essential for the *scop* (poet) working in the alliterative measure, the Anglo-Saxon poets made great use of compounds. Of special interest is the kenning, a sort of condensed metaphor in which (a) is compared to (b) without (a) or the point of the comparison being made explicit; thus one might say of the camel 'The desert-ship lurched on'. So the sea is *hwæl-weġ* (masc.) 'whale-way', a ship *ȳþ-hengest* (masc.) 'wave-horse', and a minstrel *hleahtor-smiþ* (masc.) 'laughter-smith'.

We find too that many set phrases inherited from the days when the poetry was composed orally survive in the lettered poetry. These 'oral-formulae' are set metrical combinations which could be varied according to the needs of alliteration. Thus the phrase 'on, over, across the sea' can be expressed by one of the prepositions *on, ofer, ġeond*, followed by the appropriate case of one of the following words: *bæþ-weġ* 'bath-way', *flōd-weġ* 'flood-way', *flot-weġ* 'sea-way', *hwæl-weġ* 'whale-way' (all masc.), *hran-rād* 'whale-road', *swan-rād* 'swan-road', and *seġl-rād* 'sail-road' (all fem.). References to further discussions on these points will be found in §§265–266.

II THE ADDITION OF AFFIXES

§138 These can be divided into prefixes – elements placed at the beginning of words to qualify their meaning – and suffixes. The effect of many which survive today is obvious; we may cite the prefix *mis-* as in *mis-dǣd* (fem.) 'misdeed', prepositions or adverbs used as prefixes, e.g. *ofer-mæġen* (neut.) 'superior force' and *ūt-gān* 'go out', and, with suffixes, adjectives

---

[1] You should look up the noun 'gospel' in O.E.D. to find out why *godspel* has *ŏ* when the OE equivalent of 'good' is *gōd*.

ending in *-full*, *-isċ*, and *-leas*, e.g. *synn-full* 'sinful', *ċild-isċ* 'childish', and *feoh-lēas* 'moneyless, destitute', and nouns ending in *-dōm*, *-ere*, *-scipe* (all masc.) and *-nes*, *-nis*, *-nys* (fem.), e.g. *wīs-dōm* 'wisdom', *fisc-ere* 'fisherman', *frēond-scipe* 'friendship', and *beorht-nes* 'brightness'. Others which occur frequently but are not so easily recognizable are set out below.

Prefixes

ā-   1   Sometimes it means 'away', as in *ā-fȳsan* 'drive forth'.

2   But sometimes it seems to have no effect on the meaning, e.g. *ā-galan* 'sing'.

æ̇ġ-   It generalizes prons. and advs., e.g. *æ̇ġ-hwā* 'everyone' and *æ̇ġ-hwǣr* 'everywhere'.

be-   1   In some words *be-* is the same as the prep. 'about', e.g. *be-gān* 'surround' and *be-rīdan* 'ride round, surround'.

2   Sometimes it is a deprivative, e.g. *be-dǣlan* 'deprive' and *be-hēafdian* 'behead'.

3   It can make an intransitive verb transitive, e.g. *be-þenċan* 'think about' and *be-wēpan* 'bewail'.

for-   It is an intensifier, e.g. *for-bærnan* 'burn up, consume', *forelorenness* (fem.) 'perdition', and *for-heard* 'very hard'.

ġe-   1   In some nouns it has the sense of 'together', e.g. *ġe-fēra* (masc.) 'companion' and *ġe-brōþru* (masc. pl.) 'brothers'.

2   In verbs, it sometimes has a perfective sense, e.g. *ġe-āscian* 'find out' and *ġe-winnan* 'get by fighting, win'; hence its frequent use in past ptcs.

on-, an-   1   In verbs like *on-bindan* 'unbind' and *on-lūcan* 'unlock', it has a negative sense.

2   Sometimes it means 'against', as in *on-rǣs* (masc.) 'attack'.

or-   1   This is a deprivative in *or-mōd* 'without courage, despairing' and *or-sorg* 'without care, careless'.

2   It can also mean 'early, original, primaeval' (cf. *or* (neut.) 'beginning, origin'), e.g. *or-eald* 'of great age', *or-ieldu* (fem.) 'extreme old age', and *or-þanc* (masc.) 'inborn thought, ingenuity, skill'.

tō-   1   Sometimes it is the same as the prep. *tō*, e.g. *tō-cyme* (masc.) 'arrival' and *tō-weard* (prep.) 'towards'.

2   But with verbs it frequently means separation, e.g. *tō-drīfan* (trans.) 'drive apart, disperse, scatter' and *tō-faran* (intrans.) 'go apart, disperse'.

un-   1   This is sometimes a negative prefix, e.g. *un-friþ* (masc.) 'un-peace, war' and *un-hold* 'unfriendly'.

2   Sometimes it is pejorative, as in *un-ġiefu* (fem.) 'evil gift' and *un-weder* (neut.) 'bad weather'.

wan-   This is a deprivative or negative prefix, e.g. *wan-hāl* 'not hale, ill' and *wan-hoga* (masc.) 'thoughtless man'.

wiþ-   Its primary sense in compounds is 'against', e.g. *wiþ-cēosan* 'reject', *wiþ-cweþan* 'reply, contradict', *wiþ-drīfan* 'repel', and *wiþ-feohtend* (masc.) 'enemy, opponent, rebel'.

ymb-   This means 'around', e.g. *ymb-gang* (masc.) 'circuit, circumference' and *ymb-lǣdan* 'lead round'.

Suffixes

Nouns

-aþ, -oþ   This forms masc. nouns, e.g. *herg-aþ* 'plundering' and *fisc-oþ* 'fishing'.

-end   This equals '-er', as in *Hǣl-end* (masc.) 'Healer, Saviour' and *wīg-end* (masc.) 'fighter, warrior'. It derives from the pres. ptc. ending *-ende*.

-hād   This introduces masc. nouns and equals MnE '-hood', as in *ċild-hād* 'childhood' and *woruld-hād* 'secular life'.

-ing   1   In masc. nouns it means 'son of', e.g. *Ælfred Æþelwulf-ing* 'Alfred son of Æthelwulf', or 'associated with', e.g. *earm-ing* 'wretch' and *hōr-ing* 'adulterer, fornicator'.
             2   In fem. nouns, it equals *-ung*; see below.

-mǣl   1   The noun *mǣl* (neut.) 'measure, fixed time' appears in compound nouns, e.g. *fōt-mǣl* (neut.) 'foot's length, foot' and (with the dat. pl. used adverbially; see §191.3) *floc-mǣlum* 'in (armed) bands' and *ġēar-mǣlum* 'year by year'.
             2   In the sense 'mark, sign', it appears in compound nouns, e.g. *fȳr-mǣl* (neut.) 'fire-mark', and also in compound adjectives; see below.

-rǣden   This forms fem. abstract nouns, e.g. *hierd-rǣden* 'guardian-ship, care, guard'.

-þ(o), -þ(u)   This is used to form fem. abstract nouns, e.g. *fǣh-þ(o)* 'hostility' and *ierm-þ(u)* 'misery, poverty'. Note that *ġeogoþ* 'youth' is fem.

-ung, -ing   This is found in fem. abstract nouns formed from verbs, e.g. *bod-ung* 'preaching' and *rǣd-ing* 'reading'.

Adjectives

-en   1   This is the ending of past ptcs. of strong verbs.
             2   It is also found in adjectives with an *i*-mutated vowel in the stem, e.g. *ǣttr-en* 'poisonous' and *ġyld-en* 'golden'.

-*iġ*	This equals MnE '-y', as in *cræft-iġ* 'powerful, mighty' and *hāl-iġ* 'holy'.
-*liċ*	This, originally the same word as *līċ* (neut.) 'body', equals MnE '-ly, -like', e.g. *heofon-liċ* 'heavenly' and *ċild-liċ* 'child-like, childish'.
-*mǣl*	This element, listed above under Nouns, also occurs in compound adjectives, e.g. *grǣg-mǣl* 'of a grey colour', *hring-mǣl* 'ring-marked, ornamented with a ring', and *wunden-mǣl* 'with curved markings'.
-*sum*	This occurs in words like *wynn-sum* 'delightful, pleasant' (cf. 'winsome') and *hīer-sum* 'hear-some, obedient'.

Adverbs

See §135.

Verbs

-*an*	The most common infinitive ending for strong and weak verbs. (For the -*an* in class 1 weak verbs, which was originally **-jan*, see Appendix B.)
-*ian*	The infinitive ending for class 2 weak verbs. Verbs borrowed from Latin are usually conjugated according to this class, e.g. *declinian* 'decline' < *declināre* and *predician* 'preach' < *praedi-cāre*.
-*rian*	See §132.1.
-*sian*	This is the infinitive ending of a subclass of weak 2 verbs formed from adjectives and nouns, e.g. *clǣnsian* 'cleanse' and *rīcsian* 'be powerful, reign'.
-*ettan*	This infinitive ending is used to form a subclass of weak 1 verbs from adjectives and nouns, e.g. *lāþ-ettan* 'hate, loathe', *līc-ettan* 'pretend', and *sār-ettan* 'lament'.
-*lǣċan*	This infinitive ending is also used to form a subclass of weak 1 verbs from adjectives and nouns, e.g. *ġe-ān-lǣċan* 'unite' and *ġe-þwǣr-lǣċan* 'consent'.

5

Syntax

INTRODUCTION

§139 Syntax has been described as the study of 'the traffic rules of language'. If this is so, you are offered here only a simplified Anglo-Saxon highway code, designed to deal with constructions likely to worry the beginner. OE syntax is recognizably English; in some passages the word order at least is almost without exception that of MnE. At other times, we seem to be wrestling with a foreign language. Some of the difficulties arise from idiosyncrasies due to the Germanic ancestry of OE. Another reason, which obtains mostly in the early writings when OE prose was in a formative state, is that Alfred and his companions were struggling to develop the language as a vehicle for the expression of complicated narrative and abstract thought. They achieved no little success, but had their failures too. The breathless but vigorous account of the Battle of Ashdown (the annal for 871 in the Parker MS of the Anglo-Saxon Chronicle), which sweeps us along on a surging current of simple sentences joined by *ond*, is not untypical of the early efforts of prose writers who were not translating from Latin. There is only one complex sentence in the whole piece (the last but one). That the writer gets into trouble with it is symptomatic; cf. the account of the sea-battle of 897 in the same manuscript, where what has happened is not particularly clear on first reading. This inability to cope with complicated ideas is more apparent in the translated texts, where the influence of the Latin periodic structure often produces stilted prose, as in the story of Orpheus and Eurydice in King Alfred's translation of Boethius. Even Alfred's original prose is sometimes twisted in the same way, e.g. the sentences discussed in §172. Perhaps Latin, being the language of the Church, the language from which many works were translated, and the only model available, was accorded a status denied to it (or to any other original) today.

§140 Another source of difficulty becomes apparent from a study of the major differences between OE and MnE. It is sometimes said that OE is the period of full inflexions, ME the period of levelled inflexions (all with the vowel *e*, e.g. *-e, -es, -en*, as opposed to the endings of OE with their different vowels), and MnE the period of no inflexions. This statement points to the vital truth that MnE depends on word-order and prepositions to make distinctions which in an inflected language are made by the case endings.

A Guide to Old English, Eighth Edition. Bruce Mitchell and Fred C. Robinson.
© 2012 Bruce Mitchell and Fred C. Robinson. Published 2012 by Blackwell Publishing Ltd.

However, it needs qualification. That there are still a few inflexions in MnE is of little importance. But it might be less misleading to say that OE is a 'half-inflected' language. Firstly, it has only four cases and remnants of a fifth left of the eight cases postulated for the original IE language. Secondly, as has been pointed out in §189 note, there is often no distinction in form between nominative and accusative. Hence word-order is often the only thing which enables us to tell which is subject and which is object; consider *Enoch gestrynde Irad and Irad gestrynde Mauiahel* (and so on) 'E. begat I. and I. begat M.' (contrast *Caesarem interfecit Brutus*) and *Hi hæfdon þa ofergan Eastengle and Eastsexe* 'They had then conquered the East Anglians and the East Saxons'. These and many similar examples support the view that the Anglo-Saxons already had the feeling that the subject came first. If we did not have evidence for this, we should have to hesitate instead of automatically following the modern rule and taking *Oswald and Ealdwold* as the subject in the following lines from *Maldon*, for the order object, subject, verb, is possible in OE (see §147):

> Oswold and Ealdwold   ealle hwile,
> begen þa gebroþru,   beornas trymedon

'O. and E., the two brothers, all the time encouraged the warriors'. (More is said in §147 on the triumph of the order 'subject verb'.) Thirdly, prepositions followed by an oblique case are often used to express relationships which could be expressed by case alone; cf. *ond þa geascode he þone cyning lytle werode . . . on Merantune* 'and then he discovered the king [to be] at Merton with a small band (inst. case alone)' with *eode he in mid ane his preosta* 'he went in with one of his priests (*mid* + inst. case)'. All these things suggest a language in a state of transition. The implications of this for the future development of English are mentioned briefly in §231; here we are concerned with it as another source of difficulty.

§141   Important differences between OE and MnE are found in the following:

the position of the negative (§§144.1 and 184.4);
the use of the infinitives (§205);
the uses of moods and tenses of the verb (§§195 ff.);
the resolved tenses[1] and the function of the participles therein (§§199 ff.);
the meaning of 'modal' auxiliaries (§§206 ff.);
agreement (§187);
the meaning and use of prepositions (§§213–214).

§142   Features found in OE, but not in MnE, include

strong and weak forms of the adjective (§§63 and 64);
some special uses of cases (§§188–192);

---

[1] This term is explained in §199.

some special uses of articles, pronouns, and numerals (§§193–194);

the use of a single verb form where MnE would use a resolved tense or mood (§195);

idiomatic absence of the subject (§193.7).

But the main difficulty of OE syntax lies, not in these differences, but in the word-order of the simple sentence or clause, and in the syntax of the subordinate clauses. These fundamental topics are accordingly treated first; if any of the points mentioned in this or the preceding section cause immediate difficulty, see the Contents and read the appropriate section. The order of clauses within the complex sentence is very similar to that of MnE, and will cause little difficulty.

I   WORD-ORDER[1]

§143   If we take subject and verb as the fundamental elements of a sentence, we shall find that the following arrangements are common in OE prose:

S.V., where the verb immediately follows the subject;

S. . . . V., where other elements of the sentence come between subject and verb;

V.S., where the subject follows the verb.

The same orders are also found in the poetry. But, like their successors, the Anglo-Saxon poets used the language much more freely than the prose writers did. Hence the comments made below apply to the prose only. But the word-order in the poetry will not cause you much difficulty if you understand what follows.

§144   As in MnE, the order S.V. can occur in both principal and subordinate clauses, e.g. *he hæfde an swiðe ænlic wif* 'he had a most excellent wife' and *þe getimbrode his hus ofer sand* 'who built his house on sand'. Therefore it cannot tell us whether a clause is principal or subordinate, except in the circumstances discussed in §§150 ff. It is also found after *ond* 'and' and *ac* 'but', e.g. *ond his lic liþ æt Winburnan* 'and his body lies at W.'.

There are naturally variations of this order. Some are found in both OE and MnE. Thus an adverb precedes the verb in *Se Hælend ða het þa ðeningmen afyllan six stænene fatu mid hluttrum wætere* 'The Saviour then ordered the servants to fill six stone vessels with pure water'. The indirect object precedes the direct object in *Romane gesealdon Gaiuse Iuliuse seofon legan* 'The Romans gave Gaius Julius seven legions', but follows it in *ac he forgeaf eorðlice ðing mannum* 'but he gave earthly things to men'.

[1] In these sections, the following abbreviations are used: S. (subject), V. (verb), O. (object), Adv (adverb or adv. phrase). A MnE sentence such as 'Do you sing?' is characterized by v. (auxiliary verb) S.V. Round brackets indicate that the feature in question is optional.

Arrangements not found in MnE are

1   The position of the negative *ne* 'not' immediately before the verb. This is the rule in all three OE word-orders; see §184.4.

2   The placing of a pronoun O., which would be unstressed, between S. and V. when a noun O., which would carry some stress, would follow V. Thus *we hie ondredon* 'we feared them' is an idiomatic variation of the order S.V. rather than an example of S. . . . V.

3   The possibility that an infinitive or a participle may have final position, e.g. *he ne meahte ongemong oðrum monnum bion* 'he could not be among other men' and *Eastengle hæfdon Ælfrede cyninge aþas geseald* 'The East Angles had given King Alfred oaths'. On the order S.V. in non-dependent questions, see §160.

§145   The order S. . . . V. is most common in subordinate clauses, e.g. *se micla here, þe we gefyrn ymbe spræcon* 'the great army which we spoke about before' and *gif hie ænigne feld secan wolden* 'if they wished to seek any open country', and after *ond* 'and' and *ac* 'but', e.g. *Ac ic þa sona eft me selfum andwyrde* 'But again I immediately answered myself'. But it also occurs in principal clauses, e.g. *Ða reðan Iudei wedende þone halgan stændon* 'The cruel Jews in their rage stoned the saint' and *Stephanus soðlice gebige-dum cneowum Drihten bæd . . .* 'Stephen however on bended knees besought the Lord . . .'. Hence the order S. . . . V. does not certify that a clause is subordinate. With this order, the verb need not have final position, but may be followed by an adverbial extension, e.g. *ær he acenned wæs of Marian . . .* 'before He was born of Mary' and *. . . þæt hi wel wyrðe beoð þære deoflican ehtnysse . . .* 'that they will be worthy of devilish persecution'. On this order in non-dependent questions, see §160.

§146   The order V.S. occurs in MnE in questions with the verbs 'to have' and 'to be', e.g. 'Have you the book?' and 'Are you there?', and in a few other set phrases or constructions, e.g. 'said he', 'Long live the King!', 'be he alive or be he dead', and 'Had I but plenty of money, I would be in Bermuda'. It must not be confused with the normal interrogative word-order of MnE, which is v. S.V., e.g. 'Have you found him?', 'Is he coming?', and 'Do you see him?' In OE the order V.S. is found in

1   Positive non-dependent questions either with or without interrogative words, e.g. *Hwær eart þu nu, gefera?* 'Where are you now, comrade?' and *Gehyrst þu, sælida?* 'Do you hear, seaman?'

2   Negative non-dependent questions, e.g. *ne seowe þu god sæd on þinum æcere?* 'Did you not sow good seed in your field?'

3   Positive statements, e.g. *Wæs he Osrices sunu* 'He was Osric's son' and *Hæfde se cyning his fierd on tu tonumen* 'The king had divided his army in two'.

4   Negative statements, e.g. *Ne com se here* 'The army did not come'.

5   In subordinate clauses of concession and condition, e.g. *swelte ic, libbe ic* 'live I, die I', i.e. 'whether I live or die'.

6 In principal clauses introduced by certain adverbs; cf. MnE 'Then came the dawn'. On the value of this word-order for distinguishing principal from subordinate clauses, see §§150 ff.

Notes

1 The orders described in 3 and 4 above are NOT necessarily emphatic.

2 In Matthew 20:13, we read: *Eala þu freond, ne do ic þe nænne teonan; hu, ne come þu to me to wyrcenne wið anum peninge?* 'Friend, I do thee no wrong; lo, didst thou not come to me to work for one penny?' Here exactly the same word-order is used first in a statement (order 4 above) and then in a question (order 2 above).

§147 Other word-orders may, of course, occur. Some which are used for emphasis are also found in MnE, e.g. *Gesælige hi wurdon geborene* . . . 'Blessed they were born', *Micelne geleafan he hæfde* . . . 'Great faith he had', and (with a MnE preposition replacing the OE dative case) *þam acennedan Cyninge we bringað gold* . . . 'To the newborn King we bring gold' and *Gode ælmihtgum sie ðonc* 'To God Almighty be thanks'. But the order O.V.S. found in *deman gedafenað setl* 'a seat is the proper place for a judge' would be impossible today because, in a MnE sentence of the pattern 'Man flees dog', what precedes the verb must be the subject. Consider what happens to the meaning of the spoken sentence if the word-order is altered. 'Dog flees man', 'Fleas dog man', and even 'Fleas man dog', all mean something different. The absence of endings and the interchangeability of MnE parts of speech have left word-order the only guide and the absolute master. The gradual triumph of this order S.V.O. is one of the most important syntactical developments in English. Its beginnings can be seen in OE. Thus in Matthew 7:24 *ælc þæra þe þas min word gehyrð and þa wyrcð, bið gelic þæm wisan were, se his hus ofer stan getimbrode*, the two subordinate clauses have S. . . . V. But in Matthew 7:26 *And ælc þæra þe gehyrð þas min word, and þa ne wyrcð, se bið gelic þam dysigan men, þe getimbrode his hus ofer sandceosel*, they both have S.V. This suggests that any difference there may have been between these orders was disappearing. Again, the old preference for V.S. after an adverb (compare modern German) is at times conquered by the new preference for S.V., e.g. *Her cuomon twegen aldormenn* 'In this year two chiefs came' but *Her Hengest 7 Æsc fuhton wiþ Brettas*[1] 'In this year H. and A. fought against the Britons'. Of course, in OE, where the distinction between the nominative and accusative is not always preserved, freedom sometimes leads to ambiguity, e.g. *Ðas seofon hi gecuron* . . . , where only the context tells us that *hī* is the subject. In MnE 'these seven they chose' is unambiguous because of 'they' and because, while the order O.S.V. is possible, the order S.O.V. is not.

---

[1] 7 is a common MS abbreviation for *ond* which is often reproduced by editors.

II SENTENCE STRUCTURE

Three difficulties in sentence structure must now be discussed.

Recapitulation and Anticipation

§148   The first is this. In their attempts to explain complicated ideas, Anglo-Saxon writers often had recourse to a device similar to that used by some modern politician who has the desire but not the ability to be an orator, viz. the device of pausing in mid-sentence and starting afresh with a pronoun or some group of words which sums up what has gone before. A simple example will be found in Alfred's Preface to the translation of the *Cura Pastoralis*. Alfred, having written (or dictated) *Ure ieldran, ða ðe ðas stowa ær hioldon* 'Our ancestors who previously occupied these places' pauses as it were for thought and then goes on *hie lufodon wisdom* 'they loved wisdom', where *hīe* sums up what has gone before and enables him to control the sentence. Compare with this the orator's gesture-accompanied 'all these things' with which he attempts to regain control of a sentence which has run away from him. Other examples of recapitulatory pronouns will be found in *7 þæt unstille hweol ðe Ixion wæs to gebunden, Leuita cyning, for his scylde, ðæt oðstod for his hearpunga. 7 Tantalus se cyning ðe on ðisse worulde ungemetlice gifre wæs, 7 him ðær ðæt ilce yfel filgde ðære gifernesse, he gestilde* 'And the ever-moving wheel to which Ixion, King of the Lapithae, was bound for his sin, [that] stood still for his (Orpheus') harping. And King Tantalus, who in this world was greedy beyond measure and whom that same sin of greed followed there, [he] has rest'. More complicated examples will be found in *hergode he his rice, þone ilcan ende þe Æþered his cumpæder healdan sceolde* 'He (Hæsten) ravaged his (Alfred's) kingdom, that same province which Æthered, his son's godfather, had the duty of holding', where *his rīce* is qualified by the rest of the sentence, and in the second passage discussed in §172.

The common use of a pronoun to anticipate a noun clause may be compared with this. A simple example is

> þa þæt Offan mæg   ærest onfunde,
> þæt se eorl nolde   yrhðo geþolian

lit. 'When the kinsman of Offa first learned that thing (the first *þæt*), that the leader would not tolerate cowardice'. We have perhaps all had this experience at the hand of some leader, but MnE would dispense with the tautologic *þæt* in giving it expression. In *þæs ic gewilnige and gewysce mid mode, þæt ic ana ne belife æfter minum leofum þegnum.* 'That thing I desire and wish in my mind, that I should not remain alone after my beloved thanes', the pronoun *þæs* anticipates the following *þæt* clause. It is in the genitive after the verbs *ġwilnian* and *ġewyscan*. The pronoun *hit* is sometimes found similarly used, e.g.

> þæt is micel wundor
> þæt hit ece God   æfre wolde
> þeoden þolian,   þæt wurde þegn swa monig
> forlædd be þam lygenum . . .

Here the first *þæt* is in apposition with the *þæt* clause in l. 2 while *hit* anticipates the *þæt* clause in l. 3: lit. 'That is a great wonder that eternal God the Lord would ever permit it, that so many a thane should be deceived by those lies'. Dependent questions may be similarly anticipated, e.g. *Men þa þæs wundrodon, hu þa weargas hangodon* lit. 'Men then wondered at that, how the criminals hung' (where *þæs* is genitive after *wundrodon*) and

> Hycgað his ealle,
> hu ge hi beswicen

lit. 'All [of you] take thought about it, how you may deceive them' (where *his* is genitive after *hycgað*).

Note

It is possible that in the sentence 'He said that he was ill', 'that' was originally a demonstrative – 'He said that: he was ill' – which gradually became a part of the noun clause. If so, the introduction of the second *þæt* or of *hit* illustrates how our ancestors proceeded in collecting and expressing complicated thoughts.

The Splitting of Heavy Groups

§149 The second thing which sometimes helps to make OE seem a foreign language is a tendency to split up heavy groups. Thus we say today 'The President and his wife are going to Washington'. But the more common OE arrangement was 'The President is going to Washington, and his wife'. Examples of this tendency are common. We find

1 A divided subject in *eower mod is awend, and eower andwlita* 'your mind and your countenance are changed'. Note here the word-order S.V. and the singular verb; cf. MnE 'Tom was there and Jack and Bill and all the boys'.

2 A divided object in *þa he þone cniht agef 7 þæt wif* 'when he returned the child and the woman'.

3 A divided genitive group in *Inwæres broþur 7 Healfdenes* 'the brother of I. and H.'.

4 Divided phrases in *þa þe in Norþhymbrum bugeað ond on East Englum* 'those who dwell in Northumbria and East Anglia'.

5 Separation of adjectives governing the same noun in *þæt hi næfre ær swa clæne gold, ne swa read ne gesawon* 'that they never before saw such pure, red gold'.

But such groups are not always divided, e.g. *Her Hengest 7 Horsa fuhton wiþ Wyrtgeorne þam cyninge* 'In this year, H. and H. fought against King W.'.

Correlation

§150 The third thing which makes us feel that OE is a foreign language is its marked fondness for correlation. This may have its origin in, and so be a more sophisticated manifestation of, the same feeling of insecurity in the face of the complicated sentence which produced the awkward repetitions already discussed. But it later becomes a very important stylistic device which such an outstanding writer as Ælfric exploited to the full. Consider the following sentence from his Homily on the Passion of St. Stephen: *þider ðe Stephanus forestop, mid Saules stanum oftorfod, þider folgode Paulus, gefultumod þurh Stephanes gebedu* 'Where Stephen went in front, stoned by the stones of Saul, there Paul followed, helped by the prayers of Stephen'. Note:

1 that both the principal and subordinate clause contain the same elements;

2 the word-order S.V. in the subordinate clause *þider ðe Stephanus forestop* and V.S. in the principal clause *þider folgode Paulus*. This is regular OE (see §151) but produces a chiasmus;

3 that the word-order 'prepositional phrase + particle' in the first clause is reversed in the second. Again, both are good OE, but the change produces another chiasmus;

4 the change from *Saules* to *Paulus* – a sermon in itself.

It is (we can say) certain beyond all doubt that Ælfric was influenced by Latin prose style; it is hard to see how it could have been otherwise. But it is equally important to realize that this powerful and moving sentence – parallel yet doubly chiastic and with the effective contrast between Saul and Paul – contains nothing which is not 'good Old English'. It follows therefore that we must avoid the tendency (often found in critics of Milton's *Paradise Lost*) to rush around slapping the label 'Latinism' on anything which deviates in the slightest from our preconceived notions of the norms of ordinary speech.

§151 Much of the difficulty with correlative pairs arises from the fact that (with a few exceptions such as *gif . . . þonne* 'if . . . then') the conjunction and the adverb have the same form, e.g. *þa* can mean both 'when' and 'then'. For the interrogatives (with the possible exception of *hwonne* 'when, until') were not used to introduce adjective or adverb clauses in OE; see §159 n. 2. Sometimes the indeclinable particle *þe* is added to the conjunction, e.g. in the passage discussed in §150 *þider ðe* means 'whither' and *þider* 'thither'. But this is by no means the rule. Sometimes the context helps, e.g. we can safely translate *þa se cyng þæt hierde, þa wende he hine west* as 'When the king heard that, then he turned (reflexive) west'. But the word-order is an even more useful and reliable guide, for it may be taken as a pretty safe rule for prose that, when one of two correlative *þa* clauses has the word-order V.S., it must be the principal clause and *þa* must mean 'then'. The temporal clause introduced by *þa* 'when' may have the order S. . . . V., e.g. *þa he on* *lichoman wæs* 'when he was in the flesh', or S.V., e.g. *þa þunor ofslog XXIIII heora fodrera* 'when thunder killed twenty-four of their foragers'. The adverb *þā* may be repeated within the subordinate clause, e.g. *þa he þæt þa sumre tide dyde* 'when he did that on one particular occasion', where it need not of course be translated. Doubled *þā*, as in *ða þa seo boc com to us* 'when the book came to us' and *þa þa Dunstan geong man wæs* 'when Dunstan was a young man' usually introduces a subordinate clause, as the word-order in these examples testifies. Ælfric is very fond of this device.

§152   Other correlative pairs with which we can use word-order to determine which of the clauses is principal are

> *þonne . . . þonne* 'when . . . then'
> *þǣr . . . þǣr* 'where . . . there'
> *þider . . . þider* 'whither . . . thither'

On the distinction between *þā* and *þonne*, see §168, s.v. *þonne*.

Note

Correlative pairs to which this rule does not regularly apply include: *ǣr . . . ǣr, nū . . . nū, siþþan . . . siþþan, swā . . . swā, þanon . . . þanon, þēah . . . þēah*; on these, see §168. *þeah . . . hwæþre* 'though . . . yet' and *gif . . . þonne* 'if . . . then' present no problems. It should also be noted that the word-order S.V. often occurs after adverbs other than those discussed above; see §147 for an example after *Hēr*, and note *nu todæg hi under-fengon Stephenum* 'now today they received Stephen' and *On deaðe he wæs gesett . . .* 'he was placed in death . . .'. S.V. seems to be more common in such sentences when the subject is an unstressed pronoun, as in the last two examples, but often occurs with a noun subject, as in the example in §147. Compare §144.2.

Exceptions to the rule do exist. But you should view with suspicion any you meet, for the punctuation of some modern editions is sometimes at fault. Remember, however, that the rule does not apply to the poetry and that correlation is not essential, e.g.

> *þa he þa wið þone here þær wæst abisgod wæs, 7 þa hergas wæron þa gegaderode begen to Sceobyrig on Eastseaxum, 7 þær gcweorc worhtun, foron begen ætgædere up be Temese*

'When he was occupied against the army there in the west, and the [other] Danish armies were assembled at Shoebury in Essex, and had made a fortress there, they both went together up along the Thames'.

§153   The value of this rule can be demonstrated from the following complicated passage in the Old English version of Bede's account of the poet Cædmon (selection 9, paragraph 2):

> *Ond he for þon oft in gebeorscipe, þonne þær wæs blisse intinga gedemed, þæt heo ealle sceolden þurh endebyrdnesse be hearpan singan, þonne he geseah þa hearpan him nealecan, þonne aras he for scome from*

þæm symble ond ham eode to his huse. Þa he þæt þa sumre tide dyde, þæt he forlet þæt hus þæs gebeorscipes ond ut wæs gongende to neata scipene, þara heord him wæs þære neahte bedoden, þa he ða þær in gelimplicre tide his leomu on reste gesette ond onslepte, þa stod him sum mon æt þurh swefn ond hine halette ond grette ond hine be his noman nemnde.

We can begin by underlining the verbs in the second sentence: *dyde, forlēt . . . ond ūt wæs gongende, wæs . . . beboden, gesette ond onslēpte, stōd . . . ond . . . hālette . . . ond grētte . . . ond nemnde.* Now the corresponding conjunctions for these five verbs or groups of verbs are *þā . . . þā, þæt, þāra, þā . . . ðā,* and *þā. þæt* introduces a noun clause (§155) and *þāra* an adjective clause (§162). From our word-order rule, we know that '*þā* subject *þā*' introduces a subordinate clause, '*þā* V.S.' a principal clause. Hence the last *þā* means 'then', the syntax of the sentence is clear, and we can translate fairly literally: 'When he did that on one particular occasion, namely left the feast-hall and went out to the stall of the cattle, the care of which had been entrusted to him for that night [and] when in due time he stretched his limbs on the bed there and fell asleep, then a certain man appeared to him in a dream and saluted him and greeted him and called upon him by name'.

Similarly, in the first sentence, we have three *þonne* clauses, viz. *þonne þær wæs . . . , þonne hē geseah . . . þonne ārās hē. . . .* The rule instantly tells us that the last is the principal clause 'then he arose . . .'.

III NOUN CLAUSES

Introduction

§154 This heading traditionally comprehends dependent statements, desires (commands, wishes, etc.), questions, and exclamations. The OE patterns conform very closely to those of MnE, apart from the use of *þæt* and *hit* to anticipate a noun clause (see §148).

Dependent Statements and Desires

§155 Dependent statements are introduced by *þæt*, e.g. *ða ðohte he ðæt he wolde gesecan helle godu* 'then he thought that he would seek the gods of hell', or *þætte* (= *þæt þe*), e.g. *ic wene ðætte noht monige begiondan Humbre næren* 'I believe that there were not many beyond the Humber'. *þæt(te)* is sometimes repeated, as in the second sentence discussed in §172, and is sometimes not expressed, e.g. *Swa ic wat he minne hige cuðe* 'So I know he perceived my intention'.

Dependent desires are also introduced by *þæt*, e.g. *bæd þæt hyra randas rihte heoldon* '[he] requested that they should hold their shields properly', or *þætte*.

þæt clauses arc, however, more common in OE than their equivalent in MnE, for they are often found where we should use an accusative and infinitive (as in the last example, where we should say 'commanded them to hold their shields properly') or some other construction.

§156   The verb of the *þæt* clause may be indicative or subjunctive. Two questions arise – first, 'What is the significance of the two moods?' and second 'When must the subjunctive be represented in translation?' The first is usually answered in some such way as this:

The *indicative* is used when the content of the noun clause is presented as a fact, as certain, as true, or as a result which has actually followed or will follow.

When the *subjunctive* occurs, some mental attitude towards the content of the noun clause is usually implied; one of the following ideas may be present – condition, desire, obligation, supposition, perplexity, doubt, uncertainty, or unreality.

There is some truth in this. Thus the subjunctive is the natural mood in dependent desires, e.g. *ic ðe bebiode ðæt ðu do* . . . 'I command that you do . . .'. But the indicative sometimes occurs after verbs of commanding, compelling, and thc like, e.g. *he bebead Tituse his suna þæt he towearp þæt templ* and *and ðurh ðine halige miht tunglu genedest þæt hi ðe to hera ð*. Here the indicative cmphasizes that the action desired actually took place; hence the translations might read 'Titus carried out his father's command and destroyed the temple' and 'through your holy power you compel the stars to worship you'. These and similar clauses could be called result clauses or noun clauses with the indicative showing that the event actually took place.

Similarly, in dependent statements, the indicative shows that the speaker is certain of the factuality of what he says and is vouching for its truth, e.g. *ic wat þæt þu eart heard mann* 'I know that you are a hard man', . . . *ðe cyðan . . . ðæt me com swiðe oft on gemynd* . . . 'to make known to you that it has often come into my mind . . .', and *þonne wite he þæt God gesceop to mæran engle þone þe nu is deofol* 'let him know therefore that God created as a great angel the creature who is now thc devil'. But the subjunctive appears when no certainty is implied about a happening in the future, e.g. *Hit wæs gewitegod þæt he on ðære byrig Bethleem acenned wurde* 'It was prophesied that He should be born in the city of Bethlehem', when the truth of another's statement is not vouched for, e.g. *Be þæm Theuhaleon wæs gecweden . . . þæt he wære moncynnes tydriend, swa swa Noe wæs* 'About that Deucalion it was said that he was the father of mankind, as Noah was', or when it is denied, e.g. *Nu cwædon gedwolmen þæt deofol gesceope sume gesceafta, ac hi leogað* 'Now heretics said that some creations were the work of the devil but they lie'. This distinction between the indicative and the subjunctive is seen clearly in *Ne sæde þæt halige godspel þæt se rica reafere wære, ac wæs uncystig and modegode on his welum* 'The holy gospel did not say that the rich man was a robber, but that he was mean and exulted in his wealth'.

However, the rule does not tell the whole truth. The indicative does not always state a fact, e.g. *And gif hit gelimpþ þæt he hit fint* 'And if it happens that he finds it', nor does the subjunctive always imply uncertainty, doubt, or the like, e.g. *Mine gebroða, uton we geoffrian urum Drihtne gold, þæt we andettan þæt he soð Cyning sy, and æghwær rixige* 'My brothers, let us offer our Lord gold, that we may confess that He is [the] true King and rules everywhere'; they all believe this. Again, in *Se wisa Augustinus . . . smeade hwi se halga cyðere Stephanus cwæde þæt he gesawe mannes bearn standan æt Godes swyðran* 'The wise Augustine . . . enquired why the holy martyr Stephen said that he saw the Son of Man standing at God's right hand', the subjunctive *gesāwe* does not mean that Augustine is casting doubt on Stephen's statement; it is probably due in part to the 'attraction' of the subjunctive form *cwæde* and in part to the influence of the verb *cweðan* itself. For, when introducing a dependent statement, *cweðan* prefers the subjunctive, *cyðan* the indicative. This may reflect some original difference in meaning such as 'I (think and) give it as my opinion' as against a more objective 'I (know and) make it known'. Perhaps originally *cweðan* always had the subjunctive and *cyðan* the indicative, and perhaps this situation would have continued if language were always a strictly logical activity in which verbs of thinking took the subjunctive and verbs of knowing the indicative. But it is not. We tend to say 'I think he may come' and 'I know he will come'. But 'I know he may be here in ten minutes, but I can't wait' and 'I think that he is without doubt the cleverest boy in the school' show that no hard and fast rules can be laid down. Each situation must be judged on its merits.

Hence we may say that, while the rule set out above often works, fluctuation between the subjunctive and the indicative in OE noun clauses is often of little significance. It is just as dangerous to place too much reliance on the presence of a subjunctive in OE as it would be to draw firm conclusions about a modern speaker's attitude from the fact that he started his sentence with 'I know that . . .' rather than 'I think that . . .'.

So the answer to our second question 'When must the subjunctive be represented in translation?' can only be something indefinite like 'When the situation demands it'. It is, for example, unnecessary to bring out the fact that a verb of denying or supposing is followed by a subjunctive referring to some past act, for the verb 'to deny' or 'to suppose' is in itself enough to give a modern reader the necessary information. The subjunctive which will be most frequently represented in MnE is that in which some doubt or uncertainty arises over an action which, at the time of speaking, is still in the future. Such a subjunctive, of course, occurs most commonly in dependent desires.

Dependent Questions

§157 Questions fall into two main divisions – those in which the questioner seeks new information, e.g. *Hwær eart þu?* 'Where are you?' and *Hwy stande ge ealne dæg idele?* 'Why do you stand idle all day?', and those in which he asks his hearer to choose between alternatives expressed or implied in the question, e.g. *'Wilt þu we gað and gadriað hie?' Ða cwæð he: 'Nese'* ' "Do you wish us to go and gather them?" And he answered "No".' [But he could have answered 'Yes'.] Rhetorical questions may, of course, be of either type.

§158   Those questions which seek new information present little difficulty. The dependent question will include the interrogative word of the non-dependent question. This may be a pronoun (e.g. *hwā* 'who' and *hwæt* 'what'), an adjective (e.g. *hwelċ* 'which, what sort of'), or an adverb (e.g. *hū* 'how' and *hwær* 'where'). Other common adverbs are *hwider* 'whither', *hwanon* 'whence', *hwonne* 'when' (see §159 n. 2), *hwȳ* and *hwæt* 'why', and combinations of a preposition + an oblique case of *hwæt*, e.g. *tō hwæs* 'whither', *for hwon* and *for hwȳ* 'why'. These questions may be anticipated by a demonstrative or personal pronoun; see §148.

Note
Some of these interrogative words can also be used indefinitely, e.g. *hwā* can mean 'someone, anyone' and *hwær* 'somewhere, anywhere'.

§159   In MnE many of these interrogative words can also be used as relative pronouns, e.g. 'The man who . . .', 'The place where . . .', and so on. This use seems to stem (in part at least) from OE sentences of the type 'I know you, what you are' and 'Consider the lilies of the field, how they flourish', in which the main verb has as objects both a noun (or pronoun) and a clause containing a dependent question. A convenient OE example is a possible reading of *The Wanderer* ll. 23b–27

> ond ic hean þonan
> wod wintercearig   ofer waþema gebind,
> sohte sele dreorig   sinces bryttan,
> hwær ic feor oþþe neah   findan meahte
> þone þe in meoduhealle   mine wisse

'and I, miserable, with winter in my heart, made my way thence over the frozen expanse of the waves, sadly seeking the hall of a giver of treasure, [sadly seeking] far and near where I might find one who in the mead-hall might know of my origins'.

Here the two objects of *sōhte* are *sele* and the *hwær* clause.

Note 1
The first object of *sōhte* is *sinces bryttan* in our text (piece 16), where the attractive compound *seledrēorig* 'sad for a hall' is accepted. But the fact that this interpretation is possible emphasizes that the *hwær* clause is interrogative, not adjective. It could not qualify *bryttan*.

Similarly in

> Ne meahte hire Iudas . . .
> sweotole gecyþan   be ðam sigebeame
> on hwylcne se hælend   ahafen wære

hwylċne is strictly an interrogative introducing a noun clause, object of *gecȳþan*, and the literal sense is 'Nor could Judas . . . tell her beyond doubt about the victorious tree, [tell her] on which tree the Saviour was raised up'.[1] It is easy to see how such juxtaposition of noun and interrogative would lead to the use of the interrogative as a relative. But this stage has not been reached in OE.

Note 2
Hwonne 'when, until' is perhaps furthest advanced of all the OE interrogatives on the way to becoming a word which could introduce adverb and adjective clauses. Those who are interested may care to look at the ways in which *hwonne* is used in the following examples: *Andreas* l. 136 (noun clause); *Riddle* 31 l. 13 (adjective clause); *Genesis* l. 2603 (adverb clause of time 'when'); *Genesis* l. 1028 (adverb clause of time 'whenever'); and *Andreas* l. 400 (adverb clause of time 'until'). We have put in brackets the interpretation which seems to offer the most convenient translation. But careful consideration will show that an Anglo-Saxon might have regarded all these as noun clauses – if he or she ever thought about it.

§160   Non-dependent questions inviting a choice between alternatives (i.e. yes-or-no questions) can be asked in two ways in OE:

1   by the word-order V.S. (as in MnE) – for examples see §§146.1 and 146.2;
2   with *hwæþer* (*þe*) and the word-order S. . . . V., e.g. *Hwæþer þe þin eage manful is?* 'Is your eye evil?', or S.V., e.g. *Hwæðer ic mote lybban oðþæt ic hine geseo?* 'May I live until I see him?'

As in MnE, dependent questions of this type are normally introduced by an interrogative word – either *hwæþer* 'whether', e.g. *Lætaþ þæt we geseon hwæðer Elias cume* 'Let us see whether E. comes', or *gif* 'if', e.g. *frægn gif him wære niht getæse* 'asked if the night had been pleasant to him'. An occasional example like 'He asked was anybody there' occurs (e.g. *Elene* ll.157 ff.); in these the original word-order is retained but the tense has been changed.
   In the examples cited above, the alternative 'or not' is implied. But it is occasionally expressed, e.g. *Anra gehwylc wat gif he beswuncgen wæs oððe na*

---

[1] The OE relative construction occurs in

> . . . ond geflitu ræran
> be ðam sigebeame   on þam soðcyning
> ahangen wæs . . .

'to stir up controversy about the victorious tree on which the true King was crucified . . .'. Note the difference in mood – *wære* above but *wæs* here.

'Each man knows whether he was beaten, or not'. An unusual example of the type of question under discussion here occurs in *Genesis* ll. 531 ff., where the conjunctions are *þēah . . . þe* 'whether . . . or'.

The remarks made about mood in dependent statements also apply in general to dependent questions.

The Accusative and Infinitive

§161 This construction, well known in Latin, e.g. *Solon furere se simulavit* 'Solon pretended to be mad', and in MnE, e.g. 'I know him to be dead', is also an OE idiom. The subject accusative may be expressed, as in

> Het þa hyssa hwæne   hors forlætan,
> feor afysan,   and forð gangan

'He then ordered each of the warriors to release his horse [and] drive it away, and to go forth', but is often left unexpressed, as in *ond ðe cyðan hate* lit. 'I order [someone] to make known to you . . .', and *he het hi hon on heam gealgum* lit.'he ordered [someone] to hang them on the high gallows' (where *hī* is the object of *hōn*). In the last two examples, the subject accusative is not expressed, either because everybody knows or because nobody cares who is to perform the action. In these, it is very convenient to translate the infinitives *cyðan* and *hōn* as if they were passive – 'I order you to be told' (or '. . . that you be told . . .') and 'he ordered them to be hanged'. Much time has been spent in idle controversy over the question whether these infinitives were actually passive; what is important is that, when the subject accusative of the accusative and infinitive is not expressed, the active infinitive can usually be *translated* as a passive.

IV ADJECTIVE CLAUSES

Definite Adjective Clauses

§162 Definite adjective clauses are those which refer to one particular antecedent, e.g. 'This is the man *who did it*' as opposed to indefinite clauses whose antecedent is unspecified, e.g. '*Whoever did it* will be caught'. As in Latin, the relative pronoun agrees with its antecedent (expressed or implied) in number and gender, but takes its case from the adjective clause. There are various ways of expressing it in OE.

1   The indeclinable particle *þe* is very common when the relative is the subject, e.g. *Ic geseah þa englas þe eower gymdon* 'I saw the angels who took care of you', *ælc þæra þe ðas min word gehyrð* 'each of those who hears these my words', and *swa swa hit gewunelic is þæm ðe on wuda gað oft* 'as is customary among those who frequently go in the wood'. It occurs fairly often when the

relative is the object, e.g. *her onginneð seo boc þe man Orosius nemneð* 'here begins the book which one calls Orosius'. It very occasionally functions as a relative in the genitive or dative. Examples are *of ðæm mere ðe Truso standeð in staðe* 'from the sea *on whose* shore Truso stands' and *oð ðone dæg þe hi hine forbærnað* 'until the day *on which* they burn him'.

2 In these last two examples, however, the case of the relative pronoun is not immediately clear because *þe* is indeclinable. So the appropriate case of the third person pronoun was sometimes added. Thus there is no ambiguity in *Eadig bið se wer, þe his tohopa bið to Drihtne* 'Blessed is the man whose hope is in the Lord' or in

þæt se mon ne wat

þe him on foldan   fægrost limpeð

'That (object) the man for whom it goes very pleasantly on the earth does not know'.

Note

This combination sometimes occurs when the relative is nominative, e.g. *Paris Psalter* 67 l. 4 (*þe hē*) and, with first person pronouns, *Riddle* 12 l. 14 (*þe ic*) and *Christ* l. 25 (*þe wē*). With the second person pronoun the regular combination is *þū þe* or *gē þe*; see *The Review of English Studies* 15 (1964), 135–7.

3 The appropriate case of the demonstrative *se, sēo, þæt* is often used as a relative, e.g. *se hearpere, ðæs nama wæs Orfeus, hæfde an wif, seo wæs haten Eurydice* 'the harper, whose name was Orpheus, had a wife who was called Eurydice', *eall þæt ic geman* 'all that I remember', and *fif Moyses boca, ðam seo godcunde æ awriten is* 'five (of the) books of Moses in which the divine law is written'. Here there is no ambiguity about case and number, but we cannot always be sure whether the pronoun is demonstrative or relative.

4 But there is no ambiguity for us in sentences like . . . *and wæs se soþa Scyppend, seþe ana is God, forsewen* '. . . and the true Creator, who alone is God, was rejected', in which both antecedent and relative have the same case, for *þe* certifies that we have a relative pronoun and *se* tells us its case. This can be called the *seþe* relative. Again, there is no ambiguity for us in sentences like *þa com he on morgenne to þam tungerefan, se þe his ealdormon wæs* 'Then he came in the morning to the steward, who was his superior' and *þystre genip, þam þe se þeoden self sceop nihte naman* 'the cloud of darkness, for which the Lord Himself made the name "night"', for the presence of the particle *þe* after *se* and *þām* makes it clear that we have to do with a relative pronoun, while *se* and *þām* tell us its case. This pattern, in which the *se* element has the case required by the adjective clause only, can be called the *'seþe* relative. In both these patterns, although the elements are written sometimes together, sometimes separately, by the scribes, the *se* element tells us the case of the relative pronoun.

Note

In the nominative, these combinations can mean 'he who' or 'the one who' or 'whoever'; cf. §164.

5   So far, then, we can say that the OE relatives are the indeclinable particle *þe*, to which the personal pronoun can be added to remove ambiguities of case, and the demonstrative pronoun *se, sēo, þæt* in the case required by the *adjective* clause, either alone or followed by the indeclinable particle *þe* to make clear that we have a relative and not a demonstrative pronoun.

§163 The comments which follow may be useful when you have mastered §162.

1   Another example of the *'seþe* type like those in §162.4 is

> Se wæs Hroþgare   hæleþa leofost
> rice randwiga,   þone ðe heo on ræste abreat

'That man was the most beloved of heroes to Hrothgar, a mighty shield-warrior whom she (the monster) killed in his resting-place'. But a word of warning is necessary here, because you are likely to meet sentences which seem to contain this combination, but do not. Thus in *gedo grenne finul XXX nihta on ænne croccan þone þe sie gepicod utan* 'put green fennel for thirty nights into a jar which is covered with pitch on the outside' and in

> syððan hie gefricgeað   frean userne
> ealdorleasne,   þone ðe ær geheold
> wið hettendum   hord ond rice

'when they learn our lord to be dead, he who in the past guarded our treasure and kingdom against enemies', *þone þe* is not an accusative relative, for *þone* has the case of the *principal* clause agreeing with its antecedent. Formally, *þone* belongs to the principal clause and we can therefore say that the relative in these examples is *þe*. But they differ from the second and third sentences quoted in §162.1 (where the demonstrative is the only antecedent) in that there is already an antecedent and the demonstrative is therefore superfluous. In earlier times *þone* was no doubt stressed in such sentences – 'our lord . . . that one . . . he'. But there may be some truth in the view that in our sentences *þone* belonged rhythmically to the adjective clause and was felt as part of the relative; hence we can (if we wish) distinguish the relative in which the demonstrative has the case of the principal clause but is not the antecedent, as the *se'þe* relative. There is no real difficulty in the pattern seen in the *ðā ðe* clause in example B in §172, where the two clauses require different cases (acc./nom.) but where *ðā* can be either nominative or accusative. But you should be on the alert for examples of this *se'þe* type. Its forms can be difficult, except for *þāra þe* 'of those who' (18a/785 and 843).

Notes

1   Examples in which real ambiguity occurs are rare. But there is one in *Beowulf* ll. 2291–3:

> Swa mæg unfæge   eaðe gedigan
> wean and wræcsið   se ðe Wealdendes
> hyldo gehealdeþ.

If the relative pronoun is *se'þe, hyldo* (indeclinable feminine) is the subject of the adjective clause, *ðe* is accusative, and the translation would read 'So may an undoomed man whom the favour of the Almighty protects easily survive both woe and banishment'. If the relative pronoun is *seþe*, it is nominative, *hyldo* is accusative, and the translation would read 'So may an undoomed man who retains the favour of the Almighty . . .'.

2   Sometimes, when the relative pronoun is in a case other than the nominative, the personal pronoun follows a relative of the *se'þe* type. This enables us to tell immediately the case of the relative pronoun, e.g.

> se biþ leofast   londbuendum
> se þe him God syleð   gumena rice

'that one is most beloved by land-dwellers to whom God gives the kingdom of men' and *se, se þe him ær geþuhte þæt him nan sæ wiþhabban ne mehte þæt he hine mid scipum afyllan ne mehte, eft wæs biddende anes lytles troges æt anum earman men, þæt he mehte his feorh generian* 'he to whom it once had seemed that no sea was so great (lit. could stop him) that he could not fill it with ships, finally asked a wretched man for one little boat so that he could save his life'. See also *Dream of the Rood* ll. 85–6.

2   A not uncommon idiom is found in the sentence about Tantalus quoted in §148. The antecedent *Tantulus* is followed by two adjective clauses joined by *ond*. In the first, *ðe . . . gīfre wæs*, the relative pronoun is nominative. The second is *him . . . ðære gīfernesse*. Here the relative pronoun is [*þe*] *him* 'whom'. But it is idiomatic not to repeat the *þe*; *him* warns us of the change of case from nominative to dative.

Another idiom is found in

> Nis nu cwicra nan
> þe ic him modsefan   minne durre
> sweotule asecgan.

Here the antecedent is *nān cwicra*. The relative pronoun is *þe him*. *Ic* is the subject of the adjective clause. So we have 'There is no one alive to whom I dare reveal my thoughts'. When the relative pronoun is *þe* + personal pronoun and another pronoun is the subject of the adjective clause, the latter comes between the two elements of the relative. So *þe ic him*.

3   The indeclinable relative *þe* always precedes any preposition which governs it; see the sentence about Ixion quoted in §148.

4   The adjective clause need not immediately follow the antecedent.

5   *þæt* often combines antecedent and relative pronoun. It must then be translated 'what', e.g. *he hæfde ðeah geforþod þæt he his frean gehet* 'he had, however, done what he promised his lord'. This survived into eMnE, e.g. in the King James Version John 13:27 'That thou doest, do quickly'. In

> gode þancode
> mihtigan drihtne,   þæs se man gespræc,

þæs is genitive after *þancode* and we might expect *þe*: 'thanked God for that which the man spoke'. But this is probably an example of *þæt* 'what' – 'thanked God, the mighty Lord, for what the man spoke'.

6   In MnE the difficulty of combining an adjective clause and a verb of saying or thinking often produces a 'grammatical error', e.g. 'This is the man whom they thought would revolutionize the teaching of English' where we should have '. . . who, they thought, . . .'. The same problem arises in OE and often results in what seems to us a somewhat incoherent arrangement, e.g. *Đa eode he furður oð he gemette ða graman gydena ðe folcisce men hatað Parcas, ða hi secgað ðæt on nanum men nyton nane are, ac ælcum men wrecen be his gewyrhtum, þu hi secgað ðæt walden ælces mannes wyrde* 'Then he went on further until he met the terrible goddesses whom the people of that land call the Parcae, who (they say) show no mercy to any man, but punish each man according to his deserts; these (they say) control each man's fate'. A result acceptable in MnE can be obtained in these examples by omitting the *ðæt*. Sometimes, however, the subject is expressed twice, e.g. *in þære cirican seo cwen gewunade hire gebiddan, þe we ær cwædon þæt heo Cristen wære*. Here we need to omit *þæt hēo* to get the sense: 'in that church the queen who, we said formerly, was Christian, was wont to say her prayers'. But even this is clumsy and needs polishing.

7   Attempts have been made to lay down the rules which governed the use of the various relative pronouns in OE. They have not succeeded, largely because the vital clue of intonation is denied to us.

Indefinite Adjective Clauses

§164   The relative pronouns used in definite adjective clauses also appear in the indefinite ones, e.g.

> þa wæs eaðfynde   þe him elles hwær
> gerumlicor   ræste sohte

'Then it was easy to find whoever (= the man who) sought a bed for himself elsewhere, further away',

> heold hyne syðþan
> fyr ond fæstor   se þæm feonde ætwand

'thereafter kept himself further away and in greater safety whoever escaped the enemy', *sægde se þe cuþe* . . . 'he who knew said . . .' (the *seþe* relative; see §162.4), and *Se þe gewemð Godes tempel, God hine fordeð* 'Whoever defiles God's temple, God will destroy him' (the *'seþe* relative; see again §162.4).

As has already been noted, the interrogatives *hwā* 'who', *hwǣr* 'where', and the like, are not used alone in OE as relatives; see §159. But they are used in the indefinite relatives *swā hwā swā* 'whoever', *swā hwæt swā* 'whatever', *swā hwǣr swā* 'wherever', and so on. One example will suffice – *swa hwa swa þe genyt þusend stapa, ga mid him oðre twa þusend* 'whoever compels thee [to go] one mile, go with him two'.

Mood

§165 The adjective clause usually has its verb in the indicative, even when it is in dependent speech. But the subjunctive may occur in the following situations:

1 When the principal clause contains an imperative or a subjunctive expressing a wish, e.g. Matthew 5:42 *syle þam ðe þe bidde* Authorized Version 'Give to him that asketh thee'. However, the fact that the indicative is found in such circumstances, e.g. Matthew 19:21 *becyp eall þæt þu ahst* Authorized Version 'sell that thou hast', shows that the mood varies with the speaker's attitude and not with any automatic 'law of symmetry'. In the first example, there is uncertainty because the asker is as yet unknown and indeed may not exist; we could translate 'Give to anyone who may ask'. In the second, the young man's possessions exist and are known to him. For, as the story tells us, 'he went away sorrowful, for he had great possessions'.

2 When the principal clause contains a negative, e.g. the second sentence discussed in §163.2. But this again is no automatic rule. The subjunctive is found only when the content of the adjective clause is put forward as unreal; in the example, there is no such person in existence nor probably could there be. But in *Beowulf* ll. 1465–7

> Huru ne gemunde   mago Ecglafes
> eafoþes cræftig,   þæt he ær gespræc
> wine druncen

'However, the son of Ecglaf, powerful in his might, did not remember what he had said before, when drunk with wine', Unferth (*mago Ecglāfes*) actually had spoken the words, but he did not now remember them; the poet could have said that he had forgotten them. In this example, the *ne* negates merely the verb of the principal clause, not the whole idea which follows; hence the indicative in the adjective clause.

3 When the principal clause contains a rhetorical question, e.g.

> Hwa is on eorðan   nu unlærdra
> þe ne wundrige   wolcna færeldes . . . ?

'Who is there on earth among the unlearned who does not wonder at the motion of the clouds . . . ?' The answer demanded is, of course, 'No one'. Such examples are exactly parallel to those discussed in 2 above, for the poet could easily have said 'There is no one on earth . . .'.

4 When a limiting adjective clause[1] has as antecedent a genitive depending on a superlative, e.g.

> Niwe flodas   Noe oferlað,
>
> . . .
>
> þone deopestan   drencefloda
> þara ðe gewurde   on woruldrice.

Here the poet is saying that Noah sailed over the deepest deluge that could ever be or have been. Similar examples occur in *Beowulf* ll. 2129 ff., *Genesis* ll. 626 ff., and *Daniel* ll. 691 ff. In these the subjunctive is used to imply that all the possible examples of floods, griefs, women, and cities, respectively are being considered – those which the writer knows about, those which have happened without his knowledge, and those which may yet happen. That the 'superlative + genitive' does not automatically cause the subjunctive is shown by examples like

> . . . ond hi þa gesette   on þone selestan
> foldan sceata,   þone fira bearn
> nemnað neorxnawong . . .

'and then he placed them in the best regions of the earth, which the sons of men call Paradise', where the non-limiting adjective clause has the indicative.

V ADVERB CLAUSES

Introduction

§166 The conventional classification will serve us here. It distinguishes eight types – place, time, purpose, result, cause, comparison, concession, condition. On the whole, you will find that these clauses are fundamentally very similar to their counterparts in MnE. The main differences to be noted are:

1 the conjunctions themselves;
2 the methods of correlation, linked with
3 the word-order within the clauses. On these two points, see §§150–153;
4 a more frequent use of the subjunctive mood. Sometimes it is used by rule and is of little significance for us, sometimes it makes an important distinction. On this, see §§173–180.

§§167–171 contain a discussion of the conjunctions and alphabetical lists of non-prepositional and prepositional formulae with their main uses.

---

[1] In the sentence 'The soldiers who (that) were tired lay down' the adjective clause does not merely describe the soldiers; it limits the action of lying down to a particular group – those who were tired. Hence it is a 'limiting' clause. But in 'The soldiers, who were tired, lay down' the adjective clause merely tells us something more about all the soldiers. Hence it is 'non-limiting'.

§§173–180 discuss each type of clause in turn, outlining briefly the conjunctions and moods used in them and any other points of special interest.

§167 If we adopt a purely formal classification, we can detect in MnE at least five types of conjunction. Consider the following series of clauses:

1   Christ died, *that* his followers might live.
2   Christ died, *so that* his followers might live.
3   *So* boldly did Christ speak, *that* all men listened.
4
5
6   Christ died, *to the end that* his followers might live.
7   *To this end* Christ died, *that* his followers might live.

In OE, we can find comparable examples to these and can fill in the missing items 4 and 5:

1   . . . *he biþ geseald hæþnum mannum þæt hie hine bysmrian* '. . . he will be given to heathen men that they may mock him'.

2   *Hæfde se cyning his fierd on tu tonumen, swa þæt hie wæron simle healfe æt ham, healfe ute* 'The king had divided his army into two, so that at any one time half were at home, half in the field'.

3   *He . . . swa anræd þurhwunode þæt he nolde abugan to bismorfullum leahtrum* 'he . . . remained so resolute that he was unwilling to turn aside to shameful sins'.

4   . . . *ond ðæs ðe ðu gearo forwite hwam ðu gemiltsige, ic eom Apollonius, se Tyrisca ealdormann* '. . . and, so that you may know who is receiving your mercy, I am Apollonius, Prince of Tyre'.

Note: This use of *ðæs ðe* is a rare one, but it is included to complete the series.

5   *Ic wat þæt nan nis þæs welig þæt he sumes eacan ne þyrfe* 'I know that there is no man so wealthy that he does not need more of something'.

6   *And ic hyne nyste, ac ic com and fullode on wætere, to þam þæt he wære geswutelod on Israhela folce* 'And I knew him not, but I came and baptized [him] in water, to the end that he might be manifested to the people of Israel'.

7   [the Heavenly King] *þe to ði com on middangeard þæt he of eallum ðeodum his gecorenan gegaderode* . . . '[the Heavenly King] who to this end came into the world that he might gather his chosen from all nations'.

So we find

	MnE	OE
1	'that'	*þæt*
2	'so that'	*swā þæt*

3	'so . . . that'	*swā . . . þæt*
4		*þæs þe*
5		*þæs . . . þæt*
6	'to this end that'	*tō þām þæt*
7	'to this end . . . that'	*tō þī . . . þæt*

On the variations *þe*/*þæt* in 4 and 5 and *þām*/*þī* in 6 and 7, see §169.

We can therefore speak of prepositional conjunctions (6 and 7) and non-prepositional conjunctions (1–5). We can speak of simple conjunctions (1), grouped conjunctions (2, 4, and 6), and divided conjunctions (3, 5, and 7). MnE has no exact equivalent for types 4 and 5. Their real force cannot be brought out literally today because *þæs* is the genitive of *þæt* used adverbially and we no longer have a genitive of 'that' to use in this way. So we must translate them either 'so that' and 'so . . . that', which brings out the adverbial force only, or 'to the end that' and 'to the end . . . that', which brings out the adverbial force and at the same time demonstrates the important truth that a good many functions of the OE cases have been taken over by MnE prepositions. Other examples of this type in OE include:

(*a*) *þȳ . . . þȳ* (the instrumental of *þæt*) in comparisons, the ancestor of MnE, '*the* more, *the* merrier' (lit. 'by that much . . . by that much');

(*b*) *þā hwīle þe* 'while'; where we have an accusative of duration of time turned into a conjunction by the addition of the indeclinable particle *þe*;

(*c*) *þȳ lǣs* (*þe*) MnE 'lest'. On the use of *þe* in (*b*) and (*c*), see §169.

For practical purposes, the best grouping is a twofold one – non-prepositional conjunctions, simple, grouped and divided (i.e. items 1–5), and prepositional conjunctions or formulae, grouped and divided (items 6–7). The following sections contain separate alphabetical lists of the most important OE conjunctions in these two groups, with any comments necessary on their use. Examples are often given from poems you are likely to read.

Non-Prepositional Conjunctions

§168 Non-Prepositional conjunctions include *ǣr* 'before', *būtan* 'but, except that, unless', *gif* 'if', *hwonne* 'when', *nefne, nemne* 'unless', *nū*, 'now that', *oð* 'until', *sam . . . sam* 'whether . . . or', *siþþan* 'after, since', *swā* 'so, as', *swā þæt* 'so that', *swelce* 'such as', *þā* 'when', *þā hwīle þe* 'as long as, while', *þanon* 'whence', *þǣr* 'where', *þæs* 'after', *þæt* 'that, so that', *þēah* 'although', *þenden* 'while', *þider* 'whither', *þonne* 'whenever, when, then,' *þȳlǣs* (*þe*) 'lest'.

Prepositional Conjunctions

§169 Basically these consist of a preposition + an oblique case of *þæt* (+ *þæt* or *þe*).

Note

The case used depends on the preposition. Thus, since *for* governs the dat. or inst., we find in the manuscripts *for þæm, for þam, for þan, for þon, for þy, for þi* – all variant spellings of the dat. or inst. (*ð* may appear instead of *þ* in any of these spellings). The formulae are sometimes written together, e.g. *forþon*. In the discussions which follow, one particular form of the prepositional formula (such as *for þæm*) includes all these variant spellings unless the contrary is specifically stated. *To* sometimes governs the gen. instead of the dat. or inst.; so we find *to þæs* in addition to *to þæm* etc.

These conjunctions probably grew out of an originally adverbial use of a prepositional phrase such as occurs in *ond for ðon ic ðe bebiode ðæt ðu . . .* 'and for that (= 'therefore') I command you that you . . .' and in *for þan wearð her on felda folc totwæmed . . .* 'because of that the army here in the field was divided . . .' Such phrases were then used as conjunctions by the addition of *þe* or *þæt* to indicate the new function, e.g. *. . . ond he hi him eft ageaf, for þæm þe hiora wæs oþer his godsunu . . .* 'and he afterwards returned them to him, because one of them was his godson . . .'. Here *þe* warns us that the combination is a conjunction. We can call *þe* (if we wish) a subordinating particle. This is the general function of *þe* and its use as a relative pronoun is probably a special adaptation; see §162. We can perhaps get nearest to its original force by translating it as 'namely'. So, in the example above, we have 'and he afterwards returned them to him, for that [reason], namely, one of them was his godson'.

These formulae can be used in two ways. Thus *for þæm* sometimes refers *back* to a reason already given as in the second example above – '[Some fled.] Therefore the army was divided'. Here it is equivalent to MnE 'therefore'. But sometimes it refers *forward* to a reason yet to be given, as in the third example above, where the *þe* warns us not to relax because something – the reason – is still to come, and so tells us that *for þæm* means 'because' and not 'therefore'.

Sometimes *þæt* is used instead of *þe*, e.g. *forþan þæt he wolde Godes hyrde forlætan* 'because he wished to desert God's flock'. This use of *þæt* becomes more common as we move from OE to ME and still survives in Chaucer's metrically useful 'if that', 'when that', and the like.

So far we have distinguished *for þæm* adverb 'therefore' from *for þæm þe* conjunction 'because'. But this distinction was not long preserved by the Anglo-Saxons. They could distinguish adverb and conjunction by the context, word-order, and intonation, just as we can distinguish the use of 'who' in 'The man who did that is a fool' from its use in 'The soldiers, who were tired, lay down'. So they sometimes dispensed with the subordinating particle and used the formula as a conjunction without *þe* or *þæt*, e.g. *Wuton agifan ðæm esne his wif, forðæm he hi hæfð geearnad mid his hearpunga* 'let us give the man back his wife, because he has earned her with his harping'.

Like other adverbs and conjunctions such as *þā* (see §§150 ff.), pre-positional conjunctions may be used correlatively. Examples are *forðæm we*

*habbað nu ægðer forlæten ge ðone welan ge ðone wisdom forðæmðe we noldon to
ðæm spore mid ure mode onlutan* 'and for that reason we have now lost both
the wealth and the wisdom, because we would not bend to the track with
our minds', and, without *þe* in the conjunction, *For þon nis me þæs þearf . . .
to secgenne, for þon hit longsum is, ond eac monegum cuð* 'For this reason, there
is no need for me . . . to speak of it, because it is long and also known to many'.

So now we have

> *for þǣm* adv. 'therefore'
> *for þǣm þe* conj. 'because'
> *for þǣm* conj. 'because'

and the correlative combination *for þǣm . . . for þǣm* (*þe*), 'for this reason
. . . because'.

One further variation needs to be recorded. We have already seen that con
junctions can be divided. An OE example of a divided prepositional conjunction
is *þa comon for ðy on weg ðe ðara oðerra scipu asæton* lit. 'those (men) got
for that away, namely, the ships of the others had gone aground' and so 'those
escaped because the others' ships were aground'. The causal conjunction is
for ðȳ . . . ðe, divided by *on weg*.

§170   Since all these arrangements are possible with the prepositional
conjunctions, it follows that, when in your reading you meet *for þæm* or some
such combination, it may be

1   an adverb used alone;
2   a conjunction used alone;
3   an adverb used correlatively with a prepositional conjunction;
4   the first part of a divided prepositional conjunction. If it is this, you
will need to find the following *þe* or *þæt*.

The combination *for þǣm þe* is almost always a conjunction. But sometimes
MnE 'for' will be a better translation than 'because'.

§171   The remarks made in §170 about *for þǣm* and *for þǣm þe* apply
to all the prepositional conjunctions set out in the list which follows. It
contains all that you are likely to meet. You should note, however, that these
combinations may occur 'in their own right' and may not be true prepositional conjunctions. Thus *mid þǣm þæt* does not mean 'while' or 'when' in
ealles swiþost mid þæm þæt manige þara selestena cynges þegna forðferdon; we
must translate 'most of all by the fact that (lit. "with that, namely") many of
the king's best thanes died'.

æfter + dat., inst.
Adv. and conj. 'after'.

Note
æfter is never used alone in OE as a conj. But it does occur as an adv.

ǣr + dat., inst.
   Adv. and conj. 'before'.

betweox + dat., inst.
   Conj. 'while'.

for + dat., inst.
   See §§169–170 above. *For* alone as a conj. is late.

mid + dat., inst.
   Conj. 'while, when'.

oþ + acc.
   Conj. 'up to, until, as far as' defining the temporal or local limit.
   It appears as *oþþe*, *oþþæt*, and *oð ðone fyrst ðe* 'up to the time at which' (a good example of how *þe* can turn a phrase into a conj.).

tō + dat., inst.
   Conj. 'to this end, that' introducing clauses of purpose with subj. and of result with ind.

tō + gen.
   Conj. 'to the extent that, so that'.

wiþ + dat., inst.
   Conj. lit. 'against this, that'. It can be translated 'so that', 'provided that', or 'on condition that'.

An Exercise in Analysis

§172   Now you are in a position to 'try your strength' by analysing and translating the following sentences *before* consulting the key given below:

A. Ond for ðon ic ðe bebiode ðæt ðu do swæ ic geliefe ðæt ðu wille, ðæt ðu ðe ðissa woruldðinga to ðæm geæmetige, swæ ðu oftost mæge, ðæt ðu ðone wisdom ðe ðe God sealde ðær ðær ðu hiene befæstan mæge, befæste.

B. Forðy me ðyncð betre, gif iow swæ ðyncð, ðæt we eac sume bec, ða ðe niedbeðearfosta sien eallum monnum to wiotonne, ðæt we ða on ðæt geðiode wenden ðe we ealle gecnawan mægen, ond gedon, swæ we swiðe eaðe magon mid Godes fultume, gif we ða stilnesse habbað, ðætte eall sio gioguð ðe nu is on Angelcynne friora monna, ðara ðe ða speda hæbben ðæt hie ðæm befeolan mægen, sien to liornunga oðfæste, ða hwile ðe hie to nanre oðerre note ne mægen, oð ðone first ðe hie wel cunnen Englisc gewrit arædan.

In A, we have

1   three noun clauses introduced by *ðæt* – one the object of *bebīode*, one
the object of *ġelīefe*, and one which is perhaps most simply explained as being
in explanatory apposition to the clause *ðæt ðū dō*.

2   an adjective clause introduced by *ðe*.

3   two prepositional formulae –
for ðon adverb used alone 'thereafter' and
tō ðæm . . . ðæt used as a divided prepositional conjunction.

4   two *swā* clauses, one of comparison (*swæ iċ ġelīefe*) and the other of
time (*swæ ðū oftost mæġe*).

5   an adverb clause of place introduced by *ðær ðær*.

In B, we have

1   two noun clauses –
the *ðæt* clause subject of *ðyncð* 'seems', which begins after *ðyncð* and
has *ðæt*, the subject, and the object, repeated after *wiotonne*. It has two
verbs – *wenden* and *ġedōn*;
the *ðætte* clause object of *ġedōn*.

2   four adjective clauses –
the *ðā ðe* clause, where the relative pronoun does not clearly tell us its
case (see §163.1);
two *ðe* clauses, excluding that mentioned in 7;
the *ðāra ðe* clause.

3   two conditional clauses introduced by *ġif*.

4   a *swā* clause of comparison.

5   a clause of purpose or result introduced by *ðæt* (following *hæbben*).

6   a clause of time introduced by *ðā hwīle ðe*. Here we must understand
oðfæste wesan.

7   two prepositional formulae –
for ðȳ adverb 'therefore';
the temporal conjunction *oð ðone first ðe*, where *ðe* can be described as
a relative pronoun 'until the time at which'.

These and similarly complicated sentences in Alfred's Preface to the *Cura
Pastoralis* show the problems which faced a person writing in English prose
about difficult and complicated subjects. But they and later writers overcame
them, often triumphantly.

Clauses of Place

§173   The main conjunctions are:

1   *þær* 'where', 'whither', *þider* 'whither', and *þanon* 'whence'. These may
introduce both definite and indefinite clauses.

2   *swā hwǣr swā* 'wherever' and *swā hwider swā* 'wherever, whitherso-
ever'.

The prevailing mood is the indicative. In examples like *Beowulf* l.1394 *ga
þær he wille*, the subjunctive reflects the subjunctive in the principal clause,
the indefiniteness of the adverb clause, and probably also the fact that
the whole expression means 'no matter where he goes' and therefore has a
concessive force. For other examples see *Genesis* ll. 2723–4 and a passage from
Gregory's *Dialogues* where MS C reads *Far þu þider þe þu wille* and MS H
Far þu nu swa hwider swa þu wille 'Go wherever you wish'.

Clauses of Time

§174   1   Conjunctions whose primary meaning is 'when' or 'while' are:
þā, *þonne*, *mid þām* (*þe*), *þā hwīle* (*þe*), *þenden*, and *swā lange swā*.
     2   Conjunctions whose primary meaning is 'after' are: *siððan* and *þæs þe*.
Æfter is not used alone as a conjunction in OE.
     3   'Before' is rendered by *ǣr* either alone or introducing a prepositional
formula.
     4   Conjunctions whose primary meaning is 'until' are: *oð*, *oð þe*, *oð þæt*,
and *hwonne*; on the last, see §159 n. 2.

All these conjunctions usually take the indicative with the exception of
ǣr, which prefers the subjunctive, and *hwonne*, which always seems to take
the subjunctive (except in *Exodus* l. 251, which is therefore suspect).

Note
Doubtless the fact that both *ǣr* and *hwonne* clauses refer to a time AFTER the action
of the verb of the main clause has something to do with the subjunctive, but the same
is true of *oð þæt* which prefers the indicative. The interrogative origin of *hwonne* is
also relevant. There are other factors too, but when they have all been investigated,
we have to fall back on 'the attitude of the speaker' to explain some variations in mood.

The conjunctions which prefer the indicative may take the subjunctive if
circumstances demand. Thus cf. *Beowulf* l. 1374 and l. 1485, in both of which
þonne, while frequentative and/or indefinite and referring to the future, has
the indicative after an indicative principal clause, with Luke 14:13 *Ac þonne
þu gebeorscype do, clypa þearfan* 'Whenever you make a feast, call the poor',
where the imperative *clypa* imparts to the sentence a further element of wishing and uncertainty which is reflected in the subjunctive *dō*. Again, while *þonne*
frequentative in the past is followed by the preterite indicative, e.g. *Beowulf*
ll. 1580 ff., it has the subjunctive when the time reference was to the future
at the time of speaking. (We may call this the 'future-in-the-past'.) In these
circumstances, the reference may be to a single act, e.g. *þa bæd he hine
þæt he him þæs arwyrþan treos hwylcne hwego dæl brohte, þonne he eft ham*

come 'he asked him to bring a little bit of that precious tree when he came home again' – *þonne*, the conjunction appropriate to a single act in the future, is retained for the future-in-the-past – or to a series of acts, e.g. *He þa . . . geworhte anes fearres anlicnesse of are, to ðon, þonne hit hat wære, 7 mon þa earman men oninnan don wolde, hu se hlynn mæst wære þonne hie þæt susl þæron þrowiende wæron* 'He then made the likeness of a boar in brass with the object [of showing] how, when it was hot and the wretches had been put inside it, the noise would be greatest when they were undergoing the torture'.

Clauses of Purpose and Result

§175 Since a result is often a fulfilled purpose and a purpose a yet-to-be-completed result, these two have much in common. Both can be introduced by the following conjunctions: *þæt, þætte, swā þæt,* and *swā . . . þæt,* though the last two are rare in purpose clauses. *þæs . . . þæt* and *tō þæs . . . þæt* occasionally introduce result clauses, more commonly in the poetry than in the prose. *þȳ læs (þe)* 'lest' is found only in negative clauses of purpose.

It is generally agreed that purpose clauses take the subjunctive, result clauses the indicative. This proposition cannot be proved, for it is only by classifying all clauses with the subjunctive as purpose and all clauses with the indicative as result that we can deduce the rule. This is clearly a circular agreement. But it seems likely enough when we think of MnE usage.

Causal Clauses

§176 The main causal conjunctions are the *for* formulae, *nū,* and *þæs (þe). þe, þȳ,* and *þȳ þe* are sometimes found.

When the true cause is given, the causal clause has an indicative verb. The subjunctive is regularly used for a rejected reason, e.g. *Ne cwæþ he þæt na forþon þe him wære ænig gemynd þearfendra manna, ah he wæs gitsere . . .* 'He said that, not because he cared at all about needy men, but because he was a miser . . .'

Clauses of Comparison

§177 1 Comparisons involving 'than' are expressed in OE by *þonne* or (occasionally and only after a negative principal clause) *þon mā þe.* There is a strong tendency for the *þonne* clause to have the subjunctive when the principal clause is positive, e.g. *Ic Ælfric munuc and mæssepreost, swa þeah wacre þonne swilcum hadum gebyrige, wearþ asend . . .* 'I Ælfric, monk and mass-priest, though weaker than is fitting for such orders, was sent . . .', and the indicative when the principal clause is negative, e.g. *Beowulf* ll. 247–9. However, exceptions are not uncommon.

   2   Comparisons involving 'as' may be expressed by

     (*a*) *swā* 'as' or *swā swā* 'just as';

     (*b*) *swā* . . . *swā* 'so . . . as, as . . . so';

     (*c*) *swā* + superlative;

     (*d*) *swylċe* 'such as';

     (*e*) *swylċe* . . . *swā* 'such . . . as';

     (*f*) *þæs* (*þe*), e.g. *Beowulf* l. 1341 and (with a superlative) *Beowulf* l. 1350.

The prevailing mood in these clauses is the indicative.

   3   Comparisons involving 'the . . . the' are expressed by *þȳ* . . . *þȳ*, e.g. *Maldon* ll. 312–13. The verbs are in the indicative.

   4   Comparisons involving hypothesis are expressed by *swā* or *swilċe* 'as if' followed by the subjunctive. When the time reference is to the past, the preterite subjunctive is found in the 'as if' clause, e.g. *Wanderer* l. 96 and *Finnsburh* l. 36. When it is to the present, we find the present subjunctive in the 'as if' clause, e.g. *Christ* ll. 179–81 and ll. 1376–7. The preterite subjunctive is not used of the present as it is in OE type 3 Conditions (see §179.4) or in MnE 'He runs as if he were tired'; the MnE equivalent of the OE idiom would be 'He runs as if he be tired'.

Clauses of Concession

§178   1   Simple concessive clauses are usually introduced by *þēah* (*þe*) 'though'. The prevailing mood is the subjunctive, whether the concession is one of fact or hypothesis.

Note

Sometimes we have *þēah* . . . *eall*, as in *Beowulf* l. 680 *þeah ic eal mæge*. Here *eall* is an adverb, perhaps with the sense 'easily'. But this probably represents a stage in the development of 'although'; see *OED* s.v. *all* C adv. II 10, and note that in such ME examples as *The Pardoner's Prologue* lines 371, 449, and 451 (line references to Robinson's edition), *al* is still an adverb and the concession is expressed by the word-order V.S.

   2   Disjunctive concessions are expressed by *sam* . . . *sam* 'whether . . . or'. In such clauses, the subjunctive is the rule, e.g. *sam hit sy sumor sam winter* 'whether it be summer or winter'.

   3   As in MnE, an element of concession is often present in indefinite adjective clauses (e.g. *Beowulf* ll. 942 ff. and ll. 142–3) or in indefinite adverb clauses of place (e.g. *Genesis* ll. 2723 ff.) or time (e.g. *Genesis* ll. 1832 ff.). On the possibility that there was a special OE idiom expressing indefinite concession, see Klaeber's note on *Beowulf* l. 968.

4 Concession can sometimes be expressed by putting the verb first without any conjunction. The two most common types are *swelte ic, libbe ic* 'whether I live or die', and *hycge swa he wille* 'let him think as he will', 'no matter what he thinks'. The first type often occurs in the form *wylle ic, nylle ic* 'willy nilly'.

Clauses of Condition

§179 1 In earlier versions of this *Guide*, we classified conditional clauses according to a system traditionally used for Latin and Greek. We have abandoned this because it does not really fit OE. We now distinguish these three types:

1 (a) conceded and (b) denied conditions, e.g. (a) 'If you think that [and you have said that you do], you are wrong', and (b) 'Seek if you dare [but you do not]'.

(2) open conditions, e.g. 'If you think that [and I do not know whether you do or not], you are wrong', 'If you thought that [and you might], you would be wrong', and 'Seek if you dare [and you may or may not]'.

(3) unfulfilled or rejected or imaginary conditions, e.g. 'If you believed this [but you do not], you would be wrong', 'If you had believed this [but you did not], you would have been wrong', and 'If [= Imagine that] you saw a mouse ruling over men, you would think it strange'.

In OE, conditions of all three types may be introduced by *gif* 'if'. *þǣr* 'if' sometimes introduces type 3 conditions.

2 Conditions of types 1 and 2 fall into two main groups – those in which both clauses have the indicative, e.g. *Maldon* ll. 34–5 and ll. 36–41, and those in which the verb of the principal clause is imperative or expresses a wish in the subjunctive. In these latter sentences, the 'if' clause usually has the subjunctive, e.g. *sec, gif þu dyrre* 'seek if you dare'. This point is well illustrated by the two almost parallel *gif* clauses in *Beowulf* ll. 445–53.

3 It is not always immediately clear whether a condition belongs to type 1 or 2, e.g. *Fed ðonne min sceap gif ðu me lufige* (cf. John 21:15–17) – here Peter says that he does love Christ and ultimately proves that he does – and *sec, gif þu dyrre* (quoted above from *Beowulf* l. 1379) – here Beowulf does dare when the time comes.

4 Type 3 conditions regularly have the preterite subjunctive in both clauses, e.g. *ac hit wǣre to hrǣdlic, gif he ða on cild-cradole acweald wurde . . .* 'it would have been too early if He (Christ) had been killed in His cradle . . .' and perhaps (with *þǣr* and in dependent speech)

and þæt wiste eac   weroda Drihten,
þæt sceolde unc Adame   yfele gewurðan
ymb þæt heofonrice,   þær ic ahte minra handa geweald

'and the Lord of Hosts also knew that things would turn out badly between Adam and me about that heavenly kingdom, if I had control of my hands'.

Note

In MnE we can distinguish unreality in the past, present, and future, by means of
the verb alone, e.g.

> If he had been here, it wouldn't have happened.
> If he were here, it wouldn't be happening.
> If he were coming, it wouldn't happen.

But (as is pointed out in more detail in §§195–198) the OE verb was not as flexible
an instrument as the MnE verb. Hence an Anglo-Saxon had to use the preterite subjunctive in all these examples. In other words, he could say that a thing was unreal
or impossible, but he was unable to say when it could not happen unless he used an
adverb or some other device.

Thus both the OE examples cited in this section have the preterite subjunctive.
But the first refers to something which did not happen in the past, while the second
might refer to something which is impossible at the time when Satan spoke – the
implication being 'if only I had control of my hands now, but I haven't'. But it could
also be translated 'God knew that trouble would arise between Adam and me if
I were to have control of my hands'.

This raises a further difficulty. Does this interpretation mean that there was a
possibility that Satan might have control of his hands (type 2 condition) or that such
a thing was impossible when God spoke? The issue here is complicated by questions
of God's foreknowledge, though perhaps our own knowledge of the story enables us
to dismiss the latter possibility. But enough has been said to make it clear that the
Anglo-Saxon 'rule' that 'unreality is timeless' is not without its advantages.

A clearer example is *Beowulf* ll. 960–1, discussed in §198.

5   *Būtan* and *nympe, nemne, nefne* both have two meanings – 'unless' and
'except that'. If they take the subjunctive, they usually mean 'unless', e.g.
Beowulf l. 966 and l. 1056. If they take the indicative, they usually mean
'except that', e.g. *Beowulf* l. 1560 and l. 1353.

6   'On condition that' may be expressed by *gif* or by the *wiþ* formula
(see §171).

7   Conditions expressed by the word-order V.S. without a conjunction
– e.g. 'Had I plenty of money, I would be lying in the sun in Bermuda' –
occasionally occur in OE prose, e.g. *eaðe mihte þes cwyde beon lǣwedum
mannum bediglod, nǣre seo gastlice getacning* 'this saying could easily be concealed from laymen were it not [for] its spiritual meaning'. The only certain
example in the poetry is *Genesis* ll. 368–70; here it is arguable whether a line
is missing or whether the poet deliberately left the *þonne* clause unfinished
to obtain a dramatic effect.

8   On comparisons involving hypothesis, see §177.4.

Adverb Clauses Expressing Other Relationships

§180   The divisions outlined above are for convenience only and are far
from being watertight, for one relationship often involves another. Thus, while
clauses of time with *oþ* (*þæt*) often shade into result, and *þæt* after verbs of

motion can often be translated 'until', other temporal clauses may contain elements of cause or of condition. Similarly, indefinite adjective clauses are often the equivalent of conditional clauses, e.g. *Beowulf* ll. 1387–8. See also §178.3.

Note

This latter relationship is very clearly seen in some ME sentences which contain an adjective clause which must be rendered by a conditional clause in MnE, e.g. Hall *Selections from Early Middle English*, p. 54 l. 11 and l. 21 (cf. p. 54 l. 16) and *Sir Gawain and the Green Knight* l. 1112.

Other Ways of Expressing Adverbial Relationships

§181   1   Parataxis; examples will be found in §§182–186.

2   Participles; see §204.

3   Infinitives; see §205.

4   Prepositional phrases, e.g. *mid* expressing condition *mid Godes fultume* 'with God's help, if God helps us'; *þurh* expressing cause *þurh þæs cyninges bebod* 'by command of the king'; and *þurh* expressing time *þurh swefn* 'in a dream, while he dreamt'.

VI   PARATAXIS

Introduction

§182   The Anglo-Saxons were far from primitive. At the time of the Norman Conquest, England – although she no longer led western Europe in monastic learning, as she had in the eighth century – was fruitful ground for new forms of devotion, was famous for her craftsmen, and had a well-developed economy and the most advanced administration north of the Alps. It is of special interest here that her language was far more developed for the expression of both prose and poetry than any other contemporary European vernacular and that authors using it sometimes rose to very great heights. Look for example at the poem *The Dream of the Rood* and at the magnificent passage beginning *Ne forseah Crist his geongan cempan* in Ælfric's Homily on the Nativity of the Innocents.

Some of the reasons for the impression that Old English was a primitive language have been discussed in §§148–152. Another is the frequent use of parataxis. Some writers, steeped in the periodic structure of Latin and Greek, seem unable or unwilling to believe that parataxis can be anything but a clumsy tool used by people who did not know any better. Certainly, S. O. Andrew (in *Syntax and Style in Old English*) does well to draw our attention to inconsistencies in the editorial punctuation of Old English texts. But he allows himself to be swayed too much by his conviction that good writing must necessarily be periodic. Today, when the long and complicated sentence is losing favour in English, we will perhaps be more in sympathy with the constructions described in the following paragraphs, more able to appreciate the effect they produced, and less likely to believe that the juxtaposition of two simple sentences was necessarily less dramatic or effective than one complex sentence. During his journey to the Underworld in search of Eurydice, Orpheus met the Parcae. *Ða ongon he biddan heora miltse; ða ongunnon hi wepan mid him*, the story continues. Here the word-order supports the view that the two sentences are independent (see §151), and suggests that the writer is giving equal prominence to the two ideas. The effect he was after can perhaps be achieved by the translation 'Then he asked for their pity and they wept with him'. At the end of the same story, the final disappearance of Eurydice is related thus: *Ða he forð on ðæt leoht com, ða beseah he hine under bæc wið ðæs wifes; ða losade hio him sona* 'When he came into the light, he looked back towards his wife. Straightway she disappeared from his sight'. Here a powerful dramatic effect would be lost if we took only one of the clauses with *þā* + V.S. as principal.

§183   The term 'parataxis', with its adjective 'paratactic', has been abandoned by some writers because of its ambiguity. Here it is used in a purely formal sense to mean a construction in which sentences are not formally subordinated one to the other. 'Asyndetic' and 'syndetic' mean respectively without and with conjunctions such as *ond* and *ac*. The term 'co-ordinating' (often used for the MnE equivalents 'and', 'but', and so on) is avoided here because in OE *ond* and *ac* are frequently followed by the order S. . . . V. (see §145), which is basically a subordinate order. The opposite of 'parataxis' is 'hypotaxis', which implies the use of one or more of the conjunctions discussed in §§154–180. Examples follow.

Hypotaxis: When I came, I saw. When I saw, I conquered.
Asyndetic Parataxis: I came. I saw. I conquered.
Syndetic Parataxis: I came and I saw and I conquered.

List of Conjunctions and Adverbs Commonly Used

§184   On word-order after these words, see §§144 and 145.

1   Those meaning 'and', 'both . . . and', etc. (traditionally called 'cumulative'):

> *and, ond* 'and' (see below);
> *ǣghwæþer* (*ġe*) . . . *ġe* . . . (*ġe*) '(both) . . . and . . . (and)';
> (*ǣġþer*) (*ġe*) . . . *ġe* . . . (*ġe*) '(both) . . . and . . . (and)';
> *ēac* 'also, and'; *ġe* 'and'; *ġe . . . ġe, ǣġþer . . . and* 'both . . . and'.

The *ond* clause can of course imply more than mere continuity and is often the equivalent of an adverb clause. Thus *ofer Eastron gefor Æþered cyning; ond he ricsode V gear* could be translated 'During Easter Æthered died after ruling five years'. This of course often happens today, especially in conversation.

2 Those meaning 'but', 'however', etc. (traditionally called 'adversative'):

ac 'but, on the contrary'; *furþum* 'also, even';
hūru 'however, indeed', etc.;
hwæþere 'however, yet'; *swāþeah* 'however, yet';
þeah 'however, yet' (see also §178);
þeahhwæþere 'however, yet'.

3 Those meaning 'either . . . or' (traditionally called 'alternative'):

hwīlum . . . hwīlum 'at one time . . . at another time';
(*ǣgþer*) *oþþe . . . oþþe*; *swā . . . swā*; *þe . . . þe*.

4 Those involving a negative:

nā, ne, nō 'not';
(*nāhwæðer ne*) . . . *ne* . . . (*ne*) '(neither) . . . nor . . . (nor)';
nalles, nealles 'not at all, not';
(*nāðor ne*) . . . *ne* . . . (*ne*) '(neither) . . . nor . . . (nor)';
nǣfre 'never'; *næs* 'not' (a short form of *nalles*).

An example of 'not only . . . but also' will be found in *na þæt an þæt he wolde mann beon for us, ðaða he God wæs, ac eac swylce he wolde beon þearfa for us, ðaða he rice wæs* 'not only was He willing to become man for us when He was God, but He was also willing to become poor for us when He was rich'.
The following points should be noted:

(*a*) The OE verb is normally negated by *ne* immediately preceding it. But if the negative is stressed, as in *Wanderer* l. 96 and *Seafarer* l. 66, *nā* (= *ne* + *ā*) or *nō* (= *ne* + *ō*) is used. In *Phoenix* l. 72 the MS *no* is unstressed and should probably be emended to *ne* as a scribal anticipation of *o*.

(*b*) The arrangement seen in *Ne com se here* – *Ne* + V.S. – is common in negative principal clauses; see §146.4.

(*c*) Contraction of the negative *ne* with a following word beginning with a vowel, *h*, or *w*, produces *nis* from *ne is*, *næfde* from *ne hæfde*, *noldon* from *ne woldon*, and so on.

(*d*) *Ne* not before a finite verb is a conjunction, e.g. *ne tunge ne handa* 'neither tongue nor hands', *ne leornian ne tæcan* 'neither to learn nor to teach'.

(*e*) *Nā* and *nō* are used to negate words other than finite verbs, e.g. *He wæs Godes bydel ond na God* 'He was God's messenger and not God'.

(*f*) One negative does not cancel out another, as it does in formal MnE. The OE use is similar to that seen in such non-standard sentences as 'I didn't do nothing to nobody'; cf. *on nanum men nyton nane are* '[they] show mercy to no-one'. This could be added to the list of things which make some people think of OE as a primitive language; see §182.

(*g*) On a 'semi-subordinating' use of *ne*, see §185.2.

5 Those meaning 'for' (traditionally called 'illative'). A useful article by T. B. Haber on MnE 'for' (*American Speech* 30 (1955), 151) states: 'The only practical conclusion is that the conjunction has two uses, subordinating and co-ordinating, and that punctuation is of no significance in identifying either'. In other words, MnE 'for' can sometimes be replaced by 'because'. In OE, the situation is even more complicated, for *forþon* can mean, not only 'for' and 'because', but also 'therefore'. No rule can be laid down for distinguishing these uses; see §§169–170.

Parataxis without Conjunctions

§185 Two main types of asyndetic parataxis may be distinguished.

1 Here the two sentences are of equal status, as in the well-known *Veni. Vidi. Vici.* Examples are especially common in the poetry, e.g. *Beowulf* ll. 1422–4 and *Maldon* ll. 301–6.

2 Examples of the second type occur in *Eadmund cyning awearp his wæpnu, wolde geæfenlæcan Cristes gebysnungum* and *þa comon þeofas eahta, woldon stelan þa maðmas*, where the clauses beginning with *wolde* and *woldon* respectively could be translated 'wishing to imitate Christ's example' and 'intending to steal the treasures'. Note

> (*a*) These clauses do not themselves contain a grammatically expressed subject.
>
> (*b*) They are actually, though not formally, subordinate to the clause which precedes them; for this reason they are sometimes said to be in 'semi-subordination'.
>
> (*c*) They explain the motive for the action of the principal clause and are the equivalent of an adverb clause of purpose or cause.

This idiom occurs with verbs other than *willan*, e.g. *he sæt on ðæm muntum, weop ond hearpode* which can conveniently be translated 'he sat on the mountains, weeping and harping'. Similar examples occur with an initial negative, e.g. *Beowulf* ll. 1441–2 'Beowulf arrayed himself in princely armour without (or "not") worrying about his life'.

Some Special Idioms

§186 . . . *wæs gehāten* '. . . was called' is frequently used independently of the rest of the sentence, e.g. *mid heora cyningum, Rædgota ond Eallerica wæron hatne* 'with their kings, [who/they] were called R. and E.' (note the change from the dative to the nominative case) and *þa wæs sum consul, þæt we heretoha hataþ, Boetius wæs gehaten* 'there was a certain consul – we use

the word *heretoha* – [who/he] was called B.'. Cf., with the verb 'to be' only,
. . . *gefor Ælfred, wæs æt Baðum gerefa,* 'A., [who/he] was reeve at Bath, died'.

VII CONCORD

§187 The main rules of agreement in OE are set out below. They will present little difficulty to any reader with a knowledge of an inflected language.

1. Nouns, Pronouns and their Modifiers

(*a*) They agree in number, gender, and case, e.g. *se Ælmihtiga Hælend* 'the Almighty Saviour', *ðæs eadigan apostoles* 'of the blessed apostle', and *and þe cwicne gebindaþ* 'and will bind you alive'.

Note
The masc. ending *-e* in nom. acc. pl. of strong adjectives is often used for fem. and neut., especially in later texts.

(*b*) The participle in a participial phrase usually shows similar agreement, e.g. *Hinguar and Hubba, ge-anlæhte þurh deofol* 'H. and H., united by the devil'. But it need not, e.g. *Abraham geseah þær anne ramm betwux þam bremelum be þam hornum gehæft* 'A. saw there a ram caught among the brambles by his horns', where *gehæftne* would be the norm.

(*c*) *Gehāten* 'called' with a noun usually has the nominative irrespective of the case of the word with which it is in apposition, e.g. *into anre byrig, Gaza gehaten* 'into a city called Gaza'; cf. *for ðy hit man hæt Wīslemūða* 'therefore we call (lit. 'one calls') it W.' where the nominative *Wīslemūða* is the equivalent of the modern italics or inverted commas, and the second example in §186.1.

(*d*) After *wesan* and *weorþan* the participle often agrees with the subject, e.g. *hie wurdon ofslægene* 'they were slain' and *þe mid him ofslægene wæron* 'who were killed with them'. But it need not, e.g. *þa wurdon hiora wif swa sarige on hiora mode ond swa swiðlice gedrefed* . . . 'then their wives became so sorrowful and so greatly distressed in mind . . .'. See further §§201–203. So too with adjectives.

(*e*) After *habban*, the participle may agree with the object or may remain uninflected; see §200.

2. Pronouns and their Antecedents

(*a*) They agree in number and gender, e.g. *to þæm cyninge . . . he . . . his feores* 'to the king . . . he . . . for his life'; *anne flotan . . . se* 'a pirate . . . he (lit. "that")'; and *se hearpere . . . ðæs nama* 'the harper, whose name'.

(*b*) The main exceptions arise from the conflict between natural and grammatical gender, e.g. *ðæs hearperes wif* (neut.) . . . *hire sawle* 'the harper's wife . . . her soul' and *an swiðe ænlic wif, sio wæs haten Eurydice* 'a most excellent wife, who was called E.'. Similarly, in a passage from the Preface to the *Cura Pastoralis* (selection 5, end of first paragraph) we find *ðone wīsdōm* followed first by the grammatically right masculine *hiene* and then by the neuter *hit* which seems appropriate to us. Thus there are already signs that the feeling for grammatical gender is weakening.

Note
Agreement in case between pronoun and antecedent is a matter of chance, not principle, despite Quirk and Wrenn *An Old English Grammar* §121(*c*). In the examples they cite, *rōde* and *hēo* do not agree in case and the relative *ðāra þe* would have to be replaced by the acc. pl. *þā* of the declined relative *se*, i.e. *ðāra* has the case of the principal clause; see §163.1.

(*c*) Special uses of *hit, þæt, hwæt*, and the like, in which these neuter pronouns are used without regard to the number and gender of the noun to which they refer, should be noted, e.g. *þæt wæron eall Finnas* 'they were all Lapps' and *Hwæt syndon ge* . . . ? 'Who are you . . . ?'

3.   Subject and Verb

(*a*) Subject and verb agree in number and person. Dual pronouns are followed by plural verbs.

(*b*) Collective nouns and indefinite pronouns cause much the same problems as they do today, e.g. *an mægð* . . . *hi magon cyle gewyrcan* 'a tribe . . . they can make cold' and *þonne rideð ælc, and hit motan habban* 'then each man rides, and [they] can have it'.

(*c*) with *ond þæs ymb XIIII niht gefeaht Æþered cyning ond Ælfred his broður, where gefeaht* is singular, cf. 'Here comes Tom, and Jack, and all the boys'.

(*d*) When the relative pronoun *þāra þe* means 'of those who', the verb of the adjective clause can be singular or plural.

VIII   THE USES OF THE CASES

These will not present much difficulty to those familiar with an inflected language. On the cases used after prepositions, see §§213–214.

Nominative

§188   The case of the subject, of the complement, and of address, e.g. *Gehyrst þū sælida?* 'Do you hear, seaman?' See also §187.1(*c*).

Accusative

§189   1   The case of the direct object.

2   It also expresses duration of time, e.g. *ealne dæg* 'all day, *manega gēar* 'many years', and extent of space, e.g. *fleon fotes trym* 'to flee one foot's pace'.

Note

It is important to realize that already in OE the nominative and accusative are frequently the same. In the plural they are always the same except in the 1st and 2nd pers. pron. In the singular, many nouns have the same form in the nominative and accusative, and the distinction depends on the form of any demonstrative or possessive adjective, or on that of any adjective, which may qualify the noun. See further §140.

Genitive

§190   1   The case of possession, e.g. *Hæstenes wif* 'Hæsten's wife'.

2   The subjective genitive – *þæs cyninges bebod* 'the king's command', i.e. 'the king commanded' – differs in function from the objective genitive – *metodes ege* 'fear of the Lord', i.e. 'we fear the Lord'.

3   The genitive may describe or define, e.g. *swete hunig and wynsumes swæcces* 'honey sweet and of pleasant taste', *ðreora daga fæsten* 'a fast of three days', and *an lamb anes geares* 'a one-year-old lamb'.

4   The partitive genitive is common, e.g. *an hiora* 'one of them' and *þreora sum* 'one of three'. See also §194.

5   The genitive is used adverbially, e.g. *dæges ond nihtes* 'by day and night', *micles to beald* 'much too bold', *upweardes* 'upwards', *þæs* 'therefore, so, after that'.

6   The genitive occurs with some adjectives, e.g. *þæs gefeohtes georn* 'eager for the fight', and with some verbs, e.g. *fanda min* 'try me' and *hie þæs fægnodon* 'they rejoiced at that'. The glossary gives you this information when you need it.

Dative

§191   1   The case of the indirect object, e.g. *ond he hi him eft ageaf* 'and he afterwards gave them back to him'.

2   It may express possession, e.g. *him on heafod* 'on his head'.

3   It may express time, e.g. *hwilum* 'at times' and *ðære ylcan nihte* 'in the same night'. Other adverbial uses include *flocmælum* 'in (armed) bands' and *gearmælum* 'year by year'.

4   The dative absolute is used in imitation of the Latin ablative absolute, e.g. *gewunnenum sige* 'victory having been gained'.

5   The dative occurs after some adjectives, e.g. *ise gelicost* 'most like to ice', sometimes after comparatives, e.g. *sunnan beorhtra* 'brighter than the sun',

and after some verbs, e.g. *þæt he him miltsian sceolde* 'that he should have mercy on him'. Here too the glossary will help you.

6 It may express comparison, e.g. *Ic eom stāne heardra* 'I am harder than stone.'

Instrumental

§192 Where there is no special instrumental form (and sometimes when there is), the dative serves.

1 The instrumental expresses means or manner, e.g. *þone ilcan we hataþ oþre naman æfensteorra* 'we call the same by another name – evening star', *fægere ende his lif betynde* 'closed his life with a fair end' (but cf. the dative in *geendode yflum deaþe* 'ended with an evil death'), and *hlutre mode* 'with a pure mind'.

2 It expresses accompaniment, e.g. *lytle werode* 'with a small band'.

3 It expresses time, e.g. *þy ilcan geare* 'in the same year'.

IX ARTICLES, PRONOUNS, AND NUMERALS

Articles and Pronouns

§193 1 There are no definite 'articles' as such in OE. The demonstrative *se* does duty for 'the' and 'that', the demonstrative *þes* means 'this', e.g. *Her on þysum geare for se micla here, þe we gefyrn ymbe spræcon* . . . 'In this year went the great army which we spoke about before . . .'. Sometimes, however, *se* can be translated 'this', e.g. *anne æþeling se wæs Cyneheard haten – 7 se Cyneheard wæs þæs Sigebryhtes broþur* 'a princeling who was called C. and this C. was the brother of the S. already mentioned'.

2 The demonstrative is frequently not used in OE where we would use it or a definite article today, e.g. *wælstowe gewald* 'command of the battlefield', and, from the poetry (where its absence is even more common), *fram beaduwe* 'from the battle' and *Oddan bearn* 'the sons of Odda'. But the reverse is sometimes true, e.g. *sio lar* 'learning'.

3 In examples like *Æþered cyning* we have either absence of a demonstrative pronoun 'Æthered the King' or (more likely in view of *Iohannes se godspellere* 'John the Evangelist') a different arrangement of appositional elements 'King Æthered'. Hence *Æþelwulf aldormon* might be the equivalent of 'General Smith'.

4 The indefinite article is even rarer; thus we find *holtes on ende* 'at the edge of a wood', *to wæfersyne* 'as a spectacle', and *on beorg* 'onto a mountain'. *Ān* is sometimes used, e.g. *to anum treowe* 'to a tree' and *an wulf* 'a wolf'. But usually *ān* and *sum* mean something more, e.g. *an mægð* 'a certain tribe' and *sum mon* 'a certain man'. Sometimes these words have an even stronger sense, e.g. *þæt wæs an cyning* 'that was a peerless King', 'that wás a King',

and *eower sum* 'a particular one among you', 'your leader'. In this sense, and as the numeral 'one', *ān* is strong. Meaning 'alone', it is usually weak, e.g. *he ana*, but may be strong, e.g. *ðone naman anne* 'the name alone'.

5   *Se* is also used as a relative pronoun; see §162.3. Sometimes, as in *Beowulf* l. 1296, it may be either demonstrative or relative. But the uncertainty is of little practical consequence.

6   The third-person pronoun is sometimes used ambiguously, so that we cannot readily tell to whom it is referring. A well-known series of examples is found in the story of Cynewulf and Cyneheard (selection 6, third paragraph). But this is rather the result of inexperience in handling the language than of defects in the language itself, for later in its development, OE managed to make the meaning clear with no more pronouns at its disposal. The same is, of course, true of MnE.

7   A pronoun subject is frequently not expressed. Often the subject not expressed is the same as that of the preceding clause. But the absence of a subject does not certify that it has not changed; see, e.g. *Maldon* ll. 17–21, where the subject changes twice in l. 20 without any pronoun. A pronoun object may be similarly unexpressed, e.g. the sentence quoted in §167.6. Sometimes, however, *sē* is used instead of *hē* to make clear that a subject has changed, e.g. *Maldon* ll. 150 and 227. This avoids the ambiguity which could arise from a repeated or an absent *hē*, e.g. *Maldon* l. 286 and *Beowulf* l. 57.

Numerals

§194   The cardinal numerals can be used

1   as adjectives agreeing with a noun, e.g. *þrim gearum ær he forþferde* 'three years before he died' and *mid XXXgum cyningum* 'with thirty kings';
2   as nouns followed by a partitive genitive, e.g. *to anre þara burga* 'to one of the cities' and *þritig cyninga* 'thirty kings'.

X   VERBS

On the detailed uses of the indicative and subjunctive in subordinate clauses, see the discussions of the appropriate clause.

The Uses of the Present and Preterite Tenses

§195   As we have seen in §89, the OE verb distinguished only two tenses in conjugation – the present and the preterite. Hence, despite the fact that the beginnings of the MnE resolved tenses are found in OE (see §199), the two simple tenses are often used to express complicated temporal relationships. This is one of the things which made Professor Tolkien once say in a lecture that most people read OE poetry much more quickly than did the Anglo-Saxon minstrel, reciting or reading aloud as he was to an audience which needed time to pick up the implications of what he was saying. And this would apply, not only to the subject-matter, especially to the hints and allusions which frequently had great significance, but also to the relationships between paratactic sentences such as those discussed in §§182–185 and to the actual relationship in time between two actions both of which were described by a simple tense of a verb. Thus it is important for us to understand what these simple tenses could imply.

§196   The present expresses, not only a continuing state as in *Wlitig is se wong* 'The plain is beautiful', and *ðeos woruld nealæcð þam ende* 'this world is drawing near to its end', but also the passing moment, the actual 'now' for which MnE often uses a continuous tense, e.g. *hwæt þis folc segeð* 'what this people are saying, say now'. It is also used for the future, e.g. *þas flotmenn cumaþ* 'these seamen will come', and (as in equivalent examples in MnE) for the future perfect, e.g. *seþe þæt gelæsteð, bið him lean gearo* 'a reward will be ready for him who does (shall have done) that', and (with a subjunctive *gefeohte* as explained in §179.2) *gif hwa gefeohte on cyninges huse, sie he scyldig ealles his ierfes* 'if anyone fight (shall have fought) in the king's house, let him forfeit all his property'.

In the principal clause in the last sentence, the subjunctive *sīe* expresses a command and could be translated 'he shall forfeit'. The present subjunctive can also express a wish, e.g. *abreoðe his angin* 'may his enterprise fail', or a prayer, e.g. *God þe sie milde* 'May God be merciful to you'.

The only verb which has a special future form is the verb 'to be', where *bið* and its forms are used for the future, e.g. *bið him lean gearo* above, and for the statement of an eternal truth (a use sometimes called 'gnomic'), e.g. *wyrd bið ful aræd* 'Fate is quite inexorable' and *þonne bið heofena rice gelic þæm tyn fæmnum* 'Then the Kingdom of Heaven is like unto (the) ten virgins'. *Is* and its forms are normally used to refer to current conditions, e.g. *seo stow to dæge is nemned Godmundingaham* 'today the place *is* called Godmundingaham'.

The historic present rarely, if ever, occurs.

§197   The preterite indicative is used

1   of a single completed act in the past;
2   of an act continuing in the past. Both of these are exemplified in *soðlice þa ða men slepon, þa com his feonda sum* 'truly, while men were sleeping, one of his enemies came';
3   for the perfect, e.g. *ic mid ealre heortan þe gewilnode* 'I have wished for Thee with all my heart';
4   for the pluperfect, e.g. *sona swa hie comon* 'as soon as they had come' and (with a strengthening *ǣr*) *and his swura wæs gehalod þe ær wæs forslægen* 'and his neck, which had been cut through, was healed'. (Cf. the use of *ǣrur* in *Dream of the Rood* l. 108.) But see *Anglo-Saxon England* 4 (1975), 17–20.

§198 The preterite subjunctive may refer to the past, e.g. *ond ge wiðsocon þæt in Bethleme bearn cenned wære* 'and you denied that a child was born in Bethlehem', or to the future-in-the-past, e.g. the two sentences quoted at the end of §174.

It has already been pointed out in §179.4 that unreality is timeless in OE. An interestingly ambiguous example of this is seen in *Beowulf* ll. 960–1

Uþe ic swiþor
þæt ðu hine selfne   geseon moste . . . !

Here Beowulf might be saying to Hrothgar either

'I could wish that you could see Grendel now'; in other words 'I wish that he hadn't got away'

or 'I could wish that you could have seen Grendel yesterday'; in other words 'I wish that you had been at the fight and had seen how badly wounded he was'

or 'I could wish that you could see Grendel tomorrow'; in other words 'I wish that we could find his body and so know that he is dead'.

But the context strongly suggests the second.

The Resolved Tenses

Introduction

§199 This term is used to mean tenses made up from a participle (present or past) or an infinitive together with the verb 'to be', the verb 'to have', or one of the 'modal' verbs (see §206), e.g. MnE 'He is coming', 'He is come', 'He has come', 'He will come'. The beginnings of these forms are seen in OE, with one important difference which throws light on their origin. A MnE example will explain this. In Ephesians 6:14, the Revised Version reads 'Stand therefore, having girded your loins with truth'. If we parsed 'having girded', we would perhaps call it the perfect participle of the verb 'to gird', with 'your loins' its object; at any rate, we would say that it was part of the verb 'to gird'. But the King James Version reads 'Stand therefore having your loins girt about with truth'. Here 'your loins' is the object of the participle 'having' and 'girt about with truth' is a phrase describing 'your loins'; hence 'girt' is adjectival rather than verbal. That this was its original function in such phrases in OE becomes clear when we study the agreement of some of the examples cited below; to make this point, it will be convenient if we take first the ancestor of the MnE perfect tense with 'have'.

The Verb 'to have' as an Auxiliary

§200 Examples in which the participle is adjectival are *he us hafað þæs leohtes bescyrede* 'he has us deprived of that light' (where the present tense of *habban* is followed by *bescyrede* a past participle acc. pl. strong, agreeing with *ūs*) and *ac hi hæfdon þa heora stemn gesetenne and hiora mete genotudne* 'but then they had their term of service finished and their food used up' (where a past tense of *habban* is followed by two participles both of which are declined acc. sg. masc. strong, agreeing with *stemn* and *mete*, the objects of *hæfdon*). These are clearly the ancestors of the MnE perfect and pluperfect respectively.

But examples also occur in which there is no such declining of the past participle to agree with the object, e.g. *Eastengle hæfdon Ælfrede cyninge aþas geseald* 'The East Anglians had oaths given to King Alfred' and *Hæfde se cyning his fierd on tu tonumen* 'The king had his army divided in two'; cf. §187.1(*b*). This was of course, a necessary stage in the development of the MnE perfect and pluperfect tenses. The modern arrangement in which the participle precedes the object instead of having final position is found in such examples as *Nu ðu hæfst ongiten ða wanclan truwa þæs blindan lustes* 'Now you have perceived the fickle loyalty of blind pleasure'.

The Verb 'to be' as an Auxiliary of Tense

§201 1 It is found with the present participle as the ancestor of the MnE continuous tenses. But here too the participle was originally adjectival rather than verbal. It should also be noted that the OE combination is not the exact equivalent of the modern usage. Often it means the same as the corresponding simple tense, e.g. *þa wæs se cyning openlice andettende þam biscope* 'Then the king openly confessed to the bishop', though it may give greater vividness. (This construction is now agreed to be of native rather than of Latin origin.) But sometimes it implies that an action continued for some time, e.g. *ond hie þa . . . feohtende wæron* 'and then they kept on fighting' and *ða ða se apostol þas lare sprecende wæs* 'while the apostle was explaining this teaching'. In these examples, it comes close to the modern use.

2 The verb 'to be' is also found with the past participle forming the perfect and pluperfect of intransitive verbs, e.g. *Swæ clæne hio* [= *lar*] *wæs oðfeallenu on Angelcynne* 'So completely was learning fallen away in England' (where the participle is declined nom. sg. fem. strong, agreeing with the subject) and *hu sio lar Lædengeðiodes ær ðissum afeallen wæs* 'how the learning of Latin was fallen away before this' (where the participle is not declined). Here too the participle was originally adjectival rather than verbal.

The Passive

§202 Only one OE verb had a synthetic passive, viz. *hātte* 'is called', 'was called', e.g. *se munuc hatte Abbo* 'the monk was called A.'. Otherwise the idea was expressed by the impersonal *man* 'one' with the active voice, e.g. *Her mon mæg giet gesion hiora swæð* 'Here one can still see their track', or by the verbs 'to be' or 'to become' with the past participle, e.g. *to bysmore synd getawode þas earman landleoda* 'the miserable people of this land are (have been) shamefully ill-trcated', *Æfter þæm þe Romeburg getimbred wæs* 'After Rome was (had been) built', and *æfter minum leofum þegnum þe on heora bedde wurdon mid bearnum and wifum færlice ofslægene* 'after my beloved thanes who became (have been) suddenly killed in their beds with their wives and children'. The inflexions in the first and third of these examples show that here too the participle is adjectival rather than verbal. But again the participle was not always declined, e.g. *hie beoð ahafen from eorðan* 'they are raised from the earth'. (Can we definitely say it is not declined in the example about Rome?)

§203 The difference between the forms with *wesan* and those with *weorðan* is not well defined. The former sometimes seem to emphasize the state arising from the action, e.g. *he eall wæs beset mid heora scotungum* 'he was completely covered with their missiles' and (showing the continuing state by the use of *hið*) *ne bið ðær nænig ealo gebrowen* 'nor is any ale brewed there', and the latter the action itself, e.g. *þær wearþ se cyning Bagsecg ofslægen* 'there King B. was killed' (lit. 'became slain'). But this does not always hold; cf. e.g. *on þæm wæron eac þa men ofslægene* 'on it too the men were slain'. Such fluctuations are natural in a developing language. The fact that the *weorðan* form of the idiom disappeared suggests that the language found other ways of making the distinction when it was necessary, e.g. *þær se cyning ofslægen læg* 'whcre the king lay slain'; it was, claims J. M. Wattie, 'the only false start' in the development of the MnE verb.

Other Uses of the Present and Past Participles

§204 1 Present and past participles are found as nouns, e.g. *brimliþendra* 'of the seamen' and *He is se frumcenneda* 'He is the first-born', and as adjectives, e.g. *þinne ancennedan sunu* 'your only son'.

2 They also introduce phrases which may be the equivalent of adjective clauses, e.g. the sentences quoted in §187.1(*b*), or which may express various adverbial relationships, such as time, e.g. *þæt man his hlaford of lande lifigendne drife* 'that one should drive his lord from the land while he still lives', or cause, e.g. *me þearfendre* 'to me in my need'. (What sex is the last speaker?)

3 Together with a noun or a pronoun, a participle may be inflected in the dative case in imitation of a Latin ablative absolute; see §191.4.

4 Sometimes the exact grammatical status of such a phrase is not certain. Thus the first two words in *astrehtum handum to Gode clypode* 'with outstretched hands called to God' are taken by some as an absolute and by others as a dative of 'attendant circumstances'. Perhaps they are both. At any rate, such ambiguities are merely terminological.

The Uses of the Infinitives

§205 This section sets out the normal uses of the OE uninflected and inflected infinitives. Exceptional uses of the one in the functions here allotted to the other, however, do occur.

1   The uninflected infinitive is usual after the auxiliaries mentioned in §206 and after *uton* 'let us', *þurfan* 'need', and **durran* 'dare'. The infinitive of a verb of motion is frequently not expressed in such circumstances, e.g. *ær he in wille* 'before he will go in'.

As in MnE, there are circumstances in which either the infinitive without *tō* or a present participle can be used, e.g. *Ic geseah ða englas dreorige wepan and ða sceoccan blissigende on eowerum forwyrde* 'I saw the angels weep bitterly and the demons rejoicing at your destruction'.

On the accusative and infinitive, see §161.

2   As in MnE the inflected infinitive with *tō* is common in the following functions:

(a)   To express purpose, e.g. *an wulf wearð asend to bewerigenne þæt heafod* 'a wolf was sent to guard the head' and, with a passive sense, *bindað sceafmælum to forbærnenne* 'bind them in sheaves for burning, to be burnt'. But the simple infinitive also occurs, e.g. *ut eode ahyrian wyrhtan* 'went out to hire workers'.

(b)   With the verb 'to be' to express necessity or obligation, e.g. *Is eac to witanne* 'It must also be noted'.

(c)   To complete the sense of a verb, e.g. *and begunnon ða to wyrcenne* 'and then [they] began to work'. But cf. *ða ongan ic ða boc wendan on Englisc* 'then I began to translate the book into English', where the infinitive without *tō* occurs.

(d)   To complete the sense of a noun, e.g. *anweald to ofsleanne and to edcucigenne* 'power to kill and to restore to life', or of an adjective, e.g. *wæron æþelingas . . . fuse to farenne* 'the nobles were eager to depart'.

(e)   As the subject, or as the complement, of a sentence, e.g. *to sittanne on mine swyðran healfe . . . nys me inc to syllanne* 'to sit on my right hand is not for me to give to you two'.

The 'Modal' Auxiliaries

Introduction

§206   Some forms of the OE verbs *cunnan*, *willan*, **sculan*, *magan*, and **mōtan* still survive as auxiliaries today, viz. 'can', 'will', 'would', 'shall', 'should', 'may', 'might', and 'must'. As in OE, they are followed by the infinitive without 'to'. Their semantic history is a complicated one and even today the uses of some, especially 'shall' and 'will' and 'should' and 'would', cause great confusion to very many foreign speakers of English. Readers of OE too will find difficulties with them, but of a different sort, for the range of meanings they had in OE was wide, just as it is now.

Magan

§207   The primary meaning of *magan* is 'to be able to, can': e.g. *þæt he ealle þa tid mihte ge sprecan ge gangan* 'so that all the time he could both talk and walk'. Similarly in *Dream of the Rood* ll. 37–38: *Ealle ic mihte feondas gefyllan* 'I could have destroyed all his enemies'. Occasionally it means 'to be permitted to' as in Luke 16:2: *ne miht þu leng tunscire bewitan* 'you may no longer hold the stewardship'. In *Andreas* ll. 544ff

> Nænig manna is . . .
> ðætte areccan mæg   oððe rim wite . . .

it almost has the meaning of modern *may*: 'There is no man . . . [of such a sort] that he may (or can) relate or know the number.' The proper mood of the verb in such clauses is the subjunctive (see §175.2); hence *wite*. But parallel to it in the poem is *areccan mæg* 'may relate, may tell', which is indicative.

In *eorðe mæg wið ealra wihta gehwilce* 'the earth prevails against every creature', *magan* means 'prevail against' and has the force of an independent verb. Usage of *magan* as an independent verb with the meaning 'to prevail against' is very rare.

Thus *magan* has shades of meaning which cannot always be accurately distinguished. Does *Genesis B* ll. 436–7 mean 'what we can win by our own strength' or 'what God will allow us to win'? Consider too *ðu miht* in *Dream of the Rood* l. 78.

When it means 'to be permitted to' *magan* is a rival of **mōtan* 'to be allowed to'; cf. Luke 16:2 quoted above with Matthew 20:15 *ne mot ic don þæt ic wylle?* where the Authorized Version has 'Is it not lawful for me to do what I will?', and *Maldon* ll. 14 and 235 with *Maldon* ll. 83 and 95.

But in the sense of 'to be able to' it frequently comes close to *cunnan*; cf. Cædmon's statement (in the second paragraph of selection 9) *Ne con ic noht singan* 'I do not know how to sing anything' with the dream-figure's reply *Hwæðre þu meaht me singan*[1] 'Yet you can sing to me'. Here, as the Latin original *nescio cantare* suggests, *cunnan* may have its full sense of 'to know how to'. But it comes close to the modern sense of 'to be able to'.

*Mōtan

§208   The preterite of **mōtan* 'to be allowed to' is *mōste*, the ancestor of MnE 'must'. In *Maldon* l. 30 the present tense *þū mōst* comes close to meaning 'you must'. But it may be a very formal and ceremonious extension of the permissive use, perhaps with ironical overtones: 'The Danes bid me say that they are graciously pleased to allow you to send tribute in exchange for protection'. The sense of 'to be allowed to, may' is the prevailing one for **mōtan* in OE.

---

[1]   So some MSS. MS T lacks *me*; so some read *þu me aht singan* 'you must sing to me'. But here (i) we might expect an infl. inf. after *aht*; (ii) that *aht* could mean 'must' is uncertain.

Cunnan

§209   For an example of *cunnan* 'to know how to' shading into 'to be able, can' (its MnE sense), see §207 above.

*Sculan

§210   The most important function of **sculan* is to express necessity or obligation. Thus it must be translated 'must' in *Se byrdesta sceall gyldan* 'The wealthiest must pay', expressing a general obligation, and 'has had to' in *Wanderer* l. 3, where *sceolde* has no future reference at all. In *Maldon* l. 60 too, *sceal* means 'must', but here the reference is more clearly to one specific act which must take place in the future.

   Whether **sculan* ever represents the simple future is a matter of some dispute. Cædmon's reply to the comment of the angel quoted at the end of §207 was *Hwæt sceal ic singan?* Some of you may be tempted to translate this 'What shall I sing?' But the Latin has *Quid debeo cantare?* which demands the translation 'What must I (ought I to) sing?' Here then **sculan* clearly does not represent a simple future. And on the whole it will be safer for you to assume that it always has an idea of obligation, except in examples like those discussed in the next two paragraphs. When Ælfric in his grammar equates *lecturus sum cras* with *ic sceal rædan tomerigen*, it might seem a clear case of 'I shall read tomorrow'. But it probably means 'I must read tomorrow', for elsewhere Ælfric equates *osculaturus* with *se ðe wyle oððe sceal cyssan*. This does not mean that *wyle* and *sceal* mean the same thing, but that *osculaturus* has two possible meanings for Ælfric – futurity 'He is going to kiss' (see §211) and obligation 'He has to kiss'. So the OE version of Matthew 20:10 *And þa þe þær ærest comon wendon þæt hi sceoldon mare onfon*, which represents the Latin *Venientes autem et primi, arbitrati sunt quod plus essent accepturi*, is perhaps best translated 'And those who had come there first thought that they ought to receive more'.

   *Sculan can also express what is customary, e.g. *And ealle þa hwile þe þæt lic bið inne, þær sceal beon gedrync and plega* 'And all the time the body is within, there shall be drinking and playing'.

   In *ðæs nama sceolde bion Caron* 'whose name is said to be C.', *sceolde* shows that the reporter does not believe the statement or does not vouch for its truth. You will probably meet other examples of this.

Willan

§211   The original function of *willan* seems to have been the expression of wish or intention, e.g. *ic wille sellan* 'I wish to give', *þe þær beon noldon* 'who did not wish to be there', and *he wolde adræfan anne æþeling* 'he wanted to expel a princeling'. In these (with the possible exception of the second), there is some future reference. How far *willan* had gone along the road to simple futurity is difficult to determine, but examples like *Hi willað eow to gafole garas syllan* 'They want to (will) give you spears as tribute',

> æghwylc gecwæð,
> þæt him heardra nan   hrinan wolde

'everyone said that no hard thing would touch him', and *þa Darius geseah, þæt he oferwunnen beon wolde* 'When D. saw that he would be conquered' (note the passive infinitive), come pretty close to it.

Willan, like MnE 'will', is sometimes found 'expressing natural disposition to do something, and hence habitual action' (*OED* s.v. 'will' 8), e.g. *He wolde æfter uhtsange oftost hine gebiddan* 'He would most often pray after matins'.

On paratactic *wolde*, see §185.2 and cf. the *þæt* clause with *willan* in

> Geseah ic þa frean mancynnes
> efstan elne mycle   þæt he me wolde on gestigan

'I saw the Lord of mankind hasten with great zeal in His wish to climb on to me'.

Impersonal Verbs

§212   These are more common in OE than in MnE, but should not cause you much trouble if you notice that the subject 'it' is often not expressed, e.g. *me ðyncð betre* 'it seems better to me' and *hine nanes ðinges ne lyste* lit. 'it pleased him in respect of nothing'. But *hit* does appear, e.g. *hit gelamp* 'it happened'.

XI PREPOSITIONS

§213   The most important prepositions, with their meanings and the cases they govern, are set out below in alphabetical order. For their use in prepositional conjunctions, see §171.

Those marked with a dagger † govern both accusative and dative, the distinction usually being accusative of motion, e.g. *and heo hine in þæt mynster onfeng* 'and she received him into the monastery', and dative of rest, e.g. *on þam huse* 'in that house'. However, this distinction is not always observed.

Prepositions often follow the word they govern, e.g. *him to* 'against them' and *him biforan* 'before him'.

Sometimes words which often occur as prepositions are used without a noun or pronoun, e.g. *þa foron hie to* 'then they went thither' and *het þa in beran segn* 'then [he] ordered [them] to carry in the banner'. Here we have something similar to the separable prefixes of modern German.

List of Prepositions

§214   (Note: Some prepositions may be followed by the dative or the instrumental. As there is no significance in this variation, the instrumental has not been included in the list.)

æfter		dat. (acc.) 'after, along, according to'
ǣr		dat. (acc.) 'before'
æt		dat. 'at, from, by'; (acc. 'as far as, until')
be		dat. (acc.) 'by, along, alongside, about'
beforan		dat. acc. 'before, in front of'
betweox		dat. acc. 'among, between'
binnan	†	'within, into'
bufan	†	'above, upon'
būtan		dat. acc. 'except, outside, without'
ēac		dat. 'besides, in addition to'
for		dat. acc. 'before (of place), in front of, because of'
fram		dat. 'from, by (of agent)'
ġeond		acc. (dat.) 'throughout'
in	†	'in, into'
innan	†	'in, within'; (occasionally gen.)
mid		dat. acc. 'among, with, by means of'
of		dat. 'from, of'
ofer	†	'above, over, on'
on	†	'in, into, on'
on-ġēan		dat. acc. 'against, towards'
oþ		acc. (dat.) 'up to, until'
tō		gen. 'at, for, to such an extent, so'
		dat. 'towards, to, at, near'
		dat. 'as', in the idiom seen in *to frofre* 'as a consolation' and *to menniscum men* 'as a human being'; (acc. 'towards')
tō-ġēanes		dat. 'against, towards'
þurh		acc. (dat. gen.) 'through, throughout, by means of'
under	†	'under, beneath'
wiþ		acc. gen. dat. 'towards, opposite, against, along, in exchange for'
ymb(e)		acc. (dat.) 'after, about or concerning'

6

An Introduction to Anglo-Saxon Studies

I SOME SIGNIFICANT DATES

§215   If the Anglo-Saxon period is taken as beginning in 449 (as the venerable Bede tells us) and ending in 1066, it lasted for 617 years. It may help you to put this in perspective if you realize that this is some hundred years more than the period of time which separates us from Columbus' voyage of 1492 or, in literary terms, roughly the period between the birth of Chaucer and the deaths of Robert Frost and T. S. Eliot.

§216   See pp. 112–5.

II HISTORY

§217   The Germanic settlements in Britain[1], which (recent archaeological finds suggest) may have begun at least half a century earlier than the traditional A.D. 449, did not result in the immediate subjugation of the whole island under one Germanic king. Indeed, there is much evidence to suggest a vigorous revival of British fortunes, culminating about the time of the victory of Mons Badonicus (c. 490–517), which led to a renewed British predominance in some western and south-midland areas formerly overrun by the invaders. Only with the battles that the Chronicle associates with the West-Saxon leaders Ceawlin, Cuthwulf, Cutha, and Cuthwine (especially Biedcanford 571 and Dyrham 577), was Saxon control re-established in the Chilterns and Cotswolds. Romano-British elements, of course, still survived extensively in the population of Anglo-Saxon England.

The invading English, therefore, lived in independent kingdoms – there were ten south of the Humber in 600 – cut off from one another by geographical barriers and by hostile British. It is in such conditions of isolation that sound-changes flourish, and hence peculiarities which were originally individual or tribal and which would have been eliminated in a larger

[1] Britain, British refer to the Celtic people who populated England before the island was invaded by Germanic tribes – the Angles, Saxons, Jutes, and Frisians. England, English refer to these Germanic invaders after they took possession of the country and became the English.

A Guide to Old English, Eighth Edition. Bruce Mitchell and Fred C. Robinson.
© 2012 Bruce Mitchell and Fred C. Robinson. Published 2012 by Blackwell Publishing Ltd.

§216   TABLE OF DATES

Date	Lay	Religious	Literary
410	The Romans are no longer in Britain; Romanized Celts are left to defend themselves.		
449	Traditional date of coming of Angles, Saxons, and Jutes.		The legend of Arthur may rest on a British leader who resisted the invaders.
560–616	Æthelbert King of Kent.		*c.* 547 Gildas writes *De Excidio Britanniae.*
c. 563		St. Columba brings Celtic Christianity to Iona.	
597		St. Augustine brings Roman Christianity to Kent.	
616–632	Edwin King of Northumbria.		
c. 625	Earliest possible date for Sutton Hoo ship burial.		
625	Æthelbert's daughter marries King Edwin in Northumbria.		
627		Edwin converted to Christianity.	
632	Edwin killed by heathen King Penda of Mercia.		
635		Aidan settles in Lindisfarne, bringing Celtic Christianity.	
635		King Cynegils of Wessex converted.	
641	Oswald King of Northumbria killed by Penda.		
654	Penda killed by Oswy King of Northumbria.		
664		Synod of Whitby establishes supremacy of Roman Christianity.	

664	St. Chad becomes bishop.	
657–680	Hild Abbess of Whitby.	Cædmon uses Germanic alliterative verse for religious subjects during this period.
c. 673	Birth of Bede.	
c. 678	English missions to the continent begin.	
680		Approximate earliest date for composition of *Beowulf*.
c. 700		Date of first linguistic records.
709	Death of Aldhelm, Bishop of Sherborne.	
731		Bede completes *Historia Ecclesiastica Gentis Anglorum*.
735	Death of Bede. Birth of Alcuin.	
757–796	Offa King of Mercia.	
782	Alcuin settles at Charlemagne's court.	
793	Sacking of Lindisfarne. Viking raids begin.	
796		*fl.* 796 Nennius, author or reviser of *Historia Britonum*.
800	Four great kingdoms remain – Northumbria, Mercia, East Anglia, Wessex.	
780–850		Cynewulf probably flourishes some time in this period.
804	Death of Alcuin.	
851	Danes first winter in England.	
865	Great Danish Army lands in East Anglia.	

Date	Lay	Religious	Literary
867	Battle of York. End of Northumbria as a political power.		
869	King Edmund of East Anglia killed by Danes. East Anglia overrun.		
871	Alfred becomes King of Wessex.		
874	Danes settle in Yorkshire.		
877	Danes settle in East Mercia.		
880	Guthrum and his men settle in East Anglia. Only Wessex remains of the four kingdoms.		
?886	Boundaries of Danelaw agreed with Guthrum. Alfred occupies London.		The period of the Alfredian translations and the beginning of the Anglo-Saxon Chronicle.
892	Further Danish invasion.		
896	Alfred builds a fleet.		
899	Death of King Alfred.		
899–954	The creation of the English kingdom.		
c. 909		Birth of Dunstan.	
937	Battle of Brunanburh.		Poem commemorates the battle.
954	The extinction of the Scandinavian kingdom of York.		
959–975	Edgar reigns.		
959		Dunstan Archbishop of Canterbury. The period of the Monastic Revival.	

Date	Event	Literature
c. 971	The Blickling Homilies.	
978 or 979	Murder of King Edward.	
950–1000		Approximate dates of the poetry codices – Junius MS, Vercelli Book, Exeter Book, and *Beowulf* MS.
978 or 979–1016	Ethelred reigns.	
988	Death of Dunstan.	
991	Battle of Maldon.	Poem commemorates the battle.
990–992		*Ælfric's Catholic Homilies.*
993–998		*Ælfric's Lives of the Saints.*
1003–1023	Wulfstan Archbishop of York.	
c. 1014		*Sermo Lupi ad Anglos.*
1005–c. 1012	Ælfric Abbot of Eynsham.	
1013	Sweyn acknowledged as King of England.	
1014	Sweyn dies.	
1016	Edmund Ironside dies.	
1016–1042	Canute and his sons reign.	
1042–1066	Edward the Confessor.	
1066	Harold King.	
	Battle of Stamford Bridge.	
	Battle of Hastings.	
	William I King.	

community flourished unchecked. Thus by *c.* 700, the date of the earliest linguistic records, the four dialects mentioned in §2 – Northumbrian, Mercian, West-Saxon, and Kentish – can be distinguished in a language which at the time of the invasions may have been spoken in much the same way by all those who came to England.

The two hundred or so years after the English victory at the unidentified Biedcanford are not well documented and the history of the period is often obscure. There was certainly much fighting between the various kingdoms, with now one, now another, temporarily 'top-dog' under some powerful warrior-king, though there was a period of comparative peace during the late seventh and the eighth centuries in which the northern civilization which produced Bede, Alcuin, and the like, flourished. By 800, however, four great kingdoms survived, Northumbria, Mercia, Wessex, and East Anglia.

Then came the Danes. First they made what might be called 'smash-and-grab' raids in the summer, taking their booty back home with them. In 851 they are recorded as wintering on the Isle of Thanet. In 865 they ravaged Kent. In 867 they moved from East Anglia to York. Over the next few years there was intense activity. One by one, the kingdoms of Northumbria, East Anglia, and Mercia, ceased to exist as independent kingdoms and in 878 Wessex too was nearly extinguished, for in that year King Alfred was taking refuge in Æthelney 'with a small band' while the Danes plundered his kingdom. But Alfred was equal to the challenge. His grasp of the principles of war as revealed by a study of his campaigns against the Danes, and his activities in education, learning, and administration, over the next twenty years until his death in 899, are such that, for some people at any rate, his only rival for the title 'The greatest Englishman of all' is Sir Winston Churchill. The Anglo-Saxon Chronicle has two simple, but revealing, phrases in its account of this period. In 878, it says, the whole of Wessex surrendered to the Danes *buton þam cyninge Ælfrede* 'except King Alfred'. He escaped and rallied his forces. Men flocked to his banner *and his gefægene wærun* 'and were glad of him'.

By 880, then, only Wessex remained of the four kingdoms existing in 800. The subsequent years were a period of uneasy peace in which the Danes settled and ploughed and in which the boundaries of Danelaw were established. The arrival of another Danish army from France in 892 led to more bitter fighting in which the invaders were helped by those in Northumbria and East Anglia. But gradually Wessex, under Alfred and his successors, won back land from the settled Danes and reconciled them to English rule. In 954 the Scandinavian kingdom of York ceased to exist and the permanent unification of England as one kingdom began. As a result England was able to enjoy a period of comparative peace in the second half of the tenth century in which the great revival of Benedictine monasticism took place, and in which England began to achieve nationhood – a short passage in *The Battle of Maldon* (ll. 51–4) may perhaps contain the beginnings of a sense of patriotism. Nevertheless, in the Laws of Canute we still find a threefold division into Wessex, Mercia, and Danelaw, which reflects the divisions of the earlier period.

The subsequent history of Anglo-Saxon England is well known – the reigns of Ethelred the Unready, of the Danish dynasty, and of Edward the Confessor, were followed by Harold's victory at Stamford Bridge and his defeat at Hastings.

§218　The fortunes of Christianity fluctuated in Anglo-Saxon England, and students of its literature must grasp the implications of this fact, which are discussed in §§243–245. The Christianity of Roman Britain was not accepted by the pagan invaders, who brought with them the Germanic heroic code, which was in many ways no ignoble way of life. St. Columba and his followers brought Celtic Christianity to the north, while St. Augustine and his followers from Rome spread their teaching from the south until in 664 the Synod of Whitby established the supremacy of Rome. But heathenism was never very far away. King Edwin of Northumbria was killed by the pagan Penda, King of Mercia, in 632. Throughout the Anglo-Saxon period, preachers inveighed against paganism. Alcuin asked his famous question 'What has Ingeld to do with Christ?' in 797, in a letter condemning the recitation of heathen poetry to monks. The invading Danes brought their paganism with them. Both King Alfred and King Ethelred stood sponsor at the baptism of some of their foes, and in 1012, during the lifetime of Ælfric and Wulfstan, Ælfeah Archbishop of Canterbury was murdered by drunken Danes. It is therefore possible that any Christian poet writing in Old English between 680 and 850, when most of the extant poetry was probably written, could have been a convert from paganism or the son of a pagan. Early Christian poetry adapts pagan symbolism to its own use. This crucial ambivalence is seen in the Benty Grange helmet (§244) and in the Sutton Hoo ship burial, which could be a memorial either to the pagan King Rædwald or to one of his early Christian successors. But the Christian faith and the Christian culture were preserved and strengthened by the faithful and were not submerged by the new brand of paganism introduced by the Scandinavian invaders.

III ARCHAEOLOGY

Introduction

§219　The belief that Anglo-Saxon civilization was decadent before the Norman Conquest dies hard, despite recent attempts to refute it. But it is without foundation. By 1066, English missionaries had preached Christianity in Scandinavia and, despite two centuries of Danish attacks, political unity had been achieved. The idea of nationhood had developed among the people; in its account of the dispute between Earl Godwine and Edward the Confessor over Count Eustace, the Chronicle observes that 'it was hateful to almost all of them to fight against men of their own race, for there were very few on either side who were worth much, apart from Englishmen. Moreover, they did not wish to put this country at the mercy of foreigners by fighting each other' (MS D, 1052). Despite the wars and rumours of wars of this period, England in 1066 possessed (according to R. W. Chambers)

> a civilization based upon Alfred's English prose as the national official and literary language. English jewellery, metal-work, tapestry and carving were famed throughout Western Europe. English illumination was unrivalled, and so national that the merest novice can identify the work of the Winchester school. Even in stone-carving, those who are competent to judge speak of the superiority of the native English carver over his Norman supplanter. In building upon a large scale England was behind Normandy. But what little is left to us of Eleventh-Century Anglo-Saxon architecture shows an astonishing variety. Its mark is 'greater cosmopolitanism, as compared to the more competent, but equally more restricted and traditional architecture of the Normans'.

Unfortunately, space does not permit a full treatment of these points; all that can be done is to provide you with the means of testing for yourself the truth of R. W. Chambers's vividly expressed view that it seems as if 'Eleventh-Century England was getting into the Fifteenth; as if England was escaping from the Dark Ages without passing through the later Middle Ages at all'. A short Bibliography is given first. This is followed by a list of topics accompanied by brief comments and references to the books cited.

Note
The quotations given above are from R. W. Chambers *On the Continuity of English Prose from Alfred to More and his School* (Early English Text Society, 1932).

List of Abbreviated Titles

§220   For convenience, each book is given a brief title which is used in the sections which follow. The first three contain useful Bibliographies covering many of the topics discussed below. See also §258.

The Anglo-Saxons
> D. M. Wilson *The Anglo-Saxons* (3rd ed., Penguin, 1981). This includes thirty-eight figures and seventy-nine monochrome illustrations, covering all the topics listed below.

A-S England
> P. Hunter Blair *An Introduction to Anglo-Saxon England* introduction by Simon Keynes (new ed., Cambridge, 2003)

Archaeology
> *The Archaeology of Anglo-Saxon England*, ed. David M. Wilson (Methuen, 1976), now available in paperback (Cambridge, 1981)

Architecture
   E. A. Fisher *An Introduction to Anglo-Saxon Architecture and Sculpture* (Faber and Faber, 1959)

Art
   C. R. Dodwell *Anglo-Saxon Art. A New Perspective* (Manchester, 1982)

Note
David M. Wilson *Anglo-Saxon Art from the Seventh Century to the Norman Conquest* with 285 illustrations, 73 in colour (Thames and Hudson, 1984), can be recommended as an alternative. But it is perhaps less conveniently arranged for the beginner. Its chapter headings are 1. Taste, personalities and survival; 2. The seventh-century explosion; 3. The eighth and ninth centuries; 4. Influences; 5. From Alfred to the Conquest. The Index does not contain main entries under the headings architecture, buildings, carving, dress, embroidery, jewellery, metalwork, sculpture, or weapons.

Beowulf Arch.
   Leslie Webster 'Archaeology and *Beowulf*' in *Beowulf: An Edition* ed. Bruce Mitchell and Fred C. Robinson (rev. ed. Oxford, 2006), 183–94.

Beowulf Introduction
   Andy Orchard *A Critical Companion to Beowulf* (Cambridge, 2003)

Everyday Life
   R. I. Page *Life in Anglo-Saxon England* (London and New York, 1970)

An Indispensable Handbook
   Michael Lapidge and others, ed. *The Blackwell Encyclopaedia of Anglo-Saxon England* (Oxford, 1999)

Dress
   Gale R. Crocker-Owen *Dress in Anglo-Saxon England* (Manchester, 1986)

Jewellery
   R. Jessup *Anglo-Saxon Jewellery* (Faber and Faber, 1950)

Bayeux Tapestry
   Reproductions of this will be found in
   Douglas and Greenaway *English Historical Documents Volume II 1042–1189* (Eyre and Spottiswoode, 1953)
   F. Stenton and others *The Bayeux Tapestry: A Comprehensive Survey* (2nd ed., London, 1965)
   D. M. Wilson *The Bayeux Tapestry* (London, 1985)

The sections on archaeology are inevitably out of date in some places because many discoveries are not written up until years after they are made. One case in point is the timber material, knowledge of which has expanded enormously in recent years. New information can be found in the

Introduction to *Anglo-Saxons*, in the works listed in §258, in *Anglo-Saxon England*, published annually by Cambridge University Press, and in *Medieval Archaeology*, which each year offers an account of new finds under the heading *Medieval Britain in 20***. Colour slides of manuscripts, jewellery, and so on, can be obtained from Woodmansterne Colourslides, Holywell Industrial Estate, Watford, WD1 8RD, England, or from the museum which houses them.

Weapons and Warfare

§221 See *The Anglo-Saxons*, chapter IV.

It may be of interest to note here how archaeological finds prove the accuracy of the *Beowulf* poet's descriptions of swords, coats-of-mail, helmets, and the like. Thus his mention in ll. 1448–54 of a helmet with chain-mail is confirmed by the discovery in York of the Coppergate helmet, a magnificent piece of Anglo-Saxon craftsmanship in iron and brass with a curtain of mail protecting the neck of the wearer, while the helmet of ll. 1030–4 can be identified as a Romanesque helmet with a solid comb and not the ribbed helmet seen in the Bayeux Tapestry. See further *Beowulf Arch.*, pp. 57–67, and *The Coppergate Helmet* by Dominic Tweddle (York, 1984).

Other points worthy of study are the Danish strategy in the last decade of the ninth century and Alfred's methods of countering it, and the careful way in which the young Beowulf leads his 'platoon' during his journey to Denmark and his stay there. When reading *The Battle of Maldon* you should ask whether Byrhtnoth's decision to let the Danes cross the causeway unmolested was tactically right or the result of *ofermod* (a characteristic attributed only to Byrhtnoth and Satan). (It can scarcely be a misguided expression of the English sense of 'fair play'.)

Life and Dress

§222 Some knowledge of how the Anglo-Saxons dressed, lived, ate, and drank, will help you to realize more clearly that the writers and scribes whose work you read, and the warriors, priests, statesmen, and others, whose lives you study, were human beings like yourself, subject to weariness and pain, and prey to the same emotions as you are. This knowledge can be acquired from *The Anglo-Saxons*, chapter III, from *Dress*, or from *Everyday Life*, which reconstruct life in Anglo-Saxon times and often give some valuable insights into the way our ancestors lived, thought, and felt. The Bayeux Tapestry can be studied with profit. Works in Anglo-Saxon which throw light on the more personal and intimate sides of life include the *Leechdoms*, the *Charms*, and the *Riddles*. Ælfric's *Colloquy* (ed. G. N. Garmonsway, 2nd ed., Methuen, 1947) gives a picture of the life and activities of the middle and lower classes of whom we hear little elsewhere. But now and then those who are on the watch will catch momentary glimpses. Thus in the Chronicle for 897 (Parker MS), we find the names of three Frisian sailors killed in a sea-battle. The death of these men, who had been teaching the Anglo-Saxons the art of sea-fighting, is given poignancy by a few lines from the *Maxims* or *Gnomes* of the Exeter Book:

> Welcome is her beloved to the Frisian wife when the ship lies at anchor. His ship has returned and her husband, her own bread-winner, is at home. She welcomes him in, washes his sea-stained garments, gives him new clothes, and grants him on his return what his love demands.

Here are three Frisians whose garments will need no washing and who will be looked for in vain.

Architecture and Buildings

§223   Monochrome plates I and II in *Jewellery* illustrate timber huts and buildings. *Everyday Life* discusses timber huts and halls with illustrations – and supplements the remarks which follow – in chapter IX 'King's Hall, Peasant's Cottage, Town House'. See also *The Anglo-Saxons*, chapter III.

Aerial photographs taken in 1949 led to excavations of Old Yeavering, Northumberland, which revealed an Anglo-Saxon township. A large timber fort dated from the second half of the sixth century. A township outside the fort appeared to have developed in the seventh century. It included a massive timber hall with other smaller halls (one of which may have been a pagan temple later converted to Christian use) and a large timber grandstand for outdoor meetings. The large hall was replaced by an even more ambitious one and the grandstand was enlarged in the reign of King Edwin. The whole township was then destroyed by fire, probably by Cadwallon after Edwin's death in 632. The township was then rebuilt, still in timber, in what may have been Celtic style, and a Christian church was built, around which there grew a large cemetery. This township too was destroyed by fire – perhaps by Penda in 651. The great hall, two smaller halls, and the church, were rebuilt. But towards the end of the seventh century, Yeavering was abandoned in favour of a new site called Melmin, a few miles away.

At Cheddar in Somerset, another Saxon royal residence was excavated in 1960–2. In King Alfred's time, it consisted of a two-storey hall and three smaller buildings, the largest of which was probably a *bur*; see *Beowulf* ll. 140 and 1310. Later kings carried out additions and reconstructions.

The discoveries at Yeavering throw light on the hall in *Beowulf* (see *Beowulf Arch.*, pp. 68–77) and help to fill out the picture given by the poet. Those at Cheddar may serve to illustrate two interesting stories in the Chronicle – the death of King Cynewulf after being trapped in a *bur* which, like that at Cheddar, was separate from the hall, not part of it (selection 6; see note to line 11) and the escape of Archbishop Dunstan, who was left standing alone on a beam when the upper floor of a hall collapsed at Calne, Wiltshire (Laud MS, 978).

On these excavations, see Philip Rahtz *The Saxon and Medieval Palaces at Cheddar* (Oxford, 1979) and B. Hope-Taylor *Yeavering – An Anglo-British centre of early Northumbria* (HMSO, 1977).

Excavations on Cowdery's Down, Basingstoke, Hampshire, in 1978–81 revealed an ancient habitation-site re-used by the Anglo-Saxons but abandoned *c*. 800, and provided well-preserved and detailed evidence for timber architecture of the sixth and seventh centuries A.D.; see *The Archaeological Journal* 140 (1983), 192–261.

§224 Stone was used mainly for churches. But excavations in Northampton in 1981–2 revealed a rectangular stone hall *c*. 37.5 × 11.5 metres, with two rooms subsequently added to the west of the building, increasing its length by 6 metres. Tentatively dated early in the eighth century, it seems to have directly replaced a seventh-century timber hall and possibly decayed or was demolished during the Danish occupation of Northampton in the late ninth and early tenth centuries. See *Current Archaeology* 85 (1982), 38–41. *Architecture* contains a useful introduction to the study of Anglo-Saxon churches and crypts, with plans, photographs, and a bibliography. See also *The Anglo-Saxons*, pp. 50 ff. There are a large number of Saxon churches worth visiting. One which for some reason has proved particularly memorable is that of St. Peter at Bradwell-iuxta-Mare in Essex, which is built mostly of masonry from the nearby Roman fort. A visit to this, to the site of the battle of Maldon on a farm on the R. Blackwater, and to the new nuclear power-station, would make quite an interesting day!

However, wood was used for churches when stone was not readily available. The church at Greenstead, Essex, where (tradition relates) the body of King Edmund of East Anglia rested in 1013 on its way from London to Bury St. Edmunds, is a surviving example of the kind, though its timbers may not date back to Anglo-Saxon times.

Sculpture and Carving

§225 *Architecture* gives an interesting introduction, with illustrations, to works in stone. Survivals include crosses such as those at Ruthwell and Bewcastle, sundials like that at Kirkdale, sepulchral slabs, fonts, and figures like the angels in the Church of St. Lawrence at Bradford-on-Avon. The different types of ornamentation show influences from different countries and civilizations – Celtic, Mediterranean, Northern, and even Eastern.

The carved oak coffin of St. Cuthbert (late seventh-century) and the Franks Casket of whalebone carved with historical and legendary scenes framed with runes (early eighth-century) survive to show that Anglo-Saxon artists worked in media other than stone.

See further *The Anglo-Saxons*, pp. 53 ff., 152 ff., and 158 ff., and *Art*, chapter IV.

Jewellery and Metalwork

§226　A fascinating and well-illustrated account which tells where the jewels can be seen will be found in *Jewellery*. The author writes:

> Side by side with its interest for the archaeologist and the historian, Anglo-Saxon jewellery has a foremost appeal to the artist and the craftsman of today, who find in a contemplation of its design and technique the exercise of something more than a bare academic interest. To the practising jeweller especially its excellence needs no commendation, and to him it has often yielded an inspiration far from that of unalloyed sentiment.

See also *The Anglo-Saxons*, pp. 137 ff. and 161 ff., and *Art*, chapter VII.

To test the truth of this claim, those in a position to do so should view what Anglo-Saxon jewellery they can, especially the Kingston Brooch and the jewels of the Sutton Hoo Treasure in the British Museum (see §230) and the Alfred and Minster Lovell Jewels in the Ashmolean Museum, Oxford. Some of these are shown in colour in *Jewellery*. Other well-known treasures include the Pectoral Cross of St. Cuthbert (in the Cathedral Library, Durham), finger-rings which belonged to King Æthelwulf and to Queen Æthelswith, King Alfred's sister (both in the British Museum), and necklaces of amethyst, gold, or other material. *Jewellery*, *The Anglo-Saxons*, and *Art*, offer monochrome illustrations. *Art* has colour plates of an ivory crucifix and a chalice.

By viewing these beautiful objects, we are able to see that the love of beauty and craftsmanship we observe in *Beowulf* is no mere artistic pose, but an accurate reflection of the attitude of the people of his time. Like so many of their descendants, the Anglo-Saxons could combine fierceness in battle with love of the beautiful.

Embroidery

§227　'The tapestries', sings the *Beowulf* poet, 'shone gold-embroidered along the walls, many wondrous sights for those among men who gaze upon such.' Unfortunately, none survives. But rich embroideries can be found in the ninth-century chasuble now at Maaseik, Belgium, and in the early tenth-century vestments now among the relics of St. Cuthbert at Durham, which were made to the order of Queen Ælfflæd, King Æthelstan's queen. These include St. Cuthbert's stole, illustrated in colour in *Art*.

Strictly speaking, as Sir Eric Maclagan points out, the Bayeux Tapestry is 'no tapestry at all, the design being embroidered upon the material and not woven into it'. It is very possible that it was made in England within twenty years of the Conquest by English needlewomen working to the order of Bishop Odo of Bayeux.

See further *Art*, chapters V and VI.

Coins

§228   See *Archaeology*, pp. 349–372.

Manuscripts and Runic Inscriptions

§229   On illuminations and decorations, see *The Anglo-Saxons*, pp. 148 ff. and 156 ff., and *Art*, chapter IV and the relevant colour plates.

On the contents and whereabouts of manuscripts, see

N. R. Ker *Catalogue of Manuscripts containing Anglo-Saxon* (Clarendon Press, 1957).

On handwriting, see (in addition to the above)

Michelle P. Brown *Anglo-Saxon Manuscripts* (British Library, 1991).
Christopher de Hamel *Medieval Craftsmen: Scribes and Illuminators* (British Museum, 1992).

On runes, see

R. I. Page *An Introduction to English Runes* (Methuen, 1973).

The Sutton Hoo Ship-Burial

§230   In 1939, the excavation of a barrow at Sutton Hoo, Suffolk, revealed the ship-burial of an East Anglian King. See Martin Carver *Sutton Hoo: A Seventh-Century Princely Burial Ground and its Context* (London, 2005), which contains colour plates, including one of the great gold buckle (5.2 inches long weighing 14.6 ounces) which is portrayed on the cover of this *Guide*. It must not be thought that the poem *Beowulf* was composed to illustrate the ship-burial or that the burial was intended to illustrate *Beowulf*. However, while, in Sir David Wilson's words, 'what Sutton Hoo really illuminates is the general culture of the seventh century', the burial and *Beowulf* can be said to illuminate one another. Both show a mixture of cremation and inhumation. The burial affects the dating and genesis of *Beowulf*. It helps to explain why so much matter concerning the Swedes and other Scandinavian peoples should appear in an English poem and why there is a blend of pagan and Christian elements. It tells us that war gear and treasures of gold and gems like those described by the *Beowulf* poet existed in Anglo-Saxon times and that the poet and his audience shared the pride and joy in them which he portrays.

Further Archaeological Finds

Anglo-Saxon archaeology is a dynamic field that is constantly making new revelations about early England. A treasure hoard recently discovered in Staffordshire (1,500 artifacts) has been described as the largest collection of Anglo-Saxon gold objects ever found. A royal burial site in Prittlewell, Southend, Essex – probably contemporary with Sutton Hoo – has been excavated and continues to be evaluated. A seventh-century gold cross was discovered on a farm in Nottinghamshire, and at Aughton, South Yorkshire, a gold aestel like those referred to in selection 5, ll. 75–77 below was unearthed in 2008. In the parish of Flixborough in Lincoln an exceptionally large find with artefacts and animal remains (studied since 1989 and still being published) reveals much about Anglo-Saxon life in this area in the late seventh through the early ninth centuries and after. Such discoveries continue to enhance our understanding and appreciation of the rich culture of the Anglo-Saxons. Archeology also gives us a window into the culture that the Anglo-Saxons encountered and to some extent assimilated when they invaded England. A find unearthed in Hoxne in Suffolk in 1992 is the richest Roman hoard ever discovered in England and tells us much about the Romano-Celtic culture which the Anglo-Saxons found in place when they came to Britain. The latest coins at Hoxne were minted in A.D. 407–408, thus dating this hoard to the time just before the arrival in force of the Anglo-Saxons.

IV LANGUAGE

See first Preliminary Remarks on the Language (§§1–4).

Changes in English

§231 It has already been pointed out in §140 that Old English was in process of changing from an inflected to an uninflected language. It has also been shown in the discussions on syntax that the distinction between subject and object – originally made by the contrast between nominative and accusative endings – was increasingly brought out by word-order and that prepositions more and more took over the function of the oblique cases as the inflexional endings became reduced. These changes in accidence and syntax, and in the pronunciation of unstressed vowels, affected the English language far more fundamentally than the later changes in spelling and in the pronunciation of vowels in stressed syllables.

The primitive Germanic languages developed a stress accent on the first syllable of words in place of the shifting stress of the original IE language which is seen, for example, in classical Greek and which has already been

mentioned in §§90 and 105–106. As a result, differences in the pronunciation of unstressed syllables which had been important for making distinctions of meaning gradually disappeared. An important example in the
endings of verbs has already been mentioned in §113.3, and there are
occasional spellings which suggest that the nom. pl. ending -*as* and the gen.
sg. ending -*es* of strong masc. and neut. nouns were not always clearly
distinguished in late OE.

Before the case endings finally disappeared, we can see the same job being
done twice. In *he ofsloh ge þone cyning ge ða cwene* 'he slew both the king
and the queen', we see subject and object distinguished by word-order and
case-ending. In *mid ealre þære fierde* 'with the whole army', a preposition is
followed by an oblique case. This stage was necessary before one of the two
devices doing the same job could disappear. But once they existed together,
the disappearance of one of them became very likely, for few human beings
like doing the same job twice. The increasing use of, and finally complete
reliance on, word-order and prepositions made possible the ultimate disappearance of noun inflexions, apart from the genitive ending -*s* and the
distinction between singular and plural. Similarly, new ways were found of
distinguishing tense and mood in the verb; see the article by J. M. Wattie
mentioned in §256.

The Danish Invasions

§232   These tendencies were already apparent in OE before the influence
of the dialects spoken by the Danish invaders of the ninth century could have
made itself felt and may well have been more advanced in colloquial OE than
in the more conservative forms of the language recorded in the manuscripts.
But the Danish invasions and settlements must in fact have hastened the
process and perhaps caused it to be more complete than it might otherwise
have been. OHG (the ancestor of Modern German) and OE were very
similar in their grammatical structure. Yet today, while German has many
inflexions and retains the three word-orders S.V., V.S., and S. . . . V., and
other typically Germanic grammatical devices such as the distinction
between strong and weak forms of the adjective, English has dispensed
with them. Why? The Norman Conquest used to be blamed. As we shall
see below, it was certainly not without effect here, although its influence on
the language was felt more powerfully elsewhere. But the language of the
invading Danes was, like Old English, a Germanic language. The roots of
many words were similar, but the inflexional endings differed. When a
Dane married an Anglo-Saxon woman, it must have been very confusing
for their offspring to hear the one say *segls, segli*, where the other said *segles,
segle*, or to find that one said *nema nemir nemi* for the present subjunctive
singular form of the verb 'to take' while the other used *nime* for all persons.
Some confusion of endings was inevitable as a result of the fixing of the main

stress (already mentioned in §231) in all Germanic languages, but this confusion must have been greater in bilingual communities of Danes and Anglo-Saxons.

The Norman Conquest

§233   Since King Ethelred had married a Norman wife in 1002, the influence of French began before the Conquest. But with the Conquest, and its subsequent use as the language of the court and of administration, Norman French became more important. Certain developments already under way in English may have been reinforced by similar tendencies in Norman French and also in Central French, which began to influence English after the accession of the Angevin Henry II in 1154. These are the standardization of word-order as S.V.O. and the loss of inflexions, which resulted in the development of the simple case system of Modern English. The commencement of parallel trends is attested in continental French of the twelfth century, although their completion was long drawn out and varied from region to region. Again, the fact that many French words had plurals in -*s* must have helped the native -*s* ending of *stanas* to oust its rival, the -*n* ending of *naman*, and to become the plural ending of Modern English nouns. But perhaps the most important influences of French were on vocabulary (see §234), on spelling, and on English prose. The French scribes abandoned the conservative English spelling, which often made distinctions which no longer existed, and introduced their own system. As a result it appears that sound-changes which had occurred gradually over the centuries had happened all at once. A similar situation might arise today if English were to be respelt phonetically by foreign scribes who used their own alphabet with the addition of a few English letters. After the Conquest, English prose gradually ceased to be used for official purposes and for history, but was still used for sermons and other religious works. Further reading on this topic is suggested in §259.

Vocabulary

§234   The vocabulary of OE was basically Germanic and the language was less hospitable to borrowings than it is today, frequently preferring to make its own compounds rather than admit foreign words; see §137. But some were admitted. Up to the time of the Norman Conquest, the following groups can be distinguished:

1   Latin
   (*a*) words borrowed in Pr. Gmc. times;
   (*b*) pre-650 borrowings in Britain;
   (*c*) post-650 borrowings in Britain.

2 Greek
    (*a*) direct borrowings, mostly by the Goths;
    (*b*) borrowings through Latin.
3 Celtic.
4 Scandinavian.
5 French.

References to books which deal with this subject will be found in §261. If you do study them, you will find it interesting to note how the words borrowed from the different languages reflect the relationships which existed between the two peoples concerned and so throw light on the history of the period.

Some Questions

§235 If, while studying OE, you consciously note the differences between OE and MnE, you will make your task easier and more interesting. Questions you might like to answer with the help of one of the histories of the language mentioned in §253 are:

1 Where did the *-s* plural of MnE come from? Did French have any influence here? (This has already been touched on in §233.)
2 Where did the *-s* of the MnE genitive singular come from?
3 How did 'of' become a sign of possession, as in 'The mast of the ship'?
4 When did *-eth* disappear as the ending of 3rd sg. pres. ind.?
5 Why do we find in Chaucer the ending *-en* for the pres. ind. pl. when OE has *-að*? Where did this *-en* ending come from?

V LITERATURE

Introduction

§236 As has been pointed out in §218, the Germanic tribes who settled in England in the fifth century brought with them the Germanic heroic code. What we learn of it from Old English literature generally confirms the observations of Tacitus in his *Germania*. The salient points are these. The Germanic warrior was a member of a *comitatus*, a warrior-band. Life was a struggle against insuperable odds, against the inevitable doom decreed by a meaningless fate – *Wyrd*, which originally meant 'what happens'. There is no evidence in their literature that the pagan Anglo-Saxons believed in a life after death like that of Valhalla, the hall in Scandinavian mythology reserved for dead heroes, though there are references to the worship of heathen gods such as Woden, and the practice of placing coins, weapons, and other goods, with the bodies of the dead in both inhumation and cremation burials, suggests a belief in some kind of after-life where they could be used. On this see *The Anglo-Saxons*, pp. 35–6. It is, however, a different kind of immortality which is stressed in their literature. This was *lof*, which was won by bravery in battle and consisted of glory among men, the praise of those still living. These two ideas of *wyrd* and *lof* acquired Christian overtones; see §§244–245. So the reference of passages like those from *Beowulf* which follow is unlikely to be entirely pagan:

> Swa sceal man don,
> þonne he æt guðe   gegan þenceð
> longsumne lof;   na ymb his lif cearað

'So must a man do when he thinks to win enduring fame in battle; he will show no concern for his life' and

> Wyrd oft nereð
> unfægne corl,   þonne his ellen deah!

'Fate often spares an undoomed man when his courage is good'.

§237 An heroic warrior brought up in this tradition would show a reckless disregard for his life. Whether he was doomed or not, courage was best, for the brave man could win *lof* while the coward might die before his time. This is the spirit which inspired the code of the *comitatus*. While his lord lived, the warrior owed him loyalty unto death. If his lord were killed, the warrior had to avenge him or die in the attempt. The lord in his turn had the duty of being generous to his warriors. He had to be a great fighter to attract men, a man of noble character and a generous giver of feasts and treasures to hold them. So we read in *The Battle of Finnsburh*

> Ne gefrægn ic næfre wurþlicor   æt wera hilde
> sixtig sigebeorna   sel gebæran,
> ne nefre swanas hwitne medo   scl forgyldan
> ðonne Hnæfe guldan   his hægstealdas

'I have never heard it said that sixty conquering warriors bore themselves better or more worthily in mortal combat, or that any retainers repaid the shining mead better than Hnæf's retainers repaid him'.

The whole code receives one of its last and finest expressions in *The Battle of Maldon*, especially in the oft-quoted lines spoken by the old warrior Byrhtwold:

> Hige sceal þe heardra,   heorte þe cenre,
> mod sceal þe mare,   þe ure mægen lytlað

'Courage must be the firmer, heart the bolder, spirit the greater, the more our strength wanes' (or 'our force diminishes'). Here we see a noble manifestation of 'man's unconquerable mind'.

§238 Sometimes a conflict arose between loyalty to *comitatus* and loyalty to kin. The annal for 755 in the Parker MS of the Chronicle (selection 6 below) tells us of warriors who, in reply to offers of safe-conduct and money from kinsmen in a hostile force, said 'that no kinsman was dearer to them than their lord, and they would never follow his slayer'. This seems to have been the proper attitude. But, as Dorothy Whitelock points out, the fact that the Laws of Alfred allow a man to fight in defence of a wronged kinsman only if it did not involve fighting against his lord suggests that the claims of kin sometimes existed alongside the duty to a lord.

§239 A woman given in marriage as a *freoðuwebbe* 'a peace-weaver' to patch up a blood feud was often involved in such a conflict between loyalty to her lord, her husband, on the one hand, and to her family on the other. Freawaru was in this position, Hildeburh may have been; both appear in *Beowulf.* Sigemund's sister Signy was also involved in such a conflict of loyalties, although in her case the feud arose after the marriage. Thus the 'eternal triangle' of Anglo-Saxon literature is based on loyalty rather than on sexual love (though such poems as *The Wife's Lament* and *The Husband's Message* show that such love existed – if we need any assuring on the point). No woman inspired the hero Beowulf, as far as we know. The great love of heroic literature is that of man for man in the noblest sense, the loyalty of warrior to warrior and of warrior to lord. This is not peculiar to the Anglo-Saxons. In the *Chanson de Roland*, Roland's betrothed Aude receives passing mention – even that is perhaps unusual – but Roland's great love is for Charlemagne. Before his last battle, Roland cries to his companion Oliver:

> For his liege lord a man ought to suffer all hardship and endure great heat and great cold and give both his body and his blood. Lay on with thy lance, and I will smite with Durendal, my good sword which the King gave me. If I die here, may he to whom it shall fall say 'This was the sword of a goodly vassal'.

Again, in his book *Island of the Dragon's Blood*, Douglas Botting tells the story of a sixteenth-century battle between the Portuguese and Arabs on the island of Socotra. The Portuguese leader, Tristan da Cunha, after killing the Arabs' leader, offered the Arabs terms. The story goes on:

> But the Arabs replied that they were much obliged to the worthy chief captain for wishing to spare their lives but that, in telling them of their captain's death, he had given them a sufficient reason for declining to receive the favour, for the Fartaquins [Mahri Arabs] were not accustomed to return alive to their land and leave their captain dead on the field, especially as he was the son of their King. Therefore he might do as he pleased for they were not going to yield.

But it is important to grasp that this loyalty is fundamental to much Old English poetry. Of course, the time was not far distant when the interest of writers switched from the 'heroic' love of man for man to the 'romantic' love of man for woman. C. S. Lewis characterizes the change which then came over European literature as a revolution compared to which 'the Renaissance is a mere ripple on the surface of literature'.

§240 Among the members of the *comitatus*, there was an insistence on decorum and etiquette – *cuþe he duguðe þeaw* 'he knew the usages of noble warriors', observes the *Beowulf* poet at one point – a respect for well-tried weapons, a love of precious jewels and beautiful things, joy in ships and in warriors marching, in horse races and beer, and in feasting and music in the hall. There was too a pride in being a well-governed people. The hall was an oasis of comradeship, order, warmth, and happiness, in sharp contrast to the threatening and chaotic world of discomfort and danger which lay outside. Old English poetry is not made up entirely of gloomy moments. Sometimes there is laughter and mirth.

§241 But there is also a great awareness of the transitoriness of life – *þis læne lif* 'this transitory life' sings the poet. Some critics of Old English literature sometimes talk as if this were an idea peculiar to Germanic or Anglo-Saxon paganism. But other peoples have grasped the idea that life is transitory. Numerous passages could be cited from Latin and Greek authors. Rider Haggard quotes a Zulu saying that life is 'as the breath of oxen in winter, as the quick star that runs along the sky, as the little shadow that loses itself at sunset'. A famous passage in The Wisdom of Solomon, chapter V, compares the passing of the things of this earth to the passage of a shadow, of a ship in the waves, and of a bird or an arrow through the air. In James, chapter IV, we read that life is 'a vapour that appeareth for a little time, and then vanisheth away'. You should therefore view with suspicion any comment on such poems as *The Wanderer* and *The Seafarer* which draws unreal distinctions between pagan and Christian elements as a result of failure to realize that the transience of life is a perpetual human theme peculiar to no civilization, age, or culture.

This theme of transience receives frequent expression in Old English poetry. Three fine examples are *The Wanderer* ll. 92–110, *The Seafarer* ll. 80–93, and a passage from the less-known *Solomon and Saturn*:

> Lytle hwile   leaf beoð grene;
> ðonne hie eft fealewiað,   feallað on eorðan
> and forweorniað,   weorðað to duste

'For a little while the leaves are green. Then they turn yellow, fall to the earth and perish, turning to dust.' But while the theme is universal, the response is often different. In both *The Wanderer* and *The Dream of the Rood*, the passing of friends is lamented. But whereas in *The Wanderer* the thought provokes the famous response 'Where are they now?', the dreamer who has gazed upon the Cross affirms triumphantly that they live now in Heaven with the King of Glory.

§242 The transitoriness of all joys was brought home with special force to the man without a lord, always a figure of misery in Old English literature. He may have survived his lord because he was a coward who ran away from battle, like the sons of Odda in *The Battle of Maldon*, or by the fortune of war which decreed that he was badly wounded, but not killed, like the two survivors of the fights in the already-mentioned annal for 755. He may even have betrayed his lord, like Ceolwulf, the foolish thane who ruled Mercia as a Danish puppet for a few years after 874. Because of this uncertainty, a lordless man was suspect wherever he went. We can perhaps to some extent conceive his misery if we ponder the state of mind of people who find themselves in one of the following situations today – a trade-unionist expelled from his union and unable to earn money by his only skill; an army officer or an administrator suddenly expelled without compensation from a former colonial territory where he had made his career; a discharged convict unable to find a job; or a homeless refugee from his native land who has left family and friends behind and endures life as a lonely *isolato*.

§243 To such forlorn folk as these, and indeed to all pagan Anglo-Saxons, the coming of Christianity in the sixth century with its promise of a personal afterlife and a personal relationship with a clearly defined deity must have brought considerable comfort.

§244 To be sure, conversion was neither universal nor immediate. But those who experienced it must have been a strange blend of heroic and Christian, combining the fierce courage and pride of the heroic code with the new hope derived from Christianity – a blend strikingly seen on the Benty Grange helmet which bears both the pagan boar and the Christian Cross. Something of the same (but perhaps in reverse) must, one imagines, have been part of the make-up of those Russians who were brought up Christians before the Revolution but who were consciously or unconsciously influenced by the teachings of Marx. In 1961 Nikita Krushchev, whom one would assume was a Communistic atheist, was reported as saying that the Soviet Union possessed a 100-megaton bomb 'which, God grant it, we may never have to explode'. Whether this invocation of God was deliberately cynical, the accidental result of thought-habits formed in youth, or proof that he really was a believer at heart, one cannot say. But the fact that he could call on God will help us to understand why the *Beowulf* poet could say in the same poem both

> Wyrd oft nereð
> unfægne eorl, þonne his ellen deah!

'Fate often spares an undoomed man when his courage is good' and

> Swa mæg unfæge eaðe gedigan
> wean ond wræcsið se ðe Waldendes
> hyldo gehealdeþ!

'Thus may an undoomed man whom the grace of the Almighty protects easily survive misery and banishment.'

From this it follows that a poem which contains apparently pagan and apparently Christian ideas (as opposed to one which deals with themes common to both, such as the transience of life) need not be a Christian reworking of a pagan poem. Its author may have been a converted pagan, or, like some Russians of the Soviet period, a man who, because he had lived with survivors of a past civilization, could grasp its values imaginatively and appreciate them even while he himself belonged to a new age.[1]

§245 Christian missionaries throughout the history of Christian evangelization have often used the traditions of pagan subjects to make Christian practices more acceptable to them, weaving native songs and dances into the Christian baptismal ceremony, and so on. Missionaries in Anglo-Saxon England similarly 'baptized' pagan institutions, methods, and concepts. The Yeavering excavations give evidence of a pagan temple converted to Christian use. Bede's account of the poet Cædmon tells how, between 657 and 680, Cædmon sang his famous *Hymn* and so used heroic alliterative verse for Christian purposes – a development of great importance for Old English literature. And in *The Seafarer* and other poems, we find the pagan idea of *lof* Christianized – it now consists of praise on earth and life in Heaven and is to be won by fighting against the Devil and by doing good.

If we bear all this in mind, the incongruities to which our attention is so often drawn by critics of Old English poetry will trouble us less. After all, we can today 'thank our lucky stars' and say 'By Jove!' without believing that the stars really influence our lives or that Jupiter will protect us in battle. Similarly, if we find that our own interpretation of *Beowulf* commits us to the view that its author was a passionate believer in Christianity, we need not be deterred by the fact that he speaks of the power of *wyrd*; see §218 and note that the influence of Latin and Christian thought and means of expression is apparent (in varying degrees) in most of the texts in Part Two of this book.

§246 These problems loom large in Old English literature because we know very little about the genesis of most poems. *Cædmon's Hymn* is attributed to Cædmon and four poems – *Fates of the Apostles*, *Elene*, *Juliana*, and *Christ B* – bear Cynewulf's 'signature' in runes. But this does not give us much help, for Cynewulf is little more than a name. The unfortunate fact is that we just do not know for whom, by whom, when, where, or with what aim, most of the poems were written. This inevitably creates difficulties for us when we try to elucidate them and may lead us to criticize a poem for not having a structure which appeals to us or for not being the poem we think it ought to be.

---

[1] But see D. Whitelock *The Audience of Beowulf* (Oxford, 1951), esp. pp. 22–8.

Poetry

§247   In *An Introduction to Old English Metre*, Alan Bliss makes three points which need stressing here. The first is that 'OE poetry is not at all primitive; on the contrary, it is very highly artificial and sophisticated'. The second is that 'the vocabulary of OE poetry differs widely from that of prose'. The third is that 'OE poetry varies from most other types of poetry in that the metrical patterns are . . . selected from among the patterns which occur most commonly in natural speech'. The metrical unit is the half-line. Two half-lines alliterating together form the alliterative line which originated among the Germanic peoples in prehistoric times, was used for centuries by Old High German, Old Saxon, and other Germanic, poets, as well as by the Anglo-Saxons, and which in England had a glorious flowering in the fourteenth century with such works as *Sir Gawain and the Green Knight* and *Piers Plowman*. See further §267 and Appendix C.

§248   Apart from *The Metres of Boethius* and the Metrical Version of the Psalms found in the Paris Psalter, the bulk of Old English poetry is to be found in four manuscripts all of which date approximately from the second half of the tenth century. They are the Junius MS, the Vercelli Book, the Exeter Book, and the *Beowulf* MS. Further description of these manuscripts here would be superfluous, but you may find it interesting to answer the following questions:

Why was the Junius MS so-called? And why did some people call it the Cædmon MS? Has it any connection with Milton?

How did the Vercelli Book become associated with Italy?

Why is the *Beowulf* MS known as Cotton Vitellius A.xv? What happened to it in 1731?

Where can the Exeter Book be seen? How did it get there?

There are, of course, poems which are not found in these four manuscripts. Most of them have been collected in a volume known as *The Anglo-Saxon Minor Poems*, which is referred to in §264.

§249   The extant poems can be roughly classified according to subject matter.

1. Poems treating Heroic Subjects
Beowulf. Deor. The Battle of Finnsburh. Waldere. Widsith.

2. Historic Poems
The Battle of Brunanburh. The Battle of Maldon.

3. Biblical Paraphrases and Reworkings of Biblical Subjects
The Metrical Psalms. The poems of the Junius MS; note especially *Genesis B* and *Exodus. Christ. Judith.*

4. Lives of the Saints
Andreas. Elene. Guthlac. Juliana.

5. Other Religious Poems

Note especially *The Dream of the Rood* and the allegorical poems –
The Phoenix, *The Panther*, and *The Whale*.

6. Short Elegies and Lyrics

The Wife's Lament. *The Husband's Message*. *The Ruin*. *The Wanderer*.
The Seafarer. *Wulf and Eadwacer*. *Deor* might be included here as well
as under 1 above.

7. Riddles and Gnomic Verse

8. Miscellaneous

Charms. *The Runic Poem*. *The Riming Poem*.

Note

Four poems – *The Fates of the Apostles*, *Elene*, *Christ B*, and *Juliana* – contain Cynewulf's
'signature' in runes.

Prose

§250 As has already been pointed out in §182, English prose was far from
being a primitive vehicle of expression at the time of the Norman Conquest.
You will be able to watch it developing in the Chronicle and elsewhere. One
interesting question you may try to answer for yourself is 'Whose prose do
you prefer – that of Alfred or Ælfric?'

§251 Old English prose may be said to fall into the seven main divisions
set out below.

1. The Anglo-Saxon Chronicle

The surviving manuscripts – lettered A to H – are discussed in *The Anglo-
Saxon Chronicle*, ed. Dorothy Whitelock (Eyre and Spottiswoode, 1961),
pp. xi–xviii. MS E (The Laud Chronicle) continues until the death of Stephen
in 1154. This is, to all intents and purposes, the end of historical writing in
English prose until the fifteenth century.

Dorothy Whitelock observes that 'the confident attribution of the work
to Alfred's instigation cannot be upheld'.

2. The Translations of Alfred and his Circle

King Alfred explained his educational policy in his famous Preface to
the *Cura Pastoralis*. This is perhaps the first of his translations. He also
may have translated the *De Consolatione Philosophiae* of Boethius and the
Soliloquia of St. Augustine, and was responsible for a legal code. Also, many
scholars are convinced that Alfred made the prose translation of the first
fifty psalms in the *Paris Psalter*. But the extent to which King Alfred himself translated the *Cura Pastoralis*, Boethius, the *Soliloquies*, and the prose
psalms remains a subject for lively debate. See Godden, *Medium Ævum* 76
(2007), 1–23, and Bately, *Medium Ævum* 78 (2009), 189–215.

Bishop Wærferth of Worcester translated the *Dialogues* of Gregory the Great at Alfred's request. The OE version of Bede's *Ecclesiastical History* has long been attributed to Alfred. Dorothy Whitelock, in her British Academy Lecture in 1962, finds no evidence for this, but says that it remains a probability that the work was undertaken at Alfred's instigation. The same is true of the OE version of the *Historia adversus Paganos* of Orosius, which incorporates the story of the voyages of Ohthere and Wulfstan.

3. Homiletic Writings

The most important of these are
(*a*)　*The Blickling Homilies*, 971.
(*b*)　Ælfric's *Catholic Homilies*, 990–2, and *Lives of the Saints*, 993–8.
(*c*)　*The Homilies* of Wulfstan, who died in 1023.

4. Other Religious Prose

This includes translations of portions of both the Old and New Testaments, and a version of the Benedictine Office.

5. Prose Fiction

Here we find the story of *Apollonius of Tyre*, *Alexander's Letter to Aristotle*, and *The Wonders of the East*. It has been said that these show 'that long before the Conquest the Anglo-Saxons found entertainment in the exotic romanticism of the East'.

6. Scientific and Medical Writings

7. Laws, Charters, and Wills

7

Select Bibliography

A separate Bibliography is provided for each chapter of Part One; details of the arrangement will be found in the Contents.

For convenience of reference, each section of the Bibliography has been given its own number and the section-numbers of the discussions to which the books relate have been placed in brackets after each heading in the Bibliography.

GENERAL

§252   A useful guide is

Fred C. Robinson *Old English Literature: A Select Bibliography* (Toronto, 1970).

For fuller details see

Stanley B. Greenfield and Fred C. Robinson *A Bibliography of Publications on Old English Literature to the End of 1972* (Toronto, 1980).

Two publications with annual bibliographies which appear each year:

Anglo-Saxon England (Cambridge University Press)
Old English Newsletter (Center for Medieval and Early Renaissance Studies, State University of New York at Binghamton).

OE bibliographies are now of course available online.

CHAPTER 1
PRELIMINARY REMARKS ON THE LANGUAGE (§§1–4)

§253   An excellent Introduction to Old English will be found in §§1–22 of A. Campbell's *Old English Grammar* (Clarendon Press, 1959, reprinted with corrections 1962).

On the history of the English language generally, the following books can be recommended:

Albert C. Baugh and Thomas Cable *History of the English Language* (4th ed., Prentice Hall, 1993)

A Guide to Old English, Eighth Edition. Bruce Mitchell and Fred C. Robinson.
© 2012 Bruce Mitchell and Fred C. Robinson. Published 2012 by Blackwell Publishing Ltd.

David Crystal *The Cambridge Encyclopedia of the English Language*
(Cambridge, 1995)

You will not need a dictionary initially, as a Glossary is supplied in this
volume. If you are curious, however, you should begin by using

J. R. Clark Hall *A Concise Anglo-Saxon Dictionary* (4th ed., with Supplement
by H. D. Meritt, Cambridge, 1960), reprinted in Medieval Academy
Reprints for Teaching 14 (Toronto, 1984).

The most complete dictionary, that known as *Bosworth-Toller*, is published
by the Oxford University Press, and consists of a Dictionary and Supplements. The original Dictionary was very deficient in the letters A–G. Here,
in particular, you will have to consult both Dictionary and Supplements.

Dictionary of Old English, published online, on CD-Rom, and in microfiche
for the University of Toronto by the Pontifical Institute of Mediaeval
Studies, is detailed and authoritative but complete only through *G*.

Some have found

Stephen A. Barney *Word-Hoard: An Introduction to Old English Vocabulary*
(New Haven, 1977).

a helpful guide to learning vocabulary. This lists the words which occur in
OE poetry, starting with those which are used most frequently. Most of the
first 300 words at least are very common in prose texts.

CHAPTER 2
ORTHOGRAPHY AND PRONUNCIATION (§§5–9)
AND CHAPTER 3
INFLEXIONS (§§10–135)

§254   Although A. Campbell's *Old English Grammar* (§253) is too detailed
for you to use by itself, it may be safely consulted when you are in difficulty.
By looking at the Contents (pp. vii–xi) or the Index, you will be able to find
full paradigms, lists of examples of strong verbs or anything else you want,
and lucid explanations of any difficulty you may encounter.

CHAPTER 4
WORD FORMATION (§§136–138)

§255   Very helpful discussions and lists will be found in chapter IV of
Quirk and Wrenn *An Old English Grammar* and in pp. 355–400 of Dieter
Kastovsky's discussion in his essay cited in §260 below.

CHAPTER 5
SYNTAX (§§139–214)

§256   The standard work at present is Bruce Mitchell *Old English Syntax*
(2 vols., Clarendon Press, 1985), but this work is not for beginners. There

are plenty of monographs, but many of them are in German and most of those in English are too complicated for the beginner. One which may prove useful is J. M. Wattie's article called 'Tense' in *Essays and Studies* XVI (1930); this deals with the topics discussed in §§195–211. Some articles relevant to texts in this *Guide* will be found in Bruce Mitchell *On Old English* (Blackwell, 1988).

A short comparison of Old and Modern English syntax will be found in Bruce Mitchell *An Invitation to Old English and Anglo-Saxon England* (Blackwell, 1994).

CHAPTER 6
INTRODUCTION TO ANGLO-SAXON STUDIES (§§215–251)

History (§§215–218)

§257 The following are recommended:

P. Hunter Blair *An Introduction to Anglo-Saxon England* introduction by Simon Keynes (new ed., Cambridge, 2003)
P. Hunter Blair *Roman Britain and Early England 55 BC–AD 871* (Nelson, 1963)
F. M. Stenton *Anglo-Saxon England* (3rd ed., Oxford, 1971)
Dorothy Whitelock (ed.) *English Historical Documents*, Volume 1: *c. 500–1042* (2nd ed., London, 1979)
David Hill *An Atlas of Anglo-Saxon England 700–1066* (Blackwell, 1981)
James Campbell (ed.) *The Anglo-Saxons* (Oxford, 1982; repr. Penguin, 1991)
Christine Fell *Women in Anglo-Saxon England* (London, 1984).

Archaeology (§§219–230)

§258 See §220, the section in which each topic is discussed, and

Richard N. Bailey *Viking Age Sculpture in Northern England* (London, 1980)
Rupert Bruce-Mitford *The Sutton Hoo Ship Burial*
   Vol. 1: *Excavations, background, the ship, dating and inventory* (London, 1975)
   Vol. 2: *Arms, armour and regalia* (London, 1978)
   Vol. 3: *Late Roman and Byzantine silver, hanging-bowls, drinking vessels, cauldrons and other containers, textiles, the lyre, pottery bottle and other items* (Parts I and II, London, 1983)
Rosemary J. Cramp *Early Northumbrian Sculpture* (Jarrow, 1965)
Martin Carver (ed.) *The Age of Sutton Hoo* (Woodbridge, 1992)
Robert Farrell and Carol Neuman de Vegvar (ed.) *Sutton Hoo: Fifty Years After* American Early Medieval Studies 2 (Miami University, 1992)
David A. Hinton *A Catalogue of the Anglo-Saxon Ornamental Metalwork 700–1100 in the Department of Antiquities Ashmolean Museum* (Oxford, 1974)
H. M. Taylor and Joan Taylor *Anglo-Saxon Architecture* (3 vols., Cambridge, 1965–78)

David M. Wilson *Anglo-Saxon Ornamental Metalwork 700–1100 in the British Museum* (London, 1964).

Language (§§231–235)

History of English Prose

§259 On the topics mentioned in §233, see

R. W. Chambers *On the Continuity of English Prose from Alfred to More and his School* (Early English Text Society, 1932)[1]

Bruce Mitchell 'The Englishness of Old English' in *From Anglo-Saxon to Early Middle English: Studies Presented to E. G. Stanley* edited by Malcolm Godden, Douglas Gray, and Terry Hoad (Oxford, 1994).

Some of the points raised by Chambers are discussed in

N. Davis 'Styles in English Prose of the Late Middle and Early Modern Period' in *Les Congrès et Colloques de l'Université de Liège*, Volume 21 (1961), pp. 165–84.

See also

R. M. Wilson 'English and French in England 1100–1300', *History* 28 (1943), 37–60.

Vocabulary

Word Formation

See §255.

Changes of Meaning

§260 This is a difficult subject. Dieter Kastovsky 'Semantics and Vocabulary' in *The Cambridge History of the English Language* Vol. 1 (Cambridge, 1992) provides a thorough discussion. See §4.

Borrowings

§261 See

M. S. Serjeantson *A History of Foreign Words in English* (Routledge and Kegan Paul, 1935)

A. Campbell *Old English Grammar* (see §253 above), chapter X.

---

[1] But his suggestion (p. lxxxvi) that the line between OE and ME can be drawn between the Peterborough annals for 1131 and 1132 is not now accepted; see *The Peterborough Chronicle 1070–1154*, ed. Cecily Clark (2nd ed., Oxford, 1970), pp. lii–lxiii.

Literature (§§236–251)

Topics Raised in §§236–246

§262 On the transition from Epic to Romance, see

R. W. Southern *The Making of the Middle Ages* (Hutchinson, 1953), chapter V.

On the heroic way of, and attitude to, life, see

John Niles *Old English Heroic Poems and the Social Life of Texts* (Turnhout: Brepols, 2007)

J. R. R. Tolkien *Beowulf: The Monsters and the Critics* (British Academy Lecture, 1936)

Fred C. Robinson *Beowulf and the Appositive Style* (Knoxville, 1985)

D. Whitelock *The Audience of Beowulf* (Oxford, 1951).

General Criticism

§263 Ælfric

Helmut Gneuss *Ælfric of Eynsham: His Life, Times, and Writings* (Kalamazoo: Old English Newsletter Subsidia, 2009)

R. M. Liuzza (ed.) *Old English Literature: Critical Essays* (New Haven and London, 2002)

Daniel Donoghue, *Old English Literature: A Short Introduction* (Blackwell, 2004)

Malcolm Godden and Michael Lapidge (ed.) *The Cambridge Companion to Old English Literature* (Cambridge, 1991).

Poetry Texts

§264 Good reading editions include those in the Methuen and Manchester series. The standard edition of *Beowulf* for students is *Beowulf: An Edition* ed. Bruce Mitchell and Fred C. Robinson, revised edition with corrections (Blackwell, 2006). Virtually the entire corpus of Old English poetry is available in *The Anglo-Saxon Poetic Records*, published by Columbia University Press and Routledge and Kegan Paul. The volumes are

  I   Junius MS
 II   Vercelli Book
III   Exeter Book
 IV   Beowulf and Judith
  V   The Paris Psalter and the Meters of Boethius
 VI   Anglo-Saxon Minor Poems.

These volumes contain no glossaries and are for the use of scholars rather than of beginners. *A Concordance to the Anglo-Saxon Poetic Records*, edited by Jess B. Bessinger, Jr. and programmed by Philip H. Smith, Jr., was published by Cornell University Press in 1978.

Other editions of poems which have appeared since Robinson's *Bibliography* (see §252 above) include

The Dream of the Rood edited by M. Swanton (Manchester, 1970)
A Choice of Anglo-Saxon Verse selected with an introduction by Richard Hamer (Faber, 1970)
Daniel and Azarias edited by R. T. Farrell (Methuen, 1974)
Finnsburh Fragment and Episode edited by D. K. Fry (Methuen, 1974)
T. A. Shippey *Poems of Wisdom and Learning in Old English* (Cambridge and Totowa, N.J., 1976)
The Battle of Maldon edited by E. V. Gordon with a supplement by D. G. Scragg (Manchester, 1976)
Exodus edited by P. J. Lucas (Methuen, 1977)
The Old English Riddles of the Exeter Book edited by Craig Williamson (Chapel Hill, 1977)
Christ and Satan: A Critical Edition by R. E. Finnegan (Waterloo, 1977)
Genesis A: A New Edition by A. N. Doane (Madison, 1978)
The Saxon Genesis ed. A. N. Doane (Madison, 1991)
Resignation edited by Lars Malmberg (Durham, 1979)
The Guthlac Poems of the Exeter Book edited by Jane Roberts (Oxford, 1979)
Waldere edited by Arne Zetterstein (Manchester, 1979)
The Old English Rune Poem: A Critical Edition by Maureen Halsall (Toronto, 1981)
The Battle of Maldon edited by D. G. Scragg (Manchester, 1981)
J. R. R. Tolkien *The Old English Exodus: Text Translation and Commentary* edited by Joan Turville-Petre (Oxford, 1981)
The Old English Riming Poem edited by O. D. Macrae-Gibson (Cambridge, 1983)
Old English Minor Heroic Poems edited by Joyce Hill (Durham, 1983)
'Wulf and Eadwacer: A Classroom Edition' edited by Peter S. Baker, *Old English Newsletter* 16.2 (1983), 1–8
The Old English Catalogue Poems edited by Nicholas Howe, Anglistica 23 (Copenhagen, 1985)
The Old English Physiologus edited by Ann Squires (Durham, 1988)
Bernard James Muir *Leoð: Six Old English Poems: A Handbook* (New York, 1989)
The Battle of Maldon: Text and Translation translated and edited by Bill Griffiths (Pinner, 1991)
Anne L. Klinck *The Old English Elegies: A Critical Edition and Genre Study* (Montreal and Kingston, 1992)
The Exeter Anthology of Old English Poetry edited by Bernard J. Muir (Exeter, 1994)
Judith edited by Mark Griffith (Exeter, 1997)

Beowulf: An Edition by Bruce Mitchell and Fred C. Robinson (Blackwell, 2006).

To these can be added two earlier editions of *Judith*

Judith edited by B. J. Timmer (2nd ed., London, 1961)
Sweet's Anglo-Saxon Reader in Prose and Verse revised by Dorothy
   Whitelock (Oxford, 1967), pp. 136–48, 271–2.

Appreciation of the Poetry

§265   See §137 and

Alan Bliss 'v. The Appreciation of Old English Poetry' in *An Introduction to
   Old English Metre* (Basil Blackwell, 1962)
Companion to Old English Poetry ed. Henk Aertsen and Rolf H Bremmer,
   Jr. (Amsterdam, 1994)

The Use of Oral Formulae

§266   The oral nature of Old English poetry has been much discussed
of late. But one needs to beware of the notion sometimes advanced that
formulaic poetry is necessarily 'oral' and that all poems must be either
strictly 'oral' or strictly 'literary'. Lettered or 'literary' poets certainly
carried on the techniques of their 'oral' predecessors, and there seems no real
reason why one man should not combine the two techniques. On this topic
see initially

L. D. Benson 'The Literary Character of Anglo-Saxon Formulaic Poetry'
   Publications of the Modern Languages Association 81 (1966), 334–41
Paul Acker *Revising Oral Theory: Formulaic Composition in Old English and
   Old Icelandic Verse* (New York and London, 1998)

Metre

§267   The best introduction to Old English metre for beginners is
C. S. Lewis's 'The Alliterative Metre' in *Rehabilitations and Other Essays*
(London, 1939), pp. 117–32. Fuller and more sophisticated but still
addressed to students is Alan Bliss, *An Introduction to Old English Metre* (Oxford,
1962). Bliss's 'The Appreciation of Old English Metre', in *English and Medieval
Studies: Presented to J. R. R. Tolkien . . .* ed. Norman Davis and Charles
L. Wrenn (London, 1962), pp. 27–40 shows how Old English metre relates
to Modern English metre. A fairly recent comprehensive scholarly study
of Old English metre is Geoffrey Russom, *Beowulf and Old Germanic Metre*
(Cambridge, 1998), where one can find references to most of the preceding
scholarly studies of the subject. In Appendix C below we offer a brief,
general introduction to Old English metre.

Prose Texts

§268 Editions and translations of most of the prose texts are available. Important works which have appeared since Robinson's *Bibliography* (see §252 above) include

Ælfric's Catholic Homilies edited by Malcolm Godden (Early English Text Society SS 5, 17, 18, 1979–2000)

The Old English Orosius edited by Janet Bately (Early English Text Society, 1980)

Vercelli Homilies IX–XXIII edited by Paul E. Szarmach (Toronto, 1981)

The Prose Solomon and Saturn and *Adrian and Ritheus* edited by James E. Cross and Thomas D. Hill (Toronto, 1982)

Eleven Old English Rogationtide Homilies edited by Joyce Bazire and James E. Cross (Toronto, 1982)

The Old English Herbarium and Medicina de Quadrupedibus edited by Hubert Jan de Vriend (Early English Text Society, 1984)

The Old English Life of Machutus edited by David Yerkes (Toronto, 1984)

The Anglo-Saxon Chronicle: A Collaborative Edition general editors David Dumville and Simon Keynes

Vol. 3: MS A edited by J. M. Bately (Cambridge, 1986)

Vol. 4: MS B edited by Simon Taylor (Cambridge, 1983)

Two Voyagers at the Court of King Alfred by Niels Lund, Christine Fell, and others (York, 1984)

Ohthere's Voyages edited by Janet Bately and Anton Englert (Roskilde: Viking Ship Museum, 2007)

The Vercelli Homilies and Related Texts edited by D. G. Scragg (Early English Text Society, 1992)

Old English Homilies from MS Bodley 343 edited by Susan Irvine (Early English Text Society, 1993)

Ælfric's Prefaces edited by J. Wilcox (Durham Medieval Texts 9, Durham 1994)

The Old English Version of the Gospels edited by R. M. Liuzza (Early English Text Society OS 304, 314, 1994–2000)

Byrhtferth's Enchiridion edited by Peter S. Baker and Michael Lapidge (Early English Text Society, 1995).

Sources

§269 See

Paul Szarmach et al. ed. *Sources of Anglo-Saxon Culture* (Kalamazoo, 1986) and Szarmach et al. ed. *Sources of Anglo-Saxon Literary Culture* 2 vols (Binghamton, 1990), and (Kalamazoo 2001). See also Frederick Biggs, *Sources of Anglo-Saxon Literary Culture: The Apocrypha* (Kalamazoo, 2007).

D. G. Calder and M. J. B. Allen *Sources and Analogues of Old English Poetry: The Major Latin Texts in Translation* (Cambridge and Totowa, 1976)

Daniel G. Calder, Robert E. Bjork, Patrick R. Ford, and Daniel F. Melia *Sources and Analogues of Old English Poetry II: The Major Germanic and Celtic Texts in Translation* (Cambridge and Totowa, 1983).

APPENDIX A

Strong Verbs

This Appendix, which contains some of the more common strong verbs, is intended to illustrate §§90–109 and 131–134.

You are recommended to reread §§110–113 before studying this Appendix.

As is pointed out in §92, the 3rd pers. sg. pres. ind. is not part of the gradation series, but rather these forms are the result of i-umlaut of the vowel of the infinitive and/or syncope and assimilation. For definitions of i-umlaut, syncope, and assimilation see Appendix D. For this reason, these forms are printed in italics in this Appendix.

You will find here further examples of the simplification of endings referred to in §112.2; note

drīehþ : *drēogan* (class II)

cwiþþ : *cweþan* (class V)

and　　　　*wierþ* : *weorþan* (class III).

From *bindan* (class III) we find 2nd and 3rd pers. sg. pres. ind. *bintst* and *bint*.

Verbs in which Verner's Law forms occur (see §§105–107) are marked †.

Verbs without Verner's Law forms where they might be expected (see §108) are marked ‡.

When the forms of a verb rhyme with those of the verb before it in the list, the principal parts have been left for you to fill in.[1]

The Appendix is not a complete list of Old English strong verbs. You may find it useful to note down in the appropriate place any new verbs you come across in your reading.

---

[1] The principle of 'rhyme association' is an important one. Thus most verbs borrowed into English are made weak. But the French borrowing 'strive' became strong through association with verbs like 'drive'. Similarly the Old English weak verb 'wear' became strong through association with the strong verbs 'bear' and 'tear'.

A Guide to Old English, Eighth Edition. Bruce Mitchell and Fred C. Robinson.
© 2012 Bruce Mitchell and Fred C. Robinson. Published 2012 by Blackwell Publishing Ltd.

APPENDIX A.1

Class I

Inf.	3rd Sg. Pres. Ind.	1st Pret.	2nd Pret.	Past Ptc.
bītan 'bite'	bītt	bāt	biton	biten
flītan 'contend'				
slītan 'tear'				
wītan 'blame'				
ġewītan 'go'				
wlītan 'behold'	wlītt	wlāt	wliton	wliten
wrītan 'write'				
bīdan 'await'	bītt	bād	bidon	biden
glīdan 'glide'				
rīdan 'ride'				
slīdan 'slide'				
blīcan 'shine'	blīcþ	blāc	blicon	blicen
swīcan 'fail'				
drīfan 'drive'	drīfþ	drāf	drifon	drifen
belīfan 'remain'				
grīpan 'seize'	grīpþ	grāp	gripon	gripen
hrīnan 'touch'	hrīnþ	hrān	hrinon	hrinen
scīnan 'shine'				
stīgan 'ascend'	stīġþ, stīhþ	stāg[1]	stigon	stigen
hnīgan 'bow to'				
† līþan 'go'	līþþ	lāþ	lidon	liden
† scrīþan 'glide, move'				see §108
† snīþan 'cut'				
‡ mīþan 'conceal'	mīþþ	māþ	miþon	miþen
‡ rīsan 'rise'	rīst	rās	rison	risen

Contracted Verbs (see §103.3)

† lēon 'lend'	līehþ	lāh	ligon	ligen
† tēon 'accuse'				
† þēon 'prosper'[2]				
† wrēon 'cover'				

Note

The following weak verbs are found with *ī* in the infinitive:
čīdan 'chide', *cwīþan* 'lament', *ġedīgan* 'survive', *līxan* 'gleam', *rīnan* 'rain', and *snīwan* 'snow'.

---

[1] The form *stāh* sometimes occurs as a result of unvoicing of *g*.
[2] Historically a verb of class III. See A. Campbell *Old English Grammar* §739.

APPENDIX A.2

Class II

Inf.	3rd Sg. Pres. Ind.	1st Pret.	2nd Pret.	Past Ptc.
bēodan 'command'	*bīett*	bēad	budon	boden
brēotan 'break'	*brīett*	brēat	bruton	broten
flēotan 'float'				
ġēotan 'pour'				
scēotan 'shoot'				
† ċēosan 'choose'	*ċīest*	ċēas	curon	coren
† drēosan 'fall'				
† frēosan 'freeze'				
† hrēosan 'fall'				
† lēosan 'lose'				
crēopan 'creep'	*crīepþ*	crēap	crupon	cropen
drēogan 'endure'	*drīehþ*	drēag	drugon	drogen
flēogan 'fly'				
lēogan 'tell lies'				
hrēowan 'rue'	*hrīewþ*	hrēaw	hruwon	hrowen
† sēoþan 'boil'	*sīeþþ*	sēaþ	sudon	soden
brūcan 'enjoy'	*brȳcþ*	brēac	brucon	brocen
lūcan 'lock'				
būgan 'bow'	*bȳhþ*	bēag	bugon	bogen
dūfan 'dive'	*dȳfþ*	dēaf	dufon	dofen
scūfan 'shove'				

Contracted Verbs (see §103.4)

† flēon 'flee'	*flīehþ*	flēah	flugon	flogen
† tēon 'draw'				

Note

The following weak verbs are found with *ēo* in the infinitive:
    frēogan 'love', *neōsan* (*nēosian*) 'seek out', and *sēowan* (*sēowian*) 'sew'.

APPENDIX A.3

Class III

Inf.	3rd Sg. Pres. Ind.	1st Pret.	2nd Pret.	Past Ptc.
(a) See §95.				
breġdan 'pull'[1]	*britt*[2]	bræġd	brugdon	brogden
streġdan 'strew'				
berstan 'burst'[3]	*birst*	bærst	burston	borsten
(b) See §§96–98.				
beorgan 'protect'	*hierhþ*	bearg	burgon	borgen
ċeorfan 'cut'	*ċierfþ*	ċearf	curfon	corfon
hweorfan 'go'				
sweorcan 'grow dark'	*swiercþ*	swearc	swurcon	sworcen
weorpan 'throw'	*wierpþ*	wearp	wurpon	worpen
† weorþan 'become'	*wierþ*	wearþ	wurdon	worden
feohtan 'fight'	*fieht*	feaht	fuhton	fohten
† fēolan 'press on'[4]		fealh	fulgon	folgen
(c) See §§96–97 and 99.				
delfan 'dig'	*dilfþ*	dealf	dulfon	dolfen
helpan 'help'	*hilpþ*	healp	hulpon	holpen
belgan 'be angry'	*bilhþ*	bealg	bulgon	bolgen
swelgan 'swallow'				
meltan 'melt'	*milt*	mealt	multon	molten
sweltan 'die'				
(d) See §100.				
ġieldan 'pay'	*ġielt*	ġeald	guldon	golden
ġiellan 'yell'	*ġielþ*	ġeal	gullon	gollen
ġielpan 'boast'	*ġielpþ*	ġealp	gulpon	golpen

---

[1] This verb has been taken as the basic paradigm of class III (see §95) to make explanation easier. Originally it belonged elsewhere; see A. Campbell *Old English Grammar* §736 (b).

[2] Regular forms of 3rd sg. pres. ind. do not seem to be recorded. [3] See §95 fn. 1.

[4] See §133.2. Forms of 3rd sg. pres. ind. do not seem to be recorded.

	3rd Sg.			
Inf.	*Pres. Ind.*	*1st Pret.*	*2nd Pret.*	*Past Ptc.*

(*e*) See §101.

grimman 'rage'	*grimþ*	gramm	grummon	grummen
swimman 'swim'				
ġelimpan 'happen'	*ġelimpþ*	ġelamp	ġelumpon	ġelumpen
bindan 'bind'	*bint*	band	bundon	bunden
findan 'find'[1]				
grindan 'grind'				
windan 'wind'				
drincan 'drink'	*drincþ*	dranc	druncon	druncen
scrincan 'shrink'				
swincan 'toil'				
onġinnan 'begin'	*onġinþ*	ongann	ongunnon	ongunnen
winnan 'fight'				
singan 'sing'	*singþ*	sang	sungon	sungen
springan 'spring'				
swingan 'flog'				
þringan 'crowd'				
wringan 'wring'				
birnan 'burn'[2]	*birnþ*	barn	burnon	burnen
irnan 'run'[2]				

(*f*) Exceptional

friġnan 'ask'	*friġneþ*	fræġn	frugnon	frugnen
murnan 'mourn'	*myrnþ*	mearn	murnon	

Note

The following verbs are weak:

    hringan 'ring' and *ġeþingan* 'determine'.

On *bringan* see §123.2.

---

[1] In the 1st pret. *funde* is found alongside *fand*; see §109.
[2] Originally *brinnan*, *rinnan*. But metathesis occurred; see §95 fn. 1.

APPENDIX A.4

Class IV
(See §94 fn. 1)

Inf.	*3rd Sg.* *Pres. Ind.*	*1st Pret.*	*2nd Pret.*	*Past Ptc.*
beran 'bear'	*birþ*	bær	bǣron	boren
teran 'tear'				
brecan 'break'	*bricþ*	bræc	brǣcon	brocen
cwelan 'die'	*cwilþ*	cwæl	cwǣlon	cwolen
helan 'hide'				
stelan 'steal'				
scieran 'cut'[1]	*scierþ*	scear	scēaron	scoren
niman 'take'[2]	*nimþ*	nam, nōm	nōmon, nāmon	numen
cuman 'come'[2]	*cymþ*	cōm	cōmon	cumen

APPENDIX A.5

Class V
(See §94 fn. 2)

Inf.	*3rd Sg.* *Pres. Ind.*	*1st Pret.*	*2nd Pret.*	*Past Ptc.*
† cweþan 'say'	*cwiþþ*	cwæþ	cwǣdon	cweden
etan 'eat'	*itt*	æt[3]	ǣton	eten
fretan 'devour'				
metan 'measure'	*met*[4]	mæt	mǣton	meten
‡ ġenesan 'survive'	*ġeneseþ*[4]	ġenæs	ġenǣson	ġenesen
sprecan 'speak'	*spricþ*	spræc	sprǣcon	sprecen
specan 'speak'				
wrecan 'avenge'				
tredan 'tread'	*tritt*	træd	trǣdon	treden
wefan 'weave'	*wifþ*	wæf	wǣfon	wefen
ġiefan 'give'[5]	*ġiefþ*	ġeaf	ġēafon	ġiefen
onġietan 'perceive'[5]	*onġiet*	onġeat	onġēaton	onġieten

---

[1] See §103.1.   [2] See §§103.2 and 109.   [3] See §109.
[4] Regular forms do not seem to be recorded.   [5] See §103.1.

	3rd Sg.			
Inf.	*Pres. Ind.*	*1st Pret.*	*2nd Pret.*	*Past Ptc.*

Weak Presents (see §116)

biddan 'ask'	*bitt*	bæd	bǣdon	beden
licgan 'lie'	*liġeþ, līþ*	læġ	lǣgon	leġen
† þicgan 'partake'	*þiġeþ*	þeah[1]	þǣgon	þeġen
sittan 'sit'	*sitt*	sæt	sǣton	seten

Contracted Verb (see §103.3)

| † sēon 'see' | *siehþ* | seah[1] | sāwon | sewen |

APPENDIX A.6

Class VI

	3rd Sg.			
Inf.	*Pres. Ind.*	*1st Pret.*	*2nd Pret.*	*Past Ptc.*
dragan 'draw'	*dræhþ*	drōg	drōgon	dragen
faran 'go'	*færþ*	fōr	fōron	faren
galan 'sing'	*gælþ*	gōl	gōlon	galen
hladan 'load'	*hladeþ*[2]	hlōd	hlōdon	hladen
wadan 'go'	*wadeþ*[2]			
sacan 'quarrel'	*sæcþ*	sōc	sōcon	sacen
scacan 'shake'				
standan 'stand'[3]	*stent*	stōd	stōdon	standen

Weak Presents (see §116)

hebban 'lift'	*hefeþ*	hōf	hōfon	hafen
swerian 'swear'	*swereþ*	swōr	swōron	sworen
scieppan 'create'[4]	*sciepþ*	scōp	scōpon	scapen

Contracted Verbs (see §§103.3 and 108)

| † lēan 'blame' | *liehþ* | lōh, lōg[5] | lōgon | lagen |
| † slēan 'strike' | | | | slagen, slæġen |

---

[1] See §97.
[2] Regular forms do not seem to be recorded.
[3] See §94 fn. 3.   [4] See §103.1.   [5] See §108.

APPENDIX A.7

Class VII
(See §104)

Inf.	3rd Sg. Pres. Ind.	1st Pret.	2nd Pret.	Past Ptc.
(a)				
bannan 'summon'	*benþ*	bēonn	bēonnon	bannen
spannan 'span'				
blāwan 'blow'	*blǣwþ*	blēow	blēowon	blāwen
cnāwan 'know'				
māwan 'mow'				
sāwan 'sow'				
flōwan 'flow'	*flēwþ*	flēow	flēowon	flōwen
grōwan 'grow'				
rōwan 'row'				
spōwan 'succeed'				
fealdan 'fold'	*fielt*	fēold	fēoldon	fealden
healdan 'hold'				
wealdan 'rule'				
feallan 'fall'	*fielþ*	fēoll	fēollon	feallen
weallan 'boil'				
weaxan 'grow'	*wiext*	wēox	wēoxon	weaxen
bēatan 'beat'	*bīett*	bēot	bēoton	bēaten
hēawan 'hew'	*hīewþ*	hēow	hēowon	hēawen
hlēapan 'leap'	*hlīepþ*	hlēop	hlēopon	hlēapen

Weak Present (see §116)

wēpan 'weep'	*wēpeþ*	wēop	wēopon	wōpen
(b)				
hātan 'command, call'	*hǣtt*	hēt	hēton	hāten
ondrǣdan 'fear'	*ondrǣtt*	ondrēd	ondrēdon	ondrǣden
rǣdan 'advise'[1]				
lǣtan 'let'	*lǣtt*	lēt	lēton	lǣten
slǣpan 'sleep'	*slǣpþ*	slēp	slēpon	slǣpen

Contracted Verbs (see §108)

† fōn 'seize'	*fēhþ*	fēng	fēngon	fangen
† hōn 'hang'				

---

[1] A weak preterite *rǣdde* is also found.

APPENDIX B

Some Effects of *i*-Mutation

The principle of *i*-mutation set forth in §§52–57 explains the relationship among a number of OE (and Modern English) words which otherwise may be unapparent or puzzling. Thus the *e* of the comparative and superlative forms of *old* (i.e. *elder*, *eldest*) is explained by the fact that the comparative and superlative suffixes in this adjective were originally *-ira* and *-ist*, the *i* of which caused mutation of the vowel. (See §75 for OE adjectives which follow this pattern.) Similarly, the OE suffix *-þ(o)*, *-þ(u)*, mentioned in §138 as the element that makes feminine abstract nouns out of adjectives, frequently had *i* in the suffix in pre-OE times (*-iþu*) and hence we see the effects of *i*-mutation in nouns formed from these adjectives:

> **fūl** (*foul*) + **-iþ(u)**, by *i*-mutation and subsequent loss of *i* = **fȳlþ** (*filth*)
> **hāl** (*whole, hale*) + **-iþ(u)** = **hǣlþ** (*health*)
> **lang** (*long*) + **-iþ(u)** = **lengþ** (*length*)
> **slāw** (*slow*) + **-iþ(u)** = **slǣwþ** (*sloth*)
> **strang** (*strong*) + **-iþ(u)** = **strengþ** (*strength*)
> **wrāþ** (*wroth, angry*) + **-iþ(u)** = **wrǣþþo** (*wrath*)

Most pervasive, perhaps, is the *i*-mutation in Class 1 weak verbs explained in §117 note. Weak 1 verbs are derived from nouns, adjectives, or corresponding strong verbs. The following are derived from the nouns indicated:

> **cuss** (*kiss*) + **jan**, by *i*-mutation and subsequent loss of *j* = **cyssan** (*to kiss*)
> **dōm** (*judgement*) + **jan** = **dēman** (*to judge*)
> **drēam** (*joy*) + **jan** = **drīeman** (*to rejoice*)
> **fær** (*journey*) + **jan** = **ferian** (*to carry*)
> **flēam** (*flight*) + **jan** = **(ge)flīeman** (*to put to flight*)
> **fōda** (*food*) + **jan** = **fēdan** (*to feed*)
> **frōfor** (*comfort*) + **jan** = **frēfran** (*to comfort*)
> **gelēafa** (*belief*) + **jan** = **gelīefan** (*to believe*)
> **heorte** (*heart*) + **jan** = **hiertan** (*to hearten*)
> **lāf** (*leaving*) + **jan** = **lǣfan** (*to leave*)
> **lār** (*lore*) + **jan** = **lǣran** (*to teach*)
> **lēoht** (*light*) + **jan** = **līehtan** (*to shine*)

A Guide to Old English, Eighth Edition. Bruce Mitchell and Fred C. Robinson.
© 2012 Bruce Mitchell and Fred C. Robinson. Published 2012 by Blackwell Publishing Ltd.

lust (*pleasure*) + jan = lystan (*to list, desire*)
nama (*name*) + jan = nemnan (*to name*)
sāl (*rope*) + jan = sǣlan (*to fasten*)
scrūd (*clothing*) + jan = scrȳdan (*to clothe*)
searu (*skill*) + jan = sierwan (*to plot*)
talu (*tale*) + jan = tellan (*to tell*)
þurst (*thirst*) + jan = þyrstan (*to thirst after*)
weorc (*work*) + jan = wyrċan (*to work*)

The following are derived from the adjectives indicated:

beald (*bold*) + jan = bieldan (*to embolden*)
brād (*broad*) + jan = brǣdan (*to spread*)
cōl (*cool*) + jan = cēlan (*to cool*)
cūþ (*known*) + jan = cȳþan (*to make known*)
eald (*old*) + jan = ieldan (*to delay*)
feorr (*far*) + jan = fierran (*to remove*)
full (*full*) + jan = fyllan (*to fill*)
fūs (*ready*) + jan = fȳsan (*to prepare*)
ġeorn (*eager*) + jan = ġiernan (*to be eager, yearn*)
hāl (*whole, hale*) + jan = hǣlan (*to heal*)
rūm (*roomy*) + jan = rȳman (*to make room*)
scearp (*sharp*) + jan = scierpan (*to sharpen*)
trum (*strong*) + jan = trymman (*to strengthen*)
wōd (*mad*) + jan = wēdan (*to be mad*)

The following are derived from strong verbs, imparting to the meaning of the strong verb a causative sense or a transitive function. The vowel of the weak verb is derived from the vowel of the preterite singular or 1st preterite (see §92) of the corresponding strong verb:

cwæl (pret. of cwelan, *to die*) + jan = cwellan (*to kill*)
dranc (pret. of drincan, *to drink*) + jan = drenċan (*to drench*)
fēoll (pret. of feallan, *to fall*) + jan = fiellan (*to fell*)
fōr (pret. of faran, *to go*) + jan = fēran (*to go, lead*)
hwearf (pret. of hweorfan, *to turn*) + jan = hwierfan (*to move about*)
læg (pret. of licgan, *to lie*) + jan = lecgan (*to lay*)
rās (pret. of rīsan, *to rise*) + jan = rǣran (*to rear, raise*) (Verner's Law §§105–108)
sang (pret. of singan, *to sing*) + jan = senġan (*to singe*)
sæt (pret. of sittan, *to sit*) + jan = settan (*to set*)
sprang (pret. of springan, *to spring*) + jan = sprenġan (*to break*)
swæf (pret. of swefan, *to sleep*) + jan = swebban (*to put to sleep, kill*)
swanc (pret. of swincan, *to toil*) + jan = swenċan (*to press hard*)
wand (pret. of windan, *to wind*) + jan = wendan (*to turn around, wend*)
wearp (pret. of weorpan, *to throw*) + jan = wierpan (*to recover*)

APPENDIX C

Metre
with Examples from the Poems in this *Guide*

In order to appreciate fully the often beautiful aural effects of Old English poetry, one must know something about Old English metre, which is fundamentally different from the metres of Modern English verse.[1] In Modern English there are many different metrical forms, such as iambic pentameter ('Shăll I cŏmpáre thĕe tó ă súmmĕr's dáy?'), trochaic tetrameter ('Tígĕr, tígĕr, búrnĭng bríght'), and anapestic trimeter ('Ŏf thĕ béautĭfŭl Ánnăbĕl Lée'), and a poet normally selects one of these metrical forms and uses it exclusively throughout any poem he or she is writing. In Old English there was but one system of versification which was used for all poems. That system consisted of five variations of a basic verse-scheme, and any one of these five types could be used in any verse a poet might write. The system is based upon accent, alliteration, vowel quantity, and specified patterns of unaccented and accented syllables.

ACCENT

Each line of Old English poetry consists of two half-lines or verses:

rǽd ănd rǽddĕ,   ríncŭm tǽhtĕ

(*The Battle of Maldon*, l. 18)

The two half-lines are separated by a pause, or caesura, indicated here by a space. Each half-line has two syllables which are accented. That is, in normal speech they would be pronounced with a heavier accent than the other syllables in the line. In this respect Old English and Modern English are much the same. If we translate the above line

róde ănd cóunsĕlled,   táught thĕ sóldĭers

---

[1] Accented syllables are marked with ´, unaccented with ˣ. In citing the conventions of Modern English metre we ignore so-called free verse; a game without rules is beyond systematic analysis.

A Guide to Old English, Eighth Edition. Bruce Mitchell and Fred C. Robinson.
© 2012 Bruce Mitchell and Fred C. Robinson. Published 2012 by Blackwell Publishing Ltd.

and then pronounce it aloud, we will hear immediately that the accented syllables in the Modern English line are *rode*, *coun-*, *taught*, and *sol-*. Only someone totally ignorant of English pronunciation would pronounce the line 'rŏde ánd cŏunsélled, tăught the sŏldíers'. Similarly any Anglo-Saxon would know instinctively that *rād*, *ræd-*, *rinc-*, and *tǣh-* are the heavily accented syllables in the Old English line. The metrical pattern, or 'scansion', of both Old English and Modern English lines may be described as ´ × ´ × || ´ × ´ ×.

ALLITERATION

In the Old English line just cited three of the accented syllables alliterate with each other. That is, they all begin with the same sound, *r-*. This is a required, central feature of Old English verse. The two half-lines must be bound together by alliteration: one of the two accented syllables in the first half-line must alliterate with the first accented syllable of the second half-line. It is permissible for both accented syllables in the first half-line to alliterate (as is the case here), and both often do alliterate, but in the second half-line only the first accented syllable may alliterate.

It is only alliteration of accented syllables that counts. Unaccented syllables which happen to alliterate are irrelevant to scansion and should be ignored. An important rule of alliteration in Old English is that *sp-* alliterates only with another syllable beginning with *sp-*. It does not alliterate with *s-*. The same is true of *sc-* and *st-*, each of which alliterates only with syllables beginning with the same consonant cluster. Four lines from *The Battle of Maldon*, ll. 127–37, illustrate this principle:

> <u>St</u>ōdon <u>st</u>ædefæste;   <u>st</u>ihte hī Byrhtnōð,
>
> <u>S</u>ende ðā se <u>s</u>ærinc   <u>s</u>ūðerne gār,
>
> hē <u>sc</u>ēaf þā mid ðām <u>sc</u>ylde,   þæt se <u>sc</u>eaft tōbærst,
> and þæt <u>sp</u>ere <u>sp</u>rengde,   þæt hit <u>sp</u>rang ongēan.

Any accented syllable beginning with a vowel alliterates with any other accented syllable beginning with a vowel; the vowels do not have to be the same:

> <u>ē</u>ce dryhten   <u>ō</u>r onstealde
> (Cædmon's *Hymn*, l. 4)

Here the *ē-* of *ēce* alliterates with the *ō-* of *ōr*. Since the prefix *on-* of *onstealde* is unaccented, its alliteration with the accented syllables is fortuitous and irrelevant: it is ignored in scanning the line.

VOWEL QUANTITY

In addition to accent and alliteration, vowel quantity is also functional in Old English versification. Normally the accented syllables in a line are long. That is, they have a long vowel (as in *rād, rǣd-, ēc-*) or they have a short vowel followed by two consonants (*rinc-, dryht-, scyld-*). Also, an accented word consisting of two short syllables may count as one long syllable, this being what is called 'resolved stress'. Thus *spere* in the last of the four lines quoted above from *The Battle of Maldon* is accented as if it were one syllable. Resolved stress is indicated by ‿.

THE FIVE TYPES

We have said that each half-line or verse must have two accented syllables. How many unaccented syllables may a verse have, and where may the accented and unaccented syllables fall in relation to each other? The answers to these questions are: (1) a half-line or verse must have at least two unaccented syllables, and it may have more than two, but only in certain specified positions in the verse; and (2) the relative positions of accented and unaccented syllables which are permitted are described in five basic patterns. In a moment we shall examine these five patterns or types, but first it should be noted that in addition to accented syllables and unaccented syllables there are in Old (as in Modern) English also syllables with secondary accent. That is, they are accented more than unaccented syllables but less than accented syllables. Examples of the three levels of accent may be heard in these three sentences: 'Man is mortal.' 'Blindman's buff is a game.' 'He is speaking German.' In the first sentence *man* is accented. In the second sentence *-man* in *blindman* has secondary accent. In the third sentence *-man* in *German* is unaccented. Or again, *-y* in *penny* is unaccented, while *-knife* in *penknife* has secondary accent. *Pen-* in both words is accented. We mark secondary accent with a ` .[2]

---

[2] To some extent accent may be correlated with grammatical categories:
(a) The root syllables of nouns, adjectives, participles, and infinitives are normally accented, while prefixes, suffixes, prepositions, conjunctions, pronouns, and articles are unaccented. This is the case in Modern as well as Old English; note where the accents fall when you say aloud, 'A careful driver was signalling for a turn'.
(b) Adverbs and finite verbs and the second elements of noun or adjective compounds tend to have secondary accent but can sometimes carry primary accent (when the other syllables in their vicinity are all unaccented) and sometimes are unaccented (when the other syllables in their vicinity are all accented).
(c) Some words (such as prepositions and finite verbs) receive primary accent when they are displaced from their normal position in the sentence. Thus *in* in *māðm ín héallě* (11n, l. 13) is unaccented, but it is accented in *ic him ín wúnige* (11e, l. 6).

We are now ready to examine the five accent-patterns, or verse-types, which modern scholars designate A, B, C, D, and E. In any given poem many or all of the five types will be used to shape individual verses, and they occur in any sequence. An A-verse might be followed by a D-verse, which might be followed by a B-verse. Or two or three consecutive verses might all have the same pattern. As long as a verse fits one of the five patterns, it is metrical. In marking the scansion of the five types, ˣ is used where an unaccented syllable is required; ˣ's within parentheses, indicate that up to that number of unaccented syllables *may* occur in that position. Following the scansion formula for each verse-type will be half-lines illustrating that type. The source of these examples is identified by the item-number of the poem in this volume from which the line was taken followed by the line number. Line numbers are followed by either *a* or *b* indicating that the verse is either the first or second half-line in the line.

Type A

$$\acute{}\;^{\times}\;(^{\times\,\times\,\times\,\times})\;\acute{}\;^{\times}$$

gár tŏ gúþĕ (12, l. 13a)   féor ăfýsăn (12, l. 3a)
fréan tŏ gĕféohtĕ (12, l. 12a)   hǽþĕnĕ ǣt híldĕ (12, l. 55a)
rícĕ ǽftĕr óðrŭm (13, l. 10b)   rincă mańigĕ (18, l. 728b)

Type B

$$(^{\times\,\times\,\times\,\times})\;^{\times}\;\acute{}\;^{\times}\;(\acute{})\;\acute{}$$

ŏn úrnĕ éard (12, l. 58a)   mĕ séndŏn tŏ þĕ (12, l. 29a)
mĭd his fráncăn ŏfscéat (12, l. 77b)   ănd þŏnĕ gódăn fŏrlét (12, l. 187b)
ănd tŏ þǣrĕ híldĕ stóp (12, l. 8b)   þǣt þŭ mŏst séndăn raðe (12, l. 30b)

Type C

$$(^{\times\,\times\,\times\,\times})\;^{\times}\;\acute{}\;\acute{}\;^{\times}$$

gĕdón hǽfdĕ (12, l. 197b)   ŏn búrh rídăn (12, l. 291b)
þǣt hĭ fórð éodŏn (12, l. 229b)   nĕ tŏ hrædwýrdĕ (16, l. 66b)
þŏnnĕ hit ǽnig mǣð wǣrĕ (12, l. 195b)   þǣr is blis mýcĕl (14, l. 139b)

As the last example shows, the second of the two accented syllables in type C verses may be short.[3] Other examples: *is nū sǣl cumen* (14, l. 80b), *æt*

---

[3] Note that the other accented syllable in this line (*blis*) is long because when a monosyllable ends with a consonant it is long for purposes of metre, whether the vowel be long or short. Note *grim* in the first example under Type D.

þām wīgplegan (12, l. 268b), *ne þurfon mē embe Stūrmere* (12, l. 249a). Under special circumstances short accented syllables are permitted in some other verse types.

Type D

´ (ˣ ˣ ˣ) ´ ˋ ˣ

grim gúðplègă (12, l. 61a) hríð hréosèndĕ (16, l. 102a)

Óffă þŏnĕ sǽlidăn (12, l. 286a) héaldĕ hĭs hórdcòfăn (16, l. 14a)

Other D-verses are a slight variation of this pattern, the final unaccented syllable(s) changing place with the secondary accent:

bórd órd ŏnfèng (12, l. 110b) hrím hrúsăn bònd (17, l. 32a)

éald éntă gĕwèorc (16, l. 87a) béarwăs blóstmŭm nimăð (17, l. 48a)

Type E

´ ˋ ˣ (ˣ) ´

hrímcèaldĕ sǽ (16, l. 4b) ǽschŏlt ăscéoc (12, l. 230b)

wǽlrǽstĕ gĕcéas (12, l. 113b) féala èalră gĕbád (14, l. 125b)

wýn èal gĕdréas (16, l. 36b) wýrd bĭð fùl ărǽd (16, l. 5b)[4]

The following mnemonic (a University of Melbourne *macédoine*) may be helpful in the early stages. Each half-line gives the simplest form of one of the types and alliterates on the accented syllables with the letter by which that type is known.

A.	Anna angry	´ ˣ ´ ˣ	falling-falling
B.	And Byrhtnoth bold	ˣ ´ ˣ ´	rising-rising
C.	In keen conflict	ˣ ´ ´ ˣ	clashing
D.	Ding down strongly	´ ´ ˋ ˣ	falling by stages
	Deal death to all	´ ´ ˣ ˋ	broken fall
E.	Each one with edge	´ ˋ ˣ ´	fall and rise

ANACRUSIS

Occasionally one or even two unaccented syllables are allowed to come before a line of type A or D, and these syllables are not counted in the scansion of the line but are treated as a kind of extrametrical prelude. Such

---

[4] Here, as in a few other cases, an unaccented syllable is allowed to fall between the first accented syllable and the syllable with secondary accent.

syllables are called *anacrusis* and are marked off from the verse proper by a vertical bar:

           (Type A)   (Type D)

gĕnered wið nīðĕ (18, l. 827a)   wiðhǽfdĕ heaþodèorŭm (18, l. 772a)

            (Type A)   (Type D)

gĕbiddắþ him tŏ þŷssŭm bĕacnĕ (14, l. 83a)   bĕhĕold hrĕowcèarig (14, l. 25a)

COMPLEXITY OF ALLITERATIVE METRE

The elaborate regulations for accent, vowel length, alliteration, and verse types, further complicated by anacrusis, resolved stress, and exceptions to certain regulations, all may leave some students of Old English metre wondering whether they are dealing with an impossibly complex prosody or with no systematic prosody at all.[5] Is there any short collocation with two accented syllables that *cannot* be construed as one of the five types if one invokes enough rules and exceptions to rules? If one is tempted toward such scepticism, it may be useful to consider some of the collocations of Old English words which the metrical system *does* exclude. At first glance one might think that a half-line like *in his beorht blōd* 'into his bright blood' would make an excellent Old English verse, but in fact the Anglo-Saxon ear would immediately reject it as prose, for the accent pattern ˣ ˣ ´ ´ is not one of the five types. *Tala tungena* 'utterances of tongues' might at first glance look like an acceptable type A, but it is not. The first accented syllable is short, and, moreover, A-verses never end in two unaccented syllables; only one may occur at the end of an A-verse. *Grimm and glēaw* 'fierce and wise' might seem to be a vigorous and melodious verse to a beginner, but the Old English verse system rejects it because it has only three syllables, and an Old English verse must have at least four. Study the following collocations and see if you can determine why they are not metrical:

> *ne becōm niht*   'nor did night come'
> *folc wæs fūl*   'the people were filthy'
> *gōd is his gār*   'his spear is good'
> *fela fara*   'many journeys'
> *Hygd ne oftēah*   'Hygd did not withhold'
> *scūfað scyldas tō him*   'they push shields to him'.

---

[5] The analysis of Old English metre presented here is the traditional one first made by Eduard Sievers in the late nineteenth century and generally accepted by later metrical scholars, such as John C. Pope, *The Rhythm of 'Beowulf'* (New Haven, Conn., 1942; rev. ed. 1966). Students should be aware, however, that some metrical theorists have departed from Sievers' system in details or in principles, and their scansions may differ from those presented here.

HYPERMETRIC VERSE

Occasionally Old English poets shift in the course of a poem to an expanded form of verse which we call hypermetric. Hypermetric verses have three rather than two accented syllables in each half-line; they seem to be composed of a regular verse-type with another half-verse added on. These, for example, seem to be A-verses with an additional accented and unaccented syllable at the end:

> Tíl biþ sě þě his trēowě gěhéalděþ,   ně scěal næfrě his tórn tō rýcěně
> béorn ǒf his brēostǔm ācýþǎn,   némþě hě ǽr þā bótě cúnně,
> éorl mǐd élně gěfrémmǎn.   Wél biǒ þǣm þě hǐm árě sécěǒ,
> frófrě tō Fæder ǒn heofonǔm,   þæ̌r ǔs éal sēo fæstnǔng stónděǒ.
>
> (*The Wanderer*, ll. 112–15)

For more such lines see selection 14, ll. 8–10, 20–3, 30–4, and 39–49, and selection 20 *passim*. Hypermetric lines usually occur in groups of three or more and must have had some kind of special effect for an Anglo-Saxon audience, but we do not know what that effect was.

RHYME

Rhyme has no functional role in Old English versification. In Modern English, rhyme demarcates the boundaries of verses and provides ornament. In Old English, as we have seen, these functions are served by alliteration. Rhyme was not unknown to the Anglo-Saxons; as incidental ornament it occurs, for example, in selection 12, ll. 42 and 309, in selection 13, ll. 5b and 7b, and in selection 18, ll. 726, 734, 2258, and 3172. In late Old English verse there are signs that rhyme is beginning to displace alliteration as a functional device; see selection 12, l. 271 and note.

APPENDIX D

List of Linguistic Terms
Used in this Book

ablative absolute A Latin construction in which a noun and participle or noun and adjective in the ablative case stand syntactically independent of the rest of the sentence: e.g. '*Eo opere perfecto*, praesidia disponit' ('*That work being completed*, he sets up defences'). See §191.4.

abstract noun A noun denoting an idea, quality, or state rather than a concrete object. Abstract nouns are often derived from adjectives or verbs by the addition of a suffix: e.g. *truth* (from *true*), *width* (from *wide*), *jogging* (from *jog*).

accent see **stress**

accidence see §4.

accusative case The form that a noun, pronoun, or adjective takes when it functions as the direct object of a verb or preposition. Also called **objective case**. See §189.

active voice see **voice**

adjective A word used to describe a noun or pronoun: e.g. '*pious* songs', 'I am *happy*'. By adding the suffixes *-er* and *-est* many MnE adjectives form the comparative and superlative degrees. See §74. (Like other Germanic languages, OE has a system of 'strong adjectives' and 'weak adjectives', for which see §64.)

adjective clauses are used in the same way as **adjectives** to describe a noun or pronoun: e.g. 'The girl *who spoke to us* was Ann'.

adverb A word that modifies a verb (e.g. 'She moved *awkwardly*') or an adverb ('She moved *very* awkwardly') or an adjective ('She is *very* awkward'). Some adverbs can also introduce or modify entire clauses (*therefore*, *then*, *fortunately*, etc.). Like adjectives, many adverbs can be made comparative ('He ran *faster*') or superlative ('He ran *fastest*') by the addition of the suffixes *-er*, *-est*. See §135.

adverb clauses are used in the same way as **adverbs** to modify a verb, adverb, or adjective. MnE distinguishes the eight types described in §166.

A Guide to Old English, Eighth Edition. Bruce Mitchell and Fred C. Robinson.
© 2012 Bruce Mitchell and Fred C. Robinson. Published 2012 by Blackwell Publishing Ltd.

affix A prefix or a suffix.

agreement The requirement that some words in a sentence must 'agree' with each other in form. In MnE a singular subject requires a singular verb ('He is'), a plural subject a plural verb ('They are'). In OE there must also be agreement in gender (e.g. a feminine noun requires a feminine adjective modifying it, as in *tilu giefu* 'a good gift') and in case (a feminine dative singular noun requires a feminine dative singular adjective modifying it, as in *tilre gife* '(to) a good gift'). Also called **concord**. See §187.

analogy (analogical change) The alteration of an unusual or irregular grammatical form to make it conform with a dominant, regular pattern. Because of the pattern established in the series *blouse – blouses, house – houses, spouse – spouses*, a small child or a foreigner might be led by analogy to assume a set *mouse – mouses* (instead of *mice*). From OE to MnE many strong verbs have become weak through analogy with the numerically superior weak verb: e.g. *glīdan, scūfan, helpan, wadan*. See §44.

anomalous Irregular, such as the MnE verbs *be* and *go* and the OE verbs *bēon* and *gān*, whose past tenses do not conform to any normal pattern of conjugation, either strong or weak. See §§127–129.

antecedent A word in a sentence (usually a noun) to which another word (usually a pronoun) refers. In 'She lost her purse but later found it' *purse* is the antecedent of *it*. See §187.2.

anticipation See §148.

article In MnE the articles are *the* (definite article) and *a/an* (indefinite articles). See §§15–16, 193.1, 193.4.

assimilation When two dissimilar sounds are brought adjacent to one another, for ease of pronunciation one of the sounds will often change in order to become more similar to its adjacent sound. Thus the past tense *kissed* was in ME a dissyllable and the *-d* following the unaccented vowel *e* was pronounced as a *d*. But when in early MnE the *e* was dropped through syncopation (see **syncopation** below), the *-d* became adjacent to *ss*. The voiceless *ss* adjacent to the voiced *d* was awkward to pronounce, and so the *-d* became unvoiced and was pronounced as a *-t*. Today we pronounce *kissed* as if it were spelled *kist*. This is assimilation. The English words *indecent, immoral, illegal* (all borrowed from Latin) all have the Latin prefix *in-* meaning 'not'. But the adjacent *m-* of *immoral* causes the prefix *in-* to become *im-* in order to make the two adjacent consonants easier to pronounce. And before the initial *l-* of *legal in-* becomes *il-* for the same reason. This is assimilation.

auxiliary verb See **modal auxiliary**.

back vowel In OE the vowels *u, o,* and *a*. See §§28–32.

borrowing A word adopted from another language, like MnE *pizza*, a borrowing from Italian. Also called **loanword**. See §234.

breaking See §§96–99.

cardinal number A number indicating quantity (*one, two, three*, etc.), as opposed to an **ordinal number** indicating sequence (*first, second, third*, etc.). Cf. §§82–86.

case The grammatical form of an adjective, noun, or pronoun showing its grammatical relationship to other words in the sentence: e.g. MnE *student's* is in the possessive (or genitive) case, as is shown by the case ending -*'s*. Cf. **inflexion**. See §§188–192.

causative A description of a verb whose meaning denotes *causing* something to happen. The MnE causative verb *to fell* (as in 'to fell a tree') means 'to cause to fall'. *To lay* (as in 'to lay something down') means 'to cause to lie'.

clause A grammatical construction normally containing a subject and a **finite verb** and often constituting part of a sentence. See **dependent clause** and **main clause**. See §§154–180.

closed syllable See §27.

comparative degree A form of an adjective or adverb expressing a higher degree of a quality (but not the highest). In MnE the comparative degree is often expressed by adding the suffix -*er*: *high – higher, fast – faster, sweet – sweeter*. Cf. **superlative degree**. See §§74–76, 135.

complement A noun or adjective following a verb such as *to be* and referring to the subject. Also called **predicate nominative** and **predicate adjective**. 'He is *superior*' and 'He became *president*' are examples of complements. The latter example and a sentence like 'I consider him a *hero*' are sometimes called **object complements**.

compound A word made up of two or more independent words combined. MnE *bathroom, shellfish*, and *tenderhearted* are compounds. See §137.

concord see **agreement**

conjugation A systematic arrangement of the various grammatical forms of a verb by which are identified the verb's person, number, tense, and mood. Cf. §§110–111.

conjunction A word or words used to connect clauses, phrases, sentences, and individual words. Modern English distinguishes simple conjunctions, e.g. *if*; grouped conjunctions, e.g. *so that*; divided conjunctions, e.g. *so . . . that*; prepositional conjunctions, e.g. *to the end . . . that*. See **coordinating conjunction** and **subordinating conjunction**. See §§167–171.

contraction The process of shortening a word or word group by omitting one or more sounds usually from the interior of the word or word group: e.g. *who'd* for *who would*, *I've* for *I have*, *can't* for *cannot*. Pr OE **sleahan* is contracted to OE *slēan*. See §§103.3, 184.4.c.

coordinating conjunction Conjunctions like *and*, *but*, and *or*, which connect clauses, phrases, sentences, and words of equal status and function, are coordinating conjunctions: e.g. 'They sang *and* we danced'; 'To be *or* not to be'; 'strange *but* true'.

correlation The use of two words not side by side to link two units of speech: e.g. *either . . . or, not only . . . but also, both . . . and, neither . . . nor*. See §§150–152.

dative absolute See §§191.4, 204.3.

dative case The case of the **indirect object**. In the OE 'Hēo geaf *him* wæstm' ('She gave fruit *to him*') *him* is dative. See §191 and **possessive dative**.

declension The systematic variation in the grammatical forms of a noun, pronoun, or adjective indicating its gender, number, and case function. Declensions are arranged in **paradigms** (which see).

definite article see **article**

demonstrative pronoun A pronoun which singles out the word or idea to which it refers and distinguishes that word or idea from other members of the same class. The MnE demonstrative pronouns are *that, those, this, these*. See §§16 and 17 for OE demonstratives.

dental consonant A consonant sound made by placing the tip of the tongue in the general region of the upper teeth – e.g. *t* and *d*.

dental preterite A means of forming the past tense of verbs by affixing grammatical endings containing the dental consonant *t* or *d*: e.g. MnE *heard*, OE *hīerde*, MnE *meant*, OE *mȳscte*. Weak verbs take a dental preterite.

dependent clause A clause introduced by a conjunction or relative pronoun and combining with a **main clause** to make a complete sentence. Thus dependent clauses like 'If it rains', or 'Since you are cold', or 'When he arrives' can combine with a main clause like 'we'll go into the house' to make a complete sentence. See §§154–180.

diphthong The combination of two vowels in a single syllable: *riot, neon*, and *join* all contain diphthongs. See §8.

diphthongization The process of changing a pure vowel into a diphthong. See §§96, 100.

direct object The recipient of the action of a **transitive verb**. In 'She helped him' *him* is the direct object of the transitive verb *helped*.

disyllabic Consisting of two syllables. *Baby*, *water*, and *headstrong* are all disyllabic. See §§26, 41–44, 68–69.

dual A grammatical number indicating two (as contrasted with *singular* referring to one and *plural* referring to three or more). OE *wit* 'we two' and *git* 'you two' are examples of words with dual number. See §11.

finite (of a verb form) Having a specific tense, number, and person (e.g. *helps*, *helped*); i.e. any form of a verb other than the infinitive or past or present participles.

front vowel In OE the vowels *i*, *y*, *e*, and *æ*. See §§28–32.

function word A word used to express grammatical relationships rather than lexical meaning. Prepositions, conjunctions, articles, and auxiliary verbs are function words.

future tense A verb tense describing future events: e.g. 'He will regret doing that', 'I shall do my best.' OE has only one verb (*bēon*) which has a distinctive form for the future: *bēo* 'I shall be' (vs. *ēom* 'I am'), *biđ* 'he will be' (vs. *is* 'he is'). (See §127.) Otherwise OE uses the present tense to express future acts (as in MnE. 'I am coming tomorrow'). See §196.

future-in-the-past Reference by a speaker in the past to a future event: e.g. 'King Alfred said that the Danes would attack the following week.' In OE the subjunctive is used after *þonne* to express future-in-the-past. See §174.

gender See §12.

genitive Possessive (case): e.g. 'the *man's* house', '*their* children'. See §190.

gerund A verb ending in *-ing* functioning as a noun. See **participle**.

gradation The alteration of a root vowel as a sign of changing grammatical function: e.g. the vowel of *sing* is changed to that of *sang* to indicate past tense.

high vowel In OE the vowels *i*, *y*, *e*, and *u*. See §§28–32.

hypotaxis See §183.

imperative (of verbs) The grammatical mood for expressing a command: e.g. 'Come in', 'Look!', and 'Be careful!' See §§89.2, 112.3, 112.4, and Appendix E.

impersonal verb A verb whose subject is an unspecified agent: 'It's snowing', 'It seems to be getting dark'. Here 'to snow' and 'to seem' are impersonal verbs. See §212.

i-**mutation** See §§52–60.

indefinite article see **article**

indicative (of verbs) The grammatical mood for expressing simple statements of fact: 'Jim arrived today', 'I am tired', 'Caesar conquered Gaul'. See Appendix E.

indirect object A noun or pronoun that is affected by the action of a transitive verb but is not the direct object. In 'We gave Mr Brown a cheque' *Mr Brown* is the indirect object (*cheque* is the direct object). In 'We bought her a hat', *her* is the indirect object (*hat* is the direct object).

infinitive A non-finite (see **finite**) form of a verb that in MnE is usually preceded by *to*: *to run, to speak, to weep*. In OE the infinitive usually ends in *-an* and is not preceded by *tō*, but there is also an inflected infinitive with *tō*. See §§89.2, 205.

inflexion Systematic changes in the form of a word (usually by the addition of an ending) to indicate its grammatical function: e.g. in MnE *elephants* the *-s* is an inflexional ending indicating plurality. In *faded -ed* is an inflexional ending indicating past tense. In OE *gōdne -ne* is an inflexional ending indicating accusative singular masculine. See **declension, tense**.

initial Occurring at the beginning of a word. In *home* the initial sound is *h-*.

instrumental case A grammatical form of a noun or pronoun indicating the meaning 'by means of'. In 'He made it by hand' *hand* is in an instrumental relationship. In the OE sentence 'Hē slōh þone mann þȳ stāne' ('He struck the man with the stone') *þȳ stāne* 'with the stone', 'by means of the stone' is in the instrumental case. See §192.

interjection An exclamatory word or word group: e.g. MnE *ah! alas! dear me!* OE *hwæt! lā! Ēalā!*

interrogative A description of a word, phrase, or sentence which asks a question: *Why? How many? Has he gone?*

intransitive (of a verb) Incapable of taking a direct object: e.g. 'He smiles', 'The culprit fled.' Cf. **transitive**.

late spellings OE texts from the eighth, ninth, and tenth centuries preserve on the whole the grammatical endings of words as they appear in the paradigms in the *Guide*. Eleventh-century texts, however, begin to show *late spellings* that indicate (*inter alia*) loss of distinction in some grammatical endings: e.g. the indicative/subjunctive distinction *-on/-en* is lost and both endings are spelled *-on* or *-an*. Dative plural *-um* is sometimes spelled *-on* or *-an*. Weak 2 preterite verb endings *-ode, -odon* appear as *-ede, -edon*, etc.

levelling See §§108–109. Also, see **analogy** above.

limiting adjective clause See §165 note 1.

long-stemmed See §26, fn. 1.

low vowel In OE the vowels *æ* and *a*. See §§28–32.

main clause A clause that can stand alone as an independent sentence (e.g. 'All is well') as contrasted with a **dependent clause** such as 'If he arrives in time . . .', which must combine with a main clause in order to make a sentence.

medial Occurring in the middle of a word. In OE *heofon f* is a medial consonant.

metathesis The transposition of two sounds within a word. Through metathesis OE *græs* 'grass' sometimes appears as *gærs* and OE *wæsp* 'wasp' sometimes appears as *wæps*.

modal auxiliary *Can*, *may*, *must*, *shall*, *will* are examples of modal auxiliaries, which occur together with the infinitive of other verbs without the usual *to* before the infinitive: e.g. 'I can go', 'He will speak'. Unlike other verbs, they do not take *-s* in the third person singular present form, and (except for *will*) they are incapable of combining with the suffix *-ing*. For the most part this group of verbs corresponds with the OE **preterite-present** verbs, which see. See §§206–211.

monophthong See §9 note 1.

monosyllable Consisting of only one syllable. *Yes*, *un-*, *can* are monosyllables.

moods (of the OE verb) Variant forms of a verb indicating whether the verb (1) states a fact (indicative mood), (2) issues a command (imperative mood), or (3) expresses a wish or a hypothetical situation (subjunctive mood). See **imperative**, **indicative**, and **subjunctive**. See §89.2 and Appendix E.

nasal The OE consonants *m* and *n*, which are called 'nasals' because when they are pronounced the breath passes through the nose rather than the mouth. Cf. §§101, 103.2.

nominative case See §188.

noun A word naming things, persons, or ideas. In OE nouns are inflected for number and case and serve as subjects, objects, and complements of verbs and as objects of prepositions.

noun clauses (e.g. 'He said *that it was true*') perform the function of nouns, serving as subjects, objects, and complements of verbs and as objects of prepositions. The term embraces dependent statements and desires (§§155–156) and dependent questions §§157–160).

number A grammatical indication of how many people, things, ideas, etc. are being referred to. MnE has two grammatical numbers, singular and plural. *Meat* is a singular noun and it requires a singular verb: '*Meat is* nutritious' (*Meat* and *is* are singular in form). In 'Some *meats are* too expensive' *meats* and *are* are both plural in number. See **dual**.

object See **direct object, indirect object**. Cf. §§143–147 (where *object* is represented as 'O.').

oblique cases A collective term for all the cases of nouns, pronouns, and adjectives other than the nominative. In OE the oblique cases are the genitive, accusative, dative, and instrumental cases.

open syllable See §27.

ordinal number See **cardinal number** and §§82–83.

orthography Spelling. See §§5–9.

palatal A term describing sounds made with the tip of the tongue placed in the area of the hard palate. In OE the high vowels and the consonants *ċ* and *ġ* are palatal sounds.

palatalization In OE the change of a velar consonant (such as *k* and *g*) to a palatal consonant (*ċ*, *ġ*) caused by an adjacent palatal vowel.

paradigm An orderly arrangement of all the grammatical forms of a noun, pronoun, adjective, or verb. Examples of paradigms are §§16, 33, 70, 126.

parataxis See §183.

parsing See pp. 1–2.

participle A grammatical form derived from a verb by adding the suffixes *-ed*, *-en* (past participles) or *-ing* (present participle) to the verb stem. Participles function as adjectives (*broken* promises, *baked* beans, *running* water) and are used in forming **resolved tenses** ('He has *spoken*', 'She is *working*'). (An *-ing* form of a verb functioning as a noun (*jogging* is healthy) is not a participle but is rather a *gerund*.) Cf. §199.

partitive genitive The use of the genitive case with words denoting quantity: 'a pound *of bacon*', 'a lot *of people*' (the *of*-constructions are MnE genitives). In OE the quantity word *fela* 'much, many' and numerals normally take the partitive genitive: 'fela *folca*', 'twentig *wintra*'. See §§190.4, 194.2.

parts of speech The eight grammatical classes of words: noun, pronoun, verb, adjective, adverb, preposition, conjunction, interjection.

passive voice see **voice**

person A grammatical category referring to who is performing the action of a verb. 'I speak' is first *person*; 'you speak' is second *person*; 'She speaks', 'They speak' are third *person*. See §89.4.

personal pronoun A pronoun referring to the first and second person (§21) and third person (§18) and some of the interrogative and indefinite pronouns (§20) and to be differentiated from **demonstrative pronouns** (§§15–17) and **relative pronouns**.

phonology The study of the sounds of a language, including the study of **sound-changes**.

possessive dative The OE use of the dative case to indicate possession where MnE uses the possessive (genitive) case: e.g. '*Him* æt heortan stōd ætterne ord' ('The deadly spear stood in *his* heart').

predicate That part of a sentence or clause containing a verb and supplying information about the subject. In 'Our mother baked a cake' *Our mother* is the subject and *baked a cake* is the predicate.

predicate adjective See **complement**.

predicate nominative See **complement**.

preposition A word or group of words usually placed before a noun or pronoun object to show how the object functions in the sentence. Typical prepositions are *by, in, of, on account of, out of*. See §213.

preterite Past (tense).

preterite-present verbs A group of OE verbs corresponding to the MnE **modal auxiliaries**. The term *preterite-present* refers to the fact that historically these are past-tense forms that have come to have present-tense meanings. See §130.

principal clause see **main clause**

principal parts A list of selected forms of a verb including the infinitive, third-person singular and plural past-tense forms, and the past participle. From these forms one can deduce every grammatical form that a given verb can have. See §§90–93.

pronoun A word which can substitute for a noun: e.g. *it, she, they, him*. (See **antecedent**.) See also **relative pronoun**.

proper noun The name of a specific, unique person, place, thing, or group: e.g. *Bede, Winchester, Scots, Blarney stone*. In MnE proper names are almost always capitalized.

quantity (of vowels) The relative duration of the vowel sound in a syllable – i.e. the difference between long syllables (e.g. OE *stān*) and short syllables (e.g. OE *wer*). See §26.

recapitulation and anticipation See §148.

reduplicating Repeating a syllable of a verb to indicate a change of tense. An earlier form of OE *hātan* 'command, name' was **haitan*. To form the pret. sg. the root syllable was reduplicated: **haihait*. In OE the only vestige of this process is the pret. sg. *heht*, which, however, is often simplified to *hēt*, thus removing the evidence of reduplication. See §93.

reflexive (of pronouns) Reflexive pronouns denote the same entity as that denoted by the subject: e.g. 'She blames *herself*', 'He made *himself* a sandwich'. Some verbs require a reflexive pronoun (e.g. 'He betook *himself* to the airport'). Far more OE verbs take a reflexive pronoun than do MnE verbs.

relative pronoun A pronoun that introduces a dependent clause while referring back to a preceding noun: 'The light *that* failed', 'People *who* overeat become obese', 'Blackmail, *which* is illegal, should be punished'. In OE the relative pronoun *þe*, which is invariable in form, can be used in any case function with the meaning of any of the MnE relative pronouns – 'who', 'which', 'that', 'whom', etc.

resolved tenses Tenses formed from the participle (past or present) or an infinitive of a verb together with a form of the verbs *to be*, *to have*, *to do*, or one of the **modal auxiliaries**. See §§199–203. Also called **compound tenses**.

short-stemmed See **long-stemmed**.

sound-changes Changes in a language's sound system over a period of time. For a list of OE sound-changes, see 'sound-changes (laws)' in the Index of Subjects in this book.

stem The form of a word to which inflexional endings are attached. Cf. §26, fn. 1.

stress (or **accent**) The degree of force used in pronouncing a syllable. In MnE *body* stress falls on the first syllable; *-y* is unstressed. See §6 and Appendix C.

strong verb A verb that signals tense differences by changing the root vowel: e.g. *sing, sang, sung*. See §87 and Appendix A. Cf. **weak verb**.

subjunctive The grammatical mood of a verb expressing what is (*inter alia*) hypothetical, possible, or wished for. In 'This is treason' *is* is indicative; in 'If this be treason' *be* is subjunctive. In 'The Queen lives frugally' *lives* is indicative; in 'Long live the Queen!' *live* is subjunctive. In OE the subjunctive is used in a much wider range of syntactical contexts than it is in MnE. See Appendix E.

subordinate clause See **dependent clause**.

subordinating conjunction A word that joins two clauses and indicates that one clause is dependent on the other. *Although, because, if, when, whenever* are subordinating conjunctions.

superlative degree A form of an adjective or adverb expressing the highest degree of a quality. In MnE the superlative degree is often expressed by adding the suffix *-est*: *high – highest, fast – fastest, sweet – sweetest*. See §§74–76, 135. Cf. **comparative degree**.

syncopation The contraction of a word through the loss of a medial vowel. OE *drinceþ* becomes *drincþ* through syncopation of the *e*.

syntax See §§139–142.

tense The time at which a verbal action takes place: e.g. *present* tense ('He goes'), *past* tense ('He went'), and *future* tense ('He will go').

transitive (of a verb) Capable of taking a direct object: e.g. 'We *like* him', 'She *helped* them', 'They *rejected* my request' all contain transitive verbs. Cf. **intransitive**.

verb The part of speech displaying such grammatical features as tense, voice, and mood and usually expressing an action, a process, or a state of being: e.g. *jump, understand, ponder*. For various aspects of OE verbs see 'verbs' in the Index of Subjects in this book.

voice (of a verb) The grammatical category that expresses whether the subject of a verb is the agent of the verb's action (*active voice*) or the recipient of that action (*passive voice*). 'Helen helped her friends' exemplifies the active voice; 'Helen was helped by her friends' (in which the verb is converted into a past participle combined with a form of the verb 'to be') exemplifies the passive voice.

voiced consonant Consonants pronounced while the vocal cords are vibrating. MnE *v, z, d, b, g, m, n, l* are all voiced consonants.

voiceless consonants Consonants pronounced without simultaneous vibration of the vocal cords. MnE *f, s, t, p, k* are all voiceless consonants. If one makes a prolonged pronunciation of *v* and then suddenly stops the vibration in the vocal cords, the sound becomes *f*. This process is called *unvoicing*.

weak verb A verb that forms the past tense by adding a grammatical ending containing *d* or *t* ('dental suffixes'): e.g. MnE *dress*ed, *hear*d, *mean*t; OE *frem*ede, *hīer*de, *wȳsc*te. See §§87, 115–126. Cf. **strong verb**.

word-order The relative position of grammatical elements, especially subject, verb, and object, in a sentence. In discussing word-order it is customary to use the capital letters S., V., O. to represent *subject, verb*, and *object*. See §§143–147.

APPENDIX E

The Moods of Old English

There are four moods in Old English – the indicative, the imperative, the subjunctive, and the infinitive (§89.2).

It should be noted that the inflexions of verbs are sometimes ambiguous, e.g. *þu sunge* (§113.2) and the *-on*, *-en* endings (§§118, 120).

INDICATIVE

On the functions of the indicative, see §156.

On the present indicative, see §§195 and 196.

On the preterite indicative, see §197.

The historic present rarely, if ever, occurs (§196).

IMPERATIVE

The imperative occurs only in the second person singular and plural of the present tense. Its basic function is to express a command. For example, Open the door! *Bēo þæt þū eart!* 'Be what you are!'

INFINITIVE

See §205 and, for the accusative and infinitive, §161.

SUBJUNCTIVE

The functions of the subjunctive can best be described by comparing them with those of the indicative. See §156 and Appendix D.

A Guide to Old English, Eighth Edition. Bruce Mitchell and Fred C. Robinson.
© 2012 Bruce Mitchell and Fred C. Robinson. Published 2012 by Blackwell Publishing Ltd.

APPENDIX F

Grimm's and Verner's Laws

§§105–108 (above) describe 'consonant changes that distinguish the Gmc languages from the other IE languages' (commonly known as 'Grimm's Law' and 'Verner's Law', Grimm and Verner being the scholars who first explained these changes). Here we give a more detailed account of the correspondences between the IE consonants and the Gmc consonants that evolved from them. The symbol > means 'becomes'.

Grimm's Law

Indo-European		Germanic
bh	>	b
dh	>	d
gh	>	g
b	>	p
d	>	t
g	>	k
p	>	f
t	>	þ
k	>	h

IE l, m, n, r, and s do not change.

Verner's Law

Indo-European		Germanic
p	>	b
t	>	d
k	>	g
s	>	r

A few examples will illustrate how the IE forms change into Gmc. First, Grimm's Law: IE *bhrāter* 'brother' (whose consonant structure is preserved in Sanskrit *bhrātr*) becomes OE *brōþor*, illustrating how IE *bh* becomes Gmc *b* and IE *t* becomes Gmc *þ*. The IE root *dhō-* (whose initial consonant is

A Guide to Old English, Eighth Edition. Bruce Mitchell and Fred C. Robinson.
© 2012 Bruce Mitchell and Fred C. Robinson. Published 2012 by Blackwell Publishing Ltd.

preserved in Sanskrit -*dhāmi* 'put, lay') becomes MnE *do*. IE **kērd-* 'heart' (whose consonants are preserved in Greek *kardiā* and Latin *cordis* 'of the heart') becomes MnE *heart*, thus illustrating how IE *k* becomes Gmc *h* and how IE *d* becomes Gmc *t*. IE **pek-* 'cattle' (whose consonants are retained in Latin *pecu* 'cattle' and *pecunia* 'money') becomes OE *feoh* 'cattle, wealth', which then becomes MnE *fee*. The OE form illustrates how IE *p* becomes *f* and *k* becomes *h*. MnE *fee* has lost the final -*h*.

Illustrating Verner's Law, IE **kṃtóm* 'one hundred' becomes MnE *hundred*. Following Grimm's Law, the initial *k* regularly becomes *h*, but the *t* of **kṃtóm* does not become *þ*, as Grimm's Law prescribes. Karl Verner explained that when a consonant is preceded by an unaccented syllable in IE, the consonant follows Verner's Law rather than Grimm's, *t* becoming *d* rather than *þ*. Similarly IE **altós* 'high, full-grown' has an unaccented syllable before the *t* and accordingly it becomes Gmc *d*, as prescribed by Verner's Law, thus producing the MnE cognate *old*.

Part Two
Prose and Verse Texts

NOTE

The first eighteen texts are arranged in order of increasing difficulty. The first three selections are normalized throughout, and palatal *ċ* and *ġ* are distinguished from velar *c* and *g*. The fourth selection is not normalized, but a few spelling peculiarities have been removed to ease transition to the unnormalized texts in the remainder of the readings. Students should notice that in the manuscript page (as in all other OE manuscripts) there are no commas, colons, semicolons, question marks or other modern punctuation. All the punctuation in OE texts published in modern times is introduced into the texts by modern editors and has no manuscript authority. Students should be mindful of this when reading Old English in modern editions.

I

Practice Sentences

A. Although sometimes pronounced differently from their MnE descendants, many OE words have the same form and the same basic meaning as their MnE counterparts: e.g. *bliss, colt, dung, elm, finger, fox, handle, him, land, mist, nest, of, on, rest, sprang, winter, writ.* Indeed, entire sentences can have essentially the same appearance in OE and MnE, although it must be conceded that such sentences can be composed only through a rather artificial selection of words from the OE lexicon:

> Harold is swift. His hand is strong and his word grim. Late in
> līfe hē went tō his wīfe in Rōme.
> Is his inn open? His cornbin is full and his song is writen.
> Grind his corn for him and sing mē his song.
> Hē is dēad. His bed is under him. His lamb is dēaf and blind.
> Hē sang for mē.
> Hē swam west in storme and winde and froste.
> Bring ūs gold. Stand ūp and find wīse men.

B. Many other OE words appear strange at first glance, but when pronounced according to the rules set out in §§5–9 they become immediately recognizable as MnE words in earlier dress: e.g. *bæc, biscop, ċinn, diċ, disc, ecg, feðer, hecg, hwelp, lifer, piċ, ræfter, scort, þæċ, þing, þiðer, þrescold, wecg, wofen.* Among the following sentences set out for practice in pronunciation are a number of words which will become recognizable when pronounced correctly.

> Is his þeġn hēr ġīet?
> His līnen socc fēoll ofer bord in þæt wæter and scranc.
> Hwǣr is his cȳþþ and cynn?
> His hring is gold, his disc glæs, and his belt leðer.
> Se fisc swam under þæt scip and ofer þone sciellfisc.

5

A Guide to Old English, Eighth Edition. Bruce Mitchell and Fred C. Robinson.
© 2012 Bruce Mitchell and Fred C. Robinson. Published 2012 by Blackwell
Publishing Ltd.

His ċicen ran from his horsweġe, ofer his pæð, and in his
  ġeard.

Se horn sang hlūde: hlysten wē!

Se cniht is on þǣre brycge.

Sēo cwēn went from þǣre ċiriċe.

Hēo siteþ on þǣre benċe.

10 God is gōd.

þis trēow is æsc, ac þæt trēow is āc.

Hē wolde begān wiċċecræft, and hē began swā tō dōnne.

Fuhton ġē manlīċe oþþe mānlīċe?

His smiððe is þām smiðe lēof.

  C.   After studying key paradigms 1, 2, and 4 (p. 4), you should
find most of the grammatical relationships in the following sentences
readily understandable:

15 Iċ bræc þone stān.

Se stān is miċel.

Ðæs stānes miċelnes is wundorliċ.

þes stānwyrhta ġeaf þǣm stāne hīw.

Hē slōh þone mann þȳ stāne.

20 Sēo sunne is swiðe miċel.

þǣr hēo scīnþ, þǣr biþ dæġ.

Niht is þǣre eorðan sceadu betwēonan þǣre sunnan and
  mancynne.

þis līf is lǣne, and þēos woruld drēoseþ and fealleþ.

25 Sing þisne song!

Hīe scufon ūt hira scipu and siġldon tō þǣre sǣ.

On þissum dæġe cwealdon wē þone fēond þisses folces.

Iċ ġeman þā naman þāra folca and þissa folca.

His wīfes nama wæs Elizabeþ.

30 þēos ġiefu is for ūs, and hēo līcaþ ūs.

Se dēaþ is þisses līfes ende, ac sēo sāwol is undēadliċ.

Hīe hine ne dorston þā þing āscian.

Hwæt þyncþ ēow be Crīste? Hwæs sunu is hē?

Hwæs sunu eart þū? And hwæs dohtor eart þū?

35 Hwȳ ġeworhte God þā yfelan nǣdran?

2

Two Old Testament Pieces

The Bible and its translations have had a profound influence on the English language and on English literature. Among early experiments in rendering Scripture into the vernacular is that of Ælfric, a dedicated scholar and gifted prose stylist who served as Abbot of Eynsham from 1005 until his death. He had serious reservations about the wisdom of translating the Old Testament (see selection 4 below), but at the request of his patron Æthelweard he did so, rendering the Latin Vulgate version into relatively clean prose marred only occasionally by un-English, Latinate constructions. Readers can compare this work with that of the great King James translation, corresponding excerpts of which are provided on the facing page along with the Latin version for those who might like to compare the Old English with its approximate source. Since the King James translators worked from Greek and Hebrew originals rather than from the Vulgate, the correspondence between the two English versions is inexact.

The text is basically that of Bodleian Library, Oxford, MS Laud Misc. 509, but it has been normalized throughout.

A Guide to Old English, Eighth Edition. Bruce Mitchell and Fred C. Robinson.
© 2012 Bruce Mitchell and Fred C. Robinson. Published 2012 by Blackwell Publishing Ltd.

The Fall of Man (Genesis 3:1–19)

Old English Version

Ēac swelċe sēo nǣdre wæs ġēappre þonne ealle þā ōðre nīetenu þe
God ġeworhte ofer eorðan; and sēo nǣdre cwæð tō þām wīfe: 'Hwȳ
forbēad God ēow þæt ġē ne ǣten of ǣlcum trēowe binnan Paradīsum?'. Þæt wīf andwyrde: 'Of þāra trēowa wæstme þe sind on
5 Paradīsum wē etað: and of þæs trēowes wæstme, þe is onmiddan
neorxenawange, God bebēad ūs þæt wē ne ǣten, ne wē þæt trēow
ne hrepoden þȳ lǣs þe wē swulten.' Þā cwæð sēo nǣdre eft tō þām
wīfe: 'Ne bēo ġē nāteshwōn dēade, þēah þe ġē of þām trēowe eten.
Ac God wāt sōðlīċe þæt ēowre ēagan bēoð ġeopenode on swā
10 hwelċum dæġe swā ġē etað of þām trēowe; and ġē bēoð þonne
englum ġelīċe, witende ǣġðer ġe gōd ġe yfel.' Þā ġeseah þæt wīf
þæt þæt trēow wæs gōd tō etanne, be þām þe hire þūhte, and wlitiġ
on ēagum and lustbǣre on ġesihðe; and ġenam þā of þæs trēowes
wæstme and ġeǣt, and sealde hire were: hē ǣt þā. And hira bēġra
15 ēagan wurdon ġeopenode: hīe oncnēowon þā þæt hīe nacode
wǣron, and sīwodon him fīclēaf and worhton him wǣdbrēċ.

Eft þā þā God cōm and hīe ġehīerdon his stefne, þǣr hē ēode on
neorxenawange ofer middæġ, þā behȳdde Adam hine, and his wīf
ēac swā dyde, fram Godes ġesihðe onmiddan þām trēowe neorxen-
20 awanges. God clipode þā Adam, and cwæð: 'Adam, hwǣr eart þū?'

---

3   **forbēad . . . þæt ġē ne ǣten** Since OE uses multiple negation for emphasis
(§184.4*f*), the negative sense of 'forbade' is here merely reinforced by *ne*. Translate
either 'forbade . . . that you should eat' or 'commanded . . . that you should not eat'.

5   **wē etað** literally, 'we eat', but translate 'we do eat'.

6–7   **ne wē þæt trēow ne hrepoden þȳ lǣs þe** 'nor might we touch that tree
lest . . .'. As in l. 3, the double negative *ne* conj. (§184.4*d*) . . . *ne* adv. (§184.4*a*) is for
emphasis and should not be translated as double negative in Modern English.

8   **Ne bēo ġē** 'You will not be.' For the form and meaning of *bēo* see §§111 and 196.
Cf. the form of *bēoð* in l. 10, which is also future: 'will be'.

12   **gōd tō etanne** 'good to eat'. For this use of the inflected infinitive see
§205.2*d*.

be þām þe 'as'. See glossary under *se, þæt, sēo* and §169.

hire þūhte 'it seemed to her'. Impersonal verb (§212).

14   The object of the verbs *ġeǣt, sealde,* and *ǣt* (i.e. 'fruit') is understood (§193.7).

hē ǣt þā 'he ate then'.

16   **him . . . him** Both occurrences mean 'for themselves'. Cf. note to l. 18.

17–18   **þā þā . . . þā** 'when . . . then'. See §151.

18   **hine** 'himself'. In OE the personal pronouns also serve as reflexive pronouns: cf.
the second *mē* 'myself' in l. 22.

King James Version

Now the serpent was more subtil than any beast of the field which the LORD God had made. And he said unto the woman, Yea, hath God said, Ye shall not eat of every tree of the garden?

2 And the woman said unto the serpent, We may eat of the fruit of the trees of the garden:

3 But of the fruit of the tree which *is* in the midst of the garden, God hath said, Ye shall not eat of it, neither shall ye touch it, lest ye die.

4 And the serpent said unto the woman, Ye shall not surely die:

5 For God doth know that in the day ye eat thereof, then your eyes shall be opened, and ye shall be as gods, knowing good and evil.

6 And when the woman saw that the tree *was* good for food, and that it *was* pleasant to the eyes, and a tree to be desired to make *one* wise, she took of the fruit thereof, and did eat, and gave also unto her husband with her, and he did eat.

7 And the eyes of them both were opened, and they knew that they *were* naked; and they sewed fig leaves together, and made themselves aprons.

8 And they heard the voice of the LORD God walking in the garden in the cool of the day: and Adam and his wife hid themselves from the presence of the LORD God amongst the trees of the garden.

9 And the LORD God called unto Adam, and said unto him, Where *art* thou?

Latin Vulgate Version

Sed et serpens erat callidior cunctis animantibus terrae, quae fecerat Dominus Deus. Qui dixit ad mulierem: Cur praecepit vobis Deus ut non comederetis de omni ligno paradisi? [2]Cui respondit mulier: De fructu lignorum, quae sunt in paradiso, vescimur; [3]de fructu vero ligni, quod est in medio paradisi, praecepit nobis Deus ne comederemus et ne tangeremus illud, ne forte moriamur. [4]Dixit autem serpens ad mulierem: Nequaquam morte moriemini. [5]Scit enim Deus quod in quocumque die comederitis ex eo, aperientur oculi vestri, et eritis sicut dii scientes bonum et malum. [6]Vidit igitur mulier quod bonum esset lignum ad vescendum et pulchrum oculis aspectuque delectabile, et tulit de fructu illius et comedit deditque viro suo, qui comedit. [7]Et aperti sunt oculi amborum. Cumque cognovissent se esse nudos, consuerunt folia ficus et fecerunt sibi perizomata.

[8]Et, cum audissent vocem Domini Dei deambulantis in paradiso ad auram post meridiem, abscondit se Adam et uxor eius a facie Domini Dei in medio ligni paradisi. [9]Vocavitque Dominus Deus Adam et dixit ei: Ubi

Hē cwæð: 'þīne stefne iċ ġehīerde, lēof, on neorxenawange, and iċ
ondrēd mē, for þām þe iċ eom nacod, and iċ behȳdde mē.' God
cwæð: 'Hwā sæġde þē þæt þū nacod wǣre, ġif þū ne ǣte of þām
trēowe þe iċ þē bebēad þæt þū of ne ǣte?' Adam cwæð: 'þæt wīf þæt
25 þū mē forġēafe tō ġefēran, sealde mē of þām trēowe, and iċ ǣt.' God
cwæð tō þām wīfe: 'Hwȳ dydest þū þæt?' Hēo cwæð: 'Sēo nǣdre
bepǣhte mē and iċ ǣt.'

    God cwæð tō þǣre nǣdran: 'For þām þe þū þis dydest, þū bist
āwierġed betweox eallum nīetenum and wilddēorum. þū gǣst on
30 þīnum brēoste and etst þā eorðan eallum dagum þīnes līfes. Iċ sette
fēondrǣdene betweox þē and þām wīfe and þīnum ofspringe and
hire ofspringe; hēo tōbrȳt þīn hēafod and þū sierwst onġēan hire hō.'

    Tō þām wīfe cwæð God ēac swelċe: 'Iċ ġemaniġfealde þīne
iermða and þīne ġeēacnunga; on sārnesse þū ācenst ċild and þū
35 bist under weres onwealde and hē ġewielt þē.' Tō Adame hē cwæð:
'For þām þe þū ġehīerdest þīnes wīfes stefne and þū ǣte of þǣm
trēowe, þe iċ þē bebēad þæt þū ne ǣte, is sēo eorðe āwierġed on
þīnum weorce; on ġeswincum þū etst of þǣre eorðan eallum
dagum þīnes līfes. þornas and brēmelas hēo āspryt þē, and þū etst
40 þǣre eorðan wyrta. On swāte þīnes andwlitan þū brȳcst þīnes
hlāfes, oð þæt þū ġewende tō eorðan, of þǣre þe þū ġenumen
wǣre, for þām þe þū eart dūst and tō dūste wierþst.'

21–2 iċ ondrēd mē 'I was afraid.' The *mē* is reflexive and need not be translated
in Modern English. (But cf. early Modern English 'fear *thee* not'.)

22 **For þām þe** 'Because' (§§169–170). So also in ll. 28, 36, and 41–2.

29–32 **gǣst . . . etst . . . sette . . . tōbrȳt . . . sierwst** present tense used with future
meaning (§196). Several present-tense verbs in the following paragraph (e.g.
ġemaniġfealde, ācenst, ġewielt, etst, āspryt, brȳcst) should also be translated as future.

32 **tōbrȳt** The verb ending -*eþ* has disappeared through syncope and assimilation.
(See §112.2.) So also in *ġewielt, āspryt* in the following paragraph.

39 **hēo** is fem. nom. sg. agreeing in gender with its antecedent, *sēo eorðe*.

40–1 **þīnes hlāfes** The verb *brūcan* takes a genitive object here. See §190.6.

41 **þǣre þe** 'which'. *þe* combines with *þǣre* to form a compound rel. pron. See
§162.4.

10 And he said, I heard thy voice in the garden, and I was afraid, because I *was* naked; and I hid myself.

11 And he said, Who told thee that thou *wast* naked? Hast thou eaten of the tree, whereof I commanded thee that thou shouldest not eat?

12 And the man said, The woman whom thou gavest *to be* with me, she gave me of the tree, and I did eat.

13 And the LORD God said unto the woman, What *is* this *that* thou hast done? And the woman said, The serpent beguiled me, and I did eat.

14 And the LORD God said unto the serpent, Because thou hast done this, thou *art* cursed above all cattle, and above every beast of the field; upon thy belly shalt thou go, and dust shalt thou eat all the days of thy life:

15 And I will put enmity between thee and the woman, and between thy seed and her seed; it shall bruise thy head, and thou shalt bruise his heel.

16 Unto the woman he said, I will greatly multiply thy sorrow and thy conception; in sorrow thou shalt bring forth children; and thy desire *shall be* to thy husband, and he shall rule over thee.

17 And unto Adam he said, Because thou hast hearkened unto the voice of thy wife, and hast eaten of the tree, of which I commanded thee, saying, Thou shalt not eat of it: cursed *is* the ground for thy sake; in sorrow shalt thou eat *of* it all the days of thy life;

18 Thorns also and thistles shall it bring forth to thee; and thou shalt eat the herb of the field;

19 In the sweat of thy face shalt thou eat bread, till thou return unto the ground; for out of it wast thou taken: for dust thou *art*, and unto dust shalt thou return.

es? [10]Qui ait: Vocem tuam audivi in paradiso et timui eo quod nudus essem et abscondi me. [11]Cui dixit: Quis enim indicavit tibi quod nudus esses, nisi quod ex ligno, de quo praeceperam tibi ne comederes, comedisti? [12]Dixitque Adam: Mulier, quam dedisti mihi sociam, dedit mihi de ligno, et comedi. [13]Et dixit Dominus Deus ad mulierem: Quare hoc fecisti? Quae respondit: Serpens decepit me, et comedi.

[14]Et ait Dominus Deus ad serpentem: Quia fecisti hoc, maledictus es inter omnia animantia et bestias terrae: super pectus tuum gradieris et terram comedes cunctis diebus vitae tuae. [15]Inimicitias ponam inter te et mulierem, et semen tuum et semen illius; ipsa conteret caput tuum, et tu insidiaberis calcaneo eius. [16]Mulieri quoque dixit: Multiplicabo aerumnas tuas et conceptus tuos: in dolore paries filios et sub viri potestate eris et ipse dominabitur tui. [17]Adae vero dixit: Quia audisti vocem uxoris tuae et comedisti de ligno, ex quo praeceperam tibi ne comederes, maledicta terra in opere tuo: in laboribus comedes ex ea cunctis diebus vitae tuae. [18]Spinas et tribulos germinabit tibi, et comedes herbam terrae. [19]In sudore vultus tui vesceris pane, donec revertaris in terram, de qua sumptus es; quia pulvis es, et in pulverem reverteris.

Abraham and Isaac (Genesis 22:1–19)

Old English Version

God wolde þā fandian Abrahames ġehīersumnesse, and clipode his naman, and cwæð him þus tō: 'Nim þīnne āncennedan sunu Īsaac,
45 þe þū lufast, and far tō þām lande *Visionis* hraðe, and ġeoffra hine þǣr uppan ānre dūne.' Abraham þā ārās on þǣre ilcan nihte, and fērde mid twām cnapum tō þām fierlenan lande, and Īsaac samod, on assum rīdende. þā on þām þriddan dæġe, þā hīe þā dūne ġesāwon þǣr þǣr hīe tō scoldon tō ofslēanne Īsaac, þā cwæð Abra-
50 ham tō þām twām cnapum þus: 'Anbīdiað ēow hēr mid þām assum sume hwīle. Iċ and þæt ċild gāð unc tō ġebiddenne, and wē siððan cumað sōna eft tō ēow.' Abraham þā hēt Īsaac beran þone wudu tō þǣre stōwe, and hē self bǣr his sweord and fȳr. Īsaac þā āscode Abraham his fæder: 'Fæder mīn, iċ āscie hwǣr sēo offrung sīe; hēr
55 is wudu and fȳr.' Him andwyrde sē fæder, 'God foresċēawað, mīn sunu, him self þā offrunge.' Hīe cōmon þā tō þǣre stōwe þe him ġesweotolode God, and hē þǣr wēofod ārǣrde on þā ealdan wīsan, and þone wudu ġelōgode swā swā hē hit wolde habban tō his suna bærnette siððan hē ofslæġen wurde. Hē ġeband þā his sunu, and

44 **cwæð him þus tō** 'spoke to him thus'. In OE the preposition can sometimes follow the object (§213).

45 **þām lande *Visionis*** 'the land of Moriah'. The Hebrew name *Moriah* was taken by Biblical commentators to mean 'vision' etymologically, and both the Vulgate and the OE translator preserve this sacral etymology, substituting the Latin word *visionis* for the name itself. For the peculiar use of name-meanings by OE writers, see *Anglia* (1968), 14–58.

48–9 **þā dūne . . . þǣr þǣr hīe tō scoldon tō ofslēanne** 'the mountain where they must (go) to slay'. The verb of motion following *scoldon* is understood (§205.1). For *þǣr þǣr* 'where' see 168, *þǣr* 3.

50 **ēow** reflexive. OE *anbīdian* takes a reflexive object, but modern 'wait' does not. Therefore ignore *ēow* in translation.

51 **unc** The reflexive pronoun need not be translated.

54 **sīe** 'is, may be'. The present subjunctive form of the verb 'to be' is used here because there is no offering present. Cf. the contrasting use of the indicative in 'hēr *is* wudu and fȳr'. See §156.

55 **foresċēawað** pres. tense with future meaning.

57 **on þā ealdan wīsan** 'in the ancient manner'. The OE translator is concerned to emphasize that human sacrifice, although seemingly condoned by the Old Testament, is no longer an acceptable practice.

59 **ofslæġen wurde** 'had been slain'. For pret. subj. expressing future-in-the-past see §174.

King James Version

AND it came to pass after these things, that God did tempt Abraham, and said unto him, Abraham: and he said, Behold, *here* I *am.*

2 And he said, Take now thy son, thine only *son* Isaac, whom thou lovest, and get thee into the land of Mōrīah; and offer him there for a burnt offering upon one of the mountains which I will tell thee of.

3 And Abraham rose up early in the morning, and saddled his ass, and took two of his young men with him, and Isaac his son, and clave the wood for the burnt offering, and rose up, and went unto the place of which God had told him.

4 Then on the third day Abraham lifted up his eyes, and saw the place afar off.

5 And Abraham said unto his young men, Abide ye here with the ass; and I and the lad will go yonder and worship, and come again to you.

6 And Abraham took the wood of the burnt offering, and laid *it* upon Isaac his son; and he took the fire in his hand, and a knife, and they went both of them together.

7 And Isaac spake unto Abraham his father, and said, My father: and he said, Here *am* I, my son. And he said, Behold the fire and the wood: but where *is* the lamb for a burnt offering?

8 And Abraham said, My son, God will provide himself a lamb for a burnt offering: so they went both of them together.

9 And they came to the place which God had told him of; and Abraham built an altar there, and laid the wood in order, and bound Isaac his son, and laid him on the altar upon the wood.

Latin Vulgate Version

Quae postquam gesta sunt, tentavit Deus Abraham et dixit ad eum: Abraham, Abraham. At ille respondit: Adsum. [2]Ait illi: Tolle filium tuum unigenitum, quem diligis, Isaac, et vade in terram visionis, atque ibi offeres eum in holocaustum super unum montium, quem monstravero tibi. [3]Igitur Abraham de nocte consurgens stravit asinum suum ducens secum duos iuvenes et Isaac filium suum; cumque concidisset ligna in holocaustum, abiit ad locum, quem praeceperat ei Deus. [4]Die autem tertio, elevatis oculis, vidit locum procul, [5]dixitque ad pueros suos: Exspectate hic cum asino: ego et puer illuc usque properantes, postquam adoraverimus, revertemur ad vos. [6]Tulit quoque ligna holocausti et imposuit super Isaac filium suum; ipse vero portabat in manibus ignem et gladium. Cumque duo pergerent simul, [7]dixit Isaac patri suo: Pater mi. At ille respondit: Quid vis, fili? Ecce, inquit, ignis et ligna; ubi est victima holocausti? [8]Dixit autem Abraham: Deus providebit sibi victimam holocausti, fili mi. Pergebant ergo pariter: [9]et venerunt ad locum, quem ostenderat ei Deus in quo aedificavit altare, et desuper ligna composuit. Cumque alligasset Isaac filium suum, posuit eum in altare super struem lignorum [10]extenditque

60 his sword ātēah, þæt hē hine ġeoffrode on þā ealdan wīsan. Mid
    þām þe hē wolde þæt weorc beġinnan, þā clipode Godes engel
    arodlīċe of heofonum, 'Abraham!' Hē andwyrde sōna. Sē engel him
    cwæð þā tō: 'Ne ācwele þū þæt ċild, ne þīne hand ne āstreċe ofer
    his swēoran! Nū iċ oncnēow sōðlīċe þæt þū swīðe ondrǣtst God,
65 nū þū þīnne āncennedan sunu ofslēan woldest for him.'
       Þā beseah Abraham sōna underbæc and ġeseah þǣr ānne ramm
    betweox þām brēmelum be þām hornum ġehæft, and hē āhefde
    þone ramm tō þǣre offrunge and hine þǣr ofsnāð Gode tō lāce for
    his sunu Īsaac. Hē hēt þā þā stōwe *Dominus videt*, þæt is 'God
70 ġesiehð', and ġīet is ġesæġd swā, *In monte Dominus videbit*, þæt is
    'God ġesiehð on dūne.' Eft clipode se engel Abraham and cwæð, 'Iċ
    swerie þurh mē selfne, sæġde se Ælmihtiga, nū þū noldest ārian
    þīnum āncennedan suna, ac þē wæs mīn eġe māre þonne his līf, iċ
    þē nū bletsie and þīnne ofspring ġemaniġfealde swā swā steorran
75 on heofonum and swā swā sandċēosol on sǣ. Þīn ofspring sceal
    āgan hira fēonda gatu, and on þīnum sǣde bēoð ealle þēoda
    ġebletsode for þām þe þū ġehīersumodest mīnre hǣse þus.'
       Abraham þā ġeċierde sōna tō his cnapum and fērdon him hām
    swā mid heofonlicre bletsunge.

60 ġeoffrode pret. subj. 'might offer'.
60–1 Mid þām þe 'when' (§171).
63 tō see note to l. 44.
64–5 Nū iċ oncnēow ... nū þū 'Now I perceive ... now that thou'. *Nū* ... *nū* ...
are correlative conjunctions. See §§150–153.
64 ondrǣtst For this form instead of *ondrǣdest*, see §112.2.
67 ġehæft see §187(*b*).
69–70 *Dominus videt* 'The Lord sees.' *In monte Dominus videbit* 'on the mountain
the Lord will see'.

10 And Abraham stretched forth his hand, and took the knife to slay his son.

11 And the angel of the Lord called unto him out of heaven, and said, Abraham, Abraham: and he said, Here *am* I.

12 And he said, Lay not thine hand upon the lad, neither do thou any thing unto him: for now I know that thou fearest God, seeing thou hast not withheld thy son, thine only *son* from me.

13 And Abraham lifted up his eyes, and looked, and behold behind *him* a ram caught in a thicket by his horns: and Abraham went and took the ram, and offered him up for a burnt offering in the stead of his son.

14 And Abraham called the name of that place Jehōvahjīreh: as it is said *to* this day, In the mount of the Lord it shall be seen.

15 And the angel of the Lord called unto Abraham out of heaven the second time,

16 And said, By myself have I sworn, saith the Lord, for because thou hast done this thing, and hast not withheld thy son, thine only *son*:

17 That in blessing I will bless thee, and in multiplying I will multiply thy seed as the stars of the heaven, and as the sand which *is* upon the sea shore; and thy seed shall possess the gate of his enemies;

18 And in thy seed shall all the nations of the earth be blessed; because thou hast obeyed my voice.

19 So Abraham returned unto his young men, and they rose up and went together to Beershēba; and Abraham dwelt at Beershēba.

manum et arripuit gladium, ut immolaret filium suum. [11]Et ecce angelus Domini de caelo clamavit dicens: Abraham, Abraham. Qui respondit: Adsum. [12]Dixitque ei: Non extendas manum tuam super puerum, neque facias illi quidquam: nunc cognovi quod times Deum, et non pepercisti unigenito filio tuo propter me. [13]Levavit Abraham oculos suos viditque post tergum arietem inter vepres haerentem cornibus, quem adsumens obtulit holocaustum pro filio. [14]Appellavitque nomen loci illius Dominus videt. Unde usque hodie dicitur: In monte Dominus videbit.

[15]Vocavit autem angelus Domini Abraham secundo de caelo dicens: [16]Per memetipsum iuravi, dicit Dominus: quia fecisti hanc rem et non pepercisti filio tuo unigenito propter me, [17]benedicam tibi et multiplicabo semen tuum sicut stellas caeli et velut harenam, quae est in litore maris; possidebit semen tuum portas inimicorum suorum: [18]et benedicentur in semine tuo omnes gentes terrae quia oboedisti voci meae. [19]Reversusque est Abraham ad pueros suos, abieruntque Bersabee simul, et habitavit ibi.

3

A Colloquy on the Occupations

Teachers of Latin in the Middle Ages sometimes composed Latin dialogues or colloquies for their pupils to memorize, the assumption being that one learns a foreign language best by actually speaking it. Ælfric, who had already written a Latin *Grammar*, composed a *Colloquy* as a companion piece. He improved on the traditional form considerably, touching his characters with life and giving the exercise dramatic interest. His *Colloquy* is of particular value to modern readers because it offers an informal glimpse of Anglo-Saxon social structure, with representatives of various occupations explaining their function in the society in which they lived. Ælfric provides a series of questions for the Latin teacher to ask, and pupils assuming the roles of the various craftsmen then recite the assigned responses. By rotating pupils in the various roles, the teacher could be sure that each would learn a full range of vocabulary and syntactical structures.

Some time after Ælfric composed his Latin exercise, another Anglo-Saxon translated it into Old English. The charm of Ælfric's work is not wholly lost in this rendering, but as it stands the translation is inappropriate for modern students of Old English to use in learning the language, since it slavishly follows the Latin construction of the source text, thus producing unnatural, distorted syntax and phrasing. But in 1897 Henry Sweet, one of the greatest modern scholars of Old English, revised the translation into idiomatic prose. The text below is an adaptation and abbreviation of Sweet's version, which was published in his *First Steps in Anglo-Saxon* (Oxford, 1897), pp. 28–38. The text is normalized throughout.

The Monk

Hwelċne cræft canst þū?

Iċ eom munuc.

Hwæt cunnon þās þīne ġefēran?

Sume sind ierþlingas, sume scēaphierdas, sume oxanhierdas,
5 sume huntan, sume fisceras, sume fugleras, sume ċīepemenn, sume scōwyrhtan, sume sealteras, sume bæceras.

A Guide to Old English, Eighth Edition. Bruce Mitchell and Fred C. Robinson.
© 2012 Bruce Mitchell and Fred C. Robinson. Published 2012 by Blackwell Publishing Ltd.

The Ploughman

Hwæt seġst þū ierþling? Hū begǣst þū þīnne cræft?

Lā lēof, þearle iċ swince! Ǣlċe dæġe iċ sceal on dæġrǣd ūtgān. þonne sceal iċ þā oxan tō felda drīfan and tō þǣre sylh ġeocian. Nis
10 nān winter swā stearc þæt iċ dyrre æt hām lūtian: ne dearr iċ for mīnes hlāfordes eġe. Ac þonne iċ þā oxan ġeġeocod hæbbe, and þæt scear and þone culter on þǣre sylh ġefæstnod hæbbe, þonne sceal iċ fulne æcer erian oþþe māre.

Hæfst þū ǣnigne ġefēran?
15 Ġiese, iċ hæbbe cnapan: sē sceal þā oxan mid gāde þȳwan. Sē is nū hās for ċiele and hrēame.

Hwæt māre dēst þū? Hæfst þū ġīet māre tō donne?

Ġiese lēof, miċel iċ hæbbe tō donne! Iċ sceal þāra oxena binne mid hīeġe āfyllan, and hīe wæterian, and hira steall feormian.
20 Ēalā, þæt is miċel ġedeorf!

Ġiese lēof, hit is miċel ġedeorf, for þǣm þe iċ neom frēo.

The Shepherd

Hwæt seġst þū, sċēaphierde? Hæfst þū ǣniġ gedeorf?

Ġiese lēof, iċ hæbbe miċel ġedeorf! On ǣrnemerġen iċ drīfe mīn sċēap tō lǣswe. Siþþan stande iċ ofer hīe mid hundum, þȳ lǣs þe
25 wulfas hīe forswelgen. þonne lǣde iċ hīe on ǣfen onġēan tō hira locum. Iċ hīe melce tuwa on dæġe. Iċ maċie buteran and ċīese. And iċ eom mīnum hlāforde ġetrīewe.

The Oxherd

Ēalā oxanhierde, hwæt dēst þū?

Lā lēof, iċ swince þearle! þonne se ierþling þā oxan onġeocaþ,
30 þonne lǣde iċ hīe tō lǣswe; and ealle niht iċ stande ofer hīe, waċiende for þēofum; and þæs on morgenne iċ hīe betǣċe eft þǣm ierþlinge, wel ġefylde and ġewæterode.

The Hunter

Is þes mann ān of þīnum ġefērum?

Ġiese.

10–11   **for mīnes hlāfordes eġe** 'for fear of my lord'. See §190.2.

11–12   **þonne ... þonne** 'when ... then'. See §§151–152.

15   **sē** 'he'. See §§15 and 193.7. When demonstrative *se* is used in place of a personal pronoun, it is stressed and the vowel is long.

31   **þæs** 'afterwards'. A frequent idiomatic meaning of the gen. sg. of *þæt*. See §168 *þæs* 1.

35   Canst þū ǣniġ þing?

Ānne cræft iċ cann.

Hwelċne cræft canst þū?

Iċ eom hunta.

Hwæs hunta eart þū?

40   Iċ eom þæs cyninges hunta.

Hū begǣst þū þīnne cræft?

Iċ breġde mē nett, and āsette hīe on ġehæpre stōwe. Þonne ġetyhte iċ mīne hundas þæt hīe þāra wilddēora ēhten, oþ þæt hīe unwærlīċe on þā nett becumen. Þonne hīe þus ġelæht sind, þonne 45 cume iċ tō, and hīe on þǣm nettum ofslēa.

Ne canst þū būtan nettum huntian?

Ġiese, iċ cann būtan nettum huntian.

Hū?

Iċ fō þā wilddēor mid swiftum hundum.

50   Hwelċ wilddēor ġefēhst þū swīþost?

Iċ ġefō heorotas, and rān, and bāras, and hwīlum haran.

Wǣre þū tōdæġ on huntoþe?

Nese, for þǣm hit is sunnandæġ; ac ġiestrandæġ iċ wæs on huntoþe.

55   Hwæt ġefēnge þū?

Iċ ġefēng twēġen heorotas and ānne bār.

Hū ġefēnge þū hīe?

Þā heorotas on nettum iċ ġefēng, and þone bār iċ ofsticode.

Hū wǣre þū swā ġedyrstiġ þæt þū bār ofsticodest?

60   Þā hundas hine bedrifon tō mē, and iċ þǣr fæstlīċe onġēnstōd, and hine fǣrlīċe mid spere ofsticode.

Swīþe ġedyrstiġ wǣre þū þā!

Ne sceal hunta forhtmōd bēon, for þǣm missenlicu wilddēor wuniaþ on wudum.

65   Hwæt dēst þū ymb þīnne huntoþ?

Iċ selle þǣm cyninge swā hwæt swā iċ ġefō, for þǣm iċ eom his hunta.

Hwæt selþ hē þē?

Hē scrȳtt mē wel and fētt, and hwīlum hē mē hors selþ oþþe 70 bēag, þæt iċ þȳ ġeornor mīnne cræft begā.

---

42 **Iċ breġde mē nett** 'I weave nets for myself.' Compare modern colloquial English 'I bought me a hat.'

45 **cume iċ tō** 'I come up'. *Tō* here is the adverb.

69 **scrȳtt . . . fētt** 'clothes . . . feeds'. For the form of the verbs, see §112.2.

70 **þȳ ġeornor** 'the more eagerly'. This use of the instr. *þȳ* is the source of modern phrases like 'the bigger the better' or 'the more the merrier'. See §168 *þȳ*.

The Fisherman

Hwelċne cræft canst þū?

Iċ eom fiscere.

Hwæt beġietst þū of þīnum cræfte?

Bīleofan iċ mē beġiete, and scrūd, and feoh.

75 Hū ġefēhst þū þā fiscas?

Iċ gā on mīnne bāt, and rōwe ūt on þā ēa, and weorpe mīn nett on þā ēa. Hwīlum iċ weorpe angel ūt mid æse, oþþe spyrtan; and swā hwæt swā hīe ġehæftaþ iċ nime.

Hwæt dēst þū gif hit unclǣne fiscas bēoþ?

80 Iċ weorpe þā unclǣnan ūt, and nime þā clǣnan mē tō mete.

Hwǣr ċīepst þū þīne fiscas?

On þǣre ċeastre.

Hwā byġþ hīe?

þā ċeasterware. Ne mæġ iċ hira swā fela ġefōn swā iċ sellan

85 mæġe.

Hwelċe fiscas ġefēhst þū?

Ǣlas, and hacodas, and scēotan, and ealle ōþre fiscas þe on þǣm ēam swimmaþ.

For hwȳ ne fiscast þū on sǣ?

90 Hwīlum iċ dō swā, ac seldon; for þǣm hit is mē miċel rēwett tō þǣre sǣ.

Hwæt ġefēhst þū on þǣre sǣ?

Hǣringas, and leaxas, and styrian, and loppestran, and crabban, and fela ōþerra fisca.

95 Wilt þū hwæl fōn?

Niċ!

For hwȳ?

For þǣm miċel pleoh is þæt man hwæl ġefō. Lǣsse pleoh mē biþ þæt iċ tō þǣre ēa gā mid mīnum bāte þonne iċ mid manigum

100 scipum on hwælhuntoþ fare.

For hwȳ swā?

For þǣm mē is lēofre þæt iċ fisc ġefō þe iċ ofslēan mæġ þonne iċ fisc ġefō þe nealles þæt ān mē selfne ac ēac swelċe mīne ġefēran mid ānum sleġe besenċan mæġ oþþe ofslēan.

---

74   mē See note to l. 42 above.

79   unclǣne fiscas Cf. Deuteronomy 14:10: 'whatsoever [fish] hath not fins and scales ye may not eat; it is unclean unto you'. Some Anglo-Saxons scrupulously observed many of the Mosaic dietary laws.

80   mē tō mete 'for my food'. See §191.2.

84   hira . . . fela See §190.4.

102   mē is lēofre '(it) is more agreeable to me', i.e. 'I prefer'.

103   nealles þæt ān . . . ac ēac swelċe 'not only . . . but also'.

105 And þēah maniġe ġefōþ hwalas, and þǣm frēċennessum
ætberstaþ, and miċelne sceatt þanon beġietaþ.

Sōþ þū seġst; ac iċ ne dearr for þǣm iċ eom forhtmōd.

The Fowler

Hwæt seġst þū, fuglere? Hū beswīcst þū þā fuglas?

Iċ hīe on maniġfealde wīsan beswīce: hwīlum mid nettum,
110 hwīlum mid grīnum, hwīlum mid træppum, hwīlum mid līme,
hwīlum mid hwistlunge, hwīlum mid hafoce.

Hæfst þū hafocas?

Ġiese.

Canst þū temman hafocas?

115 Ġiese, iċ cann: hū scolden hīe mē nytte bēon, būtan iċ hīe
temman cūþe?

Sele mē hafoc!

Iċ þē selle lustlīċe, ġif þū mē selst swiftne hund. Hwelċne hafoc
wilt þū habban, þone māran hwæþer þe þone lǣssan?

120 Sele mē þone māran! Hū āfētst þū þīne hafocas?

Hīe hīe selfe fēdaþ on wintra ġe ēac swelċe mē, and on lenċtene
iċ hīe lǣte tō wuda ætflēogan; and iċ mē nime briddas on hærfest
and hīe ġetemme.

For hwȳ lǣtst þū þā ġetemedan hafocas þē ætflēogan?

125 For þǣm iċ nyle hīe on sumera fēdan, for þǣm þe hīe þearle
etaþ.

Ac maniġe fēdaþ þā ġetemedan ofer sumor, þæt hīe hīe eft ġearwe
hæbben.

Ġiese, hīe dōþ swā. Ac iċ nyle on swelċum ġeswince mid him
130 bēon, for þǣm iċ cann ōþre ġefōn – nealles ānne, ac maniġe.

The Merchant

Hwæt seġst þū, mangere?

Iċ secge þæt iċ eom swīþe nytt þǣm cyninge, and þǣm
ealdormannum, and þǣm weligum, and eallum folce.

Hū?

135 Iċ āstīge on mīn scip mid mīnum hlæstum, and fare ofer sǣ, and
selle mīn þing, and bycge dēorwierþu þing þe on þissum lande

---

115 **būtan** 'unless'. (So *cūðe* is subjunctive: see §179.5.)

118 **Iċ þē selle** The direct object (*hafoc*) is understood. See note to 2/14.

121 **Hīe hīe selfe fēdaþ** 'They feed themselves.' The first *hīe* is nom., the second
acc. (used reflexively).

122 **mē** 'for myself'. Cf. note to l. 42 above.

ācenned ne bēoþ; and iċ hit lǣde tō ēow hider ofer sǣ mid miċlum
plēo; and hwīlum iċ þolie forlidennesse, swā þæt mē losiaþ eall mīn
þing, and iċ self unēaþe cwic ætberste.

140 Hwelċ þing lǣtst þū ūs hider ofer sǣ?

Pællas, seoloc, seldcūþ rēaf, wyrtġemang, wīn, ele, elpendbān,
dēorwierþe ġimmas, gold, tin, mæstling, ār, seolfor, glæs, and fela
ōþerra þinga.

Wilt þū þīn þing hēr on lande sellan wiþ þæm ilcan weorþe þe
145 þū hīe þær ūte mid ġebohtest?

Niċ; hwæt fremede mē þonne mīn ġedeorf? Ac iċ wile hīe wiþ
māran weorþe hēr sellan þonne iċ hīe þær mid ġebohte, þæt iċ mæġe
mē sum ġestrēon beġietan, þe iċ mē mid āfēdan mæġe and mīn wīf
and mīn bearn.

The Shoemaker

150 þū scōwyrhta, hwæt wyrċst þū ūs tō nytte?

Mīn cræft is ēow swīþe nytt and swīþe nīedbehēfe. Iċ bycge hŷda
and fell, and hīe ġearcie mid mīnum cræfte, and wyrċc þærof
missenliċes cynnes ġescŷ, leþerhosa, þwangas, ġerǣdu, flascan,
and fætelsas; and ne mæġ ēower nān ofer winter wunian būtan
155 mīnum cræfte.

The Salter

Ēalā þū sealtere, hwæt fremeþ ūs þīn cræft?

Mīn cræft fremeþ ēow eallum þearle. Ne mæġ ēower nān
flǣscmetta brūcan būtan mīnum cræfte. Hwelċ mann mæġ
swētmetta brūcan būtan sealtes swæcce? Hwā ġefylþ his cleofan
160 and hēdærn būtan mīnum cræfte? Ēowru butere eall ēow losaþ and
ēower ċīese būtan iċ hīe mid minum cræfte ġehealde. Ne ġē ne
magon furþum ēowerra wyrta brūcan būtan mē.

The Baker

Hwæt seġst þū, bæcere? Hwǣm fremeþ þīn cræft?

Būtan mīnum cræfte ǣlċ bēod biþ ǣmettiġ ġeþūht, and būtan
165 hlāfe ǣlċ mete biþ tō wlǣttan ġehwierfed. Iċ ġestrangie manna

---

138–9 **mē losiaþ eall mīn þing** 'all my things are lost to me', i.e. 'I lose
everything'.

148 **þe . . . mid** 'with which'. See §163.3.

150 **ūs tō nytte** 'of use to us'.

154 **ēower nān** 'none of you'.

164 **biþ . . . ġeþūht** 'will seem'.

heortan: iċ eom wera mæġen; ġe furþum þā lȳtlingas nyllaþ mē forþolian.

The Cook

Hwæt secge wē be þǣm cōce? Beþurfon wē his cræftes tō āwihte?

170 Ġif ġē mē of ēowrum ġefērscipe ūtādrīfaþ, ġe etaþ ēowre wyrta grēne and ēowre flǣscmettas hrēawe; ne magon ġē furþum fætt broþ habban būtan mīnum cræfte.

Ne reċċe wē be þīnum cræfte: nis hē ūs nā nīedbehēfe, for þǣm wē magon selfe sēoþan þā þing þe tō sēoþanne sind, and brǣdan þā
175 þing þe tō brǣdanne sind.

Ġif ġē mē ūtādrīfaþ and þus dōþ, þonne bēo ġē ealle þēowas, and nān ēower ne biþ hlāford; and þēah hwæþre ġē ne magon etan būtan mīnum cræfte.

Critique of the Occupations

Ēalā munuc, iċ ġesēo þē habban gōde ġefēran and swīþe nytte;
180 hæfst þū ōþre ēac him?

Iċ hæbbe īsensmiþas, goldsmiþas, seolforsmiþas, trēowwyrhtan, and maniġe ōþre.

Hæfst þū wīsne ġeþeahtere?

Ġewisslīce iċ hæbbe: hū mæġ ūre ġefērscipe bēon ġewissod
185 būtan ġeþeahtere?

Ēalā þū wīsa ġeþeahtere, hwæt seġst þū? Hwelċ þissa cræfta is þē fyrmest ġeþūht?

Iċ þē secge, Godes þēowdōm is mē fyrmest ġeþūht betweox þissum cræftum, swā swā Crīst on his godspelle cwæþ 'Fyrmest
190 sēċaþ Godes rīċe, and þās þing eall ēow bēoþ tōġeīeċed'.

And hwelċ woruldcræft is þē fyrmest ġeþūht?

Eorþtilþ; for þǣm se ierþling fētt ūs ealle.

(Se smiþ seġþ:) Hwanon hæfþ se ierþling scear oþþe culter, oþþe furþum gāde, būtan of mīnum cræfte? Hwanon hæfþ se
195 fiscere angel, oþþe se scōwyrhta āwel, oþþe se sēamere nǣdle būtan of mīnum ġeweorce?

---

168 **secge wē** See §111.
173 **hē** The masculine pronoun agrees with the gender of its antecedent *cræfte*.
174–5 **tō sēoþanne . . . tō brǣdanne** 'to be boiled . . . to be roasted'.
179 **iċ ġesēo þē habban** 'I see you to have', i.e. 'I see that you have'.
186–7 **is þē . . . ġeþūht** 'seems to you'.
189–90 Luke 12:31 'But rather seek ye the kingdom of God; and all these things shall be added unto you.'

(Se ġeþeahtere andswaraþ:) Sōþ þū seġst; ac ūs eallum lēofre is
mid þǣm ierþlinge tō wīcianne þonne mid þē: for þǣm se ierþling
selþ ūs hlāf and drynce; ac þū, hwæt selst þū ūs on þīnre smiþþan
200 būtan īsene spearcan, and bēatendra slecga swēġ and blāwendra
bielga?

(Se trēowwyrhta seġþ:) Hwelċ ēower ne notaþ mīnes cræftes,
þonne iċ ēow eallum hūs wyrċe and scipu and missenlicu fatu?

(Se smiþ andswaraþ:) Ēalā trēowwyrhta, for hwȳ spricst þū swā,
205 þonne furþum ān þȳrel þū ne miht dōn būtan mīnum cræfte?

(Se ġeþeahtere seġþ:) Ēalā ġefēran and gōde wyrhtan, uton
hrædlīċe ġesēman þās ġeflitu, and sīe sibb and ġeþwǣrnes betweox
ēow, and fremme ǣlċ ōþrum on his cræfte! And uton weorþian
þone ierþling, of þǣm wē beġietaþ ūs selfum bīleofan and fōdor
210 ūrum horsum! And iċ ġelǣre eallum wyrhtum þisne rǣd: þæt ānra
ġehwelċ his cræft ġeornlīċe begā. For þǣm sē þe his cræft forlǣtt,
sē biþ fram þǣm cræfte forlǣten. Swā hwelċ swā þū sīc, swā
mæsseprēost, swā munuc, swā ċeorl, swā cempa, begā ġeornlīċe
þīnne cræft! And bēo þæt þæt þū eart! For þǣm hit is miċel demm
215 and miċel scand ġif man nyle bēon þæt þæt hē is and þæt þæt hē
bēon sccal.

---

207   sīe 'let there be'. Pres. subj. of *bēon* (§127).
209   of þǣm 'from whom' (§162.3).
212–13   Swā hwelċ swā ... swā ... swā 'whatsoever ... whether ... whether'.
215   þæt þæt 'that which'.

4

Two Characteristic Prose Works by Ælfric

Preface to Genesis

When a medieval scholar like Ælfric read the Bible, he saw behind the literal sense of the words a host of allegorical and typological meanings which had been discerned by biblical commentators from early Christian times to his own day. These meanings make up the 'spiritual sense' (*þæt gāstlice andgit*) as opposed to the literal meaning (*sēo nacede gerecednis*) of the Bible and are one of the means by which medieval Christians reconciled the sometimes bizarre and violent events of the Old Testament with the doctrine of the New. It is therefore understandable that when Ælfric's patron Æthelweard asked him to make the Old Testament available to the laity through translation, the devout scholar was apprehensive. What would the average Christian make of polygamy, human sacrifice, and other Old Testament practices when he read of them without a priest at hand to explain the 'real', spiritual sense of these things? In the Preface below, Ælfric explains these matters in a letter to Æthelweard, giving us a revealing example of how a medieval Christian scholar in Anglo-Saxon England analysed Scripture and applied it to his system of belief. He also makes it clear that he is at heart opposed to translation of the Old Testament (and elsewhere he even has misgivings about translating the New).

Although the prose of Ælfric's Preface is simple and straightforward and therefore seems appropriate as an early reading selection, some students may find the subject-matter unfamiliar and perplexing. Such students may prefer to read selection 7 before selection 4.

The text is that of Bodleian Library MS Laud Misc. 509, except that a few spellings have been normalized to ease transition into the unnormalized texts in the remainder of the reader, and that *and* has been replaced by a comma in l. 34.

A Guide to Old English, Eighth Edition. Bruce Mitchell and Fred C. Robinson.
© 2012 Bruce Mitchell and Fred C. Robinson. Published 2012 by Blackwell Publishing Ltd.

Incipit prefatio Genesis Anglice

Ælfrīc munuc grēt Æðelwærd ealdormann ēadmōdlīce. Þū bǣde
mē, lēof, þæt ic sceolde ðē āwendan of Lǣdene on Englisc þā bōc
Genesis. Ðā þūhte mē hefigtīme þē tō tīðienne þæs, and þū cwǣde
5 þā þæt ic ne þorfte nā māre āwendan þǣre bēc būton tō Isaace,
Abrahames suna, for þām þe sum ōðer man þē hæfde āwend fram
Isaace þā bōc oþ ende. Nū þincð mē, lēof, þæt weorc is swīðe
plēolic mē oððe ænigum men tō underbeginnenne, for þan þe ic
ondrǣde, gif sum dysig man þās bōc rǣt oððe rǣdan gehȳrð, þæt
10 hē wille wēnan þæt hē mōte lybban nū on þǣre nīwan ǣ swā swā þā
ealdan fæderas leofodon þā on þǣre tīde ǣr þan þe sēo ealde ǣ
gesett wǣre, oþþe swā swā men leofodon under Moyses ǣ. Hwīlum
ic wiste þæt sum mæsseprēost, se þe mīn magister wæs on þām
tīman, hæfde þā bōc Genesis, and hē cūðe be dǣle Lǣden
15 understandan; þā cwǣð hē be þām hēahfædere Iācōbe, þæt hē
hæfde fēower wīf – twā geswustra and heora twā þīnena. Ful sōð hē
sǣde, ac, hē nyste, ne ic þā gīt, hū micel tōdāl ys betweox þǣre
ealdan ǣ and þǣre nīwan. On anginne þisere worulde nam se
brōðer hys swuster tō wīfe, and hwīlum ēac se fæder tȳmde be his
20 āgenre dehter, and manega hæfdon mā wīfa tō folces ēacan, and
man ne mihte þā æt fruman wīfian būton on his siblingum. Gyf hwā
wyle nū swā lybban æfter Crīstes tōcyme swā swā men leofodon ǣr
Moises ǣ oþþe under Moises ǣ, ne byð se man nā Crīsten, ne hē
furþum wyrðe ne byð þæt him ǣnig Crīsten man mid ete.
25 Þā ungelǣredan prēostas, gif hī hwæt lītles understandað of þām
Lǣdenbōcum, þonne þincð him sōna þæt hī magon mǣre lārēowas

---

1 **Incipit . . . Anglice** 'Here begins the preface to Genesis in English.'
2 **grēt** For assimilation of the pres. tense ending -(*e*)*þ* both here and elsewhere
(e.g. *rǣt, stynt* below) see §112.2. Writers of letters in OE frequently begin in the third
person, as here, and then shift to the first person.
Æðelwærd was a secular patron of Ælfric, a descendant of the house of King Alfred
the Great, and the author of a Latin historical work, the *Chronicon Æthelweardi*.
4 **þūhte** Impersonal verb with subject 'it' understood. See also *þincð* in the next
sentence; cf. §212.
10 **on þǣre nīwan ǣ** 'in (the time of) the new law' (i.e. the New Testament).
10–11 **þā ealdan fæderas** 'the patriarchs' (of the Old Testament).
11 **þā** 'then'.
12 **wǣre** Subj. follows *ǣr þan þe* (§174.4).
14 **be dǣle** 'in part'.
15–16 **hē hæfde fēower wīf** See Genesis 29:16–30:13.
17 **sǣde** Originally *sægde* (§126), but between a front vowel and *d, n,* or *ð* OE *g* tends
to disappear and the preceding vowel is lengthened. Cf. *foresǣde*, l. 97 below.
20 **mā wīfa** 'more women (than one)'.
21 **on** 'from among'.
hwā 'someone' (§20).
25 **prēostas . . . hī** The repetition of subject is otiose: see §148 and cf. *hē* (l. 78).
hwæt lītles 'something of a little', i.e. 'a little something'.

bēon; ac hī ne cunnon swā þēah þæt gāstlice andgit þǣrtō, and hū
sēo ealde ǣ wæs getācnung tōweardra þinga, oþþe hū sēo nīwe
gecȳþnis æfter Crīstes menniscnisse wæs gefillednys ealra þǣra
30　þinga þe sēo ealde gecȳðnis getācnode tōwearde be Crīste and be
hys gecorenum. Hī cweþaþ ēac oft be Pētre, hwī hī ne mōton
habban wīf swā swā Pētrus se apostol hæfde, and hī nellað gehīran
ne witan þæt se ēadiga Pētrus leofede æfter Moises ǣ oþ þæt Crīst,
þe on þām tīman tō mannum cōm, began tō bodienne his hālige
35　godspel and gecēas Pētrum ǣrest him tō gefēran: þā forlēt Pētrus
þǣrrihte his wīf, and ealle þā twelf apostolas, þā þe wīf hæfdon,
forlēton ǣgþer ge wīf ge ǣhta, and folgodon Crīstes lāre tō þǣre
nīwan ǣ and clǣnnisse þe hē self þā ārǣrde. Prēostas sindon
gesette tō lāreowum þām lǣwedum folce. Nū gedafnode him þæt
40　hig cūðen þā ealdan ǣ gāstlīce understandan, and hwæt Crīst self
tǣhte and his apostolas on þǣre nīwan gecȳðnisse þæt hig mihton
þām folce wel wissian tō Godes gelēafan and wel bīsnian tō gōdum
weorcum.

We secgað ēac foran tō þæt sēo bōc is swīþe dēop gāstlīce tō
45　understandenne, and wē ne wrītað nā māre būton þā nacedan
gerecednisse. Þonne þincþ þām ungelǣredum þæt eall þæt andgit
bēo belocen on þǣre ānfealdan gerecednisse; ac hit ys swīðe feor
þām. Sēo bōc ys gehāten Genesis, þæt ys 'gecyndbōc' for þām þe
hēo ys firmest bōca and spricþ be ǣlcum gecinde (ac hēo ne spricð
50　nā be þǣra engla gesceapenisse). Hēo onginð þus: *In principio creauit
deus celum et terram*, þæt ys on Englisc, 'On anginne gesceōp God
heofenan and eorðan.' Hit wæs sōðlīce swā gedōn, þæt God
ælmihtig geworhte on anginne, þā þā hē wolde, gesceafta. Ac swā
þēah æfter gāstlicum andgite þæt anginn ys Crīst, swā swā hē self
55　cwæþ tō þām Iūdēiscum: 'Ic eom angin, þe tō ēow sprece.' Þurh þis
angin worhte God Fæder heofenan and eorþan, for þan þe hē

27　þǣrtō '(pertaining) thereto'.

31　hwī '(asking) why'.

35　him tō gefēran 'for his companion' (§191.2).

39　gedafnode '(it) would befit' (pret. subj.).

40　hig An alternative spelling of hī, hīe 'they'. Since OE *iġ* sometimes becomes *ī*,
the sound *ī* was sometimes spelled *iġ*.

47–8　feor þām 'far from that'.

48　gecynd, like Latin *genus*, means 'origin' and 'species'.

49–50　hēo . . . hēo . . . Hēo The pronoun agrees with the gender of its antecedent *bōc*
(§187.2a).

50　*In principio* . . . 'In the beginning God created Heaven and earth' (Genesis 1:1).

55　Ic eom angin, etc. Revelation 1:8, 21:6, 22:13.

gesceōp ealle gesceafta þurh þone Sunu, se þe wæs æfre of him
ācenned, wīsdōm of þām wīsan Fæder.

Eft stynt on þære bēc on þām forman ferse, *Et spiritus dei ferebatur*
60 *super aquas*, þæt is on Englisc, 'And Godes Gāst wæs geferod ofer
wæteru.' Godes Gāst ys se Hālga Gāst, þurh þone gelīffæste se
Fæder ealle þā gesceafta þe hē gesceōp þurh þone sunu, and se
Hālga Gāst færð geond manna heortan and silð ūs synna forgifenisse, ærest þurh wæter on þām fulluhte, and siþþan þurh
65 dædbōte; and gif hwā forsihð þā forgifenisse þe se Hālga Gāst sylð,
þonne bið his synn æfre unmyltsiendlic on ēcnysse. Eft ys sēo
hālige þrīnnys geswutelod on þisre bēc, swā swā ys on þām worde
þe God cwæð: 'Uton wircean mannan tō ūre ānlīcnisse.' Mid þām
þe hē cwæð, 'Uton wircean,' ys sēo þrinnis gebīcnod; mid þām þe
70 hē cwæð, 'tō ūre ānlīcnisse,' ys sēo sōðe ānnis geswutelod; hē ne
cwæð nā menifealdlīce tō ūrum ānlīcnissum, ac ānfealdlīce tō ūre
ānlīcnisse. Eft cōmon þrī englas tō Abrahame and hē spræc tō him
eallum þrīm swā swā tō ānum. Hū clipode Abēles blōd tō Gode
būton swā swā ælces mannes misdæda wrēgað hine tō Gode būtan
75 wordum? Be þisum lītlum man mæg understandan hū dēop sēo bōc
ys on gāstlicum andgite, þēah þe hēo mid lēohtlicum wordum
āwriten sig. Eft Iōsēp, þe wæs geseald tō Ēgipta lande and hē
āhredde þæt folc wið þone miclan hunger, hæfde Crīstes getācnunge þe wæs geseald for ūs tō cwale and ūs āhredde fram þām ēcan
80 hungre helle sūsle.

þæt micele geteld þe Moises worhte mid wunderlicum cræfte on
þām wēstene, swā swā him God self gedihte, hæfde getācnunge
Godes gelaðunge þe hē self āstealde þurh his apostolas mid
menigfealdum frætewum and fægerum þēawum. Tō þām geweorce
85 brōhte þæt folc gold and seolfor and dēorwirðe gimstānas and
menigfealde mærða; sume ēac brōhton gātehær, swā swā God
bebēad. þæt gold getācnode ūrne gelēafan and ūre gōde ingehygd

58 wīsdōm, i.e. Christ, the Logos.
Fæder see §60.2.
59–60 *Et spiritus* . . . 'And the spirit of God was carried over the waters'
(Genesis 1:2).
61 þurh þone 'through which' (§162.3).
67 ys '(it) is' (§193.7).
68 Uton . . . ānlīcnisse Genesis 1:26. In what follows, Ælfric (who was a grammarian)
concentrates on the significance of grammatical number in the scriptural passage.
72 Eft cōmon þrī englas, etc. Genesis 18:1–5.
73 Hū clipode Abēles blōd, etc. Genesis 4:10.
77 sig = *sī*, *sīe* 'may be'. See note to l. 40 above.
79 þe The antecedent is *Crīstes*. See §163.4.
81 ff. geteld The tabernacle is described in Exodus, chapters 35–9.

þe wē Gode offrian sceolon; þæt seolfor getācnode Godes spræca
and þā hālgan lāra þe wē habban sceolon tō Godes weorcum; þā
90 gimstānas getācnodon mislice fægernissa on Godes mannum; þæt
gātehǣr getācnode þā stīðan dǣdbōte þǣra manna þe heora sinna
behrēowsiað. Man offrode ēac fela cinna orf Gode tō lāce binnan
þām getelde, be þām ys swīðe menigfeald getācnung; and wæs
beboden þæt sē tægel sceolde bēon gehāl æfre on þām nȳtene æt
95 þǣre offrunge for þǣre getācnunge þæt God wile þæt wē simle wel
dōn oð ende ūres līfes: þonne bið se tægel geoffrod on ūrum weorcum.

Nū ys sēo foresǣde bōc on manegum stōwum swīðe nearolīce
gesett, and þēah swīðe dēoplīce on þām gāstlicum andgite, and hēo
is swā geendebyrd swā swā God self hig gedihte þām wrītere Moise,
100 and wē durron nā māre āwrītan on Englisc þonne þæt Lǣden hæfð,
ne þā endebirdnisse āwendan būton þām ānum þæt þæt Lǣden and
þæt Englisc nabbað nā āne wīsan on þǣre sprǣce fadunge. Æfre se
þe āwent oððe se þe tǣcð of Lædene on Englisc, æfre hē sceal
gefadian hit swā þæt Englisc hæbbe his āgene wīsan, elles hit bið
105 swīðe gedwolsum tō rǣdenne þām þe þæs Lǣdenes wīsan ne can.

Is ēac tō witanne þæt sume gedwolmen wǣron þe woldon
āwurpan þā ealdan ǣ, and sume woldon habban þā ealdan and
āwurpan þā nīwan, swā swā þā Iūdēiscan dōð. Ac Crīst self and his
apostolas ūs tǣhton ǣgðer tō healdenne þā ealdan gāstlīce and þā
110 nīwan sōðlīce mid weorcum. God gesceōp ūs twā ēagan and twā
ēaran, twā nosþirlu and twēgen weleras, twā handa and twēgen fēt,
and hē wolde ēac habban twā gecȳðnissa on þissere worulde geset,
þā ealdan and þā nīwan, for þām þe hē dēð swā swā hine selfne
gewyrð, and hē nǣnne rǣdboran nǣfð, ne nān man þearf him
115 cweðan tō: 'Hwī dēst þū swā?' Wē sceolon āwendan ūrne willan tō
his gesetnissum and wē ne magon gebīgean his gesetnissa tō ūrum
lustum.

Ic cweðe nū þæt ic ne dearr ne ic nelle nāne bōc æfter þissere of
Lǣdene on Englisc āwendan, and ic bidde þē, lēof ealdorman, þæt

---

92 ff.   **fela cinna orf** 'cattle of many kinds'. Leviticus 3:9 specifies that the 'whole
rump' of the sacrificial animal must be offered, but Ælfric's spiritual interpretation of the
injunction is not in the Bible.
93   **be þām** 'concerning which' (§162.3).
93–4   **wæs beboden** '(it) was commanded' (§212).
101   **būton þām ānum þæt** 'except for the one [reason, namely] that'.
102   **āne wīsan on . . . fadunge** 'one manner in the disposition of language', i.e. a
common word order and idiom. (*Fadunge* 'disposition' is adopted here from one of the
other manuscripts to the Preface since the Laud manuscript's *fandunge* 'testing' makes
little sense.)
103   **āwent** See note to 2/32 above.
106   **Is** '(It) is'.
106   **sume gedwolmen wǣron** 'there were some heretics'.
114   **gewyrð** '(it) pleases' (§212).

120 þū mē þæs nā leng ne bidde þī læs þe ic bēo þē ungehīrsum oððe
lēas gif ic dō. God þē sig milde ā on ēcnisse. Ic bidde nū on Godes
naman, gif hwā þās bōc āwrītan wylle, þæt hē hig gerihte wel be
þǣre bȳsne, for þan þe ic nāh geweald, þēah þe hig hwā tō wōge
bringe þurh lēase wrīteras, and hit byð þonne his pleoh nā mīn:
125 mycel yfel dēð se unwrītere, gif hē nele hys wōh gerihtan.

St. Edmund, King and Martyr

The preceding text exemplifies one of the dominant intellectual
concerns of Ælfric and his Anglo-Saxon audience – how to understand scriptural narrative in the 'spiritual sense'. The present text
exemplifies one of the most popular and most important literary
forms in Anglo-Saxon times – the saint's life. Ælfric wrote a series
of more than thirty *Lives of Saints* and included more saints' lives
in his two series of *Catholic Homilies*. Other Anglo-Saxon writers
have left us many more specimens in this genre, some in verse and
some in prose. The medieval saint's life was a highly conventional
form concerned not so much with presenting actual biography as
with supplying inspirational examples of Christian lives well lived
and of God's power revealed through the sometimes miraculous
accomplishments of His most devoted followers. Since saints' lives
often include heathen violence, Christian heroism, and supernatural
events, they can be lively and entertaining as well as exemplary.
Some of them treat the lives of traditional Christian saints like
St. Anthony, St. Sebastian, and St. Andrew, while others deal with
the lives of native English saints like St. Oswald, St. Swithun, and
St. Æthelthryth.

St. Edmund was a native English saint, a king of East Anglia
who was slain by heathen Vikings on 20 November 869. Ælfric's
account of St. Edmund is characteristic of the genre: after giving his
source for the narrative (ll. 126–36), he describes King Edmund's
exemplary qualities – his piety, his charity, and his kindness to his
people (ll. 137–46). Then there is a detailed account of his martyr-
dom, this being the culminating event of his holy life (ll. 147–222).
The long, final section of the narrative tells of the disposition of the
dead saint's body and of the miracles which occurred before and after
his burial. The miracles are carefully recorded because these
provide divine verification of Edmund's sainthood. The miracle of

---

120 **þæs** gen. obj. of *bidde*: 'ask me for that'.
123–4 **þēah þe . . . wrīteras** 'although someone might bring it (the book) to error
through false scribes'.

the protective wolf, for example, is important witness to the fact that the saint's charismatic power extended even into the animal realm of God's kingdom, a common proof of saintliness. Also, Ælfric explains, the miracles reveal God's power and presence in Anglo-Saxon England, an important domestication of the conventional Christian verities.

At the beginning of his account Ælfric tells us that his source is a Latin narrative by Abbo of Fleury, a French monk who had learned the story on a visit to England and recorded it in his *Passio Sancti Eadmundi*. But Ælfric's Old English rendering is far more than a mechanical translation. He removes Abbo's elaborate rhetorical flourishes, shortens the speeches, and makes the narrative more brisk. His most daring innovation is the prose style he uses. After giving the introduction in sober, utilitarian prose (ll. 126–36), in l. 137 Ælfric shifts into alliterative prose, an ornamental style which he devised early in his career and used in many of his works. Alliterative prose consists of four-stressed units bound by alliteration. Ælfric borrowed these features from Old English poetry, which is composed in long lines with four stresses and alliteration. The difference between Ælfric's prose and Old English verse is that he avoids the distinctive poetic vocabulary characteristic of verse (see §247) and ignores the strictly ordered stress-patterns of verse (see Appendix C). But alliterative prose is sufficiently similar to verse that modern editors usually print it in verse lines like poetry. We decline to follow this practice here for reasons set forth in Bruce Mitchell *Old English Syntax* (Oxford, 1985), II, §§3974–3975, but it may be well to print a few sentences lineated as verse in order to make clear the form that Ælfric is using:

Éadmund se Éadiga   Éastengla cýning
wæs snótor and wúrðful   and wúrðode sýmble
mid ǽþelum þéawum   þone ǽlmihtigan Gód.
He wæs éadmod and geþúngen   and swa ánræd þurhwúnode
þæt he nólde abúgan   to býsmorfullum léahtrum
ne on náþre héalfe   he ne ahýlde his þéawas
ac wæs sýmble gemýndig   þære sóþan láre.
'þu eart to héafodmen gesét?   Ne ahéfe þu ðé
ac béo betwux mánnum   swa swa an mán of hím'.

(ll. 137–43)

Here alliterating sounds are underlined and the four syllables bearing primary stress in each line are marked with an acute accent.

The text presented here is essentially that of British Library MS Cotton Julius E.vii, but a few spellings have been normalized, and occasionally we adopt a reading from one of the other manuscripts.

Sum swȳðe gelæred munuc cōm sūþan ofer sæ fram Sancte Benedictes stōwe on Æþelredes cyninges dæge tō Dūnstāne ærcebisceope þrim gēarum ær hē forðfērde, and se munuc hātte Abbo. þā
wurdon hī æt spræce oþ þæt Dūnstān rehte be Sancte Ēadmunde,
130 swā swā Ēadmundes swurdbora hit rehte Æþelstāne cyninge, þā þā
Dūnstān geong man wæs and se swurdbora wæs forealdod man. þā
gesette se munuc ealle þā gereccednysse on ānre bēc and eft, ðā þā
sēo bōc cōm tō ūs binnan fēawum gēarum, þā āwende wē hit
on Englisc, swā swā hit hēræfter stent. Se munuc þā Abbo binnan
135 twām gēarum gewende hām tō his mynstre and wearð sōna tō
abbode geset on þām ylcan mynstre.

Ēadmund se ēadiga, Ēastengla cyning, wæs snotor and wurðful
and wurðode symble mid æþelum þēawum þone ælmihtigan God.
Hē wæs ēadmōd and geþungen and swā ānræd þurhwunode þæt
140 hē nolde ābūgan tō bysmorfullum leahtrum, ne on nāþre healfe hē
ne āhylde his þēawas, ac wæs symble gemyndig þære sōþan lāre,
'þū eart tō hēafodmen geset? ne āhefe þū ðē, ac bēo betwux
mannum swā swā ān man of him'. Hē wæs cystig wædlum and
widewum swā swā fæder and mid welwillendnysse gewissode his
145 folc symle tō rihtwīsnysse and þām rēþum stȳrde and gesǣliglīce
leofode on sōþum gelēafan.

Hit gelamp ðā æt nēxtan þæt þā Deniscan lēode fērdon mid
sciphere hergiende and slēande wīde geond land swā swā heora

126–7   **Sancte Benedictes stōwe** The French monastery of Fleury, now called
St.-Benoit-sur-Loire.

127–8   **Dūnstāne ærcebisceope** St. Dunstan, who became Archbishop of
Canterbury in 959, was an adviser to several Anglo-Saxon kings and a prime mover in
the tenth-century monastic reforms which helped revitalize English intellectual life. In
making his reforms he sought counsel from the monks at Fleury.

128   **þrim gēarum** For the dative used with expressions of time see §191.3.

se munuc hātte Abbo See §202. Abbo, who became Abbot of Fleury in 988, spent
two years in England as an adviser on monastic reform.

129   **wurdon hī æt spræce** 'they came into conversation'.

132   **on ānre bēc** i.e. in the *Passio Sancti Eadmundi*.

133   **āwende wē hit** 'we translated it'. See §111 for the form of *āwende*. For *sēo bōc . . .
hit* see §187.2(b).

137   According to later sources, Edmund ascended the throne in 855, when he was
fourteen years old.

139   **Hē . . . swā ānræd þurhwunode** See §167.3.

140–1   **ne on nāþre healfe . . . þēawas** 'neither did he turn away from his good
practices' (lit. 'nor did he turn away on either side from his good practices'). The turn of
phrase was suggested by Abbo's *nec declinabat ad dexteram, extollendo se de meritis, nec ad
sinistram, succumbendo vitiis humanae fragilitatis.*

142–3   **bēo betwux . . . of him** 'be among people as (if you were) one of them'
(Ecclesiasticus 32:1).

148   **sciphere** The Scandinavian attack fleets terrorized the Anglo-Saxons and the
peoples along the coasts of Europe from approximately 800 to 1050. This particular naval
force is discussed at some length in the Anglo-Saxon Chronicle (see piece 7 below), as
is Hinguar, the leader. Hinguar and Hubba are the sons of the renowned Viking leader
Ragnar Lothbrok ('Shaggy-Britches').

gewuna is. On þām flotan wǣron þā fyrmestan hēafodmen Hinguar
150 and Hubba, geānlǣhte þurh dēofol, and hī on Norðhymbra lande
gelendon mid æscum and āwēston þæt land and þā lēoda ofslōgon.
þā gewende Hinguar ēast mid his scipum and Hubba belāf on
Norðhymbra lande, gewunnenum sige mid wælhrēownysse. Hinguar þā becōm tō Ēastenglum rowende, on þām gēare þe Ælfred
155 æðeling ān and twentig gēara wæs, se þe, Westsexena cyning,
siþþan wearð mǣre; and se foresǣda Hinguar fǣrlīce swā swā wulf
on lande bestalcode and þā lēode slōh, weras and wīf and þā
unwittigan cild, and tō bysmore tūcode þā bilewitan Crīstenan.
Hē sende ðā sōna syððan tō þām cyninge bēotlic ǣrende þæt hē
160 abūgan sceolde tō his manrǣdene gif hē rōhte his fēores. Se
ǣrendraca cōm þā tō Ēadmunde cyninge and Hingwares ǣrende
him arodlīce ābēad: 'Hingwar ūre cyning, cēne and sigefæst on sǣ
and on lande, hæfð fela lēoda geweald and cōm nū mid fyrde fǣrlīce
hēr tō lande þæt hē hēr wintersetl mid his werode hæbbe. Nū hǣt
165 hē þē dǣlan þīne dīgelan goldhordas and þīnra yldrena gestrēon
arodlīce wið hine, and þū bēo his undercyning, gif ðū cwic bēon
wylt, for ðan þe ðū nǣfst þā mihte þæt þū mage him wiðstandan.'
Hwæt þā Ēadmund cyning clypode ǣnne bisceop þe him þā
gehendost wæs, and wið hine smēade hū hē þām rēþan Hingware
170 andwyrdan sceolde. Þā forhtode se bisceop for þām fǣrlican
gelimpe and for þæs cyninges līfe, and cwæð þæt him rǣd þūhte
þæt hē tō þām gebūge þe him bēad Hinguar. Þā swīgode se cyning
and beseah tō þǣre eorþan and cwæð þā æt nēxtan cynelīce him tō,
'Ēalā þū bisceop, tō bysmore synd getāwode þās earman landlēoda,
175 and mē nū lēofre wǣre þæt ic on gefeohte fēolle, wið þām þe mīn
folc mōste heora eardes brūcan'; and se bisceop cwæð, 'Ēalā þū
lēofa cyning, þīn folc līð ofslagen and þū nǣfst þone fultum þæt þū

150   **geānlǣhte þurh dēofol** See §187.1(b). This emphasizes that they are
pagans.

153   **gewunnenum sige** See §191.4. Abbo's Latin has an ablative absolute here.

154–6   **Ælfred . . . Westsexena cyning . . . mǣre** This is King Alfred the Great,
who became King of the West Saxons in April of 871, when he was twenty-three years
old. For more on King Alfred see §217 and selection 5.

160   **abūgan . . . manrǣdene** 'submit to his service', i.e. submit to being an underking to the pagan Hinguar.

rōhte his fēores 'cared for his life'. See §190.6.

163   **fyrde** Normally *fyrd* is used for the English army and *here* for the Vikings.
The unusual use of *fyrd* here to refer to the Vikings may be for the sake of
alliteration.

171   **him rǣd þūhte** 'seemed [good] counsel to him', i.e. 'seemed advisable to him'.

172   **þæt hē . . . Hinguar** 'that he should submit to that which Hinguar demanded'
of him.

174   **tō bysmore . . . landlēoda** See §202.

175   **wið þām þe** 'provided that', 'so long as'.

feohtan mæge, and þās flotmen cumað and þē cwicne gebindað,
būtan þū mid flēame þīnum fēore gebeorge, oððe þū þē swā
180 gebeorge þæt þū būge tō him.' Þā cwæð Ēadmund cyning swā swā
hē ful cēne wæs, 'Þæs ic gewilnige and gewīsce mid mōde, þæt ic āne
ne belīfe æfter mīnum lēofum þegnum þe on heora bedde wurdon mid
bearnum and wīfum færlīce ofslagene fram þysum flotmannum.
Næs mē næfre gewunelic þæt ic worhte flēames, ac ic wolde
185 swiðor sweltan gif ic þorfte for mīnum āgenum earde; and se
ælmihtiga God wāt þæt ic nelle ābūgan fram his biggengum
æfre, ne fram his sōþan lufe, swelte ic, lybbe ic.'

Æfter þysum wordum hē gewende tō þām ærendracan þe
Hingwar him tō sende and sæde him unforht, 'Witodlīce þū wære
190 wyrðe sleges nū, ac ic nelle āfȳlan on þīnum fūlum blōde mīne
clǣnan handa, for ðan þe ic Crīste folgie, þe ūs swā gebȳsnode; and
ic blīðelīce wille bēon ofslagen þurh ēow, gif hit swā God forescēawað. Far nū swīþe hraðe and sege þīnum rēþan hlāforde, "Ne
ābīhð næfre Ēadmund Hingware on līfe, hæþenum heretogan,
195 būton hē tō Hǣlende Crīste ǣrest mid gelēafan on þysum lande
gebūge."'

Þā gewende se ærendraca arodlīce āweg and gemētte be wege
þone wælhrēowan Hingwar mid eallre his fyrde, fūse tō Ēadmunde, and sæde þām ārlēasan hū him geandwyrd wæs. Hingwar
200 þā bebēad mid bylde þām sciphere þæt hī þæs cyninges ānes ealle
cēpan sceoldon, þe his hǣse forseah, and hine sōna bindan. Hwæt
þā Ēadmund cyning, mid þām þe Hingwar cōm, stōd innan his
healle, þæs Hǣlendes gemyndig, and āwearp his wǣpnu: wolde
geæfenlǣcan Crīstes gebȳsnungum, þe forbēad Petre mid wǣpnum
205 tō winnenne wið þā wælhrēowan Iūdēiscan. Hwæt þā ārlēasan þā
Ēadmund gebundon and gebysmrodon huxlīce and bēoton mid
sāglum, and swā syððan lǣddon þone gelēaffullan cyning tō ānum
eorðfæstum trēowe and tīgdon hine þærtō mid heardum bendum,

---

178   **cumað** Translate present as future. See §196.
þē cwicne gebindað Present with future meaning. See also §187.1(a).
179–80   **þē swā gebeorge . . . būge** 'save yourself by submitting' (lit. 'save yourself in that you submit').
181–2   '**þæs ic . . . þegnum . . .**' This construction is explained in §148.
182   **on heora bedde** 'in their beds'. In OE the singular (*bedde*) is often used when
each person in a group has one of the same thing. Cf. the singular *lichaman* in l. 321 below.
187   **swelte ic, lybbe ic** See §178.4.
189–90   **wære wyrðe sleges** 'were worthy of death', i.e. 'you deserve to be killed'.
191   **þe ūs swā gebȳsnode** 'who thus set an example for us'.
198   **fūse** 'hastening'. The acc. pl. no doubt refers to Hinguar and his men together.
200   **þæs cyninges ānes** 'only the king'. *Cēpan* takes a genitive object.
201–4   **Hwæt þā Ēadmund . . . gebȳsnungum** See §185.2.
204–5   **Crīstes gebȳsnungum . . . Iūdēiscan** See John 18:10–11.

and hine eft swungon langlīce mid swipum; and hē symble clypode
210 betwux þām swinglum mid sōðum gelēafan tō Hǣlende Crīste; and
þā hǣþenan þā for his gelēafan wurdon wōdlīce yrre, for þan þe hē
clypode Crīst him tō fultume. Hī scuton þā mid gafelucum, swilce
him tō gamenes, tō, oð þæt hē eall wæs beset mid heora scotungum,
swilce igles byrsta, swā swā Sebastiānus wæs. þā geseah Hingwar,
215 se ārlēasa flotman, þæt se æþela cyning nolde Crīste wiðsacan, ac
mid ānrǣdum gelēafan hine ǣfre clypode: hēt hine þā behēafdian,
and þā hǣðenan swā dydon. Betwux þām þe hē clypode tō Crīste
þā gīt, þā tugon þā hǣþenan þone hālgan tō slege and mid ānum
swencge slōgon him of þæt hēafod, and his sāwl sīþode gesǣlig tō
220 Crīste. þǣr wæs sum man gehende, gehealden þurh God behȳd
þam hǣþenum, þe þis gehȳrde eall and hit eft sǣde swā swā wē hit
secgað hēr.

   Hwæt ðā se flothere fērde eft tō scipe and behȳddon þæt hēafod
þæs hālgan Ēadmundes on þām þiccum brēmelum þæt hit
225 bebyrged ne wurde. þā æfter fyrste, syððan hī āfarene wǣron,
cōm þæt landfolc tō, þe þǣr tō lāfe wæs þā, þǣr heora hlāfordes līc
læg būtan hēafde, and wurdon swiðe sārige for his slege on mōde,
and hūru þæt hī næfdon þæt hēafod tō þām bodige. þā sǣde se
scēawere þe hit ǣr geseah, þæt þā flotmen hæfdon þæt hēafod mid
230 him, and wæs him geðūht, swā swā hit wæs ful sōð, þæt hī
behȳddon þæt hēafod on þam hōlte forhwega.

   Hī ēodon þā ealle endemes to þām wuda, sēcende gehwǣr,
geond þȳfelas and brēmelas, gif hī āhwǣr mihten gemētan þæt
hēafod. Wæs ēac micel wundor þæt ān wulf wearð āsend þurh
235 Godes wissunge tō bewerigenne þæt hēafod wið þā ōþre dēor ofer
dæg and niht. Hī ēodon þā sēcende and symle clypigende, swā
swā hit gewunelic is þām ðe on wuda gāð oft, 'Hwǣr eart þū nū,
gefēra?', and him andwyrde þæt hēafod, 'Hēr! Hēr! Hēr!', and swā

---

212   **him tō fultume** See §191.2.
212–13   **scuton . . . tō** 'shot at'. See §213.
213   **him tō gamenes** See §191.2 and §168 p. 86.
214   **Sebastiānus** St. Sebastian was a martyr in the days of Diocletian. When it was
discovered that he was a Christian, the Emperor ordered his archers to kill him.
Although they shot innumerable arrows into his body and left him for dead, he recovered.
Later Diocletian ordered him cudgelled to death. He is always depicted tied to a stake
with many arrows protruding from his body.
216   **hēt hine þā behēafdian** See §161.
219   **slōgon him of þæt hēafod** 'struck the head from him', i.e. 'beheaded him'.
220–1   **gehealden þurh God . . . hǣþenum** 'kept hidden from the heathens by God'.
227   **on mōde** modifies *sārige*.
228–9   **se scēawere** i.e. the witness mentioned in ll. 220–2.
230   **wæs him geðūht** '[it] seemed to him'.
234–5   **ān wulf . . . þæt hēafod** See §205.2(a).
236–7   **swā swā hit . . . oft** See §162.1.

gelōme clypode, andswarigende him eallum swā oft swā heora ænig
240 clypode, oþ þæt hī ealle becōmon þurh ðā clypunga him tō. Þā læg
se grǣga wulf þe bewiste þæt hēafod and mid his twām fōtum
hæfde þæt hēafod beclypped, grǣdig and hungrig, and for Gode ne
dorste þæs hēafdes onbyrian ac hēold hit wið dēor. Þā wurdon hī
ofwundrode þæs wulfes hyrdrǣdenne, and þæt hālige hēafod hām
245 feredon mid him, þancigende þām Ælmihtigan ealra his wundra;
ac se wulf folgode forð mid þām hēafde, oþ þæt hī tō tūne cōmon,
swylce hē tam wǣre, and gewende eft siþþan tō wuda ongēan. Þā
landlēoda þā siþþan legdon þæt hēafod tō tō þām hālgan bodige and
bebyrigdon hine swā swā hī sēlost mihton on swylcere hrǣdinge,
250 and cyrcan ārǣrdon sōna him onuppon.

Eft þā on fyrste, æfter fela gēarum, þā sēo hergung geswāc and
sibb wearð forgifen þām geswenctan folce, þā fēngon hī tōgædere
and worhton āne cyrcan wurðlīce þām hālgan, for þān ðe gelōme
wundru wurdon æt his byrgene æt þām gebedhūse þǣr hē
255 bebyrged wæs. Hi woldon þā ferian mid folclicum wurðmynde
þone hālgan līchaman and lecgan innan þǣre cyrcan. Þā wæs micel
wundor þæt hē wæs eallswā gehāl swilce hē cwic wǣre, mid
clǣnum līchaman, and his swūra wæs gehālod, þe ǣr wæs
forslagen, and wæs swylce ān seolcen þrǣd embe his swūran rǣd,
260 mannum tō swutelunge hū hē ofslagen wæs. Ēac swilce þā wunda
þe þā wælhrēowan hǣþenan mid gelōmum scotungum on his lice
macodon, wǣron gehǣlede þurh þone heofonlican God; and hē
līð swā ansund oþ þisne andwerdan dæg, andbīdigende ǣristes and
þæs ēcan wuldres. His līchama ūs cȳð, þe līð unformolsnod, þæt
265 hē būtan forligre hēr on worulde leofode and mid clǣnum līfe tō
Crīste sīþode.

Sum widewe wunode, Ōswyn gehāten, æt þæs hālgan byrgene on
gebedum and fæstenum manega gēar syððan, sēo wolde efsian ælce
gēare þone sanct and his næglas ceorfan sýferlīce mid lufe and on
270 scrȳne healdan tō hāligdōme on wēofode.

Þā wurðode þæt landfolc mid gelēafan þone sanct, and Þēodred
bisceop þearle mid gifum on golde and on seolfre gegōdode þæt
mynster þām sancte tō wurðmynte. Þā cōmon on sumne sǣl
ungesǣlige þēofas eahte on ānre nihte tō þām ārwurðan hālgan:
275 woldon stelan þā māðmas þe men þyder brōhton, and cunnodon
mid cræfte hū hī in cuman mihton. Sum slōh mid slecge swīðe þā
hæpsan, sum heora mid fēolan fēolode abūtan, sum ēac underdealf

242   **for Gode** 'because of God'.
249   **swā swā . . . hrædinge** 'as best they could in such haste'.
258–9   **his swūra . . . forslagen** See §197.4.
259   **swylce** 'as it were'.
268   **manega gēar** See §189.2.

þā duru mid spade, sum heora mid hlǣddre wolde unlūcan þæt
ēagðȳrl, ac hī swuncon on īdel and earmlīce fērdon swā, þæt se
280 hālga wer hī wundorlīce geband, ǣlcne swā hē stōd strūtigende mid
tōle, þæt heora nān ne mihte þæt morð gefremman, ne hī þanon
āstyrian, ac stōdon swā oð mergen. Men þā þæs wundrodon hū þā
weargas hangodon, sum on hlǣddre, sum lēat tō gedelfe, and ǣlc
on his weorce wæs fæste gebunden. Hī wurdon þā gebrōhte tō þām
285 bisceope ealle and hē hēt hī hōn on hēagum gealgum ealle, ac hē
næs nā gemyndig hū se mildheorta God clypode þurh his wītegan
þās word þe hēr standað: *eos qui ducuntur ad mortem eruere ne cesses*
'þā þe man lǣt tō dēaðe, ālȳs hī ūt symble'; and ēac þā hālgan canōnas
gehādodum forbēodað, ge bisceopum ge prēostum, tō bēonne
290 embe þēofas, for þan þe hit ne gebyrað þām þe bēoð gecorene
Gode tō þegnigenne, þæt hī geþwǣrlǣcan sceolon on ǣniges
mannes dēaðe, gif hī bēoð Drihtnes þegnas. Eft þā Ðēodred
bisceop scēawode his bēc syððan: behrēowsode mid geōmerunge
þæt hē swā rēðne dōm sette þām ungesǣligum þēofum, and hit
295 besārgode ǣfre oð his līfes ende, and þā lēode bæd georne þæt hī
him mid fæsten fullīce þrȳ dagas, biddende þone Ǣlmihtigan þæt
hē him ārian sceolde.

On þām lande wæs sum man, Lēofstān gehāten, rīce for worulde
and unwittig for Gode, se rād tō þām hālgan mid rīccetere swīðe,
300 and hēt him ætēowian orhlīce swīðe þone hālgan sanct, hwæþer hē
gesund wǣre; ac swā hraðe swā hē geseah þæs sanctes līchaman,
þā āwēdde hē sōna and wælhrēowlīce grymetode and earmlīce
geendode yfelum dēaðe. Þis is ðām gelīc þe se gelēaffulla pāpa
Gregōrius sǣde on his gesetnysse be ðām hālgan Laurentie, ðe līð
305 on Rōmebyrig – þæt menn woldon scēawian symle hū hē lāge,
ge gōde ge yfele; ac God hī gestilde, swā þæt þǣr swulton on þǣre

279 þæt 'in that'.
282 þæs See §148.
285 hē hēt . . . ealle See §161.
287 eos qui . . . cesses 'Do not fail to release those who are led to death'.
(Proverbs 24:11).
289–90 tō bēonne ýmbe þēofas has been construed as 'to have to do with thieves',
but contextually this does not fit: Christ came to call sinners, and Himself promised a
convicted thief that he would be with Him 'this day in paradise' (Luke 23:43). However,
it has been argued that clergy are forbidden *to beonne ymbe þeofas* because God's servants
must not consent to any man's death. Even passive acceptance is not an option: the preceding injunction, *Eos qui ducuntur ad mortem eruere ne cesses*, requires their active oppo-
sition. The theft at issue is the taking of life, and *to beonne ymbe þeofas* means 'to be among
thieves' in the sense of 'to be numbered among thieves'.
300 hēt him ætēowian See §161.
þone hālgan sanct and the hwæþer clause are parallel objects of *ætēowian*. See §159.
304 Laurentie St. Lawrence was martyred in 258. The story about his body is related
in a letter by Gregory the Great (*c.* 540–604).

scēawunge āne seofon menn ǣtgǣdere. Þā geswicon þā ōþre to
scēawigenne þone martyr mid menniscum gedwylde.

Fela wundra wē gehȳrdon on folclicre sprǣce be þām hālgan
310 Ēadmunde, þe wē hēr nellað on gewrite settan, ac hī wāt gehwā. On
þysum hālgan is swutel, and on swilcum ōþrum, þæt God ælmihtig
mæg þone man ārǣran eft on dōmes dæg ansundne of eorþan, se þe
hylt Ēadmunde hālne his līchaman oð þone micclan dæg, þēah ðe
hē of moldan cōme. Wyrðe is sēo stōw for þām wurðfullan hālgan
315 þæt hī man wurþige and wel gelōgige mid clǣnum Godes þēowum
tō Crīstes þēowdōme, for þan þe se hālga is mǣrra þonne men
magon āsmēagan.

Nis Angelcynn bedǣled Drihtnes hālgena, þonne on Engla
lande licgað swilce hālgan swylce þes hālga cyning, and Cūþberht
320 se ēadiga, and Æþeldrȳð on Ēlig, and ēac hire swustor, ansunde on
līchaman, gelēafan tō trymminge. Synd ēac fela ōðre on Angelcynne
hālgan þe fela wundra wyrcað (swā swā hit wīde is cūð) þām
Ælmihtigan tō lofe, þe hī on gelȳfdon. Crīst geswutelað mannum
þurh his mǣran hālgan þæt hē is Ælmihtig God þe macað swilce
325 wundru, þēah þe þā earman Iūdēi hine eallunga wiðsōcen, for þan
þe hī synd āwyrgede, swā swā hī wīscton him sylfum. Ne bēoð nāne
wundru geworhte æt heora byrgenum, for ðan þe hī ne gelȳfað on
þone lifigendan Crīst, ac Crīst geswutelað mannum hwǣr se sōða
gelēafa is, þonne hē swylce wundru wyrcð þurh his hālgan wīde
330 geond þās eorðan. Þæs him sȳ wuldor ā mid his heofonlican Fæder
and þām Hālgan Gāste. Amen.

---

307   **āne seofon menn ǣtgǣdere** 'a band of seven men together'.
310   **ac . . . gehwā** 'for everyone knows them'.
312–13   **se þe hylt . . . līchaman** lit. 'He Who keeps his [Edmund's] body whole for
Edmund'.
319   **Cūþberht** St. Cuthbert (*c.* 630–687) was bishop of Lindisfarne.
320   **Æþeldrȳð** St. Audrey (*c.* 630–679) and her sister St. Sexburga were daughters of
King Anna of East Anglia. Both were abbesses at Ely.
321   **līchaman** For the singular form see note to l. 182 above.
   gelēafan tō trymminge 'as a confirmation of the faith'. See §214 s.v. *tō*.
325–6   **for þan þe . . . āwyrgede** 'wherefore they are accursed'. See Matthew 27:25.

5

Alfred the Great's Preface to his Translation of Gregory's *Pastoral Care*

Among the achievements of King Alfred the Great (sketched briefly in §§217 and 251 above), one of the most remarkable was the cultural renaissance he initiated in his realm even while he was leading his nation in a fight for survival against Scandinavian invaders. To save a people militarily without also restoring them culturally was apparently unthinkable to Alfred, and so he conceived and implemented a far-sighted plan for teaching all free Anglo-Saxons literacy in the vernacular and for translating the more important books of the period into English for all to read. In his letter to Bishop Wærferth, which serves as a preface to the King's translation of Pope Gregory the Great's *Cura Pastoralis* (*Pastoral Care*), the first of the important books to be translated, the elements of the programme for cultural revival are set forth, following a moving lament over the decay of learning which Alfred saw in England when he ascended the throne in 871. The prose has the intensity of deep conviction, but its pace is leisurely and aristocratic, its tone rich with nostalgia for the era of England's intellectual pre-eminence during the lifetime of Bede (673–735).

The text here is based upon that in Hatton MS 20 in the Bodleian Library, although a few unusual spellings (mainly in grammatical endings) have been replaced with more usual spellings from other manuscripts of the preface.

Ælfred kyning hāteð grētan Wǣrferð biscep his wordum luflīce ond frēondlīce; ond ðē cȳðan hāte ðæt mē cōm swīðe oft on

---

1 **hāteð grētan Wǣrferð biscep** 'commands Bishop Wærferth to be greeted' (§161). For the use of the third person, see note to 4/2 above.

2 **ond** Before nasal consonants *a* often appears as *o* (§103.2). See below such spellings as *lond* (l. 12), *understondan* (l. 15), *mon* (l. 62).

ðē cȳðan hāte '(I) command you to be informed' (§161).

cōm '(it) has come'.

2–3 **mē . . . on gemynd** 'into my mind' (§191.2).

A Guide to Old English, Eighth Edition. Bruce Mitchell and Fred C. Robinson.
© 2012 Bruce Mitchell and Fred C. Robinson. Published 2012 by Blackwell Publishing Ltd.

gemynd, hwelce wiotan iū wǣron giond Angelcynn, ǣgðer ge
godcundra hāda ge woruldcundra; ond hū gesǣliglica tīda ðā
5 wǣron giond Angelcynn; ond hū ðā kyningas ðe ðone onwald
hæfdon ðæs folces Gode ond his ǣrendwrecum hīersumedon;
ond hīe ǣgðer ge hiora sibbe ge hiora siodu ge hiora onweald
innanbordes gehīoldon, ond ēac ūt hiora ēðel rȳmdon; ond hū
him ðā spēow ǣgðer ge mid wīge ge mid wīsdōme; ond ēac ðā
10 godcundan hādas, hū giorne hīe wǣron ǣgðer ge ymb lāre ge ymb
liornunga, ge ymb ealle ðā ðīowotdōmas ðe hīe Gode dōn scoldon;
ond hū man ūtanbordes wīsdōm ond lāre hieder on lond sōhte; ond
hū wē hīe nū sceoldon ūte begietan, gif wē hīe habban sceoldon.
Swǣ clǣne hīo wæs oðfeallenu on Angelcynne ðæt swīðe fēawa
15 wǣron behionan Humbre ðe hiora ðēninga cūðen understondan
on Englisc oððe furðum ān ǣrendgewrit of Lǣdene on Englisc
āreccean; ond ic wēne ðætte nōht monige begiondan Humbre
nǣren. Swǣ fēawa hiora wǣron ðæt ic furðum ānne ānlēpne ne
mæg geðencean be sūðan Temese ðā ðā ic tō rīce fēng. Gode
20 ælmihtegum sīe ðonc ðætte wē nū ǣnigne onstal habbað lārēowa.
Ond for ðon ic ðē bebīode ðæt ðū dō swǣ ic gelīefe ðæt ðū wille,
ðæt ðū ðē ðissa woruldðinga to ðǣm geǣmetige, swǣ ðū oftost
mǣge, ðæt ðū ðone wīsdōm ðe ðē God sealde ðǣr ðǣr ðū hiene
befæstan mǣge, befæste. Geðenc hwelc wītu ūs ðā becōmon for
25 ðisse worulde, ðā ðā wē hit nōhwæðer ne selfe ne lufodon, ne ēac
ōðrum monnum ne lēfdon; ðone naman ǣnne wē lufodon ðætte wē
Crīstne wǣren, ond swīðe fēawa ðā ðēawas.

Ðā ic ðā ðis eall gemunde, ðā gemunde ic ēac hū ic geseah, ǣr
ðǣm ðe hit eall forhergod wǣre ond forbærned, hū ðā ciricean

8–9 **him ðā spēow** 'they were successful then' (lit. 'it was successful to them then';
see §212).

10 **hādas, hū giorne hīe wǣron** See note to 4/25.

14 **oðfeallenu** See §201.2.

17 **ðætte** See §155.

19 **tō rīce fēng** 'succeeded to the kingdom'.

22–4 **ðæt ðū ðē ... befæste** 'that you free yourself, as often as you can, from worldly
affairs to the end that you apply the wisdom that God gave you wherever you can apply it'.
See §172.A.

24 **wītu** The 'punishments' to which King Alfred refers are the Scandinavian
invasions: see §217.

25 **hit** The antecedent is *wīsdōm*. See §187.2, and compare *sīo lār ... hit* below
(ll. 45–6), where natural gender has again displaced grammatical gender.

26 **lēfdon** 'bequeathed, passed on' (taking this to be a non-West-Saxon spelling of
lǣfdon (l. 35) from *lǣfan* rather than from *līefan* 'allow', as previous editors have
assumed). The negligent Christians neither cherished learning themselves nor bothered
transmitting it to later generations. (Cf. *lufodon ... lǣfdon* below in ll. 34–5.)

26–7. **ðone naman ǣnne ... ðā ðēawas** 'we loved only the name that we were
Christians, and very few (of us loved) the (Christian) practices'.

29 **forhergod ... ond forbærned** 'ravaged ... and burned', i.e. by the Scandinavian
invaders (§217).

30 giond eall Angelcynn stōdon māðma ond bōca gefylda, ond ēac
micel mengeo Godes ðīowa; ond ðā swīðe lȳtle fiorme ðāra bōca
wiston, for ðǣm ðe hīe hiora nānwuht ongietan ne meahton, for
ðǣm ðe hīe nǣron on hiora āgen geðīode āwritene. Swelce hīe
cwǣden: 'Ūre ieldran, ðā ðe ðās stōwa ǣr hīoldon, hīe lufodon
35 wīsdōm, ond ðurh ðone hīe begēaton welan ond ūs lǣfdon. Hēr
mon mæg gīet gesīon hiora swæð, ac wē him ne cunnon æfter
spyrigean. Ond for ðǣm wē habbað nū ǣgðer forlǣten ge ðone
welan ge ðone wīsdōm, for ðǣm ðe wē noldon tō ðǣm spore mid
ūre mōde onlūtan.'
40   Ðā ic ðā ðis eall gemunde, ðā wundrade ic swīðe swīðe ðāra
gōdena wiotena ðe giū wǣron giond Angelcynn, ond ðā bēc ealla be
fullan geliornod hæfdon, ðæt hīe hiora ðā nǣnne dǣl noldon on
hiora āgen geðīode wendan. Ac ic ðā sōna eft mē selfum andwyrde,
ond cwæð: 'Hīe ne wēndon ðætte ǣfre menn sceolden swǣ
45 reccelēase weorðan ond sīo lār swǣ oðfeallan: for ðǣre wilnunga
hīe hit forlēton, ond woldon ðæt hēr ðȳ māra wīsdōm on londe
wǣre ðȳ wē mā geðēoda cūðon.'
     Ðā gemunde ic hū sīo ǣ wæs ǣrest on Ebriscgeðīode funden,
ond eft, ðā hīe Crēacas geliornodon, ðā wendon hīe hīe on heora
50 āgen geðīode ealle, ond ēac ealle ōðre bēc. Ond eft Lǣdenware
swǣ same, siððan hīe hīe geliornodon, hīe hīe wendon ealla ðurh
wīse wealhstodas on hiora āgen geðīode. Ond ēac ealla ōðra
Crīstna ðīoda sumne dǣl hiora on hiora āgen geðīode wendon.

---

30 **stōdon māðma ond bōca gefylda** 'were full of books and of treasures'.

31–2 **ðā swīðe lȳtle . . . wiston** 'they had very little benefit from the books'
(literally, 'they knew very little use of the books').

33–4 **Swelce hīe cwǣden** '(It is) as if they had said'. See §177.4 for the meaning of
swelce.

36 **him . . . æfter** See §213.

38–9 **mid ūre mōde** 'with our mind(s)'.

40 **wundrade** Both the gen. pl. *wiotena* and the clause *ðæt hīe . . . wendan* are objects
of the verb *wundrade*.

45 **for ðǣre wilnunga** 'on purpose, deliberately'.

46–7 **ðȳ . . . ðȳ** See §167.7a.

48 **ǣ** The Old Testament, or perhaps only the Hexateuch ('the Law'), is meant.

49 The word *hīe* occurs three times in l. 49. In the first and third occurrences it is
acc. sg. fem. 'it' agreeing with the antecedent *ǣ* (l. 48). In the second, it is nom. pl. 'they'
referring to *Crēacas*.

50 The first *ealle* is acc. sg. fem. referring back to the third *hīe* in l. 49 and so to *ǣ*
(l. 48); the second *ealle* is acc. pl. fem. modifying *bēc*. Presumably *ealle ōðre bēc* refers to
the remaining books of the Bible.

51 **siððan hīe hīe geliornodon, hīe hīe wendon ealla** 'after they (*Lǣdenware*)
had learned them (*bēc*), they translated them all'. On the repetition of the subject
(*Lǣdenware . . . hīe*), see §148.

Forðȳ mē ðyncð betre, gif īow swǣ ðyncð, ðæt wē ēac sume bēc, ðā
55 ðe nīedeðearfosta sīen eallum monnum tō wiotonne, ðæt wē ðā on
ðæt geðīode wenden ðe wē ealle gecnāwan mægen, ond gedōn swǣ
wē swīðe ēaðe magon mid Godes fultume, gif wē ðā stilnesse
habbað, ðætte eall sīo gioguð ðe nū is on Angelcynne frīora monna,
ðāra ðe ðā spēda hæbben ðæt hīe ðǣm befēolan mægen, sīen tō
60 liornunga oðfæste, ðā hwīle ðe hīe tō nānre ōðerre note ne mægen,
oð ðone first ðe hīe wel cunnen Englisc gewrit ārǣdan. Lǣre mon
siððan furður on Lǣdengeðīode ðā ðe mon furðor lǣran wille ond
tō hīerran hāde dōn wille.

Ðā ic ðā gemunde hū sīo lār Lǣdengeðīodes ǣr ðissum āfeallen
65 wæs giond Angelcynn, ond ðēah monige cūðon Englisc gewrit
ārǣdan, ðā ongan ic ongemang ōðrum mislicum ond manigfealdum
bisgum ðisses kynerīces ðā bōc wendan on Englisc ðe is
genemned on Lǣden *Pastoralis*, ond on Englisc 'Hierdebōc',
hwīlum word be worde, hwīlum andgit of andgiete, swǣ swǣ ic hīe
70 geliornode æt Plegmunde mīnum ærcebiscepe, ond æt Assere
mīnum biscepe, ond æt Grimbolde mīnum mæsseprīoste, ond æt
Iōhanne mīnum mæsseprēoste. Siððan ic hīe ðā geliornod hæfde,
swǣ swǣ ic hīe forstōd ond swǣ ic hīe andgitfullīcost āreccean
meahte, ic hīe on Englisc āwende; ond tō ælcum biscepstōle on
75 mīnum rīce wille āne onsendan; ond on ælcre bið ān æstel, se bið
on fiftegum mancessa. Ond ic bebīode on Godes naman ðæt nān
mon ðone æstel from ðǣre bēc ne dō, ne ðā bōc from ðǣm mynstre
– uncūð hū longe ðǣr swǣ gelǣrede biscepas sīen, swǣ swǣ nū,
Gode ðonc, welhwǣr siendon. Forðȳ ic wolde ðætte hīe ealneg æt
80 ðǣre stōwe wǣren, būton se biscep hīe mid him habban wille, oððe
hīo hwǣr tō lǣne sīe, oððe hwā ōðre bī wrīte.

54–61   Forðȳ . . . ārǣdan See §172.B for a detailed analysis of this sentence.
55   ðæt wē Otiose restatement of ðæt wē in l. 54. See §148.
60   ðā hwīle ðe . . . ne mægen 'as long as they are competent for no other
employment'.
69   hīe acc. sg. fem. The antecedent is *Hierdebōc*.
70–2   Plegmunde . . . Assere . . . Grimbolde . . . Iōhanne These are scholars whom
King Alfred brought in from outside Wessex to help implement the cultural revival
he sought for his people. Plegmund was a Mercian who became Archbishop of
Canterbury in 890. Asser, a Welshman, became bishop of Sherborne and wrote a
Latin biography of King Alfred. Grimbold was a Frankish priest who was ultimately
canonized, and John (*Iōhannes*) a continental Saxon whom King Alfred established as
abbot of a new monastery at Athelney in Somerset.
73–4   The *swǣ swǣ* clause and the *swǣ* clause (§168 *swā* 2(b)) are coordinate and reveal
that Alfred was modestly aware of possible deficiencies both in his understanding and in
his translation of the *Cura Pastoralis*.
75–6   se bið on fiftegum mancessa 'it is worth fifty mancuses'. This use of *on* is
an idiom. For the gen. pl. *mancessa*, see §194.2.
78   uncūð '(it is) unknown'.
79–81   Forðȳ ic . . . bī write 'Therefore I have desired that they (the book and the æstel)
always remain at that place, unless the bishop wants to have them (or it, i.e. the book)
with him, or it (the book) is on loan somewhere, or someone is making a copy (from it).'

6

Cynewulf and Cyneheard

This account appears in the Anglo-Saxon Chronicle, a year-by-year record of important events in the kingdom. (See the next selection for details.) The entry for the year 755 contains a narrative which exemplifies one of the cardinal virtues of Germanic society in the heroic age: unswerving loyalty to one's sworn leader, even when that loyalty is in conflict with claims of kinship. (See §§236–240.) For a contemporary audience, the violence and tragedy of the feud between Cynewulf and Cyneheard would have been transcended by the reassuring fact that the ideal prevailed: on both sides men made the heroic choice, and they chose right. The narration is so swift and breathless, the selection of detail so deft, that some scholars have felt that the chronicler was recording a saga refined by many retellings in oral tradition. Supporting this view (and complicating the modern reader's task in following the narrative) is the tale's spontaneous syntax and free word-order, which require close attention to grammatical endings if the sentences are to be construed accurately. Readers should also be wary of the unusual spellings of some verb endings (*wǣron, -un, -an; locude* for *locode*; and the subjunctives *ūþon* and *ēodon* in lines 29 and 33, where we would expect *-en* for *-on*). See §113.3 for such spelling variations.

The text is that of Corpus Christi College, Cambridge, MS 173 except in line 29, where we adopt *cȳþde*, the reading of most manuscripts, for *cȳðdon* of our manuscript. For historical information about persons and places mentioned and chronological disturbances, see Whitelock's work cited in §251.1.

755. Hēr Cynewulf benam Sigebryht his rīces ond Westseaxna wiotan for unryhtum dǣdum, būton Hamtūnscīre; ond hē hæfde

---

1 **Hēr** i.e. 'in this year': the chronicler uses an adverb of place rather than of time because he is referring to the dated slot in the manuscript where he is making his entry.
Sigebryht King of the West Saxons before Cynewulf, his kinsman, deposed him.
1–2 **Cynewulf . . . ond Westseaxna wiotan** is the compound subject of the sentence. The verb *benam* is singular because in OE verbs normally agree only with that part of a compound subject which precedes them: see §§149.1 and 187.3c.

A Guide to Old English, Eighth Edition. Bruce Mitchell and Fred C. Robinson.
© 2012 Bruce Mitchell and Fred C. Robinson. Published 2012 by Blackwell Publishing Ltd.

þā oþ hē ofslōg þone aldormon þe him lengest wunode. Ond hiene
þā Cynewulf on Andred ādrǣfde, ond hē þǣr wunade oþ þæt hiene
5 ān swān ofstang æt Pryfetes flōdan; ond hē wrǣc þone aldormon
Cumbran. Ond se Cynewulf oft miclum gefeohtum feaht uuiþ
Bretwālum. Ond ymb xxxi wintra þæs þe hē rīce hæfde, hē wolde
ādrǣfan ānne æþeling se was Cyneheard hāten; ond se Cyneheard
wæs þæs Sigebryhtes brōþur. Ond þā geāscode hē þone cyning lȳtle
10 werode on wīfcȳþþe on Merantūne, ond hine þǣr berād ond þone
būr ūtan beēode ǣr hine þā men onfunden þe mid þām kyninge
wǣrun.

Ond þā ongeat se cyning þæt, ond hē on þā duru ēode ond þā
unhēanlīce hine werede oþ hē on þone æþeling lōcude, ond þā ūt
15 rǣsde on hine ond hine miclum gewundode; ond hīe alle on þone
cyning wǣrun feohtende oþ þæt hīe hine ofslægenne hæfdon. Ond
þā on þæs wīfes gebǣrum onfundon þæs cyninges þegnas þā
unstilnesse, ond þā þider urnon swā hwelc swā þonnc gearo
wearþ ond radost. Ond hiera se æþeling gehwelcum feoh ond

---

3   **þā** acc. sg. fem., agreeing in gender with its antecedent *Hamtūnscīre*.

þe him lengest wunode 'who had dwelt with him longest', i.e. who had remained
faithful to him longer than the rest.

4   **Andred** A large forest which extended from Kent into Hampshire (the area now
called the Weald).

5   **Pryfetes flōdan** 'the stream at Privett' (in Hampshire).

5–6   **þone aldormon Cumbran** This is the loyal *aldormon* slain by Sigebryht
(l. 3).

7   **Bretwālum** Britons (probably Cornishmen) descended from the original inhabitants of England before the Anglo-Saxon invasion (§217).

Ond ymb xxxi wintra þæs þe . . . literally 'And after 31 winters from that in
which . . .'.

wintra i.e. 'years'. The Anglo-Saxons reckoned years in terms of winters. For the case
of *wintra* see §194.2; cf. §190.4. The passage of many years in the course of this 'annal'
shows that this is not a normal chronicle entry (which would record only the events of
the year just ended) but rather is an independent tale which the chronicler has inter-
polated into his sequence of yearly reports. The *Chronicle* records the death of Cynewulf
in the annal dated 784: apparently XXXI is an error for XXIX. The 784 entry reads as
follows: *Hēr Cyneheard ofslōg Cynewulf cyning, ond hē þǣr wearþ ofslægen ond lxxxiiii monna
mid him.*

9–10   **lȳtle werode** See §192.2.

on wīfcȳþþe on Merantūne i.e. visiting a mistress in Merton.

11   **būr** i.e. the apartment where the lady receives the King. The *būr* stands inside
the stronghold (*burh*) but is separate from the main hall, where the King's retinue is housed.
The entire compound is surrounded by a wall and is entered through *gatu* (ll. 27, 36) in
the wall. The *būr* is entered through a *duru* (l. 13).

14   **æþeling** i.e. Cyneheard.

17   **on þæs wīfes gebǣrum** 'from the woman's outcries'.

18–19   **urnon . . . ond radost** literally, 'they ran, whoever became ready and
quickest', i.e. each ran to the King as quickly as he could get ready.

19   **hiera . . . gehwelcum** 'to each of them (i.e. the King's men)'.

20 feorh gebēad, ond hiera nǣnig hit geþicgean nolde; ac hīe simle
feohtende wǣran oþ hīe alle lǣgon būtan ānum Bryttiscum gīsle,
ond sē swīþe gewundad wæs.

þā on morgenne gehīerdun þæt þæs cyninges þegnas þe him
beæftan wǣrun, þæt se cyning ofslǣgen wæs. þā ridon hīe þider,
25 ond his aldormon Ōsrīc, ond Wīferþ his þegn, ond þā men þe hē
beæftan him lǣfde ǣr, ond þone æþeling on þǣre byrig mētton þǣr
se cyning ofslǣgen lǣg (ond þā gatu him tō belocen hæfdon) ond þā
þǣrto ēodon. Ond þā gebēad hē him hiera āgenne dōm fẽos ond
londes, gif hīe him þæs rīces ūþon, ond him cȳþde þæt hiera mǣgas
30 him mid wǣron, þā þe him from noldon. Ond þā cuǣdon hīe þæt
him nǣnig mǣg lēofra nǣre þonne hiera hlāford, ond hīe nǣfre
his banan folgian noldon. Ond þā budon hīe hiera mǣgum þæt
hīe gesunde from ēodon. Ond hīe cuǣdon þæt tæt ilce hiera
gefērum geboden wǣre þe ǣr mid þām cyninge wǣrun. þā cuǣdon
35 hīe þæt hīe hīe þæs ne onmunden 'þon mā þe ēowre gefēran þe mid
þām cyninge ofslǣgene wǣrun.' Ond hīe þā ymb þā gatu feohtende

20–1 **simle feohtende wǣran** i.e. 'kept on fighting'.

21 **gīsle** Presumably the hostage was taken in the course of Cynewulf's wars with the Britons (ll. 6–7).

26 **ǣr** Here as elsewhere *ǣr* combined with pret. tense signals the pluperfect (§197.4): 'and the men that he had left behind him'.

27 **þā gatu . . . hæfdon** Cyneheard's men 'had locked the gates (leading in) to them', i.e. had locked themselves in the compound. Or, alternatively, one could read, 'had locked the gates against them (King Cynewulf's men)'.

28 **hiera āgenne dōm** Cyneheard offers to let King Cynewulf's men name their own price for allowing him to assume the kingship. (Giving enemies 'their own judgment of compensation' is a common Germanic idiom and practice.)

30 **þā þe him from noldon** 'who did not want (to go) from him' (§205.1).
cuǣdon hīe 'they (Cynewulf's men) said'.

32 **Ond þā budon hīe** 'And then they (Cynewulf's men) offered'.

33 **ēodon** subj. 'might go'.

33–4 **Ond hīe cuǣdon . . . geboden wǣre** 'And they (Cyneheard's men) said that the same (thing) had been offered to their (Cynewulf's men's) comrades'.

34–5 **þā cuǣdon . . . onmunden** 'Then they (Cyneheard's men) said that they would not pay attention to that (offer of safe passage).' *Onmunan* with refl. pron. (*hīe*) takes a gen. obj. (*þæs*).

35 **þon mā þe** '(any) more than (did)'. The mid-sentence shift into direct discourse is characteristic of vivid oral narrative.
C. T. Onions, in earlier editions of Henry Sweet's *Anglo-Saxon Reader*, provided the following dialogue to clarify the rapid shifts of speaker in the foregoing passage:

> *Cyneheard.* I offer you your own choice of money and land if you will grant me the kingship; and there are kinsmen of yours with us who will not leave me (us). *Osric.* No kinsman of ours is dearer to us than our liege lord, and we will never follow his slayer. We offer a safe exit to those of them who come out. *Cyneheard.* The same offer was made to your comrades who were with the king before. We pay no more regard to the offer than your comrades did who were killed along with the king.

36 **Ond hīe** 'and they (i.e. Cynewulf's men)'.

wǣron oþ þæt hīe þǣrinne fulgon ond þone æþeling ofslōgon ond þā men þe him mid wǣrun, alle būtan ānum, se wæs þæs aldormonnes godsunu; ond hē his feorh generede, ond þēah hē
40   wæs oft gewundad.

Ond se Cynewulf rīcsode xxxi wintra and his līc līþ æt Wintanceastre, ond þæs æþelinges æt Ascanmynster; ond hiera ryhtfæderencyn gǣþ tō Cerdice.

37   **oþ þæt hīe** 'until they (i.e. Cynewulf's men)'.
38–9   **þæs aldormonnes** perhaps Cumbra, mentioned in l. 6.
39   **ond hē his feorh generede** The *hē* refers to the godson.
43   **Cerdice** the putative founder of the kingdom and royal line of the West Saxons.

7

Selections from the Anglo-Saxon Chronicle

Around A.D. 890, during the reign of King Alfred the Great, Anglo-Saxon scholars compiled a year-by-year record of important events from antiquity to their own day. Copies of this Chronicle were distributed throughout the realm, and the annual record of happenings in England was continued by various hands in various places, sometimes only a short while after the events occurred. This annalistic activity at times approaches genuine historical writing and constitutes an important stage in the development of a narrative prose independent of Latin models. The following selections suggest the nature both of the Chronicle's prose style and of the events it portrays at one dark period in England's history. Norsemen were waging a war of conquest in the land, and the English King, Æthelred the Unready, adopted the disastrous policy of paying the invaders Danegeld rather than rallying his troops for defence, as King Alfred had done in an earlier time of trial (see §217). The leading men of the realm, moreover, were often untrustworthy, and the nation was demoralized. One Anglo-Saxon leader named Brihtnoth, whose death is noted briefly in the entry for 991, rejected the prevailing pusillanimity of his times and made a desperate stand against the invaders rather than pay Danegeld. His valour and that of his men is extolled in a moving heroic poem, *The Battle of Maldon*, which appears below as selection 12.

The entries are drawn from several manuscripts of the Chronicle, and some have been abbreviated. The words *tobrocon* (l. 39), *gefēordon* (l. 50), *se* (l. 51), and *beodon* (l. 74) have been normalized to *tōbrocen*, *gefērdon*, *sēo*, and *bēodan*.

980. Hēr on þȳs gēare wæs Æþelgār abbod tō bisceope gehālgod on vi nōnas Mai tō þām bisceopstōle æt Sēolesigge. And on þām ylcan

---

1   **Hēr** See 6/1 n.

2   **vi nōnas Mai** i.e. 2 May (Latin terms are used by some chroniclers in reckoning time.) Note here and elsewhere in this text (e.g. ll. 10, 24, 63) the use of Roman numerals.

A Guide to Old English, Eighth Edition. Bruce Mitchell and Fred C. Robinson.
© 2012 Bruce Mitchell and Fred C. Robinson. Published 2012 by Blackwell Publishing Ltd.

gēare wæs Sūðhamtūn forhergod fram scipherige, and sēo burhwaru mæst ofslegen and gehæft. And þȳ ilcan gēare wæs Tenetland
5 gehergod; and þȳ ilcan gēare wæs Lēgeceasterscīr gehergod fram
norðscipherige.

981. Hēr on þis gēare wæs Sancte Petroces stōw forhergod, and
þȳ ilcan gēare wæs micel hearm gedōn gehwǣr be þām sǣriman ǣgþer
ge on Defenum ge on Wēalum.

10   982. Hēr on þȳs gēare cōmon ūpp on Dorsǣtum iii scypu
wīcinga and hergodon on Portlande. þȳ ilcan gēare forbarn
Lundenbyrig. And on þām ylcan gēare forðfērdon twēgen ealdormenn, Æþelmǣr on Hamtūnscīre and Ēadwine on Sūðseaxum.

. . . . .

988. Hēr wæs Wecedport geheregod, and Goda, se Defenisca
15 þegen, ofslagen, and mycel wæl mid him. Hēr getōr Ðunstan
arcebisceop, and Æðelgār bisceop fēng æfter him tō arcestōle, and
hē lȳtle hwīle æfter þǣm lyfodc – būtan i gēare and iii mōnþas.

. . . . .

990. Hēr Sigerīc wæs gehālgod tō arcebisceope, and Ēadwine
abbod forðfērde, and Wulfgār abbod fēng tō þām rīce.

20   991. Hēr wæs Gypeswīc gehergod, and æfter þām swīðe raðe
wæs Brihtnōð ealdorman ofslægen æt Mældūne. And on þām gēare
man gerædde þæt man geald ǣrest gafol Deniscan mannum for þām
mycclan brōgan þe hī worhtan be þām sǣriman. Þæt wæs ǣrest x
þūsend punda. Þǣne rǣd gerædde Sīrīc arcebisceop.

25   992. Hēr Ōswald se ēadiga arcebisceop forlēt þis līf and gefērde
þæt heofonlice, and Æðelwine ealdorman gefōr on þām ilcan
gēarc. Ðā gerǣdde se cyng and ealle his witan þæt man gegaderode
þā scipu þe āhtes wǣron tō Lundenbyrig. And se cyng þā betǣhte
þā fyrde tō lǣdene Ealfrīce ealdorman and Þorode eorl and
30 Ælfstāne bisceop and Æscwīge bisceop, and sceoldan cunnian
gif hī muhton þone herc āhwǣr ūtcne betrǣppen. Ðā sende se

12 **Lundenbyrig** nom. sg. Since *burg* is declined like *bōc* (§58), the normal nom. sg.
form is *-burg*, not *-byrig*. But in the Chronicle and elsewhere the form with *i*-mutation
occasionally appears as a nominative singular.

16 **fēng . . . tō arcestōle** 'succeeded to the archiepiscopal see after him'.

19 **fēng tō þām rīce** 'succeeded to the office (of abbot)'.

22 **man gerædde . . . gafol** 'advice was given so that tribute was first paid'.

Deniscan A late spelling of *Deniscum* (§65). The Anglo-Saxons used *Denisc* loosely to
refer to any and all of the Scandinavian peoples who were invading them. The Vikings
at Maldon seem to have been mainly Norwegians.

28 **āhtes** 'of any value' (gen. sg. of *āwiht*).

29 **tō lǣdene** Properly, *tō lǣdenne* 'for leading', i.e. 'as leaders'.

29–30 **Ealfrīce ealdorman . . . Æscwīge bisceop** The names of these leaders are,
correctly, in the dative case, but their titles are uninflected.

ealdorman Ælfrīc and hēt warnian þone here, and þā on þēre nihte
ðe hī on ðone dæi tōgædere cumon sceoldon, ðā sceōc hē on niht
fram þære fyrde, him sylfum tō mycclum bismore. And se here þā
35 ætbærst, būton ān scip þær man ofslōh. And þā gemætte se here ðā
scipu of Ēastenglum and of Lunden, and hī ðær ofslōgon mycel
wæl and þæt scip genāmon eall gewæpnod, and gewædod, þe se
ealdorman on wæs.

993. Hēr on ðissum gēare æs Bæbbanburh tōbrocen and mycel
40 herehūðe þær genumen; and æfter þām cōm tō Humbran mūðe se
here and þær mycel yfel gewrohtan ægðer ge on Lindesīge ge on
Norðhymbran. þā gegaderode man swīðe mycele fyrde, and þā hī
tōgædere gān sceoldan, þā onstealdon þā heretogan ærest þone
flēam – þæt wæs Fræna and Godwine and Friðegist. On þysum
45 ilcan gēare hēt se cyng āblendan Ælfgār Ælfrīces sunu ealdormannes.

994. Hēr on þisum gēare cōm Anlāf and Swegen tō Lundenbyrig
on Nativitas sancte Marie mid iiii and hundnigontigum scipum,
and hī ðā on ðā burh festlīce feohtende wæron, and ēac hī mid fȳre
50 ontendan woldon. Ac hī þār geferdon māran hearm and yfel þonne
hī æfre wēndon þæt heom ænig burhwaru gedōn sceolde. Ac sēo
hālige Godes mōdor on ðām dæge hire mildheortnisse þære
burhware gecȳðde and hī āhredde wið heora fēondum. And hī
þanon fērdon, and wrohton þæt mæste yfel þe æfre ænig here dōn
55 mihte on bærnette and hergunge and on manslihtum ægðer be ðām
særiman on Ēastseaxum and on Centlande and on Sūðseaxum and

32 **Ælfrīc** This treacherous Ælfric (whose name is spelled *Ealfrīce* in l. 29) was
ealdorman of Hampshire. He has no connection with Abbot Ælfric, author of the
Colloquy, Biblical translations, and other works.
hēt warnian (§161).
32–3 **on þēre nihte ðe hī on ðone dæi** 'in the night before the day on which they'.
(A day was regarded as going with the previous night.)
35 **ān scip . . . ofslōh** literally 'one ship where one destroyed', i.e. 'one ship which
was destroyed'.
36 **hī** The antecedent of *hī* is the collective noun *here* (l. 35).
40 **herehūðe** partitive gen. with *micel*.
41 **gewrohtan** A late spelling of *gewrohton*. The Chronicler first thinks of *here* as a
unit (*cōm*) and then pluralizes (*gewrohtan*) as he thinks of it as many men. See §187.3*b*,
and cf. ll. 61–2 below (*cōm . . . nāmon*).
45 **hēt . . . āblendan** Ælfgār (§161). This blinding of the son was presumably in
retribution for Ælfric's treachery.
47 **Anlāf and Swegen** Since it precedes the compound subject, *cōm* is singular.
(Anlāf is King Olaf Tryggvason of Norway, who ultimately converted his countrymen
to Christianity; Swegen is Sweyn Forkbeard, King of Denmark and conqueror of
England in 1013. His son Canute was King of England and Denmark 1016–35.)
48 **Nativitas sancte Marie** '(the day of) the Nativity of Saint Mary', i.e.
8 September.
49 **hī** (preceding *mid*) acc. sg. fem. (antecedent is *burh*).

on Hamtūnscīre. And æt nȳxtan nāman heom hors and ridon swā
wīde swā hī woldon and unāsecgendlice yfel wircende wǣron. Þā
gerǣdde se cyng and his witan þæt him man tō sende and him gafol
60 behēte and metsunge wið þon þe hī þǣre hergunge geswicon. And
hī þā þet underfēngon, and cōm þā eall se here tō Hamtūne and
þǣr wintersetle nāmon. And hī man þǣr fǣdde geond eall
Westseaxna rīce, and him man geald fēos xvi þūsend punda.

. . . . .

1011. Hēr on þissum gēare sende se cyning and his witan tō ðām
65 here, and gyrndon friðes, and him gafol and metsunge behēton wið
þām ðe hī hiora hergunge geswicon. Hī Hæfdon þā ofergān (i)
Ēastengle and (ii) Ēastsexe and (iii) Middlesexe and (iv) Oxena-
fordscīre and (v) Grantabricscīre and (vi) Heortfordscīre and (vii)
Buccingahamscīre and (viii) Bedefordscīre and (ix) healfe Hunta-
70 dūnscīre and micel (x) on Hāmtūnscīre, and be sūþan Temese ealle
Kentingas and Sūðsexe and Hǣstingas and Sūðrige and Bearrocscīre and Hamtūnscīre and micel on Wiltūnscīre.
Ealle þās ungesǣlða ūs gelumpon þuruh unrǣdas, þæt man
nolde him ā tīman gafol bēodan oþþe wið gefeohtan; ac þonne hī
75 mǣst tō yfele gedōn hæfdon, þonne nam mon frið and grið wið hī.
And nā þē lǣs for eallum þissum griðe and gafole hī fērdon
ǣghweder flocmǣlum, and heregodon ūre earme folc, and hī
rȳpton and slōgon.

57   **nāman heom** Late spellings of *nāmon him*. For the function of the pronoun see
note to 3/42.
58   **unāsecgendlice** a late form of acc. pl. neut. *-licu*.
73   **unrǣdas** See below, p. 253 n. 1.
þæt 'in that'.
74   **him** i.e. the Danes.
ā tīman 'in time'.
75   **mǣst tō yfele** 'the most for harm', i.e. 'the most to (our) injury'.

8

Bede's Account of the Conversion of King Edwin

Saint Bede the Venerable – scientist, historian, philologist, and one of the Church Fathers – lived in the north of England from c.673 to 735. His important work as a theologian earned him a place in the fourth heaven of Dante's *Paradiso*, but it is his work as a historian that has established his reputation among modern readers. At a time when most 'historical' writing was a mish-mash of fact and fiction, Bede's *Ecclesiastical History of the English People* (written, like virtually all his works, in Latin) maintained a high standard of accuracy, order, and verification of sources. It is also well written and has sustained the interest of readers both during and after the Middle Ages.

Sometime during the reign of King Alfred the Great (871–899), Bede's *History* was translated into Old English. The translation is vigorous and at times even eloquent, but one can also detect in it the struggle of a vernacular artist trying (not always successfully) to free himself from the alien syntax of his source text and to establish a native English prose style. All these features are present in the following excerpt from the Old English Bede, which recounts how Christianity was brought to the pagan Anglo-Saxons of Northumbria in 625. The first missionary work took place in 597 in Kent, and it is from there that Bishop Paulinus travelled to the court of King Edwin of Northumbria in hopes of persuading the ruler and his *witan* to renounce their pagan beliefs and accept Christianity. At the point where our excerpt begins, Paulinus has just succeeded in converting Edwin, but the King explains that he must put the matter before his *witan* before he can commit his subjects to the new faith. The deliberations of his advisers, which Bede records with deft and unobtrusive art, give us a remarkable glimpse of that pivotal moment in history when the warrior society of Anglo-Saxon England began to abandon Germanic paganism for the religion newly brought from Rome.

A Guide to Old English, Eighth Edition. Bruce Mitchell and Fred C. Robinson.
© 2012 Bruce Mitchell and Fred C. Robinson. Published 2012 by Blackwell Publishing Ltd.

The text is basically that of Corpus Christi College, Oxford, MS 279 up to -*bedo* in l. 47 and of Bodleian Library MS Tanner 10 for the rest, but we have occasionally adopted a simpler reading from another manuscript when the base text is problematic, and in l. 56 we read *þā þe* for the various and conflicting readings of the manuscripts.

Þā se cyning þā þās word gehȳrde, þā andswarode hē him and cwæð, þæt hē æghwæþer ge wolde ge sceolde þām gelēafan onfōn þe hē lærde; cwæð hwæþere, þæt hē wolde mid his frēondum and mid his wytum gesprec and geþeaht habban, þæt gif hī mid hine
5 þæt geþafian woldan, þæt hī ealle ætsomne on līfes willan Crīste gehālgade wǣran. Þā dyde se cyning swā swā hē cwæð, and se bisceop þæt geþafade.

Þā hæfde hē gesprec and geþeaht mid his witum and syndriglīce wæs fram him eallum frignende hwylc him þūhte and gesawen
10 wǣre þēos nīwe lār and þǣre godcundnesse bīgong þe þǣr lǣred wæs. Him þā andswarode his ealdorbisceop, Cēfi wæs hāten: 'Geseoh þū, cyning, hwclc þēos lār sīe þe ūs nū bodad is. Ic þē sōðlīce andette þæt ic cūðlīce geleornad hæbbe, þæt eallinga nāwiht mægenes ne nyttnesse hafað sīo æfæstnes þc wē oð ðis
15 hæfdon and beēodon, for ðon nænig þīnra þegna nēodlicor ne gelustfullīcor hine sylfne underþēodde tō ūra goda bīgange þonne ic, and nōht þon lǣs monige syndon þā þe māran gefe and fremsumnesse æt þē onfēngon þonne ic, and in eallum þingum māran gesynto hæfdon. Hwæt, ic wāt, gif ūre godo ǣnige mihte
20 hæfdon, þonne woldan hīe mē mā fultumian, for þon ic him geornlīcor þēodde ond hȳrde. For þon mē þynceð wīslic, gif þū gesēo þā þing beteran and strangran þe ūs nīwan bodad syndon, þæt wē þām onfōn.'

1   **him** i.e. Bishop Paulinus, who has just explained to the King his obligation to accept Christianity.

5   **woldan** Here and elsewhere the scribe (who made this copy in the eleventh century) uses -*an* instead of -*en* for the subj. pl. ending: cf. *wǣran* (l. 6) and *woldan* (l. 20). He also uses -*an* for -*on*: *sprǣcan* (l. 38), *beēodan* (l. 43). These spellings are characteristic of the late Old English period.

willan 'fountain', i.e. baptismal font.

9–10   **hwylc him . . . wǣre** literally 'how seemed to them and was seen (by them)'. The Latin word *videretur* 'seemed' is translated with two roughly synonymous expressions (*þūhte* and *gesawen wǣre*). This practice is common in the Old English Bede and is symptomatic of the translator's awkwardness in dealing with his Latin source. Cf. *hæfdon and beēodon* (l. 15) and *sōhte ond āhsode* (l. 53).

11   **Cēfi wæs hāten** See §186.1. (Cefi's title *ealdorbisceop* means he was a *pagan* high priest.)

19   **godo** = *godu* nom. pl. neut. Pagan gods are neuter, while the Christian God is masculine.

þæs wordum ōþur cyninges wita and ealdormann geþafunge
25 sealde, and tō þǣre sprǣce fēng and þus cwæð: 'þyslīc mē is
gesewen, þū cyning, þis andwearde līf manna on eorðan tō
wiðmetenesse þǣre tīde þe ūs uncūð is: swylc swā þū æt swǣsendum sitte mid þīnum ealdormannum and þegnum on wintertīde,
and sīe fȳr onǣlæd and þīn heall gewyrmed, and hit rīne and snīwe
30 and styrme ūte; cume an spearwa and hrædlīce þæt hūs þurhflēo,
cume þurh ōþre duru in, þurh ōþre ūt gewīte. Hwæt, hē on þā tīd þe
hē inne bið ne bið hrinen mid þȳ storme þæs wintres; ac þæt bið ān
ēagan bryhtm and þæt lǣsste fæc, ac hē sōna of wintra on þone
winter eft cymeð. Swā þonne þis monna līf tō medmiclum fæce
35 ætȳweð; hwæt þǣr foregange, oððe hwæt þǣr æfterfylige, wē ne
cunnun. For ðon gif þēos nīwe lār ōwiht cūðlicre ond gerisenlicre
brenge, þæs weorþe is þæt wē þǣre fylgen.' þeossum wordum
gelīcum ōðre aldormen and ðæs cyninges geþeahteras sprǣcan.

þā gēn tōætȳhte Cēfi and cwæð, þæt hē wolde Paulīnus þone
40 bisceop geornlīcor gehȳran be þām Gode sprecende þām þe hē
bodade. þā hēt se cyning swā dōn. þā hē þā his word gehȳrde, þā
clypode hē and þus cwæð: 'Geare ic þæt ongeat, þæt ðæt nōwiht
wæs þæt wē beēodan; for þon swā micle swā ic geornlīcor on þām
bīgange þæt sylfe sōð sōhte, swā ic hit lǣs mētte. Nū þonne ic
45 openlīce ondette, þæt on þysse lāre þæt sylfe sōð scīneð þæt ūs mæg
þā gyfe syllan ēcre ēadignesse and ēces līfes hǣlo. For þon ic þonne
nū lǣre, cyning, þæt þæt templ and þā wīgbedo, þā ðe wē būton
wæstmum ǣnigre nytnisse hālgodon, þæt wē þā hraþe forlēosen ond
fȳre forbærnen.' Ono hwæt, hē þā se cyning openlīce ondette þām
50 biscope ond him eallum, þæt hē wolde fæstlīce þām dēofolgildum
wiðsacan ond Crīstes gelēafan onfōn.

---

24 **þæs wordum . . . wita** 'To that one's words another counsellor of the King'.

25 **tō þǣre sprǣce fēng** 'took up the discussion', i.e. 'took the floor'.

25–6 **mē is gesewen** 'seems to me' (literally 'is seen by me').

27 **swylc swā** (more usually *swylce swā*) + subj. means 'as if'. The poignant simile introduced here is the subject of Wordsworth's sixteenth Ecclesiastical Sonnet, but the poet misconstrues the terms of the comparison. The anonymous counsellor compares the flight of a sparrow through a hall with the life of men on earth (*þis andwearde līf manna on eorðan*). Wordsworth thinks the comparison is with 'the human Soul . . . / While in the Body lodged, her warm abode'.

37 **þæs weorþe is þæt wē** 'it is worthy of that, (namely) that we . . .'. The pleonastic *þæs* anticipates the following clause (§148).

37–8 **þeossum wordum gelīcum** 'in words like these'.

41 **hē** i.e. Cefi.

43–4 **swā micle swā ic geornlīcor . . . swā ic . . . lǣs** 'the more eagerly I . . . the less I', literally 'by so much as I more eagerly . . . so I less'.

48 **þæt wē þā** *þæt* conj. repeats the first *þæt* in l. 47; *þā* is a recapitulatory pronoun (§148).

Mid þȳ þe hē þā se cyning from þǣm foresprecenan biscope
sōhte ond āhsode heora hālignesse þe hēo ǣr bicodon, hwā ðā
wīgbed ond þā hergas þāra dēofolgilda mid heora hegum þe hēo
55 ymbsette wǣron, hēo ǣrest āīdligan ond tōweorpan scolde, þā
ondsworede hē: 'Efne ic. Hwā mæg þā nū, þā þe ic longe mid
dysignesse beēode, tō bysene ōðerra monna gerisenlecor tōweorpan, þonne ic seolfa þurh þā snytro þe ic from þǣm sōðan Gode
onfēng?' Ond hē ðā sōna from him āwearp þā īdlan dysignesse þe
60 hē ǣr beēode, ond þone cyning bæd þæt hē him wǣpen sealde ond
stōdhors þæt hē meahte on cuman ond dēofolgyld tōweorpan, for
þon þām biscope heora hālignesse ne wæs ālȳfed þæt hē mōste
wǣpen wegan ne elcor būton on mȳran rīdan. þā sealde se cyning
him sweord þæt hē hine mid gyrde ond nom his spere on hond ond
65 hlēop on þæs cyninges stēdan ond tō þǣm dēofulgeldum ferde. þa
ðæt folc hine þā geseah swā gescyrpedne, þā wēndon hēo þæt hē
teola ne wiste, ac þæt hē wēdde. Sōna þæs þe hē nēalēhte tō þǣm
herige, þā scēat hē mid þȳ spere þæt hit sticode fæste on þǣm
herige, ond wæs swīðe gefēonde þǣre ongytenesse þæs sōðan
70 Godes bīgonges. Ond hē ðā hēht his gefēran tōweorpan ealne
þone herig ond þā getimbro, ond forbærnan. Is sēo stōw gȳt
æteawed gū þāra dēofulgilda nōht feor ēast from Eoforwīcceastre
begeondan Deorwentan þǣre ēa, ond gēn tō dæge is nemned
Gōdmundingahām, þǣr se biscop þurh ðæs sōðan Godes inbryrd-
75 nesse tōwearp ond fordyde þā wīgbed þe hē seolfa ǣr gehālgode.

Ðā onfēng Ēadwine cyning mid eallum þǣm æðelingum his
þēode ond mid micle folce Crīstes gelēafan ond fulwihte bæðe þȳ
endlyftan gēare his rīces.

52–3   **biscope . . . heora hālignesse** 'high priest . . . of their religion' (i.e. Cefi).
53   **hēo** nom. pl. refers to Edwin's pagan subjects.
55   **hēo** recapitulatory pronoun (§148).
56   **þā . . . þā þe** 'those (pagan things) . . . which'.
57   **ōðerra monna** gen. pl. Translate 'for other men'.
67   **teola ne wiste** 'did not perceive well', i.e. 'was not in his right mind'.
Sōna þæs þe 'Immediately after', i.e. 'As soon as'. For *þæs þe*, see §168 *þæs* (*þe*) and §174.2.
71–2   **Is sēo stōw . . . dēofulgilda** 'The place formerly of the idols is still pointed out.'

Bede's Account of the Poet Cædmon

Cædmon is the first English poet whose name is known to us. Yet, to say that English poetry begins with him would be misleading, for when Cædmon's Anglo-Saxon forebears migrated from the Continent to the British Isles, they brought with them a well-developed poetic tradition shaped by centuries of oral improvisation in the Germanic north. Not only was this tradition rich with legends and characters, but it also included a highly formalized poetic diction and an intricate system of versification. In the normal course of Christianization this tradition would have been displaced by new subjects and new styles derived from Christian Latin poetry, for medieval missionaries were usually anxious and intolerant in the presence of established pagan traditions. But the ancient Germanic style survived in England, for Cædmon demonstrated soon after the conversion that the old heroic tradition of poetry could be put in the service of Christian themes. The result of this wedding of Christian matter with pagan Germanic style is that unique blend of Christian and heroic elements which characterizes so much Old English poetry, such as *The Dream of the Rood*, *Andreas*, *Exodus*, and *The Fates of the Apostles*.

Bede's account in his *Ecclesiastical History* of how the illiterate cattle-herd Cædmon suddenly began singing of Christian subjects in the old heroic measure seems to capture that moment in history when two cultures began to merge. To the Anglo-Saxons, Cædmon's miracle was his instantaneous acquisition of the power of poetic composition through the agency of a divinely inspired dream. Modern readers familiar with the widely documented folk-motif of people suddenly acquiring poetic powers through a dream may dismiss Bede's story as essentially fabulous, but the nine-line *Hymn* itself attests to a minor miracle of literary history that cannot be denied: in these polished verses Cædmon demonstrated that the ancient heroic style was not incompatible with Christian doctrine and hence was worthy of preservation. The old Germanic

A Guide to Old English, Eighth Edition. Bruce Mitchell and Fred C. Robinson.
© 2012 Bruce Mitchell and Fred C. Robinson. Published 2012 by Blackwell Publishing Ltd.

poets had hailed Woden with such terms as 'Father of Armies' (cf. Old Norse *Herja-faðir* in the *Edda*) and Cædmon skilfully adapts the formula to make it reflect the Christian term for God, 'Father of Glory' (Ephesians 1:17): *Wuldorfæder*. Kings were referred to as 'guardians of the realm' in traditional Anglo-Saxon poetry (cf. *Brytenrīces weard* and *rīces weard* in other Old English poems) and Cædmon appropriates the term for Christian poetry by altering it to *heofonrīces Weard*. The metre and dignity of the phrases remain intact; only the spiritual quality has been changed. Through such expedients as these the ancient style was saved from disrepute and extinction, so that even poets who wished to treat subjects not specifically Christian (such as the poets of *Finnsburg*, *Maldon*, or *The Battle of Brunanburh*) were free to do so without reproach from the Christian establishment. And monastic scribes did not hesitate to preserve poems written in the old measure, thus making it possible for us to read today specimens of the earliest English poetry which would otherwise have been lost forever.

The text of the Old English Bede presented here is that of the Bodleian Library MS Tanner 10, although we have occasionally adopted a reading from one of the other manuscripts when these seemed preferable to Tanner, most notably in lines 32, 35, 36, 47, and 69.

In ðeosse abbudissan mynstre wæs sum brōðor syndriglīce mid godcundre gife gemǣred ond geweorðad, for þon hē gewunade gerisenlīce lēoð wyrcan, þā ðe tō æfæstnisse ond tō ārfæstnisse belumpen, swā ðætte, swā hwæt swā hē of godcundum stafum
5   þurh bōceras geleornode, þæt hē æfter medmiclum fæce in scopgereorde mid þā mǣstan swētnisse ond inbryrdnisse geglængde ond in Engliscgereorde wel geworht forþbrōhte. Ond for his lēoþsongum monigra monna mōd oft tō worulde for hogdnisse ond tō geþēodnisse þæs heofonlican līfes onbærnde
10 wæron. Ond ēac swelce monige ōðre æfter him in Ongelþēode ongunnon æfæste lēoð wyrcan; ac nænig hwæðre him þæt gelīce dōn meahte, for þon hē nales from monnum ne þurh mon gelǣred wæs, þæt hē þone lēoðcræft leornade, ac hē wæs godcundlīce gefultumed ond þurh Godes gife þone songcræft onfēng. Ond hē
15 for ðon næfre nōht lēasunge ne īdles lēoþes wyrcan meahte, ac

---

1   **ðeosse abbudissan** Abbess Hild, the woman in charge of the monastic community where Cædmon became a brother. Cf. ll. 49, 61.

9   **geþēodnisse** 'joining' of the heavenly life. This very awkward sense is probably the result of confusion (by the translator or a scribe) between Latin *appetitum* 'longing' (which is what Bede wrote in the Latin version) and *appictum*, past participle of *appingo* 'join'. 'Longing for the heavenly life' is what Bede intended.

efne þā ān þā ðe tō æfæstnesse belumpon, ond his þā æfestan tungan gedafenode singan.

Wæs hē se mon in weoruldhāde geseted oð þā tīde þe hē wæs gelȳfdre ylde, ond hē næfre nænig lēoð geleornade. Ond hē for þon
20 oft in gebēorscipe, þonne þær wæs blisse intinga gedēmed, þæt hēo ealle sceolden þurh endebyrdnesse be hearpan singan, þonne hē geseah þā hearpan him nēalēcan, þonne ārās hē for scome from þæm symble ond hām ēode tō his hūse. þā hē þæt þā sumre tīde dyde, þæt hē forlēt þæt hūs þæs gebēorscipes ond ūt wæs gongende
25 tō nēata scipene, þāra heord him wæs þære neahte beboden, þā hē ðā þær in gelimplicre tīde his leomu on reste gesette ond onslēpte, þā stōd him sum mon æt þurh swefn ond hine hālette ond grētte ond hine be his noman nemnde: 'Cedmon, sing mē hwæthwugu.' þā ondswarede hē ond cwæð: 'Ne con ic nōht singan; ond ic for þon of
30 þeossum gebēorscipe ūt ēode, ond hider gewāt, for þon ic nāht singan ne cūðe.' Eft hē cwæð, se ðe mid hine sprecende wæs: 'Hwæðre þū meaht mē singan.' þā cwæð hē: 'Hwæt sceal ic singan?' Cwæð hē: 'Sing mē frumsceaft.' þā hē ðā þās andsware onfēng, þā ongon hē sōna singan in herenesse Godes Scyppendes þā fers ond þā
35 word þe hē næfre gehȳrde, þāra endebyrdnes þis is:

> Nū wē sculon herigean   heofonrīces Weard,
> Meotodes meahte   ond his mōdgeþanc,
> weorc Wuldorfæder,   swā hē wundra gehwæs,
> ēce Drihten,   ōr onstealde.
> 40 Hē ærest sceōp   eorðan bearnum
> heofon tō hrōfe,   hālig Scyppend.
> þā middangeard   monncynnes Weard,
> ēce Drihten,   æfter tēode
> fīrum foldan,   Frēa ælmihtig.

45 þā ārās hē from þæm slæpe, ond eal þā þe hē slæpende song fæste in gemynde hæfde, ond þæm wordum sōna monig word in

---

16–17   **his þā æfestan . . . singan** '(it) befitted that pious tongue of his to sing' (§212).

19–28   **Ond hē . . . nemnde** See §153. For the semantic distinction between *þonne* and *þā*, see §168 *þonne* 2.

20   **þonne þær . . . gedēmed, þæt** 'whenever it was deemed (that there was) cause for merriment there, (namely) that . . .'. The sense of the Latin is different: 'whenever it would be decided, for the sake of merriment, that . . .'. The OE translator mistook the Latin ablative *causā* for a nominative.

21   **hēo** 'they'. So also in ll. 55, 101, 104, 106, 107, and 114.

25   **þāra heord** 'the care of which'.

32   **þū meaht mē singan** 'thou canst sing to me'. See §207 and fn.

45   **eal þā þe** 'all those (things) which'.

þæt ilce gemet Gode wyrðes songes tōgeþēodde. Þā cōm hē on
morgenne tō þǣm tūngerēfan, þe his ealdormon wæs; sægde him
hwylce gife hē onfēng. Ond hē hine sōna tō þǣre abbudissan
50 gelǣdde ond hire þā cȳðde ond sægde. Þā hēht hēo gesomnian
ealle þā gelǣredestan men ond þā leorneras, ond him ondweardum
hēt secgan þæt swefn ond þæt lēoð singan, þæt ealra heora
dōme gecoren wǣre, hwæt oððe hwonon þæt cuman wǣre. Þā
wæs him eallum gesegen, swā swā hit wæs, þæt him wǣre from
55 Drihtne sylfum heofonlic gifu forgifen. Þā rehton hēo him ond
sǣgdon sum hālig spell ond godcundre lāre word; bebudon him
þā, gif hē meahte, þæt hē in swinsunge lēoþsonges þæt gehwyrfde. Þā hē ðā hæfde þā wīsan onfongne, þā ēode hē hām
tō his hūse, and cwōm eft on morgenne, ond þȳ betstan lēoðe
60 geglenged him āsong ond āgeaf þæt him beboden wæs.

Ðā ongan sēo abbudisse clyppan ond lufigean þā Godes gife in
þǣm men; ond hēo hine þā monade ond lǣrde þæt hē woruldhād
ānforlēte ond munuchād onfēnge; ond hē þæt wel þafode. Ond hēo
hine in þæt mynster onfēng mid his gōdum, ond hine geþēodde tō
65 gesomnunge þāra Godes þēowa, ond hēht hine lǣran þæt getæl þæs
hālgan stæres ond spelles. Ond hē eal þā hē in gehȳrnesse geleornian
meahte mid hine gemyndgade, ond swā swā clǣne nēten eodorcende
in þæt swēteste lēoð gehwerfde. Ond his song ond his lēoð wǣron
swā wynsumu tō gehȳranne þætte þā seolfan his lārēowas æt his
70 mūðe wreoton ond leornodon. Song hē ǣrest be middangeardes
gesceape ond bī fruman moncynnes ond eal þæt stær Genesis (þæt
is sēo ǣreste Moyses booc); ond eft bī ūtgonge Israhēla folces of
Ægypta londe ond bī ingonge þæs gehātlandes ond bī ōðrum
monegum spellum þæs hālgan gewrites canōnes bōca, ond bī Crīstes
75 menniscnesse ond bī his þrōwunge ond bī his ūpāstīgnesse in

---

47 **Gode wyrðes songes** 'of song dear to God'. Since this sentence tells us that
Cædmon immediately added more verses to the nine lines he composed in his dream
(and presumably sang this completed version to the Abbess and her scholars), we should
regard the text which we now call 'Cædmon's Hymn' as only a fragment, the opening
lines of a much longer poem in praise of the Creator.

51–2 **him ondweardum** 'with them present', i.e. 'in their presence'.

52–3 **þæt ealra . . . cuman wǣre** 'so that it might be determined by the judgement
of them all what (that poetic skill was) or whence it had come'. The Old English is
awkward and unidiomatic because the translator is following his Latin source too
slavishly.

59–60 **ond þȳ . . . wæs** 'and sang and gave back to them what had been dictated to
him, adorned with the best poetry'.

66 **eal þā** 'all those things which'.

67 **mid hine gemyndgade** 'remembered within himself', i.e. 'mulled over'.

67 **swā swā . . . eodorcende** Biblical commentators explain that the ruminating
animals of Leviticus 11:3 symbolize pious men meditating on God.

69 **þā seolfan his lārēowas** 'the same ones his teachers', i.e. 'his very
teachers'.

heofonas ond bī þæs Hālgan Gāstes cyme ond þāra apostola
lāre; ond eft bī þǣm dæge þæs tōweardan dōmes ond bī fyrhtu þæs
tintreglican wiites ond bī swētnesse þæs heofonlecan rīces hē monig
lēoð geworhte. Ond swelce ēac ōðer monig be þǣm godcundan
80 fremsumnessum ond dōmum hē geworhte. In eallum þǣm hē
geornlīce gēmde þæt hē men ātuge from synna lufan ond māndǣda,
ond tō lufan ond tō geornfulnesse āwehte gōdra dǣda; for þon hē
wæs se mon swīþe æfæst ond regollecum þēodscipum ēaðmōdlīce
underþēoded. Ond wið þǣm þā ðe in ōðre wīsan dōn woldon, hē
85 wæs mid welme micelre ellenwōdnisse onbærned; ond hē for ðon
fægre ænde his līf betȳnde ond geendade.

For þon þā ðǣre tīde nēalǣcte his gewitenesse ond forðfōre, þā
wæs hē, fēowertȳnum dagum ǣr, þæt hē wæs līchomlicre untrymnesse þrycced ond hefgad, hwæðre tō þon gemetlīce þæt hē ealle
90 þā tīd meahte ge sprecan ge gongan. Wæs þǣr in nēaweste
untrumra monna hūs, in þǣm heora þēaw wæs þæt hēo þā untrumran ond þā ðe æt forðfōre wǣron inlǣdan sceoldon, ond him þǣr
ætsomne þegnian. þā bæd hē his þegn on ǣfenne þǣre neahte þe
hē of worulde gongende wæs þæt hē in þǣm hūse him stōwe
95 gegearwode þæt hē gerestan meahte. þā wundrode se þegn for
hwon hē ðæs bǣde, for þon him þūhte þæt his forðfōr swā nēah ne
wǣre; dyde hwæðre swā swā hē cwæð ond bibēad. Ond mid þȳ hē
ðā þǣr on reste ēode, ond hē gefēonde mōde sumu þing mid him
sprecende ætgædere ond glēowiende wæs, þe þǣr ǣr inne wǣron,
100 þā wæs ofer middeneaht þæt hē frægn hwæðer hēo ǣnig hūsl inne
hæfdon. þā ondswarodon hēo ond cwǣdon: 'Hwylc þearf is ðē
hūsles? Ne þīnre forþfōre swā nēah is, nū þū þus rōtlīce ond þus
glædlīce tō ūs sprecende eart.' Cwǣð hē eft: 'Berað mē hūsl tō.' þā
hē hit þā on honda hæfde, þā frægn hē hwæþer hēo ealle smolt mōd
105 ond būton eallum incan blīðe tō him hæfdon. þā ondswaredon hȳ
ealle ond cwǣdon þæt hēo nǣnigne incan tō him wiston, ac hēo ealle
him swīðe blīðemōde wǣron; ond hēo wrixendlīce hine bǣdon þæt
hē him eallum blīðe wǣre. þā ondswarade hē ond cwæð: 'Mīne
brōðor, mīne þā lēofan, ic eom swīðe blīðemōd tō ēow ond tō eallum

---

87   **nēalǣcte** '(it) drew near' (§212).

88   **þæt hē wæs** In a clumsy effort to control the sentence the translator introduces
these three redundant words (§148). Ignore them when rendering into modern English.

89   **tō þon gemetlīce þæt** 'to that (extent) moderately that', i.e. 'sufficiently
moderately that'.

92   **æt forðfōre** 'at (the point of) death'.

99   **þe** The antecedent is *him* in l. 98. See §163.4.

104–5   **smolt mōd . . . hæfdon** 'had a serene and friendly spirit without any rancour
towards him'.

106   **nǣnigne incan . . . wiston** 'felt no rancour towards him'.

110 Godes monnum.' Ond swā wæs hine getrymmende mid þȳ
heofonlecan wegneste ond him ōðres līfes ingong gegearwode. Þā
gȳt hē frægn, hū nēah þǣre tīde wǣre þætte þā brōðor ārīsan
scolden ond Godes lof rǣran ond heora ūhtsong singan. Þā
ondswaredon hēo: 'Nis hit feor tō þon.' Cwæð hē: 'Teala: wuton
115 wē wel þǣre tīde bīdan.' Ond þā him gebæd ond hine gesegnode
mid Crīstes rōdetācne, ond his hēafod onhylde tō þām bolstre, ond
medmicel fæc onslēpte, ond swā mid stilnesse his līf geendade. Ond
swā wæs geworden þætte swā swā hē hlūttre mōde ond bilwitre ond
smyltre wilsumnesse Drihtne þēode, þæt hē ēac swylce swā smylte
120 dēaðe middangeard wæs forlǣtende, ond tō his gesihðe becwōm.
Ond sēo tunge, þe swā monig hālwende word in þæs Scyppendes
lof gesette, hē ðā swelce ēac þā ȳtmæstan word in his herenisse, hine
seolfne segniende ond his gāst in his honda bebēodende, betȳnde.
Ēac swelce þæt is gesegen þæt hē wǣre gewis his seolfes forðfōre,
125 of þǣm wē nū secgan hȳrdon.

121–3 **Ond sēo tunge . . . betȳnde** The awkward change of subject from *sēo tunge*
to *hē* is the result of a mistranslation, the Latin ablative *illāque linguā* having been
mistaken for a nominative. The Anglo-Saxon translator ought to have written *mid þǣre
tungan*: 'And with the tongue that had composed so many salutary words . . . he then
concluded his last words', etc.

124–5 **is gesegen . . . of þǣm wē** 'it is seen from what we'.

The Goths and Boethius: Prose and Verse from the Introduction to King Alfred's Boethius Translation

Among the works which King Alfred the Great is said to have translated into Old English as part of his educational programme (see selection 5 above and §251.2) was the philosophical treatise *De consolatione philosophiae* by the Roman consul Boethius. One of the most popular writings of the entire Middle Ages, the *Consolation* was composed after its author had been falsely accused of treason and imprisoned by Theodoric, King of the Ostrogoths and ruler in Rome. The injustice which occasioned Boethius' search for consolation and the pathos of his subsequent murder give the work a special force and immediacy, and so it is not surprising that King Alfred prefaced his translation with an account of the historical background of Boethius' fate: the invasion of Rome by the Goths, Theodoric's rise to power, and the imprisonment and execution of the philosopher. Nor is it surprising that this prefatory material should be recounted first in prose and then in poetry, for much of the Latin *Consolatio* itself is written in verse, and the Old English translator has left both prose and poetic renditions of each verse passage. The existence of these dual versions of the same material affords the modern student an excellent means of becoming acquainted with the form and style of Old English poetry. In the selection which follows (containing King Alfred's preface to his translation) one sees some of the most prominent features which differentiate the language of Old English poetry from that of Old English prose: the fondness for apposition, complicated syntax, colourful compounds like *sincgeofa* and *wēalāf*, and a wealth of poetic synonyms for concepts like warrior and war.

The text for the prose (*a*) is from Bodleian Library MS 180 (except that *mið* [l. 2], *and* [l. 3], *gelæst* [l. 9], and *arwyrða wæs on* [l. 26] have been changed to *mid*, *hīþā*, *gelæste*, and *ārwyrða on*). The

A Guide to Old English, Eighth Edition. Bruce Mitchell and Fred C. Robinson.
© 2012 Bruce Mitchell and Fred C. Robinson. Published 2012 by Blackwell Publishing Ltd.

text for the verse (*b*) is from Bodleian Library MS Junius 12, except that *Gotene* [l. 5], *ealla* [l. 12], *Godena* [l. 38], *weorðmynða* [l. 51], and *hererine* [l. 71] have been changed to *Gotena, ealle, Gotena, weorðmynda*, and *hererinc.*

(*a*)

On ðǣre tīde ðe Gotan of Sciððiu mǣgðe wið Rōmāna rīce gewin ūp āhōfon and mid heora cyningum, Rǣdgōta and Eallerīca wǣron hātne, Rōmāne burig ābrǣcon, hī þā eall Ītālia rīce þæt is betwux þām muntum and Sicilia þām ēalonde in anwald gerehton; and þā
5 æfter þām foresprecenan cyningum þēodrīc fēng tō þām ilcan rīce. Se þēodrīc wæs Amulinga. Hē wæs Crīsten, þēah hē on þām Arriāniscan gedwolan þurhwunode. Hē gehēt Rōmanum his frēondscipe, swā þæt hī mōstan heora ealdrihta wyrðe bēon, ac hē þā gehāt swīðe yfele gelǣste, and swīðe wrāðe geendode mid
10 manegum māne. Þæt wæs, tō ēacan ōðrum unārīmedum yflum, þæt hē Iōhannes þone pāpan hēt ofslēan.

Þā wæs sum consul, þæt wē heretoha hātað, Bōētius wæs gehāten, se wæs in bōccræftum and on woruldþēawum se rihtwīsesta. Sē þā ongeat þā manigfealdan yfel þe se cyning
15 Ðeodrīc wið þǣm crīstenandōme and wið þām Rōmaniscum witum dyde. Hē þā gemunde þāra ēðnessa and þāra ealdrihta þe hī under þām cāserum hæfdon, heora ealdhlāfordum. Þā ongan hē smēagan and leornigan on him selfum hū hē þæt rīce þām unrihtwīsan cyninge āferran mihte and on ryhtgelēaffulra and on
20 rihtwīsra anwealde gebringan. Sende þā dīgellīce ǣrendgewritu tō

2–3   **Rǣdgōta ... hātne** '(who) were called Rǣdgota and Alaric'. See §186. The Anglo-Saxon writer is here telescoping (and confusing) actual events. The heathen Goth Radagaesius (*Rǣdgota*) was killed in battle five years before Alaric led his troops into Rome.

4   **in anwald gerehton** 'subjugated'.

4–5   The Anglo-Saxon writer here skips over many years and several reigns. Theodoric did not become King of Italy until A.D. 493 – more than eighty years after the death of Alaric.

5   **foresprecenan** The ending -*an* stands here for dat. pl. -*um*; see §65; cf. *gesceapþēotan* 11(g)/4.

8   **heora ealdrihta wyrðe bēon** 'be in possession of their ancient rights', i.e. 'regain their ancient rights'.

11   **Iōhannes ... ofslēan** In 525 Theodoric had Pope John I cast into prison, where he languished and soon died.

12–13   **Bōētius wæs gehāten** '(who) was named Boethius'.

14   **Sē þā ongeat** 'he then perceived'.

16–17   **hī under ... ealdhlāfordum** *cāserum* and *ealdhlāfordum* are in apposition: 'they had under the emperors, their ancient lords'.

17–19   **þā ongan hē ... āferran mihte** 'then he began to study and take thought within himself as to how he might remove the kingdom from the unrighteous king'. Actually Boethius denied that he had betrayed the King in this way, but his enemies claimed that he had written treasonous letters to the eastern emperor Justin I.

þām kāsere tō Constentinopolim, þǣr is Crēca hēahburg and heora
cynestōl, forþām se kāsere wæs heora ealdhlāfordcynnes. Bǣdon
hine þæt hē him tō heora crīstendōme and tō heora ealdrihtum
25 gefultumede. Þā þæt ongeat se wælhrēowa cyning Ðēodrīc, þā hēt
hē hine gebringan on carcerne and þǣrinne belūcan. Þā hit ðā
gelomp þæt se ārwyrða on swā micelre nearanessa becōm, þā wæs
hē swā micle swīðor on his mōde gedrēfed swā his mōd ǣr swīðor tō
þām woruldsǣlþum gewunod wæs; and hē þā nānre frōfre beinnan
30 þām carcerne ne gemunde, ac hē gefēoll niwol ofdūne on þā flōr, and
hine āstrehte swīðe unrōt, and ormōd hine selfne ongan wēpan and
þus singend cwæð.

(*b*)

Hit wæs geāra iū,   ðætte Gotan ēastan
of Sciððia   sceldas lǣddon,
þrēate geþrungon   þēodlond monig;
setton sūðweardes   sigeþēoda twā.
5 Gotena rīce   gēarmǣlum wēox.
Hæfdan him gecynde   cyningas twēgen,
Rǣdgōd and Alerīc;   rīce geþungon.
þā wæs ofer Muntgīop   monig ātyhted
Gota gylpes full,   gūðe gelysted,
10 folcgewinnes;   fana hwearfode
scīr on sceafte;   scēotend þōhton
Ītālia   ealle gegongan,
lindwīgende.   Hī gelǣstan swuā
efne from Muntgīop   oð þone mǣran wearoð,
15 þǣr Sīcilia   sǣstrēamum in
ēglond micel,   ēðel mǣrsað.
Ðā wæs Rōmāna   rīce gewunnen,
ābrocen burga cyst;   beadurincum wæs
Rōm gerȳmed;   Rǣdgōt and Alerīc
20 fōron on ðæt fæsten;   flēah cāsere

(*a*) 22–4 **Bǣdon hine þæt . . . gefultumede** '[the letters] bade him that he should
assist them (to return) to their Christianity and their ancient laws'. 'Their Christianity'
is the orthodox Christianity that the Romans were practising when the Arian Christian,
Theodoric, conquered them. Late in his reign he began to persecute them.

25–6 **hēt hē hine . . . belūcan** Active infinitives to be translated as passive: 'he
commanded him to be brought to prison and to be locked up therein'. See §161.

27–9 **wæs hē swā micle swīðor . . . gewunod wæs** 'he was so much the more
troubled in his mind in as much as his mind had previously been accustomed to earthly
blessings'.

(*b*) 4 **sigeþēoda twā** i.e. Rǣdgota's army and Alaric's.

mid þām æþelingum   ūt on Crēcas.
Ne meahte þā sēo wēalāf   wīge forstandan
Gotan mid gūðe;   giōmonna gestrīon
sealdon unwillum   eþelweardas,
25   hālige āðas.   Wæs gehwæðeres waa.
þēah wæs magorinca   mōd mid Crēcum,
gif hī lēodfruman   læstan dorsten.
Stōd þrāge on ðām;   þēod wæs gewunnen
wintra mænigo,   oðþæt wyrd gescrāf
30   þæt þe þēodrīce   þegnas and eorlas
hēran sceoldan.   Wæs se heretēma
Crīste gecnōden;   cyning selfa onfēng
fulluhtþēawum   Fægnodon ealle
Rōmwara bearn   and him recene tō
35   friðes wilnedon.   Hē him fæste gehēt,
þæt hȳ ealdrihta   ælces mōsten
wyrðe gewunigen   on þære welegan byrig,
ðenden God wuolde,   þæt hē Gotena geweald
āgan mōste.   Hē þæt eall ālēag.
40   Wæs þæm æþelinge   Arriānes
gedwola lēofre   þonne Drihtnes æ.
Hēt Iōhannes,   gōdne pāpan,
hēafde behēawan;   næs ðæt hærlic dæd!
Ēac þā wæs unrīm   ōðres mānes,
45   þæt se Gota fremede   gōdra gehwilcum.
Ðā wæs rīcra sum   on Rōme byrig
āhefen heretoga,   hlāforde leof,
þenden cynestōle   Crēacas wīoldon.
þæt wæs rihtwīs rinc;   næs mid Rōmwarum
50   sincgeofa sēlla   siððan longe;
hē wæs for weorulde wīs,   weorðmynda georn,
beorn bōca glēaw.   Bōītius

---

25   **Wæs gehwæðeres waa** 'It was an affliction (to the Romans) in both respects'
(to have to give both their wealth and their sacred oaths to the conquerors).

26–7   **þēah wæs … dorsten** The conquered Romans looked to the Greeks in
the Eastern Empire (in Constantinople) for rescue from their Gothic invaders. Under
duress they had given 'holy vows' for allegiance to the Goths (l. 25a), 'Yet the heart of
the (Roman) warriors was with the Greeks if they would dare to help the leader of the
people (i.e. the exiled Roman emperor).'

28   **Stōd þrāge on ðām** 'it remained thus for a time'.

31–2   **Wæs … Crīste gecnōden** 'was committed to Christ'.

34–5   **and him … wilnedon** 'and soon petitioned for peace from him'.

48   **þenden … wīoldon** 'while the Greeks controlled the throne'. Theodoric's
predecessor, Odowacer, had acknowledged the overlordship of the eastern emperor in
Constantinople, as had Theodoric when he became king, but Theodoric's relations with
the Greek emperor became strained in the closing years of his reign.

se hæle hātte;   sē þone hlīsan geþāh.
Wæs him on gemynde   mǣla gehwilce
55 yfel and edwit   þæt him elðēodge
kyningas cȳðdon;   wæs on Crēacas hold,
gemunde þāra āra   and ealdrihta,
þe his eldran mid him   āhton longe,
lufan and lissa.   Angan þā listum ymbe
60 ðencean þearflīce,   hū hē ðider meahte
Crēcas oncerran,   þæt se cāsere eft
anwald ofer hī   āgan mōste.
Sende ǣrendgewrit   ealdhlāfordum
dēgelīce,   and hī for Drihtne bæd
65 ealdum trēowum,   ðæt hī æft tō him
cōmen on þā ceastre,   lēte Crēca witan
rǣdan Rōmwarum,   rihtes wyrðe
lēte þone lēodscipe.   Đā þā lāre ongeat
Đēodrīc Amuling   and þone þegn oferfēng,
70 hēht fæstlīce   folcgesīðas
healdon þone hererinc;   wæs him hrēoh sefa,
ege from ðām eorle.   Hē hine inne hēht
on carcerne   clūstre belūcan.
Þā wæs mōdsefa   miclum gedrēfed
75 Bōētius.   Brēac longe ǣr
wlencea under wolcnum;   hē þȳ wyrs meahte
þolian þā þrāge,   þā hīo swā þearl becōm.
Wæs þā ormōd eorl,   āre ne wēnde,
ne on þām fæstene   frōfre gemunde;
80 ac hē neowol āstreaht   niðer ofdūne
fēol on þā flōre;   fela worda spræc
forþōht ðearle;   ne wēnde þonan ǣfre
cuman of ðǣm clammum.   Cleopode tō Drihtne
geōmran stemne,   gyddode þus.

---

58 **þe his eldran . . . longe** 'that his elders long had among themselves'.

64–5 **hī for Drihtne . . . trēowum** 'asked them for the sake of God, (and because of their) ancient beliefs'.

66–8 **lēte Crēca . . . lēodscipe** 'let Greek senators worthy of rule, let that nation have control over the Romans'.

71–2 'his (Boethius') mind was troubled, (in him was) fear of the leader (Theodoric)'.

72–3 **Hē hine . . . belūcan** 'He commanded him to be locked in a prison, in a cell.' *Hine* is the object of *belūcan*. See §161.

76–7 **hē þȳ wyrs . . . becōm** 'the worse he was able to endure so harsh a time when it befell'.

84 The lament which follows is the first of the Latin metres of Boethius, translated into OE.

11

Riddles

Riddles are popular in most cultures, and their presence in the Bible (e.g. Judges 14:14) and in Greek tragedy reminds us that they are more than a children's game. In the Old English period scholars like Aldhelm and Symphosius composed verse riddles in polished Latin hexameters, and the anonymous vernacular riddles presented here are sometimes based upon Latin originals. Indeed, since the Latin riddles are accompanied by their solutions (as the Old English are not), this correspondence between Latin and vernacular riddles has sometimes helped scholars to solve some knottier enigmas among the latter.

The Old English verse riddles fall into two basic types. In one type the riddler speaks in his own voice (*Ic seah, Wiga is*) describing the subject of the riddle and asking the reader to guess the answer. The description is in vague, metaphorical, deliberately misleading language with much anthropomorphizing of animals and inanimate objects. In the second type, which is equally mystifying and indirect in expression, the subject of the riddle describes itself (*Ic eom, Ic wæs*) and asks to be identified. The idea of inanimate objects speaking about themselves was not unfamiliar to Anglo-Saxons, for when they inscribed a weapon or piece of jewellery to mark possession, they often put the statement in the first person singular, as if the object itself were speaking. Thus the inscription on the King Alfred Jewel says, 'Ælfred mec het gewyrcan' ('Alfred had me made'), while another says, 'Ædred mec ah, Eanred me agrof' ('Ædred owns me, Eanred engraved me'). This habit of mind culminates in one of the grandest achievements of Old English poetry, *The Dream of the Rood* (selection 14 below), in which the cross on which Christ died recounts with agony and awe the grim details of the crucifixion. Indeed, two of the riddles printed below (texts *n* and *o*) appear to have 'cross' as their solution and so may be seen as seed stages of *The Dream of the Rood*.

The subjects of the riddles presented here are various: farm implements, weapons, animals and insects, items of food or drink,

A Guide to Old English, Eighth Edition. Bruce Mitchell and Fred C. Robinson.
© 2012 Bruce Mitchell and Fred C. Robinson. Published 2012 by Blackwell Publishing Ltd.

the Bible, the natural world. Casual and intimate, they are brief meditations on familiar objects. They are often light but rarely humorous, and sometimes the riddlers seem to forget their primary purpose of creating a puzzle as they become absorbed in the curiosities and quaint perplexities which become apparent in the objects around us when we reflect on them. They explore paradoxes both in the object described and in the language describing the objects. Thoughtful probings of both the milieu and the language, the riddles reveal quirks and moods of the Anglo-Saxons quite unlike anything we find in their other poetry.

The riddles presented here have been selected from the Exeter Book, a tenth-century manuscript which contains some of the best poetry left by the Anglo-Saxons. It is a rich poetic miscellany containing nearly a hundred verse riddles and more than thirty different poems including *The Wife's Lament*, *The Wanderer*, *The Seafarer*, and *Wulf and Eadwacer*, all four of which appear below (selections 15, 16, 17, and 19).

(*a*)

Wer sæt æt wīne mid his wīfum twām
ond his twēgen suno ond his twā dohtor,
swāse gesweostor, ond hyra suno twēgen,
frēolico frumbearn; fæder wæs þǣr inne
5 þāra æþelinga ǣghwæðres mid,
ēam ond nefa. Ealra wǣron fīfe
eorla ond idesa insittendra.

(*b*)

Wiht cwōm gongan þǣr weras sǣton
monige on mæðle, mōde snottre;
hæfde ān ēage ond ēaran twā,
ond twēgen fēt, twelf hund hēafda,
5 hrycg ond wombe ond honda twā,
earmas ond eaxle, ānne swēoran
ond sīdan twā. Saga hwæt ic hātte.

Riddle a The solution is 'Lot and his offspring'. Genesis 19:30–8 tells how Lot's two daughters, after an incestuous union with their father, each gave birth to a son. The riddle explores the complicated, overlapping kinship relations which resulted. Emendations: *Wer* for MS *wær* (l. 1), *hyra* for *hyre* (l. 3).

 6 **ēam ond nefa** This refers to the sons in relation to each other. Since Lot is the father both of the daughters and their two sons, his four offspring are siblings. Therefore each son is both uncle and nephew to each other.

Riddle b The solution is 'one-eyed garlic pedlar'. Emendation: *hrycg* for MS *hryc* (l. 5).

(c)

Moððe word fræt. Mē þæt þūhte
wrǣtlicu wyrd, þā ic þæt wundor gefrægn,
þæt se wyrm forswealg wera gied sumes,
þēof in þȳstro, þrymfæstne cwide
5 ond þæs strangan staþol. Stælgiest ne wæs
wihte þȳ glēawra, þē hē þām wordum swealg.

(d)

Hrægl mīn swīgað, þonne īc hrūsan trede,
oþþe þā wīc būge, oþþe wado drēfe.
Hwīlum mec āhebbað ofer hæleþa hyht
hyrste mīne ond þēos hēa lyft,
5 ond mec þonne wīde wolcna strengu
ofer folc byreð. Frætwe mīne
swōgað hlūde ond swinsiað,
torhte singað, þonne ic getenge ne bēom
flōde ond foldan, fērende gæst.

Riddle c Since the first word identifies the subject of the poem, this is not a riddle so much as an exploration of a paradox: the insect devours learning but is none the wiser for it. The whimsical meditation is enhanced by delicate puns on words like (*for*)*swelgan* (which can mean 'understand' as well as 'consume') and *cwide* (which can mean 'morsel' as well as 'statement').

  5 **þæs strangan staþol** 'the (very) foundation of that mighty (utterance)', i.e. the vellum on which the *cwide* is written. *Staþol* could also refer to the intellectual content of the statement (cf. *staþolung* 'ordinance').

  5–6 **ne . . . swealg** 'was not a whit the wiser in that he had swallowed (comprehended) those words'. For the *þȳ . . . þē* construction, see §167(*a*) and §177.3 and cf. 11(*k*)/11–12 note.

Riddle d The solution is 'swan'. The Anglo-Saxons believed that when the swan was aloft the feathers in its wings produced music. In typical riddling fashion the poet refers to the swan's feathers with vague, metaphorical words like *hrægl* 'raiment', *hyrst* 'equipment', and *frætwe* 'trappings'.

  5 **wolcna strengu** 'The strength of the skies' is the wind.

(*e*)

Nīs mīn sele swīge,   ne ic sylfa hlūd
ymb dryhtsele;   unc dryhten scōp
sīþ ætsomne.   Ic eom swiftra þonne hē,
þrāgum strengra,   hē þreohtigra.
5 Hwīlum ic mē reste;   hē sceal rinnan forð.
Ic him in wunige   ā þenden ic lifge;
gif wit unc gedǣlað,   mē bið dēað witod.

(*f*)

Ic eom weorð werum,   wīde funden,
brungen of bearwum   ond of bēorghleoþum,
of denum ond of dūnum.   Dæges mec wǣgun
feþre on lifte,   feredon mid liste
5 under hrōfes hlēo.   Hæleð mec siþþan
baþedan in bydene.   Nū ic eom bindere
ond swingere,   sōna weorpe
esne tō eorþan,   hwīlum ealdne ceorl.
Sōna þæt onfindeð,   se þe mec fēhð ongēan
10 ond wið mægenþisan   mīnre genǣsteð,
þæt hē hrycge sceal   hrūsan sēcan,
gif hē unrǣdes   ǣr ne geswīceð.
Strengo bistolen,   strong on sprǣce,
mægene binumen,   nāh his mōdes geweald,
15 fōta ne folma.   Frige hwæt ic hātte,
ðe on eorþan swā   esnas binde,
dole æfter dyntum   be dæges lēohte.

Riddle e   The solution is 'fish in the river'. The poet delights in the paradox of the silent, versatile fish in the rushing stream, which, though seemingly insubstantial, is essential to the fish's life and will survive its death. Emendations: *ymb dryhtsele; unc dryhten scōp* for MS *ymb unc . . . dryht scop* (l. 2), *swiftra* for *swistre* (l. 3), *rinnan* for *yrnan* (l. 5).

   1   *Eom* is understood before *ic*.

Riddle f   The solution is 'mead', an alcoholic beverage made from honey. Emendations: *bēorghleoþum* (l. 2) for MS *burghleoþum*, *weorpe* for *weorpere* (l. 7), *esne* for *efne* (l. 8).

   3   **Dæges** 'by day'. See §190.5.

   4   **feþre** The wings of the bees who gather the honey from which mead is made and bring it to the hive (*under hrōfes hlēo*).

   17   **be dæges lēohte** i.e. the morning after.

(g)

Ic þā wiht geseah   wǣpnedcynnes.
Geoguðmyrþe grǣdig   him on gafol forlēt
ferðfriþende   fēower wellan
scīre scēotan   on gesceapþēotan.
5   Mon maþelade,   se þe mē gesǣgde:
'Sēo wiht, gif hīo gedȳgeð,   dūna briceð;
gif hē tōbirsteð,   bindeð cwice.'

(h)

Agob is mīn noma   eft onhwyrfed;
ic eom wrǣtlic wiht   on gewin sceapen.
Þonne ic onbūge,   ond mē on bōsme farcð
ǣtren onga,   ic bēom eallgearo
5   þæt ic mē þæt feorhbealo   feor āswāpe.
Siþþan mē se waldend,   se mē þæt wite gescōp,
leoþo forlǣteð,   ic bēo lengre þonne ǣr,
oþþæt ic spǣte   spilde geblonden
ealfelo āttor   þæt ic ǣr gegēap.
10   Ne tōgongeð þæs   gumena hwylcum,
ǣnigum ēaþe   þæt ic þǣr ymb sprice,
gif hine hrīneð   þæt mē of hrife flēogeð,
þæt þone māndrinc   mægne gecēapaþ,
fullwer fæste   fēore sīne.
15   Nelle ic unbunden   ǣnigum hȳran
nymþe searosǣled.   Saga hwæt ic hātte.

Riddle g   The solution is 'bull calf' or 'young ox'. In related contemporary Latin riddles, the poets make much of the calf's drinking milk from the 'four fountains' of the mother. Emendation: *Geoguðmyrþe* for MS *geoguð myrwe* (l. 2).

2   **him on gafol** 'as a gift to himself'.

6–7   i.e. while alive the bull will break the ground by pulling a plough through it, while the dead bull's hide will provide leather thongs that can tie people up. The shift from the grammatical gender of *wiht* in l. 6 to the logical gender of a bull in l. 7 may be intentionally mystifying.

Riddle h   The solution 'bow' is spelled backwards in the first word in the riddle. (This reverse spelling of *boga* was corrupted to *agof* by an inattentive scribe.) The riddler speaks first of the arrow as it passes into the bosom of the arched bow as the bowman takes aim (ll. 2–5) and then of the arrow's flight to its target after it is released (ll. 6–9). Emendations besides *Agob* are *on* for MS *of* (l. 3), *gegēap* for *geap* (l. 9), and *fullwer* for *full wer* (l. 14).

2   **on gewin sceapen** A characteristic riddler's double meaning: the bow is created in the toil and strife of the arrowsmith's shop; it is also given its (arched) shape in the course of battle when the bowman bends it.

5   **þæt ic mē . . . āswāpe** 'that I may remove that mortal danger (the arrow) far from me'.

6   **se mē . . . gescōp** 'who caused me that pain' (i.e. by bending the bow).

11   The noun clause *þæt ic . . . sprice* is the subject of the verb *tōgongeð*.

(j)

Ic wæs wǣpen, wiga.   Nū mec wlonc þeceð
geong hagostealdmon   golde ond sylfore,
wōum wīrbogum.   Hwīlum weras cyssað;
hwīlum ic tō hilde   hlēoþre bonne
5   wilgehlēþan;   hwīlum wycg byreþ
mec ofer mearce;   hwīlum merehengest
fereð ofer flōdas   frætwum beorhtne;
hwīlum mægða sum   mīnne gefylleð
bōsm bēaghroden;   hwīlum ic on bordum sceal,
10   heard, hēafodlēas,   behlȳþed licgan;
hwīlum hongige   hyrstum frætwed,
wlitig on wāge,   þǣr weras drincað,
frēolic fyrdsceorp.   Hwīlum folcwigan
on wicge wegað,   þonne ic winde sceal
15   sincfāg swelgan   of sumes bōsme;
hwīlum ic gereordum   rincas laðige
wlonce tō wīne;   hwīlum wrāþum sceal
stefne mīnre   forstolen hreddan,
flȳman fēondsceaþan.   Frige hwæt ic hātte.

Riddle j The subject of the riddle, a horn, is described variously as a weapon and fighter
(while still growing on the animal's head), as an ornamental drinking horn, and as a wind
instrument (used to summon warriors to battle or to the wine-drinking, or to sound the
alarm after a robbery). Emendations: *on* supplied in ll. 9 and 14; *wrāþum* for MS *wraþþum*
(l. 17).

3 **Hwīlum weras cyssað** Supply *mec*. Men kiss the horn when they put their lips
to it either to blow it or drink from it.

6–7 **hwīlum . . . beorhtne** Again, *mec* is understood.

9–10 **hwīlum . . . licgan** 'at times I must lie on the tables, hard, headless,
plundered' – presumably plundered of its contents (mead) after its lid ('head') has been
removed.

13–14 **Hwīlum . . . wegað** *Mec* is understood.

(*k*)

Mec on þissum dagum   dēadne ofgēafon
fæder ond mōdor;   ne wæs mē feorh þā gēn,
ealdor in innan.   þā mec ān ongon,
welhold mēge,   wēdum þeccan,
5 hēold ond freoþode,   hlēosceorpe wrāh
swā ārlīce   swā hire āgen bearn,
oþþæt ic under scēate,   swā mīn gesceapu wæron,
ungesibbum wearð   ēacen gæste.
Mec sēo friþemæg   fēdde siþþan,
10 oþþæt ic āwēox,   wīddor meahte
siþas āsettan.   Hēo hæfde swæsra þȳ læs
suna ond dohtra,   þȳ hēo swā dyde

Riddle k   The cuckoo leaves its egg in the nest of other birds and flies away, leaving the foster mother to hatch and feed the fledgling along with her own brood. As the young cuckoo gains strength, it often evicts the fledglings who were hatched with it. The subject of this riddle became a legendary example of ingratitude, as in the Fool's observation in *King Lear* I. iv. 235: 'The Hedgesparrow fed The Cuckoo so long that it had it head bit off by it young.' Emendations: *ofgēafon* for MS *ofgeafum* (l. 1), *ān* supplied in l. 3, *þeccan* for *weccan* (l. 4), *swā ārlīce* for *nearlīce* (l. 6).

1   **on þissum dagum** 'in these days', i.e. 'recently'.
dēadne the egg is only apparently dead, of course.
7   **swā mīn gesceapu wæron** 'as was my destiny'.
8   **ungesibbum . . . gæste** 'among (nestlings) unrelated to me I became great with life'.
11–12   **Hēo hæfde swæsra þȳ læs . . . þȳ hēo swā dyde** A correlative use of the instrumental *þȳ*: '*by so much* as she did so . . . she had *so much* the fewer of her own dear ones.' This idiom survives in MnE 'the bigger they come, the harder they fall' and 'the more the merrier'. The word *the* in these constructions is a survival of OE *þȳ*. See §167(*a*) and 177.3 and cf. 11(*c*)/5–6 and 12/312–13.

(*l*)

Ic seah wrǣtlice   wuhte fēower
samed sīþian;   swearte wǣran lāstas,
swaþu swīþe blacu.   Swift wæs on fōre,
fuglum framra;   flēag on lyfte,
5   dēaf under ȳþe.   Drēag unstille
winnende wiga   se him wegas tǣcneþ
ofer fǣted gold   fēower eallum.

(*m*)

Wiga is on eorþan   wundrum ācenned
dryhtum tō nytte,   of dumbum twām
torht ātyhted,   þone on tēon wigeð
fēond his fēonde.   Forstrangne oft
5   wīf hine wrīð;   hē him wel hēreð,
þēowaþ him geþwǣre,   gif him þegniað
mǣgeð ond mǣcgas   mid gemete ryhte,
fēdað hine fægre;   hē him fremum stēpeð
līfe on lissum.   Lēanað grimme
10   þām þe hine wloncne   weorþan lǣteð.

Riddle l The solution is two fingers and a thumb writing with a quill pen. Emendations: *flēag on* for *fleotgan* (l. 4) and *wegas* for *wægas* (l. 6).

4   **fuglum framra** 'more swift among the birds', i.e. swifter *in the air* (when the hand darts from the writing surface to the inkwell and back again) than it is when moving across the vellum page, writing. Perhaps also with a glance back at the time when the quill was a feather in the wing of a living bird flying through the air. See §191.5.

5   **under ȳþe** i.e. into the ink.
Drēag 'persevered'.

7   **fǣted gold** 'ornamented gold' (of the illuminated manuscript page).

Riddle m The solution is 'fire'. Emendations: *forstrangne* for MS *fer strangne* (l. 4), and *þām* supplied in l. 10.

3–4   **þone on . . . fēonde** 'which foe bears against foe to his injury'. A reference apparently, to the use of fire in warfare.

5–7   **hē him wel . . . mǣcgas** 'he obeys them well, compliant, he serves them, if women and men serve him . . .'.

(*n*)

Ic seah in healle,   þær hæleð druncon,
on flet beran   fēower cynna,
wrǣtlic wudutrēow   ond wunden gold,
sinc searobunden,   ond seolfres dæl
5   ond rōde tācn,   þæs ūs tō roderum ūp
hlǣdre rǣrde,   ǣr hē helwara
burg ābrǣce.   Ic þæs bēames mæg
ēaþe for eorlum   æþelu secgan;
þær wæs hlin ond āc   ond se hearda īw
10   ond se fealwa holen: frēan sindon ealle
nyt ætgædre;   naman habbað ānne,
wulfhēafedtrēo;   þæt oft wǣpen ābæd
his mondryhtne,   māðm in healle,
goldhilted sweord.   Nū mē þisses gieddes
15   ondsware ȳwe,   se hine on mēde
wordum secgan   hū se wudu hātte.

Riddle n   The solution appears to be 'cross', although some details of the riddle remain obscure. In early Christian tradition the cross was thought to have been made from four different kinds of wood, the specific kinds varying from one authority to another. (See W. O. Stevens *The Cross in the Life and Literature of the Anglo-Saxons* Yale Studies in English 22 (New Haven, 1904), p. 10; reprinted in *The Anglo-Saxon Cross* with a new preface by Thomas D. Hill (New Haven, 1977), pp. 14–15). Ceremonial crosses were ornamented with gold, silver, and jewels. See *The Dream of the Rood* below. Emendations: *healle* for MS *heall* (l. 1), *āc* for *acc* (l. 9).

2–3   **fēower ... wudutrēow** 'wondrous forest-wood of four different kinds'.

5–6   **rōde tācn ... rǣrde** 'the sign of the cross of the One (who) raised for us a ladder to the heavens'. Following *þæs* the relative *þe* is either understood or has been omitted by a scribe.

6–7   **ǣr hē ... ābrǣce** i.e. the harrowing of Hell.

12   **wulfhēafedtrēo** 'outlaw-tree', i.e. 'gallows'. The Anglo-Saxons regularly referred to the cross as gallows.

12–14   **þæt oft ... sweord** 'that often received from his lord (owner) a weapon ...'.

15   **se hine on mēde** 'he who takes it upon himself' or 'he who presumes'.

(*o*)

Ic eom lēgbysig,   lāce mid winde,
bewunden mid wuldre,   wedre gesomnad,
fūs forðweges   fȳre gebysgad,
bearu blōwende,   byrnende glēd.
5 Ful oft mec gesīþas   sendað æfter hondum,
þæt mec weras ond wīf   wlonce cyssað.
þonne ic mec onhæbbe,   hī onhnīgaþ tō mē
monige mid miltse;   þǣr ic monnum sceal
ȳcan ūpcyme   ēadignesse.

(*p*)

Ic wæs fǣmne geong,   feaxhār cwene,
ond ænlic rinc   on āne tīd;
flēah mid fuglum   ond on flōde swom,
dēaf under ȳþe   dēad mid fiscum,
5 ond on foldan stōp;   hæfde ferð cwicu.

Riddle o This too is conjectured to be a riddle about the cross, or more specifically about *ān bēam*, the Old English words which can mean 'a cross', 'a tree', and 'a log'. Emendation: *hī onhnīgaþ* for MS *ond hi on hin gaþ* (l. 7).
   2 **bewunden mid wuldre** 'girded with splendour' (probably with reference to foliage).
   3 **fūs forðweges** 'ready for the way hence'. Usually this phrasing means 'ready for death', and this is the log's fate when afflicted by fire.
   5 **sendað æfter hondum** 'pass from hand to hand'.
   8–9 **þǣr ic . . . ēadignesse** 'there I shall increase the ascendancy of happiness among men'.

Riddle p This riddle went unsolved for many years but the answer 'barnacle goose' has now been persuasively proposed by Daniel Donoghue in *Words and Works*, ed. P. S. Baker and N. Howe (Toronto, 1998), 45–58. Emendation: *ferð* for MS *forð* (l. 5).
   2 **on āne tīd** 'at the same time', 'all at once'.

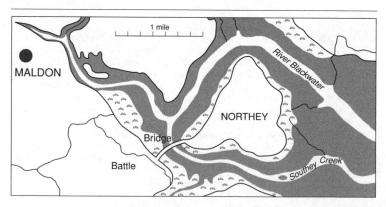

Plan of the Battle of Maldon in 991. From David Hill *An Atlas of Anglo-Saxon England* (Basil Blackwell, 1981), p. 64.

The Battle of Maldon

In August of the year 991 marauding Vikings sailed up the river Blackwater (then called 'Pante') and beached their ships on an island not far from the town of Maldon. The English ealdorman, Byrhtnoth, called out the local levy and, combining with this force the warriors from his own personal retinue, marched to the river-bank across from the island and confronted the Viking army. The ensuing battle (which is reported in the Anglo-Saxon Chronicle entry for 991 printed above in selection 7) is the subject of the poem which we are about to read.

The Battle of Maldon is the story of a military disaster suffered by the English in the course of their long and losing struggle against Scandinavian invaders. (Since 980 the Viking fleets had been raiding Southampton, Thanet, and elsewhere, and in the second decade of the eleventh century they seized the English throne.) The Anglo-Saxon king who presided over this prolonged humiliation of the English was Æthelræd (dubbed by later chroniclers 'the Unready'[1]), whose reign seems to have been characterized by demoralization in the military and, if a famous sermon by Archbishop Wulfstan is to be believed, in the populace as a whole. It is against this unhappy background that the battle of Maldon is fought by the Englishmen and celebrated by the poet. The poem is about how men bear up when things go wrong. The fighting men at Maldon, no less than those at Balaklava and Dunkirk, triumph in this test of character in a manner of which Englishmen have always been especially proud. The Anglo-Saxons who fight to the bitter end are portrayed by the poet as glorious in defeat, and their valour redeems the honour of their country. The poet of course idealizes the actual battle; his verses are poetry, not history.

To understand the action of the poem, and especially the action in ll. 62–99, one must have some idea of the geography of the battle.

---

[1] The name *Æðelræd* means 'noble counsel'. The sobriquet *unræd* means 'no counsel', i.e. 'folly'. 'Unready' is an inaccurate modernization of *unræd*.

(See map on p. 248, which shows the site which most scholars agree to be the likeliest location of the battle.) The Vikings occupy the island now called Northey, and Byrhtnoth's Anglo-Saxons array themselves across the water along the river-bank. At high tide the island is completely surrounded by water, but when the tide recedes (l. 72), an elevated road or causeway (called a *bricg* in ll. 74 and 78) is exposed, thus providing access to the island from the mainland. When the two armies first confront each other, the tide is in and the causeway is submerged (ll. 64–71). When the tide goes out, the Vikings begin to file across the causeway to the mainland, but the Anglo-Saxons block their progress from the narrow passageway to the shore (ll. 72–83). Seeing that they are at a serious disadvantage, the Vikings ask Byrhtnoth to order his troops to stand back and allow the invaders free passage to the shore (ll. 84–8). Byrhtnoth rashly agrees to give the enemy this advantage (ll. 89–95), and the battle begins.

Many of the English participants in the battle are named in the poem. (The poet seems to know nothing of the individual identities of the Vikings.) Extant documents from the period allow us to identify some of those mentioned, and it is to be assumed that all were actual Englishmen who were known to the poet's audience. Modern readers need to concern themselves with only the most important of these: the hero of the poem, Byrhtnoth (about whom a great deal is known), and his king, Æthelræd the Unready. We should also bear in mind the names of the cowardly sons of Odda: Godric, Godwig, and Godwine. Any other persons named in the poem can be assumed to be members of the Anglo-Saxon defending force – most likely members of Byrhtnoth's personal retinue, since the *fyrd*-men are generally left anonymous.

The Old English manuscript leaves containing *The Battle of Maldon* were destroyed by fire in 1731. Fortunately, a man named David Casley made a copy of the poem a few years before the fire and this copy is the basis for the present edition, except that modern conventions of punctuation, capitalization, word-division, verse-lineation, and long-vowel marking are introduced, and the following emendations are adopted: *tō hige* for MS *t hige* (l. 4), *þā* for *þ* (l. 5), *þām* for *þætam* (l. 10), *wīge* for *w . . . ge* (l. 10), *randas* for *randan* (l. 20), *hilde* for *. . ulde* (l. 33), *wē* for *þe* (l. 61), *feohte* for *fohte* (l. 103), *grimme gegrundene* for *gegrundene* (l. 109), *wearð* for *weard* (l. 113), *wearð* for *wærd* (l. 116), *gestandan* for *ge stundan* (l. 171), *Geþancie* for *ge þance* (l. 173), *wearð* for *wurdon* (l. 186), *mearh* for *mear* (l. 188), *ærndon* for *ærdon* (l. 191), *Godwine* for *godrine* (l. 192), *þearfe* for *þære* (l. 201), *forlǣtan* for *for lætun*

(l. 208), *ǣgðer* for *ægder* (l. 224), *wrǣce* for *wrece* (l. 257), *lǣge* for
lege (l. 279), *crincgan* for *crintgan* (l. 292), *Forð þā* for *forða* (l. 297),
sunu for *suna* (l. 298), *geþrange* for *geþrang* (l. 299), *oðþæt* for *od þæt*
(l. 324), *gūðe* for *gude* (l. 325).

brocen wurde.

Hēt þā hyssa hwæne   hors forlǣtan,
feor āfȳsan,   and forð gangan,
hicgan tō handum   and tō hige gōdum.
5 þā þæt Offan mæg   ǣrest onfunde,
þæt se eorl nolde   yrhðo geþolian,
hē lēt him þā of handon   lēofne flēogan
hafoc wið þæs holtes,   and to þǣre hilde stōp;
be þām man mihte oncnāwan   þæt se cniht nolde
10 wācian æt þām wīge,   þā hē tō wǣpnum fēng.
Ēac him wolde Ēadrīc   his ealdre gelǣstan,
frēan tō gefeohte,   ongan þā forð beran
gār tō gūþe.   Hē hæfde gōd geþanc
þā hwīle þe hē mid handum   healdan mihte
15 bord and brād swurd;   bēot hē gelǣste
þā hē ætforan his frēan   feohtan sceolde.
    Ðā þǣr Byrhtnōð ongan   beornas trymian,
rād and rǣdde,   rincum tǣhte
hū hī sceoldon standan   and þone stede healdan,
20 and bæd þæt hyra randas   rihte hēoldon
fæste mid folman,   and ne forhtedon nā.
þā hē hæfde þæt folc   fægere getrymmed,
hē līhte þā mid lēodon   þǣr him lēofost wæs,

1   The opening lines of the poem are lost. They must have told how the Anglo-Saxon
leader Byrhtnoth heard of the Vikings' arrival, gathered his troops, and led them to the
river shore where they could challenge the invaders.
2   The subject of *Hēt* is Byrhtnoth, referred to as *se eorl* in l. 6. Cf. §161.
4   hicgan . . . gōdum 'to give thought to their hands and to virtuous courage', i.e.
to think about courage and about the handiwork through which they can display that
courage.
5–6   For the anticipatory *þæt* see §148.
7   handon = *handum*. *-on* for *-um* appears again in l. 23 (*lēodon*), l. 129 (*Denon*),
l. 270 (*hwīlon*), l. 306 (*wordon*), etc. This is a feature of late OE.
14   þā hwīle þe 'while, as long as' (so also in ll. 83, 235, and 272).
17–24   In ll. 17–21 Byrhtnoth gives elementary instructions to the members of the
fyrd (ll. 140, 221), the home guard consisting of civilians who answer the call to arms
when the local leader summons them in an emergency. In ll. 23–4 Byrhtnoth dismounts
among his personal retinue of professional fighting men (*heorðwerod*), 'where it was most
agreeable to him' (*þār him lēofost wæs*).
20   hēoldon = *hēolden* The subjunctive plural ending of verbs is invariably spelled
-on in this poem rather than *-en*: e.g. *forgyldon* (l. 32), *dǣlon* (l. 33), *gangon* (l. 56), *syllon*
(l. 61), *ēodon* (l. 229). This coalescence in spelling is characteristic of late OE.

þǣr hē his heorðwerod   holdost wiste.

25   þā stōd on stæðe,   stīðlīce clypode
wīcinga ār,   wordum mǣlde,
se on bēot ābēad   brimlīþendra
ǣrænde tō þām eorle,   þǣr hē on ōfre stōd:
'Mē sendon tō þē   sǣmen snelle,

30   hēton ðē secgan   þæt þū mōst sendan raðe
bēagas wið gebeorge;   and ēow betere is
þæt gē þisne gārrǣs   mid gafole forgyldon,
þon wē swā hearde   hilde dǣlon.
Ne þurfe wē ūs spillan,   gif gē spēdaþ tō þām;

35   wē willað wið þam golde   grið fæstnian.
Gyf þū þat gerǣdest,   þe hēr rīcost eart,
þæt þū þīne lēoda   lȳsan wille,
syllan sǣmannum   on hyra sylfra dōm
feoh wið frēode,   and niman frið æt ūs,

40   wē willaþ mid þām sceattum   ūs tō scype gangan,
on flot fēran,   and ēow friþes healdan.'
    Byrhtnōð maþelode,   bord hafenode,
wand wācne æsc,   wordum mǣlde,
yrre and ānrǣd   āgēaf him andsware:

45   'Gehȳrst þū, sǣlida,   hwæt þis folc segeð?
Hī willað ēow tō gafole   gāras syllan,
ǣttrynne ord   and ealde swurd,
þā heregeatu   þe ēow æt hilde ne dēah.
Brimmanna boda,   ābēod eft ongēan,

50   sege þīnum lēodum   miccle lāþre spell,
þæt hēr stynt unforcūð   eorl mid his werode,
þe wile gealgean   eþel þysne,
Æþelrēdes eard,   ealdres mīnes,
folc and foldan.   Feallan sceolon

55   hǣþene æt hilde.   Tō hēanlic mē þinceð
þæt gē mid ūrum sceattum   tō scype gangon
unbefohtene,   nū gē þus feor hider
on ūrne eard   in becōmon.
Ne sceole gē swā sōfte   sinc gegangan;

---

30 **hēton ðē secgan** Cf. 5/1, 10(*a*)/72–3, etc., and ll. 62 and 101 below. Cf. §161.
31 **wið** 'in exchange for'. Cf. ll. 35, 39.
31–3 **betere . . . þon . . .** See §168 *þonne* 3(*c*). (*þon* = *þonne*.)
34 **gif gē . . . tō þām** 'If you are sufficiently rich for that (i.e. for the purpose of paying us off).'
38 **on hyra . . . dōm** 'according to their own stipulation'. Cf. 6/28.
50 **miccle lāþre spell** 'a much more unpleasant report (than they expect)'.

60 ūs sceal ord and ecg ǣr gesēman,
grim gūðplega, ǣr wē gofol syllon.'
    Hēt þā bord beran, beornas gangan,
þæt hī on þām ēasteðe ealle stōdon.
Ne mihte þǣr for wætere werod tō þām ōðrum;
65 þǣr cōm flōwende flōd æfter ebban,
lucon lagustrēamas. Tō lang hit him þūhte,
hwænne hī tōgædere gāras bēron.
Hī þǣr Pantan strēam mid prasse bestōdon,
Ēastseaxena ord and se æschere.
70 Ne mihte hyra ǣnig ōþrum derian,
buton hwā þurh flānes flyht fyl genāme.
Se flōd ūt gewāt; þā flotan stōdon gearowe,
wīcinga fela, wīges georne.
Hēt þā hæleða hlēo healdan þā bricge
75 wigan wīgheardne, se wæs hāten Wulfstān,
cāfne mid his cynne, þæt wæs Cēolan sunu,
þe ðone forman man mid his francan ofscēat
þe þǣr baldlīcost on þā bricge stōp.
    Þǣr stodon mid Wulfstāne wigan unforhte,
80 Ælfere and Maccus, mōdige twēgen,
þā noldon æt þām forda flēam gewyrcan,
ac hī fæstlīce wið ðā fȳnd weredon,
þā hwīle þe hī wǣpna wealdan mōston.
    Þā hī þæt ongēaton and georne gesāwon
85 þæt hī þǣr bricgweardas bitere fundon,
ongunnon lytegian þā lāðe gystas,
bǣdon þæt hī ūpgangan āgan mōston,
ofer þone ford faran, fēþan lǣdan.
    Ðā se eorl ongan for his ofermōde
90 ālȳfan landes tō fela lāþere ðēode.
Ongan ceallian þā ofer cald wæter

60–1 ǣr . . . ǣr . . . 'first . . . before . . .'.
  66 **lucon lagustrēamas** i.e. the rising tide submerges the causeway, completely encircling the island.
  67 **hwænne** 'when, until'. See §159, note 2.
  71 **hwā** 'someone'. Cf. 5/81.
  81 **þām forda** see §62. **flēam gewyrcan** 'flee, yield'.
  89–90 **ofermōde** 'pride'. The national pride and manly defiance which Byrhtnoth has expressed so eloquently in his answer to the Viking messenger (ll. 45–61) have been carefully noted by the invaders, who play on Byrhtnoth's *ofermōd* to persuade him to grant them free access to 'too much land' (*landes tō fela*). The poet acknowledges that Byrhtnoth makes a tactical error here, but at a time when many Anglo-Saxons are seen as cowardly, he probably half admires this display of rash pride.

Byrhtelmes bearn   (beornas gehlyston):
'Nū ēow is gerȳmed,   gāð ricene tō ūs,
guman tō gūþe;   God āna wāt
95   hwā þǣre wælstōwe   wealdan mōte.'
Wōdon þā wælwulfas   (for wætere ne murnon),
wīcinga werod,   west ofer Pantan,
ofer scīr wæter   scyldas wēgon,
lidmen tō lande   linde bǣron.
100 þǣr ongēan gramum   gearowe stōdon
Byrhtnōð mid beornum;   hē mid bordum hēt
wyrcan þone wīhagan,   and þæt werod healdan
fæste wið fēondum.   þā wæs feohte nēh,
tīr æt getohte.   Wæs sēo tīd cumen
105 þæt þǣr fǣge men   feallan sceoldon.
þǣr wearð hrēam āhafen,   hremmas wundon,
earn ǣses georn;   wæs on eorþan cyrm.
Hī lēton þā of folman   fēolhearde speru,
grimme gegrundene   gāras flēogan;
110 bogan wǣron bysige,   bord ord onfēng.
    Biter wæs se beadurǣs,   beornas fēollon
on gehwæðere hand,   hyssas lāgon.
Wund wearð Wulfmǣr,   wælrǣste gecēas,
Byrhtnōðes mǣg;   hē mid billum wearð,
115 his swustersunu,   swīðe forhēawen.
þǣr wearð wīcingum   wiþerlēan āgyfen.
Gehȳrde ic þæt Ēadweard   ānne slōge
swīðe mid his swurde,   swenges ne wyrnde,
þæt him æt fōtum fēoll   fǣge cempa;
120 þæs him his ðēoden   þanc gesǣde,
þām būrþēne,   þā hē byre hæfde.
Swā stemnetton   stīðhicgende
hysas æt hilde,   hogodon georne
hwā þǣr mid orde   ǣrost mihte
125 on fǣgean men   feorh gewinnan,
wigan mid wǣpnum;   wæl fēol on eorðan.
Stōdon stædefæste;   stihte hī Byrhtnōð,
bæd þæt hyssa gehwylc   hogode tō wīge
þe on Denon wolde   dōm gefeohtan.

---

92   **Byrhtelmes bearn** i. e. Byrhtnoth.

115   **swustersunu** The relationship between a man and his sister's son was peculiarly close in Germanic society (Tacitus comments on it in *Germania*), and so this opening scene of killing and vengeance reveals the Anglo-Saxons' adherence to ancient traditions of loyalty, both familial and military. Note that it is Byrhtnoth's personal chamberlain (*būrþegn*) who instantly avenges his leader's heavy loss.

130   Wōd þā wīges heard,   wǣpen ūp āhōf,
      bord tō gebeorge,   and wið þæs beornes stōp.
      Ēode swā ānrǣd   eorl tō þām ceorle,
      ægþer hyra ōðrum   yfeles hogode.
      Sende ðā se sǣrinc   sūþerne gār,
135   þæt gewundod wearð   wigena hlāford;
      hē scēaf þā mid ðām scylde,   þæt se sceaft tōbærst,
      and þæt spere sprengde,   þæt hit sprang ongēan.
      Gegremod wearð se gūðrinc;   hē mid gāre stang
      wlancne wīcing,   þe him þā wunde forgeaf.
140   Frōd wæs se fyrdrinc;   hē lēt his francan wadan
      þurh ðæs hysses hals,   hand wīsode
      þæt hē on þām fǣrsceaðan   feorh gerǣhte.
      Ðā hē ōþerne   ofstlīce scēat,
      þæt sēo byrne tōbærst;   hē wæs on brēostum wund
145   þurh ðā hringlocan,   him æt heortan stōd
      ætterne ord.   Se eorl wæs þē blīþra,
      hlōh þā, mōdi man,   sǣde Metode þanc
      ðæs dægweorces   þe him Drihten forgeaf.
         Forlēt þā drenga sum   daroð of handa,
150   flēogan of folman,   þæt sē tō forð gewāt
      þurh ðone æþelan   Æþelrēdes þegen.
      Him be healfe stōd   hyse unweaxen,
      cniht on gecampe,   se full cāflīce
      brǣd of þām beorne   blōdigne gār,
155   Wulfstānes bearn,   Wulfmǣr se geonga,
      forlēt forheardne   faran eft ongēan;
      ord in gewōd,   þæt sē on eorþan læg
      þe his þēoden ǣr   þearle gerǣhte.
      Ēode þā gesyrwed   secg tō þām eorle;

130   **wīges heard** evidently refers to some Viking, while *þæs beornes* (l. 131) refers to Byrhtnoth. The transition is so abrupt here that we might suspect the loss of a line or two introducing the Viking who is *wīges heard* 'bold in battle'.

134   **sūþerne gār** 'spear of southern make'. Vikings prized weapons produced in lands to the south of them, such as England and France.

135   **wigena hlāford** Byrhtnoth.

136–7   With a thrust of his shield Byrhtnoth knocks away the spear that the Viking had hurled into his body. Specifically, his shield breaks the spear-shaft in such a way that it 'forced out' (*sprengde*) the spear, which 'sprang back' (*sprang ongēan*) from the wound.

142   **feorh gerǣhte** 'reached the life'. That is, Byrhtnoth's hand guided the spear so that it reached (and thus extinguished) the life in the Viking. The phrase is strikingly Homeric. Cf. l. 226.

143   **Ðā hē . . . scēat** 'Then he (Byrhtnoth) swiftly pierced another (Viking).'

157   **sē** refers to the Viking who had wounded Byrhtnoth.

159   **gesyrwed secg** The 'armoured warrior' is yet another Viking.

160 hē wolde þæs beornes   bēagas gefecgan,
rēaf and hringas   and gerēnod swurd.
þā Byrhtnōð brǣd   bill of scēðe,
brād and brūneccg,   and on þā byrnan slōh.
Tō raþe hine gelette   lidmanna sum,
165 þā hē þæs eorles   earm āmyrde.
Fēoll þā tō foldan   fealohilte swurd;
ne mihte hē gehealdan   heardne mēce,
wǣpnes wealdan.   þā gȳt þæt word gecwæð
hār hilderinc,   hyssas bylde,
170 bæd gangan forð   gōde gefēran;
ne mihte þā on fōtum leng   fæste gestandan.
Hē tō heofenum wlāt:
'Geþancie þē,   ðēoda Waldend,
ealra þǣra wynna   þe ic on worulde gebād.
175 Nū ic āh, milde Metod,   mǣste þearfe
þæt þū mīnum gāste   gōdes geunne,
þæt mīn sāwul tō ðē   sīðian mōte
on þīn geweald,   þēoden engla,
mid friþe ferian.   Ic eom frymdi tō þē
180 þæt hī helscēaðan   hȳnan ne mōton.'
        Ðā hine hēowon   hǣðene scealcas
and bēgen þā beornas   þe him big stōdon,
Ælfnōð and Wulmǣr   bēgen lāgon,
ðā onemn hyra frēan   feorh gesealdon.
185 Hī bugon þā fram beaduwe   þe þǣr bēon noldon.
Þǣr wearð Oddan bearn   ǣrest on flēame,
Godrīc fram gūþe,   and þone gōdan forlēt
þe him mænigne oft   mearh gesealde;
hē gehlēop þone eoh   þe āhte his hlāford,
190 on þām gerǣdum   þe hit riht ne wæs,
and his brōþru mid him   bēgen ærndon,
Godwine and Godwīg,   gūþe ne gȳmdon,
ac wendon fram þām wīge   and þone wudu sōhton,
flugon on þæt fæsten   and hyra fēore burgon,

---

172   The second half of this line is missing. A few words may be lost, but since there
are other metrical irregularities in the poem (e.g. in ll. 45, 75, 183, 271) it is also possible
that this metrical defect is a feature of the later, looser style of *The Battle of Maldon*.
    173   **Geþancie þē** '(I) thank Thee.'
    179   **Ic eom frymdi tō þē** 'I am suppliant to Thee', i.e. 'I beg Thee.'
    180   **hī** acc. sg. fem. referring to *sāwul* (l. 177).
    190   **þe hit riht ne wæs** Either 'as it was not right (to do)' (see §168 s.v. *þe* 6), or
'which was not right' (assuming *þe hit* to be a compound relative introducing an adjective clause). Or *þe* may be a scribal error for *þēah* or *þēh* 'although', but in that case one
might expect the subjunctive.

195 and manna mā   þonne hit ænig mǣð wǣre,
gyf hī þā geearnunga   ealle gemundon
þe hē him tō duguþe   gedōn hæfde.
Swā him Offa on dæg   ǣr āsǣde
on þām meþelstede,   þā hē gemōt hæfde,
200 þæt þǣr mōdelīce   manega sprǣcon
þe eft æt þearfe   þolian noldon.
   þā wearð āfeallen   þæs folces ealdor,
Æþelrēdes eorl;   ealle gesāwon
heorðgenēatas   þæt hyra heorra læg.
205 þā ðǣr wendon forð   wlance þegenas,
unearge men   efston georne;
hī woldon þā ealle   ōðer twēga,
līf forlǣtan   oððe lēofne gewrecan.
Swā hī bylde forð   bearn Ælfrīces,
210 wiga wintrum geong,   wordum mælde,
Ælfwine þā cwæð,   hē on ellen spræc:
'Gemunu þā mǣla   þe wē oft æt meodo sprǣcon,
þonne wē on bence   bēot āhōfon,
hæleð on healle,   ymbe heard gewinn;
215 nū mæg cunnian   hwā cēne sȳ.
Ic wylle mīne æþelo   eallum gecȳþan,
þæt ic wæs on Myrcon   miccles cynnes;
wæs mīn ealda fæder   Ealhelm hāten,
wīs ealdorman,   woruldgesǣlig.
220 Ne sceolon mē on þǣre þēode   þegenas ætwītan
þæt ic of ðisse fyrde   fēran wille,
eard gesēcan,   nū mīn ealdor ligeð
forhēawen æt hilde.   Mē is þæt hearma mǣst;
hē wæs ǣgðer mīn mǣg   and mīn hlāford.'

198 **Swā him . . . āsǣde** 'Thus Offa had told him (earlier) in the day.' Evidently Byrhtnoth had called a meeting (*gemōt* l. 199) earlier that day to plan strategy with his *heorðwerod*, who had vowed to support him loyally in the field, as was their solemn obligation. See §237.

203–4 **ealle . . . heorðgenēatas** Byrhtnoth's personal retainers (*heorðgenēatas*), who would have been fighting close by him, could all see that their leader had fallen. Members of the *fyrd* fighting at a greater distance could not see this (ll. 239–42).

212 **Gemunu þā mǣla** '(I) remember the occasions.' Unexpressed subjects are entirely permissible in Old English when they can be readily inferred from the context (see §193.7), but their repeated use in direct discourse here (173, 212, 215) is probably a stylistic device aimed at suggesting the hurried speech of men talking to one another during the rush of battle.

215 **nū mæg . . . sȳ** 'now (one) can find out who is brave'. Cf. preceding note.

221 **fyrde** The aristocrat Ælfwine, kinsman of Byrhtnoth, identifies himself with the *fyrd*, the common militia. Distinctions between upper-class retainers and the levy are forgotten as aristocracy of rank is superseded by an aristocracy of courage.

225   þā hē forð ēode,   fǣhðe gemunde,
        þæt hē mid orde   ānne gerǣhte
        flotan on þām folce,   þæt sē on foldan læg
        forwegen mid his wǣpne.   Ongan þā winas manian,
        frȳnd and gefēran,   þæt hī forð ēodon.
230   Offa gemǣlde,   æscholt āscēoc:
        'Hwæt þū, Ælfwine, hafast   ealle gemanode
        þegenas tō þearfe,   nū ūre þēoden līð,
        eorl on eorðan.   Ūs is eallum þearf
        þæt ūre ǣghwylc   ōþerne bylde
235   wigan tō wīge,   þā hwīle þe hē wǣpen mæge
        habban and healdan,   heardne mēce,
        gār and gōd swurd.   Ūs Godrīc hæfð,
        earh Oddan bearn,   ealle beswicene.
        Wēnde þæs formoni man,   þā hē on mēare rād,
240   on wlancan þām wicge,   þæt wǣre hit ūre hlāford;
        forþan wearð hēr on felda   folc tōtwǣmed,
        scyldburh tōbrocen.   Ābrēoðe his angin,
        þæt hē hēr swā manigne   man āflȳmde!'
            Lēofsunu gemǣlde   and his linde āhōf,
245   bord tō gebeorge;   hē þām beorne oncwæð:
        'Ic þæt gehāte,   þæt ic heonon nelle
        flēon fōtes trym,   ac wille furðor gān,
        wrecan on gewinne   mīnne winedrihten.
        Ne þurfon mē embe Stūrmere   stedefæste hælǣð
250   wordum ætwītan,   nū mīn wine gecranc,
        þæt ic hlāfordlēas   hām sīðie,
        wende fram wīge,   ac mē sceal wǣpen niman,
        ord and iren.'   Hē ful yrre wōd,
        feaht fæstlīce,   flēam hē forhogode.
255   Dunnere þā cwæð,   daroð ācwehte,
        unorne ceorl,   ofer eall clypode,
        bæd þæt beorna gehwylc   Byrhtnōð wrǣce:
        'Ne mæg nā wandian   se þe wrecan þenceð
        frēan on folce,   ne for fēore murnan.'
260   Þā hī forð ēodon,   fēores hī ne rōhton;
        ongunnon þā hīredmen   heardlīce feohtan,
        grame gārberend,   and God bǣdon

---

239   **þæs** gen. obj. of *wēnan* anticipating the *þæt* clause in l. 240. See §148.
241   **felda** see §62.
242   **Ābrēoðe his angin** 'Damn his behaviour!'
255–9   The brief, simple speech of Dunnere befits his status as a 'simple churl' (*unorne
ceorl*), and yet its mere appearance here puts him in the company of the noblest men in
the region, all now united in common loyalty to the code of honour which requires that
fighting men avenge their slain leader or die in the attempt.

þæt hī mōston gewrecan   hyra winedrihten
and on hyra fēondum   fyl gewyrcan.

265 Him se gȳsel ongan   geornlīce fylstan;
hē wæs on Norðhymbron   heardes cynnes,
Ecglāfes bearn,   him wæs Æscferð nama.
Hē ne wandode nā   æt þām wīgplegan,
ac hē fȳsde forð   flān genehe;

270 hwīlon hē on bord scēat,   hwīlon beorn tǣsde,
æfre embe stunde   hē sealde sume wunde,
þā hwīle ðe hē wǣpna   wealdan mōste.
    þā gȳt on orde stōd   Ēadweard se langa,
gearo and geornful,   gylpwordum spræc

275 þæt hē nolde fleogan   fōtmǣl landes,
ofer bæc būgan,   þā his betera leg.
Hē bræc þone bordweall   and wið þā beornas feaht,
oðþæt hē his sincgyfan   on þām sǣmannum
wurðlīce wrec,   ǣr hē on wæle lǣge.

280 Swā dyde Æþerīc,   æþele gefēra,
fūs and forðgeorn,   feaht eornoste.
Sībyrhtes brōðor   and swīðe mænig ōþer
clufon cellod bord,   cēne hī weredon;
bærst bordes lǣrig,   and sēo byrne sang

285 gryrelēoða sum.   þā æt gūðe slōh
Offa þone sǣlidan,   þæt hē on eorðan fēoll,
and ðǣr Gaddes mǣg   grund gesōhte.
Raðe wearð æt hilde   Offa forhēawen;
hē hæfde ðēah geforþod   þæt hē his frēan gehēt,

290 swā hē bēotode ǣr   wið his bēahgifan
þæt hī sceoldon bēgen   on burh rīdan,
hāle tō hāme,   oððe on here cringcan,
on wælstōwe   wundum sweltan;
hē læg ðegenlīce   ðēodne gehende.

271 'Ever and anon he gave one (of the Vikings) a wound'. Since *st*- alliterates only with *st*- in the Germanic verse system, this line lacks alliteration altogether, but, like l. 282, it has rhyme to link the two half-lines. These lines anticipate the Middle English period, when rhyme displaces alliteration almost completely.

277 **Hē bræc þone bordweall** 'He penetrated the wall of shields.' Apparently Eadweard broke through the phalanx of the Vikings and fought individually with enemy warriors until he was overwhelmed and slain.

283 **cellod** occurs nowhere else, and its meaning is obscure. It is evidently an adjective describing the shield (*bord*).

285-6 **þā æt gūðe . . . sǣlidan** 'Then Offa struck that Viking in the fight so that he fell to the earth.' What Viking? It has been reasonably suggested that a line or two has been lost between ll. 283 and 284, telling us who it was whose shield's rim was broken (l. 284), and this person would be *þone sǣlidan* of l. 286.

295   Đā wearð borda gebræc.   Brimmen wōdon
        gūðe gegremode;   gār oft þurhwōd
        fæges feorhhūs.   Forð þā ēode Wīstān,
        þurstānes sunu,   wið þās secgas feaht;
        hē wæs on geþrange   hyra þrēora bana,
300   ær him Wīgelines bearn   on þām wæle læge.
        þær wæs stīð gemōt;   stōdon fæste
        wigan on gewinne,   wīgend cruncon,
        wundum wērige.   Wæl fēol on eorþan.
        Ōswold and Ēadwold   ealle hwīle,
305   bēgen þā gebrōþru,   beornas trymedon,
        hyra winemāgas   wordon bædon
        þæt hī þær æt ðearfe   þolian sceoldon,
        unwāclīce   wæpna nēotan.
        Bryhtwold maþelode,   bord hafenode
310   (se wæs eald genēat),   æsc ācwehte;
        hē ful baldlīce   beornas lærde;
        'Hige sceal þē heardra,   heorte þē cēnre,
        mōd sceal þē māre,   þē ūre mægen lȳtlað.
        Hēr līð ūre ealdor   eall forhēawen,
315   gōd on grēote.   Ā mæg gnornian
        se ðe nū fram þīs wīgplegan   wendan þenceð.
        Ic eom frōd fēores;   fram ic ne wille,
        ac ic mē be healfe   mīnum hlāforde,
        be swā lēofan men,   licgan þence.'
320   Swā hī Æþelgāres bearn   ealle bylde,
        Godrīc tō gūþe.   Oft hē gār forlēt,
        wælspere windan   on þā wīcingas,
        swā hē on þām folce   fyrmest ēode,
        hēow and hȳnde,   oðþæt hē on hilde gecranc.
325   Næs þæt nā se Godrīc   þe ðā gūðe forbēah

*   *   *

300   'before the son of Wigelin lay down in the carnage'. (The same use of reflexive pronoun with *licgan* appears in ll. 318–19 and need not be translated.) *Wīgelines bearn* seems clearly to refer to Wistan, but how can he be the son both of *þurstān* (l. 298) and *Wīgelin*? A metronymic is possible, Wigelin being Wistan's mother.

312–13   'Our resolve must be so much the firmer, our hearts so much the bolder, our courage so much the greater, by so much as our (physical) strength diminishes.' See §168 *þȳ* I.; cf. 11(*k*)/11–12 note.

325   The closing lines of the poem are lost. We know from other accounts of the battle that the Vikings were victorious.

The Ruin

'Where are those who lived before us?' In every age and culture people have raised this haunting question, especially when prompted to such thoughts by an ancient ruin or some other relic of the past. In both their poetry and their prose the Anglo-Saxons were very given to reflection on former civilizations and the people who built them, so much so that their language had a word for such meditation: *dūstscēawung* 'contemplation of the dust'. This theme occurs often as an incidental motif in longer works (e.g. *The Wanderer* ll. 73–110 and *Beowulf* ll. 2255–66), but *The Ruin* is an entire poem devoted to the depiction of an ancient ghost town and to the thoughts which the scene evokes.

The poet draws no explicit moral from his description of Roman ruins. He records rather the simple wonder with which the scene fills him: wonder at the ingenuity of the people who built the city, and wonder at the power of *wyrd* 'fate', which has laid it all waste. Although the poem is for the most part an admiring catalogue of artefacts and architecture, the objects described are all closely associated with the people who had made and used them. The poet marvels at how the builders conceived of such structures, he imagines how the inhabitants filled the city with life and joy, he muses over the fact that their gaze had fallen on the very objects he is studying, and he reflects on the powerful fate (*wyrd sēo swīþe*) that has swept them all into oblivion. Buildings and people alike have fallen (*crungon, gecrong*) and though the artefacts have survived their creators, their deteriorated state bears eloquent witness to the perishability of everything on earth. The transience of earthly things is emphasized by the repeated contrast between the ruins the poet sees and the city in its prime, which the poet re-creates with lively imagination. His details are so persuasive that some scholars have thought they could identify the city he describes as the Roman city of Bath, where thermal springs were skilfully channelled into stone baths much like those described in ll. 38–46. But other sites have also been suggested, and it could well be that the scene is a composite of various Roman ruins that the poet had seen.

A Guide to Old English, Eighth Edition. Bruce Mitchell and Fred C. Robinson.
© 2012 Bruce Mitchell and Fred C. Robinson. Published 2012 by Blackwell Publishing Ltd.

The poem survives in the Exeter Book (see selection 11, Riddles). Damage done to the later pages of the book have left *The Ruin* something of a ruin itself. Aside from a tentative reconstruction of l. 12, no effort is made to restore the damaged verses. Losses in the text are indicated by series of dots. Emendations include normalization of *þæs* to *þes* in ll. 9 and 30, deletion of *torras* (mechanically repeated from l. 3) in l. 4 following *hrīmgeat*, and the change of MS *gehēapen* to *gehēawen* (l. 12), *secgrof* to *secgrōfra* (l. 26), *rof* to *hrōf* (l. 31), and *gefrætweð* to *gefrætwed* (l. 33).

<blockquote>

Wrǣtlic is þes wealstān;   wyrde gebrǣcon
burgstede burston;   brosnað enta geweorc.
Hrōfas sind gehrorene,   hrēorge torras,
hrīmgeat berofen   hrīm on līme
5 scearde scūrbeorge   scorene, gedrorene,
ældo undereotone.   Eorðgrāp hafað
waldendwyrhtan,   forweorone, geleorene,
heard gripe hrūsan,   oþ hund cnēa
werþēoda gewitan.   Oft þes wāg gebād
10 rǣghār ond rēadfāh   rīce æfter ōþrum,
ofstonden under stormum;   stēap gēap gedrēas.
Wunað gīet se wealstān   wederum gehēawen
fel on . . . .
grimme gegrunden . . . .
15 . . . . scān   hēo . . . .
. . . . g orþonc   ærsceaft . . . .
. . . . g   lāmrindum bēag
mōd mo . . . .   yne swiftne gebrægd
hwætrēd in hringas,   hygerōf gebond
20 weallwalan wīrum   wundrum tōgædre.

</blockquote>

1–2 **wyrde . . . burston** 'the fates broke, smashed the city'.

enta geweorc 'the work of giants'. The Anglo-Saxons used this expression to refer to the impressive stone buildings left by the Romans. Cf. *Wanderer* l. 87.

3–5 **Hrōfas sind . . . gedrorene** The verb *sind* should be carried over, in both singular and plural senses, in the ensuing verses: 'The roofs are fallen, the towers [are] in ruins, the frosty gate [is] despoiled . . .'.

6–7 **undereotone** and **forweorone** are past participles with -*on*- for -*en*-, a rare but attested spelling.

9 **gewitan** = *gewiton* '[shall] have passed away'. See §198.

9–11 **Oft þes wāg . . . stormum** 'Often this wall, red-stained and grey with lichen, unmoved beneath the storms, has survived kingdom after kingdom.'

11 **stēap . . . gedrēas** *stēap* and *gēap* modify *wāg* (cf. l. 9), the understood subject of *gedrēas*.

13–18 It is best to skip over the fragmentary words and phrases, of which little sense can be made. Resume in l. 18 with *swiftne gebrægd*.

18–20 **swiftne gebrægd . . . tōgædre** '. . . put together (*gebrægd*, past ptc.) a swift, quick plan in rings; one strong in intelligence (*hygerōf*) bound the wall-braces together marvellously with wires.'

Beorht wǣron burgrǣced,　burnsele monige,
hēah horngestrēon,　hereswēg micel,
meodoheall monig　mondrēama full,
oþþæt þæt onwende　wyrd sēo swīþe.
25　Crungon walo wīde,　cwōman wōldagas,
swylt eall fornōm　secgrōfra wera;
wurdon hyra wīgsteal　wēstenstaþolas,
brosnade burgsteall.　Bētend crungon
hergas tō hrūsan.　Forþon þās hofu drēorgiað,
30　ond þes tēaforgēapa　tigelum scēādeð
hrōstbēages hrōf.　Hryre wong gecrong
gebrocen tō beorgum,　þǣr iū beorn monig
glædmōd ond goldbēorht　gleoma gefrætwed,
wlonc ond wīngāl　wīghyrstum scān;
35　seah on sinc, on sylfor,　on searogimmas,
on ēad, on ǣht,　on eorcanstān,
on þās beorhtan burg　brādan rīces.
Stānhofu stōdan,　strēam hāte wearp
wīdan wylme;　weal eall befēng
40　beorhtan bōsme,　þǣr þā baþu wǣron,
hāt on hreþre.　þæt wæs hȳðelic.
Lēton þonne gēotan . . . .
ofer hārne stān　hāte strēamas
un . . . .
45　.þþæt hringmere　hāte . . . .
. . . . þǣr þā baþu wǣron.
þonne is . . . .
. . . . re;　þæt is cynelic þing,
hūse . . . . burg . . . . .

27　**wurdon . . . wēstenstaþolas** 'their sanctuaries (places of idols) became waste places'. *Wīgsteal* could also mean 'war places', but a possible Biblical source in Amos 6:9 ('and the sanctuaries of Israel shall be laid waste') has been suggested, and this would support the meaning 'places of idols, sanctuaries'.

28–9　**Bētend . . . hrūsan** 'The tenders (i.e. repairmen), the armies fell to the earth.' *Hergas* could also mean 'idols, temples', and reference could be to the *wīgsteal* of l. 27: 'The tenders, the idols, fell to the earth.'

30–1　**ond þes tēaforgēapa . . . hrōf** 'and this red-curved roof of the vault splits from the tiles'.

32　**gebrocen tō beorgum** 'broken into rubble-heaps'.

34　**wīghyrstum scān** 'shone in his war-trappings'. (The subject is *beorn monig* 'many a warrior'.)

38–9　**strēam hāte . . . wylme** 'the flowing water threw out heat, a great billow'.

40　**beorhtan bōsme** 'within its bright bosom', i.e. in the interior of the encircling wall that holds the hot bath-water.

41　**hāt on hreþre** 'hot to the core', i.e. 'very hot'.

42–3　**Lēton þonne . . . strēamas** 'They let the hot streams gush over the grey stone.' From here to the end the text is too fragmentary to translate, except for l. 48b.

14

The Dream of the Rood
or
A Vision of the Cross

This, the earliest dream-vision poem in the English language, is the central literary document for understanding that resolution of competing cultures which was the presiding concern of the Christian Anglo-Saxons. The Germanic heroic tradition which the Anglo-Saxons brought with them to England celebrated courage, mastery, and aggressive action. The Christian outlook which the Anglo-Saxons in due course adopted stressed virtues like loving kindness and self-sacrifice. (See §§218, 236–246). Finding a proper adjustment of the two competing ideals was a constant spiritual struggle. The poet of *The Dream of the Rood* discovered in the central event of Christian history an opportunity for using his people's native poetic tradition to encompass and naturalize the alien ideals of the new faith. In so far as the crucifixion required great courage of the Saviour, it offered the poet ample opportunity for displaying how the heroic diction of Old English poetry could serve to extol Christ's passion, especially since early Christianity perceived Christ in more heroic terms than later Christianity was to do: he was a warrior-king doing battle with the Devil (as one can readily see by reading the sources and analogues of the poem in D. G. Calder and M. J. B. Allen's *Sources and Analogues of Old English Poetry* (Cambridge, 1976), pp. 53–8). But there is a gentle, passive side to the character of Christ that is absent from the pagan heroic ethos. Under provocation he turns the other cheek. He forgives his tormentors. He accepts physical defeat for the sake of spiritual victory. He allows his adversaries to kill him. The poet of *The Dream of the Rood* accommodates the intermingled passivity and heroism of Christ by his daring and imaginative device of giving human characteristics and the power of speech to the inanimate cross on which Christ died. Possibly this literal personification of the cross was suggested to him by the Old English verse riddles, where

A Guide to Old English, Eighth Edition. Bruce Mitchell and Fred C. Robinson.
© 2012 Bruce Mitchell and Fred C. Robinson. Published 2012 by Blackwell Publishing Ltd.

various inanimate objects are made to speak out and describe their essential qualities. (See especially riddles *n* and *o* above.) The example of the riddles would have been reinforced by Classical rhetorical exercises in prosopopoeia, which were prescribed in the schools. Whatever the source of the device, the poet uses it to portray a cross which is the passive, plangent sufferer in the crucifixion while Christ is left to be active and heroic – a figure reminiscent of the awesome Byzantine mosaics of Christ the King and also of Germanic heroes like Beowulf.

On a literary level the poem resolves not only the pagan–Christian tensions within Anglo-Saxon culture but also current doctrinal discussions concerning the nature of Christ, who was both God and man, both human and divine. But throughout its imaginative poeticizing of theological issues, *The Dream of the Rood* remains a stirring Germanic poem with an exciting plot, vivid martial imagery which makes heroic all that happens, startling effects such as the gory, talking cross whose drops of blood sur-realistically congeal into beautiful gems and then become blood again. The characterization of the cross is also basically Germanic: it presents itself as a loyal retainer (all creatures on earth being members of God's retinue) who is forced by his very loyalty to become the instrument of his beloved Lord's execution.

That this poem gripped the imagination of its Anglo-Saxon audience is suggested by the fact that a large, ornamented Anglo-Saxon stone cross in the town of Ruthwell has been inscribed with excerpts from *The Dream of the Rood* written in the ancient runic alphabet of the Germanic peoples (§229). Each passage quoted is from portions of the poem spoken by the animate cross. One of the pas-sages, quoted here in the Northumbrian dialect of the inscription (slightly restored), may be compared with ll. 44–5 of the poem:

> Ahof ic riicnæ kyninc
> haefunæs hlafard   hælda ic ni dorstæ

A silver reliquary cross in Brussels is also inscribed with verses which echo lines spoken by the cross in *The Dream of the Rood*.[1] The poem and the idea of a speaking cross evidently met with cordial responsiveness in the imaginations of the Anglo-Saxons.

Like virtually all Old English poems, *The Dream of the Rood* has no title in its original manuscript (The Vercelli Book), its present title being an invention of modern scholars. It has also been called *A Vision of the Cross*, which is perhaps more suitable. Following are emendations which have been adopted in the text which follows:

---

[1]   Rod is min nama; geo ic ricne cyning bær byfigynde, blode bestemed. Cf. ll. 44 and 48.

hwæt for MS *hæt* (l. 2), *eaxl* for *eaxle* (l. 9), *geweorðod* for *geweorðode* (l. 15), *bewrigen* for *bewrigene* (l. 17), *Wealdendes* for *wealdes* (l. 17), *sorgum* for *surgum* (l. 20), *ænigum* for *nænigum* (l. 47), *sorgum* supplied in l. 59, *grēotende* for *reotende* (l. 70), *stefn* for *syððan* (l. 71), *holtwudu* for *holmwudu* (l. 91), *anforht* for *unforht* (l. 117), *þām* for *þan* (l. 122), *mē* for *he* (l. 142).

> Hwæt, ic swefna cyst   secgan wylle,
> hwæt mē gemætte   tō midre nihte,
> syðþan reordberend   reste wunedon.
> þūhte mē þæt ic gesāwe   syllicre trēow
5   on lyft lædan   lēohte bewunden,
> bēama beorhtost.   Eall þæt bēacen wæs
> begoten mid golde;   gimmas stōdon
> fægere æt foldan scēatum,   swylce þær fīfe wæron
> uppe on þām eaxlgespanne.   Behēoldon þær engel Dryhtnes
> ealle
10   fægere þurh forðgesceaft;   ne wæs ðær hūru fracodes gealga,
> ac hine þær behēoldon   hālige gāstas,
> men ofer moldan   and eall þēos mære gesceaft.
> Syllic wæs se sigebēam,   and ic synnum fāh,
> forwunded mid wommum.   Geseah ic wuldres trēow

1–2   **swefna cyst** in l. 1 and the clause introduced by *hwæt* in l. 2 are parallel objects of the verb *secgan*: 'to tell the best of dreams, (to tell) what . . .'. See §159.

2   **mē gemætte** 'came to me in a vision', i.e. 'I dreamed' *gemætan* (like *þūhte* in l. 4) is an impersonal verb with dative of person. See §212.

4   **syllicre** is often said to be an absolute comparative ('exceedingly rare'), but some comparative meaning can also be implicit: 'a rarer tree (than all the others)'. Cf. ll. 90–4 below.

5   **on lyft lædan** 'lifted into the air'. The infinitive following *gesāwe* has a passive sense. See §161. So also *þenian* following *geseah* in l. 52.

8   **foldan scēatum** Either 'at the surface of the earth' (i.e. at the foot of the cross) or 'at the corners of the earth', the cross being seen as extending across the sky to four points on the horizon. With this verse begins the first of several groups of hypermetric lines which appear periodically throughout this poem (in ll. 8–10, 20–3, 30–4, 39–43, 46–9, 59–69, 75, and 133) and occasionally in other poems as well (e.g. *The Wanderer*, ll. 111–15, *The Seafarer*, ll. 106–9). Obviously some special effect was achieved by shifting from normal to hypermetric verses, but we cannot be sure what that effect was. The hypermetric verses seem to be systematic variations on the regular verse-types, most of them being expanded A-verses. The effect of hypermetric verses was exclusively aural and not visual, since the Anglo-Saxons wrote poetry continuously across the page from margin to margin just like prose and did not lineate their poems into separate verses.

9–10   **Behēoldon . . . forðgesceaft** 'All those fair by eternal decree gazed on the angel of the Lord (i.e. Christ or possibly the cross) there.' 'Those fair by eternal decree' are the *hālige gāstas* of l. 11 – the loyal angels who were predestined to remain in Heaven. Line 9b is long even for a hypermetric line and therefore has often been emended. But since it makes sense as it stands and none of the emendations is entirely satisfactory, we retain the manuscript reading.

11   **hine** refers to the nearest masculine antecedent, *gealga* 'the cross'.

15   wædum geweorðod   wynnum scīnan,
      gegyred mid golde;   gimmas hæfdon
      bewrigen weorðlīce   Wealdendes trēow.
      Hwæðre ic þurh þæt gold   ongytan meahte
      earmra ǣrgewin,   þæt hit ǣrest ongan
20 swǣtan on þā swīðran healfe.   Eall ic wæs mid sorgum gedrēfed;
    forht ic wæs for þǣre fægran gesyhðe;   geseah ic þæt fūse
        bēacen
    wendan wǣdum and blēom: hwīlum hit wæs mid wǣtan
        bestēmed,
    beswyled mid swātes gange,   hwīlum mid since gegyrwed.
          Hwæðre ic þǣr licgende   lange hwīle
25   behēold hrēowcearig   Hǣlendes trēow,
      oð ðæt ic gehȳrde   þæt hit hlēoðrode;
      ongan þā word sprecan   wudu sēlesta:
          'þæt wæs geāra iū   – ic þæt gȳta geman –
      þæt ic wæs āhēawen   holtes on ende,
30 āstyred of stefne mīnum.   Genāman mē ðǣr strange fēondas,
    geworhton him þǣr tō wǣfersȳne,   hēton mē heora wergas
        hebban;
    bǣron mē þǣr beornas on eaxlum,   oð ðæt hīe mē on beorg
        āsetton;
    gefæstnodon mē þǣr fēondas genōge.   Geseah ic þā Frēan
        mancynnes
    efstan elne micle,   þæt hē mē wolde on gestīgan.
35   þǣr ic þā ne dorste   ofer Dryhtnes word
      būgan oððe berstan,   þā ic bifian geseah
      eorðan scēatas.   Ealle ic mihte
      fēondas gefyllan,   hwæðre ic fæste stōd.

---

15 **wǣdum geweorðod** 'adorned with garments'. 'Garments' is a poetic reference to the gold and jewelled adornments. In l. 22 it refers to these and the blood covering the cross as well.

19 **earmra ǣrgewin** 'ancient hostility of wretched ones', i.e. those who crucified Christ. *Ǣrgewin* and the following *þæt* clause are parallel objects of *ongytan*.

20 **on þā swīðran healfe** 'on the right side'. According to Christian tradition, it was Christ's right side that the centurion pierced with a spear.

31 **geworhton . . . wǣfersȳne** 'they made (me) into a spectacle for themselves there'. This refers to the Romans' use of crosses for the public (and ignominious) execution of felons.

33 **gefæstnodon . . . genōge** 'Enemies enough (i.e. many enemies) secured me there.'

34 **þæt hē . . . gestīgan** '(in) that he wanted to ascend onto me', i.e. 'in his wish to ascend onto me'. See §211.

36–7 **þā ic bifian . . . scēatas** 'when I saw the surface of the earth tremble'. Matthew 27:51 says that the earth trembled at the crucifixion.

37–8 **Ealle . . . gefyllan, hwæðre . . .** 'I was able to fell (i.e. could have felled) all the adversaries, but . . .'.

Ongyrede hine þā geong hæleð   – þæt wæs God ælmihtig! –
40   strang and stīðmōd;   gestāh hē on gealgan hēanne,
mōdig on manigra gesyhðe,   þā hē wolde mancyn lȳsan.
Bifode ic þā mē se beorn ymbclypte;   ne dorste ic hwæðre
       būgan tō eorðan,
feallan tō foldan scēatum,   ac ic sceolde fæste standan.
Rōd wæs ic ārǣred;   āhōf ic rīcne Cyning,
45   heofona Hlāford;   hyldan mē ne dorste.
þurhdrifan hī mē mid deorcan næglum;   on mē syndon þā dolg
       gesīene,
opene inwidhlemmas;   ne dorste ic hira ǣnigum sceððan.
Bysmeredon hīe unc būtū ætgædere;   eall ic wæs mid blōde
       bestēmed,
begoten of þæs guman sīdan   siððan hē hæfde his gāst onsended.
50   'Feala ic on þām beorge   gebiden hæbbe
          wrāðra wyrda: geseah ic weruda God
          þearle þenian.   þȳstro hæfdon
          bewrigen mid wolcnum   Wealdendes hrǣw,
          scīrne scīman;   sceadu forð ēode,
55   wann under wolcnum.   Wēop eal gesceaft,
          cwīðdon Cyninges fyll: Crīst wæs on rōde.
          Hwæðere þǣr fūse   feorran cwōman
          tō þām Æðelinge;   ic þæt eall behēold.
Sāre ic wæs mid sorgum gedrēfed,   hnāg ic hwæðre þām secgum
       tō handa
60   ēaðmōd, elne mycle.   Genāmon hīe þǣr ælmihtigne God,
āhōfon hine of ðām hefian wīte;   forlēton mē þā hilderincas
standan stēame bedrifenne;   eall ic wæs mid strǣlum
       forwundod.
Ālēdon hīe ðǣr limwērigne;   gestōdon him æt his līces hēafdum;
behēoldon hīe ðǣr heofenes Dryhten,   and hē hine ðǣr hwīle
       reste,
65   mēðe æfter ðām miclan gewinne.   Ongunnon him þā moldern
       wyrcan
beornas on banan gesyhðe,   curfon hīe ðæt of beorhtan stāne;

49   **begoten** 'drenched' modifies *ic* in l. 48.
51–2   See note to l. 5 above.
54   **scīrne scīman** 'the bright radiance' is in apposition with *Wealdendes hrǣw*.
57   **fūse** 'eager ones'. In view of John 19:38–9, the eager ones would appear to be Joseph of Arimathea and Nicodemus, who came to claim the body of Jesus.
59   **þām secgum tō handa** 'to the hands of the men'. Poss. dat. See §191.2.
62   **strǣlum** 'with arrows'. The cross is referring to the hostile nails of l. 46.
63   **gestōdon ... hēafdum** 'they positioned themselves at his body's head'. Dat. pl. *hēafdum* with singular meaning is an OE idiom. Cf. *brēostum* in l. 118.
66   **banan** 'of the slayer'. The cross refers to itself as Christ's slayer.

gesetton hīe ðǣron sigora Wealdend.   Ongunnon him þā
    sorhlēoð galan
earme on þā ǣfentīde,   þā hīe woldon eft sīðian,
mēðe fram þām mǣran þēodne;   reste hē ðǣr mǣte weorode.
70   Hwæðere wē ðǣr grēotende   gōde hwīle
        stōdon on staðole;   stefn up gewāt
        hilderinca;   hrǣw cōlode,
        fæger feorgbold.   Þā ūs man fyllan ongan
        ealle tō eorðan;   þæt wæs egeslic wyrd!
75 Bedealf ūs man on dēopan sēaþe;   hwæðre mē þǣr Dryhtnes
    þegnas,
        frēondas gefrūnon,
        gyredon mē   golde and seolfre.
        'Nū ðū miht gehȳran,   hæleð mın se lēofa,
        þæt ic bealuwara weorc   gebiden hæbbe,
80   sārra sorga.   Is nū sǣl cumen
        þæt mē weorðiað   wīde and sīde
        menn ofer moldan   and eall þēos mǣre gesceaft,
        gebiddaþ him tō þyssum bēacne.   On mē Bearn Godes
        þrōwode hwīle;   for þan ic þrymfæst nū
85   hlīfige under heofenum,   and ic hǣlan mæg
        ǣghwylcne ānra   þāra þe him bið egesa tō mē.
        Iū ic wæs geworden   wīta heardost,
        lēodum lāðost,   ǣr þan ic him līfes weg
        rihtne gerȳmde,   reordberendum.
90   Hwæt, mē þā geweorþode   wuldres Ealdor
        ofer holtwudu,   heofonrīces Weard,
        swylce swā hē his mōdor ēac,   Marīan sylfe,
        ælmihtig God   for ealle menn
        geweorðode   ofer eall wīfa cynn.
95   'Nū ic þē hāte,   hæleð mīn se lēofa,
        þæt ðū þās gesyhðe   secge mannum;
        onwrēoh wordum   þæt hit is wuldres bēam,

---

69 **mǣte weorode** 'with little company'. Germanic understatement meaning 'alone'. So also in l. 124.

70 **wē** i.e. the three crosses.

76 The second half of this line is lost, but the sense is clear: the cross was buried, and then many years later St. Helena recovered it and adorned it as a precious relic.

79–80 **þæt ic bealuwara . . . sārra sorga** 'that I have suffered distress from dwellers in iniquity, from sore sorrows'. *Bealuwara* and *sorga* are parallel genitives dependent on *weorc*.

86 **þāra þe . . . tō mē** 'of those in whom is fear of me'. See §162.1 and 2.

92 **swylce swā** 'just as'.

se ðe ælmihtig God   on þrōwode
for mancynnes   manegum synnum
100   and Adomes   ealdgewyrhtum;
dēað hē þǣr byrigde.   Hwæðere eft Dryhten ārās
mid his miclan mihte   mannum tō helpe.
Hē ðā on heofenas āstāg.   Hider eft fundaþ
on þysne middangeard   mancynn sēcan
105   on dōmdæge   Dryhten sylfa,
ælmihtig God   and his englas mid,
þæt hē þonne wile dēman,   se āh dōmes geweald,
ānra gehwylcum,   swā hē him ǣrur hēr
on þyssum lǣnum   līfe geearnaþ.
110   Ne mæg þǣr ǣnig   unforht wesan
for þām worde   þe se Wealdend cwyð:
frīneð hē for þǣre mænige   hwǣr se man sīe,
se ðe for Dryhtnes naman   dēaðes wolde
biteres onbyrigan,   swā hē ǣr on ðām bēame dyde.
115   Ac hīe þonne forhtiað,   and fēa þencaþ
hwæt hīe tō Crīste   cweðan onginnen.
Ne þearf ðǣr þonne ǣnig   anforht wesan
þe him ǣr in brēostum bereð   bēacna sēlest;
ac ðurh ðā rōde sceal   rīce gesēcan
120   of eorðwege   ǣghwylc sāwl,
sēo þe mid Wealdende   wunian þenceð.'
      Gebæd ic mē þā tō þām bēame   blīðe mōde,
elne mycle,   þǣr ic āna wæs
mǣte werede.   Wæs mōdsefa
125   āfȳsed on forðwege,   feala ealra gebād
langunghwīla.   Is mē nū līfes hyht
þæt ic þone sigebēam   sēcan mōte
āna oftor   þonne ealle men,
well weorþian.   Mē is willa tō ðām
130   mycel on mōde,   and mīn mundbyrd is
geriht tō þǣre rōde.   Nāh ic rīcra feala
frēonda on foldan,   ac hīe forð heonon

98   **se ðe . . . þrōwode** 'on which almighty God suffered'. See §163.1.

107–9   **þæt hē þonne . . . geearnaþ** 'in that He who has power of judgement will wish to pass judgement then on each of those even as he shall have earned for himself (while) here in this transitory life'. *Ǣrur* with the present (with future meaning) *geearnaþ* yields a future perfect in meaning. Similarly *ǣr . . . bereð* in l. 118.

124–6   **Wæs mōdsefa . . . langunghwīla** '(My) mind was inspired with longing (*āfȳsed*) for the way hence (to the next world), it has experienced in all (*ealra*) many periods of longing (for the next life).'

129–30   **Mē is willa . . . on mōde** 'The desire for that is intense in my heart.'

gewiton of worulde drēamum,   sōhton him wuldres Cyning;
lifiaþ nū on heofenum   mid Hēahfædere,
35 wuniaþ on wuldre;   and ic wēne mē
daga gehwylce   hwænne mē Dryhtnes rōd,
þe ic hēr on eorðan   ǣr scēawode,
on þysson lǣnan   līfe gefetige,
and mē þonne gebringe   þǣr is blis mycel,
40 drēam on heofonum,   þǣr is Dryhtnes folc
geseted tō symle,   þǣr is singāl blis;
and mē þonne āsette   þǣr ic syþþan mōt
wunian on wuldre,   well mid þām hālgum
drēames brūcan.   Sī mē Dryhten frēond,
45 se ðe hēr on eorðan   ǣr þrōwode
on þām gealgtrēowe   for guman synnum;
hē ūs onlȳsde,   and ūs līf forgeaf,
heofonlicne hām.   Hiht wæs genīwad
mid blēdum and mid blisse,   þām þe þǣr bryne þolodan.
50 Se Sunu wæs sigorfæst   on þām sīðfate,
mihtig and spēdig,   þā hē mid manigeo cōm,
gāsta weorode,   on Godes rīce,
Anwealda ælmihtig,   englum tō blisse
and eallum ðām hālgum   þām þe in heofonum ǣr
55 wunedon on wuldre,   þā heora Wealdend cwōm,
ælmihtig God,   þǣr his ēðel wæs.

133 **him** This reflexive dative (with *sōhton*) need not be translated.

135–8 **ic wēne mē . . . gefetige** 'I look forward each day to (the time) when the cross of the Lord . . . will fetch me.' The *mē* in l. 135 is reflexive and need not be translated. On *hwænne* introducing a clause, see §159 note 2.

144 **Sī mē Dryhten frēond** 'May the Lord be a friend to me.' Cf. ll. 131–2.

146 **for guman synnum** 'for men's sins'. *Guman* is a late gen. pl. (for *gumena*).

148–9 **Hiht wæs genīwad . . . þolodan** This sentence refers to Christ's harrowing of hell when, following the crucifixion, he descended to the nether regions and rescued from the burning fires all good people who had died since the creation.

150–6 These verses refer to Christ's ascension into heaven with all the souls he had rescued in the harrowing. The ascension actually takes place forty days later.

153 **englum tō blisse** 'to the delight of the angels'.

The Wife's Lament

The Wife's Lament is a woman's account of how she became estranged from her young husband through the machinations of his relatives. Forced to live alone in a settlement far away from him, she suffers pitifully, yearning for him day and night. The details of the plot are somewhat sketchy, the poet's main attention being on the speaker's sadness and love-longing. It has been conjectured that the woman speaking in the poem was a character known to the audience from other narratives and that by knowing her story beforehand they would have been better able to understand what is going on in *The Wife's Lament*. It is true that we are told nothing about why her husband originally had to leave her and make a sea journey, about why and how his relatives persuaded him to reject her, or about the identities of any of the principal characters. But the general sequence of actions is fairly clear in the poem as it is presented here. Her husband leaves, and the wife, smitten with longing for him, joins him (ll. 6–10). His kinsmen, who want to separate the couple from each other, get the husband to send her back to his homeland where he orders her to live in a cave or hovel in the midst of a forbidding grove of trees (ll. 11–32). (Sad recollections of their former devotion to one another contrasted with the husband's hostile state of mind at present intervene at ll. 18–22.) Lines 32–41 are a poignant account of the abandoned wife's longing and sorrow. The final section (ll. 42–53) seems to be the wife's speculations as to the husband's present circumstances and her assurances to herself that he must feel as sad as she when he recalls their former life together. She closes with a gnomic observation about the suffering of parted lovers.

    Since thousands of lines of Old English poetry deal primarily with women (e.g. *Elene, Judith, Juliana*), it is not surprising to find in *The Wife's Lament* a concern with exploring the psychology of a suffering woman. Yet some scholars have doubted that this is a woman's monologue and try to interpret it as the lament of a man,

A Guide to Old English, Eighth Edition. Bruce Mitchell and Fred C. Robinson.
© 2012 Bruce Mitchell and Fred C. Robinson. Published 2012 by Blackwell
Publishing Ltd.

much like *The Wanderer*. Such interpretations have to begin by altering or explaining away the grammatical endings in *gēomorre* (l. 1) and *mīnre sylfre* (l. 2), which make it clear that the speaker is feminine. Other interpretations have sought to introduce a love-triangle by suggesting that some of the speaker's references to her lord and lover are to one man (her husband) and others are to another (her lover). Yet other scholars have suggested that the monologue is spoken by the Heavenly Bride (i.e. the Church), who is commanded by Christ to remain in this world of sorrow until the Second Coming. Another suggests it is a voice from the grave. The narrative is sufficiently cryptic and the language of Old English poetry sufficiently flexible that a case can be made for a variety of different situations in the poem. As in much literary interpretation, the only available curb to ever more ingenious speculations about *The Wife's Lament* is common sense.

The text here is that of the Exeter Book, except that modern conventions of punctuation, capitalization, word-division, verse-lineation, and long-vowel marking are introduced, and the following emendations are adopted: *āwēox* for MS *weox* in l. 3, *hycgendne* for *hycgende* in l. 20, *nǣfre* for *no* in l. 24, *sceal* for *seal* in l. 25, and *sittan* for *sittam* in l. 37.

> Ic þis giedd wrece   bī mē ful geōmorre,
> mīnre sylfre sīð.   Ic þæt secgan mæg,
> hwæt ic yrmþa gebād,   siþþan ic ūp āwēox,
> nīwes oþþe ealdes,   nō mā þonne nū.
> 5   Ā ic wīte wonn   mīnra wræcsīþa.
>   Ǣrest mīn hlāford gewāt   heonan of lēodum
> ofer ȳþa gelāc;   hæfde ic ūhtceare
> hwǣr mīn lēodfruma   londes wǣre.
> Ðā ic mē fēran gewāt   folgað sēcan,
> 10   winelēas wrǣcca,   for mīnre wēaþearfe,
> ongunnon þæt þæs monnes   māgas hycgan
> þurh dyrne geþōht,   þæt hȳ tōdǣlden unc,
> þæt wit gewīdost   in woruldrīce
> lifdon lāðlicost,   ond mec longade.

---

2   sīð is acc. sing., parallel with *giedd*. 'I narrate this poem, . . . (narrate) my own experience' lit. '[the] experience of myself' – a strange pattern rare in OE.

8   hwǣr . . . wǣre '(as to) where in the land my leader of men might be'. *Londes* (like *nīwes oþþe ealdes* in l. 4) is adverbial genitive (§190.5).

9–10   Ðā . . . wēaþearfe 'When, because of my woeful need, I set out, a friendless stranger, to visit the retinue'. Her husband, who has just been described as 'a leader of men' (*lēodfruma*, l. 8) is travelling with his retainers, and it is this group that she must seek out when she goes to visit him.

11–14   'The man's kinsmen began plotting that they would separate us, so that we two have lived most miserably, most far apart in the world, and longing has afflicted me.'

15 Hēt mec hlāford mīn   herheard niman,
   āhte ic lēofra lȳt   on þissum londstede,
   holdra frēonda,   for þon is mīn hyge geōmor.
   Ðā ic mē ful gemæcne   monnan funde,
   heardsæligne,   hygegeōmorne,
20 mōd mīþendne,   morþor hycgendne
   blīþe gebæro.   Ful oft wit bēotedan
   þæt unc ne gedælde   nemne dēað āna
   ōwiht elles;   eft is þæt onhworfen,
   is nū swā hit   næfre wære,
25 frēondscipe uncer.   Sceal ic feor ge nēah
   mīnes felalēofan   fæhðu drēogan.
       Heht mec mon wunian   on wuda bearwe,
   under āctrēo   in þām eorðscræfe.
   Eald is þes eorðsele,   eal ic eom oflongad,
30 sindon dena dimme,   dūna ūphēa,
   bitre burgtūnas,   brērum beweaxne,
   wīc wynna lēas.   Ful oft mec hēr wrāþe begeat
   fromsīþ frēan.   Frȳnd sind on eorþan,
   lēofe lifgende,   leger weardiað,
35 þonne ic on ūhtan   āna gonge
   under āctrēo   geond þās eorðscrafu.
   þǣr ic sittan mōt   sumorlangne dæg;
   þǣr ic wēpan mæg   mīne wræcsīþas,
   earfoþa fela;   forþon ic ǣfre ne mæg
40 þǣre mōdceare   mīnre gerestan,
   ne ealles þæs longaþes   þe mec on þissum līfe begeat.
       Ā scyle geong mon   wesan geōmormōd,

15 OE *eard niman* means 'to take up an abode', so *herheard niman* means 'to take up
(my) abode in a *herh*'. *Herh* (or *hearh*) refers either to a grove or a part of a pagan sanctuary or temple grounds. In view of l. 27b, it probably means 'grove' here.

18 'Then I found the man (who had been) very suitable to me . . .'.

22–3 ne . . . ōwiht 'naught, nothing': 'that naught but death alone should separate
us'.

24 'it is now as if it had never been'.

27 **Heht mec mon** 'I was commanded (by my husband).'

32 **mec hēr wrāþe begeat** 'took hold of me cruelly here', i.e. 'caused me pain'.

34 **leger weardiað** 'occupy their bed', i.e. 'are in bed together'.

39–41 Forþon . . . longaþes 'Therefore I can never rest from that sorrow of mine
nor from all that longing.'

42–52 Here the speaker seems to speculate over what might be the present state of
her estranged spouse and to assure herself that whatever his circumstances he will certainly be sharing her sorrow over their separation.

42–3 Ā scyle . . . geþōht 'it may be that the young man must always be sorrowful
(and) his heart's thought stern.' The subjunctive *scyle* suggests that she is only specu-
lating about his state of mind, but the shift to indicative *sceal* indicates certainty ('at the
same time he *must* have a cheerful demeanour along with his breast-cares'), since she has
observed at first hand in ll. 20–1 that this is a characteristic of the young man.

heard heortan geþōht,   swylce habban sceal
blīþe gebǣro,   ēac þon brēostceare,
45 sinsorgna gedreag.   Sȳ æt him sylfum gelong
eal his worulde wyn,   sȳ ful wīde fāh
feorres folclondes,   þæt mīn frēond siteð
under stānhliþe   storme behrīmed,
wine wērigmōd,   wætre beflōwen
50 on drēorsele,   drēogeð se mīn wine
micle mōdceare;   hē gemon tō oft
wynlicran wīc.   Wā bið þām þe sceal
of langoþe   lēofes ābīdan.

45-7   **Sȳ ... sȳ** ... The two subjunctives are used correlatively to introduce
alternative speculations: 'Whether he is dependent (solely) upon himself for all his joy
in the world, or whether he is outlawed far from his remote inheritance so that my dear
one sits . . .'.

50-1   **drēogeð ... mōdceare** 'that lover of mine will experience great sorrow at heart'.
This is the main clause upon which the preceding subordinate clauses depend.

The Wanderer

The Wanderer is one of several great meditative poems from the
Exeter Book. It is a dramatic monologue briefly introduced by the
Christian poet and briefly concluded by him with a terse exhortation to seek comfort in God the Father. The monologue itself is
spoken by a heroic-age nobleman whose assessment of life's meaning shows no awareness of Christian enlightenment. The only outside forces of which he has knowledge are fate, the forces of nature,
and a 'creator of men' (*ælda scyppend*, l. 85) whose only action in
the poem is to lay waste all that men have made. The wanderer who
speaks the monologue is in the worst possible circumstances for an
Anglo-Saxon warrior in the heroic age: he is a retainer who has lost
his lord and comrades and who therefore finds himself with no place
in society, no identity in a hostile world. He is man *in extremis*, alone
with his memories and naked to his enemies. This plight moves him
to strenuous and painful reflection.

He begins by acknowledging the noble precept that a suffering
man must bear up silently and, indeed, all that he says is spoken *on
mōde* 'in his mind', i.e. 'silently to himself' (l. 111). He is *āna* (l. 8),
and what we hear are his inmost thoughts. The depth of his feeling
for his dead lord and lost comrades is dramatized by the unceasing
sorrow that seems to attend his vain wanderings, and by his reveries
of the past, which at times lead to hallucinatory illusions that his
dead friends have returned and which leave him even deeper in
sadness after his return to reality. At l. 58 he begins to move from
his personal sorrow into a sense of the sorrowful state of the entire
world, where all is transient and meaningless. Like the sparrow in
Bede's story of the conversion of Edwin (8, ll. 24–38), men leave
the hall at the end of life (l. 61) and pass into darkness and
oblivion. With poetic imagination he evokes and laments a ruined
city (ll. 75–110) and concludes with the hopeless observation that
'all the foundation of this earth will become empty'. He has summoned the full range of heroic-age wisdom to his meditation on
existence, and the conclusion to which this wisdom brings him is

A Guide to Old English, Eighth Edition. Bruce Mitchell and Fred C. Robinson.
© 2012 Bruce Mitchell and Fred C. Robinson. Published 2012 by Blackwell
Publishing Ltd.

that all is empty and without meaning. When his thoughts have run their course, the Christian poet returns and offers his terse comment: our only security lies with the Father in Heaven; we must seek consolation from Him.

Some modern readers have found a troubling imbalance in the monologue and authorial comment. The wanderer's hopeless situation and despairing scrutiny of the meaning of existence seems too briefly answered by the Christian poet's assertion that all our hope is in God the Father. But this assertion is in fact all that is needed since the wanderer's philosophizing – strong in feeling, high in dignity, and wisely reflective – demonstrates its own impotence before the transience and sorrow of the world. The poet can safely assume that if such an eloquent enquirer as the wanderer can find no more satisfying answer than 'eal þis eorþan gesteal īdel weorþeð' (l. 110), then the Christian invitation to consolation requires no elaboration. This after all is the logic of the nameless nobleman who counselled King Edwin to accept Christianity: if our pagan faith offers nothing more than the meaninglessness of a sparrow's flight through a hall, then let us turn to the God whom Paulinus is proclaiming.

Later Christian poets have followed a similar course in presenting the superiority of Christianity to a noble but unavailing pagan alternative. Throughout the five books of *Troilus* Chaucer involves his readers in the beauties and disasters of love in the pagan Classical world, only to end with the brief but moving palinode exhorting his readers, 'Repeyreth hom fro worldly vanyte!' An even closer parallel is Samuel Johnson's *The Vanity of Human Wishes*, in which the poet gives eloquent expression throughout most of the poem to the Juvenalian commentator who surveys the world with stoic insight and learns from his survey nothing more than that helpless man must 'roll darkling down the torrent of his fate'. At this point the poet as Christian moralist interrupts with the command 'Enquirer cease!' and closes the poem with the solemn observation that only Christian faith offers hope and meaning to man. In all these poems it is the powerful and unavailing pagan perspective that moves the reader and makes the Christian's point, so that no Christian insistence is needed. And yet each poet leaves us permanently fascinated by the outlook he deftly rejects: Chaucer's Homeric milieu, Johnson's Roman stoicism, and the pre-Christian creed of the Anglo-Saxon wanderer.

The following emendations have been adopted: *healde* for MS *healdne* (l. 14), *mīnne* for *mine* (l. 22), *waþema* for *waþena* (l. 24), *frēondlēasne* for *freond lease* (l. 28), *wenian* for *weman* (l. 29), *mōdsefa* for *mod sefan* (l. 59), *weorþan* for *wearþan* (l. 64), *ealre* for *ealle* (l. 74), *deorce* for *deornce* (l. 89), *hrūsan* for *hruse* (l. 102).

Facsimile of the opening page of *The Wanderer*, from the Exeter Book, folio 76b, lines 1–33a. Reproduced by kind permission of the Dean and Chapter of Exeter Cathedral.

Students should notice that in this manuscript page (as in all other OE manuscripts) there are no commas, colons, semicolons, question marks or other modern punctuation. All the punctuation in OE texts published in modern times is introduced into the texts by modern editors and has no manuscript authority. Students should be mindful of this when reading OE texts in modern editions.

Oft him ānhaga   āre gebīdeð,
metudes miltse,   þēah þe hē mōdcearig
geond lagulāde   longe sceolde
hrēran mid hondum   hrīmcealde sǣ,
5   wadan wræclāstas. Wyrd bið ful ārǣd!

Swā cwæð eardstapa,   earfeþa gemyndig,
wrāþra wælsleahta,   winemǣga hryre:
'Oft ic sceolde āna   ūhtna gehwylce
mīne ceare cwīþan. Nis nū cwicra nān
10   þe ic him mōdsefan   mīnne durre
sweotule āsecgan. Ic tō sōþe wāt
þæt biþ in eorle   indryhten þēaw,
þæt hē his ferðlocan   fæste binde,
healde his hordcofan,   hycge swā hē wille.
15   Ne mæg wērig mōd   wyrde wiðstondan,
ne se hrēo hyge   helpe gefremman.
Forðon dōmgeorne   drēorigne oft
in hyra brēostcofan   bindað fæste;
swā ic mōdsefan   mīnne sceolde,
20   oft earmcearig,   ēðle bidǣled,
frēomǣgum feor   feterum sǣlan,
siþþan geāra iū   goldwine mīnne
hrūsan heolstre biwrāh,   ond ic hēan þonan
wōd wintercearig   ofer waþema gebind,
25   sōhte seledrēorig   sinces bryttan,
hwǣr ic feor oþþe nēah   findan meahte
þone þe in meoduhealle   mīne wisse,
oþþe mec frēondlēasne   frēfran wolde,

1–5   **Oft him ānhaga . . . ful ārǣd!** Because *gebīdeð* can mean both 'waits for' and
'experiences', this sentence has been variously interpreted. We suggest: 'The solitary
man always waits for prosperity, for the favour of fate, although he, sad at heart, has long
had to stir the ice-cold sea with his hands, traverse throughout the water-ways the paths
of an exile. Fate is wholly inexorable!' *Oft* literally means 'often', but in poetry is
frequently an understatement for 'always'. The pronoun *him* (l.1) is dative of interest:
'for himself'.

7   **winemǣga hryre** (= hryra) 'of the deaths of kinsmen'. This is but one of several attempts by scholars to interpret the grammar of *hryre*.

9–11   **Nis nū . . . āsecgan** See §163.2.

11   **tō sōþe** 'for a truth', 'truly'.

14   **hycge . . . wille** 'think as he will', 'whatever he may want to think'.

17   **drēorigne** 'sorrowful (mind)', with *hyge* understood from l. 16.

22–3   **siþþan geāra iū . . . biwrāh** 'since years ago I concealed (i.e. buried) my lord
in earth's darkness'. The subject of *biwrāh* is *ic*, understood from l. 19.

25   **sōhte seledrēorig** 'sad for the lack of a hall, I sought'. See §159.

27   **mīne wisse** 'might know of my own (i.e. my origins or people)'. Only if a lord
has prior knowledge of the man's tribal affiliations will he be willing to accept the
wanderer into his retinue.

wenian mid wynnum. Wāt se þe cunnað
30 hū slīþen bið   sorg tō gefēran
þām þe him lȳt hafað   lēofra geholena:
warað hine wræclāst,   nales wunden gold,
ferðloca frēorig,   nalæs foldan blæd.
Gemon hē selesecgas   ond sincþege,
35 hū hine on geoguðe   his goldwine
wenede tō wiste.   Wyn eal gedrēas!

Forþon wāt se þe sceal   his winedryhtnes
lēofes lārcwidum   longe forþolian:
ðonne sorg ond slæp   somod ætgædre
40 earmne ānhogan   oft gebindað,
þinceð him on mōde   þæt hē his mondryhten
clyppe ond cysse   ond on cnēo lecge
honda ond hēafod,   swā hē hwīlum ǣr
in geārdagum   giefstōlas brēac.

45 Ðonne onwæcneð eft   winelēas guma,
gesihð him biforan   fealwe wēgas,
baþian brimfuglas,   brǣdan feþra,
hrēosan hrīm ond snāw   hagle gemenged.

þonne bēoð þȳ hefigran   heortan benne,
50 sāre æfter swǣsne.   Sorg bið genīwad.
þonne māga gemynd   mōd geondhweorfeð,
grēteð glīwstafum,   georne geondscēawað
secga geseldan;   swimmað oft on weg.

29–30 **Wāt se þe cunnað . . . gefēran** 'He who has experience knows how cruel sorrow is as a companion.'

32 **warað hine wræclāst** 'the path of an exile claims him'.

37–44 **Forþon wāt . . . brēac** The long sentence in ll. 39–44 is the direct object of *wāt* (l. 37): 'He who must long forgo his beloved lord's counsels knows (that) when sorrow and sleep both together constrain the wretched solitary, it seems to him . . .'.

43–4 **swā hē hwīlum . . . brēac** 'just as from time to time he used to make use of the throne in days of old'. (*Giefstōlas* is a late spelling of gen. sg. *giefstōles*.) 'Making use of the throne' by embracing the lord, placing hand and head on his knees, etc. is evidently a ritual confirming the close ties between the lord and his retainer.

46–7 **gesihð him biforan . . . brimfuglas** 'sees before him the fallow waves (sees) the seabirds bathing', etc.

51–3 **þonne māga gemynd . . . geseldan** Either 'whenever the memory of kinsmen passes through his mind, he greets joyfully (and) eagerly scrutinizes the companions of men' or 'whenever the mind passes through the memory of kinsmen, it greets joyfully (and) eagerly scrutinizes the companions of men'. *Secga geseldan* (and the *flēotendra ferð* of l. 54) appear to refer both to the birds the wanderer sees when he is awake and to the remembered kinsmen, whom he imagines he sees before him in his dreams and reveries.

53 **swimmað oft on weg** 'they always drift away'. Just as in the next line *nō . . . fela* means (by ironic understatement) 'none', here *oft* 'often' means 'always'. Cf. l. 1 above.

Flēotendra ferð   nō þǣr fela bringeð
55 cūðra cwidegiedda.   Cearo bið genīwad
þām þe sendan sceal   swīþe geneahhe
ofer waþema gebind   wērigne sefan.
    Forþon ic geþencan ne mæg   geond þās woruld
for hwan mōdsefa   mīn ne gesweorce
60 þonne ic eorla līf   eal geondþence,
hū hī fǣrlīce   flet ofgēafon,
mōdge maguþegnas.   Swā þes middangeard
ealra dōgra gehwām   drēoseð ond fealleþ;
forþon ne mæg weorþan wīs   wer, ǣr hē āge
65 wintra dǣl in woruldrīce.   Wita sceal geþyldig,
ne sceal nō tō hātheort   ne tō hrædwyrde,
ne tō wāc wiga   ne tō wanhȳdig,
ne tō forht ne tō fægen,   ne tō feohgīfre
ne nǣfre gielpes tō georn,   ǣr hē geare cunne.
70 Beorn sceal gebīdan,   þonne hē bēot spriceð,
oþþæt collenferð   cunne gearwe
hwider hreþra gehygd   hweorfan wille.
Ongietan sceal glēaw hæle   hū gǣstlic bið,
þonne ealre þisse worulde wela   wēste stondeð,
75 swā nū missenlīce   geond þisne middangeard
winde biwāune   weallas stondaþ,
hrīme bihrorene,   hryðge þā ederas.
Wōriað þā wīnsalo,   waldend licgað
drēame bidrorene,   duguþ eal gecrong,
80 wlonc bī wealle.   Sume wīg fornōm,
ferede in forðwege,   sumne fugel oþbær

58–9 **Forþon ic geþencan . . . gesweorce** 'Wherefore I cannot think for all this
world why my mind does not grow dark.' The highly metaphorical *mōdsefa . . . gesweorcan*
'mind darken' obviously means more than simply 'become sad', since the speaker has
been sad ever since his wanderings began. Probably 'despair' or 'lose the light of reason'
or something equally critical is intended.

61 **flet ofgēafon** lit. 'left the floor (of the meadhall)', i.e. 'died'.

66–9 **ne sceal . . . geare cunne** 'must not be wrathful at all, nor precipitate of speech',
etc. Although the literal sense is that a wise man 'must not be too wrathful, nor too precipitate in speech', etc., it is obvious that these are qualities to be avoided altogether. The
use of *tō* 'too' here seems to be a rhetorical expression growing out of the Anglo-Saxons'
predilection for understatement rather than absolute assertion. (An infinitive meaning
'be' should be understood following each *sceal*, this omission being characteristic of gnomic
utterances in OE.)

70–2 'Whenever he makes a vow, a stout-hearted warrior must wait until he knows
precisely where the thoughts of his heart will tend.' Both here and in l. 69 the speaker
is warning against rash vows (*gielp*, *bēot*) uttered in public, since a man would earn contempt if he failed to carry out what he boasted he would do.

73 **bið** 'it will be'.

80–4 **Sume wīg fornōm** 'War destroyed several' is followed by a description of
the fate met by the corpses of individual members of the slain (*sumne* being acc. sg.

ofer hēanne holm,   sumne se hāra wulf
dēaðe gedǣlde,   sumne drēorighlēor
in eorðscræfe   eorl gehȳdde.

85 Ȳþde swā þisne eardgeard   ælda scyppend
oþþæt burgwara   breahtma lēase
eald enta geweorc   īdlu stōdon.

   Se þonne þisne wealsteal   wīse geþōhte
ond þis deorce līf   dēope geondþenceð,

90 frōd in ferðe,   feor oft gemon
wælsleahta worn,   ond þās word ācwið:
'Hwǣr cwōm mearg? Hwǣr cwōm mago?   Hwǣr cwōm
   māþþumgyfa?
Hwǣr cwōm symbla gesetu?   Hwǣr sindon
   seledrēamas?
Ēalā beorht bune!   Ēalā byrnwiga!

95 Ēalā þēodnes þrym!   Hū sēo þrāg gewāt,
genāp under nihthelm,   swā hēo nō wǣre.
Stondeð nū on lāste   lēofre duguþe
weal wundrum hēah,   wyrmlīcum fāh.
Eorlas fornōman   asca þrȳþe,

100 wǣpen wælgīfru,   wyrd sēo mǣre,
ond þās stānhleoþu   stormas cnyssað,
hrīð hrēosende   hrūsan bindeð,
wintres wōma,   þonne won cymeð,
nīpeð nihtscūa,   norþan onsendeð

105 hrēo hæglfare   hæleþum on andan.'
Eall is earfoðlic   eorþan rīce,
onwendeð wyrda gesceaft   weoruld under heofonum.
Hēr bið feoh lǣne,   hēr bið frēond lǣne,
hēr bið mon lǣne,   hēr bið mǣg lǣne,

---

masc.). The bird of prey which carries off the body (piecemeal) and the wolf are a familiar
motif in Old English battle poetry. Cf. 12/106–7.

86–7 **oþþæt burgwara . . . stōdon** 'until the ancient works of giants stood empty,
devoid of the revelry of their (erstwhile) inhabitants'.

87   **enta geweorc** Cf. 13/2 and note.

88   **Se** 'He who'. See §164.

92–3 **Hwǣr cwōm** 'where has gone'; loosely, 'what has become of'. This haunting
lament on the transience of earthly things may be based on *ubi sunt* passages in Latin sermons, as has been suggested, but such a universal sentiment hardly needs a specific source.

97   **on lāste lēofre duguþe** lit. 'in the track of the dear retinue', i.e. 'after (the departure, i.e. death of) the dear retinue'.

99–100 **Eorlas** is acc. pl. masc.; **þrȳþe**, **wǣpen**, and **wyrd** are nom., parallel
subjects of *fornōman*.

107   **onwendeð . . . heofonum** 'the operation of the fates changes the world under
the heavens'.

110   eal þis eorþan gesteal   īdel weorþeð!'
      Swā cwæð snottor on mōde,   gesæt him sundor æt
      rūne.
      Til biþ se þe his trēowe gehealdeþ   ne sceal næfre his
      torn tō rycene
      beorn of his brēostum ācȳþan,   nemþe hē ær þā bōte
      cunne
      eorl mid elne gefremman.   Wel bið þām þe him āre sēceð,
115   frōfre tō Fæder on heofonum,   þær ūs eal sēo fæstnung
      stondeð.

114   **Wel bið . . . sēceð** 'Well is it for the one who seeks mercy for himself'.

The Seafarer

Ever since the Anglo-Saxons migrated by ship from the Continent to the isle of Britain, Englishmen seem to have been more aware than most people of the importance and fascination of the sea and seafaring. One aspect of the seafaring life which has always captured the attention of people everywhere is the paradoxical state of mind called 'sea fever' – that irresistible call of the sea felt by experienced seamen who may on some occasions complain bitterly about the pains and trials of sea travel, but will sign on for another voyage when the opportunity presents itself. Poems and novels in many periods have treated this subject, but none has done so more convincingly than the Old English poetic monologue *The Seafarer*, which searches so deeply the thoughts and feelings of one Anglo-Saxon sailor that the poet Ezra Pound claims to have discovered in this work 'the English national chemical'.

But impressive as it is in its treatment of the physical and psychological rigours of seafaring life, the poem is about much more than that. Indeed, most of the latter half of the monologue does not mention the sea but rather is concerned with the impermanence of earthly riches and worldly fame and the import-ance of fixing one's attention on the world to come, where judgement will be severe and the rewards will be lasting. The juxtaposition of the seafarer's account of his involvement with the sea and his concerns for the future life is startling, but it is not incomprehensible. First he describes dramatically his sufferings at sea while men on land live in comfort, but he simultaneously expresses his disdain for the landlubber's life and his preference for the trials and challenges of seafaring. But then (ll. 64–6) his thoughts shift from considerations of sea voyages to his ultimate goal of union with the Lord in Heaven. To achieve this higher goal, one must forgo the pomps and joys of earthly existence and the fleeting benefits of gold and worldly goods at large. Just as the seafaring man is willing to deny himself the pleasures of life on land in order to take up the hard challenges of the sea, the devout

A Guide to Old English, Eighth Edition. Bruce Mitchell and Fred C. Robinson.
© 2012 Bruce Mitchell and Fred C. Robinson. Published 2012 by Blackwell Publishing Ltd.

Christian must be willing to renounce the pleasures of the flesh in order to arrive at his heavenly destination. Once this analogy is perceived, the vividness and force of the early description of the seafarer's lot take on in retrospect larger dimensions. The movingly expressed catalogue of pleasures that the seafarer renounces (ll. 44–7) seem on second thought like the determined exercise in self-abnegation that a Christian might practise on taking holy orders. The undefined cares which are hot in the seafarer's heart in l. 11 are echoed in ll. 64–6 when he speaks of the joys of the Lord being 'hotter' than transitory earthly existence. (And we may be reminded of Luke 24:32: 'did not our heart burn within us, while he [the Lord] talked with us by the way . . . ?') Key words like *dryhten* and *lond* take on second meanings as the initial monologue of the seafarer is placed in juxtaposition with this broader conception of man's voyage through life to an ultimate destination. Scholars have detected artful symmetries and subtle allegories at work in *The Seafarer*, but perhaps the poet's strongest statement is the question implicit in the simple analogy he has established: if we can all accept the fact that seafaring men will forgo the pleasures of life on land for the obscure enticements of a dangerous ocean journey, is it unreasonable for Christianity to require renunciation of some earthly delights for the goal of eternal salvation?

As the notes below will indicate, *The Seafarer* presents some difficulties in syntax and thought transition, partly because of its strong feeling and sometimes passionate insistence. But its hard realism combined with lofty otherworldliness repays the effort required to read the poem. The following emendations have been adopted: *hleahtre* for MS *hleahtor* (l. 21), *ne ænig* for *nænig* (l. 25), *frēfran* for *feran* (l. 26), *gewītan* for *gewitað* (l. 52), *sēftēadig* for *efteadig* (l. 56), *hwælweg* for *wælweg* (l. 63), *stondað* for *stondeð* (l. 67), *tīddege* for *tide ge* (l. 69), *bið* for *þæt* (l. 72), *fremum* for *fremman* (l. 75), *blæd* for *blæð* (l. 79), *nearon* for *næron* (l. 82), *mon* for *mod* (l. 109), *lufan* supplied in l. 112, *swīþre* for *swire* (l. 115), *wē* for *se* (l. 117).

> Mæg ic be mē sylfum   sōðgied wrecan,
> sīþas secgan,   hū ic geswincdagum
> earfoðhwīle   oft þrōwade,
> bitre brēostceare   gebiden hæbbe,
> 5   gecunnad in cēole   cearselda fela,
> atol ȳþa gewealc.   þær mec oft bigeat
> nearo nihtwaco   æt nacan stefnan,

2   **geswincdagum** 'in days of hardship'.

5   **cearselda fela** 'many a house of care'. The ship has often been a sorrowful abode for the seafarer.

6–7   **mec oft bigeat . . . stefnan** 'the anxious nightwatch often held me at the ship's prow'.

þonne hē be clifum cnossað.   Calde geþrungen
wæron mīne fēt,   forste gebunden,
10 caldum clommum,   þær þā ceare seofedun
hāt'ymb heortan;   hungor innan slāt
merewērges mōd.   þæt se mon ne wāt
þe him on foldan   fægrost limpeð,
hū ic earmcearig   īscealdne sæ
15 winter wunade   wræccan lāstum,
winemægum bidroren,
bihongen hrīmgicelum;   hægl scūrum flēag.
þær ic ne gehȳrde   būtan hlimman sæ,
īscaldne wæg.   Hwīlum ylfete song
20 dyde ic mē tō gomene,   ganetes hlēoþor
ond huilpan swēg   fore hleahtre wera,
mǣw singende   fore medodrince.
Stormas þær stānclifu bēotan,   þær him stearn oncwæð
īsigfeþera;   ful oft þæt earn bigeal,
25 ūrigfeþra;   ne ǣnig hlēomæga
fēasceaftig ferð   frēfran meahte.
     Forþon him gelȳfeð lȳt,   se þe āh līfes wyn
gebiden in burgum,   bealosīþa hwōn,
wlonc ond wīngāl,   hū ic wērig oft
30 in brimlāde   bīdan sceolde.
Nāp nihtscūa,   norþan snīwde,
hrīm hrūsan bond,   hægl fēol on eorþan,

11 **hāt'** The correct nom. pl. fem. form (modifying *ceare*) is *hāte*, but here the *-e* is elided before the vowel of *ymb*.

12–14 **þæt se mon . . . hū ic . . .** 'The man whom it befalls most pleasantly on land does not know that, (namely) how I . . .' etc. *þæt* anticipates the noun clause introduced by *hū*. See §148.

13 **þe him** See §162.2.

15 **winter** 'in the winter' (adverbial acc.). The object of *wunade* is *sæ* (l. 14).

16 A half-line appears to be missing, but the sense is unimpaired.

18 **ic ne gehȳrde būtan** 'I heard nought but'.

19–20 **ylfete song . . . tō gomene** 'I made the song of the wild swan (serve) for my entertainment'.

23 **him** i.e. the storms.

24 **þæt** is the object of *bigeal* and refers to the clamour of the storms and the tern (l. 23).

27 **Forþon** The usual meanings of *forþon* 'therefore', 'because' do not always serve well in *The Seafarer*, and it has been suggested that in this poem (as in a few other places) it may sometimes have the meaning 'indeed' or even 'and yet'.

27–9 **him gelȳfeð lȳt . . . hū ic . . .** 'he who has experienced joy of life in the cities (and) few baleful journeys little believes how I . . .' *Āh* in l. 27 is used as an auxiliary verb with past ptc. *gebiden*; *wyn* and *hwōn* are parallel objects of *āh gebiden*.

corna caldast.   Forþon cnyssað nū
heortan geþōhtas,   þæt ic hēan strēamas,
35   sealtȳþa gelāc   sylf cunnige;
monað mōdes lust   mǣla gehwylce
ferð tō fēran,   þæt ic feor heonan
elþēodigra   eard gesēce.
Forþon nis þæs mōdwlonc   mon ofer eorþan,
40   ne his gifena þæs gōd,   ne in geoguþe tō þæs hwæt,
ne in his dǣdum tō þæs dēor,   ne him his dryhten tō
      þæs hold,
þæt hē ā his sǣfōre   sorge næbbe,
tō hwon hinc dryhten   gedōn wille.
Ne biþ him tō hearpan hyge   ne tō hringþege,
45   ne tō wīfe wyn   ne tō worulde hyht,
ne ymbe ōwiht elles,   nefne ymb ȳða gewealc,
ac ā hafað longunge   se þe on lagu fundað.
Bearwas blōstmum nimað,   byrig fægriað,
wongas wlitigað,   woruld ōnetteð;
50   ealle þā gemoniað   mōdes fūsne

33–5   **Forþon cnyssað nū . . . cunnige** 'And yet the thoughts of my heart are pressing (me) now that I myself should explore the high seas, the tumult of the salt waves'. But since the seafarer has already been to sea, some have argued that *sylf* means 'alone'.

37   **ferð** is acc., direct object of *monað*.

38   **elþēodigra eard** 'land of foreigners', i.e. 'foreign lands'. Some have argued that this could mean 'Heaven', *elþēodig* referring to those who are pilgrims on earth and regard Heaven as their true home. See Hebrews 11:13–16.

39   **nis þæs . . . mon** 'there is no man so proud in spirit'. The repeated *þæs* (or *tō þæs*) in ll. 40–1 means 'so' also. See §168 *þæs . . . þæt* note 2.

40   **ne his . . . gōd** 'nor so fortunate in his gifts'.

41–3   **dryhten . . . dryhten** The first *dryhten* seems clearly to refer to the seafarer's earthly lord; the second one could have the same reference ('that he does not always have concern as to what his lord might be willing to do for him [in return for his services as a seafarer]'). But the sentence could also refer to what rewards on earth or in the next life the Lord may have in store for him. The ambiguity is probably deliberate since this is where the poet begins to make his transition between the seafarer's account of his experiences and Christian exhortation. Since Old English scribes did not capitalize the first letter of terms for the Deity (as is regularly done in Modern English), the play on the secular and religious meanings of *dryhten* was easy.

44–6   **Ne biþ him . . . gewealc** 'His thought is not for the harp nor for the ring-taking, nor his pleasure in a woman nor his delight in the world, nor (is his thought) about anything else but the rolling of the waves.' This description of how the seafarer willingly forgoes the delights of the land for a higher, harder goal establishes the analogy between the self-abnegation of seamen and that required of Christians.

48–9   **Bearwas . . . wlitigað** *Bearwas* 'groves' may be taken as the subject of *fægriað* and *wlitigað* as well as of *nimað*. But since it is odd to say that *bearwas* ('groves', 'woods') beautify cities, some have preferred to take *fægriað* and *wlitigað* as intransitive: 'the cities grow fair, the meadows become beautiful'. *Byrig* could also mean 'mulberry trees' (nom. pl. neut.).

50–1   **gemoniað . . . tō sīþe** 'urge (the one) eager of spirit, (urge) the mind to the journey'.

sefan tō sīþe			þām þe swā þenceð
on flōdwegas			feor gewītan.
Swylce gēac monað			geōmran reorde,
singeð sumeres weard,			sorge bēodeð
55	bitter in brēosthord.			Þæt se beorn ne wāt,
sēftēadig secg,			hwæt þā sume drēogað
þe þā wræclāstas			wīdost lecgað.
	Forþon nū mīn hyge hweorfeð			ofer hreþerlocan,
mīn mōdsefa			mid mereflōde
60	ofer hwæles ēþel			hweorfeð wīde,
eorþan scēatas,			cymeð eft tō mē
gīfre ond grǣdig,			gielleð ānfloga,
hweteð on hwælweg			hreþer unwearnum
ofer holma gelagu.			Forþon mē hātran sind
65	Dryhtnes drēamas			þonne þis dēade līf,
lǣne on londe.			Ic gelȳfe nō
þæt him eorðwelan			ēce stondað.
Simle þrēora sum			þinga gehwylce
ǣr his tīddege			tō twēon weorþeð;
70	ādl oþþe yldo			oþþe ecghete
fǣgum fromweardum			feorh oðþringeð.
Forþon bið eorla gehwām			æftercweþendra
lof lifgendra			lāstworda betst,

---

51 **þām þe swā þenceð** 'by which (he [*mōdes fūs*]) (or it [*sefa*]) thus thinks to travel far on the ocean ways': the *seþe* relative (§162.4) with an unexpected subject. See *Review of English Studies* 36 (1985), 535–7.

58 **Forþon** 'and yet'. (Alternatively, one can take this *Forþon* as correlative with the *forþon* in l. 64: 'Indeed . . . because . . . '.) In this sentence the mind of the speaker leaves his body and ranges like a bird over land and sea, locates his goal, and then returns to urge him on to his destination.

58–61 **hyge** and **mōdsefa** are parallel subjects of *hweorfeð*; **ēþel** and **scēatas** are parallel objects of *ofer* in l. 60.

ofer hreþerlocan 'beyond my breast'.

66 **on londe** Two senses are simultaneously operative here: 'land (as opposed to sea)' and 'earth (as opposed to heaven)'.

67 **þæt him . . . stondað** 'that worldly goods will endure forever'. The *him* is apparently reflexive and need not be translated.

68 **þinga gehwylce** 'in every circumstance', i.e. 'invariably'.

69 **tō twēon weorþeð** 'arises as an uncertainty', i.e. 'hangs in the balance'. Until the end of his days (*ǣr his tīddege*) a man can never be sure when age, sickness, or a hostile weapon might take his life from him.

72–80 Having mentioned the certainty of death, the poet seems at first to cite the traditional Germanic-heroic view that earning fame after death through valorous deeds in life is the best course for a man. But he Christianizes this admonition by specifying that the deeds should be in Christian action against the devil and that the fame that counts is fame in Heaven, which will earn him the joy of eternal life. Cf. Milton's *Lycidas*, ll. 78–84.

72–4 **bið eorla . . . hē gewyrce** 'for every man the best of reputations after death (*lāstworda*) will be the praise of posterity (*æftercweþendra*), of the living, (will be) that he should bring it about . . . '.

þæt hē gewyrce,   ǣr hē on weg scyle,
75   fremum on foldan   wið fēonda nīþ,
dēorum dǣdum   dēofle tōgēanes,
þæt hine ælda bearn   æfter hergen,
ond his lof siþþan   lifge mid englum
āwa tō ealdre,   ēcan līfes blǣd,
80   drēam mid dugeþum.
                                Dagas sind gewitene,
ealle onmēdlan   eorþan rīces;
nearon nū cyningas   ne cāseras
ne goldgiefan   swylce iū wǣron,
þonne hī mǣst mid him   mǣrþa gefremedon
85   ond on dryhtlīcestum   dōme lifdon.
Gedroren is þēos duguð eal,   drēamas sind gewitene,
wuniað þā wācran   ond þās woruld healdaþ,
brūcað þurh bisgo.   Blǣd is gehnǣged,
eorþan indryhto   ealdað ond sēarað,
90   swā nū monna gehwylc   geond middangeard.
Yldo him on fareð,   onsȳn blācað,
gomelfeax gnornað,   wāt his iūwine,
æþelinga bearn,   eorþan forgiefene.
Ne mæg him þonne se flǣschoma,   þonne him þæt feorg
        losað,
95   ne swēte forswelgan   ne sār gefēlan,
ne hond onhrēran   ne mid hyge þencan.
þēah þe grǣf wille   golde strēgan
brōþor his geborenum,   byrgan be dēadum
māþmum mislicum,   þæt hine mid wille,
100   ne mæg þǣre sāwle   þe biþ synna ful
gold tō gēoce   for Godes egsan,
þonne hē hit ǣr hȳdeð   þenden hē hēr leofað.

80–100   This declaration of the demise of the past (heroic) age, though somewhat
tinged with regret (e.g. ll. 85, 87–9), is concerned primarily to emphasize the transience
of worldly glory as contrasted with the eternal life in Heaven.

84   þonne hī . . . gefremedon 'when they performed the greatest of glorious deeds
among themselves'.

88   brūcað þurh bisgo 'live in (it) by toil'.

97–102   þēah þe grǣf . . . hēr leofað 'Although a brother may wish to strew the
grave with gold for his born (brother), bury (him) among the dead with various
treasures, which he wishes (to go) with him, gold, when he hides it here while he
lives on earth previously, cannot (be) of help before the terrible power of God to the soul
that is full of sin.' þæt (l. 99) is a neut. sg. relative pron. agreeing with *gold* (l. 97).
The familiar Christian admonition against hoarding gold and burying lavish treasures
with the dead is here introduced to stress that man is beyond earthly help when he faces
Judgement.

Micel bið se Meotudes egsa, for þon hī sēo molde
   oncyrreð;
se gestaþelade stīþe grundas,
105 eorþan scēatas ond ūprodor.
Dol biþ se þe him his Dryhten ne ondrædeþ; cymeð him
   se dēað unþinged.
Ēadig bið se þe ēaþmōd leofaþ; cymeð him sēo ār of
   heofonum,
Meotod him þæt mōd gestaþelað, forþon hē in his
   meahte gelȳfeð.
Stīeran mon sceal strongum mōde, ond þæt on
   staþelum healdan,
110 ond gewis wērum, wīsum clǣne;
scyle monna gehwylc mid gemete healdan
lufan wiþ lēofne ond wið lāþne bealo,
þēah þe hē hine wille fȳres fulne . . . .
oþþe on bǣle forbærnedne
115 his geworhtne wine. Wyrd biþ swīþre,
Meotud meahtigra þonne ǣnges monnes gehygd.
Uton wē hycgan hwǣr wē hām āgen,
ond þonne geþencan hū wē þider cumen,
ond wē þonne ēac tilien, þæt wē tō mōten
120 in þā ēcan ēadignesse,
þǣr is līf gelong in lufan Dryhtnes,
hyht in heofonum. Þæs sȳ þām Halgan þonc,
þæt hē ūsic geweorþade, wuldres Ealdor,
ēce Dryhten, in ealle tīd.

Amen.

103 **for þon hī sēo molde oncyrreð** 'before which the earth turns (itself) aside'. Revelation 20:11 'him . . . from whose face the earth and the heaven fled away' may lie behind this.

108 'The Lord establishes that (good) spirit in him, because he believes in His (the Lord's) power.'

110 **on gewis . . . clǣne** 'and (keep it) steadfast in (its) pledges, pure in (its) ways'.

111–12 'each man should hold in moderation his affection towards a friend and his enmity towards a foe'.

113–15 **þēah þe hē . . . wine** This seems to continue the sense of what precedes, but l. 113 is metrically defective, and the lines are probably corrupt: 'although he may wish him (the *lāþne* of l. 112) full of fire (in hell?) or his friend (i.e. the friend of the enemy?) consumed on a funeral pyre'.

117–18 These lines return the religious exhortation to the original seafaring imagery.

119 **þæt wē tō mōten** 'that we may (proceed) thither'.

18

Beowulf

Beowulf is the first great English heroic poem, and yet its subject is
not England but men and women from Germanic legend and
history. It takes place in northern Europe before Christianity had
reached that part of the world. The poet, who wrote centuries
later than the time of the poem's action, was a Christian and may
even have been a cleric, but he (or she) claimed for his subject
pre-Christian nations living in and around the lands from which the
Anglo-Saxons had originally migrated to England. (Throughout this
commentary we follow the customary practice of using masculine
pronouns to refer to the poet; in fact, we have no way of knowing
whether the poet was a man or a woman.) He admires the characters
he describes, especially the hero Beowulf, but there is poignancy in
his admiration, for he knows that these brave and eloquent people
were ignorant of the revelation generally believed to be essential for
Christian salvation.

The poem describes how a powerful warrior from the land of the
Geats (a Scandinavian people dwelling in southern Sweden) travels
to Denmark to do battle with a man-eating ogre who is killing King
Hrothgar's thanes in a series of nocturnal attacks. Beowulf rids the
Danes of their tormentor and returns to Geatland, where he puts
his great strength at the service of his own people in their wars with
hostile neighbours. Eventually, he becomes King of the Geats, and
years later, when he is an old man, he gives his life in the course
of slaying a dragon that had threatened to destroy the nation. His
people bury him amid forebodings of disaster, for the Geats will not
be able to withstand their enemies without Beowulf's strong
supporting hand.

Beowulf is our most sustained demonstration of the power and
range of Old English poetry. In the excerpts printed here readers
will recognize several of the themes and strains encountered

A Guide to Old English, Eighth Edition. Bruce Mitchell and Fred C. Robinson.
© 2012 Bruce Mitchell and Fred C. Robinson. Published 2012 by Blackwell
Publishing Ltd.

Facsimile of the first page of *Beowulf* with lines corresponding to verses
1–21 on the opposite page. This page occurs on fol. 129r of MS Cotton
Vitellius A.XV in the British Library, which is reproduced by the kind permission of the British Library. Note the absence of modern punctuation.

individually in the preceding poetic texts: appreciative descriptions of valour in battle, stirring speeches, elegiac reflections on man and his world, love of the past, and a keen sense of the transience of things.[1]

Prologue

The first twenty-five lines of the poem are here attended by exceptionally heavy annotation commenting on the style and content as well as on the language of the poem. This is intended to provide the student with a general introduction to *Beowulf* and the special challenges it presents, preparing the student, one hopes, for entering upon a study of the entire poem in a future course. The excerpts following the Prologue are provided with only normal annotation.

Although the Prologue opens with praise of the prowess of the Danes, Danes are not the central subject of the poem. Denmark is simply the locale where the poem's hero, a warrior from the land of the Geatas, has his first adventure. The Geatas were a Scandinavian people living in what is now southern Sweden. (The subtitle [Prologue] is supplied by the editor, as are the other subtitles given below.) As one can see from the facsimile, in the original manuscript the poem had neither title nor subtitle (nor punctuation).

---

[1] The emendations and reconstructions required in these passages from *Beowulf* are extensive and so are relegated to this footnote. 'MS' refers to MS Cotton Vitellius A.xv in the British Museum; 'A' and 'B' refer to the two transcripts of the manuscript known as the Thorkelin transcripts. Textual details and complexities are avoided here. For a thorough description of the manuscript readings, see *The Nowell Codex*, ed. Kemp Malone, Early English Manuscripts in Facsimile, vol. 12 (Copenhagen, 1963). See also Kevin Kieman, Andrew Prescott, et al. *Electronic Beowulf* (London: British Library; Ann Arbor: University of Michigan Press, 1999), 2 CDs.

The emendations and reconstructions are as follows: *eorlas* for MS *eorl* (l. 6), *aldorléase* for MS *aldor . . . ase* (l. 15), *geong guma* for MS *. . . uma* (l. 20), *bearme* for MS *. . . rme* (l. 21), *scynscaþa* for MS *synscaþa* (l. 707), *onhrān* for MS *hran* (l. 722), *hē gebolgen* for MS *. . . bolgen* (l. 723), *him* for MS *hi . . .* (l. 747), *scēata* for MS *sceat/ta* (l. 752), *wæs* for MS *he wæs* (l. 765), *betlīc* for MS *hetlic* (l. 780), *hrōf* for B *hr* (l. 836), *Sigemundes* for MS *sige munde* (l. 875), *hwæþer* for MS *hwæþre* (l. 1314), *nægde* for AB *hnægde* (l. 1318), *æþeling ærgōd* for MS *ærgod* (l. 1329), *nēodlaðum* for MS *neod laðu* (l. 1320), *hwæder* for MS *hwæþer* (l. 1331), *gefægnod* for MS *gefrægnod* (l. 1333), *onlīcnes* for MS *onlic næs* (l. 1351), *nemdon* for MS *nemdod* (l. 1354), *standeð* for MS *standeð* (l. 1362), *hafelan hȳdan* for MS *hafelan* (l. 1372), *sinnigne* for MS *fela sinnigne* (l. 1379), *wundnum* for MS *wun/dini* (l. 1382), *mōstan* for MS *mæstan* (l. 2247), *fȳra* for MS *fyrena* (l. 2250), *þāra* for MS *þana* (l. 2251), *þis līf ofgeaf* for MS *þis ofgeaf* (l. 2251), *forð bere* for MS *fe . . . r . . .* (l. 2253), *scōc* for MS *seoc* (l. 2254), *hlīðe* for MS *liðe* (or *lide*) (l. 3157), *we* for MS *. . .* (l. 3158), *hyt æror* for MS *hy . . . or* (l. 3168), *twelfe* for MS *twelfa* (l. 3170), *care* for illegible space in MS (l. 3171), *ond cyning* for MS *cyning* (l. 3171), *læded* for illegible space in MS (l. 3177), *wyruldcyninga* for MS *wyruldcyning* (l. 3180).

Hwæt wē Gār-Dene   in geārdagum,
þēodcyninga   þrym gefrūnon,
hū þā æþelinʒas   ellen fremedon.
Oft Scyld Scēfing   sceaþena þrēatum
5   monegum mægþum   meodosetla oftēah,
egsode eorlas   syððan ǣrest wearð
fēasceaft funden.   Hē þæs frōfre gebād,
wēox under wolcnum,   weorðmyndum þāh
oð þæt him ǣghwylc   þāra ymbsittendra
10   ofer hronrāde   hȳran scolde,
gomban gyldan.   Þæt wæs gōd cyning.
Ðǣm eafera wæs   æfter cenned
geong in geardum   þone god sende
folce tō frōfre;   fyrenðearfe ongeat,
15   þæt hīe ǣr drugon   aldorlēase
lange hwīle.   Him þæs līffrea

1 **Hwæt** Several OE poems begin with the interjection *Hwæt* 'lo, oh'. (See above the beginning of selection 14.) The metre in all these introductory verses makes clear that the interjection *Hwæt* is unaccented. Scholars who have suggested that regardless of the metre an interjection at the beginning of any poem must necessarily have been accented, an emphatic word calling the audience's attention to the recitation to follow – such scholars must be unfamiliar with the hymns 'Oh little town of Bethlehem' and 'Oh come all ye faithful'. *Hwæt* was merely an introductory particle: 'Now we have heard . . .'.
wē is the subject of *gefrūnon*: 'we have heard'. The gen. plurals *Gārdena* and *þeodcyninga* are in apposition and are dependent upon the acc. sg. *þrym*: 'the glory of the spear-Danes, of the kings of the people'. Such parallelism or apposition is pervasive in *Beowulf*.
In geārdagum modifies *þrym*, not *gefrūnon*.
3 **hū þā** . . . This noun clause is the direct object of *gefrūnon* and is therefore parallel with *þrym*.
4–5 **Scyld . . . oftēah** 'Scyld Scefing took away the meadhall benches from troops of warriors, from many tribes' – i.e. he conquered them.
6 **syððan** is the conjunction 'after'. The subject of *wearð* is Scyld.
7 **fēasceaft funden** 'discovered (as) a destitute (foundling)'. According to legend, Scyld arrived in Denmark as an infant alone in a boat at a time when the Danes were leaderless (*aldorlēase* l. 15) and desperate for a ruler. Scyld grows up (*wēox under wolcnum* l. 8) and becomes their illustrious king.
Hē þæs frōfre gebād 'he received consolation for that' – i.e. for having been a foundling.
10 **hronrāde** 'the whale's road', a typical kenning for 'ocean, sea'. Kennings (defined in §137) are pervasive in *Beowulf*.
10–11 **hȳran . . . gyldan** 'had to obey him, (had to) pay tribute (to him)'.
12 **Ðǣm** 'to that one' i.e. to Scyld. **æfter** the adverb 'afterwards'.
13–14 **þone god . . . frōfre** 'whom God sent to the Danish people for their consolation', an heir to their king being a comfort to the nation. The Christian poet informs his Christian Anglo-Saxon audience that it was the Christian God who gave Scyld an heir. But the pagan Danes are ignorant of the source of their consolation.
14–15 **ongeat** has two parallel objects: *fyrenðearfe* and the *þæt* clause in l. 15.
16 **Him þæs** 'To him [Scyld's son] because of that'. **Līffrea** and **wuldres wealdend** are parallel terms for the Christian deity and are the subject of **forgeaf**.

wuldres wealdend   woroldāre forgeaf:
Bēowulf wæs brēme   – blǣd wīde sprang –
Scyldes eafera   Scedelandum in.

20   Swā sceal geong guma   gōde gewyrcean
fromum feohgiftum   on fæder bearme
þæt hine on ylde   eft gewunigen
wilgesīþas   þonne wīg cume,
lēode gelǣsten: lofdǣdum sceal
in mǣgþa gehwǣre   man geþēon.

(*a*) *Beowulf's Fight with Grendel*

For twelve years the monster Grendel has left his watery abode
at night and come to the royal hall Heorot to seize and devour
some warriors of King Hrothgar's. On the occasion described in this
selection the Geatish champion Beowulf and his fourteen comrades are awaiting Grendel's attack. The monster stalks across
the moor, tears open the door to the hall and gobbles down one
of the Geatish warriors before Beowulf can do battle with him.
The two then fight, and after the fray the Danes and Geats follow
Grendel's tracks to the mere and then return to Heorot. Along the
way one of King Hrothgar's thanes celebrates Beowulf's courage by
reciting a poem about Sigemund, son of Wæls, Sigemund being the
ideal Germanic hero and a worthy figure with whom to compare
Beowulf.

16 and 25   **Him þæs Līffrēa** and **man geþēon** do not conform to any of the five
metrical types described in Appendix C; therefore they are unmetrical. But if we restore
the archaic forms of **Līffrēa** and **geþēon** (i.e. *Līffregea and *geþeohan), the two half-
lines become perfectly metrical, 16b being a C-type verse and 25b being being an A-type
verse. Many verses in *Beowulf* become metrical only when an earlier form of a word is
restored. Some scholars take this fact as proof that the poem must have been composed
long before the date of the manuscript (ca. A.D. 1000), the scribe of the manuscript
having automatically modernized the original poem's spellings, thus inadvertently making these verses unmetrical.

18   **Bēowulf** is the name of Scyld's son. This Danish Beowulf has nothing to do with
the Geatish hero of the poem, who is not introduced until l. 194.

20–25   Here as elsewhere in *Beowulf* the poet pauses in his account of events to offer
a moral generalization suggested to him by the narrative he is relating.

20–21   **gōde . . . bearme** 'bring it about by good (deeds), by generous gifts from
his father's possessions'. A successful king in the Germanic world was one who is con-
sistently generous to his retainers, thereby purchasing their loyal support when he
needs it.

22–24   **gewunigen wilgesīþas . . . lēode gelǣsten** Parallel phrases meaning
'retainers stand by (him)'. The verbs are subjunctive plurals, They are subjunctive because
they do not refer to something actually happening in the present but rather to something
that might happen in the future.

24   **lofdǣdum** 'by praiseworthy deeds' i.e. by generous gifts to his retainers.

25   **in mǣgþa gehwǣre** 'in every tribe'.

Cōm on wanre niht
scrīðan sceadugenga. Scēotend swǣfon,
þā þæt hornreced   healdan scoldon
705 ealle būton ānum   – þæt wæs yldum cūþ,
þæt hīe ne mōste,   þā metod nolde,
se scynscaþa   under sceadu bregdan –
ac hē wæccende   wrāþum on andan
bād bolgenmōd   beadwa geþinges.
710 Ðā cōm of mōre   under misthleoþum
Grendel gongan;   Godes yrre bær;
mynte se mānscaða   manna cynnes
sumne besyrwan   in sele þām hēan.
Wōd under wolcnum   tō þæs þe hē wīnreced,
715 goldsele gumena   gearwost wisse
fǣttum fāhne.   Ne wæs þæt forma sīð,
þæt he Hroþgares   ham gesōhte;
nǣfre hē on aldordagum   ǣr ne siþðan
heardran hǣle,   healðegnas fand!
720 Cōm þā tō recede   rinc sīðian
drēamum bedǣled.   Dura sōna onarn
fȳrbendum fæst,   syþðan hē hire folmum onhrān;
onbrǣd þā bealohȳdig,   ðā hē gebolgen wæs,
recedes mūþan.   Raþe æfter þon
725 on fāgne flōr   fēond treddode,
ēode yrremōd;   him of ēagum stōd
ligge gelīcost   lēoht unfǣger.
Geseah hē in recede   rinca manige,
swefan sibbegedriht   samod ætgædere,
730 magorinca hēap.   þā his mōd āhlōg:

702 3 **Cōm ... scrīðan** The threefold announcement of Grendel's approach to Heorot is each time expressed using *cōm* plus an infinitive: *cōm ... scrīðan* 'came gliding', *cōm ... gongan* 'came striding' (ll. 710–11), *Cōm ... sīðian* 'came stalking' (l. 720).

703 **sceadugenga** 'walker in darkness', i.e. Grendel (who always attacks at night).

706–7 **þæt hīe ... bregdan** 'that the demonic foe might not fling them beneath the shades when the ruler did not wish (it)', i.e. Grendel could not kill them without the consent of a higher power.

708 **hē** i.e. Beowulf.

709 **geþinges** 'result, outcome' (object of *bād*, which takes gen.).

714 **tō þæs þe** 'to (the point) where, until'.

715 **wisse** 'knew', i.e. 'recognized'.

718–19 **nǣfre hē ... fand!** 'Never did he before nor after in the days of his life find hall-thanes (and) worse luck!'

722 **hire** i.e. the door (object of *onhrān*).

726 **him of ēagum stōd** 'from his eyes shone forth' (poss. dat.; see §191.2).

mynte þæt hē gedǣlde   ǣr þon dæg cwōme,
atol āglǣca   ānra gehwylces
līf wið līce,   þā him ālumpen wæs
wistfylle wēn.   Ne wæs þæt wyrd þā gēn,
735   þæt hē mā mōste   manna cynnes
ðicgean ofer þā niht.   Þrȳðswȳð behēold
mǣg Higelāces   hū se mānscaða
under fǣrgripum   gefaran wolde.
Ne þæt se āglǣca   yldan þōhte,
740   ac hē gefēng hraðe   forman sīðe
slǣpendne rinc,   slāt unwearnum,
bāt bānlocan,   blōd ēdrum dranc,
synsnǣdum swealh;   sōna hæfde
unlyfigendes   eal gefeormod,
745   fēt ond folma.   Forð nēar ætstōp,
nam þā mid handa   higeþīhtigne
rinc on ræste,   him rǣhte ongēan
fēond mid folme;   hē onfēng hraþe
inwitþancum   ond wið earm gesæt.
750   Sōna þæt onfunde   fyrena hyrde,
þæt hē ne mētte   middangeardes,
eorþan scēata   on elran men
mundgripe māran;   hē on mōde wearð
forht on ferhðe;   nō þȳ ǣr fram meahte.
755   Hyge wæs him hinfūs,   wolde on heolster flēon,
sēcan dēofla gedræg;   ne wæs his drohtoð þǣr
swylce hē on ealderdagum   ǣr gemētte.
Gemunde þā se gōda,   mǣg Higelāces,
ǣfensprǣce,   uplang āstōd
760   ond him fæste wiðfēng;   fingras burston;
eoten wæs ūtweard,   eorl furþur stōp.

731 **mynte þæt hē gedǣlde** 'he intended to sever' (lit. 'he intended that he should sever').
734 **Ne wæs . . . gēn** 'It was not by any means destined'.
738 **under . . . wolde** 'would proceed with his sudden grips'.
740 **forman sīðe** 'at the first opportunity'.
745 **fēt ond folma** '(including) the feet and hands'.
748–9 **fēond** i.e. Grendel.
hē onfēng . . . gesæt 'he (Beowulf) received (him, i.e. Grendel) quickly with hostile purpose and sat up against (Grendel's) arm.' Beowulf seizes Grendel in an arm-lock.
750 **fyrena hyrde** 'master of crimes', i.e. Grendel.
752–3 **on elran . . . māran** 'a greater handgrip in (any) other man'.
754 **nō þȳ . . . meahte** 'none the sooner could he (get) away', i.e. 'yet he could not (get) away'.
756–7 **ne wæs his . . . gemētte** 'nor was his experience there such as (§168 *swelce* 2) he had ever before met with in the days of his life'.
760 **him** i.e. Grendel.

Mynte se mǣra,   þǣr hē meahte swā,
wīdre gewindan   ond on weg þanon
flēon on fenhopu;   wiste his fingra geweald
765 on grames grāpum.   Þæt wæs gēocor sīð,
þæt se hearmscaþa   tō Heorute ātēah.
Dryhtsele dynede;   Denum eallum wearð,
ceasterbūendum,   cēnra gehwylcum,
eorlum ealuscerwen.   Yrre wǣron bēgen,
770 rēþe renweardas.   Reced hlynsode.
þā wæs wundor micel,   þæt se wīnsele
wiðhæfde heaþodēorum,   þæt hē on hrūsan ne fēol,
fæger foldbold;   ac hē þæs fæste wæs
innan ond ūtan   īrenbendum
775 searoþoncum besmiþod.   Þǣr fram sylle ābēag
medubenc monig   mīne gefrǣge
golde geregnad,   þǣr þā graman wunnon.
þæs ne wēndon ǣr   witan Scyldinga,
þæt hit ā mid gemete   manna ǣnig
780 betlīc ond bānfāg   tōbrecan meahte,
listum tōlūcan,   nymþe līges fæþm
swulge on swaþule.   Swēg ūp āstāg
nīwe geneahhe: Norð-Denum stōd
atelīc egesa,   ānra gehwylcum
785 þāra þe of wealle   wōp gehȳrdon,
gryrelēoð galan   Godes andsacan,
sigelēasne sang,   sār wānigean
helle hæfton.   Hēold hine fæste
se þe manna wæs   mægene strengest
790 on þǣm dæge   þysses līfes.
Nolde eorla hlēo   ǣnige þinga

---

762   **se mǣra** i.e. Grendel.
þǣr hē meahte swā 'if he (Grendel) could (do) so'.
764   **wiste his ... gewcald** 'he (Grendel) realized the control of his fingers (was)'.
769   **ealuscerwen** '?terror'. A mysterious word, recorded only here.
773   **hē** i.e. the hall.
þæs 'so' (§168 *þæs* 2).
776   **mīne gefrǣge** 'as I have heard say'. Infrequently the poet enters the narrative in the first person.
778–9   **þæs ... þæt** Anticipatory pronoun followed by noun clause (§148). *þæs* is object of *wēndon*, which takes gen.
786–8   **Godes andsacan ... helle hæfton** i.e. Grendel. Cf. l. 711. The monster's screams of pain are described with grim irony as an unhappy song.
788   **Hēold hine fæste** '(Beowulf) held him (Grendel) firmly.'
791–2   **Nolde eorla hlēo ... forlǣtan** 'The protector of men (Beowulf) did not want to let the murderous visitor go alive by any means.' But the monster does break away (ll. 819–21). It is important to notice that although he is 'the strongest of men in that day of this life' (ll. 789–90), Beowulf is subject to human limitations.

þone cwealmcuman   cwicne forlǣtan,
ne his līfdagas   lēoda ǣnigum
nytte tealde.   þǣr genehost brægd
795 eorl Bēowulfes   ealde lāfe,
wolde frēadrihtnes   feorh ealgian,
mǣres þēodnes,   ðǣr hīe meahton swā.
Hīe þæt ne wiston,   þā hīe gewin drugon,
heardhicgende   hildemecgas,
800 ond on healfa gehwone   hēawan þōhton,
sāwle sēcan: þone synscaðan
ǣnig ofer eorþan   īrenna cyst,
gūðbilla nān   grētan nolde;
ac hē sigewǣpnum   forsworen hæfde,
805 ecga gehwylcre.   Scolde his aldorgedāl
on ðǣm dæge   þysses līfes
earmlic wurðan,   ond se ellorgāst
on fēonda geweald   feor sīðian.
Ðā þæt onfunde   se þe fela ǣror
810 mōdes myrðe   manna cynne,
fyrene gefremede   – hē, fāg wið God –
þæt him se līchoma   lǣstan nolde,
ac hine se mōdega   mǣg Hygelāces
hæfde be honda;   wæs gehwæþer ōðrum
815 lifigende lāð.   Līcsār gebād
atol ǣglǣca;   him on eaxle wearð
syndolh sweotol,   seonowe onsprungon,
burston bānlocan.   Bēowulfe wearð
gūðhrēð gyfeþe;   scolde Grendel þonan
820 feorhsēoc flēon   under fenhleoðu,
sēcean wynlēas wīc;   wiste þē geornor
þæt his aldres wæs   ende gegongen,

794–5 **þǣr genehost . . . lāfe** 'A warrior of Beowulf's in abundance brandished his ancient heirloom there', i.e. 'Many a warrior brandished his sword'.

800–1 **ond on healfa . . . sēcan** 'and intended to slash away on every side, to get (i.e. kill) the soul (of Grendel)'.

801–5 Grendel's invulnerability to weapons seems to be explained here as the result of his having laid a spell on them, but the meaning of *forsworen* is uncertain.

805–8 **Scolde** 'had to' is to be construed with both *wurðan* and *sīðian*.

810–11 **mōdes myrðe . . . gefremede** *myrðe* and *fyrene* are parallel gen. pl. nouns with -*e* for -*a* (cf. 16/7 note): 'had done to the race of men afflictions of spirit, crimes'.

811 **hē, fāg wið God** 'he, hostile towards God'. This phrase is parallel with and specifies *se þe* (l. 809).

817–18 **seonowe . . . bānlocan** 'the sinews sprang asunder, the joints broke (apart)', that is, Grendel's arm was torn from his body.

822–3 **his aldres . . . dægrīm** 'the number of his days, the end of his life, had run out'.

dōgera dægrīm.   Denum eallum wearð
æfter þām wælrǣse   willa gelumpen.
825   Hæfde þā gefælsod   se þe ǣr feorran cōm,
snotor ond swȳðferhð,   sele Hrōðgāres,
genered wið nīðe.   Nihtweorce gefeh,
ellenmǣrþum.   Hæfde Ēast-Denum
Gēatmecga lēod   gilp gelǣsted,
830   swylce oncȳþðe   ealle gebētte,
inwidsorge,   þe hīe ǣr drugon
ond for þrēanȳdum   þolian scoldon,
torn unlȳtel.   þæt wæs tācen sweotol,
syþðan hildedēor   hond ālegde,
835   earm ond eaxle   – þǣr wæs eal geador
Grendles grāpe –   under geapne hrōf.

　　Ðā wæs on morgen   mīne gefrǣge
ymb þā gifhealle   gūðrinc monig;
fērdon folctogan   feorran ond nēan
840   geond wīdwegas   wundor scēawian,
lāþes lāstas.   Nō his līfgedāl
sārlīc þūhte   secga ænegum
þāra þe tīrlēases   trode scēawode,
hū hē wērigmōd   on weg þanon,
845   nīða ofercumen,   on nicera mere
fǣge ond geflȳmed   feorhlāstas bær.
Ðǣr wæs on blōde   brim weallende,
atol ȳða geswing   eal gemenged,
hāton heolfre,   heorodrēore wēol;
850   dēaðfǣge dēog,   siððan drēama lēas
in fenfreoðo   feorh ālegde,
hǣþene sāwle;   þǣr him hel onfēng.

　　þanon eft gewiton   ealdgesīðas
swylce geong manig   of gomenwāþe,
855   fram mere mōdge   mēarum rīdan,
beornas on blancum.   Ðǣr wæs Bēowulfes
mǣrðo mǣned;   monig oft gecwæð,
þætte sūð ne norð   be sǣm twēonum
ofer eormengrund   ōþer nǣnig
860   under swegles begong   sēlra nǣre

---

837   **mīne gefrǣge** See l. 776 note.
847   **Ðǣr wæs ... weallende** 'There the water was surging with blood.' The men
from far and near have followed Grendel's tracks back to the mere where he had his abode.
850   **dēaðfǣge dēog** 'the one doomed to death (i.e. Grendel) had been concealed'.
The meaning of *dēog*, which occurs only here, is uncertain.

rondhæbbendra, rīces wyrðra.

Nē hīe hūru winedrihten   wiht ne lōgon,

glædne Hrōðgār,   ac þæt wæs gōd cyning.

Hwīlum heaþorōfe   hlēapan lēton,

865   on geflit faran   fealwe mēaras,

ðǣr him foldwegas   fægere þūhton,

cystum cūðe.   Hwīlum cyninges þegn,

guma gilphlæden,   gidda gemyndig,

se ðe ealfela   ealdgesegena

870   worn gemunde,   word ōþer fand

sōðe gebunden;   secg eft ongan

sīð Bēowulfes   snyttrum styrian,

ond on spēd wrecan   spel gerāde,

wordum wrixlan;   wēlhwylc gecwæð,

875   þæt hē fram Sigemundes   secgan hȳrde

ellendǣdum,   uncūþes fela,

Wælsinges gewin,   wīde sīðas,

þāra þe gumena bearn   gearwe ne wiston,

fæhðe ond fyrena,   būton Fitela mid hine,

880   þonne hē swulces hwæt   secgan wolde,

ēam his nefan,   swā hīe ā wǣron

æt nīða gehwām   nȳdgesteallan;

hæfdon ealfela   eotena cynnes

sweordum gesǣged.   Sigemunde gesprong

885   æfter dēaðdæge   dōm unlȳtel,

syþðan wīges heard   wyrm ācwealde,

hordes hyrde;   hē under hārne stān,

861   **rīces wyrðra** 'more worthy of a kingdom', i.e. 'more worthy of being a king'. This high praise leads naturally to the reassurance that they intended no dispraise of their own king (who had been unable to protect them from Grendel).

867   **cystum cūðe** 'known for their good qualities' refers to *foldwegas* nom. pl.

870–1   **word ōþer ... gebunden** '(the king's thane) found other words faithfully bound together', 'other' meaning perhaps new words for this occasion. *Gebunden* seems to refer to the alliterative linking together of words in Old English verse.

872   **sīð ... styrian** 'to engage Beowulf's undertaking skilfully'. Some such sense as 'engage' is implied, because the thane does not narrate the hero's achievement but rather celebrates it by telling other heroic stories, exalting Beowulf's victory to the status of the greatest victories of Germanic legend, such as Sigemund's slaying of the dragon.

874–97   The first part of the thane's account of Sigemund's adventures describes his expeditions with his nephew Fitela (ll. 874–84). The details of this activity are to be found in the Old Norse *Volsungasaga*, chapters 3–8. Sigemund's dragon fight (ll. 884–97) is the event renowned in Germanic legend at large, only in other accounts the dragon is slain by Sigemund's son Siegfried. Indeed, it is possible that this passage says the same, since *wīges heard ... hē* (ll. 886–7) could refer to Siegfried. The Middle High German *Nibelungenlied* is the most famous of the accounts of Siegfried, but he is also prominent in Scandinavian literature.

879   **būton Fitela mid hine** 'except for Fitela (who was) with him'.

æþelinges bearn   āna genēðde
frēcne dǣde,   ne wæs him Fitela mid;
890 hwæþre him gesǣlde,   ðæt þæt swurd þurhwōd
wrǣtlicne wyrm,   þæt hit on wealle ætstōd,
dryhtlic īren;   draca morðre swealt.
Hæfde āglǣca   elne gegongen,
þæt hē bēahhordes   brūcan mōste
895 selfes dōme;   sǣbāt gehlēod,
bǣr on bearm scipes   beorhte frætwa,
Wǣlses eafera;   wyrm hāt gemealt.

(b) Beowulf Consoles Hrothgar for Æschere's Death

The night after Beowulf's victory over Grendel, the Danes are surprised by another monstrous visitant: Grendel's mother comes to Heorot and slays Hrothgar's favourite thane, Æschere, in vengeance for her son's death. Beowulf, who has lodged in a separate building some distance from the royal hall, is brought to the King, and Hrothgar tells him of Æschere's death. He also describes to Beowulf the eerie lair where Grendel and his mother live, and this description (ll. 1357–79) is one of the most famous passages in all Old English literature. As if appalled by his own account of the monsters' dwelling place, he asks almost despairingly whether the hero will consider challenging this second monster. Beowulf's answer (ll. 1383–96) is the finest statement we have of the Germanic heroic ethos.

þā wæs frōd cyning,
hār hilderinc   on hrēon mōde,
syðþan hē aldorþegn   unlyfigendne,
þone dēorestan   dēadne wisse.
1310 Hraþe wæs tō būre   Bēowulf fetod,
sigorēadig secg.   Samod ǣrdæge
ēode eorla sum,   æþele cempa

891 **þæt hit ... ætstōd** 'so that it (the sword) stuck into the wall'. The dragon is pinned to the wall.

893 **Hæfde ... gegongen** 'By his valour the combatant (i.e. Sigemund or Siegfried) had brought it about.'

895 **selfes dōme** 'according to (his own) judgement', i.e. 'to his heart's content'.

897 **wyrm hāt gemealt** 'the hot dragon was consumed (? in its own fire)'.

1309 **þonne dēorestan ... wisse** 'knew the dearest one (to be) dead'.

1312 **eorla sum** 'a certain one of the warriors' or perhaps 'the important warrior' (i.e. Beowulf).

self mid gesīðum   þǣr se snotera bād
hwæþer him alwalda   ǣfre wille
1315   æfter wēaspelle   wyrpe gefremman.
Gang ðā æfter flōre   fyrdwyrðe man
mid his handscale   – healwudu dynede –
þæt hē þone wīsan   wordum nǣgde
frēan Ingwina,   frægn gif him wǣre
1320   æfter nēodlaðum   niht getǣse.
Hrōðgār maþelode,   helm Scyldinga:
'Ne frīn þū æfter sǣlum!   Sorh is genīwod
Denigea lēodum.   Dēad is Æschere,
Yrmenlāfes   yldra brōþor,
1325   mīn rūnwita   ond mīn rǣdbora,
eaxlgestealla,   ðonne wē on orlege
hafelan weredon,   þonne hniton fēþan,
eoferas cnysedan.   Swylc scolde eorl wesan,
æþeling ǣrgōd,   swylc Æschere wæs!
1330   Wearð him on Heorote   tō handbanan
wælgǣst wǣfre;   ic ne wāt hwæder
atol ǣse wlanc   eftsīðas tēah,
fylle gefægnod.   Hēo þā fǣhðe wræc,
þe þū gȳstran niht   Grendel cwealdest
1335   þurh hǣstne hād   heardum clammum,
forþan hē tō lange   lēode mīne
wanode ond wyrde.   Hē æt wīge gecrang
ealdres scyldig,   ond nū ōþer cwōm
mihtig mānscaða,   wolde hyre mǣg wrecan,
1340   ge feor hafað   fǣhðe gestǣled,
þæs þe þincean mæg   þegne monegum,
se þe æfter sincgyfan   on sefan grēoteþ –
hreþerbealo hearde: nū sēo hand ligeð,
se þe ēow wēlhwylcra   wilna dohte.
1345   Ic þæt londbūend,   lēode mīne,
selerǣdende   secgan hȳrde,
þæt hīe gesāwon   swylce twēgen

1313–14   bād hwæþer 'waited (to find out) whether'.
1330   Wearð him . . . handbanan 'became his slayer in Heorot'.
1340   ge feor . . . gestǣled 'and has avenged the hostility far (i.e. thoroughly)'.
1341   þæs þe 'as'. See §177.2 (*f*).
1343   hreþerbealo hearde nom. sg., in loose apposition with ll. 1338b–42.
1343–4   nū sēo hand . . . dohte 'now the hand lies low which did well by you as regards all good things'. Grammatically *sēo þe* rather than *se þe* (l. 1344) is required to agree with *sēo hand*, but the poet was no doubt thinking of the man rather than the feminine hand.
1347   swylce twēgen 'two such', i.e. Grendel and his mother.

micle mearcstapan   mōras healdan,
ellorgǣstas. Ðǣra ōðer wæs,

1350 þæs þe hīe gewislīcost   gewitan meahton,
idese onlīcnes; ōðer earmsceapen
on weres wæstmum   wræclāstas træd,
næfne hē wæs māra   þonne ænig man ōðer;
þone on gēardagum   Grendel nemdon

1355 foldbūende; nō hīe fæder cunnon,
hwæþer him ænig wæs   ǣr ācenned
dyrnra gāsta. Hīe dȳgel lond
warigeað wulfhleoþu,   windige næssas,
frēcne fengelād,   ðǣr fyrgenstrēam

1360 under næssa genipu   niþer gewīteð,
flōd under foldan. Nis þæt feor heonon
mīlgemearces,   þæt se mere standeð;
ofer þǣm hongiað   hrinde bearwas,
wudu wyrtum fæst   wæter oferhelmað.

1365 þǣr mæg nihta gehwǣm   nīðwundor sēon,
fȳr on flōde. Nō þæs frōd leofað
gumena bearna,   þæt þone grund wite.
Dēah þe hæðstapa   hundum geswenced,
heorot hornum trum   holtwudu sēce,

1370 feorran geflȳmed,   ǣr hē feorh seleð,
aldor on ōfre,   ǣr hē in wille,
hafelan hȳdan;   nis þæt hēoru stōw!

1349–51 **Ðǣra ōðer ... ōðer** 'One of them ... the other.'

1350 **þæs þe hīe gewislīcost** 'as well as they'. See §177.2 (*f*).

1351–2 **idese onlīcnes ... on weres wæstmum** 'the likeness of a woman (i.e. of a woman's shape) ... in a man's shape'.

1353 **næfne** 'except that'. See §179.5.

1355–7 **nō hīe fæder ... gāsta** 'they do not know whether they had any father born of mysterious demons'. Earlier in the poem the poet explains that the Grendelkin are the offspring of Cain, but the Danes, who know nothing of the Bible, are ignorant as to the monsters' parentage.

1357–76 The landscape described here is at once vivid and mysterious. There is a mere or pool surrounded by sheer cliffs with overhanging trees. A waterfall descends into the mere, and concealed behind this waterfall is a cave where Grendel and his mother live. The cave can be reached only by diving into the water and swimming under the waterfall. The Old Norse *Grettissaga*, which tells a story much like that of Beowulf's fight with the Grendelkin, describes the setting with precision.

1362 **mīlgemearces** 'in measurement by miles'. See §190.5.

1366 **fȳr on flōde** The fire in the water would be the fire burning in the cave of the Grendelkin (which Beowulf later sees), but to the Danes it is an inexplicable glimmering on the surface of the water.

1366–7 **þæs ... þæt** See §168 *þæs ... þæt* and note 1.

1370–1 **ǣr hē feorh ... wille** 'he will sooner give up his life, his spirit, on the shore before he will (go) in'.

þonon ȳðgeblond   ūp āstīgeð
won tō wolcnum,   þonne wind styreþ
1375 lāð gewidru,   oð þæt lyft drysmaþ,
roderas rēotað.   Nū is se rǣd gelang
eft æt þē ānum.   Eard gīt ne const,
frēcne stōwe,   ðǣr þū findan miht
sinnigne secg;   sēc gif þū dyrre!
1380 Ic þē þā fǣhðe   fēo lēanige,
ealdgestrēonum,   swā ic ǣr dyde,
wundnum golde,   gyf þū on weg cymest.'
    Bēowulf maþelode,   bearn Ecgþēowes;
'Ne sorga, snotor guma!   Sēlre bið ǣghwǣm,
1385 þæt hē his frēond wrece,   þonne hē fela murne.
Ūre ǣghwylc sceal   ende gebīdan
worolde līfes;   wyrce se þe mōte
dōmes ǣr dēaþe;   þæt bið drihtguman
unlifgendum   æfter sēlest.
1390 Āris, rīces weard,   uton hraþe fēran,
Grendles māgan   gang scēawigan.
Ic hit þē gehāte: nō hē on helm losaþ,
ne on foldan fæþm,   ne on fyrgenholt,
ne on gyfenes grund,   gā þǣr hē wille!
1395 Ðȳs dōgor þū   geþyld hafa
wēana gehwylces,   swā ic þē wēne tō.'
Āhlēop ðā se gomela,   gode þancode,
mihtigan drihtne,   þæs se man gesprǣc.

(c) The Lament of the Last Survivor

The last thousand lines of *Beowulf* describe the hero's final battle
with a fire-breathing dragon. He is an old man and, having no
progeny, the last of his line. The profoundly elegiac tone of this final
section of the poem is established by the poet just after the section
gets under way. He describes an unnamed man who is the sole
survivor of his people, a people who lived in an earlier age long
before the time of the poem's action. Since there is no one left to

1376–7 Nū is se rǣd . . . ānum 'Now the remedy is again dependent upon you
alone.'

1387–8 wyrce . . . dēaþe 'let him who is able achieve fame before death'. This is the
ruling ideal of the Germanic heroic ethos.

1392–4 hē . . . hē Grammatical gender: masc. *hē* agrees with the antecedent *māgan*
(l. 1391).

1395–6 geþyld . . . gehwylces 'have patience in each of your afflictions'.

1397–8 gode þancode . . . gesprǣc. See §163.5.

carry on the tribe's history, the heroic ideal of fame as the one means of survival beyond death is rendered meaningless. Having no other use for the treasures of his nation, he decides to bury them, and as there is no one to whom he can address his lament, he addresses it to the earth which is receiving the people's treasure. The speech prefigures the end of *Beowulf*, where the Geatish nation buries a treasure hoard with their slain king (selection 18(d) following). Compare selection 13.

'Heald þū nū, hrūse,   nū hæleð ne mōstan,
eorla æhte!   Hwæt, hyt ær on ðē
gōde begēaton.   Gūðdēað fornam,
2250   feorhbealo frēcne   fȳra gehwylcne
lēoda mīnra   þāra ðe þis līf ofgeaf:
gesāwon seledrēam.   Nāh, hwā sweord wege
oððe forð bere   fæted wæge,
dryncfæt dēore;   duguð ellor scōc.
2255   Sceal se hearda helm   hyrstedgoldc,
fætum befeallen;   feormynd swefað,
þā ðe beadogrīman   bȳwan sceoldon;
ge swylce sēo herepād,   sīo æt hilde gebād
ofer borda gebræc   bite īrena,
2260   brosnað æfter beorne.   Ne mæg byrnan hring
æfter wīgfruman   wīde fēran,
hæleðum be healfe.   Næs hearpan wyn,
gomen glēobēames,   ne gōd hafoc
geond sæl swingeð,   ne se swifta mearh
2265   burhstede bēateð.   Bealocwealm hafað
fela feorhcynna   forð onsended!'

(d) Beowulf's Funeral

The aged King Beowulf was successful in his fight with the dragon: the creature that had threatened to destroy the Geatish nation was himself destroyed by Beowulf's hand. But in the course of the fight

2247   **nū hæleð ne mōstan** For *nū* see §168 *nū* 2.
2252   **gesāwon seledrēam** Assuming that the *ge-* prefix gave perfective meaning to the verb *sāwon* here, we can translate '(they) had seen the last of joys in the hall'.
Nāh, hwā sweord wege 'I do not have anyone who can bear the sword.' Cf. 12/212 note.
2255-6   **Sceal . . . befeallen** 'Must (be) . . . deprived of'.
2258   **ge swylce** 'and likewise'.
2261   **æfter wīgfruman** 'along with the war-leader'. The corselet is personified and described as a companion of the man.
2262   **Næs** (= *Ne wæs*) 'there was no'.

Beowulf received a mortal wound. The poet describes the hero's suffering and death and records his speeches of farewell to his people. The Geats cremate his body in an impressive pagan ceremony, and then we are told in the present selection how they bury his ashes and bid him farewell. The sadness of his funeral is deepened by the people's awareness that with King Beowulf gone the entire nation faces certain destruction by their surrounding enemies, who had been kept at bay only by the protective power of their king. With Beowulf's fall the nation will fall.

       Geworhton ðā   Wedra lēode
       hlǣw on hlīðe   se wæs hēah ond brād,
       weglīðendum   wīde gesȳne,
       ond betimbredon   on tȳn dagum
3160   beadurōfes bēcn,   bronda lāfe
       wealle beworhton,   swā hyt weorðlīcost
       foresnotre men   findan mihton.
       Hī on beorg dydon   bēg ond siglu,
       eall swylce hyrsta   swylce on horde ǣr
3165   nīðhēdige men   genumen hæfdon;
       forlēton eorla gestrēon   eorðan healdan,
       gold on grēote,   þǣr hit nū gēn lifað
       eldum swā unnyt   swā hyt ǣror wæs.
       Þā ymbe hlǣw riodan   hildedēore,
3170   æþelinga bearn,   ealra twelfe,
       woldon care cwīðan,   ond cyning mǣnan,
       wordgyd wrecan,   ond ymb wer sprecan;
       eahtodan eorlscipe   ond his ellenweorc
       duguðum dēmdon.   Swā hit gedēfe bið,
3175   þæt mon his winedryhten   wordum herge,
       ferhðum frēoge,   þonne hē forð scile
       of līchaman   lǣded weorðan,
       swā begnornodon   Gēata lēode
       hlāfordes hryre,   heorðgenēatas:
3180   cwǣdon þæt hē wǣre   wyruldcyninga
       mannum mildust   ond monðwǣrust,
       lēodum līðost   ond lofgeornost.

    3161–2 **swā hyt . . . mihton** 'as splendidly as the very wise men were able to devise it'.
    3164 **eall swylce hyrsta** 'all such treasures as'.
    on horde 'from the hoard'.
    3176 **ferhðum frēoge** 'cherish (him) in (his) heart'. For the dat. pl. *ferhðum* see 14/63 note.

19

Wulf and Eadwacer

The poem to which modern scholars have given the name *Wulf and Eadwacer* is the most mysterious and tantalizing of all OE poems. Over the years it has provoked an extraordinary variety of completely diverse interpretations. We know that the speaker of the poem is feminine because of the inflexional endings of the adjectives *rēotugu* (l. 10) and *sēoce* (l. 14). She seems to be involved with two men whose names are *Wulf* and *Eadwacer* (both attested male names in Anglo-Saxon England). But even these points have been disputed. One critic has argued that *wulf* is not a proper name but the common noun 'wolf' and that the poem is a beast fable. Others think that Wulf and Eadwacer are the same person. In the following paragraph we shall propose one interpretation of the poem, an interpretation which has found favour in part or as a whole with a number of scholars. The glossing and parsing of the poem's words will then conform with the interpretation proposed here. But having read the poem in these narrow terms, the student should turn to Henk Aertsen's '*Wulf and Eadwacer*: A Woman's Cri de Coeur – For Whom? For What?' in *Companion to Old English Poetry*, ed. Henk Aertsen and Rolf H. Bremmer, Jr. (Amsterdam, 1994), pp. 119–44, which provides a skilful review of the wide range of interpretations which have been put forward along with some original reflections on the poem. Consideration of the multiple and mutually contradicting views of what this poem means will give the reader a salutary sense of just how arbitrary modern editions and modern interpreters can be in stipulating word-meanings in a text and in assigning modern punctuation to an OE text. (See above, p. 278, the editors' note.)

We may surmise that the speaker of the poem is a woman held in confinement at her home while her husband or lover, perhaps an outlaw, ranges abroad, unable to return home because of unspecified hostilities. (Cf. the speaker's situation in *The Wife's Lament* above.)

A Guide to Old English, Eighth Edition. Bruce Mitchell and Fred C. Robinson.
© 2012 Bruce Mitchell and Fred C. Robinson. Published 2012 by Blackwell Publishing Ltd.

If he dares to come out of exile and join the troop of men (her people's army or that of the 'slaughter-cruel men' of l. 6), then it will be like making them a present of his life – they will kill him. She and Wulf are on separate islands, and she sadly laments his absence from her. A warrior-guard, presumably the Eadwacer mentioned in l. 16, has on occasion 'encompassed her with limbs' – a locution usually understood as a delicate way of saying that he has made love to her. This experience she describes as giving her some pleasure but at the same time as being loathsome to her. She then calls out to Wulf by name, saying that not seeing him has left her sick (i.e. lovesick). Then, turning to her abusive ward Eadwacer, she bitterly announces that Wulf has abducted their (hers and Wulf's? hers and Eadwacer's?) child. She closes with the rueful comment that it has been easy to break up the harmony of two people who were never allowed to be united in the first place.

Besides the problems of meaning which this text presents, there are also several anomalies of verse-form here. Lines 2–3 and 7–8 are repetitions, like a refrain, and this is unusual in OE verse. Lines 17 and 19, like 3 and 8, are only half the length of a normal line, and yet the sense does not suggest any loss of text. The first half of l. 13 has only three syllables, whereas an OE verse requires at least four syllables. And yet the verse as it stands is very effective in context. We conclude that this poet is willing to violate the strict rules of OE prosody in order to achieve bold effects.

Wulf and Eadwacer is preserved in the manuscript known as the Exeter Book. We have adopted three emendations: for MS *ungelice* we read *ungelic* (to bring l. 8 into conformity with l. 3). For MS *dogode* in l. 9 we read *hogode*, since there is no evidence of a verb *dogian* in OE, while *hogode* makes good sense in context. In l. 16 we read *earmne* for MS *earne*, again for the sake of sense.

> Lēodum is mīnum   swylce him mon lāc gife;
> willað hȳ hine āþecgan   gif hē on þrēat cymeð.
>   Ungelīc is ūs.
> Wulf is on īege,   ic on ōþerre.

1   **lāc** Of this word's wide range of meanings ('gift, offering, sacrifice, play, battle') the provisional interpretation suggested here requires 'gift'.

    gife is pres. subj. after *swylce* 'as if'. The reference must be to present time ('as if one give *lāc* to them') not to the past ('as if one had given . . .'). See §177.4.

2   **willað hȳ** Inversion of subject and verb may but need not signal an interrogative sentence. (Cf. *Gehȳrest þū* l. 16.) We make the assumption here (and in l. 7) that the sentence is declarative, not a question.

3   **ūs** Pl., not dual, may mean that the reference is to more than two people (cf. *uncer* l. 19). But since *ūs* sometimes takes over the function of dual *unc* in the course of OE (see Bruce Mitchell's *Old English Syntax* (*OES*) §258), *ūs* here could refer to only two: 'It is different for the two of us'.

5 Fæst is þæt ēglond, fenne biworpen.
  Sindon wælrēowe weras þǣr on īge;
  willað hȳ hine āþecgan gif hē on þrēat cymeð.
    Ungelīc is ūs.
  Wulfes ic mīnes wīdlāstum wēnum hogode
10 þonne hit wæs rēnig weder ond ic rēotugu sæt;
  þonne mec se beaducāfa bōgum bilegde,
  wæs mē wyn tō þon, wæs mē hwæþre ēac lāð.
  Wulf, mīn Wulf! wēna mē þīne
  sēoce gedydon, þīne seldcymas,
15 murnende mōd, nales metelīste.
  Gehȳrest þū, Ēadwacer? Uncerne earmne hwelp
  bireð Wulf tō wuda.
  þæt mon ēaþe tōslīteð þætte nǣfre gesomnad wæs,
  uncer giedd geador.

9 'I thought with hopes about my Wulf's far wanderings' or 'I thought hopefully (the dative pl. being taken as adverbial)'.

10–11 **þonne** 'whenever'. The speaker refers to recurrent events (§168 *þonne* 2).

11 **beaducāfa** In the provisional interpretation suggested here, this general term for a warrior refers to the man identified as Ēadwacer (a name which means 'watcher of wealth') in l. 16. He seems to be the ward or self-appointed companion of the woman speaking.

13 **wēna mē þīne** 'my hopes for you' or 'my expectations (of your visits)'.

16 **hwelp**, like modern *whelp*, refers to the young of an animal, but here it seems to be used punningly to refer to the child of a man whose name means 'wolf'.

18 This line has been taken to refer to Matthew 19:6 'What God hath joined together let no man put asunder'.

Judith

The Old English poem *Judith* is a reshaping and retelling of the Old
Testament apocryphon 'Judith' as it is presented (in somewhat
abbreviated form) in St Jerome's Vulgate Bible. The Old English
poet is in firm command of the traditional heroic style and has
produced one of the best narrative poems in the corpus. The rather
full cast of characters in the Vulgate version is reduced by the Old
English poet to only two named characters – Judith, the radiant
Jewish heroine, and her antagonist the Assyrian commander
Holofernes. Incidents from the original Latin telling of the tale are
selected and sometimes rearranged, and the narrative is simplified
in a way that heightens the drama of the story. Favourite Old English
topics like warfare and the victors' plundering of their defeated enemy
are developed with all the traditional motifs in place. The Jewish
heroine is not only heroicized in the traditional Germanic way but
is also Christianized: she prays to the Holy Trinity and names the
Son of God. Some students of the poem have concluded that the
poet's handling of the story has been guided by Christian com-
mentaries on 'Judith'.

Although the poem as we have it makes a satisfying narrative
whole, there is text missing from the beginning of *Judith*. How much
is missing? Some have conjectured that as much as nine hundred
or more lines have been lost. This is based primarily upon the fact
that in the manuscript in which it is preserved *Judith* is segmented
into three sections (called 'fitts' by the Anglo-Saxons) and, at the
beginning, a portion of a fourth section. The three complete sections are numbered X, XI, XII. This has been taken to imply that
nine preceding sections have been lost. But this need not be the case.
Sometimes a manuscript containing several different poems will have
the sections of the poems numbered consecutively. (The poetic
manuscript Junius XI in the Bodleian Library in Oxford is a case in
point.) The manuscript in which *Judith* originally appeared may have
been numbered like this, and some of the preceding nine fitts might
have contained poems which have nothing to do with *Judith*. The

A Guide to Old English, Eighth Edition. Bruce Mitchell and Fred C. Robinson.
© 2012 Bruce Mitchell and Fred C. Robinson. Published 2012 by Blackwell
Publishing Ltd.

beheading of Holofernes and its aftermath (which are told in full in the poem as we have it) are the only significant things that happened in Judith's life. If there were originally nine fitts containing nine hundred or so lines leading up to the text before us, then this would be a long preamble to a tale indeed. After you have read *Judith*, ask yourself whether it seems that a major portion of the story is missing.

Like most Old English poems, *Judith* is anonymous and undated, although stylistic features suggest that it was composed in the latter rather than the earlier part of the Old English period. Some scholars have tried to associate the poem with some specific person or event in history. Since Judith was the name of the second wife of King Æthelwulf (Alfred the Great's father), one scholar suggests that the poem was written in her honour. Another scholar thinks it commemorates another royal personage, Æthelflæd, Lady of the Mercians. But no such impetus for the poem's composition is necessary. The story of Judith was generally popular in the early Middle Ages. Besides the poem before us, a detailed narrative of the story in rhythmic prose is to be found among Ælfric's works, and there is another verse account in Middle English. A versified version of the story is also found in a twelfth-century Middle High German manuscript. In early northern Europe the story was evidently popular among verse translators.

The style of *Judith* is distinctive. A large fraction of the poem is written in hypermetric verses, such as we encountered in *The Dream of the Rood* (see above p. 266, note to l. 8). The poet also shows an unusual fondness for end-rhymes (e.g. l. 2 *grunde:funde*, l. 29 *sīne:wīne*, l. 63 *nēosan:-lēosan*, etc.). There are also irregularities in the handling of alliteration in l. 279, where all four accented syllables alliterate, l. 55, where *sn-* alliterates with *st-*, and l. 149 (see note). These features are among the symptoms that the poem is late, since the strict metrical practice of the original alliterative verse seems to be breaking down.

At some point during its history *Judith* became detached from its original manuscript and was bound up next to the poem *Beowulf* in British Library MS Cotton Vitellius A.xv. Before the fire of 1731, which badly damaged this codex, the seventeenth-century scholar Franciscus Junius made a transcription of *Judith*, which is housed today in the Bodleian Library. In places where the fire left the original manuscript damaged, we can get the readings from Junius's transcript. The present text is based upon these two sources, and we have made no effort to record when a reading is based upon Junius rather than the Vitellius manuscript.[1]

---

[1] Junius's text is reproduced in full in *Old English Verse Texts from Many Sources: A Comprehensive Collection*, ed. Fred C. Robinson and E. G. Stanley, Early English Manuscripts in Facsimile vol. 23 (Copenhagen, 1991).

twēode
gifena in ðȳs ginnan grunde.   Hēo ðǣr ðā gearwe funde
mundbyrd æt ðām mǣran þēodne   þā hēo āhte mǣste
þearfe
hyldo þæs hēhstan Dēman,   þæt hē hīe wið þæs hēhstan
brōgan
5   gefriðode, frymða Waldend.   Hyre ðæs Fæder on
roderum
torhtmōd tīðe gefremede   þe hēo āhte trumne gelēafan
ā tō ðām Ælmihtigan.   Gefrægen ic ðā Holofernus
wīnhātan wyrcean georne   ond eallum wundrum þrymlic
girwan up swǣsendo,   tō ðām hēt se gumena baldor
10   ealle ðā yldestan ðegnas.   Hīe ðæt ofstum miclum
ræfndon, rondwiggende,   cōmon tō ðām rīcan þēodne
fēran, folces rǣswan.   Þæt wæs þȳ fēorðan dōgore
þæs ðe Iūdith hyne,   glēaw on geðonce,
ides ælfscīnu,   ǣrest gesōhte.
X   15   Hīe ðā tō ðām symle   sittan ēodon,
wlance tō wīngedrince,   ealle his wēagesiðas,
bealde byrnwiggende.   Þǣr wǣron bollan stēape
boren æfter bencum gelōme,   swylce ēac būnan ond orcas

In our text of *Judith* we have introduced the following emendations: *baldor* for MS
.aldor [with initial *b* erased] (l. 32), *gūðfreca* supplied (l. 62), *þearfendre* for MS
þearffendre (l. 85), *heorte* for MS *heorte ys* (l. 87), *hie* for MS *hie hie* (l. 134), *hēoldon* for
MS *heoildon* (l. 142), *Iūdith* for MS *iudithe* (l. 144), *forlætan* for MS *forlæton* (l. 150),
Þēodnes for MS *þeoðnes* (l. 165), *starian* for MS *stariað* (l. 179), *fyllað* for MS *fyllan*
(l. 194), *sigeþūfas* for MS *þufas* (l. 201), *wiston* for MS *westan* (l. 207), *rīcne* for MS *rice*
(l. 234), *tōbrēdan* for MS *tobredon* (l. 247), *wērigferhðe* for MS *weras ferhðe* (l. 249), *hilde*
for MS *hildo* (l. 251), *dægweorce* for MS *dæge weorce* (l. 266), *nyde* supplied (l. 287),
lindwigan for MS *lind.* (l. 297), *māre* for MS *mærra* (l. 329), *on* for MS 7 (l. 332). One
emendation to Junius's transcription: *ā* supplied in l. 345 (cf. l. 7a).

1–2   The first sentence is fragmentary, text having been lost from the poem's
beginning. Most scholars assume that a negative preceded *twēode*, the sense of the
sentence being 'she did not doubt His gifts in this wide world'. Cf. ll. 345–6.

2–12   The first group of expanded or hypermetric lines, which comprise some fifth
of the poem. See 'Hypermetric Verse', p. 162 above.

4   **hyldo** has been explained as gen. sg. dependent on *þearfe* (l. 3) or as acc. sg. in
apposition with *mundbyrd* (l. 3). The former seems more natural. *Þæt* introduces a noun
clause in apposition with *mundbyrd* (l. 3). Both are objects of *funde* (l. 2).

5–6   **ðæs . . . þe** introduces a causal clause 'for that [reason] . . . that . . .'.

7   **Holofernus** The Latin nominative form is used in the OE text for all cases – acc.
(as here), nom. (ll. 21, 46), and gen. (ll. 180, 250, but *Holofernes* l. 336). The poet takes
the initial *H-* as merely graphic: the name always alliterates with initial vowels.

9   **tō ðām** neut. pl. referring to *swǣsendo* is an ambiguous demonstrative/relative (§162.3)
'to it' or (as we assume here) 'to which'.

10   **ofstum miclum** The dat. pl. has adverbial force: 'very speedily'.

11–12   **cōmon . . . fēran** 'came travelling'.

12   **rǣswan** is probably dat. sg. in apposition with *þēodne*.

12–13   **þæt wæs . . . þæs ðe** 'It was . . . that' or 'It was . . . when'.

fulle fletsittendum;   hīe þæt fǣge þēgon,
20   rōfe rondwiggende,   þēah ðæs se rīca ne wēnde,
egesful eorla dryhten.   Ðā wearð Holofernus,
goldwine gumena,   on gytesālum;
hlōh ond hlȳdde,   hlynede ond dynede,
þæt mihten fīra bearn   feorran gehȳran
25   hū se stīðmōda   styrmde ond gylede,
mōdig ond medugāl,   manode geneahhe
bencsittende   þæt hī gebǣrdon wel.
Swā se inwidda   ofer ealne dæg
dryhtguman sīne   drencte mid wīne,
30   swīðmōd sinces brytta,   oð þæt hīe on swīman lāgon,
oferdrencte his duguðe ealle   swylce hīe wǣron dēaðe
geslegene,
āgotene gōda gehwylces.   Swā hēt se gumena baldor
fylgan fletsittendum   oð þæt fīra bearnum
neālǣhte niht sēo þȳstre.   Hēt ðā nīða geblonden
35   þā ēadigan mægð   ofstum fetigan
tō his bedreste   bēagum gehlæste,
hringum gehrodene.   Hīe hraðe fremedon,
anbyhtscealcas,   swa him heora ealdor bebēad,
byrnwigena brego,   bearhtme stōpon
40   tō ðām gysterne   þǣr hīe Iūdithðe
fundon ferhðglēawe   ond ðā fromlīce
lindwiggende   lǣdan ongunnon
þā torhtan mægð   tō træfe þām hēan
þǣr se rīca hyne   reste on symbel
45   nihtes inne,   Nergende lāð,
Hōlofernus.   Þǣr wæs eallgylden
flēohnet fæger   ond ymbe þæs folctogan

---

20   **ðæs** object of *wēnde*, refers to the Assyrians' doomed status (*fǣge* l. 19).

21b–7   Note the alliterating verbs and consider their effect here and in *Beowulf* (selection 18a) ll. 739–45a.

22   **on gytesālum** 'in (wine-)pouring joys', i.e. 'merry with drink'.

27   **gebǣrdon wel** 'should enjoy themselves thoroughly'. Encouraging one's guests to carouse and over-indulge in drink is explicitly and repeatedly condemned in OE sermons and other religious writings.

28   **ofer ealne dæg** 'over the whole day'.

30–1   **oð þæt . . . geslegene** 'until they lay in a swoon, all his cohorts inebriated as if they had been stricken with death'. We take *oferdrencte* as past ptc. with nom. pl. inflexion.

34   **nīða** gen. pl. used instrumentally 'with malice'.

42   **lǣdan ongunnon** could well mean 'began to lead'; see *OES* §678 and cf. l. 270.

44–5   **þǣr . . . inne** 'wherein'; cf. *ðǣr inne* l. 50.

46–9   **þǣr wæs . . . þurh** 'A beautiful curtain was there, all of gold and hung round the commander's bed so that the wicked man could see through [it] . . .' Previous editors' deletion of MS *ond* in l. 47 has distorted the sense of this passage.

bed āhongen   þæt se bealofulla
mihte wlītan þurh,   wigena baldor,
50 on æghwylcne   þe ðær inne cōm
hæleða bearna,   ond on hyne nænig
monna cynnes,   nymðe se mōdiga hwæne
nīðe rōfra   him þē nēar hēte
rinca tō rūne gegangan.   Hīe ðā on reste gebrōhton
55 snūde ðā snoteran idese;   ēodon ðā stercedferhðe;
hæleð heora hearran cȳðan   þæt wæs sēo hālige mēowle
gebrōht on his būrgetelde.   Þā wearð se brēma on mōde
blīðe, burga ealdor,   þōhte ðā beorhtan idese
mid wīdle ond mid womme besmītan;   ne wolde þæt
                                        wuldres Dēma
60 geðafian, þrymmes Hyrde,   ac hē him þæs ðinges
                                        gestȳrde,
Dryhten, dugeða Waldend.   Gewāt ðā se dēofulcunda,
gālferhð gūðfreca,   gumena ðrēate
bealofull his beddes nēosan   þær hē sceolde his blǣd
                                        forlēosan
ǣdre binnan ānre nihte;   hæfde ðā his ende gebidenne
65 on eorðan unswǣslicne,   swylcne hē ǣr æfter worhte,
þearlmōd ðēoden gumena   þenden hē on ðysse worulde
wunode under wolcna hrōfe.   Gefēol ðā wīne swā
                                        druncen
se rīca on his reste middan   swā hē nyste rǣda nānne
on gewitlocan.   Wiggend stōpon
70 ūt of ðam inne   ofstum miclum,
weras wīnsade,   þe ðone wǣrlogan,
lāðne lēodhatan,   lǣddon tō bedde
nēhstan sīðe.   Þā wæs Nergendes
þēowen þrymful   þearle gemyndig
75 hū hēo þone atolan   ēaðost mihte
ealdre benǣman   ǣr se unsȳfra
womfull onwōce.   Genam ðā wundenlocc
Scyppendes mægð   scearpne mēce,

51 **on hyne nænig** 'not any [could look] on him'.
52–4 **hwæne** governs *nīðe rōfra . . . rinca.*
53 **þē nēar** inst. + compar.: 'the nearer'.
57 **on mōde** 'in [his] heart' refers to *blīðe* l. 58, not to *brēma*.
62 **gūðfreca** is supplied here to complete the verse (cf. l. 224); there is no gap in the MS. An eye-skip from *gu-* to *gu-* would explain the scribe's omission.
65 **swylcne** qualifies *ende* l. 64 'such [an end] as he had striven after previously'. The acc. with *æfter* is not well attested, but see *OES* §§1179–80 and cf. *The Wanderer* (text 16) l. 50 *sāre æfter swǣsne.*

scūrum heardne,   ond of scēaðe ābrǣd
80 swīðran folme;   ongan ðā swegles Weard
be naman nemnan,   Nergend ealra
woruldbūendra,   ond þæt word ācwæð:
'Ic ðē, frymða God   ond frōfre Gǣst,
Bearn Alwaldan,   biddan wylle
85 miltse þīnre   mē þearfendre,
Ðrȳnesse ðrym.   þearle ys mē nū ðā
heorte onhǣted   ond hige geōmor,
swȳðe mid sorgum gedrēfed.   Forgif mē, swegles Ealdor,
sigor ond sōðne gelēafan,   þæt ic mid þȳs sweorde mōte
90 gehēawan þysne morðres bryttan;   geunne mē mīnra
                                          gesynta,
þearlmōd þeoden gumena.   Nāhte ic þīnre nǣfre
miltse þon māran þearfe.   Gewrec nū, mihtig Dryhten,
torhtmōd tīres Brytta,   þæt mē ys þus torne on mōde,
hāte on hreðre mīnum.'   Hī ðā se hēhsta Dēma
95 ǣdre mid elne onbryrde   swā hē dēð ānra gehwylcne
hērbūendra   þe hyne him tō helpe sēceð
mid rǣde ond mid rihte gelēafan.   þā wearð hyre rūme
                                          on mōde,
hāligre hyht genīwod;   genam ðā þone hǣðenan mannan
fæste be feaxe sīnum,   tēah hyne folmum wið hyre weard
100 bysmerlīce,   ond þone bealofullan
listum ālēde,   lāðne mannan,
swā hēo ðæs unlǣdan   ēaðost mihte
wel gewealdan.   Slōh ðā wundenlocc
þone fēondsceaðan   fāgum mēce,
105 heteþoncolne,   þæt hēo healfne forcearf
þone swēoran him   þæt hē on swīman læg,
druncen ond dolhwund.   Næs ðā dēad þā gȳt,
ealles orsāwle;   slōh ðā eornoste
ides ellenrōf   ōðre sīðe
110 þone hǣðenan hund   þæt him þæt hēafod wand
forð on ðā flōre.   Læg se fūla lēap

79 **scūrum heardne** 'hardened in the storms of battle'. Cf. *Beowulf* l. 1033, where *scūrheard* modifies swords.
80 **ongan** '[she] began'.
85 **mē þearfendre** 'to needy me' i.e. 'to me in my need'.
93–7 **torne ... hāte ... rūme** are all adverbs. Such uses can be paralleled in OE (see *OES* §1108) but adjectives are more usual in such constructions. It is as if *on mōde*, *on hreðre* were apprehended as modifiers, themselves to be modified by adverbs: 'what is in my mind painfully, in my heart searingly'.
97 '. . . in her mind abundantly'.
99 **wið hyre weard** 'toward her'. Tmesis of this kind is well attested; see *OES* §1217.
102 **swā** conj. 'so that, in such a way that'.
105–6 **þæt ... þæt** conjs. introducing clauses of result 'so that'. So also *þæt* l. 110.

gēsne beæftan;   gǣst ellor hwearf
under neowelne næs   ond ðǣr genyðerad wæs,
sūsle gesǣled   syððan ǣfre,

115   wyrmum bewunden,   wītum gebunden,
hearde gehæfted   in hellebryne
æfter hinsīðe.   Ne ðearf hē hopian nō,
þȳstrum forðylmed,   þæt hē ðonan mōte
of ðām wyrmsele   ac ðǣr wunian sceal

120   āwa tō aldre   būtan ende forð
in ðām heolstran hām   hyhtwynna lēas.

XI   Hæfde ðā gefohten   foremǣrne blǣd
Iūdith æt gūðe,   swā hyre God ūðe,
swegles Ealdor,   þe hyre sigores onlēah.

125   þā sēo snotere mægð   snūde gebrōhte
þæs herewǣðan   hēafod swā blōdig
on ðām fǣtelse   þe hyre foregenga,
blāchlēor ides,   hyra bēgea nest,
ðēawum geðungen,   þyder on lǣdde,

130   ond hit þā swā heolfrig   hyre on hond āgeaf,
higeðoncolre,   hām tō berenne,
Iūdith gingran sīnre.   Ēodon ðā gegnum þanonne
þā idesa bā   ellenþrīste
oð þæt hīe becōmon   collenferhðe,

135   ēadhrēðige mægð,   ūt of ðām herige
þæt hīe sweotollīce   gesēon mihten
þǣre wlitegan byrig   weallas blīcan,
Bēthūliam.   Hīe ðā bēahhrodene
fēðelāste   forð ōnettan

140   oð hīe glædmōde   gegān hæfdon
tō ðām wealgate.   Wiggend sǣton,
weras wæccende   wearde hēoldon
in ðām fæstenne,   swā ðām folce ǣr
geōmormōdum   Iūdith bebēad,

145   searoðoncol mægð,   þā hēo on sīð gewāt,
ides ellenrōf.   Wæs ðā eft cumen
lēof tō lēodum   ond ðā lungre hēt
glēawhȳdig wīf   gumena sumne
of ðǣre ginnan byrig   hyre tōgēanes gān

150   ond hī ofostlīce   in forlǣtan

---

122   gefohten The *ge-* is perfective: 'won by fighting'.
136   þæt conj. 'so that' shading into 'until'.
149   Here two words in the second half-line alliterate with one word in the first half-line, contrary to the rules of alliterative verse. Some editors remove this defect by reversing the order of the two half-lines.

　　þurh ðæs wealles geat,　ond þæt word ācwæð
　　tō ðām sigefolce:　'Ic ēow secgan mæg
　　þoncwyrðe þing,　þæt gē ne þyrfen leng
　　murnan on mōde.　Ēow ys Metod blīðe,
155　cyninga Wuldor;　þæt gecȳðed wearð
　　geond woruld wīde,　þæt ēow ys wuldorblæd
　　torhtlic tōweard　ond tīr gifeðe
　　þāra lǣðða　þe gē lange drugon.'
　　þā wurdon blīðe　burhsittende
160　syððan hī gehȳrdon　hū sēo hālige sprǣc
　　ofer hēanne weall.　Here wæs on lustum;
　　wið þæs fæstengeates　folc ōnette,
　　weras wīf somod,　wornum ond hēapum,
　　ðrēatum ond ðrymmum　þrungon ond urnon
165　ongēan ða þēodnes mægð　þūsendmǣlum,
　　ealde ge geonge.　Ǣghwylcum wearð
　　men on ðǣre medobyrig　mōd ārēted
　　syððan hīe ongēaton　þæt wæs Iūdith cumen
　　eft tō ēðle,　ond ðā ofostlīce
170　hīe mid ēaðmēdum　in forlēton.
　　þā sēo glēawc hēt,　golde gefrætewod,
　　hyre ðīnenne　þancolmōde
　　þæs herewǣðan　hēafod onwrīðan
　　ond hyt to bēhðe　blōdig ætȳwan
175　þām burhlēodum,　hū hyre æt beaduwe gespēow.
　　Sprǣc ðā sēo æðele　tō eallum þām folce:
　　'Hēr gē magon sweotole,　sigerōfe hæleð,
　　lēoda rǣswan,　on ðæs lāðestan
　　hǣðenes heaðorinces　hēafod starian,
180　Hōlofernus　unlyfigendes,
　　þe ūs monna mǣst　morðra gefremede,
　　sārra sorga,　ond þæt swȳðor gȳt
　　ȳcan wolde,　ac him ne ūðe God
　　lengran līfes　þæt hē mid lǣððum ūs
185　eglan mōste;　ic him ealdor oðþrong
　　þurh Godes fultum.　Nū ic gumena gehwǣne
　　þyssa burglēoda　biddan wylle,
　　randwiggendra,　þæt gē recene ēow

158　þāra lǣðða gen. pl. 'of/from those afflictions' (to be taken with *tīr* with
general sense 'triumph over those afflictions').
163　weras wīf somod 'men [and] women together'.
181　ūs monna ... morðra 'the greatest number of killings of our people'.
186b–95a　This passage is discussed in *A Note on the Punctuation of Old English Poetry*,
below, p. 341.

fȳsan tō gefeohte syððan frymða God,
190 ārfæst Cyning, ēastan sende
lēohtne lēoman. Berað linde forð,
bord for brēostum ond byrnhomas,
scīre helmas in sceaðena gemong,
fyllað folctogan fāgum sweordum,
195 fǣge frumgāras. Fȳnd syndon ēowere
gedēmed to dēaðe, ond gē dōm āgon,
tīr æt tohtan, swā ēow getācnod hafað
mihtig Dryhten þurh mīne hand.'
þā wearð snelra werod snūde gegearewod,
200 cēnra tō campe. Stōpon cynerōfe
secgas ond gesīðas, bǣron sigeþūfas,
fōron tō gefeohte forð on gerihte,
hæleð under helmum of ðǣre hāligan byrig
on ðæt dægrēd sylf; dynedan scildas,
205 hlūde hlummon. Þæs se hlanca gefeah
wulf in walde, ond se wanna hrefn,
wælgīfre fugel. Wiston bēgen
þæt him ðā þēodguman þōhton tilian
fylle on fǣgum, ac him flēah on lāst
210 earn ǣtes georn, ūrigfeðera,
salowigpāda sang hildelēoð,
hyrnednebba. Stōpon heaðorincas,
beornas tō beadowe, bordum beðeahte,
hwealfum lindum, þā ðe hwīle ǣr
215 elðēodigra edwīt þoledon,
hǣðenra hosp. Him þæt hearde wearð
æt ðām æscplegan eallum forgolden,
Assȳrium, syððan Ebrēas
under gūðfanum gegān hæfdon
220 tō ðām fyrdwīcum. Hīe ðā fromlīce
lēton forð flēogan flāna scūras,
hildenǣdran of hornbogan,
strǣlas stedehearde, styrmdon hlūde
grame gūðfrecan, gāras sendon
225 in heardra gemang. Hæleð wǣron yrre,
landbūende, lāðum cynne,
stōpon styrnmōde, stercedferhðe,

189 fȳsan 2nd pers. pres. pl. subj. (with reflexive *ēow*).
190 sende 3rd pers. sg. pret. ind. 'has sent'; see §197.3. The Vulgate Judith (14:2) has *cum exierit sol* 'when the sun shall have risen'.
209 ac not adversative here. Translate 'moreover'.
214 hwīle ǣr 'for a while before'.
216–17 hearde . . . forgolden 'fully requited'.

wrehton unsōfte   ealdgenīðlan
medowērige;   mundum brugdon
230 scealcas of scēaðum   scīrmæled swyrd
ecgum gecoste,   slōgon eornoste
Assīria   ōretmæcgas,
nīðhycgende,   nānne ne sparedon
þæs herefolces,   hēanne ne rīcne,
235 cwicera manna   þe hīe ofercuman mihton.
XII   Swā ðā magoþegnas   on ðā morgentīd
ēhton elðēoda   ealle þrāge
oð þæt ongēaton   ðā ðe grame wǣron,
ðæs herefolces   hēafodweardas,
240 þæt him swyrdgeswing   swīðlic ēowdon
weras Ebrisce.   Hīe wordum þæt
þām yldestan   ealdorþegnum
cȳðan ēodon,   wrehton cumbolwigan,
ond him forhtlīce   fǣrspel bodedon,
245 medowērigum   morgencollan,
atolne ecgplegan.   Þā ic ǣdre gefrægn
slegefǣge hæleð   slǣpe tōbrēdan
ond wið þæs bealofullan   būrgeteldes
wērigferhðe   hwearfum þringan,
250 Hōlofernus.   Hogedon āninga
hyra hlāforde   hilde bodian
ǣr ðon ðe him se egesa   on ufan sǣte,
mægen Ebrēa.   Mynton ealle
þæt se beorna brego   ond sēo beorhte mægð
255 in ðām wlitegan træfe   wǣron ætsomne,
Iūdith sēo æðele   ond se gālmōda,
egesfull ond āfor.   Næs ðēah eorla nān
þe ðone wiggend   āweccan dorste
oððe gecunnian   hū ðone cumbolwigan
260 wið ðā hālgan mægð   hæfde geworden,
Metodes mēowlan.   Mægen nēalǣhte,
folc Ebrēa,   fuhton þearle
heardum heoruwǣpnum,   hæfte guldon

238b–9   refer to the Assyrians and are the subject of *ongēaton* l. 238.

246   **ǣdre** modifies *tōbrēdan*.

252   **on . . . sǣte** are to be taken together: *on ufan sǣte* 'descended'.

259b–60   Here *geweorðan* is used impersonally: 'how it had fared for the warrior (acc.) with the holy maiden (dat.)'.

263   **hæfte** inst. sg. could be an otherwise unattested (in OE) noun meaning 'warfare' (cf. Old Icelandic *heipt* 'battle') or a metonymical use of *hæft* '(sword-)handle, hilt' referring to 'sword'. It is parallel with *fāgum swyrdum* l. 264.

hyra fyrngeflitu,   fāgum swyrdum,
265 ealde æfðoncan;   Assȳria wearð
on ðām dægweorce   dōm geswiðrod,
bælc forbīged.   Beornas stōdon
ymbe hyra þēodnes træf   þearle gebylde,
sweorcendferhðe.   Hi ðā somod ealle
270 ongunnon cohhetan,   cirman hlūde
ond grīstbitian,   gōde orfeorme,
mid tōðon torn þoligende.   þā wæs hyra tīres æt ende,
ēades ond ellendǣda.   Hogedon þā eorlas āweccan
hyra winedryhten;   him wiht ne spēow.
275 þā wearð sīð ond late   sum tō ðām arod
þāra beadorinca   þæt hē in þæt būrgeteld
nīðheard nēðde   swā hyne nȳd fordrāf.
Funde ðā on bedde   blācne licgan
his goldgifan   gǣstes gēsne,
280 līfes belidenne.   Hē þā lungre gefēoll
frēorig tō foldan,   ongan his feax teran,
hrēoh on mōde,   ond his hrægl somod,
ond þæt word ācwæð   tō ðām wiggendum
þe ðǣr unrōte   ūte wǣron:
285 'Hēr ys geswutelod   ūre sylfra forwyrd,
tōweard getācnod   þæt þǣre tīde ys
mid nīðum nēah geðrungen   þe wē sculon nȳde losian,
somod æt sæcce forweorðan: hēr līð sweorde gehēawen,
behēafdod healdend ūre.'   Hī ðā hrēowigmōde
290 wurpon hyra wǣpen ofdūne,   gewitan him wērigferhðe
on flēam sceacan.   Him mon feaht on lāst,
mægenēacen folc,   oð se mǣsta dǣl
þæs heriges læg   hilde gesǣged
on ðām sigewonge,   sweordum gehēawen,

268 **gebylde** Since *gebylde* 'emboldened, encouraged' makes no sense in this context, we take the word to be past ptc. of *gebylgan* 'provoke, trouble'.
270 **ongunnon** see l. 42 note.
cohhetan, cirman hlūde 'to cough [and] make noise loudly'.
271 **gōde orfeorme** 'without success, doing no good'. Their efforts to rouse Holofernes with coughing and noise-making having failed, the warriors gnash their teeth.
272b–3a Lit. 'then it was at an end for their glory, their success and deeds of courage'.
275–6 **tō ðām arod . . . þæt** 'to that extent/so bold . . . that'.
285–8 **Hēr ys . . . forweorðan** The text of this passage is disturbed in the MS and has been reconstructed in several ways. The sense of the passage as reconstructed here is this: 'Here is revealed, indicated, the impending destruction of ourselves, so that it draws near to the time with afflictions in which we must by necessity be lost, perish together in battle.'
290–1 **gewitan him . . . sceacan** 'went hastening away'.

295   wulfum tō willan   ond ēac wælgīfrum
      fuglum to frōfre.   Flugon ðā ðe lyfdon,
      lāðra lindwigan.   Him on lāste fōr
      swēot Ebrēa   sigore geweorðod,
      dōme gedȳrsod;   him fēng Dryhten God
300   fǣgre on fultum,   Frēa ælmihtig.
      Hī ðā fromlīce   fāgum swyrdum,
      hæleð higerōfe,   herpað worhton
      þurh lāðra gemong,   linde hēowon,
      scildburh scǣron.   Scēotend wǣron
305   gūðe gegremede,   guman Ebrisce;
      þegnas on ðā tīd   þearle gelyste
      gārgewinnes.   Þǣr on grēot gefēoll
      se hȳhsta dæl   hēafodgerīmes
      Assīria   ealdorduguðe,
310   lāðan cynnes;   lȳthwon becōm
      cwicera to cȳðða.   Cirdon cynerōfe,
      wiggend on wiðertrod,   wælscel on innan,
      rēocende hrǣw.   Rūm wæs tō nimanne
      londbūendum   on ðām lāðestan,
315   hyra ealdfēondum   unlyfigendum
      heolfrig hererēaf,   hyrsta scȳne,
      bord ond brād swyrd,   brūne helmas,
      dȳre mādmas.   Hæfdon dōmlīce
      on ðām folcstede   fȳnd oferwunnen
320   ēðelweardas,   ealdhettende
      swyrdum āswefede.   Hīe on swaðe reston,
      þā ðe him tō līfe   lāðost wǣron
      cwicera cynna.   Þā sēo cnēoris eall,
      mǣgða mǣrost,   ānes mōnðes fyrst,
325   wlanc, wundenlocc,   wǣgon ond lǣddon
      tō ðǣre beorhtan byrig   Bēthūliam,
      helmas ond hupseax,   hāre byrnan,
      gūðsceorp gumena   golde gefrǣtewod,
      māre mādma   þonne mon ǣnig
330   āsecgan mæge   searoþoncelra;
      eal þæt ðā ðēodguman   þrymme geēodon,

306–7 **þegnas ... gārgewinnes** 'the thanes were exceedingly desirous of battle on
that occasion'.

313–14 **Rūm wæs ... londbūendum** 'There was opportunity for the Hebrews to
take from the hated ones (dat. pl.)'.

329 **māre** is acc. sg. neut. used substantively with partitive gen.: 'more of the
treasures'.

cēne under cumblum   on compwīge
þurh Iūdithe   glēawe lāre,
mægð mōdigre.   Hī tō mēde hyre
335   of ðām sīðfate   sylfre brōhton,
eorlas æscrōfe,   Hōlofernes
sweord ond swātigne helm,   swylce ēac sīde byrnan
gerēnode rēadum golde,   ond eal þæt se rinca baldor
swīðmōd sinces āhte   oððe sundoryrfes,
340   bēaga ond beorhtra māðma,   hī þæt þære beorhtan idese
āgēafon gearoþoncolre.   Ealles ðæs Iūdith sægde
wuldor weroda Dryhtne   þe hyre weorðmynde geaf,
mærðe on moldan rīce,   swylce ēac mēde on heofonum,
sigorlēan in swegles wuldre,   þæs þe heo āhte sōðne
geleafan
345   ā tō ðam Ælmihtigan.   Hūru æt þām ende ne twēode
þæs lēanes þe hēo lange gyrnde.   Ðæs sȳ ðām lēofan
Drihtne
wuldor tō wīdan aldre,   þe gesceōp wind ond lyfte,
roderas ond rūme grundas,   swylce ēac rēðe strēamas
ond swegles drēamas   ðurh his sylfes miltse.

334–5 **hyre ... sylfre** 'herself' i.e. 'her'.
338–9 **eal ... sinces ... sundoryrfes** 'all of the treasure and wealth'.
341 **Ealles ðæs** 'For all of that'.
344 **þæs þe** 'since, because'.
Note: For explanations of several of the readings proposed here see Fred C. Robinson, 'Five Textual Notes on the OE *Judith*' *American Notes and Queries* 15 (2001), 47–51.

Cotton Gnomes or Maxims

Here and there in OE poetry occur succinct expressions of timeless truths which are variously denominated gnomes, maxims, apophthegms, or proverbs. Examples of gnomes used in *Beowulf* are 'It is better for a man to avenge a friend than to mourn overmuch' and 'Fate goes always as she must'.

In many early cultures gnomes were collected and offered up as valuable repositories of folk wisdom. The Old Testament book of Proverbs is an outstanding example. Other such compilations are to be found in the first seventy-seven stanzas of the Old Icelandic *Hávamál* ('Sayings of the High One [i.e. Odin]') and in several Old Irish collections. A number of OE poems are composed partly or entirely of versified gnomes. The text presented here is from the British Library's manuscript Cotton Tiberius B.1, where the gnomic verses serve as an introduction to a version of the Anglo-Saxon Chronicle (see selection 7 above, pp. 225–7), the timeless gnomic truths standing in pointed contrast with the year-by-year record of events as they happen in time.

The Cotton Gnomes, like other gnomic compilations in OE, use two verbs in senses unique to this kind of utterance: gnomic *bið* and gnomic *sceal*. Rather than their usual senses 'is' and 'must' (see §§ 196 and 210), in gnomic usage these words indicate the statement of an eternal truth. Thus the first verse below has the literal meaning 'A king must hold the power' but actually means something more like 'It is the nature of a king to hold the power.' *Wyrd byð swiðost* in the fifth line of the poem suggests 'Fate has always been and always will be most powerful'.

Some gnomes simply enunciate verities of the natural world: 'A river runs downhill' or 'Fish spawn their kind in the water'. Others make judgements about human affairs: 'Valour belongs in a nobleman' or 'It is for kings to dispense treasure in the hall'. Sometimes juxtaposed expressions seem to complement or confirm each other, a simple fact of nature mirroring a human circumstance. Line 13,

A Guide to Old English, Eighth Edition. Bruce Mitchell and Fred C. Robinson.
© 2012 Bruce Mitchell and Fred C. Robinson. Published 2012 by Blackwell Publishing Ltd.

for example, could be loosely paraphrased, 'As surely as clouds move slowly, misfortune is clinging (i.e. takes a long time to pass on)'. The degree to which the sequence of the gnomes is meaningful or random has been debated. As you translate the Cotton Gnomes, consider whether there is significance in juxtapositions such as those in ll. 50–4a.

In l. 16 the manuscript's misspelling *hellme* has been corrected to *helme*. Otherwise the text below adheres to the manuscript in all respects.

> Cyning sceal rīce healdan.   Ceastra bēoð feorran gesȳne,
> orðanc enta geweorc,   þā þe on þysse eorðan syndon,
> wrǣtlic weallstāna geweorc.   Wind byð on lyfte
>   swiftust,
> þunar byð þrāgum hlūdast.   Þrymmas syndan Crīstes
>   myccle;
> 5 wyrd byð swīðost.   Winter byð cealdost,
> lencten hrīmigost   (hē byð lengest ceald)
> sumor sunwlitegost   (swegel byð hātost)
> hærfest hrēðēadegost,   hæleðum bringeð
> gēares wæstmas   þā þe him God sendeð.
> 10 Sōð bið swicolost   sinc byð dēorost,
> gold gumena gehwām,   and gomol snoterost,
> fyrngēarum frōd,   sē þe ǣr feala gebīdeð.
> Wēa bið wundrum clibbor.   Wolcnu scrīðað.
> Geongne æþeling sceolan   gōde gesīðas
> 15 byldan tō beaduwe   and tō bēahgife.
> Ellen sceal on eorle;   ecg sceal wið helme
> hilde gebīdan.   Hafuc sceal on glōfe
> wilde gewunian;   wulf sceal on bearowe,
> earn ānhaga;   eofor sceal on holte

1b–3a **Ceastra** 'cities, towns' is an OE borrowing from Latin (*castra* 'fortified encampments, fortresses') and is often used to refer to the buildings left in England by the Romans. Constructed from stone (*weallstāna geweorc*), the Roman buildings were a source of wonder to Anglo-Saxons, who traditionally built only wooden structures. Hence the Anglo-Saxons referred to the stone structures as *enta geweorc*. Cf. *Ruin* l. 2.

10 **Sōð bið swicolost** 'Truth is most tricky' or 'most deceptive' because of the difficulty at times of distinguishing between truth and falsehood. In his *The Cambridge Old English Reader*, Marsden entitles his §33 'Truth is Trickiest'. In his note on this line Marsden, rightly rejecting the common emendation of *swicolost* to *swītolost*, translates the former as 'most deceitful', or 'trickiest'. This translation and the use of 'Truth is Trickiest' in the title fail to report the fact that in the Bloomfield Festschrift 1982 Fred C. Robinson defended the MS reading and proposed the translation 'Truth is most tricky / Truth is trickiest'.

12 **fyrngēarum frōd** 'old (and wise) through bygone years'.

19 **earn ānhaga** 'the eagle [shall be] a solitary'. Often *earn* has been emended to *earm* giving the sense 'a wretched solitary', referring to the wolf.

20   tōðmægenes trum.   Til sceal on ēðle
dōmes wyrcean.   Daroð sceal on handa,
gār golde fāh.   Gim sceal on hringe
standan stēap and gēap.   Strēam sceal on ȳðum
mecgan mereflōde.   Mæst sceal on cēole,
25   segelgyrd, seomian.   Sweord sceal on bearme,
drihtlic īsern.   Draca sceal on hlǣwe,
frōd, frætwum wlanc.   Fisc sceal on wætere
cynren cennan.   Cyning sceal on healle
bēagas dǣlan.   Bera sceal on hǣðe,
30   eald and egesfull.   Ēa ofdūne sceal
flōdgrǣg fēran.   Fyrd sceal ætsomne,
tīrfæstra getrum.   Trēow sceal on eorle,
wisdom on were.   Wudu sceal on foldan
blǣdum blōwan.   Beorh sceal on eorþan
35   grēne standan.   God sceal on heofenum,
dǣda dēmend.   Duru sceal on healle,
rūm recedes mūð.   Rand sceal on scylde,
fæst fingra gebcorh.   Fugel uppe sceal
lācan on lyfte.   Leax sceal on wǣle
40   mid scēote scrīðan.   Scur sceal on heofenum,
winde geblanden,   in þās woruld cuman.
þēof sceal gangan þȳstrum wederum.   þyrs sceal on
            fenne gewunian
āna innan lande.   Ides sceal dyrne cræfte,
fǣmne hire frēond gesēcean,   gif hēo nelle on folce
            geþēon,
45   þæt hī man bēagum gebicge.   Brim sceal sealte weallan,
lyfthelm and laguflōd   ymb ealra landa gehwylc,
flōwan firgenstrēamas.   Feoh sceal on eorðan
tȳdran and tȳman.   Tungol sceal on heofenum
beorhte scīnan,   swā him bebēad Meotud.
50   Gōd sceal wið yfele;   geogoð sceal wið yldo;
līf sceal wið dēaþe;   lēoht sceal wið þȳstrum,
fyrd wið fyrde,   fēond wið ōðrum,

---

24   **mecgan mereflōde** 'mix with the ocean current'.
25   **Sweord . . . bearme** 'A sword rests in the lap'. It has been suggested that this
refers to royal personages sitting with a sword lying across the knees and with the hands
holding either end (as pictured in some manuscript illuminations).
40b–1   **Scūr . . . cuman** 'Rain, mingled with wind in the heavens, shall come into
this world.'
43b–45a   The general sense is that a woman who has no desire to enter into marriage will typically meet covertly with a lover.
45b–7a   **Brim sceal . . . firgenstrēamas** 'The sea shall well with salt, the ocean
currents, tide and atmosphere, [shall] whirl around every land.'

lāð wið lāþe   ymb land sacan,
synne stǽlan.   Ā sceal snotor hycgean
55 ymb þysse worulde gewinn,   wearh hangian,
fǽgere ongildan   þæt hē ǽr fācen dyde
manna cynne.   Meotod āna wāt
hwyder sēo sāwul sceal   syððan hweorfan,
and ealle þā gāstas   þe for Gode hweorfað
60 æfter dēaðdæge,   dōmes bīdað
on Fæder fæðme.   Is sēo forðgesceaft
dīgol and dyrne;   Drihten āna wāt,
nergende Fæder.   Nǽni eft cymeð
hider under hrōfas,   þe þæt hēr for sōð
65 mannum secge   hwylc sȳ Meotodes gesceaft,
sigefolca gesetu,   þǽr hē sylfa wunað.

54 **synne stǽlan** 'accuse [each other] of crime'. The verb *stǽlan* has many meanings, but the similar phrase *syndǽda stǽleþ* 'accuses of crimes' cited in the Bosworth-Toller *Dictionary* s.v. *stǽlan* suggests that 'accuse, charge' is the sense here.
64b–6 **þæt** is acc. sg. direct object of *secge* and in apposition with the following clause introduced by *hwylc*: 'who can say that to people, [namely] what God's creation where he [with his] triumphant folk lives might be [like]'. See §148 above.

Sermo Lupi ad Anglos

Quando Dani Maxime Persecuti Sunt eos,
quod fuit Anno Millesimo. XIIII. ab
Incarnatione Domini Nostri Iesu Cristi*

Wulfstan was a contemporary of Ælfric's, the two of them being the most accomplished prose stylists of the late West Saxon period. Author of at least twenty-six homilies in Old English (and of others in Latin), Wulfstan wrote the *Sermo Lupi ad Anglos* during the period when the Danes were completing their conquest of Anglo-Saxon England. In his sermon he tells his countrymen that the devastating invasion of their land is God's punishment of the Anglo-Saxons for the sharp decline in their moral standards and for their craven response to the Danish challenge. He itemizes their failings of character mercilessly and exhorts them to abandon their depravity and return to good Christian behaviour. England under siege is described as a world turned upside down, with former slaves subduing their erstwhile masters and friend betraying friend and kinsman betraying kinsman. He heightens the tone of his jeremiad with emphatic rhythmic patterns and with ringing repetitions of both phrasing and subject-matter.

Wulfstan was a high-ranking churchman, serving as both bishop of Worcester and archbishop of York. Unlike Ælfric, he was also an important public servant. He was the author of tracts on both ecclesiastical and governmental matters and took part in the drafting of law-codes for both King Æthelræd and King Cnut.

The *Sermo Lupi ad Anglos* survives in five manuscripts. The following text takes as its base text British Library MS Cotton Nero A.1 with only occasional normalization of spellings. Among the linguistic features in the sermon which are characteristic of late Old English an especially prominent one is the use of *-an* to represent

* 'The Sermon of Wulfstan to the English When the Danes Persecuted them Most Severely, which was in the Year 1014 from the Incarnation of our Lord Jesus Christ' (*Lupus* 'wolf' is Wulfstan's Latin name).

A Guide to Old English, Eighth Edition. Bruce Mitchell and Fred C. Robinson.
© 2012 Bruce Mitchell and Fred C. Robinson. Published 2012 by Blackwell Publishing Ltd.

the preterite plural ending -*on* of verbs and the dative ending -*um* of adjectives and nouns.

Lēofan men, gecnāwað þæt sōð is: ðēos worold is on ofste, and hit nēalǣcð þām ende, and þȳ hit is on worolde aa swā leng swā wyrse; and swā hit sceal nȳde for folces synnan ǣr Antecrīstes tōcyme yfelian swȳþe, and hūru hit wyrð þænne egeslic and grimlic wīde
5 on worolde.

Understandað ēac georne þæt dēofol þās þēode nū fela gēara dwelode tō swȳþe, and þæt lȳtle getrēowþa wǣran mid mannum, þēah hȳ wel spǣcan, and unrihta tō fela rīcsode on lande; and næs ā fela manna þe smēade ymbe þā bōte swā georne swā man scolde,
10 ac dæghwāmlīce man īhte yfel æfter ōðrum and unriht rærde and unlaga manege ealles tō wīde gynd ealle þās þēode. And wē ēac for þām habbað fela byrsta and bysmara gebiden, and gif wē ǣnige bōte gebīdan scylan, þonne mōte wē þæs tō Gode earnian bet þonne wē ǣr þysan dydan. For þām mid miclan earnungan wē geearnedan
15 þā yrmða þe ūs onsittað, and mid swȳþe micelan earnungan wē þā bōte mōtan æt Gode gerǣcan, gif hit sceal heonanforð gōdiende weorðan. Lā hwæt, wē witan ful georne þæt tō miclan bryce sceal micel bōt nȳde, and tō miclan bryne wæter unlȳtel, gif man þæt fȳr sceal tō āhte ācwencan. And micel is nȳdþearf manna gehwilcum
20 þæt hē Godes lage gȳme heonanforð georne and Godes gerihta mid rihte gelǣste. On hǣþenum þēodum ne dear man forhealdan lȳtel ne micel þæs þe gelagod is tō gedwolgoda weorðunge; and wē forhealdað ǣghwǣr Godes gerihta ealles tō gelōme. And ne dear man

---

1 **Lēofan men** 'Dear people'. A standard form of address at the beginning of OE sermons.

2 **þȳ** 'therefore'.

2–3 **hit is . . . wyrse** 'it is ever the worse in the world the longer [the world lasts]'.

3 **synnan** (= s*ynnum*) This is the late OE spelling -*an* for -*um*, -*on*. Cf. below *wǣran* for *wǣron* and *spǣcan* for *spǣcon* (ll. 7 and 8).

Antecrīstes tōcyme According to Church Fathers, not long before the end of the world Antichrist, posing as the Messiah in His second coming, will reign cruelly before God 'shortens his days' and holds the Last Judgement.

6 **nū fela gēara** 'for many years now'.

7 **dwelode tō swȳþe** Wulfstan frequently uses *tō* with ironical understatement. That the devil should deceive people at all is the point of objection, not that the devil should refrain from deceiving them 'too much'. Cf. *unrihta tō fela* in l. 8 and the use of *tō* in *The Wanderer*, ll. 66–9.

8 **fela rīcsode** In Wulfstan *fela* as the subject of a verb is always treated as a singular.

16–17 **sceal heonanforð gōdiende weorðan** 'is to be henceforth improving' i.e. 'is to start improving'.

17–18 **sceal micel bōt nȳde** '[there] must [be] great amends'.

19 **tō āhte** 'at all'.

23 **Godes gerihta** 'God's dues'. Presumably church dues, which the Anglo-Saxons would have had difficulty paying when strapped by the need for Danegeld payments and by the expenses of the ongoing war.

gewanian on hæþenum þeodum inne ne ūte ænig þæra þinga þe
25 gedwolgodan brōht bið and tō lācum betæht bið; and wē habbað Godes
hūs inne and ūte clæne berȳpte. And Godes þēowas syndan mæþe
and munde gewelhwær bedælde; and gedwolgoda þēnan ne dear man
misbēodan on ænige wīsan mid hæþenum lēodum, swā swā man
Godes þēowum nū dēð tō wīde, þær Crīstene scoldan Godes lage
30 healdan and Godes þēowas griðian.

Ac sōð is þæt ic secge, þearf is þære bōte, for þām Godes gerihta
wanedan tō lange innan þysse þeode on æghwylcan ænde, and
folclaga wyrsedan ealles tō swȳþe, and hālignessa syndan tō griðlēase
wīde, and Godes hūs syndan tō clæne berȳpte ealdra gerihta and innan
35 bestrȳpte ælcra gerisena, and wydewan syndan fornȳdde on unriht
tō ceorle, and tō mænege foryrmde and gehȳnede swȳþe, and earme
men syndan sare beswicene and hrēowlīce besyrwde and ūt of þysan
earde wīde gesealde swȳþe unforworhte fremdum tō gewealde, and
cradolcild geþēowede þurh wælhrēowe unlaga for lȳtelre þyfþe wīde
40 gynd þās þeode, and frēoriht fornumene and þrælriht genyrwde and
ælmæsriht gewanode; and hrædest is tō cweþenne, Godes laga lāðc
and lāra forsawene; and þæs wē habbað ealle þurh Godes yrre bysmor
gelōme, gecnāwe sē þe cunne; and se byrst wyrð gemæne, þēh man
swā ne wēne, eallre þysse þeode, būtan God beorge.

45   For þām hit is on ūs eallum swutol and gesēne þæt wē ær þysan
oftor bræcan þonne wē bēttan, and þȳ is þysse þeode fela onsæge.
Ne dohte hit nū lange inne ne ūte, ac wæs here and hunger, bryne
and blōdgyte on gewelhwylcan ende oft and gelōme. And ūs stalu
and cwalu, strīc and steorfa, orfcwealm and uncoþu, hōl and
50 hete and rȳpera rēaflāc derede swȳþe þearle, and ungylda swȳðe
gedrehtan, and ūs unwedera foroft wēoldan unwæstma; for þām on
þysan earde wæs, swā hit þincan mæg, nū fela gēara unrihta fela and

---

24   **inne ne ūte** '[neither] inside nor outside (the pagan sanctuaries)'.

26–7   **Godes þēowas syndan ... bedælde** 'God's servants are everywhere
deprived of respect and protection'.

27   **þēnan** (i.e. *þegnum*) are pagan priests.

33–4   **hālignessa ... wīde** 'sanctuaries far and wide are not protected'.

37–8   **ūt of þysan earde ... gewealde** The selling of Christian English people into
foreign countries was strictly prohibited in all periods of Anglo-Saxon England since this
could put Christians at the mercy of heathens, who might even use the Christians as human
sacrifices to pagan gods.

38   **fremdum tō gewealde** 'into the possession of foreigners'.

39   **cradolcild** Some Anglo-Saxon laws stipulate that if a person steals with the full
knowledge of his or her household, then the entire family may as punishment be sent
into slavery. Thus even an infant might share in the punishment.

41   **hrædest is tō cweþenne** 'to be brief', 'in short'.

42   **þæs** 'for this', 'therefore'.

46   **fela** is nom.; *þysse þeode* is dat. sg.

47   **nū lange inne ne ūte** 'now for a long time anywhere'.

50   **ungylda** i.e. the Danegeld.

tealte getrȳwða æghwǣr mid mannum. Ne bearh nū foroft gesib
gesibban þē mā þe fremdan, ne fæder his bearne, ne hwīlum bearn
55 his āgenum fæder, ne brōþor ōþrum; ne ūre ænig his līf fadode
swā swā hē sceolde, ne gehādode regollīce, ne lǣwede lahlīce. Ac
worhtan lust ūs tō lage ealles tō gelōme, and nāþor ne hēoldan ne
lāre ne lage Godes ne manna swā swā wē scoldan; ne ænig wið ōþerne
getrȳwlīce þōhte swā rihte swā hē scolde, ac mǣst ælc swicode and
60 ōþrum derede wordes and dǣde, and hūru unrihtlīce mǣst ælc ōþerne
æftan hēaweþ mid sceandlican onscytan, dō māre, gif hē mæge. For
þām hēr syn on lande ungetrȳwþa micle for Gode and for worolde,
and ēac hēr syn on earde on mistlice wīsan hlāfordswican manege.
And ealra mǣst hlāfordswice sē bið on worolde þæt man his
65 hlāfordes sāule beswīce; and ful micel hlāfordswice ēac bið on
worolde þæt man his hlāford of līfe forrǣde, oððon of lande
lifiendne drīfe; and ǣgþer is geworden on þysan earde: Ēadweard
man forrǣdde and syððan ācwealde and æfter þām forbærnde [and
Æþelred man drǣfde ūt of his earde]. And godsibbas and godbearn
70 tō fela man forspilde wīde gynd þās þēode, and ealles tō mænege
hālige stōwa wīde forwurdan þurh þæt þe man sume men ǣr þām
gelōgode, swā man nā ne scolde, gif man on Godes griðe mǣþe witan
wolde; and Crīstenes folces tō fela man gesealde ūt of þysan earde
nū ealle hwīle; and eal þæt is Gode lāð, gelȳfe sē þe wille. And
75 scandlic is tō specenne þæt geworden is tō wīde, and egeslic is tō
witanne þæt oft dōð tō manege, þe drēogað þā yrmþe, þæt scēotað
tōgædere and āne cwenan gemǣnum cēape bicgað gemǣne, and wið
þā āne fȳlþe ādrēogað, ān æfter ānum, and ælc æfter ōðrum, hundum
gelīccast, þe for fȳlþe ne scrīfað, and syððan wið weorðe syllað of

---

54 **þē mā þe** 'any more than'.

56–7 **Ac worhtan lust ūs tō lage** 'But we have made pleasure our law'.

60 **wordes and dǣde** instr. gen. 'by word and by deed'.

mǣst ælc 'almost everyone'.

61 **dō māre, gif hē mæge** 'he would do more, if he could'.

62 **syn** looks like a form of the subj. pl. (*sien, syn*), but here and elsewhere in this sermon it seems rather to be the ind. *synd* 'are' with simplification of the final consonant cluster -*nd* to -*n*, a phonological development documented in other late OE texts as well.

for Gode and for worolde 'towards God and towards the world' i.e. 'in matters both of church and of state'.

66 **his hlāford . . . forrǣde** 'plot against his lord's life'.

67–9 **Ēadweard . . . earde** King Edward the Martyr was murdered at Corfe, Dorset, in 978, possibly by members of the household of his half-brother Æthelræd so that Æthelræd could succeed to the throne. Æthelræd was crowned one month after the murder. The manuscript used for this edition lacks *and Æþelred . . . of his earde*; it has been supplied from other manuscripts. It refers to Æthelræd's flight to refuge in Normandy after Christmas 1013. He returned the following spring.

76–7 **scēotað tōgædere** 'go in together' i.e. pool their resources.

77 **gemǣnum cēape** 'as a joint purchase'.

79 **wið weorðe** 'for a price'.

80 lande fēondum tō gewealde Godes gesceafte and his āgenne cēap,
þe hē dēore gebohte.

Ēac wē witan georne hwǣr sēo yrmð gewearð þæt fæder gesealde
bearn wið weorþe, and bearn his mōdor, and brōþor sealde ōþerne
fremdum tō gewealde; and eal þæt syndan micle and egeslice dǣda,
85 understande sē þe wille. And gȳt hit is māre and ēac mænigfealdre
þæt dereð þysse þēode: mænige synd forsworene and swȳþe forlogene, and wed synd tōbrocene oft and gelōme; and þæt is gesȳne on
þysse þeode þæt ūs Godes yrre hetelīce onsit, gecnāwe sē þe cunne.

And lā, hū mæg māre scamu þurh Godes yrre mannum gelimpan
90 þonne ūs dēð gelōme for āgenum gewyrhtum? Ðēh þrǣla hwylc
hlāforde æthlēape and of Crīstendōme tō wīcinge weorþe, and hit
æfter þām eft geweorþe þæt wǣpngewrixl weorðe gemǣne þegene
and þrǣle, gif þrǣl þæne þegen fullīce āfylle, licge ǣgylde ealre his
mǣgðe; and, gif se þegen þæne þrǣl þe hē ǣr āhte fullīce āfylle, gylde
95 þegengylde. Ful earhlice laga and scandlice nȳdgyld þurh Godes yrre
ūs syn gemǣne, understande sē þe cunne; and fela ungelimpa
gelimpð þysse þēode oft and gelōme. Ne dohte hit nū lange inne ne
ūte, ac wæs here and hete on gewelhwilcan ende oft and gelōme, and
Engle nū lange eal sigelēase and tō swȳþe geyrigde þurh Godes yrre;
100 and flotmen swā strange þurh Godes þafunge þæt oft on gefeohte
ān fēseð tȳne, and hwīlum lǣs, hwīlum mā, eal for ūrum synnum.
And oft tȳne oððe twelfe, ælc æfter ōþrum, scendað tō bysmore þæs
þegenes cwenan, and hwīlum his dōhtor oððe nȳdmāgan, þǣr hē on
lōcað, þe lǣt hine sylfne rancne and rīcne and genōh gōdne ǣr þæt
105 gewurde. And oft þrǣl þæne þegen þe ǣr wæs his hlāford cnyt swȳþe
fæste and wyrcð him tō þrǣle þurh Godes yrre. Wālā þǣre yrmðe
and wālā þǣre woroldscame þe nū habbað Engle, eal þurh Godes
yrre! Oft twēgen sǣmen oððe þrȳ hwīlum drīfað þā drāfe Crīstenra
manna fram sǣ tō sǣ ūt þurh þās þēode gewelede tōgædere, ūs
110 eallum tō woroldscame, gif wē on cornost ænige cūþon āriht
understandan. Ac ealne þæne bysmor þe wē oft þoliað wē gyldað

---

80   **his āgenne cēap** '[God's] own purchase', i.e. the rape victim, who, like all Christians, had been redeemed spiritually by God's sacrifice on the cross, but is now sold to pagans. See note to ll. 37–8 above.

91   **tō wīcinge weorþe** 'becomes a [pagan] Viking'.

95   **þegengylde** 'thane's price' i.e. the wergild of a man of the upper class. The Danes, who had by treaty gained the right to claim a thane's wergild for any Danish freeman, were claiming this payment even for English slaves who had fled their Anglo-Saxon masters and become Vikings.

97–8   **nū lange inne ne ūte** 'now for a long time anywhere'.

105   **gewurde** 'happened' The subj. is used because it is not a specific historical instance that is being described, but something that could occur at any time.

106   **him** 'for himself' The dir. obj. of *wyrcð* is *þæne þegen*.

109   **from sǣ . . . þēode** 'throughout this nation from sea to sea'.

110   **ænige** i.e. *ænige scame*.

mid weorðscipe þām þe ūs scendað. Wē him gyldað singāllīce, and
hȳ ūs hȳnað dæghwāmlīce. Hȳ hergiað and hȳ bærnað, rȳpað and
rēafiað and tō scipe lǣdað; and lā, hwæt is ǣnig ōðer on eallum þām
115 gelimpum būtan Godes yrre ofer þās þēode swutol and gesǣne?

   Nis ēac nān wundor þēah ūs mislimpe, for þām wē witan ful georne
þæt nū fela gēara menn nā ne rōhtan foroft hwæt hȳ worhtan wordes
oððe dǣde, ac wearð þes þēodscipe, swā hit þincan mæg, swȳþe
forsyngod þurh mænigfealde synna and þurh fela misdǣda: þurh
120 morðdǣda and þurh māndǣda, þurh gītsunga and þurh gīfernessa,
þurh stala and þurh strūdunga, þurh mannsylena and þurh hæþene
unsida, þurh swicdōmas and þurh searacræftas, þurh lahbrycas and
þurh ǣswicas, þurh mǣgrǣsas and þurh manslyhtas, þurh hādbrycas
and þurh ǣwbrycas, þurh siblegeru and þurh mistlice forligru.
125 And ēac syndan wīde, swā wē ǣr cwǣdan, þurh āðbricas and þurh
wedbrycas and þurh mistlice lēasunga forloren and forlogen mā
þonne scolde, and frēolsbricas and fæstenbrycas wīde geworhte oft
and gelōme. And ēac hēr syn on earde apostatan ābroþene and
cyrichatan hetole and lēodhatan grimme ealles tō manege, and ofer-
130 hogan wīde godcundra rihtlaga and Crīstenra þēawa, and hōcorwyrde
dysige ǣghwǣr on þēode oftost on þā þing þe Godes bodan bēodaþ,
and swȳþost on þā þing þe ǣfre tō Godes lage gebyriað mid rihte.
And þȳ is nū geworden wīde and sīde tō ful yfelan gewunan þæt
menn swȳþor scamað nū for gōddǣdan þonne for misdǣdan, for þām
135 tō oft man mid hōcere gōddǣda hyrweð and godfyrhte lehtreð ealles
tō swȳþe, and swȳþost man tǣleð and mid olle gegrēteð ealles tō
gelōme þā þe riht lufiað and Godes ege habbað be ǣnigum dǣle.
And þurh þæt þe man swā dēð þæt man eal hyrweð þæt man scolde
heregian and tō forð lāðet þæt man scolde lufian, þurh þæt man
140 gebringeð ealles tō manege on yfelan geþance and on undǣde, swā
þæt hȳ ne scamað nā, þēh hȳ syngian swȳðe and wið God sylfne

---

114 **hwæt . . . ōðer** 'what else is there'.
116 **Nis ēac . . . mislimpe** 'Nor is it any wonder that [things] go awry with us'.
125 **syndan** (=*sindon*) The subject is *mā þonne scolde* 'more people than there should
be' in ll. 126–7.
127 **frēolsbricas . . . geworhte** Supply *sindon* 'are'.
128 **apostatan ābroþene** 'degenerate apostates'.
130–1 **hōcorwyrde . . . on þā þing** 'deriders . . . of those things'.
133 **geworden . . . tō ful yfelan gewunan** 'come . . . to that full sorry pass'.
134 **menn swȳþor scamað** 'it causes people more shame'. *Scamað* is impersonal;
menn is acc.
137 **Godes ege habbað** 'have fear of God' i.e. are God-fearing.
137–9 **þurh þæt þe man swā dēð þæt . . . þurh þæt . . .** 'because one behaves in
this way namely that . . . therefore . . .'.
140 **gebringeð ealles tō . . . undǣde** 'leads all too many in evil thinking and mis-
behaviour'.
141 **hȳ ne scamað nā** 'it does not shame them at all'.

forwyrcan hȳ mid ealle, ac for īdelan onscytan hȳ scamað þæt hȳ
bētan heora misdǣda swā swā bēc tǣcan, gelīce þām dwǣsan þe for
heora prȳtan lēwe nellað beorgan ǣr hȳ nā ne magan, þēh hȳ eal willan.

145   Hēr syndan þurh synlēawa, swā hit þincan mæg, sāre gelēwede
tō manege on earde. Hēr syndan mannslagan and mǣgslagan and
mæsserbanan and mynsterhatan, and hēr syndan mānsworan and
morþorwyrhtan, and hēr syndan myltestran and bearnmyrðran
and fūle forlegene hōringas manege, and hēr syndan wiccan and
150   wælcyrian, and hēr syndan rȳperas and rēaferas and woroldstruderas
and, hrǣdest is tō cweþenne, māna and misdǣda ungerīm ealra. And
þæs ūs ne scamað nā, ac ūs scamað swȳþe þæt wē bōte āginnan swā
swā bēc tǣcan, and þæt is gesȳne on þysse earman forsyngodan
þēode. Ēalā, micel magan manege gȳt hērtōēacan ēaþe beþencan
155   þæs þe ān man ne mehte on hrǣdinge āsmēagan; hū earmlīce hit
gefaren is nū ealle hwīle wīde gynd þās þēode. And smēage hūru
georne gehwā hine sylfne and þæs nā ne latige ealles tō lange. Ac la,
on Godes naman, utan dōn swā ūs nēod is, beorgan ūs sylfum swā
wē geornost magan, þē lǣs wē ætgædere ealle forweorðan.

160   Ān þēodwita wæs on Brytta tīdum, Gildas hātte; sē āwrāt be
heora misdǣdum hū hȳ mid heora synnum swā oferlīce swȳþe God
gegrǣmedan þæt hē lēt æt nȳhstan Engla here heora eard gewinnan
and Brytta dugeþe fordōn mid ealle. And þæt wæs geworden, þæs
þe hē sǣde, þurh rīcra rēaflāc and þurh gītsunge wōhgestrēona, þurh
165   lēode unlaga and þurh wōhdōmas, þurh biscopa āsolcennesse and
þurh lȳðre yrhðe Godes bydela, þe sōþes geswugedan ealles tō gelōme
and clumedan mid ceaflum þǣr hȳ scoldan clypian. þurh fūlne ēac
folces gǣlsan and þurh oferfylla and mænigfealde synna heora eard
hȳ forworhtan and selfe hȳ forwurdan. Ac utan dōn swā ūs þearf is,

---

143   **bēc** reference is to penitentials, i.e. manuals for confessors.

144   **nellað beorgan . . . willan** 'will not seek a cure for their injury until they no
longer can, although they strongly wish [to do so]'.

146   **tō manege on earde** 'too many in this country' is the subject of the sentence.

151   **māna and . . . ealra** 'a countless number of all [kinds of] crimes and misdeeds'.
It is to this *ungerīm* that *þæs* refers: 'we are not ashamed *of that*'.

154   **manege** is the subject of *magan beþencan*; *micel* is direct object; *þæs* is partitive
gen. with *micel*; *micel . . . þæs þe ān man ne mehte* = 'much that one man could not'.

155–6   **hū earmlīce hit gefaren is** 'how wretchedly everything has gone'. This clause
is parallel with *micel*, object of *beþencan*.

156–7   **smēage . . . hine sylfne** 'indeed, let each examine himself earnestly'.

158   **swā ūs nēod is** 'as is our need'.

160   **Gildas** a sixth-century Briton living during the time of the Anglo-Saxon invasion of his country, wrote a Latin jeremiad (*De excidio Britanniae*) in which he tells his
fellow Britons that the invasion they are enduring is God's punishment for their sins.

163–4   **þæs þe** 'just as'.

166   **sōþes geswugedan** 'failed to speak the truth'.

169   **swā ūs þearf is** 'as is our need'.

170 warnian ūs be swilcan; and sōþ is þæt ic secge, wyrsan dǣda wē witan
mid Englum þonne wē mid Bryttan āhwār gehȳrdan. And þȳ ūs is
þearf micel þæt wē ūs beþencan and wið God sylfne þingian
georne. And utan dōn swā ūs þearf is, gebūgan tō rihte and be suman
dǣle unriht forlǣtan, and bētan swȳþe georne þæt wē ǣr brǣcan;
175 and utan God lufian and Godes lagum fylgean, and gelǣstan swȳþe
georne þæt þæt wē behētan þā wē fulluht underfēngan, oððon þā
þe æt fulluhte ūre forespecan wǣran; and utan word and weorc
rihtlīce fadian, and ūre ingeþanc clǣnsian georne, and āð and wed
wǣrlīce healdan, and sume getrȳwða habban ūs betwēonan būtan
180 uncrǣftan; and utan gelōme understandan þone miclan dōm þe wē
ealle tō sculon, and beorgan ūs georne wið þone weallendan bryne
helle wītes, and geearnian ūs þā mǣrþa and þā myrhða þe God
hæfð gegearwod þām þe his willan on worolde gewyrcað. God ūre
helpe. *Amen.*

170 be swilcan 'from such [sins]'.
180–1 þe wē ealle tō sculon 'to which we all must [go]'.
183 ūre is the gen. object of the subj. *helpe.*

Glossary

Abbreviations are the same as those on p. xv except that within entries case, number, and gender are indicated with a single initial letter (nsm = nominative singular masculine, gpf = genitive plural feminine, isn = instrumental singular neuter, etc.) and verb classes are identified with a simple numeral, Roman for strong verbs and Arabic for weak, or else with anom. for anomalous verbs and pret.-pres. for preterite present verbs. Thus if an entry word is followed by m., n. or f., this means it is a masculine, neuter or feminine noun. If it is followed by II, this means it is a second-class strong verb, while a 2 would mean it was a second-class weak verb. In analysing verb forms we use an Arabic numeral to indicate person and s or p to indicate singular or plural (3p = third person plural). When verb forms are indicative, no mood is specified, but subjunctives and imperatives are marked subj. and imp. respectively. Where it seems helpful to do so, we indicate in parenthesis the section in the *Guide* where the word or its general type is discussed. Following are abbreviations used in addition to, or instead of, those listed on p. xv:

anom.	anomalous	pres. ptc.	present participle
corr.	correlative	refl.	reflexive object
def. art.	definite article	rel.	relative
impers.	impersonal	w.a.	with accusative object
imp. p.	imperative plural	w.d.	with dative object
imp. s.	imperative singular	w.d.i.	with dative or instrumental object
indecl.	indeclinable	w.g.	with genitive object
interj.	interjection	w.i.	with instrumental object
interr.	interrogative	w. ind.	with indicative mood
num.	numeral	w. refl.	with reflexive object
pers. n.	personal name	w. refl. d.	with reflexive dative
p. ptc.	past participle	w. sg.	with singular

The letter æ follows *a*, *þ/ð* follows *t*. The prefix *ġe-* is ignored in alphabetizing words, so that *ġe*munan appears under *m*. Occurrences of words are cited by text number and line: 3/25 refers to text number 3 (*A Colloquy on the Occupations*), line 25.

Probably the most difficult element of Old English vocabulary for the beginner is the considerable number of compound conjunctions like mid þām þe and for þon. Students will find it helpful to familiarize themselves with the list of conjunctions in §§168 and 171 before reading the texts or using the glossary.

This revised glossary was prepared in collaboration with Roy Michael Liuzza of Tulane University and Philip Rusche of the University of Nevada, Las Vegas.

aa see ā

ā adv. *forever, always,* 4/121, 4/330, 11(e)/6, 12/315, 15/5, 15/42, 20/7, 20/345, āwa 17/79, 20/120, etc.; *ever* 18(a)/779, aa 22/2 [archaic MnE aye]

Abbo pers. n. *Abbo* ns 4/128, 4/134

abbod m. *abbot* 7/1, 7/19; ds abbode 4/136

abbudisse f. *abbess* ns 9/61; gs abudissan 9/1; ds 9/49

ābēag see ābūgan

Abēl pers. n. *Abel* gs Abēles 4/73

ābēodan II *announce, deliver* (*a message*) imp. s. ābēod 12/49; pret. 3s ābēad 4/162, 12/27

ābīdan I w.g. *await* inf. 15/53 [MnE abide]

ābiddan V *get by asking, receive* pret. 3s ābæd 11(n)/12

ābīhð see ābūgan

A Guide to Old English, Eighth Edition. Bruce Mitchell and Fred C. Robinson.
© 2012 Bruce Mitchell and Fred C. Robinson. Published 2012 by Blackwell Publishing Ltd.

āblendan I *blind* inf. 7/45
Abraham pers. n. *Abraham* ns 2/46, 2/52; as 2/53, 2/71; gs Abrahames 2/43, 4/6
ābrecan IV *storm, sack* pret. 3p ābrǣcon 10(a)/3; subj. 3s ābrǣce 11(n)/7; p. ptc. ābrocen 10(b)/18
ābregdan III *draw* pret. 3s ābrǣd 20/79
ābrēoðan II *fail, come to naught* pret. subj. 3s ābrēoðe 12/242 (see note); p. ptc. ābroþen *degenerate, reprobate* npm ābroþene 22/128
ābūgan II *yield, give way* inf. 4/140, 4/160, etc.; pres. 3s ābīhð 4/194; pret. 3s ābēag 18(a)/775
abūtan adv. *about, around* 4/277
ac conj. *but, however, but on the contrary, and, moreover* 1/11, 1/33, 2/9, 2/73, 3/11, etc.
āc f. *oak* ns 1/11, 11(n)/9
ācennan I *bring forth, give birth to, produce* pres. 2s ācenst 2/34; p. ptc. ācenned 3/137, 4/58, 11(m)/1, 18(b)/1356
ācsian 2 *ask* pret. 3s āhsode 8/53
āctrēo n. *oak tree* ds 15/28, 15/36
ācwealde see ācwellan
ācweccan I *shake, brandish* pret. 3s ācwehte 12/255, 12/310 [MnE quake]
ācwellan I *kill* imp. s. ācwele 2/63; pret. 3s ācwealde 18(a)/886, 22/68
ācwenċan I *quench, extinguish* inf. 22/19
ācweðan V *utter* pres. 3s ācwið 16/91; pret. 3s ācwæð 20/82, 20/151, 20/283
ācȳþan I *make known* inf. 16/113
Adam pers. n. *Adam* ns 2/18, 2/20, 2/24; as 2/20; gs Adomes 14/100
ādl f. *sickness, disease* ns 17/70
ādrǣfan I *drive out, exile* inf. 6/8; pret. 3s ādrǣfde 6/4
ādrēogan II *practice, commit* pres. 3p ādrēogað 22/78
āfāran VI *depart* p. ptc. npm āfarene 4/225
āfeallan VII *fall off, fall (in death)* p. ptc. āfeallen (*decayed*) 5/64, 12/202
āfēdan I *feed* inf. 3/148; pres. 2s āfētst 3/120
āferran see āfierran
āfētst see āfēdan
āfierran I *remove* inf. āferran 10(a)/19
āflȳman I *put to flight, cause to flee* pret. 3s āflȳmde 12/243
āfor adj. *fierce* nsm 20/257
āfȳlan I *defile, stain* inf. 4/190
āfyllan I *fill up* inf. 3/19; *slay* subj. pres. 3s āfylle 22/93, 22/94
āfȳsan I *impel* inf. 12/3 (*drive away*); p. ptc. āfȳsed 14/125
āgan pret.-pres. *possess, own, have* inf. 2/76, 10(b)/39, 10(b)/62, 12/87; pres. 1s āh 12/175; 3s 14/107, 17/27; 2p āgon 20/196; subj. 3s āge 16/64; 1p āgen 17/117; pret.

1s āhte 15/16; 3s 12/189, 20/3, 20/6, 20/339, 20/344; 3p āhton 10(b)/58. With negative: pres. 1s nāh *do not have* 4/123, 14/131; 3s 11(f)/14; pret. 1s nāhte 20/91 [MnE owe]
āġeaf see āġiefan
āgen see āgan
āgen adj. *own* asm āgenne 6/28, 22/80; dsm āgenum 4/185, 22/55; asn āgen 5/33, 11(k)/6; asf āgene 4/104; dsf āgenre 4/20; dpn āgenum 22/90
āgēotan II *drain, deprive (of)* p. ptc. npf āgotene 20/32
āġiefan V *give back* pret. 3s āgeaf 9/60, 12/44; p. ptc. āgyfen 12/116; *place, give* pret. 3s āgeaf 20/130; 3p āgēafon 20/341
āġinnan III *begin* inf. 22/152
āglǣca m. *combatant, belligerent* ns 18(a)/732, 18(a)/739, 18(a)/893; ǣglǣca 18(a)/816
agob see boga
āgotene see āgēotan
āgyfen see āġiefan
āh see āgan
āhāfen see āhebban
āhēawan VII *cut down* p. ptc. āhēawen 14/29
āhebban VI, I *raise, lift up, wage (war)* imp. s. āhefe 4/142; pres. 3p āhebbað 11(d)/3; pret. 1s āhof 14/44; 3s āhefde 2/67, āhof 12/130, 12/244; 1p āhofon 12/213; 3p 10(a)/2, 14/61; p. ptc. āhafen 12/106, āhefen 10(b)/47
āhlēapan VII *leap up* pret. 3s āhlēop 18(b)/1397
āhlēop see āhlēapan
āhliehhan VI *laugh at, deride, exult* pret. 3s āhlōg 18(a)/730
āhlōg see āhliehhan
āhof see āhebban
āhofon see āhebban
āhōn VII *hang* p. ptc. āhongen 20/48
āhreddan I *rescue, save* pret. 3s āhredde 4/79, 7/53
āhsode see ācsian
āhte see āgan
āhte see āwiht
āhtes see āwiht
āhton see āgan
āhwǣr adv. *anywhere* 4/233, 7/31, āhwār *ever* 22/171
āhyldan I *deviate from* pret. 3s āhylde 4/141
āīdliġan 2 *render useless, profane* inf. 8/55
aldor see ealdor
aldordagum see ealdordæg
aldorlēas adj. *leaderless, lacking a leader* npm aldorlēase 18/15
aldorman see ealdormann
aldorþeġn see ealdorþeġn
ālēag see ālēogan

ālecgan I *lay down* pret. 3s ālegde 18(a)/
834, 18(a)/851 (*give up*), ālede 20/100 (*lay
out*); 3p ālēdon 14/63 (see note to 4/17)
ālēogan II *leave unfulfilled* pret. 3s ālēag
10(b)/39
Alerīc see **Eallerīca**
ālimpan III *befall, come to pass* p. ptc.
ālumpen 18(a)/733
alle see **eall**
alwalda m. *all-ruler, the Lord* ns 18(b)/
1314; gs alwaldan 20/84
ālȳfan I *permit, allow* inf. 12/90; p. ptc.
ālȳfed 8/62
ālȳsan I *release* imp. s. ālȳs 4/288
Amuling pers. n. *Amuling* ns 10(b)/69; gp
Amulinga 10(a)/6
āmyrran I *wound* pret. 3s āmyrde 12/165
[MnE mar]
ān adj. (§§83, 193.4, 194) *a, an, one, only* nsm
3/33, 4/143, 11(b)/3, 11(k)/3, āne, āna *alone*
4/181, 12/94, 14/123, 14/128, 15/22,
15/35, 16/8, 21/43, 21/57, 21/62; asm ānne
2/66, 3/36, 3/56, 5/18 (ānne ānlēpne *a
single one*) ænne 4/168, 5/26, etc.; gsm ānes
4/200, dsm ānum 3/104, 4/74, 6/21, etc.;
asn 3/205, 5/16; dsn ānum 4/101, 4/207;
asf āne 4/253, 5/75, 11(p)/2; dsf ānre
2/46, 4/132, 4/274; npm āne 4/307 (see
note); apn ān 9/16; gp ānra (ānra gehwelc
each one) 3/210, 14/108; as pron. asm
ānne 12/117, 12/226; ān æfter ānum *one
after the other* 22/78
anbīdian 2 *wait, abide* pres. ptc. andbīdigende
(w.g.) 4/263; imp. p. anbīdiað (w. refl.
ēow) 2/50
anbyhtscealc m. *retainer, servant* np
anbyhtscealcas 20/38
āncenned adj. *only begotten* asm āncennedan
2/44, 2/65; dsm 2/73
and conj. *and* 1/2, 1/3, 1/5, 2/2, 2/5, etc.;
ond 5/2, 5/4, etc.
anda m. *malice, hostility* ds andan 16/105,
18(a)/708
andbīdigende see **anbīdian**
andettan I *confess* pres. 1s andette 8/13,
ondette 8/45; pret. 3s 8/49
andġit n. *meaning, sense* ns 4/46; as 4/27;
ds andgite 4/54, 4/98, andgiete 5/69
andġitfullīċe adv. *clearly, intelligibly* superl.
andgitfullīcost 5/73
andsaca m. *enemy, adversary* as andsacan
18(a)/786
andswarian 2 *answer* pres. ptc. andswarigende
4/239; pres. 3s andswaraþ 3/197, 3/204;
pret. 3s andswarode 8/1, ondsworede 8/
56, ondswarede 9/29, ondswarade 9/108;
3p ondswarodon 9/101, ondswaredon
9/114

andswaru f. *answer* as andsware 9/33, 12/44,
ondsware 11(n)/15
andweard adj. *present* asm andwerdan 4/263;
nsn andwearde 8/26
andwlita m. *face* gs andwlitan 2/40
andwyrdan I (w.d.) *answer* inf. 4/170; pret.
1s andwyrde 5/43; 3s 2/4, 2/55, 2/62,
4/238; p. ptc. geandwyrd 4/199
ānfeald adj. *simple, onefold* dsf ānfealdan 4/47
ānfealdlīce adv. *in the singular* 4/71
ānfloga m. *solitary flier* ns 17/62
anforht adj. *very frightened, terrified* nsm
14/117
ānforlǣtan VII *abandon, renounce* pret.
subj. 3s ānforlēte 9/63
angel m. *hook* as 3/77, 3/195 [MnE angle]
Angelcynn n. *the English people, England* ns
4/318; as 5/3, 5/30; ds Angelcynne 4/321,
5/14, 5/58
anġinn n. *beginning* ns angin 4/55, 12/242
(see note); ds anginne 4/18, 4/51
ānhaga m. *solitary one, one who dwells alone*
ns 16/1, 21/19
ānhoga m. *solitary one, one who contemplates
alone* as ānhogan 16/40
āninga, adv. *at once* 20/250
Anlāf pers. n. *Olaf* ns 7/47
ġeānlǣċan I *unite* p. ptc. npm geānlǣhte
4/150
ānlēpe adj. *single* asn ānlēpne 5/18
ānlīcnes f. *image* ds ānlīcnisse 4/68, 4/70;
dp ānlīcnissum 4/71. See **onlīcnes**
ānne see **ān**
ānnis f. *oneness, unity* ns 4/70
ānra see **ān**
ānrǣd adj. *resolute* nsm 4/139, 12/44,
12/132; dsm ārǣdum 4/216
ānre see **ān**
ansund adj. *whole, uncorrupted* nsm 4/263;
asm ansundne 4/312; np ansunde 4/320
Antecrīst m. *Antechrist* gs Antecrīstes 22/3
anwald see **onweald**
anwealda m. *ruler, Lord* ns 14/153
apostata m. *apostate* np apostatan 22/128
apostol m. *apostle* ns 4/32; np apostolas
4/36; gp apostola 9/76
ār n. *copper* as 3/142 [MnE ore]
ār m. *messenger* ns 12/26
ār f. *mercy, favour, prosperity* ns 17/107; as
āre 16/1, 16/114; gs 10(b)/78; gp āra
10(b)/57
ār f. *oar*
ārās see **ārīsan**
ārǣdan I *read* inf. 5/61, 5/66; p. ptc. ārǣd
predetermined, inexorable 16/5
ārǣran I *raise, erect, establish* inf. 4/312;
pret. 3s ārǣrde 2/57, 4/38; 3p ārǣrdon
4/250; p. ptc. ārǣred 14/44 [MnE rear]

arċebiscop m. *archbishop* ns arcebisceop 7/16, 7/24, 7/25; ds ærcebiscepe 4/127, 5/70, arcebisceope 7/18

arċestōl m. *archiepiscopal see* ds arcestōle 7/16

āreċċean 1 *translate, render* inf. 5/17, 5/73

ārētan 1 *gladden* p. ptc. ārēted 20/167

ārfæst adj. *merciful* nsm 20/190

ārfæstnis f. *piety* ds ārfæstnisse 9/3

ārian 2 w.d. *spare, pardon* inf. 2/72, 4/297

āriht adv. *properly, aright* 22/110

ārīsan 1 *arise* inf. 9/112; imp. s. ārīs 18(b)/ 1390; pret. 3s ārās 2/46, 9/22, 9/45, 14/101

ārlēas adj. *dishonourable* nsm ārlēasa 4/215; dsm ārlēasan 4/199; npm 4/205

ārlīċe adv. *honourably, kindly* 11(k)/6

arod adj. *bold* nsm 20/275

arodlīċe adv. *quickly* 2/62, 4/162, 4/166, 4/197

Arriān pers. n. *Arius* gs Arriānes 10(b)/40

Arriānisc adj. *Arian* dsm Arriāniscan 10(a)/7

ārweorðe adj. *honourable* dsm ārwurðan 4/274; as noun nsm ārwyrða 10(a)/26

āsǣde see āsecgan

asca see æsc

Ascanmynster n. *Axminster* as 6/42

āsceacan VI *shake* pret. 3s āsceōc 12/230

āsceōc see āsceacan

āscian 2 *ask* inf. 1/32; pres. 1s āscie 2/54; pret. 3s āscode 2/54

ġeāscian 2 *learn by asking, learn of, discover* pret. 3s geāscode 6/9

ġeāscode see ġeāscian

āsecgan 3 *say, tell* inf. 16/11, 20/330; pret. 3s āsǣde 12/198

āsendan 1 *send* p. ptc. āsend 4/234

āsettan 1 *set, set up* inf. 11(k)/11 (sīþas āsettan *to set out on journeys*); pres. 1s āsette 3/42, subj. 3s 14/142; pret. 3p āsetton 14/32

āsingan III *sing, recite* pret. 3s āsong 9/60

āsmēagan 1 *imagine, understand* inf. 4/317; *investigate* inf. 22/155

āsolcennes f. *laziness* as āsolcennesse 22/ 165

āsong see āsingan

āspryttan 1 *sprout, bring forth* pres. 3s āspryt 2/39

assa m. *ass* dp assum 2/48, 2/50

Assīrias f. pl. *Assyrians* gp Assīria 20/232, 20/309; dp Assyrīum 20/218

āstāg see āstigan

āstandan VI *stand up, get up* pret. 3s āstōd 18(a)/759

āstealde see āstellan

āstellan 1 *establish* pret. 3s āstealde 4/83

āstīgan 1 *proceed, ascend* pres. 1s āstīge 3/135, 3s āstīgeð 18(b)/1373; pret. 3s āstāg 14/103, 18(a)/782

āstōd see āstandan

āstreaht see āstreċċan

āstreċċan 1 *stretch out, extend* imp. s. āstreċe 2/63; pret. 3s āstrehte (w. refl.) 10(a)/30; p. ptc. āstreaht 10(b)/80

āstyrian 1 *remove, move* inf. 4/282; p. ptc. āstyred 14/30 [MnE stir]

āswāpan VII *sweep away, remove* pres. 1s āswāpe 11(h)/5

āswebban 1 *put to sleep* i.e. *kill* p. ptc. āswefede 20/321

ātēah see ātēon

ateliċ adj. *horrible, dreadful* nsm 18(a)/784

ātēon II *draw, unsheathe* pret. 3s ātēah 2/60, 18(a)/766 (sið . . . ātēah *took a journey*); subj. 3s ātuge 9/81

atol adj. *terrible, hateful* nsm 18(a)/732, 18(a)/816; asm atolne 20/246, atolan 20/75; nsn atol 18(a)/848, 18(b)/1332; asn 17/6

attor n. *venom* as 11(h)/9

ātuge see ātēon

ātyhtan 1 *produce, entice* p. ptc. ātyhted 10(b)/8, 11(m)/3

āð m. *oath* as 22/178; ap āðas 10(b)/25

āðbriċe m. *oath-breaking* ap āðbricas 22/125

āþecgan 1 *serve* fig. *kill* inf. 19/2, 19/7

āwa see ā

āwearp see āweorpan

āweaxan VII *grow up* pret. 1s āweox 11(k)/ 10, 15/3

āweċċan 1 *awaken, arouse* inf. 20/258, 20/273; pret. subj. 3s āwehte 9/82

āwēdan 1 *go mad* pret. 3s āwēdde 4/302

āweg see onweg

āwel m. *awl* as 3/195

āwendan 1 *translate, change, distort* inf. 4/3, 4/5, 4/101 (*change*); pres. 3s āwent 4/103; pret. 1s āwende 5/74; 1p āwende 4/133; p. ptc. āwend 4/6

āweorpan III *throw away, discard* inf. āwurpan 4/108; pret. 3s āwearp 4/203, 8/59

āweox see āweaxan

āwēstan 1 *lay waste,* pret. 3p āwēston 4/151

āwierġan 1 *curse, damn* p. ptc. āwierġed 2/29, 2/37; npm āwyrgede 4/326

āwiht n. *aught, anything* gs āhtes 7/28 (see note); ds 3/168 (to āwihte *at all*); ahte 22/19

āwrāt see āwrītan

āwrītan 1 *write* inf. 4/100, 4/122 (*copy*); pret. 3s āwrāt 22/160; p. ptc. āwriten 4/77, np āwritene 5/33

āwurpan see āweorpan

āwyrgede see āwierġan

æ f. *law, scripture* ns 4/12, 4/28, 5/48, 10(b)/
41; as 4/40; ds 4/10, 4/12, 4/23
æcer m. *cultivated field* as 3/13 [MnE acre]
ædre adv. *soon, immediately* 20/64, 20/95,
20/246
ædre f. *vein* dp ēdrum 18(a)/742
æfæst adj. *pious* nsm 9/83; asf æfæstan 9/16;
apn æfæste 9/11
æfæstnes f. *religion* ns 8/14; ds æfæstnisse
9/3, æfæstnesse 9/16
æfen m. *evening* as 3/25; ds æfenne 9/93
geæfenlæcan 1 *imitate* inf. 4/204
æfenspræc f. *evening speech* as æfenspræce
18(a)/759
æfentid f. *evening-time* as æfentīde 14/68
[archaic MnE eventide]
æfre adv. *forever, always, ever* 4/57, 4/66,
4/187, 4/216, 4/295, 5/44, 7/54, etc.
æft see eft
æftan adv. *from behind* 22/61
æfter adv. *afterwards* 9/43, 17/77, 18/12
æfter prep. w.d. *after, according to* 4/22,
4/33, 4/54, 5/36, 20/117, *along* 20/18, etc.;
w.a. *with longing for* 16/50; æfter þām
afterward 22/68
æftercweðende m. pl. (pres. ptc) *those
speaking after* (*a man's death*) gp
æftercweðendra 17/72
æfterfylġan 1 *follow, come after* pres. subj. 3s
æfterfylige 8/35
æfðonca m. *offence, insult* ap æfðoncan
20/265
æġhwæm see æġhwā
æġhwā pron. *every one, everything* dsm
æġhwæm 18(b)/1384
æġhwær adv. *everywhere* 22/23, 22/53,
22/131
æġhwæþer see æġðer
æġhwæðres see æġðer
æġhweder adv. *in all directions* 7/77
æġhwylċ pron. *each* (*one*) nsm 12/234,
18(b)/1386; asm æġhwylcne 20/50, æġhwylcne ānra *every one* 14/86; as an adj. nsf
æġhwylc 14/120; dsm æġhwylcum 20/166
æġlæca see āglæca
æġðer pron. *each, both* ns 12/133, 12/224;
gs æġhwæðres 11(a)/5; æġðer ġe . . . ġe
both . . . and 2/11, 4/37, 5/37, 7/9, etc.,
æġwæþer ġe . . . ġe 8/2 [MnE either]
ægylde adj. *without compensation, without
payment of wergild* nsm 22/93
Ægypta see Egipte
æht f. *possessions, property* as æht 13/36; ap
æhta 4/37; æhte 18(c)/2248
æl m. *eel* ap ælas 3/87
ælċ pron., adj. *each, every* nsm 3/164, 4/283;
asn ælcne 4/280; gsm ælces 4/74; dsm
ælcum 5/74; ism ælce 3/8; gsn ælces

10(b)/36; dsn ælcum 2/3, 4/49; isn ælce
4/269; dsf ælcre 5/75; gp ælcra 22/34; ælc
æfter ōðrum *each after the other* 22/78,
22/102
ælde m. pl. *men* gp ælda 16/85; 17/77; dp
yldum 18(a)/705; eldum 18(d)/3168
ældo see yldu
Ælfere pers. n. *Ælfere* ns 12/80
Ælfgār pers. n. *Ælfgar* as 7/45
Ælfnoð pers. n. *Ælfnoth* ns 12/183
Ælfred pers. n. *Ælfred* ns 4/154, 5/1
Ælfrīc see Ealfrīc
Ælfrīc pers. n. *Ælfric* gp Ælfrīces 12/209
ælfscīne adj. *beautiful as a fairy* nsf ælfscinu
20/14
Ælfstān pers. n. *Ælfstan* ds Ælfstāne 7/30
Ælfwine pers. n. *Ælfwine* ns 12/211, vs
12/231
ælmihtig adj. *almighty* nsm 2/72 (see
Ælmihtiga *the Almighty*), 4/53, 4/186,
4/311, 14/93, (se Ælmihtiga *the Almighty*)
2/72, 4/186, 14/98, 20/300, etc.; asm
ælmihtigne 14/60, ælmihtigan 4/138,
4/296; dsm Ælmihtigan 4/245, 4/323,
20/7, 20/345, ælmihtegum 5/20
geæmetiġan 2 *free, empty, disengage* pres.
subj. 2s gæmctige 5/22
æmettig adj. *empty* nsm 3/164
ænde see ende
æniġ adj. *any* nsm 4/24, 4/239, 7/54, etc.;
asm ænigne 5/20; gsm æniges 4/291,
ænges 17/116; dsm æniġum 11(h)/11,
11(h)/15, etc.; asn æniġ 3/22, 3/35, 9/
100, etc.; gsf ænigre 8/48; as pron., nsm
14/110, 14/117, 18(a)/779, hyra æniġ *any
of them* 12/70; isn ænige þinga *in any way,
by any means* 18(a)/791; as noun 18(b)/
1356
ænliċ adj. *unique, solitary, beautiful* nsm
11(p)/2
ænne see ān
ær adv. *before, previously* (§§168, 197.4), 5/34,
6/26, 8/75, 9/88, 10(b)/75, 11(f)/12,
11(h)/7, etc.; compar: see æror; superl.:
see ærest; conj. *before* 4/128, 6/11, 11(n)/
6, 12/279, 12/300, etc.; w. subj. *rather than*
12/61, *before* 17/74; prep. w.d.i. *before* 17/
69; ær þan (or þæm) (ðe) *before* 4/11,
5/28, 14/88, ær ðon ðe 20/252 [MnE ere]
ærænde see ærende
ærċebiscop see ārċebiscop
ærdæg m. *daybreak, early morning* ds ærdæge
18(b)/1311
ærende n. *message* as 4/159, 4/161, ærænde
12/28 [MnE errand]
ærendġewrit n. *letter* as 5/16, 10(b)/63;
ap ærendgewritu 10(a)/20 [MnE errand,
writ]

ǣrendraca m. *messenger, minister* ns 4/161, 4/197; ds ǣrendracan 4/188; dp ǣrend-wrecum 5/6

ǣrendwrecum see ǣrendraca

ǣrest adj. *first* nsf ǣreste 9/72, 15/6 [archaic MnE erst, erst(while)]

ǣrest adv. *first* 4/35, 4/64, 4/195, 5/48, 7/22, 9/40, 20/14, etc., ǣrost 12/124, etc.

ǣrġewin n. *ancient hostility* as 14/19

ǣrgōd adj. *good from old times, very good* nsm 18(b)/1329

ǣrist mfn. *resurrection* gs ǣristes 4/263

ǣrnan I *run, gallop* pret. 3p ǣrndon 12/191

ǣrnemerġen m. *early morning* ds 3/23

ǣror adv. *earlier* ǣrur 14/108, ǣror 18(a)/809, 18(d)/3168

ǣrsceaft n. *ancient work* ns 13/16

ǣr þan þe, ǣr ðǣm ðe see ǣr

ǣs n. *bait, food* ds ǣse 3/77; *carrion* ds ǣse 18(b)/1332, gs ǣses 12/107

æsc m. *ash (tree)* ns 1/13; *ash (spear)* as 12/43, 12/310; gp asca 16/99; dp æscum 4/151

Æscferð pers. n. *Æscferth* ns 12/267

Æschere pers. n. *Æschere* ns 18(b)/1323, 18(b)/1329

æschere m. *army in ships, Viking army* ns 12/69

æscholt n. *spear made of ash* as 12/230

æscplegan m. *spear-fight, battle* ds æscplegan 20/217 [MnE ash(wood), play]

æscrōf adj. *brave in battle* npm æscrōfe 20/336

Æscwīġ pers. n. *Æscwig* ds Æscwīġe 7/30

æstel m. *pointer used to keep one's place as one reads* ns 5/75

ǣswic m. *criminal offence* ap ǣswicas 22/123

ǣt n. *food, prey* gs ǣtes 20/210

æt prep. w.d. *at, from* 3/10/4/21, 4/129 (*into*), 5/70, 9/27 (*to*), etc.

ġeæt see ġeetan

ætberstan III *escape* pres. 1s ætberste 3/139; 3p ætberstaþ 3/105; pret. 3s ætbærst 7/35

ætēawed see atȳwan

ǣten see etan

ætēowian see ætȳwan

ætflēogan II *fly away* inf. 3/122, 3/124

ætforan prep. w.d. *in front of, before* 12/16

ætgædere adv. *together* 4/307, 9/99, 14/48, ætgædre 11(n)/11; somod ætgædre *together* 16/39, 18(a)/729

æthlēapan VII *run away, desert* pres. subj. 3s æthlēape 22/91

ætsomne adv. *together* 8/5, 9/93, 11(e)/3, 20/255, 21/31

ætstandan VI *stand fixed, stop* pret. 3s ætstōd 18(a)/891

ætsteppan VI *step forth* pret. 3s ætstōp 18(a)/745

ætstōd see ætstandan

ætstōp see ætsteppan

ætren see ættryne

ætterne see ættryne

ættryne adj. *poisoned, fatal, deadly* nsm ætren 11(h)/4, ætterne 12/146; asm ættrynne 12/47

ætwītan I w.d. *reproach* inf. 12/220, 12/250

ætȳwan I *appear, show* inf. 20/174 (*display*), ætēowian 4/300; pres. 3s ætȳweð 8/35; p. ptc. ætēawed 8/72

Æþeldrȳð pers. n. *Æthelthryth* ns 4/320

æðele adj. *noble* nsm 12/280, 18(b)/1312; æþela 4/215; asm æðelan 12/151; dpm æþelum 4/138; as noun *the noble one* nsf 20/176, 20/256

Æþelgār pers. n. *Æthelgar* ns 7/1, 7/16; gs Æþelgāres 12/320

æþeling m. *prince, atheling* ns 4/155, 6/19, 18(b)/1329; as 6/8, 6/14, 21/14; gs æþelinges 6/42, 18(a)/888; ds æþelinge 10(b)/40, 14/58; np æþelingas 18/3; gp æþelinga 11(a)/5, 17/93, 18(d)/3170; dp æðelingum 8/76, 10(b)/21

Æþelmǣr pers. n. *Æthelmær* ns 7/13 [MnE Elmer]

æþelo n. pl. *origin, descent, noble lineage* ap 12/216, æþelu 11(n)/8

Æþelred pers. n. *Æthelred* gs Æþelredes 4/127, 12/53, 12/151, 12/203

Æþelstān pers. n. *Æthelstan* ds Æþelstāne 4/130

Æðelwine pers. n. *Æthelwine* ns 7/26

Æþerīċ pers. n. *Ætheric* ns 12/280

ǣwbryċe m. *adultery* ap ǣwbrycas 22/124

bā see bēgen

ġebād see ġebīdan

baldlīce adv. *boldly* 12/311; superl. baldlīcost 12/78

baldor m. *lord* ns 20/9, 20/32, 20/49, 20/338

bana m. *slayer* ns 12/299; gs banan 14/66, 6/32 [MnE bane]

ġeband see ġebindan

bānfāg adj. *adorned with bone* asn 18(a)/780

bānloca m. *joint, body* np bānlocan 18(a)/818, ap 18(a)/742

bār m. *wild boar* as 3/56, 3/58, 3/59; ap bāras 3/51

bāt m. *boat* as 3/76; ds bāte 3/99

bāt see bītan

baþian 2 *bathe* inf. 16/47; pret. 3p baþedan 11(f)/6

baþu see bæð

Bæbbanburh f. *Bamburgh* (*Northumberland*) ns 7/39

bæc n. *back* as 12/276 (ofer bæc *away, in the rear*)

bæcere m. *baker* ns 3/162; np bæceras 3/6

bæd see biddan

bæde see biddan

bæl n. *fire, funeral pyre* ds bæle 17/114

bælċ m. *pride* as 20/267

bær see beran

ġebǣran 1 *rejoice* pret. subj. 3p gebærdon 20/27

ġebǣre n. *outcry* dp gebærum 6/17

bærnan 1 *burn* pres. 3p bærnað 22/113

bærnett n. *burning* ds bærnette 2/58, 7/55

ġebǣro n. *demeanour* as 15/44; is 15/21

bǣron see beran

bærst see berstan

bæð n. *bath* ds bæðe 8/77; np baþu 13/40, 13/46

be prep. w.d. *about, concerning,* 1/35, 3/168, 3/173, 4/31 etc., bi 9/72 etc.; *near, by* 12/152, 12/318, 12/319, big 12/182; be þām *through that* 12/9; be þām þe *as, according as* 2/12; be sūðan see sūðan

bēacen n. *beacon, sign, portent, symbol* ns 14/6, as 14/21, bēcn 18(d)/3160 (*monument*); ds bēacne 14/83; gp bēacna 14/118

bēad see bēodan

ġebēad see ġebēodan

beadogrīma m. *war-mask; helmet* as beadogrīman 18(c)/2257

beadu m. *battle* ds beaduwe 12/185, 20/175, 21/15, beadowe 20/213; gp beadwa 18(a)/709

beaducāf adj. *bold in battle* (as noun) *warrior* ns beaducāfa 19/11

beadurǣs m. *rush of battle, onslaught* ns 12/111

beadurinc m. *warrior* gp beadorinca 20/276; dp beadurincum 10(b)/18

beadurōf adj. *bold in battle* gsm beadurōfes 18(d)/3160

bēag see būgan

bēag m. *ring* (*of precious metal used for money or ornaments*) as 3/70, bēg (as plural) 18(d)/3163, ap bēagas 12/31, 12/160, 21/29; gp bēaga 20/340; dp bēagum 20/36, 21/45 [MnE (through Yiddish) bagel]

bēaggifa m. *ring-giver, lord* as bēahgifan 12/290

bēaghroden adj. *adorned with rings* nsf 11(j)/9

bēahgifu f. *ring-giving, generosity* ds bēahgife 21/15

bēahhord n. *ring-hoard, treasure* gs bēahhordes 18(a)/894

bēahhroden adj. *ring-adorned* npf bēahhrodene 20/138

beald adj. *bold* npm bealde 20/17

bealo n. *harm, injury, enmity* as (?) 17/112 [MnE bale]

bealocwealm m. *baleful death* ns 18(c)/2265

bealofull adj. *evil* nsm 20/63, bealofulla 20/48; asm bealofullan 20/100; gsm 20/248 [MnE baleful]

bealohȳdig adj. *intending evil, hostile* nsm 18(a)/723

bealosīþ m. *painful journey, bitter experience* gp bealosīþa 17/28

bealuware m. pl. *dwellers in iniquity, evildoers* gp bealuwara 14/79

bēam m. *tree, log, cross* ns 14/97; gs bēames 11(n)/7; ds bēame 14/114, 14/122; gp bēama 14/6 [MnE beam]

bearhtme adv. *instantly* 20/39

bearm m. *bosom, lap* on bearm scipes *in the hold of a ship* as 18(a)/896; ds bearme 21/25; *possessions, holdings* ds bearme 18/21

bearn n. *child, son* ns 12/92, 12/155, 12/186, 12/209, 12/238, 22/54, 22/83; as Bearn 20/84, etc.; ds bearne 22/54; np 10(b)/34, 17/77, 20/24; ap 3/148, 11(k)/6, 17/93; gp bearna 18(b)/1367, 20/51; dp bearnum 4/183, 9/40 [MnE bairn]

bearnmyrðra m. *infanticide* np bearnmyrðran 22/148

Bearrocscīr f. *Berkshire* as Bearrocscīre 7/72–3

bearu m. *grove* ns 11(o)/4; ds bearwe 15/27, bearowe 21/18; np bearwas 17/48, 18(b)/1363; dp bearwum 11(f)/2

bēatan VII *beat, pound* pres. ptc. gpm bēatendra 3/200; pres. 3s bēateð 18(c)/2265; pret. 3p bēoton 4/206, bēotan 17/23

beæftan adv. *behind* 20/112

beæftan prep. w.d. *behind* 6/24

bebēad see bebēodan

bebēodan II (w.d. of person) *command, commend* pres. ptc. bebēodende 9/123; pres. 1s bebīode 5/21, 5/76; pret. 1s bebēad 2/24, 2/37; 3s 2/6, 4/87, 4/200, 20/38, 20/144, 21/49; bibēad 9/97; 3p bebudon 9/56; p. ptc. beboden 4/94, 9/25, 9/60

bebīode see bebēodan

beboden see bebēodan

bebudon see bebēodan

bebyrgan 1 *bury* pret. 3p bebyrigdon 4/249; p. ptc. bebyrged 4/225, 4/255

bēċ see bōc

beclyppan 1 *clasp* p. ptc. beclypped 4/242

bēcn see bēacen

becōm see becuman

becuman IV *come* pres. subj. 3p becumen 3/44; pret. 3s becwōm 9/120, becōm 4/154, 10(a)/26, 10(b)/77 (*befell*), 20/310; 2p becōmon 12/58; 3p 4/240, 5/24 (*befell*), 12/58, 20/134 (*pass, escape*) [MnE become]

becwōm see **becuman**

ġebed n. *prayer* dp gebedum 4/268

bedǣlan 1 w.d. or g. *deprive* p. ptc. bedǣled 4/318, 18(a)/721; bidǣled 16/20, npm bedǣlde 22/26

bedd n. *bed* as bed 20/48; gs beddes 20/63; ds bedde 4/182, 20/72, 20/278

Bedefordscir f. *Bedfordshire* as Bedefordscīre 7/69

bedelfan III *bury* pret. 3s bedealf 14/75

ġebedhūs n. *chapel, oratory* ds gebedhūse 4/254

bedrest f. *bed* ds bedreste 20/36

bedrīfan 1 *drive, chase* pret. 3p bedrifon 3/60; *cover over, sprinkle* p. ptc. asm bedrifenne 14/62

beēode see **begān**

befæstan 1 *apply, use* inf. 5/24, pres. subj. 2s befæste 5/24

befeallan VII *fall* p. ptc. befeallen *deprived, bereft* 18(c)/2256

befēng see **befōn**

befēolan III (§133.2) w.d. *apply oneself* inf. 5/59

beflōwan VII *flow around, surround by water* p. ptc. beflowen 15/49

befōn VII *enclose* pret. 3s befēng 13/39

began see **beģinnan**

begān anom. (§128) *practise, perform, surround* inf. 1/12; imp. s. begā 3/213; pres. 2s begǣst 3/7, 3/41; subj. 1s begā 3/70; 3s 3/211; pret. 1s beēode 8/57, 3s 6/11, etc.; 1p beēodon 8/15, beēodan 8/43; 3p biēodon 8/53

begǣst see **begān**

bēgea see **bēgen**

beģeat see **beģietan**

beģēaton see **beģietan**

bēgen m. (§84) *both* np 12/183, 12/191, 12/291, 12/305, 18(a)/769, 20/207; npf bā 20/133; apm bēgen 12/182; gp bēgra 2/14, bēgea 20/128

beģeondan prep. w.d. *beyond* 8/73, begiondan 5/17

beģēotan II *drench, cover* p. ptc. nsn begoten 14/7 (*covered*); nsm 14/49

beģietan V *get, gain, acquire, lay hold of* inf. 3/148, 5/13; pres. 1s begiete 3/74; 2s begietst 3/73; 1p begietaþ 3/209; pret. 3s begeat 15/32, 15/41, bigeat 17/6; 3p begēaton 5/35, 18(c)/2249

beģinnan III *begin* inf. 2/61; pret. 3s began 1/12, 4/34

beģiondan see **beģeondan**

begnornian 2 *lament, bemoan* pret. 3p begnornodon 18(d)/3178

begong m. *circuit, compass, region* as 18(a)/860

beģoten see **beģēotan**

bēgra see **bēgen**

behātan VII *promise* pret. 3p behēton 7/65, behētan 22/176; subj. 3s behēte 7/60

behēafdian 2 *behead* inf. 4/216; p. ptc. behēaf-dod 20/289

behealdan VII *behold, gaze at, watch over* pret. 1s behēold 14/25, 14/58; 3s 18(a)/736; 3p behēoldon 14/9, 14/11, 14/64

behēawan VII *cut off* inf. behēawan 10(b)/43

behēte see **behātan**

behionan prep. w.d. *on this side of* 5/15

behlȳþan 1 *strip, despoil* p. ptc. behlȳþed 11(j)/10

behrēowsian 2 *repent* pres. 3p behrēowsiað 4/92; pret. 3s behrēowsode 4/293

behrīman 1 *cover with frost* p. ptc. behrīmed 15/48

bēhð f. *sign, indication* ds bēhðe 20/174

behȳdan 1 *hide, conceal* pret. 1s behȳdde 2/22; 3s 2/18; 3p behȳddon 4/223, 4/231; p. ptc. behȳd 4/220

beinnan adv. *within* 10(a)/28

belāf see **belīfan**

ġebelgan III *enrage* p. ptc. gebolgen 18(a)/723

belīfan I *remain behind, survive* pres. 1s belīfe 4/182; pret. 3s belāf 4/152

belimpan III *pertain* pret. 3p belumpen 9/4, belumpon 9/16

belīðan I *deprive* p. ptc. belidenne 20/280

belocen see **belucan**

belt m. *belt* ns 1/4

belūcan II *contain, lock shut* inf. 10(a)/25, 10(b)/73; p. ptc. belocen 4/47, 6/27

belumpen (= belumpon) see **belimpan**

benam see **beniman**

benæman 1 *deprive of* inf. 20/76

benċ f. *bench* ds bence 1/9, 12/213; dp bencum 20/18

benċsittend m. *guest, bench-sitter* ap bencsittende 20/27

bend mfn *bond, chain* dp bendum 4/208

Benedict pers. n. *Benedict* gs Benedictes 4/126

beniman IV *deprive* pret. 3s benam (w.a. of person and g. of thing) 6/1

benn f. *wound* np benne 16/49

bēo see **bēon**

bēod m. *table* ns 3/164

bēodan II *command, offer* inf. 7/74; pres. 3s bēodeð (*announce*) 17/54; 3p bēodaþ 22/131; pret. 3s bēad 4/172; 3p budon 6/32

*ge*bēodan II *offer* pret. 3s gebēad 6/20,
6/28; p. ptc. geboden 6/34
bēon anom. (§127) *be* inf. 3/63, 3/115,
3/130, etc.; infl. inf. (tō) bēonne 4/289; imp.
s. bēo 3/214, 4/142, 4/166; pres. 1s eom
2/22, 3/2, 3/40, etc., bēom 11(d)/8,
11(h)/4; 2s eart 1/34, 2/20, 2/42, 3/39, bist
2/28, 2/35; 3s is 1/1, 1/3, 1/4, 2/5, 2/37,
4/17 (ys), etc.; biþ 1/23, 3/98, 3/177,
4/66, etc.; byð 4/23; 2p bēoð 2/10, bēo
2/8, 3/176; 3p sind 2/4, 3/44, sindon
4/38, 19/6, siendon 5/79, syndon 8/17, syn
22/62, 22/63, etc., syndan 22/26, 22/34,
etc., bēoð 2/9, 2/76, 3/79, 3/137, 3/190,
4/290; subj. 2s sīe 3/212; 3s sīe 2/54,
3/207, 5/20, 8/12, 8/29, etc. sī 14/144, sȳ
4/330, 12/215, 21/65, bēo 4/47; 3p sien
5/55; pret. 1s wæs 3/53; 2s wǣre 2/42,
3/52, 3/59, 3/62; 3s wæs 1/29, 2/1, 2/
12, 2/73, etc., was 6/8; 3p wǣron 2/16,
4/106, 4/225, 5/18, 7/58, etc.; wǣrun
6/12, 6/16, 6/24, wǣran 11(1)/2; subj. 2s
wǣre 2/23, 4/189; 3s 4/12, 4/175, 4/257,
4/301, 5/29, 6/34, 8/10, 9/97, etc.; 3p
wǣren 5/80, wǣran 8/6. With negative:
pres. 1s neom 3/21; 3s nis 3/9, 3/173,
4/318, 9/114, 11(e)/1; 3p nearon 17/82;
pret. 3s næs 4/184, 4/286, 10(b)/43,
12/325, 20/107, 20/257; subj. 3s nǣre
6/31; 3p nǣren 5/18, nǣron 5/33
beorg m. *mound of stone* as 14/32 (*hill,
mountain*), 18(d)/3163; ds beorge 14/50;
dp beorgum 13/32; *hillock, knoll* 21/34
*ge*beorg n. *defence, protection* ns gebeorh
21/38; ds gebeorge (*peace*) 12/31, 12/131,
12/245
beorgan III (w.d.) *save, protect* inf.
18(b)/1372, 22/181; pres. subj. 3s beorge
22/44 (w. obj. *us* understood); 1p beorgan
22/158; *seek a cure for* inf. 22/144; *spare* pret.
3s bearh 22/53; 3p burgon 12/194
*ge*beorgan III (w.d.) *save, protect* pres. subj.
2s gebeorge 4/179
beorghliþ n. *mountain-slope* dp beorg-
hleoþum 11(f)/2
beorh see beorg
beorht adj. *bright* npn 13/21; nsf 16/94;
asm beorhtne 11(j)/7; asf beorhtan 13/37;
dsm 13/40, 14/66; apf beorhte 18(a)/896;
superl. beorhtost 14/6; *radiant, fair* nsf
beorhte 20/254; asf beorhtan 20/58; dsf
20/326, 20/340; gp beorhtra 20/340
beorhte adv. *brightly* 21/49
beorn m. *man, warrior* ns 10(b)/52, 13/32,
14/42, 16/70, 16/113, 17/55; as 12/270;
gs beornes 12/131, 12/160; ds beorne
12/154, 12/245, etc.; np beornas 12/92,
12/111, 14/32, etc.; ap beornas 12/17,

12/62, 12/182, etc.; gp beorna 12/257,
20/254; dp beornum 12/101
*ge*bēorscipe m. *feast, beer party* gs gebēorscipes 9/24; ds gebēorscipe 9/20, 9/30
bēot n. *vow, boast, threat* as 12/15, 12/27 (on
bēot *threateningly*), 12/213, 16/70
bēotan see bēatan
bēotian 2 *vow* pret. 3s bēotode 12/290; 1p
bēotedan 15/21
bēotlic adj. *boastful, threatening* asn 4/159
bēoton see bēatan
Bēowulf pers. n. *Beowulf* ns 18(b)/1310,
18(b)/1383; gs Bēowulfes 18(a)/795, 18(a)/
856, 18(a)/872; ds Bēowulfe 18(a)/818
bepǣċan 1 *deceive* pret. 3s bepǣhte 2/27
bera m. *bear* ns 21/29
berād see berīdan
beran IV *carry, bear, bring* inf. 2/52, 11(n)/2,
12/12, 12/62; infl. inf. (tō) berenne 20/
131; imp. p. berað 9/103, 20/191; pres. 3s
bereð 14/118, byreð 11(d)/6, 11(j)/5;
pres. subj. 3s bere 18(c)/2253; bireð 19/
17; pret. 3s bær 2/53, 18(a)/711, 18(a)/
846, etc.; 3p bǣron 12/99, 14/32, 20/201;
subj. 3p bēron 12/67; p. ptc. boren
berēofan II *destroy, ravage* p. ptc. berofen
13/4
berīdan I *ride up to, overtake* pret. 3s berād
6/11
berofen see berēofan
berstan III *burst, fall apart* inf. 14/36; pret.
3s bærst 12/284; 3p burston 13/2 (transitive: *smashed, broke*), 18(a)/760, 18(a)/818
berȳpan 1 *despoil* p. ptc. npn berȳpte 22/26;
22/34
besārgian 2 *regret* pret. 3s besārgode 4/295
beseah see besēon
besenċan 1 *cause to sink, drown* inf. 3/104
besēon V *look* pret. 3s beseah 2/66, 4/173
besettan 1 *cover, beset* p. ptc. beset 4/213
besmītan 1 *pollute, defile* inf. 20/59
besmiþian 2 *fasten* p. ptc. besmiþod 18(a)/
775
bestalcode see bestealcian
bestandan VI *stand alongside* pret. 3p bestōdon 12/68
bestealcian 2 *move stealthily, stalk* pret. 3s
bestalcode 4/157
bestēman 1 *make wet, drench* p. ptc.
bestēmed nsm 14/48, nsn 14/22
beswīcan I *ensnare, deceive, betray* pres. 1s
beswīce 3/109; 2s beswīcst 3/108; subj.
3s beswīce 22/65; p. ptc. apm beswicene
12/238; 22/37
beswillan 1 *drench, soak* p. ptc. beswyled nsn
14/23
besyrwan 1 *ensnare, entrap* inf. 18(a)/713;
p. ptc. npm besyrwde 22/37

bet adv. *better* 22/13
bētan 1 *make amends for, atone for* inf. 22/143, 22/174; pret. 1p bēttan 22/46
ġebētan 1 *improve, remedy* pret. 3s gebētte 18(a)/830
betǣċan 1 *entrust, deliver, designate* pres. 1s betǣċe 3/31; pret. 3s begtǣhte 7/28; p. ptc. betǣht 22/25 [MnE beteach]
betǣhte see betǣċan
bētend m. *tender, rebuilder, restorer* np 13/28
betera adj. (compar. of gōd; cf §76) *better* nsn betre 5/54; nsm betera (as noun *the better* [*one*]) 12/276; nsn betere 12/31; apn beteran 8/22
betimbran 1 *build* pret. 3p betimbredon 18(d)/3159
betliċ adj. *excellent, splendid* asn 18(a)/780
betræppan 1 *entrap* inf. 7/31
betre see betera
betst adj. (superl. of gōd; cf. §76) *best* nsn 17/73 (as noun); isn betstan 9/59
bēttan (= bētton) see bētan
betwēonan prep. w.d. *between, among* 1/22, 22/179
betweox, betwux prep. w.d. *between, among* 2/29, 2/31, 2/67, 3/188, 3/207, 4/17, betwux 4/142, 4/210, 10(a)/3; betwux þām þe *while* 4/217 [MnE betwixt]
betȳnan 1 *close, conclude* pret. 3s betȳnde 9/86, 9/123
beðeahte see beðeċċan
beðeċċan 1 *cover, protect* p. ptc. npm beðeahte 20/213
beþenċan 1 *call to mind* inf. 22/154, with refl. ūs 22/172 (*reflect*)
Bethulia f. *Bethulia* as Bethuliam 20/138, 20/327
beþurfan pret.-pres. w.g. *need* pres. 1p beþurfon 3/168
beweaxan VII *grow over* p. ptc. npm beweaxne 15/31
bewerian 2 *protect* infl. inf. (tō) bewerigenne 4/235
bewindan III *wind around, envelop* p. ptc. bewunden 11(0)/2, 14/5, 20/115
bewiste see bewitan
bewitan pret.-pres. *guard* pret. 3s bewiste 4/241
beworhton see bewyrcan
bewrēon I *cover* pret. 3s biwrāh 16/23; p. ptc. bewrigen 14/17, 14/53
bewunden see bewindan
bewyrcan 1 *build around, surround* pret. 3p beworhton 18(d)/3161
bī see be
bibēad see bebēodan
bicgað see bycgan

ġebicgan 1 *pay for, post dowry for* pres. 3s subj. gebicge 21/45
ġebīcnian 2 *signify, indicate,* p. ptc. gebīcnod 4/69
bīdan I w.g. *await* inf. 9/115; pres. 3p bīdað 21/60; pret. 3s bād 18(a)/709; *remain* inf. 17/30, 18(b)/1313 [MnE bide]
ġebīdan I w.g. *await, experience* inf. 16/70, 18(b)/1386, 22/13 (*obtain*); pres. 3s gebīdeð 16/1, 21/12; pret. 1s gebād 12/174, 14/125, 15/3; 3s 13/9, 18/7 (*received*), 18(a)/815, 18(c)/2258; p. ptc. gebiden 14/50, 14/79, 22/12 (*endured*), (w.a.) 17/4, 17/28, gebidenne 20/64
bidǣled see bedǣlan
biddan V *ask, bid* inf. 20/84, 20/187; pres. ptc. biddende 4/296; pres. 1s bidde 4/121; subj. 2s 4/120; pret. 2s bǣde 4/2; 3s bæd 4/295, 8/60, 10(b)/64, 12/20, 12/128, 12/170, 12/257; 3p bǣdon 9/107, 10(a)/22, 12/87, 12/262, 12/306; subj. 3s bǣde (w.g.) 9/96 [MnE bid]
ġebiddan V *pray* infl. inf. (to) gebiddenne 2/51; pres. 3p gebiddaþ (w. refl. d.) 14/83; pret. 1s gebæd (w. refl. d.) 14/122; 3s 9/115
bidrēosan II *deprive* p. ptc. bidroren nsm 17/16; npm bidrorene 16/79
bidroren see bidrēosan
bielg m. *bellows, leather bag* gp bielga 3/201 [MnE belly]
biēodon see begān
bifian 2 *shake, tremble* inf. 14/36; pret. 1s bifode 14/42
biforan prep. w.d. *in front of* 16/46 [MnE before]
big see be
bigang see bigong
biġeal see bigiellan
ġebīġean 1 *bend* inf. 4/116
biġeat see beġietan
biġġeng m. *worship, service* dp biggengum 4/186
biġiellan III *scream round about, yell against* pret. 3s bigeal 17/24
bīgong m. *worship* ns 8/10; gs bīgonges 8/70; ds bīgange 8/16, 8/44
bihōn VII *hang around (with)* p. ptc. w.i. bihongen 17/17
bihongen see bihōn
bihrēosan II *cover* p. ptc. npm bihrorene 16/77
bilecgan 1 *encompass, afflict* pret. 3s bilegde 19/11
bīleofa m. *sustenance, food* as bīleofan 3/74, 3/209
bilewit adj. *innocent* dsn bilwitre 9/118; ap bilewitan 4/158

bill n. *sword* as 12/162; dp billum 12/114
bilwitre see **bilewit**
*ġe*bind n. *binding, commingling* as 16/24, 16/57
bindan III *bind* inf. 4/201; pres. 1s binde 11(f)/16; 3s bindeð 11(g)/7, 16/102; 3p bindað 16/18; subj. 3s binde 16/13; pret. 3s bond 17/32; p. ptc. gebunden apn 18(a)/871
*ġe*bindan III *bind, hold fast* pres. 3p gebindað 4/178, 16/40; pret. 3s ġeband 2/59, 4/280, gebond 13/19; 3p gebundon 4/206; p. ptc. gebunden 4/284, 20/115; npm 17/9
bindere m. *binder* ns 11(f)/6
biniman IV *deprive* p. ptc. binumen 11(f)/14
binn f. *bin, manger* as binne 3/18
binnan prep. w.d. *within, in* 2/3, 4/92, 4/133, 20/64
binumen see **biniman**
bireð see **beran**
biscepstōl m. *episcopal see* ds biscepstōle 5/74, bisceopstōle 7/2
biscop m. *bishop, high priest* ns bisccop 4/170, 4/272, 4/293, 7/16, 7/30 (see note), 8/7; as biscep 5/1, bisceop 4/168, 8/40; ds biscepe 5/70, bisceope 4/285, 7/1, biscope 8/50, 8/52; dp bisceopum 4/289
bisgu f. *occupation, concern, care* as 17/88; dp bisgum 5/67 [MnE busy]
bismor see **bysmor**
bīsnian 2 *set an example* inf. 4/42
*ġe*bīsnian 2 *set an example* pret. 3s gebȳsnode 4/191
*ġe*bīsnung f. *example* dp gebȳsnungum 4/204
bistelan IV *deprive of* p. ptc. bistolen 11(f)/13
bitan I *bite* pret. 3s bāt 18(a)/742
bite m. *bite, cut* as 18(c)/2259
biter adj. *bitter, grim, fierce* nsm 12/111; gsm biteres 14/114; asf bitre 17/4, bitter 17/55; npm bitre 15/31; apm bitere 12/85
biþ see **bēon**
biwāune see **biwāwan**
biwāwan VII *blow upon* p. ptc. npm biwāune 16/76
biweorpan III *surround* p. ptc. nsn biworpen 19/5
biwrāh see **bewrēon**
blāc adj. *pale* asm blācne 20/278 [MnE bleak]
blāchlēor adj. *fair-cheeked* nsf 20/128 [MnE bleak, leer]
blācian 2 *grow pale* pres. 3s blācað 17/91
blanca m. *white (or grey) horse* dp blancum 18(a)/856

*ġe*blandan VII *taint, infect, corrupt* p. ptc. geblonden 11(h)/8, 20/34, geblanden 21/41
blāwan VII *blow* pres. ptc. gpm blāwendra 3/200
blæc adj. *black* npn blacu 11(l)/3
blǣd m. *glory, wealth* ns 16/33, 17/79, 17/88, 18/18; as 20/122; *life* as 20/63; *blessings* dp blēdum 14/149
blǣd f. *branch, leaf* dp blǣdum 21/34
blēdum see **blǣd**
blēo n. *colour* dp blēom 14/22
bletsian 2 *bless* pres. 1s bletsie 2/74; p. ptc. gebletsode 2/77
bletsung f. *blessing* ds bletsunge 2/79
blīcan I *shine* inf. 20/137
bliss f. *bliss, joy, happiness* ns blis 14/139, 14/141; ds blisse 14/149, 14/153; gs 9/20 *(merriment)*
blīðe adj. *friendly, cheerful, joyous* nsm 9/108, 20/58; asn 9/105, 15/44; isn 14/122, 15/21; npm 20/159; compar. blīðra *happier* nsm 12/146; *gracious* nsm 20/154 [MnE blithe]
blīðelīce adv. *gladly* 4/192
blīðemōd adj. *friendly* nsm 9/109; np blīðemōde 9/107
blōd n. *blood* ns 4/73; as 18(a)/742; ds blōde 4/190, 14/48, on blōde *bloody* 18(a)/847
blōdgyte m. *bloodshed* ns 22/48
blōdiġ adj. *bloody* asm blōdigne 12/154; asn blōdig 20/126, 20/174
*ġe*blonden see *ġe*blandan
blōstma m. *blossom* dp blōstmum 17/48
blōwan VII *bloom, burgeon* inf. 21/34; pres. ptc. nsm blōwende 11(o)/4 [MnE blow 'blossom']
bōc f. *book* 4/44, 4/133, booc 9/72; as 4/3; gs bēc 4/5; ds 4/67, 4/132, 4/293; ap 5/41, 5/50; gp bōca 4/49, 5/30, 9/75, 10(b)/52
bōccræft m. *literature, scholarship* dp bōccræftum 10(a)/13 [MnE book-craft]
bōcere m. *scholar* ap bōceras 9/5
boda m. *messenger* ns 12/49; np bodan 22/131
bodian 2 *preach* infl. inf. (tō) bodienne 4/34; pret. 3s bodade 8/41; p. ptc. bodad 8/12, 8/22; *announce* inf. 20/251; pret. 3p bodedon 20/244 [MnE bode]
bodiġ n. *body* ds bodige 4/228, 4/248
bōg m. *limb, arm,* ip bōgum 19/11 [MnE bough]
boga m. *bow* nsm agob (reverse spelling) 11(h)/1; np bogan 12/110
*ġe*bohte see *ġe*bycgan
*ġe*bohtest see *ġe*bycgan
Boētius pers. n. *Boethius* ns 10(a)/12, Boītius 10(b)/52; gs Boētias 10(b)/75

bolgenmōd adj. *enraged* ns 18(a)/709
bolla m. *cup, bowl* np bollan 20/17
bolster n. *pillow* ds bolstre 9/116 [MnE bolster]
bond see **bindan**
*ġe*bond see *ġe*bindan
bonnan VII *summon* pres. 1s bonne 11(j)/4
bord n. *board, side of a ship* as 1/2; *shield* ns 12/110; as 12/15, 12/42, 12/131, etc.; ap 12/62, 12/283, 20/192, 20/317; gs bordes 12/284; gp borda 12/295, 18(c)/2259; dp bordum 11(j)/9 (*tables*), 12/101, 20/213
bordweall m. *shield-wall* as 12/277
*ġe*boren m. p. ptc. *one born in the same family, brother* ds geborenum 17/98
bōsm m. *bosom* as 11(j)/9; ds bōsme 11(h)/3, 11(j)/15, 13/40
bōt f. *remedy, amends* ns 22/18; as bōte 16/113, 22/12, 22/16, etc.; gs 22/30 [MnE boot 'compensation']
brād adj. *broad, wide, spacious* ns 18(d)/3157; asn 12/15, 12/163; gsn brādan 13/37; apm 20/317
bræc see **brecan**
*ġe*bræc n. *crashing* ns 12/295, as 18(c)/2259
brǣcan (= **brǣcon**) see **brecan**
*ġe*brǣcon see *ġe*brecan
brǣd see **breġdan**
brǣdan 1 *roast, broil* inf. 3/174; infl. inf. (tō) brǣdanne 3/175
brǣdan 1 *spread* inf. 16/47
*ġe*brǣġd see *ġe*breġdan
brēac see **brūcan**
breahtm m. *noise, revelry* gp breahtma 16/86
brecan IV *break* pres. 3s briceð 11(g)/6; pret. 1s bræc 1/15; 3s 12/277; p. ptc. brocen 12/1; *transgress* pret. 1p brǣcan 22/46, 22/174
*ġe*brecan V *shatter, smash* pret. 3p gebrǣcon 13/1; p. ptc. gebrocen 13/32
breġdan III *weave, knit, braid* pres. 1s breġde 3/42; *pull, drag, fling, draw* (*a sword*) inf. 18(a)/707; pret. 3s brǣd 12/154, 12/162, brægd 18(a)/794; 3p brugdon 20/229
*ġe*breġdan III *weave together, conceive* pret. 3s gebrægd 13/18
brego m. *lord* ns 20/39, 20/254
brēme adj. *famous* nsm 18/8, brēma 20/57
brēmel m. *bramble, brier* ap brēmelas 2/39, 4/233; dp brēmelum 2/67, 4/224
brenġan 1 *bring* pres. subj. 3s brenge 8/37
brēost n. *breast* ds brēoste 2/30; dp (w. sg. meaning) brēostum 12/144, 14/118, 16/113, 20/192
brēostcearu f. *grief of heart* as brēostceare 15/44, 17/4

brēostcofa m. *heart* ds brēostcofan 16/18
brēosthord n. *inmost feelings* as 17/55
brēr m. *brier* dp brērum 15/31
Bretwālas m. pl. *the Britons* dp Bretwālum 6/7
briceð see **brecan**
bricg f. *bridge, causeway* as bricge 12/74, 12/78; ds brycge 1/8
bricgweard m. *guardian of the bridge* ap bricgweardas 12/85
bridd m. *young bird* ap briddas 3/122
Brihtnōð pers. n. *Brihtnoth* ns 7/21. See also **Byrhtnōð**
brim n. *sea, water* ns 18(a)/847, 21/45
brimfugol m. *seabird* ap brimfuglas 16/47
brimlād f. *sea-way, path of ocean* ds brimlāde 17/30
brimlīðend m. *seafarer, Viking* gp brimlīðendra 12/27
brimmann m. *seafarer, Viking* np brimmen 12/295; gp brimmanna 12/49
bringan 1 *bring* pres. 3s bringeð 16/54, 21/8; subj. 3s bringe 4/124; pret. 3s brōhte 4/85; 3p brōhton 4/86, 4/275, 20/335; p. ptc. brungen 11(f)/2, brōht 22/25
*ġe*bringan 1 *bring* inf. 10(a)/20, 10(a)/25; pres. subj. 3s gebringe 14/139; pret. 3s gebrōūhte 20/125; 3p gebrōhton 20/54; p. ptc. gebrōht 20/57; p. ptc. npm gebrōhte 4/284; *lead* pres. 3s gebringeð 22/140
brocen see **brecan**
*ġe*brocen see *ġe*brecan
brōga m. *terror, danger* gs brōgan 20/4; ds 7/23
brōht, brōhte, brōhton see **bringan**
brond m. *burning, fire* gp bronda 18(d)/3160 [MnE brand]
brosnian 2 *decay* pres. 3s brosnað 13/2, 18(c)/2260; pret. 3s brosnade 13/28
broþ n. *broth* as 3/172
*ġe*brōðru see **brōðor**
brōðor m. (§60) *brother* ns brōðor 12/282, 17/98, 18(b)/1324, brōðer 4/19, 9/1, brōþur 6/9; np 9/109, 9/112, brōðru 12/191, gebrōðru 12/305
brūcan II w.g. *enjoy, use, benefit from, eat* inf. 3/158, 3/159, 3/162, 4/176, 14/144, 18(a)/894; pres. 2s brȳcst 2/40; 3p brūcað 17/88; pret. 3s brēac 10(b)/75, 16/44 [MnE brook]
brugdon see **breġdan**
brūn adj. *shining* apm brūne 20/317 [MnE brown]
brūnecg adj. *with shining blade* asn 12/163
brungen see **bringan**
bryċe m. *tansgression, breach* ds 22/17
brycge see **bricg**
brȳcst see **brūcan**

bryhtm m. *blink* ns 8/33

bryne m. *burning, fire* ns 22/47; as 14/149, 22/181; ds 22/18

brytta m. *bestower, dispenser* ns 20/30, 20/93; as bryttan 16/25, 20/90

Bryttas m.pl. *Britons* gp 22/160, 22/163; dp Bryttan 22/171

Bryttisc adj. *British* dsm Bryttiscum 6/21

būan I *inhabit, dwell* pres. 1s būge 11(d)/2

Buccingahamscīr f. *Buckinghamshire* as Buccingahamscīre 7/69

budon see bēodan

būgan II *bend, turn away, submit, retreat* inf. 12/276, 14/36, 14/42; pres. subj. 2s būge 4/180; pret. 3s bēag 13/17; 3p bugon 12/185 [MnE bow]

ġebūgan II *submit, yield, turn* inf. 22/173; pres. subj. 3s gebūge 4/172, 4/196

būge see būan

ġebunden see ġebindan

bune f. *goblet, cup* ns 16/94; np bunan 20/18

būr m. *chamber, cottage* as 6/11; ds būre 18(b)/1310 [MnE bower]

burg f. *stronghold, enclosure* as burh 7/49, 12/291, burig 10(a)/3, burg 11(n)/7, 13/37 (*city*); gs byrig 20/137; ds byrig 6/26, 10(b)/37, 10(b)/46, 20/149, 20/203, 20/326; ap byrig 17/48; gp burga 10(b)/18, 20/58; dp burgum 17/28 [MnE borough]

būrġeteld n. *pavilion* as 20/276; gs būrgeteldes 20/248; ds būrgetelde 20/57

burgon see beorgan

burgrǣced n. *city building* np 13/21

burgsteall n. *city* ns 13/28

burgstede m. *city* as 13/2, burhstede 18(c)/2265 (*courtyard pavement*)

burgtūn m. *protecting hedge* np burgtūnas 15/31

burhlēode m. pl. *citizens* gp burglēoda 20/187; dp burhlēodum 20/175

burhsittend m. *citizen* np burhsittende 20/159

burhwaru f. *citizenry, population* ns 7/4, 7/51; ds burhware 7/53; gp burgwara 16/86

burig see burg

burnsele m. *bathing hall* np 13/21

būrþēn m. *servant of the bower, chamberlain* ds būrþēne 12/121

burston see berstan

būtan prep. w.d. *without, except, but, only* 3/46, 3/47, 3/158, 3/160, būton 4/45, 4/75, 6/2, etc., 7/17 (w.a. *only*)); conj. (§179.5) w. ind. *except, only* 4/5, 4/21, w. subj. *unless* 3/115, 3/161, 4/179, 4/195, 12/71, etc.

butere f. *butter* ns 3/160; as buteran 3/26

būton see būtan

būtū n. dual *both* acc. 14/48

bycgan I *buy* pres. 1s bycge 3/136, 3/151; 3s bygþ 3/83; 3p bicgað 22/77

ġebycgan I *buy* pret. 1s gebohte 3/147; 3s 22/81; 2s gebohtest 3/145

bydel m. *messenger, preacher* gp bydela 22/166

byden f. *tub* ds bydene 11(f)/6

byht n. *dwelling* ap 11(d)/3

byldan I *encourage, embolden* inf. 21/15; pret. 3s bylde 12/169, 12/209, 12/320; pres. subj. 3s bylde 12/234

ġebylde see ġebylgan

byldu f. *arrogance, boldness* ds bylde 4/200

ġebylgan I *provoke, trouble* p. ptc. npm gebylde 20/268

ġebyrað see ġebyrian

byre m. *opportunity* as 12/121

byreð see beran

byrġan I *bury* inf. 17/98

byrġen f. *burial place, grave* ds byrgene 4/254, 4/267; dp byrgenum 4/327

Byrhtelm pers. n. *Byrhtelm* gs Byrhtelmes 12/92

Byrhtnōð pers. n. *Byrhtnoth* ns 12/17, 12/42, 12/101, etc.; as 12/257; gs Byrhtnōðes 12/114. See also Brihtnōð

Bryhtwold pers. n. *Byrhtwold* ns 12/309

ġebyrian I *befit, be proper to* pres. 3s gebyrað 4/290; *belong, pertain* 3p gebyriað 22/132

byriġ see burg

byriġan I *taste* pret. 3s byrigde 14/101

byrnan III *burn* pres. ptc. nsf byrnende 11(o)/4

byrne f. *corselet, coat of mail* ns 12/144, 12/284; as byrnan 12/163, 20/337; gs 18(c)/2260; ap 20/327 [MnE byrnie]

byrnhom m. *mail-coat, corselet* ap byrnho-mas 20/192

byrnwiga m. *mailed warrior* ns 16/94; gp byrnwigena 20/39

byrnwiggend m. *mailclad warrior* np byrnwiggende 20/17

byrst f. *bristle* np byrsta 4/214

byrst m. *injury, calamity* ns 22/43; gp byrsta 22/12 [MnE burst]

bȳsen f. *exemplar, original, example* ds bȳsne 4/123, bȳsene 8/57

bysiġ adj. *busy* npm bysige 12/110

bysiġian 2 *afflict, occupy, trouble* p. ptc. gebysgad 11(o)/3 [MnE (to) busy]

bysmara see bysmor

bysmerian 2 *mock, revile* pret. 3p bysmeredon 14/48

ġebysmerian 2 *mock* pret. 3p gebysmrodon 4/206

bysmerlīċe adv. *ignominiously* 20/100

bysmor m. *disgrace, scorn, mockery* as 22/ 42, 22/111; ds bysmore 4/158, 22/102 (tō bysmore *shamefully*), bismore 7/34; gp bysmara 22/12
bysmorful adj. *shameful* dp bysmorfullum 4/190
ġebȳsnode see ġebīsnian
ġebȳsnungum see ġebīsnung
bȳwan 1 *polish, adorn, prepare* inf. 18(c)/ 2257

cāf adj. *brave, quick, vigorous* asm cāfne 12/76
cāflīċe adv. *bravely, boldly* 12/153
cald n. *(the) cold* is calde 17/8
cald adj. *cold* nsm 21/6; asn 12/91; dp caldum 17/10; superl. caldast nsn 17/33, cealdost 21/5
camp m. *battle* ds campe 20/200 [MnE camp]
ġe**camp** m. *battle* ds gecampe 12/153
cann see **cunnan**
canōn m. *canon* gs canōnes 9/74; np canōnas 4/288
canst see **cunnan**
carcern n. *prison, dungeon* as carcerne 10(a)/25; ds 10(a)/29, 10(b)/73
care see **cearo**
cāsere m. *emperor* ns 10(b)/20, 10(b)/61, kāsere 10(a)/22; ds kāsere 10(a)/21; np cāseras 17/82; dp cāserum 10(a)/17 [MnE caesar]
ċ**eafl** m. *jaw* dp ceaflum 22/167 [MnE jowl]
cealdost see **cald** adj.
ceallian 2 *call out, shout* inf. 12/91
ċ**ēap** m. *purchase* as 22/80; ds cēape 22/77 [MnE cheap]
ġeċ**ēapian** 2 *buy* pres. 3s gecēapaþ 11(h)/13
cearo f. *care, trouble, sorrow* ns 16/55; as ceare 16/9, care 18(d)/3171; np ceare 17/10
cearseld n. *abode of care* gp cearselda 17/5
ġeċ**ēas** see ġeċ**ēosan**
ċ**easter** f. *town* as ceastre 10(b)/66, ds 3/ 82; np ceastra 21/1 [MnE (Win)chester, (Man)chester, etc.]
ċ**easterbūend** m. *city-dweller* dp ceaster-būendum 18(a)/768
ċ**easterware** f. pl. *city-dwellers* np 3/84
Cedmon pers. n. *Cædmon* ns 9/28
Cēfi pers. n. *Cefi* ns 8/11, 8/39
cellod adj. see note to 12/283
cempa m. *warrior, champion* ns 3/213, 12/119, 18(b)/1312
cēne adj. *keen, brave* nsm 4/162, 4/181, 12/ 215; npm 20/332; gpm cēnra 18(a)/768, 20/200; compar. cēnre nsf 12/312
cēne adv. *boldly, bravely* 12/283

cennan 1 *beget, spawn* inf. 21/28; p. ptc. cenned 18/12
Centland n. *Kent* ds Centlande 7/56
cēol m. *ship* ds ceole 17/5, 21/24
Cēola pers. n. *Ceole* gs Cēolan 12/76
ceorfan III *carve, hew out* inf. 4/269; pret. 3p curfon 14/66
ċ**eorl** m. *peasant, yeoman, free man of the lowest rank* ns 3/213, 12/256; as 11(f)/8; ds ceorle 12/132 [MnE churl]
ġeċ**ēosan** II *choose* pret. 3s gecēas 4/35, 12/ 113; p. ptc. nsn gecoren 9/53 (*decided*); npm gecorene 4/290; dpm gecorenum (*chosen ones, disciples*) 4/31
cēpan 1 w.g. *seize* inf. 4/201
Cerdiċ pers. n. *Cerdic* ds Cerdice 6/43
ċ**icen** n. *chicken* ns 1/6
ċ**iele** m. *chill, cold* ds 3/16
ċ**īepan** 1 *sell* pres. 2s cīepst 3/81
ċ**īepemann** m. *merchant* np cīepemenn 3/5
ġeċ**ierran** 1 *return* pret. 3s gecierde 2/79
ċ**īese** m. *cheese* ns 3/161; as 3/26
ċ**ild** n. *child* ns 2/51; as 2/63; ap 3/34, 4/158
ġe**cinde** see ġe**cynd**
cinn see **cynn**
ċ**iriċe** f. *church* as cyrcan 4/250, 4/253; ds 4/256, cirice 1/10; np ciricean 5/29
ċ**irman** 1 *make noise* inf. 20/270
ċ**irran** 1 *turn back* pret. 3p cirdon 20/311
clammum see **clomm**
clǣne adj. *clean, pure* dsm clǣnum 4/258; nsm clǣne 9/67; asn 17/110; dsn clǣnum 4/265; apm clǣnan 3/80; dpm clǣnum 4/315; apf clǣnan 4/191
clǣne adv. *utterly, entirely* 5/14, 22/26, 22/34 [MnE clean]
clǣnnis f. *purity, cleanness* ds clǣnnisse 4/38
clǣnsian 2 *cleanse* inf. 22/178
cleofa m. *cellar, pantry* as cleofan 3/159
clēofan II *split, cleave* pret. 3p clufon 12/283
cleopode see **clipian**
clibbor adj. *clinging, tenacious* nsm 21/13
clif n. *cliff* dp clifum 17/8
clipian 2 *call, summon, cry out, speak out* inf. clypian 22/167; pres. ptc. clypigende 4/236; pret. 3s clipode 2/20, 2/43, 2/61, 2/71, 4/73, clypode 4/168, 4/209, 4/286, 8/42, 12/25, 12/256, cleopode 10(b)/83 [archaic MnE clepe, yclept]
clomm m. *grip, fetter* dp clommum 17/10, clammum 10(b)/83, 18(b)/1335 [MnE clam, clamp]
clumian 2 *mumble* pret. 3p clumedan 22/167
clūstor n. *prison* ds clūstre 10(b)/73
clypian see **clipian**
clypiġende see **clipian**

clyppan 1 *embrace* inf. 9/61; pres. subj. 3s clyppe 16/42 [MnE clip]

clypode see **clipian**

clypung f. *shout, calling out* ap clypunga 4/240

cnapa m. *servant, boy* as cnapan 3/15; dp cnapum 2/47, 2/50, 2/78 [MnE knave]

ġecnāwan VII *understand, acknowledge* inf. 5/56; imp. p. gecnāwað 22/1; pres. subj. 3s gecnāwe 22/43, 22/88 [MnE know]

cnēo n. *knee* as 16/42; *generation* gp cnēa 13/8

cnēoris f. *nation, tribe* ns 20/323

cniht m. *boy, youth, squire, servant* ns 1/9, 12/9, 12/153 [MnE knight]

cnōdan VII *to be committed (to)* p. ptc. gecnōden 10(b)/32

cnossian 2 *toss, dash, drive* pres. 3s cnossað 17/8

cnyssan 1 *dash against, batter* pres. 3p cynssað 16/101, 17/33 (fig. *urge, press*); pret. 3p cnysedan (*clashed*) 18(b)/1328

cnyttan 1 *bind* pres. 3s cnyt 22/105

cōc m. *cook* ds cōce 3/167

cohhetan 1 *cough (to gain attention)* inf. 20/270

cōlian 2 *cool* pret. 3s cōlode 14/72

collenferð adj. *stout-hearted* nsm 16/71; npf collenferhðe 20/134

cōm see **cuman**

cōmen see **cuman**

cōmon see **cuman**

compwīġ n. *battle* ds compwīge 20/332

con (= cann) see **cunnan**

const see **cunnan**

Constentinopolim f. *Constantinople* ds 10(a)/21

consul m. *consul* ns 10(a)/12

ġecoren see ġeċēosan

corn n. *kernel, grain* gp corna 17/33 [MnE corn]

ġecost adj. *tested, trusty* apm gecoste 20/231

crabba m. *crab* ap crabban 3/93

cradolċild n. *infant* as 22/39 [MnE cradle, child]

ġecranc see ġecringan

cræft m. *trade, skill, force* ns 3/151, 3/163; as 3/1, 3/7, 3/41, etc.; gs cræftes 3/168; ds cræfte 3/73, 3/151, 3/155, 4/81, 4/276; *cunning* inst s 21/43 [MnE craft]

Crēacas m. pl. *the Greeks, Greece* npm 5/49, 10(b)/48; ap Crēacas 10(b)/56, Crēcas 10(b)/21, 10(b)/61; gp Crēca 10(a)/21, 10(b)/66; dp Crēcum 10(b)/26

crincgan III *fall, perish* inf. 12/292; pret. 3p cruncon 12/302, crungon 13/25, 13/28 [MnE cringe]

ġecringan III *fall, perish* pret. 3s gecranc 12/250, 12/324, gecrang 18(b)/1337, gecrong 13/31 (*fell to*), 16/79

Crīst pers. n. *Christ* ns 4/33, 4/323, 4/328, 14/56; as 4/212, 4/328; gs Crīstes 4/29, 4/204, 4/210, 8/77; ds Crīste 1/33, 4/30, 4/191, 4/195, 4/266, 8/5, 10(b)/32, 14/116

Crīsten adj. *Christian* nsm 4/23, 10(a)/6; gsn Crīstenes 22/73; np Crīstne 5/27; ap Crīstenan 4/158; npf Crīstna 5/53; gpm Crīstenra 22/108, 22/130; as noun: npm Crīstene 22/29

crīstendōm m. *Christendom, Christianity* ds crīstendōme 10(a)/23, 22/91, crīstenandōme 10(a)/15

ġecrong see ġecringan

crungon see **crincgan**

cuǣdon see **cweðan**

culter m. *coulter, a cutting blade on a plough* as 3/12, 3/193

cuman IV *come* inf. 4/276, 8/61, cumon 7/33, etc.; pres. 1s cume 3/45; 2s cymest 18(b)/1382; 3s cymeð 8/34, 16/103, 17/61, etc; 1p cumað 2/52; 3p 4/178; subj. 3s cume 8/30, 18/23; 1p cumen 17/118; pret. 3s cōm 2/17, 4/34, 4/126, 4/202, 7/40, 20/50, etc., cwōm 9/59, 11(b)/1, etc.; 3p cōmon 2/56, 4/72, 4/246, 4/273, 7/10, 20/11, cwōman 13/25, etc.; subj. 3s cōme 4/314, cwōme 18(a)/731; 3p cōmen 10(b)/66; p. ptc. cuman 9/53, cumen 12/104, 14/80, 20/146, 20/168

cumbol n. *banner* dp cumblum 20/332

cumbolwiga m. *warrior* as cumbolwigan 20/259; ap 20/243

Cumbra pers. n. *Cumbra* as Cumbran 6/6

cumon see **cuman**

cunnan pret.-pres. *know, know how to, can* pres. 1s cann, 3/36, 3/47, 3/115, 3/130, con 9/29; 2s canst 3/1, 3/35, 3/37, const 18(b)/1377, etc.; 3s can 4/105; 1p cunnon 5/36, cunnun 8/36; 3p cunnon 3/3, 4/27, etc.; subj. 3s cunne 16/69 (*have knowledge*), 16/71, 16/113, 22/96, etc.; 3p cunnen 5/61; pret. 1s cūðe 9/31; 3s 4/14; 1p cūðon 5/47, 22/110; 3p 5/65; subj. 1s cūþe 3/116; 3p cūðen 4/40, 5/15

cunnian 2 *try, find out* inf. 7/30, 12/215; pres. 3s cunnað 16/29 (*knows at first hand*); subj. 1s cunnige 17/35; pret. 3p cunnedon 4/275 (*tried to discover*); p. ptc. gecunnad 17/5 (*experienced, came to know*)

ġecunnian 2 *try to discover* inf. 20/259

curfon see **ceorfan**

cūð adj. *familiar, well known* ns 4/322, 18(a)/705; npm cūðe 18(a)/867; gpn cūðra 16/55 [MnE (un)couth]

Cūþberht pers. n. *Cuthbert* ns 4/319

cūþe see **cunnan**

cūðliċ adj. *certain* compar. as cūðlicre 8/36

cūðliċe adv. *clearly* 8/13

cūðon see cunnan
cwalu f. *death* ds cwale 4/79
cwǣde see cweðan
cwǣð see cweðan
cwealdon see cwellan
cwealmcuma m. *murderous visitor* as cwealmcuman 18(a)/792
cwellan 1 *kill* pret. 2s cwealdest 18(b)/1334; 1p cwealdon 1/27 [MnE quell]
cwēn f. *woman, queen* ns 1/8
cwene f. *woman* ns 11(p)/1; as cwenan 22/77, 22/103
cweðan V *say* inf. 14/116; infl. inf. (tō) cweþenne 22/41, 22/151; pres. 1s cweðe 4/118; 3s cwyþ 14/111; 3p cweþaþ 4/31; pret. 1s cwæð 5/44; 2s cwǣde 4/4; 3s cwæð 2/2, 2/7, 2/20, 2/21, 2/44, 3/189, etc.; 1p cwǣdon 22/125; 3p cuǣdon 6/30, 6/34, cwǣdon 9/106 etc.; subj. 3p cwǣden 5/34 [archaic MnE quoth]
ġecweðan V *speak, utter* pret. 3s gecwæð 12/168, 18(a)/857, 18(a)/874
cwic adj. *alive* nsm 3/139, 4/166, 4/257; asm cwicne 4/178, 18(a)/792; nsf cwicu 11(p)/5; apm cwice 11(g)/7; gpm cwicra 16/9, 20/235, 20/311, 20/323 (*living*) [MnE quick]
cwide m. *statement, saying* as 11(c)/4
cwideġiedd n. *spoken utterance* gp cwide-giedda 16/55
cwīðan 1 *bewail, lament* inf. 16/9, 18(d)/3171; pret. 3p cwīðdon 14/56
cwōm see cuman
cyme m. *coming* ds 9/76
cymeð see cuman
ġecynd n. *species, kind, origin, lineage* ds gecinde 4/49
ġecyndbōc f. *book of origin*, i.e. *book of Genesis* ns 4/48
ġecynde adj. *proper, lawful* apm 10(b)/6 [MnE kind]
cyneliċ adj. *noble* nsn 13/48
cynelīce adv. *regally* 4/173
cynerīċe n. *kingdom* gs kynerīces 5/67
cynerōf adj. *nobly brave* npm cynerōfe 20/200, 20/311
cynestōl m. *royal seat, throne* ns 10(a)/22; ds cynestōle 10(b)/48
Cynewulf pers. n. *Cynewulf* ns 6/1, 6/4, 6/6, etc.
cyng see cyning
cyning m. *king* ns kyning 5/1, cyng 7/27, 7/45, cyning 4/137, 4/319, 8/1, 8/76, 10(a)/14, 10(a)/24, 18(a)/863, 18(b)/1306, 20/190; as 4/207, 6/9, 8/60; gs cyninges 3/40, 4/127, 4/200, 6/17, etc.; ds cyninge 3/66, 3/132, 4/130, 10(a)/19, kyninge 6/12; np cyningas 17/82, kyningas

5/5; ap cyningas 10(b)/6, kyningas 10(b)/56; gp cyninga 20/155; dp cyningum 10(a)/2, etc.
cynn n. *kin, family, kind, race* ns 1/3; as 14/94; gs cynnes 3/153, 12/217, 12/266, 18(a)/712, 18(a)/735, etc.; ds cynne 12/76, 18(a)/810, 20/226, 21/57; gp cynna 11(n)/2, 20/323, cinna 4/92
cynren n. *progeny, kind* as 21/28
ċyrċan see ċiriċe
ċyriċhata m. *persecutor of the church* np cyrichatan 22/129
cyrm m. *cry, uproar* ns 12/107
cyssan 1 *kiss* pres. 3p cyssað 11(j)/3, 11(o)/6; subj. 3s cysse 16/42
cyst f. *best* ns 10(b)/18, 18(a)/802, as 14/1; dp cystum 18(a)/867 (*good quality, excellence*)
cystig adj. *generous* nsm 4/143
cȳðan 1 *reveal, make known, inform* inf. 5/2, 20/56, 20/243; pres. 3s cȳð 4/264; pret. 3s cȳþde 6/29, 9/50; 3p cȳðdon (*manifested toward*) 10(b)/56; p. ptc. gecȳðed 20/155
ġecȳðan 1 *show, make known, declare* inf. 12/216; pret. 3s gecȳðde 7/53
ġecȳþnis f. *testament* ns 4/29; ds gecȳðnisse 4/41; ap gecȳðnissa 4/112
cȳþþ f. *kinfolk* ns 1/3; *native land* ds cȳððe 20/311 [MnE kith (and kin)]

ġedafenian 2 (impersonal verb (§212) w.d.) *befit* pret. 3s gedafenode 9/17; subj. gedafnode 4/39
dagas see dæġ
daroð m. *spear* ns 21/21; as 12/149, 12/255
dǣd f. *deed* ns 10(b)/43; as dǣde 18(a)/889; gs 22/60; np dǣda 22/84; ap 22/170; gp dǣda 9/82, 21/36; dp dǣdum 6/2, 17/41, 17/76
dǣdbōt f. *penitence, penance* as dǣdbōte 4/65
dæġ m. *day* ns 1/21, etc.; as dæg 4/236, 4/263, 4/312, 4/313, 12/198, 15/37, dǣi 7/33; gs dæges 11(f)/3 (as adv.), 11(f)/17; ds dæge 1/27, 2/10, 2/48, 3/26, etc., tō dæge *today* 8/73; np dagas 17/80; ap 4/296; gp daga 14/136; dp dagum 2/38, 11(k)/1, etc.
dæghwāmlīce adv. *every day, daily* 22/10, 22/113
dæġrǣd n. *dawn* as 3/8, dægrēd 20/204
dæġrīm n. *number of days* ns 18(a)/823
dæġweorc n. *day's work* gs dægweorces 12/148; ds dægweorce 20/266
dæi see dæġ
dǣl m. *part, portion* ns 20/293, 20/308; as 5/42, 5/53, 11(n)/4, 16/65; ds dǣle 4/14; bē ǣnigum (sumum) dǣle *to any (some) extent* 22/137, 22/173-4 [MnE deal]

dǣlan 1 *share, dispense* inf. 4/165, 21/29; pres. subj. 1p dǣlon 12/33 [MnE deal]

ġedǣlan 1 *part, separate* pres. 1p gedǣlað 11(e)/7; pret. 3s gedǣlde (*shared*) 16/83; subj. 3s 15/22, 18(a)/731

dēad adj. *dead* nsm 11(p)/4, 18(b)/1323, 20/107; nsn dēade 17/65; asm dēadne 11(k)/1, 18(b)/1309; np dēade 2/8; dp (as noun) dēadum 17/98

dēaf see dūfan

dēagan VII *conceal, be concealed* pret. 3s dēog 18(a)/850

dēah see dugan

dear see durran

dearr see durran

dēaþ m. *death* ns 1/31, 11(e)/7, 15/22, 17/106, as 14/101; gs dēaðes 14/113; ds dēaðe 4/288, 4/292, 4/303, 9/120, 16/83, 18(b)/1388, 20/196, 21/51; is 20/31

dēaðdæġ m. *death-day* ds dēaðdæge 18(a)/885, 21/60

dēaðfæġe adj. *fated to die, doomed* ns 18(a)/850

ġedēfe adj. *fitting, seemly* nsm 18(d)/3174

Defenas m. pl. *Devon, the people of Devon* dp Defenum 7/9

Defenisc adj. *Devonian, from Devon* nsm Defenisca 7/14

dēgelīce see dēogollīce

dehter see dohtor

ġedelf n. *digging* ds gedelfe 4/283

dēma m. *judge* ns 20/59, 20/94; gs dēman 20/4

dēman 1 *judge, deem* inf. 14/107; pret. 3p dēmdon 18(d)/3174 (*praised*); p. ptc. gedēmed 9/20, 20/196

dēmend m. *judge* ns 21/36

demm m. *misfortune, loss* ns 3/214

Dene m. pl. *Danes* dp Denum 12/129 (*Vikings*), 18(a)/767, 18(a)/823; gp Denigea 18(b)/1323

Denisc adj. *Danish* np Deniscan 4/147; dp 7/22

denu f. *valley* np dena 15/30; dp denum 11(f)/3

dēofol m.n. *the devil* ns 22/6; as 4/150; ds dēofle 17/76; gp dēofla 18(a)/756

dēofolcund adj. *diabolical* nsm dēofolcunda 20/61

dēofolġild n. *idol* as dēofolgyld 8/61; gp dēofolgilda 8/54; dp dēofolgildum 8/50, dēofulgeldum 8/65

dēog see dēagan

dēogol adj. *secret, hidden, mysterious* ns dīgol 21/62; asn dȳgel 18(b)/1357; apm dīgelan 4/165

dēogollīce adv. *secretly* dēgelīce 10(b)/64, dīgellīce 10(a)/20

dēop adj. *deep, profound* nsf 4/44, 4/75; dsm dēopan 14/75

dēope adv. *deeply, profoundly* 16/89

dēoplīce adv. *profoundly, deeply* 4/98

dēor n. *wild animal* ap 4/235, 4/243 [MnE deer]

dēor adj. *bold, brave* nsm 17/41; dpf dēorum 17/76

deorc adj. *dark* asn deorce 16/89; dpm deorcan 14/46

dēore adj. *dear, precious, beloved* asn 18(c)/2254; apm dȳre 20/318; superl. asm dēorestan 18(b)/1309, nsn dēorost 21/10

dēore adv. *dearly, at great cost* 22/81

ġedeorf n. *toil, hardship* ns 3/20, 3/21, 3/146; as 3/22, 3/23

Deorwente f. *the Derwent River* ds Deorwentan 8/73

dēorwierþe adj. *valuable, costly* apm 3/142, dēorwirðe 4/85; apn dēorwierþu 3/136 [archaic MnE dearworth]

derian 1 w.d. *harm, afflict* inf. 12/70; pres. 3s dereð 22/86; pret. 3s derede 22/50, 22/60

dēst see dōn

dēð see dōn

dīgol see dēogol

dīgelan see dēogol

dīgellīce see dēogollīce

ġedihtan 1 *dictate* pret. 3s gedihte 4/82

dim adj. *gloomy* npf dimme 15/30 [MnE dim]

disc m. *dish* ns 1/4

dō see dōn

dōgor n. *day* is dōgore 20/12, dōgor 18(b)/1395; gp dōgra 16/63, dōgera 18(a)/823

dohte see dugan

dohtor f. (§60) *daughter* ns 1/34; as 22/103; np 11(a)/2; ds dehter 4/20; gp dohtra 11(k)/12

dol adj. *foolish* nsm 17/106; apm dole 11(f)/17 (*dazed*)

dolg n. *wound* np 14/46

dolhwund adj. *wounded* nsm 20/107

dōm m. *judgment* as 4/294, 6/28, 12/38; gs dōmes 4/312, 9/77, 14/107, 21/60; ds dōme 9/53, 18(a)/895; dp dōmum 9/80; poet. *glory, reputation, fame* ns 18(a)/885, 20/266; as 12/129, 20/196; gs dōmes 18(b)/1388, 21/21; ds dōme 17/85; is 20/299 [MnE doom]

dōmdæġ m. *Day of Judgement* ds dōmdæge 14/105 [MnE doom(s)day]

dōmgeorn adj. *eager for glory* npm dōmgeorne 16/17

dōmlīce adv. *gloriously* 20/318

dōn anom. (§128) *do, make, take* inf. 3/205, 5/63 (*promote*), etc.; infl. inf. (tō) dōnne 1/12, 3/17; pres. 1s dō 3/90; 2s dēst 3/17, 3/28, 3/65, 3/79; 3s dēð 4/113; 2p dōþ 3/176; 3p 3/129, 4/108; subj. 2s dō 5/21; 3s 5/77, 22/61; 1p 4/96; pret. 1s dyde 17/20; 2s dydest 2/26, 2/28; 3s dyde 2/19, 8/6, 9/24, etc.; 3p dydon 4/217, dydan 22/14; p. ptc. gedōn 4/52, 12/197

*ge*dōn anom. (§128) *do* inf. 7/51, 17/43; pres. subj. 1p 5/56; *make, cause to be* pret. 3p gedydon 19/14

Dorsǣte m. pl. *Dorset, men of Dorset* dp Dorsǣtum 7/10

dorste see durran

dorston see durran

dōþ see dōn

draca m. *dragon* ns 18(a)/892, 21/26 [archaic MnE drake]

drāf f. *throng, herd* ap drāfe 22/108 [MnE drove]

*ge*drǣg n. *tumult,* (*noisy*) *company* as 18(a)/756, gedreag 15/45 (*multitude*)

drēag see drēogan

*ge*dreag see *ge*drǣg

drēam m. *joy, delight,* ns 14/140, 17/80; gs drēames 14/144; ds drēame 16/79; np drēamas 17/65, 17/86; ap 20/349; gp drēama 18(a)/850; dp drēamum 14/133, 18(a)/721 [MnE dream]

*ge*drēas see *ge*drēosan

*ge*dreccan I *oppress* pret. 3p gedrehtan 22/51

drēfan I *stir up, disturb* pres. 1s drēfe 11(d)/2

*ge*drēfan I *trouble, afflict* p. ptc. gedrēfed nsm 10(a)/27, 10(b)/74, 14/20, 14/59, nsf 20/88

drencan I *ply* (*with liquor*), *importune* pret. 3s drencte 20/29 [MnE drench]

dreng m. (*Viking*) *warrior* gp drenga 12/149

drēogan II *suffer, perform, be engaged in* inf. 15/26; pres. 3s drēogeð 15/50; 3p drēogað 17/56; pret. 3s drēag 11(l)/5; 2p drugon 20/158; 3p drugon 18/15, 18(a)/798, 18(a)/831

drēorgian 2 *grow desolate* pres. 3p drēorgiað 13/29

drēorig adj. *sad* asm drēorigne 16/17 [MnE dreary]

drēorighlēor adj. *sad-faced* nsm 16/83

drēorsele m. *desolate hall, hall of sorrow* ds 15/50

drēosan II *decline* pres. 3s drēoseþ 1/24, 16/63

*ge*drēosan II *collapse, perish* pret. 3s gedrēas 13/11, 16/36 (*perish*); p. ptc. gedroren nsf 17/86; npf gedrorene 13/5

drīfan I *drive* inf. 3/9; pres. 1s drīfe 3/23; 3p drīfað 22/108

drihten m. *lord, the Lord* ns 9/39, 12/148, dryhten 11(e)/2, 14/101, 20/21, 20/61, 20/92, 20/198, 20/299, etc.; as 14/64, 17/106; gs Drihtnes 4/292, 4/318, 10(b)/41, dryhtnes 14/9, 14/35, 14/75, 14/113, 14/136, 14/140, 17/65, 17/121; ds Drihtne 9/55, 9/119, 10(b)/64, 10(b)/83, 18(b)/1398, dryhtne 20/342, 20/346

drihtlic see dryhtlic

drincan III *drink* pres. 3p drincað 11(j)/12; pret. 3s dranc 18(a)/742 3p druncon 11(n)/1; p. ptc. nsm druncen *drunk* 20/67, 20/107

drohtoð m. *course, way of life* ns 18(a)/756

*ge*drorene see *ge*drēosan

drugon see drēogan

druncon see drincan

dryht f. *multitude, men* dp dryhtum 11(m)/2

dryhten see drihten

dryhtguma m. *retainer, warrior* ds drihtguman 18(b)/1388; ap 20/29

dryhtlic adj. *lordly, magnificent* nsn 18(a)/892, drihtlic 21/26; superl. dsm dryhtlicestum 17/85

dryhtsele m. *retainer's hall, splendid hall* ns 18(a)/767

drynce m. *drink* as 3/199

dryncfæt n. *drinking vessel, cup* as 18(c)/2254

drysmian 2 *become gloomy* pres. 3s drysmaþ 18(b)/1375

dūfan II *dive* pret. 1s dēaf 11(p)/4; 3s 11(i)/5

dugan pret.-pres. w.d. *be of use* pres. 3s 12/48; pret. 3s dohte 18(b)/1344; ne dohte hit *nothing has prospered* 22/47, 22/97

duguð f. *advantage, benefit* ds duguðe 12/197; dp duguðum 18(d)/3174 (*power, excellence, glory*)

duguð f. *troop of seasoned retainers, mature men* ns 16/79, 17/86, 18(c)/2254; ds duguþe 16/97; npf 20/31; gp duguða 20/61; dp dugeþum (*heavenly host*) 17/80; *host, army* 22/163

dumb adj. *dumb* dpm dumbum 11(m)/2

dūn f. *hill, down, mountain* as dūne 2/48; ds 2/46, 2/71; np dūna 15/30; ap 11(g)/6; dp dūnum 11(f)/3

Dunnere pers. n. *Dunnere* ns 12/255

Dūnstān pers. n. *Dunstan* ns 4/129, 4/131, 7/15; ds Dūnstāne 4/127

durran pret.-pres. *dare* pres. 1s dearr 3/10, 3/107; 3s dear 22/21, 22/23, 22/27; 1p durron 4/100; subj. 1s dyrre 3/10, durre 16/10; 2s dyrre 18(b)/1379; pret. 1s dorste 14/35, 14/42, 14/45, etc.; 3s 4/243; 3p dorston 1/32; subj. 3p dorsten 10(b)/27

duru f. *door* ns 18(a)/721; as 4/278, 6/13, 8/31

dūst n. *dust* ns 2/42; ds dūste 2/42

dwǣs adj. *foolish*, (as a noun) *fool* dp dwǣsan 22/143

dwelian 2 *deceive* pret. 3s dwelode 22/7

ġedwola m. *heresy* ns 10(b)/41; ds gedwolan 10(a)/7

ġedwolgod m. *false god, heathen god* gp gedwolgoda 22/22, 22/27; dp gedwolgodan 22/25

ġedwolmann m. *heretic* np gedwolmen 4/106

ġedwolsum adj. *misleading* nsn 4/105

ġedwyld n. *heresy* ds gedwylde 4/308

dydan see dōn

dyde see dōn

dydon see dōn

ġedȳgan 1 *survive* pres. 3s gedȳgeð 11(g)/6

dȳgel see dēogol

dynian 2 *make a din* pret. 3s dynede 20/23; 3p dynedan 20/204

dynnan 1 *resound* pret. 3s dynede 18(a)/767, 18(b)/1317

dynt m. *blow* dp dyntum 11(f)/17 [MnE dint]

dȳre see dēore

dyrne adj. *secret* nsf 21/62; asm 15/12; inst sm 21/43; gpm dyrnra 18(b)/1357

dyrre see durran

dȳrsian 2 *glorify* p. ptc. gedȳrsod 20/299

ġedyrstiġ adj. *daring, bold* nsm 3/59, 3/62

dysiġ adj. *ignorant, foolish* nsm 4/9; npm dysige 22/131 [MnE dizzy]

dysiġnes f. *folly* as dysignesse 8/59; ds 8/57 [MnE dizziness]

ēa f. *river* ns 21/30; as 3/76, 3/77; ds 3/99, 8/73; dp ēam 3/88

ēac adv. *also, and* 4/19, 4/31, 4/234, 4/277, 7/49, 14/92, etc.; prep. w.d.i. *in addition to, besides* 3/180, 10(b)/44, 12/11; ēac swā *likewise, also* 2/19; ēac swelce (swā), swelce ēac *also, moreover* 2/1, 2/33, 3/103, 3/121, 4/260, 9/79, ēac swylce 9/119; ēac þon *moreover, besides* 15/44; ne ēac *nor even* 5/25 [archaic MnE eke]

ēaca m. *increase* ds ēacan 4/20; tō ēacan w.d. *in addition to* 10(a)/10

ēacen adj. *increased, endowed, great* nsm 11(k)/8

ġeēacnung f. *child-bearing, increase* ap ġeēacnunga 2/34

ēad n. *wealth* as 13/36; *prosperity* gs ēades 20/273

ēadhrēðiġ adj. *triumphant* npf ēadhrēðige 20/135

ēadiġ adj. *blessed* nsm 17/107, ēadiga 4/33, 4/137, 4/320, 7/25; asf eadigan 20/35

ēadiġnes f. *blessedness, bliss* as ēadignesse 17/120, gs 8/46, 11(o)/9

ēadmōd adj. *humble* nsm 4/139

ēadmōdlīċe adv. *humbly* 4/2

Ēadmund pers. n. *Edmund* ns 4/137, 4/168, 4/194; as 4/206; gs Ēadmundes 4/130; ds Ēadmunde 4/129, 4/313

Ēadrīċ pers. n. *Eadric* ns 12/11

Ēadwacer pers. n. *Eadwacer* ns 19/16

Ēadweard pers. n. *Edward* ns 12/117, 12/273; as 22/67

Ēadwine pers. n. *Edwin* ns 7/13, 7/18, 8/76

Ēadwold pers. n. *Eadwold* ns 12/304

eafora m. *offspring, son* ns eafera 18/12, 18/19, ns eafora 18(a)/897

ēage n. *eye* as 11(b)/3; gs ēagan 8/33; np ēagan 2/9, 2/15; ap 4/111; dp ēagum 2/13, 18(a)/726

ēagðȳrl n. *window* as 4/279

eahte num. *eight* npm 4/271

eahtian 2 *esteem, praise* pret. 3p eahtodan 18(d)/3173

eal see eall

ēalā interj. *oh, lo* 3/20, 3/28, 3/156, 3/179, etc.

eald adj. *old, ancient* nsm 12/310, 15/29, ealda 12/218 (see **fæder**); asm ealdne 11(f)/8; nsf ealde 4/11, 4/28; asf ealdan 2/57, 2/60, 4/40, ealde 18(a)/795; npm ealde 20/166, ealdan 4/11 (see **fæder**); apm ealde 20/265; npn eald 16/87; apn ealde 12/47; ipm ealdum 10(b)/65; compar. yldra 18(b)/1324; *senior* superl. apm yldestan 20/10; dpm 20/242

ealdes adv. *long ago* 15/4

ealdfēond m. *enemy of old* dp ealdfēondum 20/315

ealdġenīðla m. *ancient enemy* ap ealdgenīðlan 20/228

ealdġeseġen f. *old tradition* gp ealdgesegena 18(a)/869

ealdġesīð m. *old comrade or retainer* np ealdgesīþas 18(a)/853

caldġestrēon n. *ancient treasure* dp ealdgestrēonum 18(b)/1381

ealdġewyrht n. or f. *deed of old, former action* dp ealdgewyrhtum 14/100

ealdhettend m. *ancient enemy* ap ealdhettende 20/320

ealdhlāford m. *lord from old times* dp ealdhlāfordum 10(a)/17, 10(b)/63

ealdhlāfordcynn n. *hereditary lordship, race of ancient kings* gs ealdhlāfordcynnes 10(a)/22

ealdian 2 *grow old* pres. 3s ealdað 17/89

ealdor m. *leader, prince* ns 12/202, 12/222, 12/314, 14/90, 17/123, 20/38, 20/58, 20/88, 20/124; gs ealdres 12/53; ds ealdre 12/11 [MnE alder(man)]

ealdor n. *life, age* ns 11(k)/3; as aldor 18(b)/
1371, ealdor 20/185; gs ealdres 18(b)/
1338, aldres 18(a)/822; ds ealdre 20/76,
āwa tō ealdre *forever* 17/79, 20/120, tō
wīdan aldre *forever* 20/347

ealdorbisceop m. *high-priest* ns 8/11

ealdordagas m. pl. *days of life* dp aldordagum 18(a)/718, ealdordagum 18(a)/757

ealdorduguð f. *nobility* gs ealdorduguðe
20/309

ealdorġedǽl n. *separation from life, death* ns
aldorgedāl 18(a)/805

ealdorman m. *nobleman, ruler* ns 4/119,
7/21, 7/29 (see note), aldormon 6/25, etc.;
as ealdormann 4/2; aldormon 6/3, 6/5; gs
ealdormannes 7/45; np ealdormenn 7/12,
aldormen 8/38; dp ealdormannum 3/133,
8/28 [MnE alderman]

ealdorþeġn m. *chief thane* as aldorþegn
18(b)/1308; dp ealdorðegnum 20/242

ealdriht n. *ancient right* gp ealdrihta 10(a)/8,
10(a)/16, 10(b)/36, 10(b)/57; dp ealdrihtum
10(a)/23

ealfela adj. *very much, a great many* as 18(a)/
869, 18(a)/883

ealfelo adj. *entirely harmful, dire*, asn
11(h)/9

Ealfrīc pers. n. *Ælfric* ns Ælfrīc 7/32; gs
Ælfrīces 7/45; ds Ealfrīce 7/29

ealgian 2 *defend* inf. 18(a)/796

*ġe*ealgian 2 *defend* inf. gealgean 12/52

Ealhelm pers. n. *Ealhelm* ns 12/218

eall adj. *all* nsm 7/61; asm ealne 8/70,
22/111; gsm ealles 15/41; nsn eall 14/6;
asn 4/221, 5/30, 14/58, 14/94, eal 22/84,
as noun *everything* 22/138; nsf 3/160,
14/12, 14/55, eal 15/46, 20/323, etc.; asf
ealle 3/30, 4/132, 5/50, 9/89, 10(b)/12,
20/31, 20/237, ealle hwīle *all the while*
22/74, 22/156; dsf eallre 4/198, 22/44, ealre
22/93; npm ealle 3/176, 4/200, 4/232,
4/240, 4/285, 7/27, 11(n)/10, 14/128,
20/16, 20/253, 20/269, alle 6/15; apm
3/87, 3/192, 5/11, 7/70, 12/320, 14/37,
etc.; gpm ealra 11(a)/6; gp ungerīm ealra *a
countless number of all kinds* 22/151, ealra
mǽst *the greatest of all* 22/64; dpm eallum
4/239, 11(l)/7, 12/233; npn ealle 2/1, eall
3/138, 3/190; apn eal 9/45; dpn eallum 2/29,
20/8 (*all sorts of*), 20/217 (*fully*); gpn ealra
4/29, 4/245; 14/125; npf ealle 2/76; apf
ealle 4/62, ealla 5/41; gpf ealra 12/174; as
pron. nsn eal 18(a)/835; asn eall 12/256,
13/26, 13/39; npm ealle 14/9; gpn ealra
20/81; gsn (adv.) ealles *entirely* 20/108,
22/11, 22/23, 22/57, 22/70, 22/129,
22/135, 22/136, 22/140, 22/157; dsn mid
ealle *entirely* 22/142, 22/163

eall adv. *all, entirely, completely* 4/213, 7/37,
12/314, 14/20, 14/48, 14/82, eal 15/29,
22/101, 22/107, 22/138, 22/144

Eallerīca pers. n. *Alaric* ns 10(a)/2; as Alerīc
10(b)/7

eallġearo adj. *entirely ready, eager* nsf 11(h)/4

eallgylden adj. *all of gold* nsn 20/46

eallswā adv. *just as* 4/257 (eallswā . . . swilce
just as . . . as if)

eallunga adv. *utterly* 4/325, eallinga 8/13

ealneġ adv. *always* 5/79

ēalond n. *island* ds ēalonde 10(a)/4

ealra see **eall**

ealuscerwen f. *dispensing of ale, distress,
terror* ns 18(a)/769 (see note)

ēam m. *uncle* ns 11(a)/6, 18(a)/881

eard m. *homeland, country* as 12/53, 12/58,
12/222, 17/38, 18(b)/1377; gs eardes
4/176; ds earde 4/185, 22/37, 22/52, etc.

eardġeard m. *city, dwelling place* as 16/85

eardstapa m. *wanderer* ns 16/6

ēare n. *ear* ap ēaran 4/111, 11(b)/3

earfeða see **earfoð**

earfoð n. *hardship* gp earfoða 15/39, earfeþa
16/6

earfoðhwīl f. *time of hardship* as earfoðhwīle
17/3

earfoðliċ adj. *full of trouble, fraught with
hardship* nsn 16/106

earh adj. *cowardly* nsn 12/238 [MnE eerie]

earhliċ adj. *base* npf earhlice 22/95

earm m. *arm* as 12/165, 18(a)/749, 18(a)/
835; ap earmas 11(b)/6

earm adj. *poor, wretched* asm earmne 16/40,
19/16; asn earme 7/77; dsf earman 22/153;
npm earme 14/68, 22/36, earman 4/174,
4/325; as noun gp earmra 14/19

earmceariġ adj. *wretched and troubled* nsm
16/20, 17/14

earmliċ adj. *miserable, pitiable* ns 18(a)/
807

earmlīċe adv. *miserably, wretchedly* 4/279,
4/302

earmsceapen adj. *wretched, miserable* nsm
18(b)/1351

earn m. *eagle* ns 12/107, 17/24, 20/210,
21/19 [MnE erne]

earnian 2 w.g. *deserve* inf. 22/13

*ġe*earnian 2 *earn, deserve* inf. 22/182; pres.
3s geearnaþ 14/109; pret. 1p geearnedan
22/14

earnung f. *deserts* dp earnungan 22/14,
22/15 [MnE earning]

*ġe*earnung f. *favour, act deserving gratitude* ap
geearnunga 12/196

eart see **beon**

ēast adv. *east* 4/152, 8/72

ēastan adv. *from the east* 10(b)/1, 20/190

Ēastdene m. pl. *the Danes* dp Ēastdenum 18(a)/828

Ēastengle m. pl. *East Anglia* ap 7/67; gp Ēastengla 4/137; dp Ēastenglum 4/154, 7/36

ēasteð n. *riverbank* ds ēasteðe 12/63

Ēastseaxe m. pl. *Essex, the East Saxons* ap Ēastsexe 7/67; dp Ēastseaxum 7/56; gp Ēastseaxena 12/69

ēaðe adv. *easily* 5/57, 11(h)/11, 11(n)/8, 19/18; superl. ēaðost *most easily* 20/75, 20/102

ēaðmēdu f. *reverence* dp ēaðmēdum 20/170

ēaðmōd adj. *humble, obedient* nsm 14/60, 17/107

ēaðmōdlīċe adv. *humbly* 9/83

eaxl f. *shoulder* as eaxle 18(a)/835, ds 18(a)/816; ap eaxle 11(b)/6; dp eaxlum 14/32

eaxlġespann n. *crossbeam, intersection* ds eaxlgespanne 14/9

eaxlġestealla m. *shoulder-companion, comrade* ns 18(b)/1326

ebba m. *ebb-tide* ds ebban 12/65

Ebrēas m. pl. *Hebrews* np 20/218; gp Ebrēa 20/253, 20/262, 20/298

Ebrisc adj. *Hebrew* npm Ebriscc 20/241, 20/305

Ebriscġeðiode n. *the Hebrew language* ds 5/48

ēċe adj. *eternal, everlasting* nsm 9/39, 9/43, 17/124; dsm ēcan 4/79; gsn ēces 8/46, ēcan 4/264, 17/79; asf ēcan 17/120; gsf ēcre 8/46; as adv. *eternally* 17/67

ecg f. *edge, sword* ns 12/60, 21/16; gp ecga 18(a)/805; dp ecgum 20/231

ecghete m. *deadly hatred, violence* ns 17/70

Ecglāf pers. n. *Ecglaf* gp Ecglāfes 12/267

ecgplega m. *sword-play* as ecgplegan 20/246

Ecgþēow pers. n. *Ecgtheow* gs Ecgþēowes 18(b)/1383

ēċnis f. *eternity* ds on ēcnysse *forever and ever* 4/66, ecnisse 4/121

ēċre see ēċe

edor m. *building* np ederas 16/77

ēdrum see ǣdre

edwit n. *reproach, disgrace* ns 10(b)/55; *abuse* as 20/215

efne adv. *even, only* 8/56, 9/16, 10(b)/14

efsian 2 *cut (the hair)* inf. 4/268

efstan 1 *hasten* inf. 14/34; pret. 3p efston 12/206

eft adv. *again, afterwards, thereupon, back* 2/7, 2/17, 2/52, 2/71, 3/31, 3/126, 5/49, etc., æft 10(b)/65; eft ongean *in reply, back again* 12/49, 12/156; eft onhwyrfed *reversed, backwards* 11(h)/1

eftsīð m. *journey back, return* ap eftsīðas tēah *returned* 18(b)/1332

eġe m. *fear, terror* ns 2/73, 10(b)/72; as 22/137; ds 3/11

eġesa m. *awe, terror* ns 14/86, 18(a)/784, 20/252, egsa 17/103; ds egsan 17/101

eġesful adj. *terrible* nsm 20/21, egesfull 20/257, 21/30

eġesliċ adj. *fearful, awesome, dreadful* nsf 14/73; nsn 22/4, 22/75; npf egeslice 22/84

Ēgipte m. pl. *Egyptians* gp Ēgipta 4/77, Ægypta 9/73

eġlan 1 *plague, torment* inf. 20/185 [MnE ail]

ēġlond n. *island* ns 10(b)/16, 19/5

eġsian 2 *terrify* pret 3s egsode 18/6

ēhtan 1 w.g. *chase, pursue* pres. subj. 3p ēhten 3/43; pret. 3p ēhton 20/237

elcor adv. *otherwise* 8/63

eldran see ieldran

eldum see ælde

ele m. *oil* as 3/141

Ēlig f. *Ely* ds Ēlig 4/320

Elizabeþ pers. n. *Elizabeth* ns 1/29

ellen n. *courage, strength* ns 21/16; as 18/3; ds elne 16/114, 18(a)/893; is elne myclc *with great zeal* 14/34, 14/60, 14/123, on ellen *valiantly* 12/211, elne 20/95

ellendǣd f. *deed of valour* dp ellendǣdum 18(a)/876; *daring deed* gp ellendǣda 20/273

ellenmǣrþu f. *fame for courage, heroic deed* dp ellenmǣrþum 18(a)/828

ellenrōf adj. *courageous* nsf 20/109, 20/146

ellenþriste adj. *courageous* npf 20/133

ellenweorc n. *valorous deed* ap 18(d)/3173

ellenwōdnis f. *zeal* gs ellenwōdnisse 9/85

elles adv. *otherwise, else* 4/104, 15/23, 17/46

ellor adv. *elsewhither* 18(c)/2254, 20/112

ellorgǣst m. *spirit from elsewhere, alien spirit* ns ellorgāst 18(a)/807; ap ellorgǣstas 18(b)/1349

elne see ellen

elpendbān n. *ivory, elephant bone* as 3/141

elra adj. *another* dsm elran 18(a)/752

elðēod f. *foreign people* gp elðēoda 20/237

elþēodiġ adj. *alien, foreign* as noun: np elðēodge 10(b)/55; gp elþēodigra 17/38, elðēodigra 20/215

embe see ymbe

ende m. *end, conclusion* ns 1/31, 18(a)/822; as 4/7, 4/96, 4/295, 18(b)/1386; ds 14/29 (on ende *from the edge*); ds 22/2; *region* ænde 22/32, ende 22/48, 22/98; is ænde 9/86

endebyrdan 1 *arrange, dispose* p. ptc. geendebyrd 4/99

endebyrdnes f. *order, (word-)order, succession, sequence* ns 9/35; as endebirdnisse 4/101, endebyrdnesse 9/21

endemes adv. *together* 4/232

ġeendian 2 *end, complete* pret. 3s geendode 4/303 (ended his life), 10(a)/9; geendade 9/86, 9/117

endlyfta adj. *eleventh* isn endlyftan 8/78

engel m. *angel* ns 2/61, 2/71; as 14/9; np englas 4/72, 14/106; dp englum 2/11, 14/153, 17/78; gp engla 4/50, 12/178

Engle m. pl. *the English* np 22/99, 22/107; gp Engla 4/318; dp Englum 22/171

Englisc adj., noun *English* ns 4/102; as 4/3, 4/51, 4/134, 5/16, 5/61, etc.

Engliscġereord n. *the English language* ds Engliscgereorde 9/7

ent m. *giant* gp enta 13/2, 16/87, 21/2

ēode see gān

ēodon see gān

eodorcan 1 *chew the cud* pres. ptc. nsn eodorcende 9/67

eofor m. *boar* ns 21/19; *figure of a boar, helmet ornamented with a boar image* 18(b)/1328

Eoforwīcċeaster f. *York* ds Eoforwīcceastre 8/72

eoh m. *horse* as 12/189

eom see bēon

eorcanstān m. *jewellery, precious stone* as 13/36

eorl m. *nobleman* ns 7/29, 10(b)/78, 12/6, 12/51, 12/89, etc.; gs eorles 12/165; ds eorle 10(b)/72, 12/28, 12/159, 16/12, 21/16; np eorlas 10(b)/30, 20/273, 20/336; ap 16/99, 18/6; gp eorla 11(a)/7, 16/60, 17/72, 18(b)/1312, 20/21, 20/257; dp eorlum 11(n)/8, 18(a)/769 [MnE earl]

eorlscipe m. *nobility* as 18(d)/3173

eormengrund m. *spacious ground, earth* as 18(a)/859

eornost f. *earnestness* as on eornost (*seriously*) 22/110

eornoste adv. *earnestly, determinedly* 12/281, 20/108, 20/231

eorðe f. *earth* as eorðan 2/30, 4/52, 4/56, 4/330, 12/126, 12/286, 12/303, etc.; gs 1/22, 2/40, 9/40, 14/37, etc.; ds 2/2, 2/38, 2/41, etc.

eorðfæst adj. *firmly rooted in the earth* dsn eorðfæstum 4/208 [MnE earthfast]

eorþgrāp f. *grip of earth* ns 13/6

eorþscræf n. *cave, grave* ds eorðscræfe 15/28, 16/84; ap eorðscrafu 15/36

eorþsele m. *cave, barrow* ns 15/29

eorþtilþ f. *farming, earth-tilling* ns 3/192

eorþweġ m. *earthly way* ds eorðwege 14/120

eorþwela m. pl. *worldly prosperity* np eorþwelan 17/67

eoten m. *giant* ns 18(a)/761; gp eotena 18(a)/883

ēow see ġē

ēowdon see īewan

ēower *of you* see ġē

ēower poss. adj. *your* nsm 3/161; dsm ēowrum 3/170; nsf ēowru 3/160; npm ēowre 6/35, ēowere 20/195; npn ēowre 2/9; apf ēowre 3/170; gpf ēowerra 3/162

erian 1 *plough* inf. 3/13

esne m. *man* as 11(f)/8; ap esnas 11(f)/16

etan V *eat* infl. inf. (tō) etanne 2/12; pres. 2s etst 2/30, 2/39; 1p etað 2/5; 2p 2/10, 3/170; 3p 3/126; subj. 3s ete 4/24; 2p eten 2/8; pret. 1s ǣt 2/25, 2/27; 2s æte 2/36, 3s ǣt 2/14; subj. 2s ǣte 2/23, 2/24, 2/37; 1p ǣten 2/6; 2p ǣten 2/3

ġeetan V *eat, devour* pret. 3s ġeǣt 2/14

eþel m. *homeland, territory* ns 14/156; as 5/8, 10(b)/16, 12/52, 17/60; ds ēðle 16/20, 20/169, 21/20

eþelweard m. *defender of the homeland* np eþelweardas 10(b)/24, ēðelweardas 20/320

ēðnis f. *ease, comfort* gp ēðnessa 10(a)/16

facen n. *crime* as 21/56

ġefadian 2 *arrange, phrase* inf. 4/104

fadung f. *arrangement, order (of words)* ds fadunge 4/102

fāh adj. *stained, guilty, outcast* nsm 14/13, 15/46, 16/98 (*decorated*), fāg 18(a)/811 (*in a state of feud with*); asm fāgne 18(a)/725, fāhne 18(a)/716; *gleaming* nsm fāh 21/22; dsm fāgum 20/104; dp 20/194, 20/264, 20/301

fana m. *banner* ns 10(b)/10 [MnE (weather)vane]

fandian 2 w.g. *test* inf. 2/43

far see faran

faran VI *go, travel, advance* inf. 12/88, 12/156, 18(a)/865; imp. s. far 2/45, 4/193; pres. 1s fare 3/135; 3s færð. 4/63, fareð 11(h)/3, 17/91 (him on fareð *overtakes him*); subj. 1s fare 3/100; pret. 3s fōr 20/297; pret. 3p fōron 10(b)/20, 20/202 [MnE fare]

ġefaran VI *proceed, act, die* inf. 18(a)/738; pret. 3s gefōr 7/15, 7/26

fatu see fæt

fæc n. *interval* ns 8/33; as 9/117; ds fæce 8/34, 9/5

fæder m. (§60) *father* ns 2/54, 2/55, 4/56, 4/144, 11(a)/4, 11(k)/2, 20/5, etc.; as 2/54, etc.; ds 4/58, 4/330, 16/115; gs 21/61; np ealdan fæderas *patriarchs* 4/11; nsm ealda fæder *grandfather* 12/218

fǣġe adj. *fated, doomed to die* nsm 12/119, 18(a)/846; dsm fǣgean 12/125; npm fǣge 12/105; apm 20/195; as noun gsm fǣges 12/297; dsm fǣgum 17/71; npm 20/19; dpm fǣgum 20/209 [archaic MnE fey] fǣgen adj. *rejoicing, happy* nsm 16/68 [MnE fain]

fǣger adj. *beautiful, pleasant* nsn 14/73, 18(a)/773, 20/47; dsf fægran 14/21; ism fægre 9/86; npm fægere 14/8, 14/10, 18(a)/866; dpm fægerum 4/84 [MnE fair]

fǣgere adv. *properly* 12/22, 21/56, fægre 11(m)/8; *generously* 20/300 [MnE fair(ly)]

fǣġernis f. *beauty, excellent feature* ap fæger nissa 4/90 [MnE fairness]

fǣġnian 2 *rejoice* pret. 3p fægnodon 10(b)/33

ġefǣġnian 2 *make glad* p. ptc. gefægnod 18(b)/1333

fǣġrian 2 *make or become beautiful, adorn* pres. 3p fægriað 17/48

fæġrost adv. superl. *most happily, most pleasantly* 17/13

fǣhðo f. *feud, battle, enmity* as fæhðe 12/225, 18(a)/879, 18(b)/1333, 18(b)/1340, 18(b)/1380, fæhðu 15/26

fǣlsian 2 *cleanse, purge* p. ptc. gefælsod 18(a)/825

fǣmne f. *maiden, woman* ns 11(p)/1, 21/44

fǣrgripe m. *sudden grip, sudden attack* dp færgripum 18(a)/738

fǣrlic adj. *sudden* dsn færlican 4/170

fǣrlīċe adv. *quickly, suddenly* 3/61, 4/156, 4/163, 16/61

fǣrsceaða m. *sudden attacker, Viking* ds færsceaðan 12/142

fǣrspel n. *dreadful news* as 20/244

fǣrð see faran

fæst adj. *fast, firm, fixed* nsm 18(b)/1364, 21/38; nsf 18(a)/722; *secure, enclosed* nsm 19/5

fæstan 1 *fast, abstain from food* pret. subj. 3p fæsten 4/296

fæste adv. *firmly, fast* 4/284, 8/68, 9/46, 10(b)/35, 11(h)/14, 12/21, 12/103, 20/99, etc.

fæsten see fæstan

fæstenbryċe m. *failure to observe fasts* ap fæstenbrycas 22/127

fæsten n. *stronghold, fortress* as 10(b)/20, 12/194; ds fæstene 10(b)/79, fæstenne 20/143

fæsten n. *fast, abstinence from food* dp fæstenum 4/268

fæstenbryċe m. *failure to observe fasts* ap fæstenbrycas 22/127

fæstengeat n. *fortress gate* gs fæstengeates 20/162

fæstlīċe adv. *steadfastly, firmly, steadily* 3/60, 8/50, 10(b)/70, 12/82, 12/254, festlīce 7/49

fæstnian 2 *fasten, establish (truce)* inf. 12/35; p. ptc. gefæstnod 3/12

ġefæstnian 2 *fasten* pret. 3p gefæstnodon 14/33

fæstnung f. *(place of) security* ns 16/115

fæt n. *vessel, utensil* ap fatu 3/203 [MnE vat]

fǣt n. *gold ornament, ornamental plate* dp fætum 18(c)/2256, fættum 18(a)/716

fǣted adj. *ornamented, plated* asn 11(l)/7, 18(c)/2253

fǣtels m. *pouch, bag* ds fætelse 20/127; ap fætelsas 3/154

fǣtt adj. *fat, rich* asn 3/171

fæðm m. *embrace* ns 18(a)/781; as 18(b)/1393 *(interior)*; ds fæðme 21/61 [MnE fathom]

fēa adv. *little* 14/115

feaht see feohtan

fĕala see fela

feallan VII *fall, fall in battle* inf. 12/54, 12/105, 14/43; pres. 3s fealleþ 1/26, 16/63; pret. 3s fēoll 1/2, 12/119, 12/166, 12/286, fēol 10(b)/81, 12/126, 12/303, etc.; 3p fēollon 12/111; subj. 1s fēolle 4/175

ġefeallan VII *fall* pret. 3s gefēoll 10(a)/29, 20/280, 20/307, gefēol 20/67

fealohilte adj. *golden-hilted* nsn 12/166

fealu adj. *tawny, dark* nsm fealwe 11(n)/10, apm 16/46, 18(a)/865 [MnE fallow]

fēasceaft adj. *destitute* nsm 18/7

fēasceaftiġ adj. *wretched, desolate* asn 17/26

fēawe pl. adj. *few* np fēawa 5/14, 5/18, 5/27, etc.; dp fēawum 4/133

feax n. *hair* as 20/281; ds feaxe 20/99

feaxhār adj. *grey-haired* nsf 11(p)/1

ġefecgan 2 *fetch, carry off* inf. 12/160

fēdan 1 *feed* inf. 3/125; pres. 3s fētt 3/69, 3/192; 3p fēdaþ 3/121, 3/127, 11(m)/8; pret. 3s fēdde 11(k)/9, fædde 7/62

ġefēhst see ġefōn

fēhð see fōn

fela pron. (usually w.g.: see §190.4) *many* 3/84 (hira . . . fela *many of them*), 3/94, 3/142, etc.; *much* 22/46

felalēof adj. *dearly loved* gsm felaleofan 15/26

ġefēlan 1 *feel* inf. 17/95

feld m. (§§61, 62), *field* ds felda 3/9, 12/241

fell n. *skin* ap 3/152

fenfreoðo f. *refuge in the fens* ds 18(a)/851

fēng see fōn

ġefēng see ġefōn

fenġelād n. *fen-path, tract of swamp* as 18(b)/1359

fengon see fōn

fenhlið n. *fen slope, marshy tract* ap fenhleoþu 18(a)/820

fenhop n. *retreat in the fen* ap fenhopu 18(a)/764

fenn m. and n. *fen* ds fenne 19/5, 21/42

feoh n. *money* ns 16/108; as 3/74, 6/19, 12/
39; gs fēos 6/28, 7/63; ds fēo 18(b)/1380;
cattle ns 21/47 [MnE fee]
feohgīfre adj. *greedy, avaricious* nsm 16/68
feohġift f. *gift of treasure, treasure-giving*
inst. p. feohgiftum 18/21
ġefeoht n. *battle, fight* ds gefeohte 4/175, 12/
12, 20/189, 20/202, 22/100; dp gefeohtum
6/6
feohtan III *fight* inf. 4/178, 12/16, 12/261;
pres. ptc. feohtende 6/16, 6/21, 7/49,
etc.; pret. 3s feaht 6/6, 12/254, 12/277,
12/281, etc.; 3p fuhton 1/13; 3p 20/262
ġefeohtan III *fight, achieve by fighting* inf.
7/74, 12/129; p. ptc. gefohten 20/122
feohte f. *battle, fight* ns 12/103
fēol see **feallan**
fēolan III *penetrate* pret. 3p fulgon 6/37
fēole f. *file* ds fēolan 4/277
fēolheard adj. *hard as a file* apn fēolhearde
12/108
fēolian 2 *file* pret. 3s fēolode 4/277
fēoll see **feallan**
ġefēoll see **ġefeallan**
fēolode see **fēolian**
ġefēon V *rejoice* pres. ptc. gefēonde (w.g. or
i. *rejoicing in*) 8/69, 9/98; pret. 3s gefeh
18(a)/827, gefeah 20/205
fēond m. (§59) *enemy* ns 11(m)/4, 18(a)/725;
as 1/27, 18(a)/748; ds fēonde 11(m)/4;
np fēondas 14/30, 14/33, fynd 20/195; ap
fȳnd 12/82, 20/319, fēondas 14/38; gp
fēonda 2/76, 17/75, 18(a)/808; dp fēondum
7/53, 12/103, 12/264 [MnE fiend]
fēondrǣden f. *enmity* as fēondrǣdene 2/31
fēondsceaþa m. *enemy, robber* as fēondsceaðan 20/104; ap fēondsceaþan 11(j)/19
feor adj. *far* nsn 4/48 (w.d. *far from*), 8/72,
9/114, etc.; gsn feorres 15/47
feor adv. *far* 11(h)/5, 12/3, 12/57, 15/25,
16/21, 16/26, etc.
fēore see **feorh**
feorg see **feorh**
feorgbold n. *life-house, dwelling of the soul,
body* ns 14/73
feorh n. *life* ns 11(k)/2, feorg 17/94, as feorh
6/20, 6/39, 12/125, 12/142, 12/184, etc.;
gs fēores 4/160, 12/260, 12/317; ds fēore
4/179, 12/194, 12/259; is 11(h)/14
feorhbealo n. *threat to life, deadly evil* ns
18(c)/2250; as 11(h)/5
feorhcynn n. *race of men* gp feorhcynna
18(c)/2266
feorhhūs n. *life-house, body* as 12/297
feorhlāst m. *bloody track* ap feorhlāstas
18(a)/846
feorhsēoc adj. *mortally wounded* nsm 18(a)/
820

feormian 2 *clean* inf. 3/19
ġefeormian 2 *consume, eat up* p. ptc. gefeormod 18(a)/744
feormynd m. *cleanser, polisher* np 18(c)/
2256
feorran adv. *from afar* 14/57, 18(a)/825,
18(a)/839, 18(b)/1370, 20/24, 21/1
fēorða num. *fourth* ism fēorðan 20/12
fēos see **feoh**
fēower num. *four* ap 4/16, 11(g)/3, 11(l)/1,
11(n)/2; dp 11(l)/7
fēowertȳne num. *fourteen* dpm fēowertȳnum
9/88
ġefēra m. *companion, comrade* ns 4/238, 12/
280; as gefēran 3/14, 8/70; ds 2/25, 4/35,
16/30; np 3/3, 3/206, 6/35; ap 3/103,
3/179, 12/170, 12/229; dp gefērum 3/33,
6/33
fēran 1 *set out, proceed, go, fare* inf. 12/41,
12/221, 15/9, 17/37, 20/12, etc.; pres.
ptc. nsm fērende 11(d)/9; pret. 3s fērde
2/47, 4/223, 8/65; 3p fērdon 2/78 (w.
refl.), 4/147, 4/279, 7/54, 18(a)/839
ġefēran 1 *reach by travel, attain, meet with*
pret. 3s gefērde 7/25; 3p gefērdon 7/50
feredon see **ferian**
fērende see **fēran**
ferhðe see **ferð**
ferhðglēaw adj. *prudent* asf ferhðglēawe
20/41
ferian 1 *go* inf. 12/179
ferian 1 *carry* inf. 4/255; pres. 3s fereð
11(j)/7; pret. 3s ferede 16/81; 3p feredon
4/245, 11(f)/4; p. ptc. geferod 4/60
[MnE ferry]
fers n. *verse* ds ferse 4/59; ap fers 9/34
ġefērscipe m. *fellowship, community* ns 3/184;
ds 3/170
ferð n. *spirit, mind* ns 16/54; as 11(p)/5,
17/26, 17/37; ds ferðe 16/90, ferhðe
18(a)/754; dp (w. sg. meaning) ferhðum
18(d)/3176
ferðfriþende adj. *life-sustaining* apf 11(g)/3
ferðloca m. *breast, heart* ns 16/33; as ferðlocan 16/13
fēsan 1 *put to flight* pres. 3s fēseð 22/101 [MnE
faze]
festlice see **fæstlice**
fēt see **fōt**
feter f. *fetter* dp feterum 16/21
fetian 2 *fetch* inf. fetigan 20/35; pres. subj.
3s gefetiġe 14/138; p. ptc. fetod 18(b)/
1310
fetigan see **fetian**
fētt see **fēdan**
fēða m. *foot-troop, infantry* as fēðan 12/88,
np 18(b)/1327
fēðelāst m. *footpath* ds fēðelāste 20/139

feðer f. *feather* np feþre 11(f)/4; ap feþra 16/47

fícléaf n. *figleaf* ap 2/16

fierlen adj. *far off, distant* dsn fierlenan 2/47

fíf num. *five* npm fífe 11(a)/6, 14/8

fífteġ num. *fifty* dp fíftegum 5/76

ġefillednys f. *fulfilment* ns 4/29

findan III *find, meet* inf. 16/26, 18(b)/1378, 18(d)/3162 (*devise*); pret. 1s funde 15/18; 3s 20/2, 20/278, fand 18(a)/719, 18(a)/870; 3p fundon 12/85, 20/41; p. ptc. funden 5/48, 11(f)/1, 18/7

finger m. *finger* np fingras 18(a)/760; gp fingra 18(a)/764, 21/38

fiorm f. *use, benefit* as fiorme 5/31

fíras m. pl. *people, human beings* gp fýra 18(c)/2250, fíra 20/24, 20/33; dp fírum 9/44

firmest see fyrmest

first m. *period of time, time* as 5/61; ds fyrste 4/225, 4/251

fírum see fíras

fisc m. *fish* ns 1/5, 21/27; as 3/102, 3/103; np fiscas 3/79; ap 3/75, 3/81, 3/86, 3/87; gp fisca 3/94; dp fiscum 11(p)/4

fiscere m. *fisherman* ns 3/72, 3/195; np fisceras 3/5

fiscian 2 *fish, catch fish* pres. 2s fiscast 3/89

Fitela pers. n. *Fitela* ns 18(a)/879, 18(a)/889

flán m. *arrow, missile* as 12/269; gs flánes 12/71; gp flána 20/221

flasce f. *flask, leather bottle* ap flascan 3/153

flǽschoma m. *covering of flesh, body* ns 17/94

flǽscmete m. *meat* ap flǽscmettas 3/171; gp flǽscmetta 3/158 [MnE fleshmeat]

fléag see fléogan

fléam m. *flight* as 7/44, 12/81, 12/254, 20/291; gs fléames 4/184; ds fléame 4/179, 12/186

fléogan II *fly* inf. 12/7, 12/109, 12/150, 12/275 (*flee*); 3s fléogeð 11(h)/12; pret. 1s fléah 11(p)/3; 3s fléag 11(l)/4, 17/17, fléah 20/209

fléohnet n. *curtain* ns 20/47 [MnE fly-net]

fléon II *flee* inf. 12/247, 18(a)/755, 18(a)/764, 18(a)/820; pret. 3s fléah 10(b)/20; 3p flugon 12/194

fléotend m. *swimmer, seafarer* (*seabird*) gp fléotendra 16/54

flet n. *floor, hall* as 11(n)/2, 16/61

fletsittend m. *hall-guest* dp flettsittendum 20/19, 20/33

ġeflit n. *dispute, rivalry, contest* as 18(a)/865; ap geflitu 3/207

flocmǽlum adv. *in* (*armed*) *bands* 7/77 [archaic MnE flockmeal]

flód m. *body of water, stream, tide* ns 12/65, 12/72, 18(b)/1361; ds flóde 11(d)/9,

11(p)/3, 18(b)/1366; ap flódas 11(j)/7 [MnE flood]

flode f. *channel, stream* ds flódan 6/5

flódgrǽg adj. *sea-grey* nsf 21/31

flódwegas m. pl. *paths of the ocean* ap 17/52 [MnE floodways]

flór m., f. *floor* asm 18(a)/725; asf 10(a)/30, flore 10(b)/81, 20/111; ds 18(b)/1316

flot n. *sea* as 12/41

flota m. *ship, seaman, Viking* as 12/227; ds flotan 4/149; np 12/72

flothere m. *sea-army, Viking band* ns 4/223

flotman m. *sailor, Viking* ns 4/215; np flotmen 4/178, 4/229; dp flotmannum 4/183

flówan VII *flow, gush* inf. 21/47; pres. ptc. flówende 12/65

flugon see fléon

flyht m. *flight* as 12/71

flýman 1 *put to flight* inf. 11(j)/19; p. ptc. geflýmed 18(a)/846, 18(b)/1370

fódor n. *fodder, food* as 3/209

ġefohten see ġefeohtan

folc n. *folk, people, nation* ns 4/86, 4/176, 8/66, 12/45, 12/241, 14/140; as 4/78, 4/145, 7/77, 11(d)/6, 12/22, 12/54; gs folces 1/27, 4/20, 20/162, 20/292, etc.; ds folce 3/133, 4/39, 4/252, 12/227, etc.; is 8/77; gp folca 1/28

folcġesíð m. *companion of the people, warrior* ap folcgesíðas 10(b)/70

folcġewinn n. *battle* gs folcgewinnes 10(b)/10

folclagu f. *public law* np folclaga 22/33

folclic adj. *vernacular, public* dsn folclicum 4/255; dsf folclicre 4/309

folclond n. *country* gs folclondes 15/47 [MnE folkland]

folcstede m. *battlefield* ds 20/319

folctoga m. *leader of the people, commander* gs folctogan 20/47; np 18(a)/839; ap 20/194

folcwiga m. *warrior* np folcwigan 11(j)/13

foldbold n. *building* ns 18(a)/773

foldbúend n. *earth-dweller, man* np foldbúende 18(b)/1355

folde f. *earth, ground* as foldan 9/44, 12/54, 18(b)/1361; gs 14/8, 14/43, 16/33, 18(b)/1393; ds 11(d)/9, 11(p)/5, 12/166, 12/227, 14/132, 17/13, 17/75, 20/281, 21/33

foldweġ m. *way, path* np foldwegas 18(a)/866

folgað m. *retinue* as 15/9

folgian 2 w.d. *follow* inf. 6/32; pres. 1s folgie 4/191; pret. 3s folgode 4/246; 3p folgodon 4/37

folme f. *hand* ds 18(a)/748, 20/80, folman 12/21, 12/108, 12/150; dp folmum 18(a)/722, 20/99; ap folma 18(a)/745; gp 11(f)/15

fōn VII *catch, seize* inf. 3/95; pres. 1s fō 3/49; 3s fēhð 11(f)/9 (fēhð ongean *struggles against*); **fōn tō rōce** *succeed to the kingdom* (or *the office*, etc.) pret. 1s fēng 5/19; 3s 7/16, 8/25 (see note), 10(a)/5, 12/10, 20/299 (fēng . . . on fultum *helped*); 3p fēngon 4/252 (fēngon tōgædere *joined together*)

ġefōn VII *catch* inf. 3/84, 3/130; pres. 1s gefō 3/51, 3/66, 3/102, 3/103; 2s gefēhst 3/50, 3/75, 3/86, 3/92; 3p gefōþ 3/105; subj. 3s gefō 3/98; pret. 1s gefēng 3/56, 3/58; 2s gefēnge 3/55, 3/57; 3s gefēng 18(a)/740

for prep. w.d.a.i. *for, because of, before* 1/32, 2/65, 2/68, 3/10, 3/16, 4/298 (*with respect to*), 7/76 (*in spite of*), 9/8, etc.; for hwon *why* 9/95–6; for hwȳ *why* 3/89, 3/101, 3/124; for þǣm *because* 3/53, 3/63, 3/66, 3/90, 3/98, 3/102, 3/107, 3/125; for þǣm þe, for ðān þe *because* 2/22, 2/28, 2/36, 2/42, 2/77, 3/21, 3/125, 4/6, 4/166; for ðon (ðe) *therefore, because, and so, wherefore* 4/325, 5/21, 8/15, 8/61, 9/96, 15/17 (*wherefore*); for ðȳ *therefore, because*; for þām *therefore* 22/11–12, 22/14, etc. See §169

fōr f. *journey, course* ds fōre 11(l)/3

ġefōr see **ġefaran**

foran tō adv. *beforehand, above* 4/44

forbarn see **forbeornan**

forbærnan 1 *burn, burn up* inf. 8/71; pres. subj. 1p forbærnen 8/49; pret. 3s forbærnde 22/68; p. ptc. forbærned 5/29, asm forbærnedne 17/114

forbēad see **forbēodan**

forbēah see **forbūgan**

forbēodan II (w.d. of person) *forbid* pres. 3p forbēodaþ 4/289; pret. 3s forbēad 2/3, 4/204

forbeornan III *burn down* pret. 3s forbarn 7/11

forbīgan 1 *abase, humble* p. ptc. forbīged 20/267

forbūgan II *flee from* pret. 3s forbēah 12/325

forceorfan III *cut through* pret. 3s 20/105

ford m. *ford* as 12/88; ds forda 12/81

fordōn anom. (§128) *destroy* inf. 22/63; pret. 3s fordyde 8/75 [MnE fordo]

fordrīfan 1 *impel, force* pret. 3s fordrāf 20/277

fore prep. w.d. *for, in place of* 17/21, 17/22

forealdian 2 *grow old* p. ptc. forealdod *elderly* 4/131

foregangan VII *precede* pres. subj. 3s foregange 8/35

foregenga m. *attendant* ns 20/127

foremǣre adj. *illustrious* asm foremǣrne 20/122

forescēawian 2 *provide, preordain* pres. 3s forescēawað 2/55, 4/193

foresecgan 3 *mention before* p. ptc. nsm foresǣda *aforementioned* 4/156; nsf 4/99; nsm 4/156

foresnotor adj. *very wise, very clever* npm foresnotre 18(d)/3162

forespeca m. *sponsor* np forespecan 22/177 [MnE forespeaker]

foresprecan V *say before* p. ptc. dsm foresprecenan *aforementioned* 8/52, dpm 10(a)/5

forġēafe see **forġīefan**

forġīefan V *give* imp. s. forgif 20/88; pret. 2s forgēafe 2/25; 3s forgēaf 12/139, 12/148, 14/147; p. ptc. forgifen 4/252, 9/55; ap forgiefene 17/93 [MnE forgive]

forgif see **forġīefan**

forġifenis f. *forgiveness* as forgifenisse 4/65

forgolden see **forgyldan**

forgyldan III *buy off* pres. subj. 2p forgyldon 12/32; *requite* p. ptc. forgolden 20/217

forhealdan VII *withhold* inf. 22/21; pres. 3p forhealdað 22/23

forheard adj. *exceedingly hard* asm forheardne 12/156

forhēawan VII *cut down* p. ptc. forhēawen 12/115, 12/223, 12/288, 12/314

forherġian 2 *ravage* p. ptc. forhergod 5/29, 7/3, 7/7

forhicgan 2 *despise, scorn* pret. 3s forhogode 12/254

forhogdnis f. *contempt* ds forhogdnisse 9/8

forht adj. *afraid* nsm 14/21, 16/68, 18(a)/754

forhtian 2 *fear* pres. 3p forhtiað 14/115; pret. 3s forhtode 4/170; subj. 3p forhtedon 12/21

forhtlīce adv. *fearfully* 20/244

forhtmōd adj. *timorous* nsm 3/63, 3/107

forhwega adv. *somewhere* 4/231

for hwon see **for**

for hwȳ see **for**

forlǣtan VII *abandon, neglect, forsake, let* (*go*) inf. 12/2, 12/208, 18(a)/792, 20/150; pres. ptc. forlǣtende 9/120; pres. 3s forlǣtt 3/211, forlǣteð 11(h)/7; pret. 3s forlēt 4/35, 7/25, 9/24, 11(g)/2, 12/149, 12/156, 12/187, etc.; 3p forlēton 4/37, 5/46, 14/61, 18(d)/3166, 20/170; p. ptc. forlǣten 3/212, 5/37

forlegene see **forlicgan**

forlēogan II *perjure, forswear* p. ptc. forlogen 22/126; npm forlogene 22/86–7

forlēosan II *destroy* pres. subj. 1p forlēosen 8/48; *lose* inf. 20/63; p. ptc. forloren 22/126 [MnE p. ptc. forlorn]

forlēt see **forlǣtan**

forlicgan V *fornicate* p. ptc. forlegen *adulterous, fornicating* npm forlegene 22/149
forlidennes f. *shipwreck* as forlidennesse 3/138
forliġer n. *fornication, wantonness* ds forligre 4/265; ap forligru 22/124
forloren see forlēosan
forma adj. *first* nsm 18(a)/716, asm forman 12/77; ds 4/59, 18(a)/740 [MnE form(er), forem(ost)]
formoni adj. *very many* (*a*) nsm 12/239
forniman IV *take away* pret. 3s fornōm 13/26, 16/80, fornam 18(c)/2249; 3p fornōman 16/99; p. ptc. npn fornumene 22/40
fornōm see forniman
fornȳdan 1 *compel* p. ptc. npf fornȳdde 22/35 (*compelled to marry*)
foroft adv. *all too often* 22/51, 22/53, 22/117
fōron see faran
forrǣdan 1 *betray* pret. 3s forrǣde 22/68; subj. 3s 22/66
forsēon V *reject, despise* pres. 3s forsihð 4/65; pret. 3s forseah 4/201; p. ptc. npf forsawene 22/41
forsihð see forsēon
forslēan VI *cut through* p. ptc. forslagen 4/259
forspillan 1 *kill* pret. 3s forspilde 22/70
forst m. *frost* is forste 17/9
forstandan VI *understand, withstand* inf. 10(b)/22; pret. 1s forstōd 5/73
forstelan IV *rob, steal* p. ptc. asn forstolen 11(j)/18 (as noun: *that which has been stolen*)
forstōd see forstandan
forstrang adj. *very strong* asm forstrangne 11(m)/4
forswelgan III *devour, eat* inf. 17/95; pret. 3s forswealg 11(c)/3; pres. subj. 3p forswelgen 3/25
forswerian VI w.d. *make useless by a spell* p. ptc. forsworen 18(a)/804, *swear falsely, forswear* p. ptc. npm forsworene 22/86 [MnE forswear]
forsyngian 2 *corrupt, ruin by sin* p. ptc. forsyngod 22/119, dsf forsyngodan 22/153
forð adv. *forth, forward* 4/246, 11(e)/5, 12/3, 12/12, 12/170, etc.; to forð *too deeply, too successfully* 12/150, *too greatly* 22/139
for þan þe see for
for þǣm see for
for þǣm þe see for
forþbringan 1 *produce, bring forth* pret. 3s forþbrōhte 9/7
forðencan 1 *despair* p. ptc. forðōht *in despair* 10(b)/82
forðfēran 1 *die* pret. 3s forðfērde 4/128, 7/19; 3p forðfērdon 7/12

forðfōr f. *forth-faring, death* ns 9/96; gs forðfōre 9/88, 9/124; ds 9/92, forþfōre 9/102
forðġeorn adj. *eager to advance* nsm 12/281
forðġesceaft f. *eternal decree* as 14/10; *future* ns 21/61
forðian 2 *carry out, accomplish* p. ptc. geforðod 12/289
forðōht see forðencan
forþolian 2 *do without, dispense with* inf. 3/167, 16/38
for þon see for
forðweġ m. *the way forth, departure* gs forðweges 11(o)/3; ds forðwege 16/81, 14/125
forðȳ adv. *therefore* 5/54, 5/79
forðylman 1 *enwrap, envelope* p. ptc. forðylmed 20/118
forwegan V *carry off, kill* p. ptc. forwegen 12/228
forweorone see forweosan
forweorðan III *perish* inf. 20/288, 22/159; pret. 3p forwurdan 22/169, *deteriorate* 22/71
forweosan I *perish* p. ptc. apm forweorone 13/7
forwundian 2 *wound sorely* p. ptc. forwunded 14/14, forwundod 14/62
forwyrcan 1 *do wrong* pres. subj. 3p 22/142; *destroy* pret. 3p forworhtan 22/169 [MnE for-, work]
forwyrd f. *destruction* as 20/285
foryrman 1 *reduce to poverty, impoverish* p. ptc. npf foryrmde 22/36
fōt m. *foot* gs fōtes 12/247; np fēt 17/9; ap 4/111, 11(b)/4, 18(a)/745; gp fōta 11(f)/15; dp fōtum 4/241, 12/119, 12/171
fōtmǣl n. *space of a foot* as 12/275
fracod adj. *vile, wicked* as noun gsm fracodes 14/10
fram prep. w.d. *from, by* 1/8, 2/19, 3/212, 7/3, etc.
fram adv. see from
framra adj. see from
franca m. *spear* as francan 12/140; ds 12/77
ġefrǣġe n. *information through hearsay* is mīne gefrǣge *as I have heard say* 18(a)/776, 18(a)/837
frǣġn see friġnan
Frǣna pers. n. *Frǣna* ns 7/44
frǣt see fretan
frǣtwan 1 *ornament, adorn* p. ptc. frǣtwed 11(j)/11
ġefrǣtwan 1 *adorn* p. ptc. gefrǣtwed 13/33, gefrǣtwod 20/171, 20/328
frǣtwe f. pl. *ornaments* np 11(d)/6; ap frǣtwa 18(a)/896; dp frǣtewum 4/84, *treasure* 21/27; ip frǣtwum 11(j)/7

frēa m. *lord, master, the Lord* ns 9/44, 20/ 300; as frēan 12/184, 12/259, 14/33, 18(b)/1319; gs 15/33; ds 11(n)/10, 12/12, 12/16, 12/289

frēadryhten m. *lord* gs frēadryhtnes 18(a)/ 796

frēċennes f. *danger, harm* dp frēċennessum 3/105

frēcne adj. *daring, dangerous, audacious* nsn 18(c)/2250, asn 18(b)/1359, asf 18(a)/889, 18(b)/1378

frēfran I *console, comfort* inf. 16/28, 17/26

fremde adj. *strange* as noun *stranger, foreigner* dp fremdum 22/38, 22/84, fremdan 22/54

fremman I *do, benefit, perpetrate* pres. 3s fremeþ 3/156, 3/163; subj. 3s fremme 3/208; pret. 3s fremede 10(b)/45; subj. 3/146; pret. 3p fremedon 20/37, *performed* 18/3

ġefremman I *bring about, provide, do, grant, perpetrate* inf. 4/281, 16/16, 16/114, 18(b)/1315; pret. 3s gefremede 18(a)/811, 20/6, 20/181; 3p gefremedon 17/84

fremsumnes f. *benefit* ap fremsumnesse 8/18; dp fremsumnessum 9/80

fremu f. *beneficial action, good deed* dip fremum 11(m)/8, 17/75

frēo adj. *free* nsm 3/21; gpm frīora 5/58

frēod f. *friendship, peace* as frēode 12/39

frēoġan 2 *love* pres. subj. 3s frēoge 18(d)/ 3176

frēoliċ adj. *free, noble, beautiful* nsn 11(j)/13; npn frēolico 11(a)/4

frēolsbriċe m. *failure to observe holy days* ap frēolsbricas 22/127

frēomǣg m. *noble kinsman* dp frēomǣgum 16/21

frēond m. (§59) *friend, lover* ns 14/144, 15/47, 16/108; as 18(b)/1385, 21/44; np frȳnd 15/33, frēondas 14/76; ap frȳnd 12/229; gp frēonda 14/132, 15/17; dp frēondum 8/3

frēondlēas adj. *friendless* asm frēondlēasne 16/28

frēondlīċe adv. *lovingly, in friendly fashion* 5/2

frēondscipe m. *friendship, love* ns 15/25; as 10(a)/8

frēoriġ adj. *frozen* nsm 16/33; *chilled, trembling* nsm 20/281

frēoriht n. *rights of freemen* np 22/40

freoþian 2 *care for, protect* pret. 3s freoþode 11(k)/5

fretan V *eat up, devour* pret. 3s fræt 11(c)/1 [MnE fret]

friġnan III *ask, enquire* pres. ptc. frignende 8/9; imp. s. frige 11(f)/15, 11(j)/19, frīn 18(b)/1322; pres. 3s frīneð 14/112; pret. 3s frægn 9/100, 9/104, etc.

ġefriġnan III *find out, learn by asking* pret. 1s gefrægn 11(c)/2, 20/246, gefrægen 20/7; 3p gefrūnon 14/76, 18/2

frīn see **friġnan**

frīneð see **friġnan**

frīora see **frēo**

frið m. *peace* as 7/75, 12/39; gs friðes 7/65, 10(b)/35, 12/41; ds friðe 12/179

Friðeġist pers. n. *Frithegist* ns 7/44

friþemǣg f. *protective woman* ns 11(k)/9

ġefriðian 2 *protect* pret. subj. 3s gefriðode 20/5

frōd adj. *old, wise, experienced* nsm 12/140, 12/317, 16/90, 18(b)/1306, etc.

frōfor f. *consolation, solace* as frōfre 16/115, 18/7; gs 10(a)/28, 10(b)/79, 20/83; ds 20/296

from adj. *active, swift, strong* compar. nsm framra 11(l)/4; *willing, generous* inst. p. fromum 18/21

from adv. *away* 6/33, fram 12/317, 18(a)/754

from prep. see **fram**

fromlīċe adv. *quickly* 20/41, 20/220, 20/ 301

fromsīþ m. *departure* ns 15/33

fromweard adj. *about to depart, passing away* dsm fromweardum 17/71

fruma m. *beginning* ds fruman 4/21, 9/71

frumbearn n. *first-born son* np 11(a)/4

frumgār m. *leader* (frum- *first*, gār *spear*) ap frumgāras 20/195

frumsceaft f. *first creation* as 9/33

ġefrunon see **ġefriġnan**

frymdi adj. *desiring, requesting, entreating* nsm 12/179 (ic eom frymdi tō þē *I beseech you*)

frymð f. *creature, created thing* gp frymða 20/5, 20/83, 20/189

frȳnd see **frēond**

fuglere m. *fowler* ns 3/109; np fugleras 3/5

fugol m. *bird* ns fugel 16/81, 20/207, 21/38; ap fuglas 3/108; dp fuglum 11(l)/4, 11(p)/3, 20/296 [MnE fowl]

fuhton see **feohtan**

fūl adj. *foul, vile* nsm fūla 20/111; asm fūlne 22/167; dsn fūlum 4/190; npm fūle 22/149

ful adv. *very, completely* 4/181, 11(o)/5, 12/253, 12/311, 15/1, 15/18, 15/21, etc., full 12/153

fulgon see **fēolan**

full adj. *full, entire, completed, filled* nsm 10(b)/9; nsf 13/23, 17/100; asm fulne 3/ 13, 17/113; asn ful 4/16; apm fulle 20/19

be fullan *completely* 5/42

fullīce adv. *entirely, fully* 4/296, 22/93, 22/94

fulluht see **fulwiht**

fulluhtþēaw m. *rite of baptism* dp fulluhtþēawum 10(b)/33
fullwēr m. *complete atonement* as 11(h)/14
fulne see full
fultum m. *help, support* as 4/177, 20/186,
20/300; ds fultume 4/212, 5/57
fultumian 2 *help, support* inf. 8/20; p. ptc.
gefultumed 9/14
ġefultumian 2 *help* pret. subj. gefultumode
10(a)/24
fulwiht m. *baptism* as fulluht 22/176; gs
fulwihte 8/77; ds fulluhte 4/64, 22/177
funde see findan
funden see findan
fundian 2 *set out* pres. 3s fundaþ 14/103,
17/47
furþum adv. *even* 3/162, 3/166, 4/24, 5/16,
etc.
furþur adv. *further, forward* 5/62, 18(a)/
761, furðor 5/62, 12/247
fūs adj. w.g. *eager, ready (for death or battle)*
nsm 11(o)/3, 12/281; asm fūsne 17/50; asn
fūse 14/21; apm 4/198; as noun npm fūse
(hastening ones) 14/57
fyl m. *fall, death* as 12/71, 12/264, fyll 14/56
fylġan 1 w.d. *follow* inf. fylgean 22/175;
pres. subj. 1p fylgen 8/37; *serve* inf. 20/33
fyllan 1 *fill, satisfy* p. ptc. apm gefylde 3/32
fyllan 1 *fell, cut down* inf. 14/73; imp. pl
20/194
ġefyllan 1 *fill, replenish* pres. 3s gefylleð
11(j)/8, gefylþ 3/159; p. ptc. npf gefylda
5/30
ġefyllan 1 *fell, kill, strike down* inf. 14/38
fyllo f. *fill, feast* gs fylle 20/209; ds 18(b)/
1333
fylstan 1 w.d. *help* inf. 12/265
fȳlþ f. *filth, foul act* as fȳlþe 22/78; ds 22/79
fȳnd see fēond
fȳr n. *fire* ns 2/55, 8/29; as 2/53, 18(b)/
1366, 22/18; gs fyres 17/113; ds fȳre
7/49; is 8/49, 11(o)/3
fȳra see fīras
fȳrbend f. *band forged with fire* dp fȳrbendum
18(a)/722
fyrd f. *national army, the English levy, army*
ns 21/31, 21/52; as fyrde 7/29, 7/42; ds
fyrde 4/163, 4/198, 7/34, 12/221, 21/52
fyrdrinc m. *warrior* ns 12/140
fyrdsceorp n. *war-ornament* ns 11(j)/13
fyrdwīc n. *camp* dp fyrdwīcum 20/220
fyrdwyrðe adj. *distinguished in war* nsm
18(b)/1316
fyren f. *crime, wickedness, sin* gp fyrena 18(a)/
750, fyrene 18(a)/811; ap 18(a)/879
fyrenðearf f. *dire distress* as fyrenðearfe
18/14
fyrgenholt n. *mountain-wood* as 18(b)/1393

fyrgenstrēam m. *mountain stream* ns 18(b)/
1359; *mighty current* np fyrgenstrēamas
21/47
fyrhtu f. *horror, fear* dsf 9/77 [MnE fright]
fyrmest adj. (superl. of forma) *foremost, first*
nsm 3/187, 3/188, 3/191, 12/323; nsf
firmest 4/49; npm fyrmestan 4/149
fyrmest adv. *first of all* 3/189
fyrnġēar n. *bygone year* dp fyrngēarum
21/12
fyrnġeflit n. *ancient quarrel* ap fyrngeflitu
20/264
fyrst see first
fyrst m. *period, space* as 20/324
fȳsan 1 *send forth, shoot* pret. 3s fȳsde 12/
269; *hasten* pres. subj. 2p (w. refl. ēow)
20/189

gād f. *goad* as gāde 3/194; ds 3/15
Gadd pers. n. *Gadd* gp gaddes 12/287
ġegaderian 2 *gather* pret. 3s gegaderode
7/27, 7/42, etc.
gafeluc m. *spear, missile* dp gafelucum
4/212
gafol n. *tribute* as 7/22, 7/59, 7/65, 11(g)/2
(him on gafol *as a gift to himself*), gofol
12/61; ds gafolc 7/76, 12/32, 12/46
galan VI *sing, sound* inf. 14/67, 18(a)/786
[MnE (nightin)gale]
gālferhð adj. *lascivious* nsm 20/62
gālmōd adj. *lecherous* nsm gālmōda (as noun)
lecher 20/256
gamen see gomen
gamol adj. *old, aged, ancient* nsm gomela
18(b)/1397, gomol (as noun) *the old one*
21/11
gān anom. (§128) *go, walk* inf. 7/43, 12/247,
20/149; imp. p. gāð 12/93; pres. 1s gā
3/76; 2s gǣst 2/29; 3s gǣþ 6/43; 1p gāð (w.
refl. unc) 2/51; 3p 4/237; subj. 1s gā 3/99;
3s 18(b)/1394; pret. 1s ēode 9/30; 3s
2/17, 6/13, 9/23, etc.; 3p ēodon 4/232,
4/236, 6/28, 20/15, 20/55, etc.; subj. 3p
6/33, 12/229
ġegān see ġegongan
ganet m. *gannet* gs ganetes 17/20
gang m. *flow* ds gange 14/23; *track* as
18(b)/1391 [MnE gang, gang(ster)]
gangan see gongan
ġegangan see ġegongan
gār m. *spear* ns 12/296; as 12/13, 12/134,
12/154, etc.; ds gāre 12/138; ap gāras
12/46, 12/67, 12/109, 20/224, 21/22
[MnE gar(fish)]
gārberend m. *spear-bearer, warrior* np 12/
262
Gār-Dene np *Danes, Spear-Danes* gp Gār-
Dena 18/1

garġewinn n. *spear-fight, battle* gs garge-winnes 20/307
gārrǣs m. *storm of spears, battle* as 12/32
gāst m. *spirit, soul, angel* ns 4/61, gǣst 11(d)/9, 20/83, 20/112; as 9/123, 14/49; gs Gāstes 9/76, gǣstes 20/279; ds gāste 4/331, 12/176, gǣste 11(k)/8; np gāstas 14/11 (*angels*), 21/59; gp gāsta 14/152, 18(b)/1357 [MnE ghost]
gāstliċ adj. *spiritual* asn gāstlice 4/27; dsn gāstlicum 4/54 [MnE ghostly]
gāstlīċe adv. *spiritually, in the spiritual sense* 4/40, 4/44, etc.
gātehǣr n. *goat-hair* as 4/86
gatu see **ġeat**
gāð see **gān**
gǣlsa m. *lasciviousness* as gǣlsan 22/168
gǣst see **gān**
gǣst see **gāst**
gǣstliċ adj. *spectral, terrifying* nsn 16/73
gǣþ see **gān**
ġe conj. *and* 3/121, 3/166, 20/166; (ǣġðer) ġe . . . ġe *both* . . . *and* 2/11, 4/289, 5/37, etc.
ġē pron. (§21) *ye, you* np 1/13, 2/3, 2/8, 2/10, 3/161, 3/170, etc.; gp ēower 3/154, 3/177, 3/202; dp ēow 1/33, 2/3, 2/50 (refl.), 2/52, 3/137, 3/157, 3/190, īow 5/54
ġēac m. *cuckoo* ns 17/53
ġeador adv. *together* 18(a)/835, 19/19
ġeaf see **ġiefan**
ġeald see **ġieldan**
ġealga m. *gallows, cross* ns 14/10; as gealgan 14/40; dp gealgum 4/285
ġealgean see **ġeealgian**
ġealgtrēo n. *gallows-tree, cross* ds gealgtreowe 14/146
ġēap adj. *deceitful* compar. nsf gēappre 2/1
ġēap adj. *spacious, wide* nsm 13/11; asm gēapne 18(a)/836; *prominent* nsm 21/23
ġeġēap see **ġeġēopan**
ġēar n. *year* as 7/17; gs gēares 21/9; ds geare 4/154, 7/21, 7/47, 7/64, etc.; is 4/269, 7/1, 7/7, 7/10, 8/78; ap gēar 4/268; gp gēara 4/155, fela gēara *for many years* 22/6, 22/52, 22/117; dp gēarum 4/128, etc.
ġeāra adv. *long ago* 10(b)/1, 14/28 (geāra iu *years ago, very long ago*), 16/22 [archaic MnE (days of) yore]
ġearcian 2 *prepare* pres. 1s gearcie 3/152
ġeard m. *yard, enclosure* as 1/6; dp geardum (*precincts, palace grounds*) 18/13
ġeārdagas m. pl. *days gone by* dp geārdagum 16/44, 18(b)/1354, 18/1
ġeare adv. *readily* 8/42, gearwe 20/2; *clearly* geare 16/71; gearwe ne . . . *not at all* 18(a)/878; superl. gearwost 18(a)/715
ġēarmǣlum adv. *year by year* 10(b)/5

ġearo adj. *ready, prepared* nsm 6/18, 12/274; npm gearowe 12/72, 12/100; apm gearwe 3/127
ġearoðoncol adj. *ready-witted, wise* dsf gearo-ðoncolre 20/341
ġearwe see **ġearo** and **ġeare**
ġeġearwian 2 *prepare* pret. subj. 2s gegear-wode 9/95; p. ptc. gegearewod 20/199, gegearwod 22/183
ġeat n. *gate* as 20/151; ap gatu 2/76, 6/27, 6/36
Ġēatas m. pl. *the Geats* gp Gēata 18(d)/3178
Ġēatmæcgas m. pl. *men of the Geats* gp Gēatmecga 18(a)/829
ġefe see **ġiefu**
gegnum adv. *directly* 20/132
ġeman 1 *take heed* pret. 3s gēmde 9/81
ġēn adv. *yet* 8/39, 11(k)/2, 18(a)/734, 18(d)/3167
ġeō adv. *formerly, of old* iū 5/3, 10(b)/1, 13/32, 14/28 (see **ġeāra**), 14/87, giū 5/41, gū 8/72, etc.
ġēoc f. *help* ds gēoce 17/101
ġeocian 2 *yoke* inf. 3/9; p. ptc. gegeoced 3/11
ġeocor adj. *grievous, sad* nsm 18(a)/765
ġeofon m. or n. *sea, ocean,* gs gyfenes 18(b)/1394
ġeogoð see **ġioguð**
ġeoguðe see **ġioguð**
ġeoguðmyrþ f. *delight of the young* (*i.e. milk*) gs geoguðmyrþe 11(g)/2
ġeōmerunge see **ġeōmorung**
ġeōmor adj. *sad* nsm 15/17, 20/87; dsf geōmorre 15/1, geōmran 17/53; dsm geōmran 10(b)/84
ġeōmormōd adj. *sad-minded, serious* nsm 15/42; ds geōmormōdum 20/144
ġeōmorung f. *sadness* ds geōmerunge 4/293
ġeond prep. w.a. *through, throughout* 4/63, 4/148, 4/233, 4/330, 7/62, 15/36, 16/3, giond 5/3, 5/30, gynd 22/11, 22/40, etc. [MnE (be)yond]
ġeondhweorfan III *pervade, visit every part* pres. 3s geondhweorfeð 16/51
ġeondscēawian 2 *survey, examine every part* pres. 3s geondscēawað 16/52
ġeondþenċean 1 *meditate on, ponder every part* pres. 1s geondþence 16/60; 3s geondþenceð 16/89
ġeong adj. *young* nsm 4/131, 11(j)/2, 12/210, 14/39, 15/42, etc., as noun geonga 12/155; as geongne 21/14; nsf 11(p)/1; npm geonge 20/166; *handmaid, attendant* compar. dsf gingran 20/132
ġeġēopan II *take to oneself, receive, swallow* pret. 1s gegēap 11(h)/9

ġeorn adj. w.g. *eager* nsm 10(b)/51, 12/107, 16/69, 20/210; npm georne 12/73, giorne 5/10

ġeorne adv. *eagerly, zealously, readily* 4/295, 12/123, 12/206, 12/84, 16/52, 20/8, 22/9, 22/17, ful georne *full well, all too well* 22/17, etc.; compar. geornor 3/70, 18(a)/821; superl. geornost *most surely* 22/159

ġeornful adj. *eager* nsm 12/274

ġeornfulnes f. *desire* ds geornfulnesse 9/82 [MnE yearnfulness]

ġeornlīċe adv. *eagerly, zealously* 3/211, 9/81, 12/265; compar. geornlīcor 8/21, 8/40, 8/43

ġēotan II *pour* inf. 13/42

gēsne adj. *dead* nsm 20/112; *deprived* w.g. asm 20/279

ġidda see ġiedd

ġiedd n. *word, speech, riddle* as 15/1, gied 11(c)/3; gs gieddes 11(n)/14; gp gidda 18(a)/868; *song*, fig. *harmonious relationship* as 19/19

ġieddian 2 *sing, recite* pret. 3s gyddode 10(b)/84

ġiefan V *give* pres. subj. 3s gife 19/1; pret. 3s geaf 1/1

ġiefstōl m. *throne* gs giefstolas 16/44

ġiefu f. *gift* ns 1/30, gifu 9/55; as gyfe 8/46, gife 9/14, 9/49, etc.; ds 9/2; ap gefe 8/17; gp gifena 17/40 (see note), 20/2; dp gifum 4/272

ġieldan III *pay, render, reward, repay* inf. gyldan 18/11; pres. 1p gyldað 22/12; subj. 3s gylde 22/94; pret. 3s geald 7/22, 7/63 [MnE yield]

ġiellan III *cry out* pres. 3s gielleð 17/62; pret. 3s gylede 20/25 [MnE yell]

ġielpes see ġyip

ġiernan 1 *yearn* pret. 3s gyrnde 20/346; *entreat, beg for* 3p gyrndon (w.g.) 7/65

ġiese adv. *yes* 3/15, 3/18, 3/21, 3/113, etc.

ġiestrandæġ m. *yesterday* ns 3/53

ġīet adv. *yet, still* 1/1, 2/70, gīt 4/17, gȳt 8/71, etc., gȳta 14/28; þā gȳt *still* 4/218, 12/168, etc.

ġif conj. *if* 2/23, 3/79, 3/118, 3/170, 4/9, gyf 4/21, etc.

ġife see ġiefu

ġifena see ġiefu

ġīfernes f. *greed, greedy deed* ap gīfernessa 22/120

ġifeðe adj. *given, granted by fate* nsm gyfeþe 18(a)/819, gifeðe 20/157

ġifheall f. *gift-hall* as gifhealle 18(a)/838

ġifre adj. *greedy, ravenous* nsm 17/62

ġifum see ġiefu

Gildas m. ns 22/160

ġilp see ġylp

ġilphladen adj. *covered with glory, proud* nsm 18(a)/868

ġimm m. *gem* ns gim 21/22; np gimmas 14/7, 14/16; ap 3/142

ġimstān m. *jewel* ap gimstanas 4/85 [MnE gemstone]

ġingran see ġeong

ġinn adj. *spacious, wide* dsm ginnan 20/2; dsf 20/149

ġioguð f. *young people, youth* ns 5/58; ds geoguðe 16/35, 17/40

ġiōmonn n. *man of yore* gp giōmonna 10(b)/23

ġiond see ġeond

ġiorne see ġeorn

girwan see ġyrwan

ġīsl m. *hostage* ns gȳsel 12/265; ds gīsle 6/21

ġit see ġiet

ġītsung f. *coveting, act of avarice* as gītsunge 22/164; ap gītsunga 22/120

ġiū see ġeō

glæd adj. *kind, gracious* asm glædne 18(a)/863 [MnE glad]

glædlīċe adv. *joyfully* 9/103 [MnE gladly]

glædmōd adj. *joyous* nsm 13/33; npf glædmōde 20/140 [MnE glad, mood]

geglæng̣de see glengan

glæs n. *glass* ns 1/4, as 3/142

glēaw adj. *wise, clear-sighted* nsm 10(b)/52, 16/73; nsf 20/13, glēawe 20/171; asf 20/333; compar. nsm glēawra 11(c)/6

glēawhȳdig adj. *wise, prudent* nsn 20/148

glēd f. *ember, burning coal* ns 11(o)/4 [MnE gleed]

glengan 1 *adorn* pret. 3s geglæng̣de 9/7, p. ptc. geglenged 9/60

glēobēam m. *harp* gs glēobēames 18(c)/2263

gleomu f. *splendour* ds gleoma 13/33

glēowian 2 *make merry, joke* pres. ptc. glēowiende 9/99

glīwstafum adv. *joyfully* 16/52

gnornian 2 *mourn, feel sorrow* inf. 12/315; pres. 3s gnornað 17/92

gōd adj. *good* nsm 1/10, 17/40, gōda 18(a)/758 (as noun); asm gōdne 10(b)/42, gōdan 12/187 (as noun); dsm gōdum 12/4; asn gōd 12/13; asf gōde 4/89, 14/70 (gōde hwīle *a long while*); npm 3/206, 4/306; apm 3/179; gpm gōdena 5/41, gōdra 10(b)/45; gpf gōdra 9/82; dpn gōdum 4/42; *stout, brave* asm gōdne 22/104

God m. *God* ns 1/10, 1/35, 2/2, 2/3, 2/55, 4/52, etc.; as 2/64, etc.; gs Godes 2/19, 2/61, 3/188, etc.; ds Gode 2/68, 4/242, 4/291, 4/299, 5/11, etc.

god n. (*pagan*) *god* np godo 8/19; gp goda 8/16

gōd n. *good, goodness, goods* as 2/11; gs gōdes 12/176; dp gōdum 9/64; *good thing* (i.e. *human faculty*) gōda 20/32; *good effect, success* ds gōde 20/271; *good deeds* inst. s. 18/20

Goda pers. n. *Goda* ns 7/14

godbearn n. *godchild* ap 22/69 [MnE god, bairn]

godcund adj. *divine, religious* gsf godcundre 9/56; dsf 9/2; npm godcundan 5/10; gpm godcundra 5/4; dpm godcundum 9/4; dpf godcundan 9/79

godcundlīce adv. *divinely* 9/13

godcundnes f. *divinity, Godhead* gs godcundnesse 8/10

gōddǣd f. *good deed* dp gōddǣdan 22/134; gp gōddǣda 22/135

godfyrht adj. *godfearing* as noun *fear of God* as godfyrhte 22/135 [MnE godfright]

gōdian 2 *improve* pres. ptc. gōdiende 22/16

ġegōdian 2 *endow* pret. 3s gegōdode 4/272

Gōdmundingahām m. *Goodmanham (Yorkshire)* ns 8/74

Godrīċ pers. n. *Godric* ns 12/187, 12/237, 12/321, 12/325

godsib m. *sponsor (at baptism)* ap godsibbas 22/69 [MnE gossip]

godspell n. *gospel* as godspel 4/35; ds godspelle 3/189

godsunu m. *godson* ns 6/39

Godwig pers. n. *Godwig* ns 12/192

Godwine pers. n. *Godwin* ns 7/44; 12/192

gofol see gafol

gold n. *gold* ns 1/4, 16/32, 17/101; as 3/142, 4/87, 11(l)/7, 11(n)/3, 14/18; ds golde 4/272, 12/35, 14/7, 14/16, 14/77, 17/97, etc.; is 11(j)/2, 20/17, 20/328, 20/338

goldbeorht adj. *bright with gold* nsm 13/33

goldġiefa m. *gold-giver, lord* as goldgifan 20/279; np goldgiefan 17/83

goldhilted adj. *gold-hilted* asn 11(n)/14

goldhord m. *hoard of gold, treasure* ap goldhordas 4/165

goldsele m. *gold-hall* as 18(a)/715

goldsmiþ m. *goldsmith* ap goldsmiþas 3/181

goldwine m. *generous lord* ns 16/35, 20/22; as 16/22

gombe f. *tribute* as gomban 18/11

gomela see gamol

gomelfeax adj. *hoary-haired* as noun nsm 17/92

gomen n. *entertainment, pastime, sport, mirth* ns 18(c)/2263; gs gamenes 4/213; ds gomene 17/20 [MnE game]

gomenwāþ f. *joyous journey* ds gomenwāþe 18(a)/854

gomol see gamol

gongan VII *go, walk* inf. 9/90, 11(b)/1, 18(a)/711, gangan 12/3, 12/40, 12/62, 12/170; pres. ptc. gongende 9/24, 9/94; pres. 1s gonge 15/35; subj. 2p gangon 12/56; pret. 3s gang 18(b)/1316

ġegongan VII *get, obtain, overrun* inf. 10(b)/12, gegangan 12/59; p. ptc. gegongen 18(a)/822, 18(a)/893; *go* inf. gegangan 20/54; pret. 3p geēodon 20/332; p. ptc. gegān 20/140, 20/219

Gota m. *Goth* ns 10(b)/9, 10(b)/45; np Gotan 10(a)/1, 10(b)/1; ap 10(b)/23; gp Gotena 10(b)/5, 10(b)/38

gram adj. *fierce, hostile* gsm grames 18(a)/765; npm grame 12/262, 20/224, 20/238; graman 18(a)/777; as noun dpm gramum 12/100

Grantabriċscir f. *Cambridgeshire* as Grantabricscire 7/68

grāp f. *grasp, claw* gs grāpe 18(a)/836; dp grāpum 18(a)/765

grǣdiġ adj. *greedy* nsm 4/242, 17/62, nsf 11(g)/2

græf n. *grave* as 17/97

grǣg adj. *grey* nsm grǣga 4/241

Gregōrius pers. n. *Gregory* ns 4/304

gremian 2 *enrage* p. ptc. nsm gegremod 12/138; npm gegremode 12/296, gegremede 20/305

Grendel pers. n. *Grendel* ns 18(a)/711, 18(a)/819; as 18(b)/1334, 18(b)/1354; gs Grendles 18(a)/836, 18(b)/1391

grēne adj. *green, raw* apf 3/171

grēot n. *dirt, dust* as 20/307; ds grēote 12/315, 18(d)/3167 [MnE grit]

grēotan II *weep* pres. ptc. grēotende np 14/70; pres. 3s grēoteþ 18(b)/1342

grēt see grētan

grētan 1 *greet, approach, touch* inf. 5/1, 18(a)/803 (*harm*); pres. 3s grēt 4/2, grēteð 16/52; pret. 3s grētte 9/27

grim adj. *fierce* nsm 12/61; np grimme 22/129 [MnE grim]

grimlic adj. *terrible* nsn 22/4

grimme adv. *grimly, fiercely* 11(m)/9, 12/109, 13/14

grīn n. *snare* dp grīnum 3/110

grindan III *grind, sharpen* p. ptc. gegrunden 13/14; apm gegrundene 12/109

gripe m. *grasp* ns 13/8

gristbītian 2 *gnash (the teeth)* inf. 20/271

grið n. *truce* as 7/75, 12/35, ds griðe 7/76; *sanctuary* ds griðe 22/72

griðian 2 *protect* inf. 22/30

griðlēas adj. *unprotected* npf griðlēase 22/33

grund m. *ground, earth, bottom* as 12/287, 18(b)/1367, 18(b)/1394; dsm grunde 20/2; ap grundas 17/104, 20/348

*ġe*grundene see grindan
grymetian 2 *roar, rage* pret. 3s grymetode 4/302
gryrelēoð n. *song of terror, terrible song* as 18(a)/786; gp gryrelēoða 12/285
ġū see ġeō
guma m. *man* ns 16/45, 18/20, 18(a)/868, 18(b)/1384; gs guman 14/49; np 12/94, 20/305; gp gumena 11(h)/10, 18(a)/715, 18(a)/878, 18(b)/1367, 20/9, 20/22, 20/32, etc., guman 14/146 (see note)
gumena see guma
gūð f. *war, battle* as gūðe 12/325; gs 10(b)/9, 12/192; ds 10(b)/23, 12/13, 12/94, 12/187, 20/123, 20/306, etc.
gūðbill n. *war-sword* gp gūðbilla 18(a)/803
gūðdēað m. *death in battle* ns 18(c)/2249
gūðfana m. *battle standard* dp gūðfanum 20/219
gūðfreca m. *warrior* ns 20/62; np gūðfrecan 20/224
gūðhrēð n. *glory in battle* ns 18(a)/819
gūðplega m. *the game of battle, conflict* ns 12/61
gūðrinc m. *warrior* ns 12/138, 18(a)/838
gūðsceorp n. *armour* as 20/328
ġyddode see ġieddian
ġyf see ġif
ġyfe see ġiefu
ġyfenes see ġeofon
ġyfeþe see ġifeþe
ġyldað, ġylde see ġieldan
gylede see ġiellan
ġylp m. *boasting, pride* as gilp 18(a)/829; gs gylpes 10(b)/9, gielpes 16/69 [MnE yelp]
ġylpword n. *boasting word* dp gylpwordum 12/274
ġȳman 1 w.g. *care about, care for, heed* pres. subj. 3s gȳme 22/20; pret. 3p gȳmdon 12/192
ġynd see ġeond
Gypeswīċ m. *Ipswich* ns 7/20
gyrdan 1 *gird* pret. 3s gyrde 8/64
gyrndon see ġiernan
ġyrwan 1 *adorn, prepare, dress* inf. girwan 20/9; pret. 3p gyredon 14/77; p. ptc. gegyred 14/16, gegyrwed 14/23
ġȳsel see ġīsl
gyst m. *stranger* np gystas 12/86 [MnE guest]
gystern n. *guest-hall* ds gysterne 20/40
ġystran adv. *yesterday* 18(b)/1334
ġȳt(a) see ġīet

habban 3 *have, hold* inf. 2/58, 3/119, 3/172, 4/112 (*keep*), etc.; pres. 1s hæbbe 3/11, 3/12, 3/15, 3/23, 8/13; 2s hæfst 3/14, 3/17, 3/22, 3/112, 3/180, hafast 12/231; 3s hæfþ 3/193, 4/100, 4/163,

etc., hafað 8/14, 13/6, etc.; 1p habbað 5/37, etc.; 3p 22/107, 22/137; subj. 3s hæbbe 4/104, 4/164; 3p hæbben 3/128, 5/59; pret. 3s hæfde 4/6, 4/14, 6/7, 8/8, etc.; 1p hæfdon 8/15; 3p 4/20, 4/36, 4/229, 6/16, etc., hæfdan 10(b)/6; subj. 8/20, 9/101. With negative: pres. 2s næfst 4/167, 4/177; 3s næfð 4/114; 3p nabbað 4/102; subj. 3s næbbe 17/42; pret. 3p næfdon 4/228
hacod m. *pike* ap hacodas 3/87 [MnE haked]
hād m. *office, order* as 18(b)/1335 (*manner*); ds hāde 5/63; np hādas 5/10; gp hāda 5/4 [MnE (mother)hood, (child)hood]
hādian 2 *ordain* p. ptc. *ordained (ones), clerics* npm gehādode 22/56; dpm gehādodum 4/289
*ge*hādode, *ge*hādodum see hādian
hafast see habban
hafela m. *head* as hafelan 18(b)/1327, ds 18(b)/1372
hafenian 2 *raise aloft* pret. 3s hafenode 12/42, 12/309
hafoc m. *hawk* ns 18(c)/2263, hafuc 21/17; as 3/117, 3/118, 12/8; ds hafoce 3/111; ap hafocas 3/112, 3/114, 3/120, 3/124
hagle see hægl
hagostealdmon m. *bachelor, warrior* ns 11(j)/2
hāl adj. *safe, unhurt* asm hālne 4/313; npm hāle 12/292 [MnE hale, whole]
*ge*hāl adj. *whole, intact* nsm 4/94, 4/257
hālettan 1 *hail* pret. 3s hālette 9/27
hālgian 2 *consecrate* pret. 1p hālgodon 8/48; p. ptc. gehālgod 7/1, gehālgade 8/6, gehālgode 8/75 [MnE hallow]
hālian 2 *heal* p. ptc. gehālod 4/258
hāliġ adj. *holy* nsm 9/41, Hālga 4/63, 4/280; asm hālgan 4/256, 4/300; gsm 4/224; dsm 4/304, 4/331; asn hālige 4/34, 4/244, hālig 9/56; gsn hālgan 9/66, 9/74; dsn 4/248, 4/309; nsf hālige 7/52; asf hālgan 20/260; dsf hāligre 20/98, hāligan 4/248, 4/309; npm 14/11, hālgan 4/288; apm 10(b)/25; apf hālgan 4/89; as noun m. *saint* ns hālga 4/316, 4/319; nsf hālige 20/160; as hālgan 4/218; gs 4/267; ds 4/253, 4/274, 4/299, 4/314; Hālgan (*God*) 17/122; np 4/322; ap 4/324; gpm hālgena 4/318; dpm hālgum 14/143, 14/154
hāliġdōm m. *relics* ds hāligdome 4/270
hāliġnes f. *religion* gs hālignesse 8/53, 8/62 [MnE holiness]
*ge*hālod see hālian
hals m. *neck* as 12/141
hālwende adj. *salutary, salvific* apn 9/121
hām adv. *homewards, home* 2/78, 4/135, 4/244, 9/23, 12/251

hām m. *home* as 14/148, 17/117, 18(a)/717, ds (or locative) hām 3/10, hāme 12/292, 20/121, 20/131

Hamtūn m. *Southampton* ds Hamtūne 7/61

Hamtūnscīr f. *Hampshire* as Hamtūnscīre 7/73; ds 6/2, 7/13, 7/57

Hāmtūnscīr f. *Northamptonshire* ds Hāmtūnscīre 7/70

hand f. *hand* ns 12/141, 18(b)/1343; as 2/63, 12/112, hond 8/64, 17/96, 18(a)/834, 20/130, 20/198; ds handa 12/149, 14/59, 18(a)/746, 21/21, honda 9/104, 9/123, 18(a)/814; ap handa 4/111, 4/191, honda 11(b)/5, 16/43; dp handum 12/4, 12/14, hondum 11(o)/5, 16/4, handon 12/7

handbona m. *slayer with the hand* ds handbanan 18(b)/1330

handscalu f. *hand-troop, companions* ds handscale 18(b)/1317

hangian 2 *hang* inf. 21/55; pres. 1s hongige 11(j)/11; 3p hongiað 18(b)/1363; pret. 3p hangodon 4/283

hār adj. *hoary, grey, grey-haired* nsm 12/169, 18(b)/1307, hāra 16/82; asm hārne 13/43, 18(a)/887; *metallic grey* apf hāre 20/327

hara m. *hare* ap haran 3/51

hās adj. *hoarse* nsm 3/16

hāt n. *heat* ds hāte 13/38 (see note)

hāt adj. *hot* nsm hāt 18(a)/897; dsm hāton 18(a)/849; npn 13/41; npf 17/11; npm hāte 13/43; 13/45; compar. hātra npm hātran 17/64; superl. hātost 21/7

ġehāt n. *promise* ap 10(a)/9

hātan VII *command, order, call, name* pres. 1s hāte 5/2, 14/95; 3s hæt 4/164, hāteð 5/1; 1p hāteð 10(a)/12; passive *be called, was called* hātte is 11(f)/15, 11(h)/16, 11(j)/19, 11(b)/7, 11(j)/19; 3s 4/128, 10(b)/53, 11(n)/16, 22/160; pret. 3s hēt 2/52, 2/69 (*named*), 4/216, 4/285, 4/300, 7/32, 9/52, 20/9 (*summoned*), 20/32, 20/147, 20/171, etc., hēht 8/70, 9/50, 9/65, 10(b)/70, etc.; 3p hēton 12/30, 14/31; subj. 3s hēte 20/53; p. ptc. gehāten 4/48, 4/267, 4/298, 10(a)/13, hāten 6/8, 12/75, 12/218; np hātne 10(a)/3 [archaic MnE hight]

ġehātan VII *promise, vow* pres. 1s gehāte 12/246, 18(b)/1392; pret. 3s gehēt 10(a)/7 10(b)/35, 12/289

hāte adv. *hotly* 20/94

hātheort adj. *angry, impulsive* nsm 16/66 [MnE hotheart(ed)]

ġehātland n. *promised land* gs gehātlandes 9/73

hātte see hātan

hæbbe see habban

hæfde see habban

hæfdon see habban

hæfst see habban

hæft m. *captive* asm hæfton 18(a)/788

hæft m. *warfare* (?), *sword* (?) is hæfte 20/263

ġehæftan 1 *catch, hold captive* pres. 3p gehæftaþ 3/78; p. ptc. asm gehæft 2/67; nsf 7/4; p. ptc. gehæfted 20/116

hæfþ see habban

hæġl m. *hail* ns 17/17, 17/32; ds hagle 16/48

hæġlfaru f. *hailstorm* as hæglfare 16/105

hǣlan 1 *heal, save* inf. 14/85; p. ptc. npf gehǣlede 4/262

hæle m. *warrior, man* ns 10(b)/53, 16/73

Hǣlend m. *Saviour* (lit. *Healer*) gs Hǣlen-des 4/203, 14/25; ds Hǣlende 4/195, 4/210

hæleþ m. *hero, warrior, man* ns 14/39, 14/78, 14/95; np 11(f)/5, 11(n)/1, 12/214, 18(c)/2247, 20/56, 20/177, 20/203, 20/225, 20/302, hælæð 12/249; ap hæleð 20/247; gp hæleða 11(d)/3, 12/74, 20/51; dp hæleþum 16/105, 18(c)/2262, 21/8

hǣlo f. *luck* as hæle 18(a)/719; *salvation* gs 8/46 [obs. MnE heal]

ġehæp adj. *suitable* dsf gehæpre 3/42 [MnE hap(py)]

hæpse f. *hasp, door-fastener* as hæpsan 4/277

hærfest m. *autumn* ns 21/8; as 3/122 [MnE harvest]

hǣring m. *herring* ap hǣringas 3/93

hærliċ adj. *noble* nsf 10(b)/43

hǣs f. *behest, command* as hǣse 4/201; gs 2/77

hǣste adj. *violent* asm hǣstne 18(b)/1335

Hǣstingas m. pl. *Hastings* (*Sussex*) ap 7/72

hǣt see hātan

hǣð f. *heath* ds hǣðe 21/29

hǣþen adj. *heathen* asm hǣðenan 20/98, 20/110; gsm hǣðenes 20/179; dsm hǣþenum 4/194, 4/221; npm hǣðene 12/181; apm 22/121; gpm hǣðenra 20/216; asf hǣþene 18(a)/852; dpf hǣþenum 22/21, 22/24; as noun npm hǣþenan 4/211, 4/217, 4/218, 4/261, hæþene 12/55

hǣþstapa m. *heath-stalker, stag* ns 18(b)/1368

hē, hēo, hit pron (§18) *he, she, it* pl. *they* nsm hē (*he*) 1/12, 1/19, 1/33, 2/14, etc.; asm hine (*him*) 1/34, 2/18 (refl.), 2/45, 3/60, 3/61, 6/14 (refl.), etc., hiene 5/23, 6/3, etc.; gsm his 1/1, 1/2, 1/3, 1/29, etc.; dsm him 2/55, 2/56, 2/76, etc.; nsn hit (*it*) 3/21, 3/53, etc., hyt 18(d)/3168; asn 2/58, 4/130, 4/294, etc.; nsf hēo (*she*) 1/9, 1/21, 1/30, 2/26, 2/32, hīo 5/81; asf hīe 5/49, 5/80, hī 4/315, etc.; gsf hire (*her*) 2/14, 2/32, 7/52, etc.; dsf 2/12, 9/50, etc.; np hīe (*they*) 1/26, 1/32, 2/15, 2/17,

2/48, 2/49, 2/56, 3/42, 3/43, 3/121, hī
4/26, 4/129, 7/49, hȳ 19/2, 19/7, hig
4/40, 4/41, hēo 9/55, 9/104, 9/106,
etc.; ap hīe (*them*) 3/19, 3/25, 3/26, 3/
30, 3/121 (refl.), 3/123, 3/161, hī 4/310,
7/53; gp hira (*their*) 1/26, 2/14, 2/76,
3/84, heora 4/148, 4/226, hiora 5/7,
5/18, 7/66, hiera 6/19, hyra 11(a)/3; dp
him (*them*) 2/16, 3/180, 4/143, 5/36,
19/1, heom 7/57, etc.
hēa see **hēah**
hēafod n. *head* ns 20/110; as 2/32, 4/219,
4/223, 4/238, 9/116, 16/43, 20/126,
20/173, 20/179; gs hēafdes 4/243; ds
hēafde 4/227, 4/246, 10(b)/43; dp hēafdum
14/63 (w. ds meaning: see note); gp heafda
11(b)/4
hēafodġerīm m. *muster-role* gs hēafod-
gerīmes 20/308
hēafodlēas adj. *headless* nsm 11(j)/10
hēafodman m. *leader* ds hēafodmen 4/142;
np 4/149 [MnE headman]
hēafodweard m. *leader* np hēafodweardas
20/239
hēagum see **hēah**
hēah adj. *high* nsm 16/98, 18(d)/3157;
nsn 13/22; nsf hēa 11(d)/4; asm hēanne
14/40, 16/82, 20/161; dsm hēan 18(a)/
713, dsn 20/43; apm hēan 17/34; dpm
hēagum 4/285; compar. hīerra (§75) dsm
hīerran 5/63; superl. nsm hēhsta 20/
94, hȳhsta (*great*) 20/308; gsm hēhstan
20/4
hēahburg f. *chief city* ns 10(a)/21
hēahfæder m. *patriarch* ds hēahfædere 4/15;
14/134 (*God the father*)
healdan VII *keep, observe, hold, stand firm*
inf. 4/270, 12/14, 12/19, 12/41 (w.d. of
person and g. of thing), 12/74, etc.,
healdon 10(b)/71; infl. inf. (tō) healdenne
4/109; pres. 3s hylt 4/313; 3p healdaþ
17/87; subj. 3s healde 16/14 (*keep closed*);
pret. 3s hēold 4/243, 11(k)/5 (*foster,
cherish*), 18(a)/788; 3p hēoldon 20/142,
hīoldon 5/34 (*occupied*); subj. 3p hēoldon
12/20
*ġe*healdan VII *hold, maintain, preserve* inf.
12/167; pres. 3s ġehealdeþ 16/112, subj.
1s ġehealde 3/161; pret. 3p gehīoldon 5/8;
p. ptc. gehealden 4/220
healdend m. *ruler, lord* ns 20/289
healf adj. *half* asm healfne 20/105; asf healfe
7/69
healf f. *side* (w.d. of person) as healfe 14/20;
ds 4/140, 12/152, 12/318, 18(c)/2262; gp
healfa 18(a)/800
heall f. *hall* ns 8/29; ds healle 4/203, 11(n)/1,
11(n)/13, 12/214, 21/28, 21/36

healðegn m. *hall-thane* ap healðegnas
18(a)/719
healwudu m. *wood of a hall* ns 18(b)/1317
hēan adj. *dejected, wretched, lowly* nsm 16/23;
asm hēanne 20/234
hēanliċ adj. *humiliating, shameful* nsn 12/55
hēanne see **hēah**
hēap m. *band, multitude* as 18(a)/730; dp
hēapum 20/163 [MnE heap]
heard adj. *hard, resolute, bitter, fierce, brave*
nsm 11(j)/10, 12/130, 13/8, 15/43, 18(a)/
886 hearda 11(n)/9, 18(c)/2255; asn hearde
18(b)/1343, heard 12/214; asm heardne
12/167, 12/236; asf hearde 12/33; gsn
heardes 12/266; gp heardra (*cruel ones*)
20/225; dp heardum 4/208; dpm 18(b)/
1335, *sturdy, sharp* 20/263; compar. heardra
nsm 12/312, heardran asf 18(a)/719; superl.
heardost nsn 14/87
hearde adv. *firmly, fully* 20/116, 20/216
heardhicgende adj. *brave-minded* npm
18(a)/799
heardlīċe adv. *fiercely* 12/261 [MnE hardly]
heardsæliġ adj. *unfortunate, unhappy, ill-
fated* asm heardsæligne 15/19
hearm m. *damage, harm, grief, sorrow* ns 7/8;
as 7/50; gp hearma 12/223
hearmscaþa m. *pernicious enemy* ns 18(a)/
766
hearpe f. *harp* as hearpan 9/22; gs 18(c)/
2262, ds 9/21, 17/44
hearra m. *lord* ds hearran 20/56 [German
Herr]
heaþodēor adj. *brave in battle* dpm heaþodēorum 18(a)/772
heaðorinc m. *warrior* gs heaðorinces 20/179;
np heaðorincas 20/212
heaðorōf adj. *brave in battle* npm heaþorōfe
18(a)/864
hēawan VII *hew, cut down, kill* inf. 18(a)/800;
pres. 3s hēaweþ 22/61; pret. 3s hēow
12/324; 3p hēowon 12/181, 20/303; p.
ptc. gehēawen 13/12
*ġe*hēawan VII *kill* inf. 20/90; p. ptc.
gehēawen (*hack, cut down*) 20/288, 20/
294
hebban VI *raise up, lift* inf. 14/31 [MnE heave]
hēdærn n. *storeroom* as 3/160
hefian see **hefiġ**
hefiġ adj. *heavy, oppressive* dsn hefian 14/61;
compar. npf hefigran 16/49
hefiġan 2 *weigh down, burden* p. ptc. hefgad
9/89
hefigtīme adj. *burdensome, troubling* nsn 4/4
heġe m. *fence, enclosure* dp hegum 8/54
[MnE hedge]
hēhsta see **hēah**
hēht see **hātan**

hell f. *hell* ns hel 18(a)/852; gs helle 4/80, 18(a)/788, 22/182
hellebryne m. *hell-fire* ds 20/116
helm m. *protection, cover, helmet* ns 18(b)/1321 (*lord*), 18(c)/2255; as 18(b)/1392, 20/337; ap helmas 20/193, 20/317, 20/327; dp helmum 20/203
help f. *help* as helpe 16/16; ds 14/102, 20/96
helpan 111 w.g. *help* subj. pres. 3s helpe 22/184
helsceaða m. *thief from hell, devil* np helsceaðan 12/180
helwaru f. pl. *inhabitants of hell* gp helwara 11(n)/6
*ġe***hende** prep. w.d. *near to, beside* 12/294; adv. gehende *nearby* 4/220, superl. gehendost 4/169
hēo see **hē**
heofon m. *heaven* as 9/41, heofenan 4/52, 4/56; gs heofenes 14/64; ap heofonas 9/76, 14/103; gp heofona 14/45; dp heofonum 2/62, 2/75, 12/172, 14/85, 14/134, etc.
heofonlić adj. *heavenly* asm heofonlicne 14/148, heofonlican 4/262; dsm 4/330; asn heofonlice 7/26; gsn heofonlican 9/9, heofonlecan 9/78; isn heofonlecan 9/111; nsf heofonlic 9/55; dsf heofonlicre 2/79
heofonrīċe n. *kingdom of heaven* gs heofonrīces 9/36, 14/91
heold see **healdan**
heolfor m. or n. *blood, gore* ds heolfre 18(a)/849
heolfrig adj. *gory* asn 20/130, 20/316
heolstor adj. *dark* dsm heolstran 20/121
heolstor m. *darkness, hiding-place* as 18(a)/755; ds heolstre 16/23 [MnE holster]
heom (= him) see **hē**
heonanforð adv. *henceforth* 22/16, 22/20
heonon adv. *hence, from here* 12/246, 14/132, 15/6, 17/37, 18(b)/1361
heora (= hira) see **hē**
heord f. *care, custody* ns 9/25 [MnE herd]
hēore adj. *safe, pleasant, good* nsf hēoru 18(b)/1372
heorodrēor m. *battle-blood* ds heorodrēore 18(a)/849
heorot m. *deer, stag* ns 18(b)/1369; ap heorotas 3/51, 3/56, 3/58 [MnE hart]
Heorot m. *Heorot* ds Heorute 18(a)/766, Heorote 18(b)/1330
heorra m. *lord* ns 12/204
heorte f. *heart* ns 12/312, 20/87; as heortan 17/11; ds 12/145; gs 15/43, 16/49, 17/34 ap 3/166, 4/63
Heortfordscīr f. *Hertfordshire* as Heortfordscīre 7/68
heorðġenēat m. *hearth-companion, retainer* np heorðgenēatas 12/204, 18(d)/3179

heorðwerod n. *body of household retainers* as 12/24
heoruwǣpen n. *sword* dp heoruwǣpnum 20/263
hēow see **hēawan**
hēr adv. *here* 1/1, 2/50, 2/54, 3/144, etc.
hēran see **hīeran**
hēræfter adv. *hereafter* (i.e. *in the following pages*) 4/134
hērbūend m. *dweller on earth* gp hērbūendra 20/96 [MnE here]
here m. *invading army* ns 7/34, 7/41; as 7/31, 22/162; gs heriges 20/293; ds herige 20/135; *host, army* ns here 20/161; *devastation* ns 22/47, 22/98
herefolc n. *army* gs herefolces 20/234, 20/239
hereġeatu f. *heriot, war-equipment* as 12/48
hereġian see **heriġean**
herehūð f. *booty, plunder* gs herehūðe 7/40
herenes f. *praise* ds herenesse 9/34, herenisse 9/122
herepād f. *coat of mail* ns 18(c)/2258
hererēaf n. *booty* as 20/316
hererinc m. *soldier, hero* as 10(b)/71
heresweġ m. *noise of an army, martial sound* ns 13/22
heretēma m. *ruler* ns 10(b)/31
heretoga m. *military leader, commander* ns 10(b)/47, heretoha 10(a)/12; ds heretogan 4/194; np 7/43
hēreð see **hīeran**
herewǣða m. *warrior* gs herewǣðan 20/126, 20/173
herġas see **heriġ**
herġen see **heriġean**
herġian 2 *ravage* inf. heregian 22/139; pres. ptc. npm herġiende 4/148; pret. 3p hergodon 7/11, heregodon 7/77; p. ptc. gehergod 7/5, 7/20, geheregod 7/14 [MnE harry]
herġung f. *ravaging, harrying* ns 4/251; ds hergunge 7/55, 7/60
herheard m. *abode in a grove* as 15/15
heriġ m. *pagan sanctuary, fane* as 8/71; ds herige 8/68; np hergas 13/29; ap 8/54
heriġean 1 *praise* inf. 9/36; pres. subj. 3s herge 18(d)/3175, 3p hergen 17/77
herpað m. *passage for an army, inroad* as 20/302
hērtōēacen adv. *besides* 22/154
hēt see **hātan**
hetelīċe adv. *violently, excessively* 22/88
heteþoncol adj. *hateful* asm heteðoncolne 20/105
hetol adj. *hostile, hate-filled* npm hetole 22/129

hō see hē

hicgan 3 *think, plan, be intent upon* inf. 12/4 (see note), hycgan 15/11, 17/117; pres. ptc. asm hycgendne 15/20; pres. subj. 3s hycge 16/14

hider adv. *hither* 3/137, 3/140, 12/57, 14/103, 21/64, hieder 5/12

hīe see hē

hieder see hider

hīeg n. *hay* ds hīege 3/19

hiene (= hine) see hē

hiera see hē

hīeran 1 w.d. *obey, hearken to, hear* inf. hēran 10(b)/31, hȳran 11(h)/15; 3s hēreð 11(m)/5; pret. 1s hȳrde 8/21; 18(b)/1346; 1p hȳrdon 9/125; 3s hȳrde 18(a)/875

ġehīeran 1 *hear* inf. gehīran 4/32, gehȳran 8/40, 14/78, 20/24; infl. inf. (tō) gehȳranne 9/69; pres. 2s gehȳrst 12/45, gehȳrest 19/16; 3s gehȳrð 4/9; pret. 1s gehīerde 2/21, gehȳrde 12/117, 14/26, 17/18; 2s gehīerdest 2/36; 3s gehȳrde 4/221, 8/1, 8/41, etc.; 3p gehīerdon 2/17, gehīerdun 6/23, gehȳrdon 4/309, 18(a)/785, 20/160, gehȳrdan 22/171

hierdebōc f. *shepherd book* as 5/68

hīerran see hēah

hīersumian 2 *be obedient, obey* pret. 3p hīersumedon 5/6

ġehīersumian 2 *obey* pret. 2s gehīersumodest (w.g.) 2/77

ġehīersumnes f. *obedience* gs gehīersumnesse 2/43

hiġ (= hīe) see hē

hiġe m. *mind, heart, courage, thought* ns 12/312, 20/87, hyge 15/17, 16/16, 17/44, 17/58, 18(a)/755; ds 12/4, 17/96

Higelāc see Hygelāc

hiġerōf adj. *brave-minded* npm hiġerōfe 20/302

higeþīhtig adj. *strong-hearted, determined* asm higeþīhtigne 18(a)/746

hiġeðoncol adj. *prudent, wise* dsf higeðoncolre 20/131

hiht see hyht

hild f. *battle* as hilde 12/33, 20/251; 21/17; ds 11(j)/4, 12/8, 12/48, 12/55, 12/123, 20/293, etc.

hildedēor adj. *brave in battle* nsm 18(a)/834; npm hildedēore 18(d)/3169

hildelēoð n. *battle-song* as 20/211

hildemecg m. *warrior* np hildemecgas 18(a)/799

hildenædre f. *battle-snake, arrow* ap hildenædran 20/222 [MnE adder]

hilderinc m. *warrior* ns 12/169, 18(b)/1307; np hilderincas 14/61; gp hilderinca 14/72

hine see hē

hinfūs adj. *eager to get away* nsm 18(a)/755

Hinguar pers. n. *Hingwar* ns 4/149, 4/151; as 4/198; gs Hingwares 4/161; ds Hingware 4/169, 4/194

hinsīð m. *journey hence, death* ds hinsīðe 20/117

hīo (= hīe) see hē

ġehioldon see ġehealdan

hiora see hē

hira see hē

ġehīran see ġehīeran

hire see hē

hīredmann m. *retainer, warrior* np hīredmen 12/261

his see hē

hit see hē

hīw n. *shape, form* as 1/18 [MnE hue]

ġehladan VI *load* pret. 3s gehlēod 18(a)/895

hlāf m. *bread* as 3/199; gs hlāfes 2/41; ds hlāfe 3/165 [MnE loaf]

hlāford m. *lord, master* ns 3/177, 6/31, 12/135, 12/189, etc.; as 14/45; gs hlāfordes 3/11, 4/226, 18(d)/3179; ds hlāforde 3/27, 4/193, 10(b)/47, 12/318, 20/251, etc.

hlāfordlēas adj. *lordless, without a lord* nsm 12/251

hlāfordswica m. *traitor* np hlāfordswican 22/63

hlāfordswice m. *treachery* ns 22/64, 22/65

hlanc adj. *lean* nsm hlanca 20/205 [MnE lank]

hlæder f. *ladder* as hlædre 11(n)/6; ds hlæddre 4/278, 4/283

hlæst m. *load, freight* dp hlæstum 3/135

hlæstan 1 *adorn* p. ptc. asf gehlæste 20/36

hlæw m. *mound, barrow, cave* as 18(d)/3157, 18(d)/3169; ds hlǣwe 21/26

hleahtor m. *laughter* ds hleahtre 17/21

hlēapan VII *leap, gallop* inf. 18(a)/864; pret. 3s hlēop 8/65

ġehlēapan VII *leap upon, mount* pret. 3s gehlēop 12/189

hlēo n. *protection, shelter, protector* ns 12/74, 18(a)/791; as 11(f)/5 [MnE lee]

hlēomæg m. *protecting kinsman* gp hlēomæga 17/25

hlēop see hlēapan

hlēosceorp n. *protecting garment* ds hlēosceorpe 11(k)/5

hlēoðor n. *sound, cry, voice* as 17/20; is hlēoþre 11(j)/4

hlēoðrian 2 *make a noise, speak* pret. 3s hlēoðrode 14/26

hliehhan VI *laugh, exult* pret. 3s hlōh 12/147, 20/23

hlīfian 2 *tower, rise up* pres. 1s hlīfige 14/85

hlimman III *roar, resound* inf. 17/18; pret. 3p hlummon 20/205

hlin m. *maple* ns 11(n)/9
hlīsa m. *fame, reputation* as hlīsan 10(b)/53
hlīðe n. *cliff* ds hlīðe 18(d)/3157
hlōh see hliehhan
hlūd adj. *loud* nsm 11(e)/1; superl. hlūdast 21/4
hlūde adv. *loud, loudly* 1/8, 11(d)/7, 20/205, 20/223, 20/270
hlummon see hlimman
hlūttor adj. *pure* isn hlūttre 9/118
hlȳdan 1 *bellow* pret. 3s hlȳdde 20/23
hlynnan 1 *shout* pret. 3s hlynede 20/23
hlynsian 2 *resound* pret. 3s hlynsode 18(a)/770
hlystan 1 *listen* pres. subj. 1p hlysten 1/8
ġehlystan 1 *listen* pret. 3p gehlyston 12/92
hnāg see hnīgan
hnǣgan 1 *bring low, humble* p. ptc. gehnǣged 17/88
hnīgan I *bow down* pret. 1s hnāg 14/59
hnītan I *strike, clash together* pret. 3p hniton 18(b)/1327
hō see hōh
hocor n. *derision* ds hocore 22/135
hocorwyrde adj. *derisive,* as noun: *derider* npm 22/130
hof n. *building* np hofu 13/29
hogian 2 *think, give thought* pret. 3p hogodon 12/123; subj. 3s hogode 12/128; *intend* pret. 3s hogode 12/133; 3p hogedon 20/250, 20/273; *think about* pret. 1s hogode 19/9 [Late WS for hicgan]
hōh m. *heel* ds hō 2/32
hōl n. *malice, envy* ns 22/49
ġehola m. *protector, close friend* gp geholena 16/31
hold adj. *loyal, friendly, gracious* nsm 10(b)/56, 17/41; gpm holdra 15/17; superl. holdost asn 12/24
holen m. *holly* ns 11(n)/10
holm m. *sea* as 16/82; gp holma 17/64
Holofernus pers. n. ns 20/21, 20/46, as 20/7; gs 20/180, 20/250, Holofernes 20/36
holt n. *wood, forest* gs holtes 12/8, 14/29; ds holte 4/231, 21/19
holtwudu m. *tree of the forest, forest* as 14/91, 18(b)/1369
hōn VII *hang, be hanged* inf. 4/285
hond see hand
hongiað see hangian
hongige see hangian
hopian 2 *hope* inf. 20/117
hord n. *hoard, treasure* gs hordes 18(a)/887; ds horde 18(d)/3164
hordcofa m. *heart* as hordcofan 16/14
horing m. *adulterer, fornicator* np horingas 22/149

horn m. *horn* ns 1/8; dp hornum 2/67, 18(c)/1369
hornboga m. *horn-tipped bow* dp hornbogan 20/222
horngestrēon n. *abundance of gables* ns 13/22
hornreced adj. *gabled house* as 18(a)/704
hors n. *horse* as 3/69, 12/2; dp horsum 3/210
horsweġ m. *bridle path, horseway* ds horsweġe 1/6
hosp m. *insult, abuse* as 20/216
hraðe adj. *quick* superl. radost 6/19
hraðe adv. *quickly, soon* 2/45, 4/193, 4/301, 8/48, raðe 7/20, 12/30, 12/164, 12/288, etc. [MnE rath(er), archaic MnE rathe]
hræd adj. *quick* superl. hrædest *quickest* hrædest is tō cweþenne *to be brief,* 22/41, 22/151
hræding f. *haste* ds hrædinge 4/249, on hrædinge *quickly* 22/155
hrædlīċe adv. *forthwith, swiftly* 3/207, 8/30
hrædwyrde adj. *hasty of speech* nsm 16/66
hræġl n. *dress, garment* ns 11(d)/1; as 20/282 [archaic MnE rail]
hrǣw n. *corpse* ns 14/72; as 14/53; ap 20/313
hrēam m. *shouting* ns 12/106; ds hrēame 3/16
hrēaw adj. *raw* apm hrēawe 3/171
hreddan 1 *save, rescue* inf. 11(j)/18
hrefn m. *raven* ns 20/206; np hremmas 12/106
hremm see hrefn
hrēoh adj. *troubled* nsm 10(b)/71, 20/282, hrēo 16/16; asf 16/105 (*fierce*); dsn hrēon 18(b)/1307
hrēoriġ adj. *ruinous* npm hrēorge 13/3
hrēosan II *fall* inf. 16/48; pres. ptc. nsf hrēosende 16/102; p. ptc. npm gehrorene 13/3
hrēowcearig adj. *sorrowful, troubled* nsm 14/25
hrēowigmōd adj. *sad at heart* npm hrēowigmōde 20/289 [MnE rue, mood]
hrēowliċe adv. *cruelly* 22/37
hrepian 2 *touch* pret. subj. 1p hrepoden 2/7
hrēran 1 *set in motion, stir* inf. 16/4
hrēðēadig adj. *exultant, glorious* superl. hrēðēadegost nsm 21/8
hreþer n. *heart* as 17/63; ds hreþre 13/41, 20/94; gp hreþra 16/72
hreðerbealo n. *distress* as 18(b)/1343
hreðerloca m. *enclosure of the heart, breast* as hreðerlocan 17/58
hrif n. *belly, womb* ds hrife 11(h)/12
hrīm m. *frost* ns 13/4, 17/32; as 16/48; is hrīme 16/77 [archaic MnE rime]
hrīmceald adj. *ice-cold* asf hrīmcealde 16/4

hrīmġeat n. *frosty gate* ns 13/4
hrīmġicel m. *icicle* dp hrīmgicelum 17/17
hrīmig adj. *frosty, rimy* superl. hrīmigost nsm 21/6
hrīnan I *touch* 3s hrīneð 11(h)/12; p. ptc. hrinen 8/32
hrinde adj. *covered with frost* nsm 18(b)/1363
hring m. *ring* ns 1/4, 18(c)/2260 (*ring-mail, armour*); ds hringe 21/22; ap hringas 12/161, 13/19; dp hringum 20/37
hringloca m. *ring-mail shirt, corselet* ap hringlocan 12/145
hringmere m. *circular pool* as 13/45
hringþegu f. *receiving of rings* (*by a retainer from his lord*) ds hringþege 17/44
hrīð f. *snowstorm* ns 16/102
gehroden (p. ptc. of *hrēodan*) *adorned* asf gehrodene 20/37
hrōf m. *roof* ns 13/31, as 18(a)/836; gs hrōfes 11(f)/5; ds hrōfe 9/41, 20/67; np hrōfas 13/3; ap 21/64
hronrād f. *ocean, whale's road* ds hronrāde 18/10
hrōstbēag m. *circle formed by inner roofwork, ceiling-vault* gs hrōstbēages 13/31
gehrorene see hrēosan
Hrōðgār pers. n. *Hrothgar* ns 18(b)/1321; as 18(a)/863; gs Hrōðgāres 18(a)/717, 18(a)/826 [MnE Roger]
hrūse f. *earth* ns 18(c)/2247; as hrūsan 11(d)/1, 11(f)/11, 13/29, 16/102, 17/32, 18(a)/772; gs 13/8, 16/23
hrycg m. *back* as 11(b)/5, is hrycge 11(f)/11 [MnE ridge]
hryre m. *ruin, fall* ns 13/31, as 18(d)/3179; gp 16/7 (see note)
hrȳðig adj. *snow-swept, exposed to storms* npm hrȳðge 16/77
hū adv. *how* 3/7, 3/41, 3/48, 3/57, 3/75, etc.; conj. 4/169, 4/199, 4/260, 16/30, 16/35, 16/61, etc.
Hubba pers. n. *Hubba* ns 4/150, 4/152
huilpe f. *curlew* gs huilpan 17/21 [dialectal MnE whaup]
Humbre f. *the Humber River* gs Humbran 7/40; ds Humbre 5/15
hund m. *dog* as 3/118, 20/110; ap hundas 3/43; dp hundum 3/24, 3/49, 18(b)/1368, 22/78 [MnE hound]
hund num. *hundred* ns 11(b)/4, 13/8
hundnigontiġ num. *ninety* dp hundnigontigum 7/48
hungor m. *hunger, famine* ns hungor 17/11; as hunger 4/78; ds hungre 4/80
hungrig adj. *hungry* nsm 4/242
hunta m. *huntsman* ns 3/38, 3/39, 3/40, etc.; np huntan 3/5

Huntadunscīr f. *Huntingdonshire* as Huntadunscīre 7/70
huntian 2 *hunt* inf. 3/46, 3/47
huntoþ m. *hunting, game* as 3/65 (*game*); ds (on) huntoþe (*on a*) *hunt* 3/52, 3/54
hupseax n. *short sword* ap 20/327
huru adv. *certainly, especially, indeed* 4/228, 14/10, 22/4, etc.
hūs n. *house* ns 9/91; as 3/202, 8/30, 9/24; ds hūse 9/23, 9/94; ap hūs 22/26, 22/34
hūsl n. *Eucharist, the consecrated bread and wine for Holy Communion* as 9/100, 9/103; gs hūsles 9/102
huxlīċe adv. *shamefully* 4/206
hwā, hwæt pron. (§20) *who, what, someone, something* ns hwā 2/23, 3/83, 3/159, 4/21 (*someone*), 4/65 (*someone*), 8/56, etc.; as hwæne 12/2 (*each one*), 20/52 (*someone*); gs hwæs 1/34, 3/39; nsn hwæt 1/33, 8/35; asn 3/3, 3/7, 3/17, 3/22, 3/28, 3/55, 3/65, 3/66 (see swā), 3/73, 3/78 (see swā), 3/92, 4/25 (*something*), 4/40, etc.; dsn hwǣm 3/163; isn hwon 9/96 (see for), 17/43 (to hwon *to what, as to what*); hwȳ *why* 1/35, 2/2, 2/26, hwī 4/31, for hwȳ (see for)
ġehwā pron. *each, everyone* nsm 4/310; as ġehwæne 20/186; gsn ġehwæs 9/38; dsm ġehwām 16/63, 17/72, 21/11; dsf ġehwǣre (in mǣgþa ġehwǣre *in each of tribes* i.e. *in every tribe*) 18/25
hwanon adv. *whence* 3/193, 3/194, hwonon 9/53
hwæder see hwider
hwæl m. *whale* as 3/95, 3/98; gs hwæles 17/60; ap hwalas 3/105
hwælhuntoþ m. *whale-hunt* as 3/100
hwælweg m. *path of the whale, the sea* as 17/63
hwǣne pron. see hwā
hwænne conj. *until the time when* 12/67, 14/136
hwǣr adv. *where* 1/3, 2/20, 3/81, 5/81 (*somewhere*), etc.; conj. 2/54, 4/328, 15/8, 16/26
ġehwǣr adv. *everywhere* 4/232, 7/8
ġehwǣre see ġehwā
hwæs see hwā
ġehwæs see ġehwā
hwæt interj. *lo!* 4/168, 4/201, 4/223, 8/19, 8/31, 12/231, 14/1, 18(c)/2248, 22/17
hwæt pron. see hwā
hwæt adj. *vigorous, quick, active* nsm 17/40
hwæthwugu pron. *something* as 9/28
hwætrēd m. *ingenuity, quick design* as 13/19

hwæðer conj. *whether* 4/300, 9/100, 18(b)/
 1314, 18(b)/1356, hwæþer 9/104. See
 hwæþer þe
ġehwæðer indef. adj. *either* nsm 18(a)/814
 asf gehwæðere 12/112
hwæþere adv., conj. *however, nevertheless,
 yet, but* 8/3, hwæðre 9/11, 9/32, 9/89,
 14/18, 14/38, 14/42, etc.
ġehwæðeres adv. *in both respects* 10(b)/25
hwæþer þe conj. *or* 3/119
hwæþre see hwæþere
hwealf adj. *concave, hollow* dsf hwealfum
 20/214
hwearf n. *crowd, flock* dp hwearfum 20/249
hwearfian 2 *wave* pret. 3s hwearfode 10(b)/
 10
hwelċ interrogative pron. and adj. *which,
 what, what kind of* nsm 3/186, 3/212
 (swa hwelc swa *whatsoever*), þræla hwylc
 some slave 22/90; asm hwelcne 3/1, 3/37,
 3/71, 3/118; dsm hwelcum (see swa)
 2/10; dsm hwylcum 11(h)/10 (each, any);
 swā hwelc(um) (. . . swā) swā *whoever* see
 swā; nsf hwylc 8/9, 21/65 (*of what sort*),
 hwelc 8/12, hwylc 9/101; asf hwylce
 9/49; npn hwelc 5/24; apn 3/50, 3/140
ġehwelċ pron., adj. *each* nsm 3/211 (ānra
 gehwelc *each one*), gehwylc 12/128, 12/
 257; as gehwylcne 20/95; gs gehwylces
 20/32; dsm gehwelcum 6/19, gehwilcum
 10(b)/45, 22/19, gehwylcum 14/108; ism
 gehwylce 14/136, 16/8; isn 17/36, 17/68
hwelp m. *whelp, cub* as 19/16
hweorfan III *turn, go* inf. 16/72, 21/58;
 pres. 3s hweorfeð 17/58, 17/60; pret. 3s
 hwearf 20/112
ġehwerfde see ġehwierfan
hwettan 1 *whet, incite* pres. 3s hweteð 17/63
hwī see hwā
hwider adv. *whither, in which direction* 16/72,
 hwæder 18(b)/1331, hwyder 21/58
hwierfan 1 *turn, change* p. ptc. gehwierfed
 3/165
ġehwierfan 1 *turn* pret. 3s gehwerfde 9/68;
 subj. 3s gehwyrfde 9/57
hwīl f. *time, while* as hwīle 2/51, 7/17, etc.;
 dp hwīlum *sometimes* 3/51, 3/69, 3/77,
 3/90, 3/109, 3/110, 3/111, 4/12 (*once,
 at one time*), 4/19, hwīlon 12/270, etc.;
 ðā hwīle ðe conj. *while, as long as* 5/60,
 12/14, 12/83, 12/235, etc.; ealle hwīle *all
 the time* 22/74, 22/156
ġehwilċum see ġehwelċ
hwīlon see hwīl
hwīlum see hwīl [archaic MnE whilom]
hwistlung f. *whistling* ds hwistlunge 3/111
hwon see hwā
hwōn adj. (as noun) *little, few* as w.g. 17/28

hwonon see hwanon
hwȳ see hwā
hwyder see hwider
hwylc see hwelc
ġehwylċ see ġehwelċ
hwylce see hwelc
ġehwyrfde see ġehwierfan
hycgan see hicgan
hycgendne see hicgan
hȳd f. *hide, skin* ap hȳda 3/151
hȳdan 1 *hide, hoard* inf. hȳdan 18(b)/1372;
 pres. 3s hȳdeð 17/102
ġehȳdan 1 *conceal* pret. 3s gehȳdde 16/84
ġehygd f. *thought, intention* ns 16/72, 17/116
hyge see hige
hygegeōmor adj. *sad at heart* asm hygegeōmorne 15/19
Hygelāc pers. n. *Hygelac* gs Higelāces 18(a)/
 737, 18(a)/758, Hygelāces 18(a)/813
hygerōf adj. *resolute* as noun nsm 13/19
hȳhsta see hēah
hyht m. *hopeful joy, bliss* ns 14/126, 17/45,
 17/122, hiht 14/148; *hope* ns 20/97
hyhtwynn f. *joy of hope* gp hyhtwynna
 20/121
hyldan 1 *bow, bend* inf. 14/45 (w. refl.)
hyldo f. *grace, favour* gs 20/4
hylt see healdan
hȳnan 1 *injure, lay low, kill* inf. 12/180; pret.
 3s hȳnde 12/324; *abase, humiliate* pres.
 3p hȳnað 22/113; p. ptc. npf gehȳnede
 22/36
hȳra see hē
hȳran see hīeran
ġehȳran see ġehīeran
hȳrde see hīeran
hyrde m. *guardian, keeper* ns 18(a)/750,
 20/60; as 18(a)/887 [MnE (cow)herd,
 (shep)herd]
ġehȳrde see ġehīeran
ġehȳrdon see ġehīeran
hyrdrǣden f. *guardianship* ds hyrdrǣdenne
 4/244
hyrnednebb adj. *horny-beaked* nsm hyrnednebba 20/212
ġehȳrnes f. *hearing* ds gehȳrnesse 9/66
hyrst f. *ornament, trapping* np hyrste 11(d)/4;
 ap hyrsta 18(d)/3164, 20/316; ip hyrstum
 11(j)/11
hyrstedgold n. *fairly wrought gold* ds hyr-
 stedgolde 18(c)/2255
ġehȳrð see ġehīeran
hyrwan 1 *deride* pres. 3s hyrweð 22/135,
 22/138
hys (= his) see hē
hyse m. *warrior, youth* ns 12/152; gs hysses
 12/141; np hyssas 12/112, hysas 12/123;
 ap hyssas 12/169; gp hyssa 12/2, 12/128

hyt see **hē, hēo, hit**
hȳþelic adj. *convenient* nsn 13/41

Iācōb pers. n. *Jacob* ds Iācōbe 4/15
iċ pron. (§21) *I* ns 1/17, 1/30, 2/21, 2/22, 3/
2, 3/23, etc.; as mē 2/25, 2/72, 3/103, mec
16/28, 17/6, 19/11; gs mīn (*of me*) 2/73;
ds mē 2/25, 2/27, 3/74 (*for myself*),
3/80, 3/122
īdel adj. *idle, worthless, vain* nsm 16/110; gs
īdles 9/15; asf īdlan 8/59; npn īdlu 16/87;
on īdel *in vain* 4/279
ides f. *woman* ns 20/14, 20/109, 20/128,
20/146, 21/43; as idese 20/55, 20/58;
gs 18(b)/1351; np idesa 20/133; gp
11(a)/7
īeċan 1 *add, pile up* pret. 3s īhte 22/10
īeg f. *island* ds īege 19/4, īge 19/6
ieldran m. pl. (§75) *elders, ancestors* np
5/34, eldran 10(b)/58; gp yldrena 4/
165
iermðu f. *misery* ap iermða 2/34
ierþling m. *ploughman, farmer* ns 3/7, 3/29,
3/192; as 3/209; ds ierþlinge 3/32, 3/198;
np ierþlingas 3/4 [MnE earthling]
īewan 1 *disclose, show* pres. subj. 3s ȳwe
11(n)/15; pret. 3p ēowdon 20/240
īge see **īeg**
igl m. *hedgehog* gs igles 4/214
ilca adj., pron. *same, the same* asn ilce 6/33,
9/47; dsn ilcan 3/144, 4/136, 7/26, 7/45,
10(a)/5, ylcan 7/2, 7/12; isn ilcan 7/4,
7/8; dsf 2/46 [MnE ilk]
in prep. w.d. *in*, w.a. *into* (§213) w.d. 9/5, 9/7,
9/34, 9/61, 9/90, etc.; w.a. 1/2, 9/10,
9/46, 9/64, 9/76, etc.
in adv. *in, inside* 12/58, 12/157, 18(b)/1371,
20/150, 20/170
inbryrdnes f. *inspiration* as inbryrdnesse
8/74, mbryrdnisse 9/6
inca m. *rancour* as incan 9/106; ds 9/105
indryhten adj. *very noble, aristocratic* nsm
16/12
indryhto f. *nobility* ns 17/89
inġehygd f. *intention, conscience* as 4/87
inġeþanc m. *conscience* as 22/178
ingong m. *immigration, entry* as 9/111; ds
ingonge 9/73
Ingwine m. pl. *the Danes* gp Ingwina 18(b)/
1319
inlǣdan 1 *bring in* inf. 9/92
inn n. *chamber* ds inne 20/70 [MnE inn]
innan prep. w.d. *within* 4/202, 4/256, 21/43,
22/34
innan adv. *from within* 17/11, 18(a)/774; in
innan *inside* 11(k)/3; *inside* 22/34
innanbordes adv. *at home, within the nation*
5/8

inne adv. *inside, within* 8/32, 9/99, 11(a)/4,
10(b)/72, inne ne ūte *at home or abroad,*
anywhere 22/24, 22/47, 22/97, inne and ūte
everywhere 22/26
insittende adj. *sitting within* as noun: gpm
insittendra 11(a)/7
intinga m. *cause* ns 9/20
inwidda m. *wicked one* nsm 20/28
inwidhlemm m. *malicious wound* np inwidhlemmas 14/47
inwidsorh f. *evil care or sorrow* as inwidsorge
18(a)/831
inwitþanc m. *hostile purpose* dp inwitþancum
18(a)/749
Iōhannes pers. n. *John* as 10(a)/11, 10(b)/42
Iōsēp pers. n. *Joseph* ns 4/77
iow (= ēow) see **ġē**
īren n. (*iron*) *sword* ns 12/253, 18(a)/892; gp
īrenna 18(a)/802, īrena 18(c)/2259
īrenbend f. *iron band* dp īrenbendum 18(a)/
774
irnan III *run* inf. rinnan (*hasten, flow*) 11(e)/
5; pret. 3s ran 1/6; 3p urnon 6/18, 20/164
is see **bēon**
Īsaac pers. n. *Isaac* ns 2/47, 2/53; as 2/44,
2/52, 2/69; ds Īsaace 4/5
īsceald adj. *ice-cold* asm īscealdne 17/14,
īscaldne 17/19
īsen adj. *iron* ap īsene 3/200; ns īsern *iron*
weapon, sword 21/26
īsensmiþ m. *blacksmith* ap īsensmiþas 3/181
īsern see **īsen**
īsigfeþera adj. *having icy feathers* nsm 17/
24
Israhēlas m. pl. *Israelites* gp Israhēla 9/73
Ītālia m. pl. the *Italians, Italy* ap 10(b)/12;
gp 10(a)/3
iū see **ġēo**
Iūdēi m. pl. *Jews* np 4/325
Iūdēiscan adj. pl. *Jewish* (*people*), *the Jews* np
4/108; ap 4/205; dp Iūdēiscum 4/55
Iudith pers. n. *Judith* ns 20/13, 20/123,
20/132, 20/168, etc.; as Iudithðe 20/40; gs
Iudithe 20/333
iūwine m. *friend* (*or lord*) *of former days* ap
17/92
īw m. *yew* ns 11(n)/9

kāsere see **cāsere**
Kentingas m. pl. *Kent* ap 7/71
kynerīċes see **cynerōċe**
kyning see **cyning**

lā interj. *lo! oh!* 3/8, 3/29, etc.; lā hwæt *for*
lo 22/17
lāc n. *sacrifice, offering* ds lāce 2/68, 4/92; *gift*
as 19/1; dp lācum 22/24
ġelac n. *rolling, tumult* as 15/7, 17/35

lācan VII *sport, contend, fight* inf. 21/39; pres. 1s lāce 11(o)/1

lāf f. *remnant, heirloom, inheritance* as lāfe 18(a)/795, 18(d)/3160; ds tō lāfe wæs *was left* 4/226

lāge see **licgan**

*ge*lagian 2 *assign by law, ordain* p. ptc. gelogod 22/22

lāgon see **licgan**

lagu m. *sea, water* as 17/47

lagu f. *law* as lage 22/29; gs 22/20; ds 22/57; np laga 22/41; dp lagum, 22/175; etc.

laguflōd m. *ocean wave, tide* ns 21/46

*ge*lagu n. pl. *expanse (of ocean)* ap 17/64

lagulād f. *sea-way* ap lagulāde 16/3

lagustrēam m. *water, river* np lagustrēamas 12/66

lahbryċe m. *lawbreaking* ap lahbrycas 22/122

lahlīċe adv. *in accordance with secular laws* 22/56

*ge*lamp see *ge*limpan

lāmrind f. *crust of mud* dp lāmrindum 13/17

land n. *land, country* as 4/148, 21/53 lond 5/12, 18(b)/1357; gs londes 6/29, 15/8, landes 12/90, 12/275; ds lande 2/45, 2/47, 3/136, 4/77, etc.

landbuēnd m. pl. *earth-dwellers, inhabitants* ap londbuēnd 18(b)/1345; *in-dwellers of the land* (i.e. *Hebrews*) np landbūende 20/226; dp londbūendum 20/314

lang adj. *long, tall* nsm langa 12/273; asf lange 14/24, 18/16 (lange hwīle *for a long time*); nsn tō lang *too long (a time)* 12/66; compar. nsf lengre 11(h)/7, gsn lengran 20/184

*ge*lang see *ge*long

lange adv. *long, for a long time* longe 5/78, 8/56, 10(b)/50, 10(b)/58, etc., lange 18(b)/1336, etc.; compar. leng *longer* 4/120, 12/171, 20/153; superl. lengest 6/3, 21/6

langlice adv. *for a long time* 4/209

langoþ m. *longing* gs longaþes 15/41; ds langoþe 15/53

langung f. *longing, yearning* as longunge 17/47

langunghwīl f. *time of longing, time of spiritual desire* gp langunghwīla 14/126

lār f. *teaching, doctrine* ns 5/45, 5/64, 8/10; as lāre 5/10, 10(b)/68, 20/333, as 22/58; gs 4/141, 9/56; ds 4/37, 9/76; np lāra 22/42; ap lāra 4/89 [MnE lore]

lārcwide m. *counsel* dp lārcwidum 16/38

lārēow m. *teacher* np lārēowas 4/26, 9/69; gp lārēowa 5/20; dp lārēowum 4/39

lāst m. *track* np lāstas 11(l)/2; ap 18(a)/841; ds on lāste (see note) 16/97; dp lastum 17/15; *the rear* as him . . . on lāst *behind them* 20/209, on lāst *from behind* 20/291; ds him on lāste *behind them* 20/297

lāstword n. *reputation left behind* gp lāstworda 17/73

late adv. *belatedly* 20/275

latian 2 *delay* pres. subj. 3s þæs . . . latige *delay doing it* 22/157

lāð adj. *hateful, hostile* nsm 18(a)/815, 20/45; nsn 19/12, 22/74; asm lāðne 20/72, 20/101; gsm lāþes 18(a)/841; gsn lāðan 20/310; dsn lāðum 20/226; dsf lāðere 12/90; npm lāðe 12/86; apm lāð 18(b)/1375; gpm lāðra 20/297, 20/303; as a noun nsm 21/53; asm lāþne 17/112; dsm lāðe (*foe*) 21/53; compar. lāðre asn 12/50; superl. lāðost nsm 14/88, 20/322; gsm lāðestan 20/178; dpm lāðestan 20/314; *hated* npf 22/41 [MnE loathe(some)]

lāðettan 1 *hate* pres. 3s lāðet 22/139

laðian 2 *invite, summon* pres. 1s laðige 11(j)/16

lāðlicost adv. (superl. of **lāðlice**) *in most wretched fashion* 15/14

lāðost see **lāð**

lāðre see **lāð**

*ge*laðung f. *church, congregation* gs gelaðunge 4/83

Laurentius pers. n. *Lawrence* ds Laurentie 4/304

læċċan 1 *capture, catch* p. ptc. gelæht 3/44 [colloquial MnE latch (onto)]

lædan 1 *lead, bring, lift, carry off* inf. 12/88, 14/5 (see note), 20/42; infl. inf. (tō) lædene 7/29 (see note); pres. 1s læde 3/25, 3/30, 3/137; 2s lætst 3/140; 3s læt 4/288; 3p lædað 22/114 pret. 3s lædde 20/129; 3p læddon 4/207, 10(b)/2, 20/72, 20/325; p. ptc. læded nsm 18(d)/3177

*ge*lædde 1 *lead* pret. 3s gelædde 9/50

Læden n. *Latin* ns 4/100, 4/101; as 4/14, 5/68; gs Lædenes 4/105; ds Lædene 4/3, 5/16

Lædenbōc f. *Latin book* dp Lædenbōcum 4/26

Lædenġeðīode n. *the Latin language* as 5/62; gs Lædengeðīodes 5/64

Lædenware m. pl. *the Romans* npm 5/50

læfan 1 *leave, bequeath* pret. 3s læfde 6/26; 3p lēfdon 5/26, læfdon 5/35

læg see **licgan**

lægon see **licgan**

*ge*læht see **læċċan**

læn n. *loan* de læne 5/81

lǣne adj. *temporary, transitory* nsm 16/108, 16/109 (twice); nsn 1/24, 16/108, 17/66; dsn lǣnum 14/109, lǣnan 14/138

lǣran 1 *teach, advise* inf. 5/62, 9/65; pres. 1s lǣre 8/47; subj. 3s lǣre 5/61; pret. 3s lǣrde 8/3, 9/62, 12/311; p. ptc. lǣred 8/10

ġelǣran 1 *teach, advise, urge* pres. 1s gelǣre 3/210; p. ptc. nsm gelǣred 4/126, 9/12; npm gelǣrede 5/78; superl. apm gelǣredestan *most learned* 9/51

ġelǣredestan see *ġelǣran*

lǣrig m. *rim of a shield* ns 12/284

lǣs indeclinable noun *less, fewer* apm 22/101

lǣs adv. *less* 8/44, 11(k)/11; nōht þon lǣs *nevertheless* 8/17; þȳ lǣs þe *lest* 2/7, 3/24, 4/120, þē lǣs *lest* 22/159

lǣs f. *pasture* ds lǣswe 3/24, 3/30

lǣssa adj. (compar. of lȳtel; cf. §76) *less, smaller* asm lǣssan 3/119; nsn lǣsse 3/98

lǣsst adj. (superl. of lȳtel; cf. §76) adj. *least, smallest* nsn lǣsste 8/33

lǣstan 1 w.d. *follow* inf. 10(b)/27, 18(a)/812 (*do service, avail*) [MnE last]

ġelǣstan 1 *perform, carry out, continue, stand by, support* inf. 12/11 (w.d.), 22/175; subj. pres. 3s gelǣste 22/21 (*pay*); 3p gelǣsten 18/24; pret. 3s 10(a)/9, 12/15; 3p gelǣstan 10(b)/13; p. ptc. gelǣsted 18(a)/829

lǣswe see *lǣs*

lǣt see *lǣdan*

lǣtan VII *let, allow* pres. 1s lǣte 3/122; 2s lǣtst 3/124; 3s lǣteð 11(m)/10; pret. 3s lēt (*cause*, w. verb of motion) 12/7, 12/140, 22/162; 3p lēton 12/108, 13/42, 18(a)/864, 20/221; subj. 3s lēte 10(b)/66, 10(b)/68; *consider* pres. 3s lǣt 22/104

lǣtst see *lǣdan*

læðð f. *affliction, wrong* gp lǣðða 20/158; dp lǣððum 20/184

lǣwede adj. *unlearned, lay* dsn lǣwedum 4/39; as noun *layman* npm 22/56 [MnE lewd]

ġelēafa m. *belief, faith* ns 4/329; as gelēafan 4/87, 20/6, 20/89, 20/344; gs 4/321; ds 4/42, 4/146, 4/195, 8/2, 8/77, 20/97

ġelēafful adj. *faithful* nsm gelēaffulla 4/303; asm gelēaffullan 4/207

leahtor m. *sin, vice* dp leahtrum 4/140

lēan n. *reward* gs lēanes 20/346

lēan VI *blame, find fault with* pret. 3p lōgon 18(a)/862

lēanian 2 w.d. *repay, reward* pres. 1s lēanige 18(b)/1380; 3s lēanað 11(m)/9

lēap m. *torso, carcase* ns 20/111

lēas adj. w.g. *devoid of, without* nsm 18(a)/850, 20/121; nsn 15/32; npn lease 16/86 [MnE (home)less, (bottom)less, etc.]

lēas adj. *faithless, false to God* nsm 4/121

lēasung f. *lying, fable, fiction* gs lēasunge 9/15; ap lēasunga 22/126

lēat see *lūtan*

leax m. *salmon* ns 21/39 ap leaxas 3/93 [MnE (through Yiddish) lox]

lecgan 1 *lay, place* inf. 4/256; pres. 3p lecgað 17/57; subj. 3s lecge 16/42; pret. 3p legdon 4/248

lēfdon see *lǣfan*

lēgbysig see *līgbysig*

legdon see *lecgan*

Lēġeċeasterscīr f. *Cheshire* ns 7/5

leġer n. *bed* ap 15/34 [MnE lair]

lehtrian 2 *revile* pres. 3s lehtreð 22/135

lencten m. *spring* ns 21/6 ds lenctene 3/121 [MnE lent]

ġelendan 1 *land, arrive* pret. 3p gelendon 4/151

leng see *lange*

lengest see *lange*

lengran see *lang*

lengre see *lange*

lēod m. *man, member of a tribe or nation, prince* ns 18(a)/829

lēode f. or m. pl. *people* np 4/147, 18/24, 18(d)/3156, 18(d)/3178; ap lēoda 4/151, 12/37, lēode 4/157, 4/295, 18(b)/1336, 18(b)/1345; gp lēoda 4/163, 18(a)/793, 20/178, lēode 22/165; dp lēodum 12/23, 12/50, 14/88, 15/6, 18(b)/1323, 18(d)/3182, 19/1, 20/147, 22/28, lēodon 12/23, leodum . . . minum *to my people* 19/1

lēodfruma m. *leader of a people, lord* ns 15/8; ds lēodfruman 10(b)/27

lēodhata m. *tyrant* as lēodhatan 20/72; np 22/129

lēodon see *lēode*

lēodscipe m. *nation* as 10(b)/68

lēof adj. *beloved, dear, pleasant, agreeable, (in direct address) sir, sire* ns 2/21, 3/8, 3/18, 3/21, 3/23, 3/29, 4/3, lēofa 4/177, 14/78, etc.; nsf lēof 20/147; asm lēofne 12/7, 12/208, 17/112 (as noun); gsm lēofes 15/53 (as noun), 16/38; dsm lēofan 12/319, 20/346; dsf lēofre 16/97; npm lēofan 9/109, lēofe 15/34 (as noun); gpm lēofra 15/16 (as noun), 16/31; dpm lēofum 4/182; compar. lēofre *more agreeable, preferable* nsn 3/102, 3/197, 4/175; nsm 10(b)/41 lēofra *dearer* 6/31; superl. lēofost *most pleasing, most agreeable* nsm 12/23 [archaic MnE lief]

lēofað see *libban*

leofede see *libban*

leofode see *libban*

leofodon see *libban*

Lēofstān pers. n. *Leofstan* ns 4/298

Lēofsunu pers. n. *Leofsunu* ns 12/244
lēoht adj. *bright, radiant* asm lēohtne 20/191
[MnE light]
lēoht n. *light* ns 18(a)/727, 21/51; ds lēohte
11(f)/17, 14/5
lēohtlīċ adj. *apparently easy* dpn lēohtlicum
4/76
lēoma m. *light* as lēoman 20/191
leomu see **lim**
*ġe***lēoran** II *depart* p. ptc. apm geleorene
13/7
leornere m. *scholar* ap leorneras 9/51 [MnE
learner]
leornian 2 *learn, study* inf. leornigan 10(a)/
18; pret. 3s leornade 9/13; 3p leornodon
9/70
*ġe***leornian** 2 *learn* inf. 9/66; pret. 1s geliornode 5/70; 3s geleornode 9/5, geleornade
9/19; 3p geliornodon 5/49; p. ptc.
geliornod 5/42, geleornad 8/13
lēoð n. *song, poem, poetry* ns 9/68; as 9/19,
9/52, etc.; gs lēoþes 9/15; is lēoðe 9/59; ap
lēoð 9/3, 9/11, 9/79
lēoðcræft m. *poetic art* as 9/13
leoþo see **liþ**
lēoþsong m. *song, poem, poetry* gs lēoþsonges
9/57; dp lēoþsongum 9/8
lēt see **lǣtan**
lēte see **lǣtan**
lēton see **lǣtan**
*ġe***lettan** 1 *hinder, prevent* pret. 3s gelette
12/164
leðer m. *leather* ns 1/4
leþerhose f. *leather gaiter* ap leþerhosa
(*leggings*) 3/153
lēw f. *injury* ds lēwe 22/144
*ġe***lēwed** adj. *injured* np gelēwede 22/145
libban 3 *live* inf. lybban 4/10, 4/22; pres. ptc.
asm lifigendan 4/328, lifiendne (*alive*)
22/67; npm lifgende 15/34, lifigende
18(a)/815; gp lifgendra 17/73; pres. 3s
lifað 18(d)/3167, leofað 17/102, 17/107,
18(b)/1366; 3p lifiaþ 14/134; subj. 1s
lybbe 4/187, lifge 11(e)/6; 3s 17/78; pret.
3s leofede 4/33, leofode 4/146, 4/265,
lyfode 7/17; 1p lifdon 15/14; 3p leofodon
4/11, 4/22, lifdon 17/85, lyfdon 20/296
(*survive*)
līċ n. *body* ns 4/226, 6/41; gs līċes 14/63; ds
līċe 4/261, 18(a)/733
*ġe***līċ** adj. w.d. *like, similar to* nsn 4/303;
np gelīċe 2/11, 22/143; dp gelīcum 8/38;
superl. gelīccast *just like* 22/79
*ġe***līċe** adv. w.d. *like* 9/11; superl. gelīcost
just like, most like unto nsn 18(a)/727
licgan V *lie, lie dead* inf. 11(j)/10, 12/319,
20/278; pres. ptc. licgende nsm 14/24;
pres. 3s līþ 4/177, 4/262, 4/304, 6/41,

12/232, 12/314, 20/288; ligeð 12/222,
18(b)/1343, subj. licge 22/93; 3p licgað
4/319, 16/78; pret. 3s læg 4/227, 4/240,
6/27, 12/157, 12/204, 12/227, 20/106,
20/111, 20/293, leg 12/276, etc.; 3p
lægon 6/21, lāgon 12/112, 12/183, 20/30;
subj. 3s lāge 4/305, lǣge 12/279, 12/
300
līchama m. *body* ns 4/264, līchoma 18(a)/
812; as līchaman 4/256, 4/301; ds 4/258,
4/313, 4/321, 18(d)/3177
līchomlīċ adj. *bodily* ds līchomlicre 9/88
līcian 2 *please* pres. 3s līcaþ 1/30 [MnE like]
līcsār n. *bodily pain, wound* as 18(a)/815
lidmann m. *sailor, Viking* np lidmen 12/99;
gp lidmanna 12/164
*ġe***līefan** 1 *believe, trust in* pres. 1s gelīefe
5/21, gelȳfe 17/66; 3s gelȳfeð (w. refl. d.)
17/27, 17/108; 3p gelȳfað 4/327, subj. 3s
gelȳfe 22/74; pret. 3p gelȳfdon 4/323
līf n. *life* ns 1/24, 2/73, 8/26, 8/34, etc.; as
7/25, 9/86, 9/117, etc.; gs līfes 1/31,
2/30, 2/39, 4/295, 8/5, etc.; ds līfe 4/
171, 4/194 (on līfe *alive*), 4/265, 11(m)/9,
14/109, 14/138, 15/41, 20/322 (*in life, in
their lifetime*)
līfdagas m. pl. *life-days, life* ap 18(a)/793
lifdon see **libban**
*ġe***līffǣstan** 1 *bring to life* pret. 3s gelīffǣste
4/61
līffrēa m. *lord of life* i.e. *God* ns 18/16
lifge see **libban**
līfgedǣl n. *parting from life, death* ns 18(a)/
841
lifgende, lifiendne see **libban**
lifiaþ see **libban**
lifte see **lyft**
līġ m. *flame, fire* gs līġes 18(a)/781; ds ligge
18(a)/727
līġbysiġ adj. *beset by flames, flammable* nsm
lēġbysiġ 11(o)/1
ligeð see **licgan**
līhtan 1 *alight, dismount* pret. 3s līhte 12/
23
lim n. *limb* ap leomu 9/26
līm m. *sticky material, birdlime* ds līme 3/110,
13/4 (*cement*)
*ġe***limp** n. *occurrence, misfortune* ds gelimpe
4/171; dp gelimpum 22/115
limpan III impers. w.d. *befall, happen* pres.
3s limpeð 17/13
*ġe***limpan** III *befall* inf. 22/89; pres. 3s
gelimpð 22/97; pret. 3s gelamp 4/147,
gelomp 10(a)/26; 3p gelumpon 7/73; p. ptc.
gelumpen 18(a)/824
*ġe***limplīċ** adj. *suitable* isf gelimplicre 9/26
limwēriġ adj. *weary of limb, exhausted* asm
limwērigne 14/63

lind f. *shield* (*of linden-wood*) as linde 12/ 244; ap 12/99, 20/191, 20/303; dp lindum 20/214

Lindesīġ f. *Lindsey* ds Lindesīge 7/41

lindwiga m. *shield-warrior* ap lindwigan 20/297

lindwīgend m. *warrior* np lindwīgende 10(b)/13, 20/42

līnen adj. *linen, made of flax* nsn 1/2

ġeliornod see ġeleornian

liornung f. *learning* as liornunga 5/11; ds 5/60

liss f. *kindness, joy* gp lissa 10(b)/59; dp lissum 11(m)/9

list f. *art, skill, cunning* ds liste 11(f)/4; dp listum 10(b)/59, 18(a)/781, 20/101 (adv. *skilfully*)

lītel see lӯtel

līþ see licgan

liþ n. *limb* ap leoþo 11(h)/7

līþe adj. *gentle, kind* superl. līðost nsm 18(d)/3182 [MnE lithe]

loc n. *enclosure, sheepfold* dp locum 3/26 [MnE lock]

lōcian 2 *look* pres. 3s lōcað 22/104; pret. 3s lōcude 6/14

lōcude see lōcian

lof n. *praise* ns 17/73, 17/78; as 9/121; ds lofe 4/323

lofdǣd f. *praiseworthy deed* inst. p. lofdǣdum 18/24

lofgeorn adj. *eager for praise, eager for fame* superl. lofgeornost nsm 18(d)/3182

ġelōgian 2 *place, put, arrange* pres. subj. 3s gelōgige 4/315; pret. 3s gelōgode 2/58; *lodge, install* 22/72

lōgon see lēan

ġelōme adj. *frequent* dpf gelōmum 4/261; adv. gelōme *frequently* 4/239, 4/253, 20/18, 22/43, 22/180, etc.; calles tō gelōme *all too often* 22/23, etc.; oft ond gelōme *again and again* 22/48, 22/87, etc.

ġelomp see ġelimpan

lond see land

londbūend see landbūend

londstede m. *country* ds 15/16

ġelong adj. *belonging to, dependent on* nsn 17/121; nsf 15/45; nsm gelang 18(a)/1376

longaþes see langoþ

longe see lange

longian 2 impers. w.a. *afflict with longing* pret. 3s longade 15/14

longunge see langung

loppestre f. *lobster* ap loppestran 3/93

losian 2 *escape, be lost, perish* inf. 20/287; pres. 3s losaþ 3/160 (*spoil, go bad*), 17/94, 18(b)/1392; 3p losiaþ 3/138 [MnE lose]

lūcan II *lock, join, enclose* pret. 3p lucon 12/66

lufian 2 *love* inf. 22/139, 22/175, lufigean 9/61; pres. 2s lufast 2/45; 3p lufiað 22/135; pret. 1p lufodon 5/25, 5/26

luflīce adv. *affectionately* 5/1 [obs. MnE lovely]

lufu f. *love* gs lufan 10(b)/59; ds lufan 9/81, 9/82, 17/121; ds lufe 4/187, 4/269

ġelumpon see ġelimpan

Lunden f. *London* ds 7/36

Lundenbyriġ f. *London* ns 7/12 (see note); ds 7/28, 7/47

lungre adv. *quickly, forthwith* 20/147, 20/280

lust m. *desire, pleasure* ns 17/36; as 22/57; dp lustum 4/117, on lustum (*joyful*) 20/161 [MnE lust]

lustbǣre adj. *desirable, pleasant* nsn 2/13

ġelustfullīce adv. *willingly* compar. gelustfullīcor 8/16

lustlīce adv. *gladly, willingly* 3/118 [MnE lust(i)ly]

lūtan II *bend, stoop* pret. 3s lēat 4/283

lūtian 2 *skulk, lurk* inf. 3/10

lybban see libban

ġelӯfað see ġelīefan

ġelӯfdon see ġelīefan

ġelӯfed adj. *advanced* gsf gelӯfdre 9/19

ġelӯfeð see ġelīefan

lyfode see libban

lyft f. *air, sky, breeze* ns 11(d)/4, 18(b)/1375; ds lyfte 11(l)/4, lifte 11(f)/4; as 20/347, on lyft *into the air, aloft* 14/5; on lyfte *in the air, in the sky* 21/3, 21/39

lyfthelm m. *atmosphere, mist* ns 21/46

lӯsan 1 *release, redeem, ransom* inf. 12/37, 14/41

ġelystan 1 impers. w.a. of person and g. of thing *desire* pret. 3s gelyste 20/306

ġelysted adj. *desirous of* nsm 10(b)/9

lӯt noun indecl. w.g. *few, little* as 15/16, 16/31; as adv. 17/27

lytegian 2 *use guile, deceive* inf. 12/86

lӯtel adj. *little, few* asf lӯtle 7/17; dsf lӯtelre (*petty*) 22/38; npf lӯtle 22/7; gsn lӯtles 4/25; isn lӯtle 6/9; (as noun) asn lӯtel 22/22; dpn lītlum (*little things*) 4/75

lӯthwōn n. w.g. *few* ns 20/310

lӯtlian 2 *diminish, grow less* pres. 3s lӯtlað 12/313

lӯtling m. *child* np lӯtlingas 3/165 [MnE dialect littling]

lӯðre adj. *base* asf 22/166

mā adj., noun, adv. *more* as (noun indecl.) 5/47, 18(a)/735; np 12/195; ap 4/20; adv. 8/20, 15/4, þon mā þe *any more than* 6/35 [archaic MnE mo]

macian 2 *make* pres. 1s macie 3/26; pres. 3s macað 4/324; pret. 3p macodon 4/262

Maccus pers. n. *Maccus* ns 12/80

māga m. *relative, kin* gs māgan 18(b)/1391

magan pret.-pres. *be able, can, be competent* pres. 1s mæg 3/84, 3/102, etc.; 2s miht 3/205; 3s mæg 3/104, 3/154, 3/184, 4/75, etc.; 1p magon 3/174, 5/57; 2p 3/162, 3/171; 3p 4/26, 4/317, magan 22/154, 22/159; subj. 1s mæge 3/85, 3/147; 2s 4/178, 5/23, 20/330, mage 4/167; 3s mæge 22/61; 1p mægen 5/56; 3p 5/60; pret. 1s meahte 5/74, 14/18, mihte 14/37; 3s meahte 9/12, 9/15, etc., mihte 4/21, 7/55, etc.; 3p mihton 4/41, 4/249, 4/276, meahton 5/32, etc.; subj. 3s meahte 9/57, mihte 4/281, mehte 22/155; 3p mihten 4/233, 20/24, muhton 7/31, etc. [MnE may]

māge f. *kinswoman* ns mēge 11(k)/4

magister m. *teacher* ns 4/13 [MnE master]

mago m. *young man, youth* ns 16/92

magon see **magan**

magorinc m. *warrior* gp magorinca 10(b)/26, 18(a)/730

maguþegn m. *young retainer* np maguþegnas 16/62, magoþegnas 20/236

man see **mann**

man indefinite pron. *one, they* ns 3/98, 3/215, 4/21, 4/75, mon 5/61, 19/1, etc.

*ġe*man see *ġe*munan

mān n. *crime* gs mānes 10(b)/44; ds māne 10(a)/10; gp māna 22/151

mancess m. *mancus (a gold coin worth 30 silver pence)* gp mancessa 5/76

mancynn n. *mankind* as 14/104, mancyn 14/41; gs mancynnes 14/33, 14/99, monncynnes 9/42; ds mancynne 1/23

māndǣd f. *evil deed* ap māndǣda 22/120 gp māndǣda 9/81

māndrinc m. *evil drink, poison, deadly drink* as 11(h)/13

manega see **maniġ**

mangere m. *merchant* ns 3/131 [MnE (fish)monger]

manian 2 *exhort, urge, admonish* inf. 12/228; pres. 3s monað 17/36, 17/53; pret. 3s monade 9/62, manode 20/26

*ġe*manian 2 *exhort, urge, remind* pres. 3p gemoniað 17/50; p. ptc. apm gemanode 12/231

maniġ adj., pron. *many, many a* (w. sg. noun) nsm mænig 12/282; asm mænigne 12/188, manigne 12/243; asn monig 10(b)/3; dsn manegum 10(a)/10; np manega 4/20, 12/200, manige 3/127, monige 5/17, 8/17, 9/10, 11(b)/2, mænege 22/36, manege 22/63 etc.; ap manige 3/130, 3/182, apf manege 22/11; apn manega 4/268, monig 9/46, 9/78, mænigo 10(b)/29; gp monigra 9/8; dpn manigum 3/99; dpf manegum 14/99; monegum 18/5; gp manigra 14/41; ealles tō mænege *all too many* 22/70

maniġeo see **menigu**

maniġfeald adj. *manifold, various* nsf menigfeald 4/93; apf manigfealde 3/109, menigfealde 4/86, mænigfealde 22/119, 22/168; apm manigfealdan 10(a)/14; dpm menigfealdum 4/84; dpf manigfealdum 5/66; compar. nsn mænigfealdre 22/85

*ġe*maniġfealdan 1 *multiply, increase* pres. 1s gemanigfealde 2/33, 2/74

manlīċe adv. *manfully, nobly* 1/13

mānlīċe adv. *wickedly* 1/13

mann m. *person, man* ns 3/33, 3/158, man 4/143, 4/288, mon 5/77, etc.; as man 4/312, mann 1/19, mannan 4/68, 20/98, 20/101, mon 9/12, monnan 15/18; gs mannes 4/74, 4/292; ds men 4/8, 9/62, 20/167; np 4/22, 4/275, 4/282, 6/25, menn 4/307, 5/44; ap men 9/81, 22/71; etc.; gp manna 3/165, 4/63, 8/26, monna 5/58, 8/34, etc., monna cynnes *of the race of men, of mankind* 20/52; dp mannum 4/34, 4/143, 4/260, monnum 5/26, 9/12, 11(o)/8, etc.; used indefinitely: *one, a man* ns 4/288, 18/25, 19/1, 20/291, 20/329

mannslaga m. *manslayer, murderer* np mannslagan 22/146

mannsylen f. *slavetrading* ap mannsylena 22/121

manslyht m. *manslaughter* ap manslyhtas 22/123

mānswora m. *perjuror* np mānsworan 22/147

manrǣden f. *service, tribute* ds manrǣdene 4/160

mānscaða m. *wicked, ravager, evil-doer* ns 18(a)/712, 18(a)/737, 18(b)/1339

mansliht m. *manslaughter, slaying* dp manslihtum 7/55

māra adj. (compar. of **micel** §76) *more, larger* asm māran 3/119, 3/120, 7/50, 18(a)/753; nsn māre 12/313; asn māre 2/73, 3/13, 3/17, 4/5, 4/45, 20/329, dsn māran 3/147; asf māran 8/17, 8/19

Maria pers. n. *Mary* as Marian 14/92

martyr m. *martyr* as 4/308

maðelian 2 *speak, make a speech* pret. 3s maðelode 12/42, 12/309, 18(b)/1321, 18(b)/1383, maþelade 11(g)/5

māðm m. *treasure* as 11(n)/13; ap māðmas 4/275, mādmas 20/318; gp māðma 5/30, 20/340, mādma 20/329; dp māðmum 17/99

māþþumgyfa m. *giver of treasure* ns 16/92

ġemǣc adj. *suitable* asm gemǣcne 15/18

mæcg m. *man* np mæcgas 11(m)/7

mæg m. *kinsman* ns 6/31, 12/5, 12/114, 12/224, 12/287, 16/109, etc.; as 18(b)/1339; np mǣgas 6/29, māgas 15/11; gp māga 16/51; dp mǣgum 6/32

mæg see **magan**

mæġen n. *strength, power* ns 3/166, 12/313; gs mæġenes 8/14; ds mæġene 11(f)/14, 18(a)/789; is mæġne 11(h)/13; *armed force, army* ns mæġen 20/253, 20/261 [MnE (might and) main]

mæġenēacen adj. *mighty* nsn 20/292

mæġenþise f. *force, violence* ds mæġenþisan 11(f)/10

mǣgrǣs m. *attack on a kinsman* ap mǣgenrǣsas 22/123

mǣgslaga m. *slayer of a kinsman* np mǣgslagan 22/146

mǣġð f. *tribe, nation* ds mǣġðe 10(a)/1; gp mǣgþa 18/25; dp mǣgþum 18/5; *kindred* ds mǣgðe 22/94

mǣġð f. *maiden, woman* ns 20/78, 20/125, 20/145, 20/254; as 20/35, 20/43, 20/165, 20/260; gs 20/334; np 20/135, mæġeð 11(m)/7; gp mæġða 11(j)/8

mǣl n. *time, occasion* ap mǣla 12/212; gp 10(b)/54, 17/36

mǣlan 1 *speak* pret. 3s mǣlde 12/26, 12/43, 12/210 [MnE (black)mail]

ġemǣlan 1 *speak* pret. 3s gemǣlde 12/230, 12/244

Mǣldūn m. *Maldon* ds Mǣldūne 7/21

mǣnan 1 *speak of, relate, bemoan* inf. 18(d)/3171; p. ptc. mǣned 18(a)/857

gemǣne adj. *common* nsm 22/43; nsn 22/92 (wǣpengewrixl weorðe gemǣne *a conflict takes place*); *in common* asf 22/96; ds gemǣnum ċēape *as a joint purchase* 22/77

mæniġ see **maniġ**

mæniġe see **meniġu**

mæniġfealde see **maniġfeald**

mǣran 1 *make famous* p. ptc. gemǣred 9/2

mǣran see **mǣre**

mǣre adj. *famous, illustrious, glorious, notorious* nsm 4/156, 18(a)/762 (as noun); dsm mǣran 14/69, 20/3; nsf mǣre 14/12, 14/82, 16/100; asm mǣran 10(b)/14; gsm mǣres 18(a)/797; np mǣre 4/26; apm mǣran 4/324; compar. mǣrra nsm 4/316; superl. mǣrost nsf 20/324

mǣrsian 2 *proclaim, mark out* pres. 3s mǣrsað 10(b)/16

mǣrðu f. *glorious thing, fame, glory* ns mǣrðo 18(a)/857; as mǣrðe 20/343; ap mǣrða 4/86, 22/182; gp mǣrþa 17/84

mæsseprēost m. *mass-priest* ns 3/213, 4/13; ds mæsseprīoste 5/71

mæsserbana m. *slayer of a priest* np mæsserbanan 22/147

mǣst adj. *most, greatest* nsm mǣsta 20/292; asm mǣst 20/181; asn mǣste 7/54; asf mǣstan 9/6, mǣste 12/174, 20/3

mǣst adv. *mostly* 7/4

mǣst n. *most, greatest* ns 12/223; as 7/75, 17/84

mæst m. *(ship's) mast* ns 21/24

mæstling m. *brass* as 3/142

ġemǣtan 1 impers. w.d. of person *dream* pret. 3s gemǣtte 14/2

mǣte adj. *small, limited* isn 14/69 (see note), 14/124

ġemǣtte see ġemǣtan, ġemētan

mǣð f. *propriety, fitness, respect* ns 12/195; as mǣþe 22/72, ds 22/26

mæðel n. *assembly* ds mæðle 11(b)/2

mǣw m. *mew, seagull* as 17/22

mē see **iċ**

meahte (n.) see **miht**

meahte (v.) see **magan**

meahtigra see **mihtig**

mearc f. *boundary, region, border* ap mearce 11(j)/6

mearcstapa m. *wanderer in the wasteland, border-haunter* ap mearcstapan 18(b)/1348

mearg see **mearh**

mearh m. *horse* ns 18(c)/2264, mearg 16/92; as mearh 12/188; ds mēare 12/239; ap mēaras 18(a)/865; dp mēarum 18(a)/855 [MnE mare]

mec see **iċ**

mēċe m. *sword* as 12/167, 12/236, 20/78; ds 20/104

mecgan 1 *mix, mingle* inf. 21/24

mēd f. *reward* as mēde 20/343; ds 20/334 [MnE meed]

mēdan 1 *presume* (?) pres. subj. 3s mēde 11(n)/15

medmiċel adj. *moderate, brief* asn 9/117; dsn medmiclum 8/34, 9/5

medubenċ f. *mead-bench* ns medubenc 18(a)/776

medoburh f. *mead-city, festive city* ds medobyrig 20/167

medodrinc m. *mead* ds medodrince 17/22

medowērig adj. *besotted with mead* apm medowērige 20/229, dp medowērigum 20/245

medugāl adj. *drunk with mead* nsm 20/26

mēġe see **māge**

mehte (meahte) see **magan**

melcan III *milk* pres. 1s melce 3/26

ġemeltan III *melt* pret. 3s gemealt 18(a)/897

men see **mann**

ġemengan 1 *mingle* p. ptc. gemenged 16/48, 18(a)/848

menġeo see **meniġu**
menifealdlīċe adv. *in the plural* 4/71 [MnE manifoldly]
meniġfeald see **maniġfeald**
meniġu f. *multitude* ns mengeo 5/31; ds mænige 14/112, manigeo 14/151
menn see **mann**
mennisc adj. *human* dsn menniscum 4/308
menniscnis f. *incarnation* ds menniscnisse 4/29, menniscnesse 9/75 [MnE mannishness]
meodo m. *mead* ds 12/212
meodoheall f. *mead-hall* ns 13/23; ds meoduhealle 16/27
meodosetl n. *mead-hall seat* gp meodosetla 18/5
meotod m. *creator* ns 17/108, meotud 17/116, metod 18(a)/706, 12/175, 20/154, 21/57; gs meotodes 9/37, 21/65, metudes 16/2, meotudes 17/103, metodes 20/261; ds metode 12/147
mēowle f. *maiden* ns 20/56; as mēowlan 20/261
Merantūn m. *Merton* ds Merantūne 6/10
mere m. *pool, lake* ns 18(b)/1362; as 18(a)/845; ds 18(a)/855 [MnE mer(maid), mere]
mereflōd m. *sea-tide, ocean* ds mereflōde 17/59, 21/24
merehengest m. *sea-horse (ship)* ns 11(j)/6
merewēriġ adj. *sea-weary* gs merewērges 17/12 (as noun)
mergen see **morgen**
ġemet n. *measure, metre* as 9/47; mid gemete *with moderation, in proper measure* 11(m)/7, 17/111, 18(a)/779 (*in any way*)
mētan I *meet, encounter* pret. 1s mētte 8/44; 3s 18(a)/751; 3p mētton 6/26
ġemētan I *meet, find* inf. 4/233; pret. 3s gemētte 4/197, 18(a)/757, gemǣtte 7/35
mete m. *food* ns 3/165; ds 3/80 [MnE meat]
metelīst f. *lack of food* np metelīste 19/15
ġemetlīċe adv. *moderately* 9/89
metod see **meotod**
metsung f. *provisions* as metsunge 7/60; 7/65
mētte see **mētan**
mētton see **mētan**
mēðe adj. *weary, tired* nsm 14/65, npm 14/69
meðelstede m. *meeting-place, assembly* ds meþelstede 12/199
micclan see **micel**
miccle adv. *much* 12/50
miċel adj. *great, large, much* nsm 1/16, 3/214; asm micelne 3/106, miclan 4/78, micclan 4/313; gsm miccles 12/217; dsm mycclum 7/34; ism micle 8/77, 14/34 (elne micle *with great zeal*), etc.; nsn 3/20, 3/21, 3/98, 4/17, etc.; asn 3/23, mycel 7/15, 7/36, 7/39, etc.; dsn miclum 3/137;

isn micle 8/43; nsf 1/20, 3/214; asf 15/51; gsf micelre 9/85; npm myccle 21/4; npf micle (*grave*) 22/84; dpn miclum 6/6; dpf 20/10, 20/70, miclan 22/14, 22/15, etc.; (as noun) asn micel 22/22 [MnE dialect mickel]. See **miccle, miclum**
miċel n. *much, a great part* as 3/18, 7/70, 7/72
miċelnes f. *size* ns 1/17
miċlan (miċlum) see **miċel**
miclum adv. *greatly, severely* 6/15, 10(b)/74
mid prep. w.d.a.i. *with, amid, among, by means of* 2/47, 2/50, 2/79, 3/15, 4/24, etc.; as adv. *in attendance, at the same time* 11(a)/5, 14/106; mid þām þe *when* 2/60, 4/69, 4/202; mid þȳ (þe) *when* 8/52, 9/97
midd adj. *middle, mid* dsf midre 14/2
middan see **onmiddan**
middanġeard m. *world, middle earth* ns 16/62; as 9/42, 9/120, 14/104, 16/75, 17/90; gs middangeardes 9/70, 18(a)/751
middǣġ m. *midday, noon* as 2/18
Middelseaxe m. pl. *Middlesex* ap Middelsexe 7/67
middeneaht f. *midnight* as 9/100
mid þām þe see **mid**
mid þȳ see **mid**
miht f. *power, might* as mihte 4/167, 8/19, meahte 9/37, 17/108; ds mihte 14/102
miht (v.) see **magan**
mihte (n.) see **miht**
mihte (v.) see **magan**
mihten see **magan**
mihtiġ adj. *mighty, powerful* nsm 14/151, 18(b)/1339; dsm mihtigan 18(b)/1398; compar. meahtigra nsm 17/116
mihton see **magan**
milde adj. *merciful, kind* nsm 4/121; nsm 12/175; superl. mildust nsm 18(d)/3181 [MnE mild]
mildheort adj. *merciful* nsm mildheorta 4/286 [MnE mildheart(ed)]
mildheortnes f. *mercy, pity* as mildheortnisse 7/52 [MnE mildheart(ed)ness]
mīlġemearc n. *measure by miles* gs mīlgemearces 18(b)/1362
milts f. *mercy, favour, reverent joy* as miltse 16/2, 20/349; gs 20/85, 20/92; ds 11(o)/8
mīn poss. adj. *my, mine* nsm 2/54, 2/55, 19/13; asm mīnne 3/70, 3/76, etc.; gsm mīnes 3/11; dsm mīnum 3/27, 3/172; isn mīne gefrǣge *as I have heard tell* 18(a)/776, 18(a)/837; asn mīn 3/76, 3/135; nsf mīn 14/130; as mīne 20/198; gsf mīnre 2/77; dsf 11(j)/18; npm mīne 9/109; apm 3/43, 3/103; dpm mīnum 3/135; npn mīn 3/138; apn 3/23, 3/135, 3/149; apf mīne 4/190

mīn (pron.) see ič
mīne 16/27 see note
misbēodan II w.d. *ill-use* inf. 22/28
misdǣd f. *misdeed* np misdǣda 4/74 gp
22/119, 22/151; dp misdǣdum 22/161,
misdǣdan 22/134, etc.
mislič adj. *various* apf mislice 4/90, mistlice
22/126, etc.; dpm mislicum 17/99; dpf
5/66
mislimpan III (impers. w.d.) *go awry*
22/116
missenlič adj. *various, manifold* gsn missen-
lices 3/153; npn missenlicu 3/63; apn 3/
203
missenlīče adv. *in various places* 16/75
misthliþ n. *misty hill, cover of darkness* dp
misthleoþum 18(a)/710
mistliče see misliče
mīþan I *conceal* pres. ptc. asm mīþendne
15/20
mōd n. *spirit, courage, mind* ns 10(b)/26,
12/313, 13/18, 16/15, 16/51, 18(a)/730,
19/15, 20/167; as 9/104, 15/20, 17/12,
17/108; gs mōdes 11(f)/14, 17/36, 17/50,
18(a)/810; ds mōde 4/181, 4/227, 5/39,
10(a)/27, 11(b)/2, 14/130, 16/41, 16/
111, 17/109, 18(a)/753, 18(b)/1307, *heart*
20/57, 20/93, 20/97, 20/154, 20/282;
is 9/98, 9/118, 14/122; np 9/8 [MnE
mood]
mōdcearig adj. *troubled in thought* nsm 16/2
mōdcearu f. *grief of heart* as mōdceare
15/51; gs 15/40
mōdġeþanc m. *conception, purpose* as 9/37
mōdiġ adj. *brave, bold, arrogant* nsm 14/
41, 20/26, mōdiga 20/52, mōdi 12/147,
mōdega 18(a)/813; gsf mōdigre 20/334;
npm mōdige 12/80, mōdge 16/62, 18(a)/
855 [MnE moody]
mōdiġlīče adv. *boldly, bravely* mōdelice
12/200 [MnE moodily]
mōdor f. *mother* ns 7/52, 11(k)/2; as 14/92
mōdsefa m. *heart, spirit* ns 10(b)/74, 14/
124, 16/59, 17/59; as mōdsefan 16/10,
16/19
mōdwlonc adj. *proud of heart, spirited* nsm
17/39
molde f. *earth* ns 17/103; as moldan 14/12,
14/82; gs 20/343; ds 4/314
moldern n. *earth-house, sepulchre* as 14/65
mon see man, mann
ġemon see ġemunan
monade see manian
monað see manian
mōnað m. *month* gs monðes 20/324; ap
mōnþas 7/17
mondrēam m. *joy of men, revelry, festivity*
gp mondrēama 13/23

mondryhten m. *liege lord* as 16/41; ds
mondryhtne 11(n)/13
monegum, monig see manig
ġemong m. *troop, horde* as 20/193, 20/303,
gemang 20/225
ġemoniað see ġemanian
moniġ see maniġ
monn see mann
monnan see mann
monncynnes see mancynn
mōnþas see mōnað
monðwǣre adj. *gentle, kind* superl. monð-
wǣrust nsm 18(d)/3181
mōr m. *moor, marsh, wasteland* ds mōre
18(a)/710; ap mōras 18(b)/1348
morgen m. *morning* as 18(a)/837, mergen
4/282; ds morgenne 3/31, 6/23, 9/48,
9/59 [MnE morn]
morġencolla m. *morning attack* as morgencollan 20/245
morġentīd f. *morning* as 20/236
morð n. *crime* as 4/281
morðdǣd f. *murder* ap morðdǣda 22/120
morðorwyrhta m. *murderer* np morðor-
wyrhtan 22/148
morþor n. *crime, violence, torment* as 15/20;
gs morðres 20/90; ds morðre 18(a)/892; gp
morðra 20/181 [MnE murder]
mōste see mōtan
ġemōt n. *meeting, council, encounter* ns 12/301;
as 12/199
mōtan pret.-pres. *may, be allowed to* pres. 1s
mōt 14/142; 2s mōst 12/30; 3p mōton
4/31; subj. 1s mōte 14/127, 20/89; 3s
20/118; 1p mōten 17/119, 3p mōton
12/180; pret. 3s mōste 8/62, 12/272,
18(a)/706, 18(a)/735; 3p mōston 12/83;
subj. 3s mōste 4/176, 10(b)/39, 10(b)/62,
20/185; 3p mōstan 10(a)/8, 12/87,
12/263, mōsten 10(b)/36
moððe f. *moth* ns 11(c)/1
Moyses pers. n. *Moses* gs 4/12, 9/72,
Moises 4/23
muhton see magan
ġemunan pret.-pres. *remember* pres. 1s
geman 1/28, 14/28, gemunu 12/212; 3s
gemon 15/51, 16/34, 16/90; pret. 1s
gemunde 5/28, 5/40; 3s 10(a)/16 (w.g.),
10(a)/29, 10(b)/57, 10(b)/79, 12/225,
18(a)/758, 18(a)/870; subj. 3p gemundon
12/196
mund f. *hand* dp mundum 20/229; *security,
protection* ds munde 22/27
mundbyrd f. *protection, hope of protection* ns
14/130; as 20/3
mundgripe m. *hand-grip* as 18(a)/753
munt m. *mountain* dp muntum 10(a)/4
[MnE mount]

Muntġiop m. *the Alps* as 10(b)/8; ds 10(b)/14 [MnE mount, Jove]

munuc m. *monk* ns 3/179, 3/213, 4/2, etc.

munuchād m. *monastic orders* as 9/63 [MnE monkhood]

murnan III *mourn, care about* inf. 12/259; 20/154; pres. ptc. murnende 19/15; pres. subj. 3s murne 18(b)/1385; pret. 3p murnon 12/96

mūð m. *mouth* ns 21/37; as mūþan 18(a)/724; ds mūðe 7/40, 9/70

mycclan see **miċel**

myċel see **miċel**

myltestre f. *prostitute* np myltestran 22/148

ġemynd n. *mind, remembrance* as 5/3, 16/51; ds gemynde 9/46, 10(b)/54

ġemyndgian 2 *remember* pret. 3s gemyndgade 9/67

ġemyndig adj. w.g. *mindful* nsm 4/141, 4/203, 4/286, 16/6, 18(a)/868; *concerned* nsf 20/74

mynster n. *church, monastery* as 4/273, 9/64; ds mynstre 4/135, 5/77, 9/1 [MnE (West)minster]

mynsterhata m. *persecutor of monasteries* np mynsterhatan 22/147

myntan 1 *intend, think* pret. 3s mynte 18(a)/712, 18(a)/731, 18(a)/762; *assume* pret. 3p mynton 20/253

Myrce m. pl. *the Mercians* dp Myrcum 12/217

myre f. *mare* ds myran 8/63

myrhð f. *joy* as myrhða 22/182

myrðu f. *disturbance, trouble, affliction* gp myrðe 18(a)/810

nā adv. *no, by no means, not at all, never* 3/173, 4/5, 4/23, etc., nō 15/4, 16/54, etc.; nā þē lǣs *nevertheless* 7/76

nabbað see **habban**

naca m. *boat, ship* gs nacan 17/7

nacod adj. *naked* nsm 2/22, 2/23; asf nacedan (*bare, literal*) 4/45; np nacode 2/15

nāh see **āgan**

nāht see **nānwuht**

nahte see **āgan**

nalæs see **nealles**

nales see **nealles**

nam see **niman**

ġenam see **ġeniman**

nama m. *name* ns 1/29, 12/267, noma 11(h)/1; as naman 2/44, 11(n)/11; ds 4/122, 5/76, 14/113, 20/81; noman 9/28; ap naman 1/28

ġenamon see **ġeniman**

nān (= ne ān) pron., adj. *none, not one, not any, no* nsm 3/10, 3/154, 3/177, etc.; asm nǣnne 4/114, 5/42, nānne 20/68, 20/233; nsn nān 18(a)/803; asf nāne 4/118; gsf nānre 10(a)/28; npn nāne 4/326

nānne see **nān**

nānwuht pron. *nothing* as 5/32, nōht 9/15, 9/29, nāht 9/30

nāp see **nīpan**

nāteshwōn adv. *not at all* 2/8

nāþor adj. *neither* dsf nāþre 4/140; nāþor ne . . . ne *neither . . . nor* 22/57

nāwiht n. *nothing* ns nōwiht 8/42; as 8/14 [MnE naught]

næbbe see **habban**

nǣdl f. *needle* as nǣdle 3/195

nǣdre f. *snake, serpent* ns 2/1, 2/2, 2/26; ds nǣdran 2/28; as nǣdran 1/35 [MnE (a)n adder]

nǣfdon (= ne hæfdon) see **habban**

næfne see **nefne**

nǣfre adv. *never* 4/184, 4/195, 6/31, 9/15, 9/19, 9/35, etc.

næfst (= ne hæfst) see **habban**

næfð (= ne hæfð) see **habban**

nǣgan 1 *accost, address* pret. 3s nǣgde 18(b)/1318

nægl m. *nail, fingernail* ap næglas 4/269; dp næglum 14/46

nǣnig pron. *none, no one* ns 6/20, 6/31, 8/15, 9/11, etc.; as 9/19

nǣnne see **nān**

nǣren (= ne wǣren) see **bēon**

næs (= ne wæs) see **bēon**

næs adv. *by no means* 18(c)/2262

næss m. *headland, bluff* ap næssas 18(b)/1358; gp næssa 18(b)/1360; *chasm, ground* as næs 20/113

ġenǣstan 1 *contend, grapple* pres. 3s genǣsteð 11(f)/10

ne adv., conj. *not, nor* 1/34, 2/3, 3/63, 3/84, 3/161 (ne . . . ne *nor*), 4/23, 4/24, etc.

nēah adv. *near* 15/25, 16/26, nēh 12/103; compar. nēar 18(a)/745; predicate adj. *near, imminent* 9/96, 9/112; superl. nīehsta dsn nēxtan 4/147, nȳxtan 7/57 (æt nȳxtan *at last, eventually*), 22/162 (æt nȳhstan *at last*) [MnE nigh]

ġeneahhe adv. *often, very, frequently* 16/56, 18(a)/783, 20/26, genehe 12/269; superl. genehost 18(a)/794

neahte see **niht**

nēalēċan 1 *draw near* inf. 9/22; pres. 3s nēalǣcð 22/2 pret. 3s nēalēhte 8/67, nēalǣcte 9/87, nēalǣhte 20/34, 20/261

nealles adv. *not at all* nales 9/12, 16/32, 19/15, nalæs 16/33, nealles (þæt) ān . . . ac *not only . . . but* 3/103, 3/130

nēan adv. *from near, near* 18(a)/839

nearo adj. *narrow, close, anxious* nsf 17/7

nearolīce adv. *sparely* 4/97 [MnE narrowly]

nearon see **bēon**

nearones f. *distress, strait* ds naranessa
10(a)/26 [MnE narrowness]

nēat n. *cattle, neat* gp nēata 9/25

ġenēat m. *retainer, comrade* ns 12/310

nēawest f. *neighbourhood* ds nēaweste 9/90

nefa m. *nephew* ns 11(a)/6; ds nefan 18(a)/881

nefne conj. *except, but* 17/46, næfne 18(b)/
1353. See **nemne**

nēh see **nēah**

ġenehe see ġeneahhe

ġenehost see ġeneahhe

nēhsta adj. *last* dsm nēhstan 20/73

nelc (= ne wile) see **willan**

nellað (= ne willað) see **willan**

nelle (ne wille) see **willan**

nemnan I *call, name*, inf. 20/81; pret. 3s
nemnde 9/28; 3p nemdon 18(b)/1354;
p. ptc. genemned 5/68, nemned 8/73

nemne conj. *except* 15/22. See **nefne**

nemþe see **nymþe**

nēod f. *need* ns 22/158

nēodlaðu f. *desire (or urgent summons?)* dp
nēodlaðum 18(b)/1320

nēodlīce adv. *diligently* compar. nēodlīcor
8/15

neom (= ne eom) see **bēon**

neorxenawang m. *Paradise* gs neorxena-
wanges 2/19; ds neorxenawange 2/6,
2/18, 2/21

nēosan I w.g. *go to* inf. 20/63

nēotan II w.g. *use, make use of* inf. 12/308

neowol adj. *prostrate* nsm 10(b)/80, niwol
10(a)/29; *deep* asm neowolne 20/113

nerġend m. *saviour* as 20/81; gs nergendes
20/73; ds nergende 20/45

nerian I *save* pres. ptc. nsm nergende
(*saving, salvific*) 21/63

ġenerian I *save, protect* pret. 3s generede
6/39; p. ptc. genered 18(a)/827

nese adv. *no* 3/53

nest n. *food* as 20/128

nēten see **nīeten**

nett n. *net* 3/76; ap 3/42, 3/44; dp nettum
3/45, 3/46, 3/109, etc.

nēðan I *venture* pret. 3s nēðde 20/277

ġenēþan I *venture (on)* pret. 3s genēðde
18(a)/888

nēxtan see **nēah**

niċ adv. *no, not* I 3/96, 3/146

nicor m. *sea-monster* gp nicera 18(a)/845

nīedbehēfe adj. *necessary* nsm 3/151, 3/
173

nīedbeðearf adj. *necessary, essential* superl.
npf nīedbeðearfosta 5/55

nīehst see **nēah**

nīeten n. *beast, cattle* ns nēten 9/67; ds
nytene 4/94; np nietenu 2/1

niht f. *night* ns 1/22, 18(b)/1320, 20/34; as
3/30, 4/236, 7/33 (on niht by *night*), 18(a)/
736; gs neahte 9/93; nihtes (adv. *at night*)
20/45; ds nihte 2/46, 4/274, 7/32, 14/2,
neahte 9/25, niht 18(a)/702, 18(b)/1334,
nihte 20/64; gp nihta 18(b)/1365

nihthelm m. *cover of night* as 16/96

nihtscūa m. *shadow of night* ns 16/104,
17/31

nihtwaco f. *night-watch* ns 17/7

nihtweorc n. *night-work* ds nihtweorce
18(a)/827

niman IV *take* inf. 12/39, 12/252, 15/15;
imp. s. nim 2/44; pres. 1s nime 3/78, 3/
80, 3/122; 3p nimað 17/48; pret. 3s nam
4/18, 7/75, nom 8/64, etc.; 3p naman
7/57, namon 7/62; p. ptc. genumen 2/41,
7/40

ġeniman IV *take, seize* pret. 3s genam 2/13,
20/77, 20/98; 3p genamon 7/37, 14/30,
14/60; subj. 3s gename 12/71; p. ptc.
genumen nsm 18(d)/3165

ġenip n. *darkness, mist* ap genipu 18(b)/1360

nīpan I *grow dark* pres. 3s nīpeð 16/104; pret.
3s nāp 17/31

ġenīpan I *grow dark* pret. 3s genāp 16/96

nis (= ne is) see **bēon**

nīþ m. *hatred, malice, trouble, affliction* as 17/
75; ds nīðe 18(a)/827; is 20/53 (*in malice*);
gp nīða 18(a)/845, 18(a)/882, 20/34
(*iniquity*); dp nīðum 20/287

niþer adv. *downwards* 10(b)/80, 18(b)/1360
[MnE nether]

nīðheard adj. *daring* nsm 20/277

nīðhēdig adj. *hostile* npm nīðhedige 18(d)/
3165

nīðhycgend m. *evil-schemer* ap nīðhycgende
20/233

nīðwundor n. *fearful wonder, portent* as
18(b)/1365

ġenīwad see **nīwian**

nīwan adv. *newly* 8/22

nīwe adj. *new* nsm 18(a)/783; nsf 4/28, 8/10;
dsf nīwan 4/10, 4/18

nīwes adv. *recently* 15/4

nīwian 2 *restore, renew* p. ptc. genīwad nsm
14/148; nsf 16/50, 16/55; genīwod 18(b)/
1322, 20/98

niwol see **neowol**

nō see **nā**

ġenōg adj. *enough* npm genōge 14/33 (*many*)

ġenōh adv. *quite, exceedingly* 22/104 [MnE
enough]

nōht adv. *not, not at all* 5/17, 8/72, nāwiht
8/14; nōht þon læs *nevertheless* 8/17

nōht see **nānwuht**

nōhwæðer conj. *neither* 5/25 (nōhwæðer ne
. . . ne *neither . . . nor*)

nolde (= ne wolde) see **willan**
noldest (= ne woldest) see **willan**
noldon (= ne woldon) see **willan**
nom see **niman**
noman see **nama**
norð adv. *northwards* 18(a)/858
norðan adv. *from the north* 16/104, 17/31
Norðdene m. pl. *the Danes* dp Norðdenum 18(a)/783
Norðhymbre m. pl. *Northumbria* gp Norðhymbra 4/150, 4/153; dp Norðhymbran 7/42, Norðhymbron 12/266
norðsciphere m. *northern fleet, attack fleet of the Northmen* ds norðscipherige 7/6
nosþyrl n. *nostril* ap nosþirlu 4/111
notian 2 w.g. *use, enjoy* pres. 3s notaþ 3/202
notu f. *employment* ds note 5/60
nōwiht see **nāwiht**
nū adv., conj. *now that, now* adv. 2/64, 2/74, etc.; conj. 2/64 (nū . . . nū *now . . . now that*), 2/27, 12/57, etc.
ᵹenumen see **niman**
nȳd f. *need, necessity* ns 20/277; ds nȳde *by necessity* 20/287, 22/3, 22/18
nȳdᵹestealla m. *comrade in battle* np nȳdgesteallan 18(a)/882
nȳdᵹyld n. *forced tribute* np 22/95
nȳdmāge f. *near kinswoman* as nȳdmāgan 22/103
nȳdþearf f. *need, necessity* ns 22/19
nȳhst see **nēah**
nyle (= ne wyle) see **willan**
nymþe conj. *unless, except* 11(h)/16, 18(a)/781, nemþe 16/113
nyrwan 1 *diminish, narrow* p. ptc. npn genyrwde 22/40
nyste (= ne wyste) see **witan**
nytene see **nieten**
nytnisse see **nyttnes**
nytt adj. *useful* nsm 3/132, 3/151; npm nytte 3/115; apm 3/179, 18(a)/794; npn nyt 11(n)/11
nytt f. *use, utility* ds nytte 3/150, 11(m)/2
nyttnes f. *usefulness, benefit* gs nyttnesse 8/14, nytnisse 8/48
nyðerian II *prostrate, abase* p. ptc. genyðerad 20/113
nȳxtan see **nēah**

Odda pers. n. *Odda* gs Oddan 12/186, 12/238
of prep. w.d. *from* 2/3, 2/14, 2/25, 3/33 (*of*), 4/3, etc.
ofdūne adv. *down, downhill* 10(a)/27, 10(b)/80, 20/290, 21/30
ofer prep. w.d.a. *over, after* 1/2, 1/5, 2/2, 2/18, 2/64, 3/24, etc., *contrary to* 14/35; ofer bæc see **bæc**

ōfer m. *river-bank, shore* ds ōfre 12/28, 18(b)/1371
ofercuman IV *overcome* inf. 20/235; p. ptc. ofercumen 18(a)/845
oferdrenċan 1 *inebriate* p. ptc. npf oferdrencte 20/31
oferfēng see **oferfōn**
oferfōn VII *seize* pret. 3s oferfēng 10(b)/69
oferfyll f. *gluttony* as oferfylla 22/168 [MnE over, fill]
ofergān anom. (§128) *overrun* p. ptc. ofergān 7/66 [MnE overgo]
oferhelmian 2 *overhang, overshadow* pres. 3s oferhelmað 18(b)/1364
oferhoga m. *despiser* np oferhogan 22/129–30
oferlīċe adv. *excessively* 22/161 [MnE overly]
ofermōd n. *pride, arrogance, overconfidence* ds ofermōde 12/89
oferwinnan III *conquer* p. ptc. oferwunnen 20/319
Offa pers. n. *Offa* ns 12/198, 12/230, 12/286, 12/288; gs Offan 12/5
offrian 2 *offer* inf. 4/89; pret. 3s offrode 4/93
ᵹeoffrian 2 *sacrifice, offer up* imp. s. geoffra 2/45; pret. subj. 3s geoffrode 2/60; p. ptc. geoffrod 4/97
offrung f. *offering, sacrifice* ns 2/54; as offrunge 2/56; ds 2/69
ofġīefan V *abandon* pret. 3s ofgeaf 18(c)/2251; 3p ofgēafon 11(k)/1, 16/61
oflongian 2 *seize with longing* p. ptc. oflongad 15/29
ofostlīċe see **ofstlīċe**
ofscēotan II *shoot, kill with a missile* pret. 3s ofscēat 12/77
ofslagen see **ofslēan**
ofslæġen see **ofslēan**
ofslēan VI *slay, destroy* inf. 2/65, 3/102, 10(a)/10; infl. inf. (tō) ofslēanne 2/49; pres. 1s ofslēa 3/45; pret. 3s ofslōg 6/3, ofslōh 7/35; 3p ofslōgon 4/151, 6/37, 7/36; p. ptc. ofslagen 2/59, 4/177, 4/192, 4/260, 7/15, ofslæġen 6/24, 6/27, 7/21, ofslegen 7/4, asm ofslæġenne 6/16; npm ofslagene 4/183
ofslegen see **ofslēan**
ofslōg see **ofslēan**
ofsnað see **ofsnīðan**
ofsnīðan 1 *slaughter* pret. 3s ofsnāð 2/68
ofspring m. *offspring* ns 2/75; as 2/74; ds ofspringe 2/31
ofst f. *haste* dp ofstum 20/10, 20/35, 20/70; ds on ofste *hastening* 22/1
ofstang see **ofstingan**
ofstician 2 *stab to death* pret. 1s ofsticode 3/58, 3/61; 2s ofsticodest 3/59

ofstingan III *stab to death* pret. 3s ofstang
6/5

ofstlīċe adv. *quickly* 12/143, ofostlīċe 20/150,
20/169

ofstondan VI *remain standing* p. ptc. ofstonden 13/11

oft adv. *often* 4/237, 5/2, 6/6, 18/4, etc.; compar. oftor 14/128; superl. oftost 5/22

oftēon II *take away from, deprive* pret 3s
oftēah 18/5

ofwundrian 2 *be astonished* p. ptc. npm
ofwundrode 4/244

oll n. *scorn* ds olle 22/136

on adv. *on, onward* 8/61, 17/91

on prep. w.d.a. *on, onto, upon, in, into* w d
(*on, in*) 1/9, 1/11, 1/29, 2/4, 2/9, 2/17,
2/21, 3/26 (*during*), 4/132, 6/17 (*from*),
etc.; w.a. (*onto, upon, into*) 3/44, 3/76,
3/122, 6/15 (*against*), etc.; 22/131 (*of*),
22/72 (*for*)

onarn see onirnan

onǣlan 1 *kindle* p. ptc. onǣlæd 8/29
[archaic MnE anneal]

onbærnan 1 *kindle, inspire* p. ptc. npm
onbærnde 9/9, onbærned 9/85

onbreġdan III *swing open* pret. 3s onbrǣd
18(a)/723

onbryrdan 1 *inspire* pret. 3s onbryrde 20/
95

onbūgan II *bend* pres. 1s onbūge 11(h)/3

onbyriġan 1 w.g. *taste* inf. 14/114, onbyrian
4/243

oncierran 1 *turn* inf. oncerran 10(b)/61;
pres. 3s oncyrreð (w. refl.: *change direction,
turn aside*) 17/103

oncnāwan VII *recognize, perceive, acknowledge* inf. 12/9; pret. 1s oncnēow 2/64; 3p
oncneowon 2/15

oncnēow see oncnāwan

oncnēowon see oncnāwan

oncweðan V w.d. *answer* pret. 3s oncwæð
12/245, 17/23

oncyrreð see oncierran

oncȳðð f. *grief, distress* as oncȳþðe 18(a)/830

ond see and

ondette see andettan

ondrǣdan VII *be afraid, dread* pres. 1s
ondrǣde 4/9; 2s ondrǣtst 2/64; 3s
ondrǣdeþ 17/106; pret. 1s ondrēd (w.
refl.) 2/22

ondrēd see ondrǣdan

ondswarodon see andswarian

ondsworede see andswarian

ondweard adj. *present* dp ondweardum 9/51

onemn prep. w.d.a. *alongside* 12/184

ōnettan 1 *hasten on, be active* pres. 3s ōnetteð
17/49; pret. 3s ōnette 20/162; 3p ōnettan
20/139

onfēng see onfōn

onfēngon see onfōn

onfindan III *discover, realize* pres. 3s
onfindeð 11(f)/9; pret. 3s onfunde 12/5,
18(a)/750, 18(a)/809; 3p onfundon 6/17;
subj. 3p onfunden 6/11

onfōn VII w.d.a. *receive, accept, take up* inf.
8/2, 8/51; pres. subj. 1p 8/23; pret. 1s onfēng 8/59; 3s 8/76, 9/14, etc.; 3p onfēngon
8/18; subj. 3s onfēnge 9/63; p. ptc. asf
onfongne 9/58

onga m. *arrow, dart* ns 11(h)/4

ongan see onġinnan

ongēan prep. w.d.a. *against* 2/32, 11(f)/9,
12/100; *toward* 20/165

ongēan adv. *again, back* 3/25, 4/247, 12/49,
12/137, 12/156 18(a)/747 (*out*)

ongēanstandan VI *stand opposite, withstand*
pret. 1s ongēanstōd 3/60

ongeat see onġietan

Ongelþēod f. *the English people, England* ds
Ongelþēode 9/10

ongemang prep. w.d. *among* 5/66

ongeocian 2 *unyoke* pres. 3s ongeocaþ 3/29

onġietan V *understand, perceive* inf. 5/32,
16/73, ongytan 14/18; pret. 1s ongeat
8/42; 3s 6/13, 10(a)/14, 10(a)/24, 10(b)/
68, 18/14; 3p ongēaton 12/84, 20/168,
20/238

onġildan III *pay, make amends* inf. 21/56

onġinnan III *begin* pres. 3p onginð 4/50; subj.
3p onginnen 14/116; pret. 1s ongan 5/66;
3s 9/61, 10(a)/17, 10(a)/30, 12/12, 12/
17, 12/89, 12/91, ongon 11(k)/3, angan
10(b)/59, ongan 20/80, 20/281, etc.; 3p
ongunnon 9/11, 12/86, 12/261, 14/65,
14/67, 15/11, 20/42, 20/270

ongon see onġinnan

ongunnon see onġinnan

ongyrwan 1 *unclothe, strip* pret. 3s ongyrede
14/39

onġytan see onġietan

onġytenes f. *knowledge* gs ongytenesse 8/69

onhæbbe see onhebban

onhǣtan 1 *inflame* p. ptc. onhǣted 20/87

onhebban VI *raise up, exalt* pres. 1s (w. refl.)
onhæbbe 11(o)/7

onhnīgan 1 *bend, bow down* pres. 3p
onhnīgað 11(o)/7

onhrēran 1 *stir, move* inf. 17/96

onhrīnan 1 *touch* w.g. pret. 3s onhrān 18(a)/
722

onhweorfan III *change* p. ptc. onhworfen
15/23

onhworfen see onhweorfan

onhwyrfan 1 *turn around* p. ptc. onhwyrfed
11(h)/1

onhwyrfed see onhwyrfan

onhyldan I *lower, incline* pret. 3s onhylde 9/116

oninnan prep. w.a. *into* 20/312

onirnan III *give away, spring open* pret. 3s onarn 18(a)/721

onlēon I w.d. of person and g. of thing *grant* pret. 3s onlēah 20/124

onlīcnes f. *image* ns onlīcnes 18(b)/1351. See ānlīcnes

onlūtan II *bow, incline, bend down* inf. 5/39

onlȳsan I *liberate, redeem* pret. 3s onlȳsde 14/147

onmēdla m. *pomp, magnificence* np onmēdlan 17/81

onmiddan prep. w.d. *in the middle of* 2/5, 2/19, on . . . middan *upon, onto* 20/68 [MnE amid]

onmunan pret.-pres. w.g. *pay attention to* pret. subj. 3p onmunden 6/35

onmunden see onmunan

ono hwæt interj. *lo and behold!* 8/49

onsǣġe adj. *assailing* nsn 22/46

onscyte m. *attack, calumny* dp onscytan 22/61, 22/142

onsendan I *send, send forth* inf. 5/75; pres. 3s onsendeð 16/104; p. ptc. onsended 14/49, 18(c)/2266

onsittan V *oppress* pres. 3s onsit 22/88; 3p onsittað 22/15

onslēpan I *fall asleep* pret. 3s onslēpte 9/26, 9/117

onspringan III *spring asunder* pret. 3p onsprungon 18(a)/817

onstal m. *supply* as 5/20

onstellan I *institute, set the example for, establish* pret. 3s onstealde 9/39; 3p onstealdon 7/43

onsȳn f. *appearance, face* ns 17/91

ontendan I *kindle, burn* inf. 7/50

onuppon prep. w.d. *above* 4/250

onwæcnan VI *awaken* pres. 3s onwæcneð 16/45; pret. 3s subj. onwōce 20/77

onweald m. *authority, power, jurisdiction, command* as onwald 5/5, anwald 10(a)/4, 10(b)/62; ds onwealde 2/35, anwealde 10(a)/20

onweġ adv. *away* 16/53, āweg 4/197

onwendan I *change* pres. 3s onwendeð 16/107; pret. 3s onwende 13/24

onwōce see onwæcnan

onwrēon I *reveal, disclose* imp. s. onwrēoh 14/97

onwrīðan I *unwrap* inf. 20/173 [MnE unwrithe]

open adj. *open* npm opene 14/47

openian 2 *open* p. ptc. npn geopenode 2/9, 2/15

openlīċe adv. *openly* 8/45, 8/49

ġeopenode see openian

ōr n. *beginning* as 9/39

orc m. *flagon, pitcher* np orcas 20/18

ord m. *point, spear, vanguard* ns 12/60, 12/69, 12/146, 12/157, etc.; as 12/47, 12/110; ds orde 12/124, 12/226, 12/273

ōretmæcg m. *warrior* ap ōretmæcgas 20/232

orf n. *cattle, livestock* as 4/92

orfcwealm m. *epidemic of cattle* ns 22/49

orfeorme adj. *deprived of,* i.e. *without* npm 20/271

orhlīċe adv. *insolently* 4/300

orlege n. *war, battle, strife* ds orlege 18(b)/1326

ormōd adj. *despondent, sad* nsm 10(a)/30, 10(b)/78

orsāwle adj. *lifeless* nsm 20/108 [MnE -soul]

orðanc adj. *skilful* nsn 21/2

orþonc m. *skill, intelligence* ns 13/16

Ōsrīċ pers. n. *Osric* ns 6/25

Ōswold pers. n. *Oswold* ns 12/304

Ōswyn pers. n. *Oswyn* ns 4/267

oð prep. w.a. *up to, as far as, until* 4/7, 4/96, 4/282, 4/295, 5/61, etc.; conj. *until* 6/3, oþ þæt *until* 3/43, 4/33, 4/129, 18/9, etc.

oðberan IV *carry away* pret. 3s oþbær 16/81

ōðer adj., pron. *other, another, next* nsm 4/6, etc.; asm ōþerne 12/143; dsm ōþrum 3/208, 12/64, 12/70, 12/133, 18(a)/814, 21/52, 22/55; dsn 13/10, 22/10; gsn ōðres 9/111; asf ōðre 5/81, 9/84; ōþre . . . ōþre *one . . . the other* 8/31; npm ōþre 4/307, 4/321; ōðre 9/10; apm ōþre 3/87, 3/130, 3/180; gpm ōþerra 3/94, 8/57; dpm ōðrum 4/311, 5/26; npn ōðre 2/1; apn 4/235, ōðer 9/79; gpn ōþerra 3/143; dpn ōðrum 10(a)/10; npf ōðra 5/52; apf ōðre 5/50; asn ōðer twēga *one of two things* 12/207; *second* ism ōðre 20/109

oðfæstan I *set (to a task)* p. ptc. np oðfæste 5/60

oðfeallan VII *fall away, decline* p. ptc. oðfeallan 5/45; nsf oðfeallenu 5/14

ōðre see ōðer

oððon conj. *or* 22/66, 22/176

oþþe conj. *or* I/13, 3/13, 3/69, 3/77, 3/104, 4/9, etc.

oððringan III w.d. of person and a. of thing. *press out, deprive* pres. 3s oðþringeð 17/71; pret. IS oðþrong 20/185

ōwiht pron. *anything* nsn 15/23; as 8/36, 17/46. See āwiht [MnE aught]

oxa m. *ox* ap oxan 3/9, 3/11, 3/29; gp oxena 3/18

oxanhierde m. *oxherd* ns 3/28; np oxanhierdas 3/4

Oxenafordscīr f. *Oxfordshire* as Oxena-fordscīre 7/67

pāpa m. *pope* ns 4/303; as pāpan 10(a)/11, 10(b)/42
Pante f. *the river Blackwater in Essex* as Pantan 12/68, 12/97
Paradīsus m. *Paradise* ds Paradīsum 2/3, 2/5
Paulīnus pers. n. *Paulinus* as 8/39
pæll m. *purple garment, silk robe* ap pællas 3/141 [MnE pall]
pæð m. *path* as 1/6
Petroces stōw f. *Padstow (Cornwall)* ns 7/7
Pētrus pers. n. *Peter* ns 4/32, 4/33; as Pētrum 4/35; ds Pētre 4/31, 4/204
pleoh n. *danger, risk* ns 3/98, 4/124; ds plēo 3/138
plēolic adj. *dangerous* nsn 4/8
Portland n. *Portland (Dorset)* ds Portlande 7/11
prass m. *array, military force* ds prasse 12/68
prēost m. *priest* np prēostas 4/25, 4/38; dp prēostum 4/289
prȳte f. *pride* ds prȳtan 22/144
pund n. *pound* gp punda 7/24, 7/63

rā m. *roebuck* ap rān 3/51 [MnE roe]
rād see rīdan
gerād adj. *skilful, apt* asn gerāde 18(a)/873
radost see hraðe
ramm m. *ram* as 2/66
ran see irnan
rān see rā
ranc adj. *brave, proud* asm rancne 22/104 [MnE rank 'outright']
rand m. *shield-boss, shield* ns 21/37; ap randas 12/20
randhæbbend m. *shield-bearer, warrior* gp rondhæbbendra 18(a)/861
randwiggend m. *shield-bearing warrior* np rondwiggende 20/11, 20/20; gp randwiggendra 20/188
raðe see hraðe
rǣcan 1 *reach (out)* pret. 3s rǣhte 18(a)/747
gerǣcan 1 *obtain* inf. 22/16; *reach, wound* pret. 3s gerǣhte 12/142, 12/158, 12/226
rǣd see rēad
rǣd m. *advice* ns 4/171, 18(b)/1376; as 3/210, 7/24; ds 20/97; *sense, reason* gp rǣda 20/68
rǣdan 1 *read* inf. 4/9; infl. inf. (tō) rǣdenne 4/105; pres. 3s rǣt 4/9; *instruct, give counsel, rule* inf. 10(b)/67; pret. 3s rǣdde 12/18
gerǣdan 1 *decide* pres. 2s gerǣdest 12/36; pret. 3s gerǣdde 7/22, 7/24, 7/27, 7/59
rǣdbora m. *advisor* ns 18(b)/1325; as rǣd-boran 4/114

Rǣdgōd pers. n. *Radagaisus* ns Rǣdgōt 10(b)/19, Rǣdgōta 10(a)/2; as 10(b)/7
gerǣdu n. pl. *harness, trappings* ap 3/153; dp gerǣdum 12/190
ræfnan 1 *carry out, do* pret. 3p ræfndon 20/11
ræghār adj. *grey with lichen* nsm 13/10
rǣhte see rǣcan
gerǣhte see gerǣcan
rǣran 1 *lift up, offer up* inf. 9/113; pret. 3s rǣrde 11(n)/6 *(raised)*, 22/10 *(committed)* [MnE rear]
rǣsan 1 *rush* pret. 3s rǣsde 6/15
rǣste see rest
rǣswa m. *leader* ds rǣswan 20/12; np 20/178
rǣt see rǣdan
rēad adj. *red* nsm rēd 4/259; dsn rēadum 20/338
rēadfāh adj. *stained with red* nsm 13/10
rēaf n. *armour* as 12/161; *clothes* ap 3/141
rēafere m. *robber* np rēaferas 22/150 [MnE reaver]
rēafian 2 *rob, ravage* pres. 3p reafiað 22/114 [MnE reave]
rēaflāc n. *robbery, plunder* ns 22/50; ap 22/164
reccan 1 w.g. *care about, care* pres. 1p recce 3/173; pret. 3s rōhte 4/160; 3p rōhton 12/260, rohtan 22/117 [archaic MnE reck]
reccan 1 *explain, relate* pret. 3s rehte 4/129, 4/130; 3p rehton 9/55
gereccan 1 *wield, control* pret. 3p gerehton 10(a)/4
gereccednyss see gerecednis
recceleas adj. *negligent, careless* npm reccelēase 5/45 [MnE reckless]
reced m. *building, hall* ns 18(a)/770; gs recedes 18(a)/724, 21/37; ds recede 18(a)/720, 18(a)/728
gerecednis f. *narrative* as gerecednisse 4/46, gereccednysse 4/132; ds 4/47
recene adv. *quickly* 10(b)/34, ricene 12/93, rycene 16/112, recene 20/188
geregnad adj. *ornamented, decorated* nsm 18(a)/777; asn gerēnod 12/161; asf gerē-node 20/338
regollic adj. *regular, according to (monastic) rule* dpm regollecum 9/83
regollīce adv. *in accordance with ecclesiastical rule* 22/56
rehton see reccan
rēnig adj. *rainy* nsn 19/10
gerēnod see geregnad
renweard m. *guardian of the house* np renweardas 18(a)/770
rēocan II *reek* pres. ptc. rēocende 20/313
reord f. *voice* ds reorde 17/53
gereord n. *speech, voice* dp gereordum 11(j)/16

reordberend m. *speech-bearer, man* np 14/3; dp reordberendum 14/89

rēotan II *weep* pres. 3p rēotað 18(b)/1376

rēotig adj. *lamenting, tearful* nsf rēotugu 19/10

rest f. *rest, resting place* as reste 9/98, 14/3; ds 9/26, ræste 18(a)/747; *bed, couch* as reste 20/54; ds 20/68

restan I *rest, lie, remain* pres. 1s reste (w. refl.) 11(e)/5; pret. 3s reste 14/64 (w. refl.), 14/69, 20/44 (w. refl.); 3p reston 20/321

*ġe*restan I *rest* inf. 9/95, 15/40

rēþe adj. *fierce, cruel, furious* asm rēðne 4/294; dsm rēþan 4/169, 4/193; npm 18(a)/770; ap reðe 20/348; dpm rēþum 4/145

rēwett n. *rowing* ns 3/90

rīċċeter n. *arrogance* ds rīċċetere 4/299

rīċe n. *kingdom, reign* ns 10(b)/5; as 3/190, 6/7, 7/63, 10(a)/3, 10(a)/18, 13/10, 14/119, 21/1 (*power*), etc.; gs rīċes 6/1, 6/29, 8/78, 13/37, 17/81, 18(a)/861, 18(b)/1390; ds rīċe 5/19, 5/75, 10(a)/1, 10(a)/5, 10(b)/7, 16/106, 20/343 [MnE (bishop)ric, German Reich]

rīċe adj. *powerful, great* nsm 4/298, rīċa 20/20, 20/44, 20/68; asm rīċne 14/44, 20/234, 22/104; dsm rīċan 20/11; npm 10(b)/7; gp rīċra 10(b)/46 (as noun), 14/131, 22/164; superl. rīċost *most powerful, richest* nsm 12/36

ricene see **recene**

rīcost see **rīċe**

rīcsian 2 *reign* pret. 3s rīcsode 6/41; *prevail* 22/8

rīdan I *ride* inf. 8/63, 12/291, 18(a)/855; pres. ptc. rīdende 2/48; pret. 3s rād 4/299, 12/18, 12/239; 3p ridon 6/24, 7/57, riodan 18(d)/3169

rīdende see **rīdan**

ridon see **rīdan**

riht adj. *fitting, right* nsn 12/190; asm rihtne 14/89; dsn ryhte 11(m)/7; dsm rihte *true* 20/97

riht n. *justice, right* as 22/137; gs rihtes 10(b)/67; ds rihte (*what is right*) 22/173, 22/21 (mid rihte *properly*), etc.

*ġe*rihtan I *correct* inf. 4/125; pres. subj. 3s gerihte 4/122; p. ptc. nsf geriht 14/131 (*directed*) [MnE right]

rihte adv. *properly, correctly* 12/20, 22/59

*ġe*rihte n. *straight direction* ds on gerihte *directly, straightaway* 20/202; *rights, privileges* gp gerihta 22/34; Godes gerihta *God's dues* np 22/31, ap 22/20, 22/23

rihtlagu f. *just law* gp rihtlaga 22/130 [MnE right, law]

rihtġelēaffull adj. *orthodox* gpm ryhtgelēaffulra 10(a)/19

rihtlīċe adv. *rightly* 22/178

rihtwīs adj. *righteous, upright* nsm 10(b)/49; gpm rihtwīsra 10(a)/19; superl. rihtwīsesta nsm 10(a)/14

rihtwīsnys f. *righteousness,* ds rihtwīsnysse 4/145

rīnan I *rain* pres. subj. 3s rīne 8/29

rinc m. *man, warrior* ns 10(b)/49, 11(p)/2, 18(a)/720; as 18(a)/741, 18(a)/747; ap rincas 11(j)/16; gp rinca 18(a)/728, 20/54, 20/338; dp rincum 12/18

rinnan see **irnan**

riodan see **rīdan**

*ġe*risene n. *decent thing, what belongs* gp gerisena 22/35

*ġe*risenliċ adj. *suitable, proper, honourable* apn gerisenlice 9/3; compar. asn gerisenlicre 8/36

*ġe*risenlīċe adv. *fittingly* compar. gerisenlecor 8/57

rōd f. *rood, cross* ns 14/44, 14/136; as rōde 14/119; gs 11(n)/5; ds 14/56, 14/131 [MnE rood]

rōdetācn n. *sign of the cross* ds rōdetācne 9/116 [MnE rood token]

rodor m. *sky, heaven* np roderas 18(b)/1376; ap 20/348; dp roderum 11(n)/5, 20/5

rōf adj. *strong* npm rōfe 20/20; gp rōfra 20/53

rōhte see **reċċan**

rōhton see **reċċan**

Rōm f. *Rome* ns 10(b)/19; ds Rōme 10(b)/46

Rōmane pl. *Romans* gp 10(a)/1, 10(b)/17, Rōmane 10(a)/3; dp Rōmanum 10(a)/7

Rōmanisc adj. *Roman* dp Rōmaniscum 10(a)/15

Rōmeburg f. *Rome* ds Romebyrig 4/305

Rōmwara pl. *Romans* gp 10(b)/34; dp Rōmwarum 10(b)/49, 10(b)/67

rondhæbbendra see **randhæbbend**

rondwiggend see **randwiggend**

rōtlīċe adv. *cheerfully* 9/102

rōwan VII *row* pres. ptc. rōwende 4/154; pres. 1s rōwe 3/76

rūm adj. *spacious* nsf 21/37; apm rūme 20/348

rūm n. *opportunity* ns 20/313 [MnE room]

rūme adv. *abundantly* 20/97

rūn f. *secret meditation* ds rūne 16/111, tō rūne *for private consultation* 20/54

rūnwita m. *confidant, trusted counsellor* ns 18(b)/1325

rycene see **recene**

ryhte see **riht**

ryhtfæderencyn n. *direct paternal ancestry* ns 6/42

rȳman I *extend* pret. 3p rȳmdon 5/8

ġerȳman 1 *open* (*a way*) pret. 1s gerȳmde
14/89; p. ptc. gerȳmed 10(b)/19, 12/93
(ēow is gerȳmed *passage is granted to you*)
rȳpan 1 *plunder* pres. 3p rȳpað 22/113 pret.
3p rȳpton 7/78
rȳpere m. *robber, plunderer* np rȳperas 22/
150; gp rȳpera 22/50

sacan VI *fight, contend* inf. 21/53 [MnE
(for)sake]
sacu f. *battle* ds sæcce 20/288
saga see secgan
sāgol m. *cudgel, staff* dp sāglum 4/207
salowigpād adj. *dark-coated* nsm salowigpāda 20/211
same see swā
samed see samod
samod adv. *too, at the same time* 2/47,
18(a)/729, samed 11(l)/2, somod 16/39,
20/282; prep. w.d. *simultaneously with*
18(b)/1311; *together* 20/163, 20/269,
20/288
sanct m. *saint* as 4/269, 4/271, 4/300; gs
sancte 4/126, 7/7, 7/48, sanctes 4/301; ds
sancte 4/129, 4/273
sandċēosol m. *sand, grains of sand* as 2/75
sang see singan
sang see song
sār n. *pain, wound* as 17/95, 18(a)/787
sār adj. *sore, painful, grievous* npf sāre 16/50;
gpf sārra 14/80, 20/182
sāre adv. *sorely, grievously* 14/59, 22/37,
22/145
sārig adj. *sorrowful* npm sārige 4/227 [MnE
sorry]
sārliċ adj. *painful, sad* nsn 18(a)/842
sārnes f. *pain* ds sārnesse 2/34 [MnE
soreness]
sāule see sāwol
ġesawen see ġesēon
sāwol f. *soul* ns 1/31, sāwul 12/177, sāwl 4/
219, 14/120, sawul 21/58; as sāwle 18(a)/
801, 18(a)/852, sāule 22/65; ds 17/100
sǣ f. and m. *sea* as 4/126, 16/4, 17/14, 17/
18; ds 1/28, 2/75, 3/89, 3/91; dp sǣm
18(a)/858
sǣbāt m. *sea-boat, ship* as 18(a)/895
sǣcce see sacu
sǣd n. *seed, offspring* ds sǣde 2/76
sǣde see secgan
sǣfor f. *sea-voyage* ds sǣfōre 17/42
sǣġan 1 *lay low, slay* p. ptc. gesǣged 18(a)/
884, 20/293
ġesǣġd see secgan
sǣġde see secgan
ġesǣġde see secgan
sǣl m. or f. *time, occasion* ns 14/80; as 4/273;
happiness, joy dp sǣlum 18(b)/1322

sǣl n. *hall* as 18(c)/2264
sǣlan 1 *bind, fasten* inf. 16/21; p. ptc.
gesǣled 20/114
ġesǣlan 1 *befall, chance, turn out favourably*
pret. 3s gesǣlde 18(a)/890
sǣlida m. *sailor, Viking* ns 12/45; as sǣlidan
12/286
ġesǣliġ adj. *blessed* nsf 4/219 [MnE silly]
ġesǣliġliċ adj. *blessed, happy* npf gesǣliglica
5/4
ġesǣliġlīċe adv. *blessedly, happily* 4/145
sǣmann m. *sailor, Viking* np sǣmen 12/29,
22/108; dp sǣmannum 12/38, 12/278
ġesǣne see ġesīene
sǣrima m. *coast* ds sǣriman 7/8, 7/23, 7/56
[MnE sea rim]
sǣrinc m. *sea-going warrior, Viking* ns 12/134
sǣstrēam m. *ocean current* dp sǣstrēamum
10(b)/15
sǣt see sittan
scamian 2 (impers. w. acc. of person) *cause
shame* pres. 3s scamað 22/134, 22/141,
22/142, ūs . . scamað *it causes us shame, we
feel ashamed* 22/152
scamu f. *shameful consequence, shames* 22/89
scān see scīnan
scand f. *shame, disgrace* ns 3/215
scandliċ adj. *shameful* nsn 22/75; npm scand-
liċe 22/95; dpm sceandliċan 22/61
scǣron see scieran
sceacan VI *flee, hasten away* pret. 3s sceōc
7/33, scōc 18(c)/2254 [MnE shake]
scead n. *shade* ap sceadu 18(a)/707
sceādan VII *part* pres. 3s sceādeð 13/30
sceadu f. *shadow, shade, darkness* ns 1/22,
14/54
sceadugenga m. *walker in darkness* ns 18(a)/
703
scēaf see scūfan
sceaft m. *staff, shaft* ns 12/136; ds sceafte
(*staff*) 10(b)/11
ġesceaft f. *creation, creature* ns 14/12, 14/55,
14/82, 16/107 (wyrda gesceaft *ordained
course of events*); ap gesceafta 4/53, 4/57,
4/62; *condition, situation* ns 21/65
sceal see sculan
scealc m. *man, warrior* np scealcas 12/181,
20/230
sceandliċan see scandliċ
scēap n. *sheep* ap 3/24
ġesceap n. *creation* ds gesceape 9/71; np
gesceapu *destiny, fate* 11(k)/7
ġesceapþēote f. *appointed channel* dp
gesceapþēotan 11(g)/4
sceapen see scieppan
ġesceapenis f. *creation* ds gesceapenisse 4/50
scēaphierde m. *shepherd* ns 3/22; np scēaphierdas 3/4

scear n. *ploughshare* as 3/12, 3/193
sceard adj. *cut, mutilated, chipped* npf scearde 13/5
scearp adj. *sharp* asm *scearpne* 20/78
scēat m. *surface, region* ap scēatas 14/37, 17/61, 17/105; ds scēate 11(k)/7 (*fold, bosom*); gp scēata 18(a)/752; dp scēatum 14/8, 14/43
scēat see **scēotan**
sceatt m. *money, payment* as 3/106; dp sceattum 12/40, 12/56 [MnE (through Old Norse) scot(free)]
scēað f. *sheath, scabbard* ds scēaðe 20/79; dp scēaðum 20/230
sceaða n. *enemy* gp 18/4, sceaðena 20/193
scēawere m. *observer* ns 4/229
scēawian 2 *see, behold, look at* inf. 4/305, 18(a)/840, scēawigan 18(b)/1391; infl. inf. (tō) scēawigenne 4/308; pret. 1s scēawode 14/137; 3s w.d. 4/293, 18(a)/843 [MnE show]
scēawung f. *viewing, examination* ds scēawunge 4/307 [MnE showing]
Scedeland n. *the southernmost part of the Swedish peninsula (now Skåne), which was ruled by the Danes; generally, the Scandinavian lands* dp Scedelandum 18/19
Scēfing *son of Scef* (an appellation of King Scyld) ns 18/4
sceld see **scield**
scendan 1 *insult* pres. 3p scendað 22/102, 22/112
scēōc see **sceacan**
sceolde see **sculan**
sceole see **sculan**
sceolon see **sculan**
scēōp see **scieppan**
scēota m. *trout* ds scēota 21/40; ap scēotan 3/87 [MnE shoat]
scēotan II *thrust, shoot, throw* inf. 11(g)/4; pret. 3s scēat 8/68, 12/143, 12/270; 3p scuton 4/212 (scuton . . . tō *shot at*); *pay, contribute* pres. 3p scēotað 22/76
scēotend m. *warrior, bowman* np 10(b)/11, 18(a)/703, 20/304
scēð f. *sheath* ds scēðe 12/162
sceððan VI *injure* inf. 14/47 [MnE (through Old Norse) scathe]
scield m. *shield* ns Scyld (a Danish king and founder of the Danish dynasty) 18/4; gs Scyldes 18/9; ds scylde 12/136, 21/37; np scildas 20/204; ap sceldas 10(b)/2, scyldas 12/98
sciellfisc m. *shellfish* as 1/5
scieppan VI *create* pret. 3s scēōp 9/40, scōp 11(e)/2; p. ptc. sceapen 11(h)/2 [MnE shape]

ġescieppan VI *create* pret. 3s gescēōp 4/51, 4/110, 20/347, gescōp 11(h)/6
scieppend m. *creator* ns Scyppend 9/41, 16/85; gs Scyppendes 9/34, 9/121, 20/78
scieran IV *rend, tear* p. ptc. npf scorene 13/5; *cleave* pret. 3p scǣron 20/304 [MnE shear]
scildas see **scield**
scildburh see **scyldburh**
scile see **sculan**
scīma m. *light, radiance* as scīman 14/54
scīnan I *shine* inf. 14/15, 21/49; pres. 3s scīnþ 1/23, scīneð 8/45; pret. 3s scān 13/15, 13/34
scīnþ see **scīnan**
scip n. *ship* as 1/5, 3/135, 7/37; gs scipes 18(a)/896; ds scipe 4/223, scype 12/40, 12/56; np scypu 7/10; ap scipu 1/26, 3/203, 7/28; dp scipum 3/100, 4/152, 7/48
scipen n. *shed* ds scipene 9/25
sciphere m. *fleet, naval attack force* ds 4/148, 4/200, scipherige 7/3
scīr adj. *gleaming, resplendent* nsm 10(b)/11; asn 12/98; asm scīrne 14/54; apm scīre 11(g)/4, 20/193 [MnE sheer]
scīrmǣled adj. *brightly adorned* apn 20/230
Sciððia f. *Scythia* gs Sciððiu 10(a)/1, Sciððia 10(b)/2
scōc see **sceacan**
scoldon see **sculan**
scomu f. *shame* ds scome 9/22
scōp see **scieppan**
ġescōp see **ġescieppan**
scopgereord n. *poetic language* ds scopgereorde 9/6
scorene see **scieran**
scotung f. *missile, shooting* dp scotungum 4/213, 4/261
scōwyrhta m. *shoemaker* ns 3/150, 3/195; np scōwyrhtan 3/6 [MnE shoe, wright]
ġescrāf see **ġescrīfan**
scranc see **scrincan**
scrīfan I *care (about)* pres. 3p scrīfað 22/74
ġescrīfan I *ordain* pret. 3s gescrāf 10(b)/29 [MnE shrive]
scrincan III *shrink* pret. 3s scranc 1/2
scrīþan I *glide, move slowly* inf. 18(a)/703, 21/40; pres. 3p scrīðað 21/13
scrūd n. *clothing* as 3/74 [MnE shroud]
scrȳdan 1 *clothe* pres. 3s scrȳtt 3/69
scrȳn n. *chest, coffer* ds scrȳne 4/270 [MnE shrine]
scrȳtt see **scrȳdan**
scūfan II *shove, push* pret. 3s scēaf 12/136, 3p scufon 1/26

sculan pret.-pres. *must, have to, ought to* pres. IS sceal 3/8, 3/9, 3/13; 3s sceal 3/15, 3/63, 3/216, etc.; gnomic sceal (see introduction to selection 21) 18/24; 1p sculon 9/36; 2p sceole 12/59; 3p sceolon 4/291, 12/54, 12/220, sceolan 21/14; subj. 3s scyle 15/42, 17/111, 17/74 (on weg scyle *must depart*), scile 18(d)/3176; 1p scylan 22/13; pret. IS sceolde 4/3, 17/30; 3s 4/160, 8/2, 12/16, etc.; 3s scolde 22/9, etc.; 3p scoldon 2/49 (*had to* [*go*]), sceoldon 4/201, 12/19, 12/105, 12/291, etc.; subj. 3s sceolde 4/297, 7/51; 3p scolden 3/115, 9/113, sceoldon 5/13, sceoldan 7/30 (*ought to have*), sceoldon 7/33, etc.; sceolden 9/21 [MnE *shall*]

scūr m. *shower, storm* ns 21/40; dp scūrum 17/17; *storm of battle* ap scūras 20/221; dp scūrum 20/79

scūrbeorg f. *protection from storms* (i.e. *buildings*) np scūrbeorge 13/5

scuton see scēotan

*ge*scȳ n. pl. *shoes, footwear* ap 3/153

scyld see scield

scyldburh f. *wall of shields* ns 12/242, as scildburh 20/304

scyldiġ adj. w.g. *guilty* ns ealdres scyldig *having forfeited his life* 18(b)/1338

Scyldingas m. pl. *descendants of Scyld*, i.e. *the Danes* gp Scyldinga 18(a)/778, 18(b)/1321

scyle see sculan

scȳne adj. *beautiful* apf 20/316 [MnE *sheen*]

scynscaþa m. *demonic foe, hostile demon* ns 18(a)/707

scyp see scip

scyppend see scieppend

scypu see scip

*ge*scyrpan I *accoutre, equip* p. ptc. asn gescyrpedne 8/66

se, þæt, sēo dem. pron., def. art. (§16) m., n., f. *that, the, he, she, it, who, which* (§162.3) nsm se 1/5, 1/8, 1/9, 1/18, 1/33, 2/55, 3/15 (*he*), etc.; asm þone 1/5, 1/15, 1/27, 2/52, 3/12, þæne 7/24; gsm þæs 1/17, 3/40, etc.; dsm þæm 1/18, 3/66; ism þȳ 8/32; nsn þæt 2/4, 2/11, tæt 6/33, etc.; asn 1/2, 1/5, 1/11, 2/6, þet 7/61, þat 12/36, etc.; gsn þæs 2/5, 4/105, 6/29, *after, afterward* 3/31, 6/7, etc.; dsn þām 2/2, 2/10, 2/12 (be þām þe *as*), 4/39, 4/101; isn þȳ 9/59 (w. compar.) 3/70 (see note), 11(c)/6, 11(k)/11–12, (þȳ læs þe *lest*) 2/7, 3/24, 22/2 (*therefore*), 22/133 (*therefore*), 22/171 (*therefore*) þan 4/8, þon 6/35 (see note), 9/114, etc., þē (w. compar.) *the, by that* 11(c)/6, 12/146, 12/312–13, 22/54, 22/159; nsf sēo 1/8, 1/33, 2/1, 2/2, 2/26,

sīo 5/45; asf þā 2/30, 2/56, 3/76, 6/3; gsf þære 1/22, etc.; dsf 1/9, 1/8, 1/22, 1/26, 2/41 (þære þe *which*), 3/9, þēre 7/32; np þā 3/60, 3/166, 18/3, etc.; ap 1/28, 3/9, 3/11, 3/29, 3/44, 3/49, 3/58, 3/75, 3/80, 3/108, 8/48, etc.; gp þāra 1/28, 2/4, 3/18, 3/43, þæra 4/29, etc.; dp þām 2/67, 4/145, 4/237, þæm 3/87, 3/105, etc.

seah see sēon

*ge*seah see *ge*sēon

sealde see sellan

sealt n. *salt* gs sealtes 3/159; ds sealte 21/45

sealtere m. *salter, salt-maker* ns 3/156; np sealteras 3/6

sealtȳþ f. *salt seawave, ocean wave* gp sealtȳþa 17/35

sēamere m. *tailor* ns 3/195

searacræft m. *treachery* ap searacræftas 22/122

sēarian 2 *grow sere, wither, fade* pres. 3s sēarað 17/89

searobunden adj. *cunningly fastened* asn 11(n)/4

searogim n. *precious stone* ap searogimmas 13/35

searosæled adj. *skilfully bound* nsf 11(h)/16

searoþonc m. *ingenuity, skill* dp searoþoncum 18(a)/775

searoðoncol adj. *clever, wise* nsf 20/145; gp searoðoncelra 20/330

sēaþ m. *pit* ds sēaþe 14/75

Sebastianus pers. n. *Sebastian* 4/214

sēcan I *seek, search for, visit* inf. 11(f)/11, 14/104, 14/127 (*resort to*), 15/9, 18(a)/756, 18(a)/801, sēcean 18(a)/821; pres. ptc. sēcende 4/232, 4/236; imp. s. sēc 18(b)/1379; imp. p. sēcaþ 3/190; pres. 3s sēceð 16/114, 20/96; subj. 3s sēce 18(b)/1369; pret. IS sōhte 8/44, 16/25; 3s 5/12, 8/53; 3p sōhton 12/193, 14/133

*ge*sēcan I *seek, seek out, visit* inf. 12/222, 14/119, gesecean 21/44; pres. subj. IS gesēce 17/38; pret. 3s gesōhte 12/287, 18(a)/717, 20/14

secg m. *man, warrior* ns 12/159, 17/56, 18(a)/871, 18(b)/1311; as 18(b)/1379; np secgas 20/201; ap secgas 12/298; gp secga 16/53, 18(a)/842; dp secgum 14/59

secgan 3 *say, tell* inf. 9/52, 11(n)/8, 11(n)/16, 12/30, 14/1, 15/2, 17/2, 18(a)/875, etc.; imp. s. saga 11(b)/7, 11(h)/16, sege 4/193, 12/50; pres. IS secge 3/132; 2s segst 3/7, 3/22, 3/107, 3/108, 3/197; 3s segþ 3/193, segeð 12/45; 1p secge 3/168, secgað 4/44, 4/222; subj. 2s secge 14/96; 3s 21/65; pret. 3s sægde 2/23, 2/72, 20/341, sǣde 4/17, 4/189, 4/199, 12/147, etc.; 3p sægdon 9/56; p. ptc. gesǣgd 2/70

*ġe*secgan 3 *say* pret. 3s gesægde 11(g)/5,
gesǣde (þanc gesǣde *gave thanks*) 12/120
secgrōf adj. *sword-valiant, brave* gpm secgrōfra 13/26
sefa m. *heart* ns 10(b)/71; as sefan 16/57,
17/51; ds 18(b)/1342
sēftēadig adj. *blessed with comfort* nsm 17/56
sege see secgan
segelgeard m. *sail-yard, cross-pole on a mast*
ns segelgyrd 21/25
*ġe*seġen see *ġe*sēon
seġnian 2 *bless, cross (oneself)* pres. ptc. segniende 9/123
*ġe*seġnian 2 *bless, cross (oneself)* pret. 3s
gesegnode (w. refl.) 9/115
segst see secgan
segþ see secgan
*ġe*selda m. *companion* ap geseldan 16/53
seldcūþ adj. *rare* apn 3/141
seldcyme m. *infrequent visit* np seldcymas
19/14 [MnE seldom, come]
seldon adv. *seldom* 3/90
sele m. *hall, house* ns 11(e)/1; as 18(a)/826;
ds 18(a)/713
seledrēam m. *revelry in the hall* as 18(c)/
2252; np seledrēamas 16/93
seledrēorig adj. *sad at the loss of a hall* nsm
16/25
selerǣdend m. *counsellor in the hall* ap
selerǣdende 18(b)/1346
selesecg m. *retainer* ap selesecgas 16/34
sēlest adj. (superl. of gōd; cf. §76) *best* nsm
sēlesta 14/27; asn w.g. sēlest 14/118; nsn
18(b)/1389; adv. sēlost 4/249
self pron., adj. *self, himself, herself,* etc., *same,
very* nsm 2/53, 2/56, 4/38, 4/83, seolfa 8/
58, 8/75, sylfa 11(e)/1, 21/66; asm selfne
2/72, 3/103 (*myself*), sylfne 8/16, seolfne
9/123; gsm seolfes 9/124; dsm selfum
5/43, sylfum 7/34, 9/55, 17/1; asf sylfe
14/92; gsf sylfre 15/2; dsf sylfre 20/335;
nsn sylfe 8/45; asn 8/44, 20/204 (*very*); npm
selfe 3/174 (*ourselves*), 5/25 (*ourselves*),
seolfan 9/69; apm selfe 3/121; gpm sylfra
12/38; dpm sylfum 4/326
sēlla see sēlra
sellan 1 *give, sell* inf. 3/84, 3/144, syllan
8/46, 12/38, 12/46; imp. s. sele 3/117,
3/120; pres. 1s selle 3/66, 3/118, 3/136;
2s selst 3/118, 3/199; 3s selþ 3/68, 3/69,
3/199, silð 4/63, sylð 4/65, seleð 18(b)/
1370 (*give up*); subj. 1p syllon 12/61; pret.
3s sealde 2/14, 2/25, 5/23, 8/63, etc.; 3p
sealdon 10(b)/24; subj. 3s sealde 8/60; p. ptc.
geseald 4/77, npm gesealde 22/38
*ġe*sellan 1 *give, give up* pret. 3s gesealde
12/188; pret. 3p gesealdon 12/184
sēlost see sēlest

sēlra adj. (compar. of gōd; cf. §76) *better*
nsm 18(a)/860, sēlla 10(b)/50; nsn sēlre
18(b)/1384
selþ see sellan
*ġe*sēman 1 *reconcile, settle (a dispute)* inf.
3/207, 12/60
sendan 1 *send* inf. 12/30, 16/56; pres. 3s
sendeð 21/9; pres. 3p sendað 11(o)/5;
pret. 3s sende 4/159, 4/189, 7/31, 10(a)/
20, 10(b)/63, 12/134, 20/190; 3p sendon
12/29, 20/224; subj. 3s sende 7/59
*ġe*sēne see *ġe*sīene
sēo see se
*ġe*sēo see *ġe*sēon
sēoc adj. *sick* asf sēoce 19/14
seofen num. *seven* np 4/307
seofian 2 *lament, sigh* pret. 3p seofedun
17/10
seolcen adj. *silken, made of silk* nsm 4/259
Sēolesīġ f. *Selsey (Sussex)* ds Sēolesigge 7/2
seolfa see self
seolfne see self
seolfor n. *silver* as 3/142, 4/85, sylfor 13/35;
gs seolfres 11(n)/4; ds seolfre 4/272; is
14/77, sylfore 11(j)/2
seolforsmiþ m. *silversmith* ap seolforsmiþas
3/181
seoloc m. *silk* as 3/141
seomian 2 *hang, be attached* inf. 21/25
sēon V *look, see* inf. 18(b)/1365; pret. 1s seah
11(l)/1 11(n)/1; 3s 13/35
*ġe*sēon V *see* inf. 20/136, gesion 5/36; imp.
s. geseoh 8/12; pres. 1s gesēo 3/179; 3s
gesiehð 2/70, 2/71, gesihð 16/46; subj. 2s
gesēo 8/21; pret. 1s geseah 5/28, 11(g)/1,
14/14, 14/21, 14/33, etc.; 3s 2/11, 2/66,
4/214, 4/301, 8/66, etc.; 3p gesāwon
2/49, 12/84, 12/203; subj. 1s gesāwe
14/4; p. ptc. gesawen 8/9, gesewen 8/26,
1s gesegen *seems* 9/124, wæs gesegen
seemed 9/54
seonu f. *sinew* np seonowe 18(a)/817
sēoþan II *boil* inf. 3/174; infl. inf. (tō)
sēoþanne 3/174 [MnE seethe]
*ġe*set n. *seat* np gesetu 16/93, 21/66
*ġe*setnis f. *decree, narrative* ds gesetnysse
4/304; ap gesetnissa 4/116; dp gesetnissum
4/116
*ġe*sett see settan
settan 1 *set, put, establish, appoint, set out, go,
set down, compose* inf. 4/310; pres. 1s sette
2/30; pret. 3s 4/294; 3p setton 10(b)/4;
p. ptc. gesett 4/12, 4/98, geset 4/112,
4/136, 4/142, geseted 9/18, 14/141; npm
gesette 4/39
*ġe*settan 1 *set down, put, compose* pret. 3s
gesette 4/132, 9/26, 9/122; 3p gesetton
14/67

ġesewen see ġesēon
sī see bēon
ġesib adj. (used as noun) *kinsman* ns gesib
  22/53; ds gesibban 22/54 [MnE sib(ling)]
sibb f. *peace, concord* ns 3/207, 4/252; as sibbe
  5/7
sibbeġedriht f. *band of kinsmen* as 18(a)/729
sibleġer n. *act of incest* ap siblegeru 22/124
sibling m. *kinsman, sibling* dp siblingum
  4/21
Sībyrht pers. n. *Sibyrht* gs Sībyrhtes 12/
  282
Siċilia f. *Sicily* ns 10(b)/15; ds 10(a)/4
sīd adj. *large, ample* asf sīde 20/337
sīde f. *side* ds sīdan 14/49; ap 11(b)/7
sīde adv. *widely* wīde and sīde *far and wide*
  14/81, 22/133
sīe see bēon
ġesiehð see ġesēon
sīen see bēon
siendon see bēon
gesīene adj. *evident, visible* nsn gesȳne 18(d)/
  3158, 22/88, 22/153, gesǣne 22/115,
  gesēne 22/45; npn gesīene 14/46; npf
  gesȳne 21/1 (*seen*)
sierwan 1 *contrive, plot* pres. 2s sierwst 2/32
siġ (= sīe) see bēon
siġe m. *victory* ds 4/153
siġebēam m. *tree of victory, cross* ns 14/13;
  as 14/127
Siġebryht pers. n. *Sigebryht* as 6/1
siġefæst adj. *victorious* nsm 4/162
siġefolc n. *victorious people* ds sigefolce
  20/152; gp sigefolca 21/66
siġelēas adj. *without victory, in defeat* asm
  sigelēasne 18(a)/787; npm sigelēase 22/
  99
Siġemund pers. n. *Sigmund* gs Sigemundes
  18(a)/875, ds Sigemunde 18(a)/884
Siġerīċ pers. n. *Sigeric* ns 7/18, Sīrīc 7/24
sigerōf adj. *victorious* np sigerōfe 20/177
siġeþēod f. *victorious nation* np sigeþēoda
  10(b)/4
siġeðūf m. *triumphal banner* ap sigeðūfas
  20/201
siġewǣpen n. *weapon of victory* dp sigewǣpnum 18(a)/804
siġewong m. *field of victory* ds sigewonge
  20/294
siġlan 1 *sail* pret. 3p sigldon 1/26
siġle n. *jewel, brooch, necklace* ap siglu 18(d)/
  3163
sigor m. *victory* as 20/89; gs sigores 20/124;
  ds sigore 20/298; gp sigora 14/67
sigorēadig adj. *victorious* nsm 18(b)/1311
sigorfæst adj. *triumphant, victorious* nsm
  14/150
sigorlēan n. *reward for victory* as 20/344

ġesihð f. *sight, vision, presence* ds gesihðe
  2/13, 2/19, 9/120, gesyhðe 14/21, 14/41,
  14/66; as 14/96
silð see sellan
simle adv. *always* 4/95, 6/20, 17/68, symble
  4/138, 4/141, 4/288, symle 4/145, 4/236,
  4/305
sīn poss. pron. *his, her, its* isn sīne 11(h)/14;
  apm 20/29; dsn sīnum 20/99; dsf sīnre
  20/132
sinc n. *treasure* ns 21/10 as 11(n)/4, 12/59,
  13/35; gs sinces 16/25, 20/30, 20/339; ds
  since 14/23
sincfāg adj. *decorated with treasure, richly
  adorned* nsm 11(j)/15
sincġeofa see sincġyfa
sincġyfa m. *one who gives treasure, lord* ns
  sincgeofa 10(b)/50; as sincgyfan 12/278;
  ds 18(b)/1342; as 12/278
sincþegu f. *receiving of treasure* as sincþege
  16/34
sind see bēon
sindon see bēon
singāl adj. *perpetual, everlasting* nsf 14/141
singālīċe adv. *continually* 22/112
singan III *sing, resound* inf. 9/17, 9/21, etc.;
  pres. ptc. singend nsm 10(a)/31; asm
  singende 17/22; imp. s. sing 1/25, 9/28;
  pres. 3s singeþ 17/54, 3p singað 11(d)/8;
  pret. 3s sang 1/7, 20/211, song 9/45,
  9/70, etc.
sinnig adj. *sinful* asm sinnigne 18(b)/1379
sinsorg f. *constant sorrow* gp sinsorgna 15/45
sīo see se
siodu m. *morality* as 5/7
ġesīon see ġesēon
Sīrīc see Siġerīċ
siteþ see sittan
sittan V *sit* inf. 15/37, 20/15; pres. 3s siteþ
  1/9, 15/47; subj. 2s sitte 8/28; pret. 3s sæt
  11(a)/1, 19/10; subj. sǣte 20/252; 3p
  sǣton 11(b)/1, 20/141
ġesittan V *sit* pret. 3s gesæt 16/111, 18(a)/
  749 (*sat up*)
sīð adv. *tardily* 20/275
sīð m. *journey, fate, lot, venture* ns 18(a)/765;
  as 11(e)/3, 15/2, 18(a)/872, 20/145; ds
  sīþe 17/51; ap sīþas 11(k)/11, 17/2, sīðas
  18(a)/877; *time, occasion* ns 18(a)/716; ds
  18(a)/740, 20/73, is 20/109
ġesīþ m. *companion* np gesīþas 11(o)/5,
  21/14; np gesīðas 20/201; dp gesīþum
  18(b)/1313
sīðfæt m. *journey, expedition* ds sīðfate 14/
  150, 20/335
sīðian 2 *travel* inf. 11(l)/2, 12/177, 14/68,
  18(a)/720, 18(a)/808; pres. subj. 1s sīðie
  12/251; pret. 3s sīþode 4/219, 4/266

siððan adv. *afterwards, later* 2/51, 3/24, 4/64, 4/156, 5/62, syððan 4/159, 4/268, etc.; syððan æfre *forever after* 20/114; conj. *after, since, when* 2/59, 15/3, syðþan 14/3, 18/6, etc.

sīwian 2 *sew, stitch together* pret. 3p sīwodon 2/16

slāt see **slītan**

slǣp m. *sleep* ns 16/39; ds slǣpe 9/45; is slǣpe 20/247

slǣpan VII *sleep* pres. ptc. slǣpende 9/45; asm slǣpendne 18(a)/741

slēan VI *strike, beat, attack* pres. ptc. slēande 4/148; pret. 3s slōh 1/19, 4/157, 4/276, 12/163, 12/285, 20/103, 20/108; 3p slōgon 4/219, 7/78; subj. 3s slōge 12/117; p. ptc. npf geslegene 20/31 [MnE slay]

slecg m. *sledge-hammer* ds slecge 4/276; gp slecga 3/200

sleġe m. *blow, stroke, slaughter* gs sleges 4/190; ds slege 3/104, 4/218, 4/227

slegefæge adj. *doomed to perish* apm 20/247

slitan I *tear, rend* pret. 3s slāt 17/11, 18(a)/741 [MnE slit]

slīðen adj. *cruel* nsf 16/30

slōgon see **slēan**

slōh see **slēan**

smēagan 1 *think, examine* inf. 10(a)/18 (*take thought*); pres. subj. 3s smēage 22/156 (*examine*); pret. 3s smēade 22/9 (*gave thought*), 4/169 (*considered, discussed*)

smiþ m. *blacksmith* ns 3/193, 3/204; ds smiðe 1/14

smiððe f. *smithy* ns 1/14; ds smiþþan 3/199

smolt adj. *peaceful, serene* asn 9/104

smylte adj. *serene* ism 9/119; dsf smyltre 9/119

snāw m. *snow* as 16/48

snell adj. *keen, bold* npm snelle 12/29; gp snelra (*bold ones*) 20/199

snīwan 1 *snow* pres. subj. 3s snīwe 8/29; pret. 3s snīwde 17/31

snottor adj. *wise* nsm 16/111, snotor 4/137, 18(a)/826, 18(b)/1384, snotera 18(b)/1313; npm snottre 11(b)/2; nsf snotere 20/125; asf snoteran 20/55; superl. nsm snoterost 21/11; as a noun *wise person* nsm snotor 21/54

snūde adv. *quickly* 20/55, 20/125, 20/199

snytro f. *wisdom* as 8/58; dp snyttrum 18(a)/872

socc m. *sock* ns 1/2

sōfte adv. *easily* 12/59

sōhte see **sēcan**

ġesomnian 2 *gather, assemble* inf. 9/50; p. ptc. gesomnad 11(o)/2; *unite* p. ptc. gesomnad 19/18

ġesomnung f. *community* ds gesomnunge 9/65

somod see **samod**

sōna adv. *immediately* 2/52, 2/62, 2/78, 4/26, etc. [MnE soon]

song m. *song, cry* ns song 9/68; as song 1/25, 17/19, sang 18(a)/787; gs songes 9/47

songcræft m. *poetic art* as 9/14

sorg f. *sorrow, grief, trouble* ns 16/30, 16/39, 16/50, sorh 18(b)/1322; as sorge 17/42, 17/54; gp sorga 14/80, 20/182; dp sorgum 14/20, 14/59, 20/88

sorgian 2 *sorrow, grieve, care* imp. s. sorga 18(b)/1384

sorh see **sorg**

sorhlēoþ n. *song of sorrow, dirge* as 14/67

sōþ adj. *true* nsm sōða 4/328; as sōðne 20/89, 20/344; gsm sōðan 8/69; dsm 8/58, sōþum 4/146, 4/210; nsn sōð 4/230; gsf sōþan 4/141; dsf 4/187 [archaic MnE sooth]

sōþ n. *truth* ns 21/10, 22/1, 22/31, 22/170; as 3/107, 3/197, 4/16, etc., for sōð *truly, for sure* 21/64; gs sōðes 22/166; ds tō sōþe *as a fact* 16/11;

sōðe adv. *truly, faithfully* 18(a)/871

sōðgied m. *lay of truth, story about actual events* as 17/1

sōðlīċe adv. *truly* 2/9, 2/64, 4/52, etc. [archaic MnE soothly]

spadu f. *shovel, spade* ds spade 4/278

sparian 2 *spare* pret. 3p sparedon 20/233

spæcan see **sprecan**

spǣtan 1 *spit* pres. 1s spǣte 11(h)/8

spearca m. *spark* ap spearcan 3/200

spearwa m. *sparrow* ns 8/30

spēd f. *means, opportunity, wherewithal* as on spēd *successfully* 18(a)/873; ap spēda 5/59

spēdan 1 *be prosperous, be wealthy* pres. 2p spēdað 12/34 [MnE speed]

spēdiġ adj. *successful* nsm 14/151

spell n. *story, message* as 9/56, 12/50, spel 18(a)/873; gs spelles 9/66; dp spellum 99/74

spēow see **spōwan**

spere n. *spear* as 8/64, 12/137; ds 3/61; is 8/68; ap speru 12/108

spild m. *destruction* ds spilde 11(h)/8

spillan 1 *destroy* inf. 12/34

spor n. *track, trail* ds spore 5/38 [MnE spoor]

spōwan VII *succeed* (impersonal w.d.) pret. 3s spēow 5/9, 20/274

ġespōwan VII *succeed* (impersonal w.d.) pret. 3s gespēow 20/175

sprǣċ f. *utterance, speech, language* gs sprǣċe 4/102; ds 4/129, 4/309, 8/25, 11(f)/13; ap sprǣca 4/88

sprǣcan (= sprǣcon) see sprecan
ġesprec n. *conference, discussion* as 8/4
sprecan V *speak, say* inf. 9/90, 14/27, 18(d)/3172; infl. inf. tō specenne 22/75 (*to say*); pres. ptc. sprecende 8/40, 9/31, 9/99, etc.; pres. 1s sprece 4/55, sprice 11(h)/11; 2s spricst 3/204; 3s spricð 4/49, spriceð 16/70; pret. 3s sprǣc 4/72, 10(b)/81, 12/211, 12/274, 20/160, 20/176; 1p sprǣcon 12/212; 3p sprǣcan 8/38, sprǣcon 12/200, 12/212, spǣcan 22/8
ġesprecan V *say* pret. 3s gesprǣc 18(b)/1398
sprengan 1 *break, cause to spring or quiver* pret. 3s sprengde 12/137
spricst see sprecan
springan III *spring (away)* pret. 3s sprang 12/137; *spread, become widely known* 18/18
ġespringan III *spring forth, arise* pret. 3s gesprong 18(a)/884
spyriġean 1 *follow, follow in the footsteps of* inf. 5/37
spyrte f. *basket, eel basket* as spyrtan 3/77
stafum see stæf
stalu f. *stealing* ns 22/48; as stala 22/121
stān m. *stone* ns 1/16; as 1/15, 13/43, 18(a)/887; gs stānes 1/17; ds stāne 1/18, 14/66; is 1/19
stānclif n. *rocky cliff, crag* ap stānclifu 17/23
standan VI *stand, remain* inf. 12/19, 14/43, 14/62; pres. 1s stande 3/24, 3/30; 3s stent 4/134, stynt 4/59, 12/51, standeð 18(b)/1362, stondeð 16/74, 16/97, 16/115; 3p standað 4/287, stondaþ 16/76, 17/67; pret. 1s stōd 14/38; 3s 4/202, 4/280, 10(b)/28, 12/25, 12/28, 12/145, etc., stōd him ... æt *appeared to him* 9/27; 1p stōdon 14/71; 3p 4/282, 5/30, 12/63, 12/72, 12/79, 12/100, etc.
ġestandan VI *stand up* inf. 12/171; pret. 3p gestōdon 14/63 (w. refl., see note)
stang see stingan
stānhliþ n. *cliff* ds stānhliþe 15/48; ap stānhleoþu 16/101
stānhof n. *stone building* np stānhofu 13/38
stānwyrhta m. *stone-mason* ns 1/18
starian 2 *gaze* inf. 20/179 [MnE stare]
ġestaðelian 2 *establish, make steadfast* pres. 3s gestaþelað 17/108; pret. 3s gestaþelade 17/104
staðol m. *fixed position* as 11(c)/5 (*foundation*); ds staðole 14/71; dp staðelum *in place* 17/109
stædefæste see stedefæst
stæf m. *letter* dp stafum 9/4 [MnE staff]
stǣlan 1 *accuse* inf. 21/54; *avenge* p. ptc. gestǣled 18(b)/1340

stælgiest m. *thievish guest, thieving stranger* ns 11(c)/5
stær n. *history* as 9/72; gs stæres 9/66
stæð n. *bank, shore* ds stæðe 12/25
ġesteal n. *foundation* ns 16/110
steall m. *stall* as 3/19
stēam m. *moisture* ds stēame 14/62 [MnE steam]
stēap adj. *high* nsm 13/11, 21/23; npm stēape 20/17 [MnE steep]
stearc adj. *severe* nsm 3/10 [MnE stark]
stearn m. *tern* ns 17/23
stēda m. *stallion* as stēdan 8/65 [MnE steed]
stede m. *place, position* as 12/19 [MnE stead]
stedefæst adj. *steadfast, unyielding* npm stedefæste 12/249; stædefæste 12/127
stedehearde adj. *sturdy, strong* apm 20/223
stefn m. *trunk, stem, root* ds stefne 14/30
stefn f. *voice* ns 14/71; as stefne 2/17, 2/21, 2/36; is 11(j)/18; stemne 10(b)/84
stefna m. *prow or stern of a ship* ds stefnan 17/7
stelan IV *steal* inf. 4/275
stemn see stefn
stemnettan 1 *stand firm* pret. 3p stemnetton 12/122
stent see standan
steorfa m. *pestilence* ns 22/49
steorra m. *star* ap steorran 2/74
stēpan 1 w.d. *exalt* pres. 3s stēpeð 11(m)/8
steppan VI *step, advance* pret. 1s stōp 11(p)/5; 3s 12/8, 12/78, 12/131, 18(a)/761; pret. 3p stōpon 20/39, 20/69, 20/200, 20/212, 20/227
stercedferhð adj. *hardhearted, stern* npm stercedferhðe 20/55, 20/227
stician 2 *stick* pret. 3s sticode 8/68
stīeran 1 w.d. *steer, control, punish* inf. 17/109; pret. 3s stȳrde 14/145
ġestīgan I *climb up, mount, ascend* inf. 14/34; pret. 3s gestāh 14/40
stihtan 1 *direct, command, exhort* pret. 3s stihte 12/127
ġestillan 1 *restrain, stop* pret. 3s gestilde 4/306
stilnes f. *peace* as stilnesse 5/57; ds 9/117 [MnE stillness]
stingan III *stab, pierce* pret. 3s stang 12/138 [MnE sting]
stīð adj. *stern, firm, hard* nsn 12/301; as stīðan 4/91; apm stīþe 17/104
stīðhicgende adj. *firm of purpose, resolute* npm 12/122
stīðlīce adv. *sternly, loudly* 12/25
stīðmōd adj. *resolute, brave* nsm 14/40, *fierce* stīðmōda 20/25
stōd see standan
stōdhors n. *stallion* as 8/61 [MnE studhorse]
stōdon see standan

stondaþ see **standan**

stōp see **steppan**

storm m. *storm* ds storme 15/48, is 8/32; np stormas 16/101, 17/23; dp stormum 13/11

stōw f. *place* ns 4/314, 8/71, 18(b)/1372; as stōwe 2/69, 18(b)/1378; ds stōwe 2/53, 2/56, 3/42, etc.; np stōwa 22/71; ap stōwa 5/34; dp stōwum 4/97 [MnE stow]

strang adj. *strong* nsm 14/40, strong 11(f)/13; gsm strangan 11(c)/5; dsm strongum 17/109; npm strange 14/30; compar. nsm strengra 11(e)/4; apn strangran 8/22; superl. strengest nsm 18(a)/789

ġestrangian 2 *strengthen* pres. 1s gestrangie 3/165

strǣl m. or f. *arrow* ap strǣlas 20/223; dp strǣlum 14/62

strēam m. *stream, spring* ns 13/38; ap strēamas 13/43; *river* as 12/68, 21/23; *sea* ap 17/34, 20/348

strēġan 1 *strew, spread* inf. 17/97

strengra see **strang**

strengu f. *strength, power* ns 11(d)/5; ds strengo 11(f)/13

ġestrēon n. *wealth, profit, treasure* as 3/148, 4/165, 18(d)/3166, gestrīon 10(b)/23

strīċ n. *plague* ns 22/49

strong see **strang**

strūdung f. *robbery* ap strūdunga 22/121

strutian 2 *struggle* pres. ptc. strutigende 4/280 [MnE strut]

stund f. *time, short while* as stunde 12/271

Stūrmere m. *village of Sturmer (Essex)* as 12/249

stynt see **standan**

ġestȳran 1 w.d. of person and g. of thing *prevent* pret. 3s gestȳrde 20/60 [MnE steer]

stȳrde see **stīeran**

styria m. *sturgeon* ap styrian 3/93

styrian 1 *stir up* inf. 18(a)/872 (*treat of, engage*); pres. 3s styreþ 18(b)/1374

styrman 1 *storm* pres. subj. 3s styrme 8/30; pret. 3s styrmde 20/25; 3p styrmdon 20/223

styrnmōd adj. *stern of mood* npm styrnmōde 20/227

sulh f. *plough* ds sylh 3/9, 3/12

sum pron., adj. (§193.4) *a certain, some* nsm 4/6, 4/126, 4/220, 9/1, 10(a)/12, 10(b)/46, 12/149, 12/164, etc.; asm sumne 4/273, 5/53, 16/81, 16/82, etc.; gsm sumes 11(c)/3, 11(j)/15; nsn sum 17/68; asn 3/148, 9/55, 12/285, sume 2/50; nsf sum 4/267, 11(j)/8; asf sume 12/271; dsf sumre 9/23; npm sume 3/4, 3/5, 3/6, 17/56 (þā sume *those particular ones*); apm 16/80; apf 5/54; apn sumu 9/98

sumor m. *summer* ns 21/7; as 3/127; gs sumeres 17/54; ds sumera 3/125

sumorlang adj. *long as in summer* asm sumorlangne 15/37

sumu see **sum**

ġesund adj. *unharmed, whole, uncorrupted* nsm 4/301; npm gesunde 6/33 [MnE (safe and) sound]

sundor adv. *apart* 16/111 [MnE (a)sunder]

sundoryrfe m. *personal inheritance, wealth* gs sundoryrfes 20/339

sunnandæġ m. *Sunday* ns 3/53

sunne f. *sun* ns 1/20; ds sunnan 1/22

sunu m. *son* ns 1/33, 1/36, 12/76, 12/298, 14/150; as 2/44, 2/59, 2/65, 2/69, 4/57, 7/45; gs suna 2/58; ds 2/73, 4/6; np suno 11(a)/2, 11(a)/3; gp suna 11(k)/12

sunwlitiġ adj. *radiant with sunshine* superl. nsm sunwlitegost 21/7

sūsl f. *torment* gs sūsle 4/80; ds sūsle 20/114

sūð adv. *south(wards)* 18(a)/858

sūðan adv. *from the south* be sūðan *south of* 4/126, 5/19, 7/70

sūðerne adj. *southern, of southern design* asm 12/134

Sūðhamtūn m. *Southampton* ns 7/3

Sūðriġe pl. *Surrey* ap 7/72

Sūðseaxe m. pl. *Sussex, the South Saxons* ap Sūðsexe 7/72; dp Sūðseaxum 7/13, 7/56

sūðweardes adv. *southwards* 10(b)/4

swā adv. (§168 s.v. swā) *thus, so* 1/12, 2/70, 3/10, 3/59, 3/101, swǣ 5/14, 5/78 (*such*); swǣ same *likewise, similarly* 5/51; conj. *as* 3/84 (swā fela . . . swa *as many as*), 4/239 (swā oft swā *as often as*), 15/24 (w. subj. *as if*), 7/58 (swā wīde swā *as far as*); ēac swā *likewise, also* 2/19; swā hwæt swā *whatsoever* 3/66, 3/77, 9/4; swā hwelc swā *whoever* nsm 6/18; swā hwelc swā . . . swā . . . swā *whatsoever . . . whether . . . or* 3/212; swā hwelcum . . . swā *whatsoever* 2/9; swā swā *just as* 2/58, 2/75, 3/189, 4/10, 4/22, 5/73, etc., *as* 22/61, etc., *such as* 5/78; swā þēah *however* 4/27

ġeswāc see **ġeswīcan**

swam see **swimman**

swān m. *swineherd* ns 6/5

swǣse see **swǣs**

swāt m. *sweat* gs swātes (*blood*) 14/23; ds swāte 2/40

swātiġ adj. *bloody* asm swātigne 20/337 [MnE sweaty]

swaþu see **swæð**

swaþul m. or n. *flame, heat* ds swaþule 18(a)/782

swǣ see **swā**

swæcc m. *taste, flavour* ds swæcce 3/159

swǣs adj. *beloved* asm swǣsne 16/50; npf
swāse 11(a)/3; gpm swǣsra 11(k)/11

swǣsendu n. pl. *banquet* ap swǣsendo 20/9;
dp swǣsendum 8/27

swǣtan 1 *bleed* inf. 14/20 [MnE sweat]

swæð n. *track, swath* as 5/36; np swaþu
11(l)/3; *trail, footprint* ds swaðe 20/321

swealg see swelgan

sweart adj. *dark, black* npm swearte 11(l)/2
[MnE swart]

swefan V *sleep, sleep in death* inf. 18(a)/729;
pres. 3p swefað 18(c)/2256; pret. 3p swǣũ
fon 18(a)/703

swefn n. *dream* as 9/27, 9/52; gp swefna
14/1

swēġ m. *sound, din* ns 18(a)/182; as 3/200,
17/21

Sweġen pers. n. *Swein* ns 7/47

swegl n. *sky, heaven* ns swegel 21/7; gs
swegles 18(a)/860, 20/80, 20/88, 20/124,
20/344, 20/349

swelċ adj. *such* dsn swelcum 3/129; dsf
swylcere 4/249; dpm swilcum ōðrum *in
other such* 4/311; apn swilce 4/324, swylce
4/329; swylc . . . swylc *such . . . as* nsm
18(b)/328–9; npm swilce . . . swylce 4/
319; pron. *such* gsn swulces 18(a)/880; rel.
pron. *such as* npm 17/83

swelċe adv. *likewise* swylce 14/8, 15/43; ēac
swelce, swelce ēac *also, likewise* 2/1, 2/33,
3/103, 3/121, 9/79, ēac swilce 4/260,
swylce ēac 20/18, 20/337, 20/343, 20/
348; conj. *as if* 5/33, swilce 4/212, 4/257,
swylce 19/1, 20/31; *like* swilce 4/214,
swylce 4/259; swylce swā *just as* 14/92

swelgan III w.d. *swallow, imbibe* inf. 11(j)/15;
pret. 3s swealg 11(c)/6, swealh 18(a)/743;
sub 3s swulge 18(a)/782

sweltan III *die, perish* inf. 4/185, 12/293;
pres. subj. 1s swelte 4/187; pret. 3s swealt
18(a)/892; 3p swulton 4/306; subj. 1p
swulten 2/7

swencan 1 *press hard, harass, afflict* p. ptc.
geswenced 18(b)/1368, dsn geswenctan
4/252

sweng m. *blow, stroke* gs swenges 12/118; ds
swencge 4/219

swēora m. *neck* ns swūra 4/258; as swēoran
2/64, 11(b)/6, 20/106; ds swūran 4/259

ġesweorcan III *grow dark, become obscured* pres.
subj. 3s gesweorce 16/59

sweorcendferhð adj. *sombre, downcast* npm
sweorcendferhðe 20/269

sweord n. *sword* ns swurd 12/166, 18(a)/
890; as sweord 2/53, 2/59, 8/64, 11(n)/
14, 20/336, swurd 12/15, 12/161, etc.; ds
swurde 12/118; is sweorde 20/89, 20/288;
ap swurd 12/47, swyrd 20/230, 20/317;

dp sweordum 18(a)/884, 20/194, 20/294,
swyrdum 20/264, 20/301, 20/321

sweostor f. (§60) *sister* ns swustor 4/320; as
swuster 4/19; np gesweostor 11(a)/3 (see
§138 Prefixes, ġe-); ap geswustra 4/16

sweostersunu m. *sister's son* ns swustersunu
12/115

swēot n. *army* ns 20/298

sweotol adj. *clear, manifest* nsn 18(a)/817,
18(a)/833, swutel 4/311, swutol 22/45,
22/115

sweotole adv. *openly* 20/177

ġesweotolian 2 *reveal, show* pres. 3s geswutelað 4/323, 4/328; pret. 3s gesweotolode
2/56; p. ptc. geswutelod 4/67, 4/70, 20/
285

sweotollīċe adv. *clearly* 20/136

sweotolung f. *manifestation, evidence* ds
swutelunge 4/260

sweotule adv. *openly* 16/11

swerian VI *swear* pres. 1s swerie 2/72

swēte adj. *sweet* asn 17/95 (as noun); superl.
asn swēteste 9/68

swētmete m. *sweetmeat* gp swētmetta 3/159

swētnis f. *sweetness* as swētnisse 9/6; ds
swētnesse 9/78

ġeswīcan 1 *cease, desist* pres. 3s geswiceð
11(f)/12; pret. 3s geswāc 4/251; 3p
geswicon 4/307; subj. 7/60, 7/66

swicdōm m. *betrayal* ap swicdōmas 22/122

swician 2 (w.d.) *be treacherous toward, cheat*
pret. 3s swicode 22/59

swicol adj. *tricky, deceptive* superl. nsn
swicolost 21/10

swift adj. *swift* nsm 11(l)/3, swifta 18(c)/
2264; asm swiftne 3/118, 13/18; dpm
swiftum 3/49; compar. nsf swiftre 11(e)/3;
superl. swiftust nsm 21/3

swīge adj. *silent, still* nsm 11(e)/1

swīgian 2 *be quiet, fall silent* pres. 3s swīgað
11(d)/1; pret. 3s swīgode 4/172; 3p
swugedan 22/166

swilċe see swelċe

swīma m. *swoon* ds swīman 20/30, 20/106

swimman III *swim* pres. 3p swimmaþ 3/88,
16/53; pret. 1s swom 11(p)/3, 3s swam 1/5

ġeswinc n. *toil, hardship* ds geswince 3/129;
dp geswincum 2/38 [archaic MnE swink]

swincan III *labour, toil, struggle* pres. 1s
swince 3/8, 3/29; pret. 3p swuncon 4/
279

ġeswincdagas m. pl. *days of toil* dp geswincdagum 17/2

ġeswing n. *vibration, swirl, surf* ns 18(a)/848

swingan III *beat, fly* pres. 3s swingeð 18(c)/
2264; pret. 3p swungon 4/209

swingel f. *blow, stroke* dp swinglum 4/210

swingere m. *beater, scourger* ns 11(f)/7

swinsian 2 *sing, sound melodiously* pres. 3p swinsiað 11(d)/7
swinsung f. *melody* ds swinsunge 9/57
swipu f. *whip, scourge* dp swipum 4/209
swīþ adj. *mighty* nsf swīþe 13/24; compar. swīþre nsf 17/115; asf swīðran 14/20; dsf 20/80 (*right* [*hand*]); superl. swīðost nsf 21/5
swīðe adv. *very, exceedingly* 1/20, 3/62, 3/151, 3/179, 4/7, 4/193, 4/276 (*mightily*), 4/299 (*fiercely*), 11(l)/3, 12/115 (*cruelly*), swȳðe (*greatly*) 22/7, 22/15, 22/36, etc.; swīðe swīðe *very much* 5/40; compar. swīðor *more, rather* 4/185, swȳðor 20/182; superl. swīþost 3/50 (*especially*), swȳþost 22/132, 22/136, etc.; ealles tō swȳþe *all too much* 22/33
swīðferhð adj. *strong-minded, brave* nsm 18(a)/826
swīðlić adj. *violent* asn 20/240
swīðmōd adj. *arrogant* nsm 20/30, 20/339
swīðran see swīðe
swiðrian 2 *diminish, lessen* p. ptc. geswiðrod 20/266
swōgan VII *resound, make a noise* pres. 3p swōgað 11(d)/7 [MnE sough]
swom see swimman
swuā see swā
swugedan see swigian
swulge see swelgan
swulten see sweltan
swungon see swingan
swūra see swēora
swurd see sweord
swurdbora m. *swordbearer* ns 4/130, 4/131
swuster see sweostor
swustersunu see sweostersunu
ġeswustra see sweostor
swutel see sweotol
ġeswutelað see ġesweotolian
ġeswutelod see ġesweotolian
swutelunge see sweotolung
swylce see swelċe
swylt m. *death* ns 13/26
swyrdgeswing n. *sword-play* as 20/240
swȳðe see swīðe
sȳ (= sīe) see bēon
sȳferlīċe adv. *neatly, cleanly* 4/269
ġesyhðe see ġesihð
sylf see self
sylfor see seolfor
sylh see sulh
syll f. *sill, floor* ds selle 18(a)/775
syllan see sellan
syllic adj. *marvellous, wondrous* nsm 14/13; compar. syllicre asn 14/4 (see note)
symbel n. *feast* ds symble 9/23, symle 14/141, 20/15; gp symbla 16/93

symbel n. *perpetuity* as 20/44 (on symbel *always*)
symble, symle see simle
symle see symbel
syndolh n. *very great wound* ns 18(a)/817
syndon see bēon
syndriġlīċe adv. *individually, separately, especially* 8/8, 9/1 [archaic MnE sundrily]
ġesȳne see ġesīene
syngian 2 *sin, commit sin* pres. subj. 3p 22/141
synlēaw f. *sin, affliction of sin* ap synlēawa 22/145
synn f. *sin, crime* as 21/54; ap synna 22/119, 22/168; gp 4/63, 9/81; dp synnum 14/13, 14/99, 14/146, 22/101, 22/161, synnan 22/3
synscaða m. *malefactor, miscreant* as synscaðan 18(a)/801
synsnæd f. *huge* or *sinful gobbet* dp synsnædum 18(a)/743
ġesyntu f. *prosperity, success* as gesynto 8/19; gp gesynta 20/90
ġesyrwed adj. *armed* nsm 12/159
syððan see siððan

tācn n. *sign, token* ns tācen 18(a)/833; as tācn 11(n)/5
tācnian 2 *indicate, betoken* p. ptc. getācnod 20/197, 20/286
ġetācnian 2 *prefigure, betoken* pret. 3s getācnode 4/30, 4/87, 4/88
ġetācnung f. *prefiguration, signification, type* ns 4/28; as getācnunge 4/78 [MnE tokening]
tam adj. *tame* nsm 4/247
ġetāwian 2 *harass, mistreat* p. ptc. npm getāwode 4/174
tǣċan I *teach, show, direct* pres. 3s tǣċð 4/103; pret. 3s tǣhte 4/41, 12/18; 3p tǣhton 4/109; subj. pres. 3p tǣcan 22/143, 22/153
tǣcnan I *point out, signify, direct* pres. 3s tǣcneð 11(l)/6
tæġel m. *tail* ns 4/94
tǣhte see tǣċan
ġetæl n. *account, sequence* as 9/65
tǣlan I *ridicule* pres. 3s tǣleð 22/136
tǣsan I *lacerate, tear apart* pret. 3s tǣsde 12/270 [MnE tease]
ġetǣse adj. *agreeable* nsf 18(b)/1320
tæt (= þæt) see sē
tēaforgēap adj. *red-curved* nsm tēaforgēapa 13/30
tēah see tēon
teala adv., interj. *well, so* 9/114, teola 8/67
tealt adj. *wavering, unsteady* np tealte 22/53 [MnE tilt]

ġeteld n. *tabernacle* ns 4/81; ds getelde 4/93
tellan 1 *account, reckon, consider* pret. 3s
  tealde 18(a)/794 [MnE tell]
Temese f. *the Thames* ds 5/19, 7/72
temman 1 *tame* inf. 3/114, 3/116; p. ptc. apm
  getemedan 3/124, 3/127
ġetemman 1 *tame* pres. 1s getemme 3/123
templ n. *temple* as 8/47
Tenetland n. *Thanet* ns 7/4
ġetenge adj. w.d. *near to, resting on* nsm
  11(d)/8
teola see teala
tēon n. *injury, harm* as 11(m)/3
tēon 2 *adorn, create* pret. 3s tēode 9/43
tēon II *draw, drag, take (a trip or journey)*
  pret. 3s tēah 18(b)/1332, 20/99, 3p tugon
  4/218
teran IV *tear* inf. 20/281
tīd f. *time* ns 12/104, as 8/31, 9/90, 11(p)/2
  (on āne tīd *at the same time*), 17/124, tīde
  9/18, tīd 20/306; gs tīde 8/27, 9/115; ds
  4/11, 9/23, 9/87, 9/112, 20/286; np tīda
  5/4; dp tīdum 22/160 [MnE tide]
tīddeg m. *span of life, final hour* ds tīddege
  17/69
tīgan 1 *tie, fasten* pret. 3p tīgdon 4/208
tiġel f. *tile* dp tigelum 13/30
til adj. *good* nsm 16/112, as noun *good man*
  21/20
tilian 2 *strive, endeavour* pres. subj. 1p tilien
  17/119; w.d. of person and g. of thing
  provide inf. 20/208
tīma m. *time* ds tīman 4/14, 4/34, 7/74
ġetimbre n. *building, structure* ap getimbro
  8/71
tin n. *tin* as 3/142
tintreġliċ adj. *tormenting* gsn tintreglican
  9/78
tīr m. *glory* ns 12/104, 20/157; as 20/197; gs
  tīres 20/93, 20/272
tīrfæst adj. *assured of glory, set on glory* as noun
  man set on glory gpf tīrfæstra 21/32
tīrlēas adj. *inglorious, vanquished* gsm tīrlēases 18(a)/843
tīð f. *boon* as tīðe 20/6 [MnE tithe]
tīðian 2 w.d. of person and g. of thing *grant*
  infl. inf. (tō) tīðienne 4/4
tō prep. w.d. *to, into, for, as a* 1/28, 2/2, 2/7,
  2/25, 2/68, 3/9, 3/150 (tō nytte *of use*),
  4/5, 4/92 (tō lace *as an offering*), 7/1, 8/34,
  12/10 (fōn tō *take up*), etc.; adv. cume . . .
  tō *arrive* 3/45, 4/213 (scuton . . . tō *shot at*);
  with infl. inf. (§205.2) 2/12 (tō etanne *for
  eating, to eat*), 2/49, 2/51, 3/17, etc.; as adv.
  thither 17/119
tō adv. *too* 12/55, 12/66, 12/90, etc.
tōætȳcan 1 *add* pret. 3s tōætȳhte 8/39
tōætȳhte see tōætȳcan

tōberstan III *break apart, shatter* pres. 3s
  tōbirsteð 11(g)/7; pret. 3s tōbærst 12/136,
  12/144
tōbrecan IV *destroy, break apart, violate* inf.
  18(a)/780; p. ptc. tōbrocen 7/39, 12/242;
  p. ptc. npn tōbrocene 22/87
tōbrēdan III w. inst. *shake off* inf. 20/247
tōbrȳtan 1 *crush* pres. 3s tōbrȳt 2/32
tōcyme m. *coming, advent* ds 4/22, 22/3
tōdāl n. *distinction, difference* ns 4/17
tōdæġ adv. *today* 3/52
tōdǣlan 1 *part, separate* pret. 3p subj. tōdǣl-
  den 15/12
tōgædere adv. *together* 4/252, 7/33, 7/43,
  12/67, tōgædre 13/20, etc.
tōġēanes prep. w.d. *against* 17/76; *toward*
  20/149
tōġeīeċan 1 *increase, add to* p. ptc. tōgeīeced
  3/190
tōġeþēodan 1 *add* pret. 3s tōgeþēodde 9/
  47
tōgongan VII w.g. *pass away* (impers.) pres.
  3s tōgongeð 11(h)/10
ġetoht n. *battle* ds getohte 12/104
tohte f. *battle* ds tohtan 20/197
tōl n. *tool* ds tōle 4/281
tōlūcan II *pull asunder, destroy* inf. 18(a)/781
torht adj. *bright, splendid* nsm 11(m)/3; asf
  torhtan 20/43
torhte adv. *brightly, splendidly* 11(d)/8
torhtlic adj. *splendid* nsm 20/157
torhtmōd adj. *glorious* nsm 20/6, 20/93
torn n. *resentment, grief, affliction* as 16/112,
  18(a)/833, 20/272
torne adv. *grievously* 20/93
torr m. *tower* np torras 13/3
tōslītan 1 *sever, tear apart* pres. 3s tōslīteð
  19/18
tōtwǣman 1 *divide, break up* p. ptc. tōt-
  wǣmed nsn 12/241
tōð m. *tooth* dp tōðon 20/272
tōðmæġen n. *strength of tusk, tusk-power* gs
  tōðmægenes 21/20 [MnE tooth, main]
tōweard adj. *coming, future, imminent* nsm
  20/157, 20/286; gsm tōweardan 9/77; gpn
  tōweardra 4/28 [MnE toward]
tōwearde adv. *beforehand, in advance* 4/30
tōwearp see tōweorpan
tōweorpan III *throw down, demolish* inf.
  8/55, 8/57, 8/61, 8/70; pret. 3s tōwearp
  8/75
træf n. *tent, pavilion* as 20/268; ds træfe
  20/43, 20/255
træppe f. *trap* træppum 3/110
tredan V *tread on, trample* pres. 1s trede
  11(d)/1; pret. 3s træd 18(b)/1352
treddian 2 *step, go* pret. 3s treddode 18(a)/
  725

trēow n. *tree* ns 1/11, 2/12; as 2/6, 14/4, 14/ 14, 14/17, 14/25, etc.; gs trēowes 2/5; ds trēowe 2/3, 2/8, 2/10, etc.; gp trēowa 2/4

trēow f. *faith, trust, loyalty* ns 21/32; as trēowe 16/112; dp trēowum 10(b)/65 (*beliefs*) [MnE tru(th)]

*ġe*trēowð f. *loyalty* np getrēowþa 22/7, getrȳwþa 22/53; ap 22/179

trēowwyrhta m. *carpenter* ns 3/202; ap trēowwyrhtan 3/181

*ġe*trīewe adj. *faithful* nsm 3/27 [MnE true]

trodu f. *track, footprint* ap trode 18(a)/843

trum adj. *strong, firm* nsm 18(b)/1369, 21/20; asm trumne 20/6

*ġe*trum n. *troop, band* ns 21/32

trym n. *step, pace* as 12/247

trymedon see trymian

trymian 1 *array, draw up, encourage* inf. 12/17; pret. 3p trymedon 12/305; p. ptc. getrymmed asn 12/22

*ġe*trymman 1 *strengthen* pres. ptc. getrymmende 9/110 [MnE trim]

*ġe*trymmed see trymian

trymming f. *confirmation* ds trymminge 4/321

*ġe*trȳwþa see *ġe*trēowþ

tūcian 2 *mistreat, torment* pret. 3s tūcode 4/158

tugon see tēon

tūn m. *town, village* ds tūne 4/246

tunge f. *tongue* ns 9/121; as tungan 9/17

tūnġerēfa m. *town reeve, overseer of an estate* ds tūnġerēfan 9/48

tungol n. *star, heavenly body* ns 21/48

tuwa adv. *twice* 3/26

twā see twēġen

twām see twēġen

twēġen num. (§84) *two* npm 7/12, 11(a)/2, 11(a)/3, 12/80; apm 3/56, 10(b)/6, 11(b)/ 4, 18(b)/1347; dpm twām 2/47, 2/50, 4/241, 11(m)/2; apn twā 4/111; dpn 4/135, 11(a)/1; gpn twēga 12/207; npf twā 10(b)/4, 11(a)/2; apf 4/16, 11(b)/3, 11(b)/5, 11(b)/7 [archaic MnE twain]

twelf num. *twelve* npm 4/36, 11(b)/4, twelfe 18(d)/3170, 22/102

twentig num. *twenty* npm 4/155

twēo m. *doubt, uncertainty* ds twēon 17/69 (tō twēon weorþeð *becomes an occasion for uncertainty*)

twēode see twēogan

twēogan 2 w.g. *doubt* pret. 3s twēode 20/1, 20/345

twēone num. *two* dp be sǣm twēonum *between the seas, on earth* 18(a)/858

tȳdran 1 *propagate, spawn* inf. 21/48

*ġe*tyhtan 1 *train, urge on, incite* pres. 1s getyhte 3/43

tȳman 1 *propagate, beget offspring* inf. 21/48; pret. 3s tȳmde 4/19 [MnE teem]

tȳn num. *ten* npm tȳne 22/102; apm 22/101; dpm 18(d)/3159

þā adv. *then* (§151 and §168 s.v. þonne) 2/7, 2/11, 2/13, 2/15, 2/20, 2/46, 2/49, 2/56, 2/59, 2/61, 4/4, etc.; conj. *when* 8/66, 15/ 9, þā þā *when* 2/17, 4/130, etc.; þā . . . þā *then . . . when* 2/48, *when . . . then* 5/28, 5/40, 8/1, 9/23, 9/33, 9/57, etc.; þā gȳt *still* 12/168, 12/273

þā pron. see se

þafian 2 *consent to* pret. 3s þafode 9/63

*ġe*þafian 2 *consent to* inf. 8/5, 20/60; pret. 3s geþafade 8/7

þafung f. *consent* as þafunge 22/100

*ġe*þafung f. *assent* as geþafunge 8/24

*ġe*þāh see *ġe*þicgan

þan see þon

þanc see þonc

*ġe*þanc n. *thought, thinking, intention* as 12/13; ds geþance 22/140

*ġe*þancie see *ġe*þoncian

þancigende see þoncian

þancode see þoncian

þancolmōd adj. *attentive* asf þancolmōde 20/172

þanon adv. *thence, therefrom* 3/106, 4/281, 7/54, 18(a)/763, 18(a)/844, 18(a)/853, þonan 10(b)/82, 16/23, 18(a)/819, 18(b)/ 1373, ðonan 20/118, ðanonne 20/132

þār see þǣr

þās see þes

þǣm, þām see se

þǣne (= þone) see se

þǣnne see þonne

þǣr adv., conj. (§152, §168) adv. *there* 2/46, 2/57, 3/60, 3/145, etc.; conj. *where* 2/17, 4/254, 6/26, etc.; *when* 22/184; *whereas* 22/28; *while* 22/103; þǣr . . . þǣr *where . . . there* 1/21; þǣr þǣr *there where, where* 2/49, *wherever* 5/23

þǣra see se

þǣre see se

þǣrfe see þearfe

þǣrinne adv. *therein* 6/37, 10(a)/25

þǣrof adv. *thereof, from that* 3/152

þǣron adv. *therein* 14/67

þǣrrihte adv. *immediately* 4/36

þǣrtō adv. *thereto* 4/27, 4/208, 6/28

þæs adv. (gs of þæt) *afterwards, therefore* 3/31 (þæs on morgenne *next morning*), 4/330; conj. 6/7 (þæs þe *after*)

þæs pron. see se

þæt conj. *that, so that* 2/3, 2/6, 2/9, 2/23, 2/37, 2/60, 2/64, 3/43, 3/59, 8/68, 10(b)/30 (þæt þe), etc.

þæt pron. see **se**

þætte (= þæt þe) conj. (§155) *that* ðætte
5/17, 5/26, etc.

þe indeclinable relative particle (§162) *which,
who, that* 2/1, 2/4, 2/5, 2/22, 2/36, 2/45
(whom), 2/56, 3/87, etc.; *as* 12/313; sē þe
he who 3/211; þe him *to whom* 16/10,
17/13

þē see **þū**

þē (= þȳ, isn of **se**) see **se**

þēah adv. *though, yet, however, nevertheless*
3/105, 4/98, 6/39, etc.; swā þēah *however*
4/27; conj. þēah (þe) *although* 2/8, 4/313

þēah hwæþre adv. *moreover, nevertheless*
3/177

geþeaht n. *counsel, deliberation* as 8/4

geþeahtere m. *counsellor, adviser, manager* ns
3/185, 3/197; as 3/183; np geþeahteras
8/38

þearf f. *need, stress, danger* ns 9/101, 12/233,
22/31, 22/169, etc.; as þearfe 12/175, 20/
3, 20/92; ds 12/232, 12/307, þærfe 12/201

þearf see **þurfan**

þearfende adj. *needy* dsf þearfendre 20/85

þearflīce adv. *profitably, with good effect*
10(b)/60

þearl adj. *severe* nsf 10(b)/77

þearle adv. *severely, exceedingly* 3/8, 3/29,
20/74, 20/86, 20/262, 20/268, 20/306,
3/125 (*ravenously*), 3/157 (*greatly*), 4/272,
10(b)/82, 12/158, 14/52 (*violently*)

þearlmōd adj. *fierce, stern* nsm 20/66, 20/91

þēaw m. *custom, practice* ns 9/91, 16/12;
ap ðēawas 4/141, 5/27; gp þēawa 22/130;
dp þēawum 4/84, 4/138, ðēawum *way*
20/129

þeċċan I *cover* inf. 11(k)/4; pres. 3s þeceð
11(j)/1

þeġen see **þeġn**

þeġengyld n. *wergild for a thane* ds
þegengylde 22/95

þeġenlīce adv. *loyally, nobly* 12/294

þeġn m. *nobleman, thane, retainer, warrior* ns
1/1, 6/25, 18(a)/867; þegen 7/15, 22/94;
as þegen 9/93, 10(b)/69, þegen 12/151; gs
þegenes 22/103; ds þegne 18(b)/1341,
þegene 22/92; np þegnas 4/292, 6/17,
10(b)/30, 14/75 (*disciples*), þegenas 12/
205, 12/220, ap 12/232, 20/10, 20/306;
gp þegna 8/15; dp þegnum 4/182, 8/28,
þēnan 22/27 (*servants, devotees*)

þeġnian 2 w.d. *serve* inf. 9/93; infl. inf.
(tō) þegnigenne 4/291; pres. 3p þegniað
11(m)/6

þēgon see **þicgan**

þēh see **þēah**

þēnan see **þeġn**

geþencan see **geþenċean**

þenċean I *think, intend* inf. 10(b)/60,
þencan 17/96; pres. 1s þence 12/319; 3s
þenceð 12/258, 12/316, 14/121, 17/51; 3p
þencaþ 14/115; pret. 3s þōhte 18(a)/739,
getrȳwlīċe þōhte *showed loyal intentions*
22/59; 3p þōhton 10(b)/11, 18(a)/800,
20/208

geþenċean I *think, ponder, consider* inf. 5/19,
geþencan 16/58, 17/118; imp. s. geðenc
5/24; pret. 3s geþōhte 16/88

þenden conj. *while* 10(b)/38, 10(b)/48,
11(e)/6, 17/102

þenian I *stretch out* inf. 14/52 (see note)
[MnE thin]

ðēning f. *divine service* ap ðēninga 5/15

þēod f. *people, nation* ns 10(b)/28; as þēode
22/6, 22/11, 22/40, etc.; gs 8/77; ds 12/
90, 12/220, 22/32, 22/86, 22/88, 22/97,
22/131; np þēoda 2/76, þīoda 5/53; gp
þēoda 12/173; dp þēodum 22/21, 22/24,
etc.

geþēodan I *join* pret. 3s geþēodde 9/64

þēodcyningas npm *kings of the people* gp
þēodcyninga 18/2

þēodde see **þēowan**

geþēode n. *language* as geðīode 5/33, 5/52,
etc.; gp geðēoda 5/47

þēoden m. *prince, lord* ns 12/120, 12/178,
12/232, 20/66, 20/91; as 12/158; gs
þēodnes 16/95, 18(a)/797, 20/165, 20/
268; ds þēodne 12/294, 14/69, 20/3,
20/11

þēodguma m. *man of the nation* (i.e. *Hebrew*)
np þēodguman 20/208, ðēodguman 20/
331

þēodland n. *nation* as þēodlond 10(b)/3

geþēodnis f. *joining* ds geþēodnisse 9/9

þēodred pers. n. *Theodred* ns 4/271, 4/292

þēodrīċ pers. n. *Theodoric* ns 10(a)/5, 10(a)/
15, 10(a)/24, 10(b)/69; ds þēodrīce 10(b)/
30

þēodscipe m. *discipline* dp þēodscipum
9/83; *nation* ns 22/118

þēodwita m. *wise man, man of learning* ns
22/160

þēof m. *thief* ns 11(c)/4, 21/42; np þēofas
4/274; ap 4/290; dp þēofum 3/31, 4/294

þēon III *flourish, prosper* pret 3s þāh 18/8

geþēon III *flourish, succeed, prosper* inf.
18/25, 21/44; pret. 3p geþungon 10(b)/7;
p. ptc. geþungen 4/139 (*virtuous*), 20/129
(*excellent*)

þēos see **þes**

ðēosse (= ðisse) see **þes**

þeossum (= þissum) see **þes**

þēow m. *slave, servant, minister* np þēowas
3/176, 22/26; ap 22/30; gp ðīowa 5/31,
þēowa 9/65; dp þēowum 4/315, 22/29

þēowan 1 w.d. *serve* pret. 1s þēodde 8/21, 3s þēode 9/119

þēowdōm m. *service* ns 3/188; ds þēowdōme 4/316

þēowen f. *handmaid* ns 20/74

þēowian 2 w.d. *serve* pres. 3s þēowaþ 11(m)/6 *enslave* p. ptc. npn geþēowede 22/39

þēre (= þǣre) see se

þes m., þēos f., þis n. dem. pron. *this* þās pl. *these* (§17) nsm þes 1/18, 3/33; asm þisne 1/25, 3/210, þysne 12/52; dsm þissum 1/27; nsn þis 1/11, 4/303; asn 2/28, 4/55, etc.; gsn þisses 1/27, 1/31; dsn þissum 3/136, 5/64, þysson 14/138, þisum 7/47, þysan 22/14, 22/45, 22/73, etc.; isn þȳs 7/1, 20/2, þīs 7/7; nsf þēos 1/30; asf þās 4/9; gsf þisere 4/18, þisre 4/67, ðeosse 9/1, þysse 21/55; dsf þissere 4/112; ðisse 5/25, þysse 8/45; gsf þisse 16/74; np þās 3/3, 7/73; ap 16/91, 16/101; gp þissa 1/28, 3/186, 5/22, þyssa 20/187; dp þisum 4/75; þyssum 4/183, 4/188, þeossum 8/37

þet (= þæt) see se

þicce adj. *thick, dense* dpm þiccum 4/224

þicgan V *receive, partake of, eat* inf. ðicgean 18(a)/736; pret. 3p þēgon 20/19

geþicgan V *receive, gain* pret. 3s geþāh 10(b)/53

geþicgean V *accept* inf. 6/20

þider adv. *thither* 6/18, 10(b)/61, 17/118 þyder 4/275, 20/129

þīn poss. adj. *thy, thine* asm þīnne 2/44, 2/65, 2/74, 3/7, 3/41, 3/65; gsm þīnes 2/40; dsm þīnum 2/31, 3/73; asn þīn 2/32; gsn þīnes 2/30, 2/36, 2/39; dsn þīnum 2/30, 2/73; asf þīne 2/21, 2/63; dsf þīnre 3/199; npm þīne 3/3; apm 3/81, 3/120; gpm þīnra 8/15, 4/165; dpm þīnum 3/33; apn þīn 3/144; apf þīne 2/33; *of you* np þīne 19/13

þinčan, þinčeð see þynčan

þīnen f. *handmaid* as ðīnenne 20/172; ap þīnena 4/16

þing n. *thing, deed* ns 13/48; as 3/35, 20/153; gs ðinges 20/60; np 3/139, 3/190; ap 1/34, 3/136, 3/139, 8/22, 9/98; gp þinga 3/143, 4/30, 17/68 (þinga gehwylce *in all circumstances*), 18(a)/791 (ænige þinga *in any way, by any means*); dp þingum 8/18

geþinge n. *result, issue* gs geþinges 18(a)/709

þingian 2 *ask, pray* inf. ūs . . . þingian wið *address ourselves to, pray to* 22/172

ðīod see þēod

geþīode see geþēode

þīow see þēow

þīowotdōm m. *service* ap ðīowotdōmas 5/11

þis see þes

þisere see þes

þissa see þes

þisse see þes

geþōht m. *thought* ns 15/43, as 15/12, np geþōhtas 17/34

geþōhte see geþenčean

þōhton see þenčean

þolian 2 *suffer, endure* inf. 10(b)/77, 12/201, 12/307, 18(a)/832; pres. ptc. þoligende 20/272; pres. 1s þolie 3/138, 1p þoliað 22/111; pret. 3p þolodan 14/149, þoledon 20/215

geþolian 2 *endure, tolerate* inf. 12/6

þon adv. *than* 12/33

þon is of þæt (see se) *the* (used with comparatives) 8/17; for þon see for; wið þon þe see wiþ; tō þon *to an extent* 19/12

þonan see þanon

þonc m. w.d. of person and g. of cause *thanks* (*for*) ns 5/20, 5/79, 17/122; as þanc 12/120, 12/147

geðonc m. *thought* ds geðonce 20/13

þoncian 2 w.d. of person and g. of cause *thank* pret. 3s þancode 18(b)/1397

geþoncian 2 w.d. of person and g. of cause *thank, give thanks to* pres. ptc. þancigende 4/245; pres. 1s geþancie 12/173

þoncwyrðe adj. *thankworthy, worthy of gratitude* asn 20/153

þone see se

þonne adv. *then* (§§151–152, 168 s.v. þonne) 2/10, 3/9, 3/12, 3/25, 3/30, 3/42, 3/44, 3/146, þænne 22/4, etc.; conj. *when, whenever* 3/11, 3/30, 3/44, 3/205, 4/318, 4/329, etc.; conj. w. compar. (§177) *than* 2/1, 2/73, 3/99, 3/146, 3/198, 4/316, 8/18, 11(h)/7, 12/195, etc.

þorfte see þurfan

þorn m. *thorn* ap þornas 2/39

þorod pers. n. *Thorod* ds þorode 7/29

þrāg f. *time, interval* ns 16/95; as þrāge 10(b)/77, 20/237 ealle þrage (*continuously*); ds þrāge *for a time* 10(b)/28; dp þrāgum *sometimes, at times* 11(e)/4, 21/4

geþrang n. *throng, crowd* ds geþrange 12/299

þrǣd m. *thread* ns 4/259

þrǣl m. *slave* ns 22/93, 22/105; as 22/94; ds þrǣle 22/93, 22/106; gp þrǣla hwylc *some slave or other* 22/90 [MnE thrall]

þrǣlriht n. *the rights of a slave* np 22/40 [MnE thrall, right]

þrēanȳd f. *distress, sad necessity* dp þrēanȳdum 18(a)/832

þrēat m. *host, troop* as 19/2, 19/7; is þrēate 10(b)/3, ðrēate 20/62; dp ðrēatum 18/4, 20/164 [MnE threat]

þreohtig adj. *enduring* compar. nsm þreohtigra 11(e)/4

þridda num. *third* dsm þriddan 2/48

þrīe num. *three* np þrȳ 22/108; ap þrȳ
4/296; gp þrēora 12/299, 17/68 (þrēora sum
one of three things); dp þrim 4/73, 4/128

þrim see þrīe

þringan III *throng, press forward* inf. 20/249;
pret. 3p þrungon 20/164; *approach, draw*
(near) p. ptc. geðrungen 20/287

*ge*þringan III *oppress, pinch, constrict* pret.
3p geþrungon 10(b)/3; p. ptc. geþrungen
npm 17/8

þrīnnys f. *trinity* ns 4/67; gs ðrȳnesse 20/86
[archaic MnE threeness]

þrōwian 2 *suffer* pret. 1s þrowode 17/3, 3s
14/84, 14/98, 14/145

þrōwung f. *passion, suffering* ds þrōwunge
9/75

*ge*þrungen see *ge*þringan

þrȳ see þrīe

þryċċan 1 *oppress* p. ptc. þrycced 9/89

þrym m. *majesty, glory* ns 16/95, 20/86;
as 18/2; gs þrymmes 20/60; *courage* is
þrymme 20/331; *troop* dp ðrymmum
20/164; *power* np þrymmas 21/4

þrymfæst adj. *glorious* nsm 14/84; asm
þrymfæstne 11(c)/4

þrymful adj. *glorious* nsf 20/74

þrymliċ adj. *sumptuous* apn 20/8

ðrȳnes see þrīnnys

þrȳð f. *power, force* np þrȳþe 16/99

þrȳðswȳð adj. *strong, mighty* nsm 18(a)/736

þū pron. *thou, you* ns 1/36, 2/20, 2/23, 2/24,
2/26, 2/40, 3/1, 3/7, etc.; as þē 2/35,
2/74, 3/179, 4/142; ds þē 2/23, 2/24,
2/31, 2/37, 2/39, 2/74, 3/68, 3/124
(*from you*), 4/4 (*for you*)

*ge*þūht see þynċan

þūhte see þynċan

þunor m. *thunder* ns þunar 21/4

*ge*þungon see *ge*þēon

þurfan pret.-pres. *need* pres. 3s þearf 4/114,
14/117, ðearf 20/117; 1p þurfe 12/34; 3p
þurfon 12/249; pret. 1s þorfte 4/5, 4/185;
pres. 2p subj. þyrfen 20/153

þurh prep. *through, by, by means of* 2/72,
4/64, etc., þuruh 7/73, 9/21 (*in*), 9/27 (*in*);
þurh þæt þe *because* 22/71, 22/138, þurh
þæt *therefore* 22/139

þurhdrīfan I *pierce, drive through* pret. 3p
þurhdrifan 14/46

þurhflēon II *fly through* pres. subj. 3s þurhflēo 8/30

þurhwadan VI *pierce, pass through* pret. 3s
þurhwōd 12/296, 18(a)/890

þurhwunian 2 *persist, remain* pret. 3s þurhwunode 4/139, 10(a)/7

þurstān pers. n. *Thurston* gs þurstānes 12/
298

þuruh see þurh

þus adv. *thus, in this way, as follows* 2/44,
2/50, 2/77, 3/44, 3/176, etc.

þūsend num. *thousand* ns 7/24, 7/63

þūsendmǣlum adv. *in thousands* 20/165

þwang m. *thong, strap* ap þwangas 3/153

*ge*þwǣre adv. *gently, obediently* 11(m)/6

*ge*þwǣlǣcan 1 *be a party to, assent to* inf.
4/291

*ge*þwǣrnes f. *concord, tranquillity* ns 3/207

þȳ see se

þȳ lǣs þe see lǣs

þyder see þider

þȳfel m. *bush* ap þȳfelas 4/233

þȳfþ f. *theft* dsf lȳtelre þȳfþe *petty theft*
22/39

*ge*þyld f. *patience* as 18(b)/1395

*ge*þyldiġ adj. *patient* nsm 16/65

þynċan 1 (impers. verb [§212] w.d.) *seem* inf.
þincean 18(b)/1341, swā hit þincan mæg
so it seems 22/52, 22/118, 22/145; pres. 3s
þyncþ 1/33, þincð 4/7, 4/26, þynceð
8/21, þinceð 12/55, 16/41; pret. 3s þūhte
2/12, 4/4, 9/96, 11(c)/1, 12/66, 14/4,
18(a)/842; 3p þūhton 18(a)/866; p. ptc.
geþūht 3/164 (biþ geþūht *will seem*),
3/187 (is geþūht *seems*), 3/191, 4/230
[archaic MnE (me)thinks]

þȳrel n. *hole* as 3/205 [MnE (nos)tril]

þyrfen see þurfan

þyrs m. *giant, ogre* ns 21/42

þysan (þissum) see þes

þyslīċ adj. *such* nsn 8/25

þȳstre adj. *dark, gloomy* nsf 20/34; dp
þȳstrum 21/42

þȳstro f. *darkness, shadow* ds 11(c)/4, np
14/52, dp þȳstrum 20/118, 21/51

þȳwan 1 *drive, urge, goad* inf. 3/15

ufan adv. *from above* 20/252

ūhta m. or f. *period just before dawn* ds ūhtan
15/35; gp ūhtna 16/8

ūhtcearu f. *grief before dawn* as ūhtceare 15/7

ūhtsong m. *matins* as 9/113

unārīmed adj. *countless* dp unārīmedum
10(a)/10

unāsecgendliċ adj. *unspeakable* ap unāsecgendlice 7/58

unbefohten adj. *unopposed, without a fight* npm
unbefohtene 12/57

unbindan III *unbind, loosen* p. ptc. unbunden
11(h)/15

unc see wit

uncer see wit

unclǣne adj. *unclean* npm 3/79; apm unclǣnan 3/80

uncoþu f. *disease* ns 22/49
uncræft m. *subterfuge, duplicity* dp uncræftan 22/180
uncūð adj. *unknown, strange* ns 5/78, 8/27; gsn uncūðes 18(a)/876 [MnE uncouth]
undǣd f. *wicked deed, misbehavior* ds undǣde 22/140
undēadliċ adj. *immortal* nsf 1/31 [archaic MnE undeadly]
under prep. w.d.a. *under* 1/5, 2/35, 4/12, etc.
underbǣc adv. *behind, back* 2/66
underbeġinnan III *undertake* infl. inf. (tō) underbeginnenne 4/8
undercyning m. *underking* ns 4/166
underdelfan III *dig under* pret. 3s underdealf 4/277 [MnE delve under]
underetan V *eat under, undermine* p. ptc. npf undereotone 13/6
underfēngon see underfōn
underfōn VII *accept, receive* pret. 1p underfēngan 22/176; 3p underfēngon 7/61
understandan VI *understand* inf. 4/15, 4/40, 4/75; infl. inf. (tō) understandenne 4/45; imp. p. understandaō 22/6; pres. 3p understandaō 4/25; subj. 3s understande 22/85, 22/96; *appreciate, feel* inf. 22/111
underþēodan I *subject, devote* pret. 3s underþēodde 8/16; p. ptc. underþēoded 9/84
unearh adj. *undaunted, not cowardly* npm unearge 12/206
unēaþe adv. *with difficulty, hardly* 3/139
unfæġer adj. *horrible* nsn 18(a)/727
unforcūð adj. *noble, of unblemished reputation* nsm 12/51
unforht adj. *unafraid* nsm 4/189, 14/110; npm unforhte 12/79
unformolsnod adj. *undecayed* nsm 4/264
unforworht adj. *innocent* npm unforworhte 22/38
unġehīrsum adj. *disobedient* nsm 4/120
unġelǣred adj. *unlearned, ignorant* npm ungelǣredan 4/25; dpm ungelǣredum 4/46
unġelīc adj. *different* nsn 19/3, 19/8
unġelimp. n. *misfortune* gp ungelimpa 22/96
unġerīm n. *a countless number* ns 22/151
unġesǣliġ adj. *unfortunate, wretched* npm ungesǣlige 4/274; dpm ungesǣligum 4/294
unġesǣlþ f. *misfortune* np ungesǣlða 7/73
unġesibb adj. *unrelated* dsm ungesibbum 11(k)/8
unġetrȳwþ f. *disloyalty* np ungetrȳwþa 22/62
unġylde n. *excessive tax* np ungylda 22/50 [MnE un-, yield]

unhēanlīċe adv. *not ignobly, valiantly* 6/14
unlagu f. *violation of the law, injustice* ap unlaga 22/11, 22/39, 22/165 [MnE unlaw]
unlǣd adj. *wretched, accursed* gsm unlǣdan 20/102
unlifġende adj. *not living, dead* gsm unlyfigendes 18(a)/744, unlyfigendes 20/180; asm unlyfigendne 18(b)/1308; dsm unlifgendum 18(b)/1389, unlyfigendum 20/315
unlūcan II *unlock, open* inf. 4/278
unlȳtel adj. *great, not little* nsm 18(a)/885; nsn 22/18; asn 18(a)/833
unmyltsiendliċ adj. *unforgivable* ns 4/66
unnan pret.-pres. w.d. of person and g. of thing *grant, allow* pret. 3s ūðe 20/123, 20/183; pret. subj. 3p ūþon 6/29
ġeunnan pret.-pres. w.d. of person and g. of thing *grant* imp. s. geunne 20/90; pres. subj. 2s 12/176
unnyt adj. *useless* nsm 18(d)/3168
unorne adj. *simple, humble* nsm 12/256
unrǣd m. *ill advice, foolish policy* gs unrǣdes 11(f)/12; ap unrǣdas 7/73
unriht n. *injustice, wrong-doing* as 22/10, 22/174, on unriht *wrongfully* 22/35; gp unrihta 22/8 [MnE unright]
unrihtlīċe adv. *wrongly* 22/60 [MnE unrightly]
unrihtwīs adj. *unjust, wicked* dsm unrihtwīsan 10(a)/19 [MnE unrighteous]
unsidu m. *vice* ap unsida 22/122
unrīm n. *countless number* ns 10(b)/44
unrōt adj. *sad, despondent* nsm 10(a)/30; npm unrōte 20/284
unryht adj. *unjust, wrongful* dpf unryhtum 6/2 [MnE unright]
unsofte adv. *roughly, harshly* 20/228
unstille adv. *not still, restlessly* 11(l)/5
unstilnes f. *disturbance* as unstilnesse 6/18 [MnE unstillness]
unswǣslic adj. *violent* asm unswǣslicne 20/65
unsȳfre adj. *impure* nsm unsȳfra 20/76
untrum adj. *infirm, sick* gp untrumra 9/91; compar. ap untrumran 9/91
untrymnes f. *infirmity* ds untrymnesse 9/88
unþinged adj. *unprepared for, unexpected* nsm 17/106
unwāclīċe adv. *not weakly, bravely* 12/308
unwærlīċe adv. *unawares* 3/44 [MnE unwar(i)ly]
unwǣstm m. *crop failure* gp unwǣstma 22/50
unwearnum adv. *irresistibly* 17/63, 18(a)/741 (*eagerly, greedily*)

unweaxen adj. *not fully grown* nsm 12/152
unweder n. *bad weather, bad season* np unwedera 22/50 [MnE un-, weather]
unwillum adv. *unwillingly* 10(b)/24
unwittig adj. *stupid, ignorant* nsm 4/299; apn unwittigan 4/158 (*innocent*)
unwrītere m. *inaccurate scribe* ns 4/125
ūp see ūpp
ūpāstīġnes f. *ascension* ds ūpāstīġnesse 9/75
ūpcyme m. *up-springing, ascendancy* as 11(o)/9
ūpganga m. *landing, passage to land* as ūpgangan 12/87
ūphēah adj. *lofty* npf ūphēa 15/30
ūplang adj. *upright* nsm 18(a)/759
ūpp adv. *up* 7/10, up 10(a)/2, 11(n)/5, 12/130, 14/71, 15/3, etc.
uppan prep. w.d. *upon, on* 2/46
uppe adv. *up, above* 14/9, 21/38
ūprodor m. *heaven above* as 17/105
ūre poss. adj. *our* nsm 3/184, 4/162, 12/232, etc.; asm ūrnc 4/87, 12/58; nsn 12/313; asn ure 7/77; asf 4/87; dsf 4/68; dpm ūrum 12/56; npm ūre 5/34; npn 8/19; gpn ūra 8/16; dpn ūrum 3/210; dpf 4/71; *of us* nsm ūre 22/55
ūrigfeþra adj. *dewy-feathered* nsm 17/25, ūrigfeðera 20/210
urnon see irnan
ūs see wē
ūsic see wē
ūt adv. *out* 1/28, 3/76, 3/77, 3/80, 4/288, 5/8 (*outward*), etc.
ūtādrīfan I *drive out, expel* pres. 2p ūtādrīfaþ 3/170, 3/176
ūtan adv. *from without, on the outside* 6/11, 18(a)/774, ūtene 7/31
ūtanbordes adv. *from abroad* 5/12
ūte adv. *outside, abroad* 3/145, 5/13, etc.
ūtene see ūtan
ūtgān anom. (§128) *go out* inf. 3/8
ūtgong m. *exodus, emigration* ds utgongc 9/72
uton, wuton (1p pl. subj. of wītan used w. inf) *let us* 3/206, 3/208, 4/68, 4/69, 17/117, 18(b)/1390, wuton 9/115, utan 22/158, 22/169
ūtweard adj. *turning outward, striving to escape* nsm 18(a)/761
ūðe, ūþon see unnan
uuiþ see wiþ

Visionis see note to 2/45

wā m. *woe, affliction* ns waa 10(b)/25; as interj. 15/52; cf. wēa
wāc adj. *slender* asm wācne 12/43; *weak* nsm 16/67; compar. npm wācran (as noun) 17/87

wācian 2 *weaken, turn coward* inf. 12/10
wacian 2 *watch, keep awake* pres. ptc. waciende 3/31 [MnE wake]
wadan VI *go, advance, trudge* inf. 12/140, 16/5 (*travel*); pret. 1s wōd 16/24; 3s 12/130, 12/253, 18(a)/714; pret. 3p wōdon 12/96, 12/295 [MnE wade]
ġewadan VI *pass, penetrate* pret. 3s gewōd 12/157
wado see wæd
wāg m. *wall of a building* ns 13/9; ds wāge 11(j)/12
wālā interj. (w.g.) *alas* 22/106, 22/107
wald m. *forest* ds walde 20/206
waldend see wealdend
waldendwyrhta m. *master builder, the king's builder* ap waldendwyrhtan 13/7
walo see wæl
wand see windan
wandian 2 *flinch, draw back* inf. 12/258; pret. 3s wandode 12/268
wanhygdig adj. *foolhardy, reckless* nsm 16/67
wanian 2 *diminish, lessen* pret. 3s wanode 18(b)/1337; 3p wanedan 22/32 [MnE wane]
ġewanian 2 *curtail, diminish* inf. 22/23; p. ptc. npn gewanode 22/41
wāniġean 2 *bewail* inf. 18(a)/787
wann adj. *dark, black* nsm won 16/103, wanna 20/206; nsn won 18(b)/1374; nsf wann 14/55; dsf wanre 18(a)/702 [MnE wan]
warian 2 *attend, hold* pres. 3s warað 16/32; 3p warigeað 18(b)/1358 (*guard, occupy, inhabit*)
warnian 2 *warn* inf. 7/32, warnian ūs *warn ourselves, take warning* 22/170
wāt see witan
ġewāt see ġewitan
waðum m. *wave* gp waðema 16/24, 16/57
wæċċan 2 *keep awake, watch* pres. ptc. nsm wæccende 18(a)/708; npm 20/142 (*on watch*). See wacian
wæd n. *water, sea* ap wado 11(d)/2
wǣd f. *clothing, covering* dp wēdum 11(k)/4, wǣdum 14/15, 14/22 [MnE (widow's) weeds]
wǣdbrēċ f. pl. *breeches* ap 2/16
wǣdian 2 *equip* p. ptc. gewǣdod 7/37
wǣdla m. *poor person, beggar* dp wǣdlum 4/143
wǣfersȳn f. *spectacle* ds wǣfersȳne 14/31
wǣfre adj. *wandering* nsm 18(b)/1331
wǣg m. *wave* as 17/19; ap wēgas 16/46
wǣge n. *cup, flagon* as 18(c)/2253
wǣgun see wegan

wæl n. *slaughter, carnage* ns 7/15, 12/126, 12/303; as 7/37; ds wæle 12/279, 12/300 (*field of slaughter, battlefield*); np walo 13/25 (*slaughtered men, the slain*)

wæl n. *pool, river* ds wæle 21/39

wælċyrie f. *sorceress* np wælcyrian 22/150 [MnE walkyrie]

wælgǣst m. *murderous spirit* ns 18(b)/1331

wælġīfre adj. *greedy for slaughter* nsm 20/207; npn wælgīfru 16/100; dp wælgīfrum 20/295

wælhrēow adj. *fierce, bloodthirsty* nsm wælhrēowa 10(a)/24; asm wælhrēowan 4/198; npm 4/261; apm 4/205; *cruel* apf wælhrēowe 22/39

wælhrēowlīċe adv. *horribly* 4/302

wælhrēownys f. *bloodthirstiness, cruelty* ds wælhrēownysse 4/153

wælrǣs m. *murderous conflict* ds wælrǣse 18(a)/824

wælræst f. *bed of death, death in battle* as wælræste 12/113

wælrēow adj. *slaughter-cruel* npm wælrēowe 19/6

Wæls pers. n. *Wæls* gs Wælses 18(a)/897

wælscel n.(?) *carnage* as 20/312

Wælsing pers. n. *son of Wæls, i.e. Sigemund* gs Wælsinges 18(a)/877

wælsleaht m. *battle, slaughter* gp wælsleahta 16/7, 16/91

wælspere n. *deadly spear* as 12/322

wælstōw f. *place of slaughter, battlefield* gs wælstōwe 12/95; ds 12/293

wælwulf m. *wolf of slaughter* (*Viking*) np wælwulfas 12/96

wǣpen n. *weapon* ns 11(j)/1, 12/252; as 8/60, 8/63, 11(n)/12, 12/130, 12/235; gs wǣpnes 12/168; ds wǣpne 12/228; np wǣpen 16/100; ap wǣpnu 4/203, wǣpen 20/290; gp wǣpna 12/83, 12/272, 12/308, dp wǣpnum 4/204, 12/10 (tō wǣpnum fēng *took up arms*), 12/126

wǣpenġewrixl n. *conflict* ns 22/92

wǣpnedcynn n. *the male sex* gs wǣpnedcynnes 11(g)/1

wǣpnian 2 *arm* p. ptc. gewǣpnod 7/37

wǣre see **bēon**

wǣrlīċe adv. *carefully* 22/179

wǣrloga m. *perjuror, scoundrel* as wǣrlogan 20/71

wǣron see **bēon**

wǣrun (= wǣron) see **bēon**

wæs see **bēon**

wæstm m. *fruit, result* ds wæstme 2/4, 2/5; ap wæstmas 21/9; dp wæstmum 8/48, 18(b)/1352 (*growth, stature, form*)

wǣta m. *moisture, blood* ds wǣtan 14/22

wæter n. *water* ns 22/18; as 1/2, 4/64, 12/91, 12/98, 18(b)/1364; ds wætere 12/64, 12/96, 21/27 wætre 15/49; ap wæteru 4/61

wæterian 2 *water, give water to* inf. 3/19; p. ptc. apm gewæterode 3/32

wē pron. *we* np 1/27, 2/5, 2/6, 4/45, etc.; ap ūsic *us* 17/123; dp ūs 1/30, 2/6, 3/140, 3/173, 3/197, etc.

wēa m. *woe, misery* ns 21/13; gp wēana 18(b)/1396

wēaġesīð m. *companion in evil* np wēagesīðas 20/16

weal m. *wall* ns 13/39, 16/98; as weall 20/161; gs wealles 20/151; ds wealle 16/80, 18(a)/785, 18(a)/891, 18(d)/3161; np weallas 16/76; ap 20/137

wēalāf f. *survivors, woeful remnant* ns 10(b)/22

Wēalas m. pl. *Cornwall, Cornishmen* dp Wēalum 7/9 [MnE Welsh]

ġewealc n. *rolling, tossing* as 17/6, 17/46 [MnE walk]

ġeweald n. *control, dominion, power* as 4/123, 4/163, 10(b)/38, 11(f)/14, 12/178, 14/107, 18(a)/764, 18(a)/808; *possession* ds gewealde 22/38, 22/80, 22/84

wealdan VII w.g. *wield, control* inf. 12/83, 12/95, 12/168, 12/272; w.d. pret. 3p wīoldon 10(b)/48; *cause* pret. 3p wēoldan 22/51 [MnE wield]

ġewealdan VII *rule, control* w.g. inf. 20/103; pres. 3s w.a. ġewielt 2/35

wealdend m. *ruler, the Lord* ns 14/111, 14/155, waldend 11(h)/6, Waldend 12/173, 18/17, 20/5, 20/61; as 14/67; gs wealdendes 14/17, 14/53; ds wealdende 14/121; np waldend 16/78

wealgat n. *wall-gate* ds wealgate 20/141

wealhstod m. *translator* ap wealhstodas 5/52

weallan VII *well, surge, boil* inf. 21/45; pres. ptc. weallende 18(a)/847, asm weallendan 22/181; pret. 3s wēol 18(a)/849

weallwala m. *wall-brace* ap weallwalan 13/20

wealstān m. *masonry* ns 13/1; gp wealstāna 21/3

wealsteal m. *foundation* as 16/88

weard m. *guardian* ns 9/42, 14/91, 17/54, 18(b)/1390; as 9/36, 20/80 [MnE ward]

weard f. *watch, guard* as wearde 20/142

weard adv. (*to*)*ward* wið . . . weard 20/99 (*toward*)

weardiġan 2 *occupy* pres. 3p weardiað 15/34

wearh m. *criminal, felon* ns 21/55; np weargas 4/283; ap wergas 14/31

Glossary

wearoð m. *shore* as 10(b)/14

wearp see **weorpan**

wearþ see **weorðan**

wēaspel n. *tidings of woe* ds wēaspelle 18(b)/1315

wēaþearf f. *grievous need* ds wēaþearfe 15/10

weaxan VII *grow* pret. 3s wēox 10(b)/5, 18/8 [MnE wax]

Weċedport m. *Watchet (Somerset)* ns 7/14

wed f. *pledge, covenant* np 22/87; as 22/178

wēdan 1 *be insane, rave* pret. 3s wēdde 8/67

wedbryċe m. *breaking of a pledge* ap wedbrycas 22/126

weder n. *wind, storm, (bad) weather* ns 19/10; is wedre 11(o)/2; dp wederum 13/12

Wederas m. pl. *the Geats* gp Wedra 18(d)/3156

wēdum see **wǣd**

weġ m. *way, path, road* as 14/88, 17/74, 18(a)/763, 18(a)/844, 18(b)/1382; ds wege 4/197; ap wegas 11(l)/6

wegan V *carry* inf. 8/63; pres. 3s wigeð 11(m)/3; 3p wegað 11(j)/14; subj. 3s wege 18(c)/2252; pret. 3p wǣgun 11(f)/3, wēgon 12/98, wǣgon 20/325 [MnE weigh]

wēgas see **wǣg**

weglīðend m. *seafarer* dp weglīðendum 18(d)/3158

weġnest n. *viaticum, provision for a journey* isn wegneste 9/111

wel adv. *well* 3/32, 3/69, 4/42, 4/315, 9/63 *(readily)*, 22/8 *(fairly)*, well 14/129, etc.

wela m. *prosperity, riches* ns 16/74; as welan 5/35 [MnE weal]

weler m. *lip* ap weleras 4/111

welhold adj. *very kind* nsf 11(k)/4

welhwǣr adv. *well-nigh everywhere* 5/79

ġewelhwǣr adv. *well nigh everywhere* 22/27

welhwylċ adj. *every (one)* gpm welhwylcra 18(b)/1344; pron. asn welhwylc *everything* 18(a)/874

ġewelhwylc adj. *nearly every* dsm gewelhwylcan 47, 22/98

weliġ adj. *rich, well-to-do* dsf welegan 10(b)/37; dp weligum 3/133

wellan see **wille**

welm m. *fervour* ds welme 9/85

welwan 1 *huddle* p. ptc. apf gewelede 22/109

welwillendnys f. *benevolence* ds welwillendnysse 4/144

wēn f. *expectation, hope* ns 18(a)/734; np (w.g. of thing hoped for) wēna 19/13; dp wēnum 19/9

wēnan 1 w.g. *think, expect* inf. 4/10; pres. 1s wēne 5/17, 14/135 (ic wēne mē *I look forward to*), 18(b)/1396; subj. 3s 22/44; pret. 3s wēnde 10(b)/78, 10(b)/82, 12/239, 20/20; 3p wēndon 5/44, 7/51, 8/66, 18(a)/778 [archaic MnE ween]

wendan 1 *wend one's way, go, turn, translate, change* inf. 5/43, 5/67, 12/316, 14/22; pres. 3s went *(goes)* 1/8; subj. 1s wende 12/252; pret. 3p wendon 5/49, 12/193, 12/205

ġewendan 1 *return, turn* pres. subj. 2s gewende 2/41, pret. 3s 4/135, 4/152, etc.

wēndon see **wēnan**

wenian 1 *accustom* inf. 16/29 *(entertain)*; pret. 3s wenede 16/36

went see **wendan**

wēofod n. *altar* as 2/57; ds wēofode 4/270

wēop see **wēpan**

weorc n. *work, task, deed* ns 4/7; as 2/61, 9/38, 14/79; ds weorce 2/38, 4/284; ap weorc 22/177; dp weorcum 4/43

ġeweorc n. *labour, workmanship, handiwork* ns 13/2; ds geweorce 3/196, 4/84; np geweorc 16/87

weorode see **werod**

weorpan III *throw, cast* pres. 1s weorpe 3/76, 3/77, 3/80, 11(f)/7; pret. 3s wearp 13/38; 3p wurpon 20/290 [MnE warp]

weorþ n. *worth, price* ds weorþe 3/144, 3/147

weorð, -e adj. *worthy, dear, valuable, in possession of* nsm wyrðe 4/24, 4/190, weorð 11(f)/1; gsn wyrðes 9/47, 10(b)/67; nsf wyrðe 4/314, weorðe 8/37; np wyrðe 10(a)/8, 10(b)/37; compar. nsm wyrðra 18(a)/861

weorðan III *become, happen* inf. 5/45, 11(m)/10, 16/64, wurðan 18(a)/807; pres. 2s wierþst *(wilt return)* 2/42; 3s weorþeð 16/110, 17/69, wyrð 22/4, 22/43, etc.; pret. 3s wearþ 4/156, 6/19, 11(k)/8, 12/113, 12/186 (wearð . . . on fleame *took to flight*), 12/295; 3p wurdon 4/129, 4/254, 13/27; w. p. ptc. forming passive (§202) inf. 18(d)/3177; 3s wearð 4/234, 12/106, 12/114, 12/116, 12/135, 12/138, etc.; 3p wurdon 2/15, 4/243; subj. 3s wurde 2/59, 4/225, 12/1; p. ptc. geworden 9/118, 14/87, 22/133 (geworden . . . tō *reached*), 22/75 *(come about, occurred)*, 22/163, etc.

ġeweorðan III *please* pres. 3s gewyrð (impers.: *it pleases*) 4/114; *become* subj. pres. 3s geweorþe 22/91

weorðful adj. *honourable, venerable* nsm wurðful 4/137; dsm wurðfullan 4/314

weorþian 2 *respect, honour* inf. 3/208, 14/129; pres. 3p weorðiað 14/81; subj. 3s wurþige 4/315; pret. 3s wurðode 4/138, 4/271 ġeweorþian 2 *honour, exalt* pret. 3s geweorðode 14/90, 14/94, geweorþade 17/123; p. ptc. geweorðad 9/2, asm geweorðod 14/15, nsn 20/298

weorþlīċe adv. *splendidly, in splendid fashion* 14/17, wurðlīce 4/253, 12/279; superl. weorðlīcost 18(d)/3161 [MnE worthily]

weorðmynd n. or f. *honour, dignity* as weorðmynde 20/342; ds wurðmynde 4/255, wurðmynte 4/273; gp weorðmynda 10(b)/51; dp weorðmyndum 18/8

weorðscipe m. *respect, honour* ds 22/12 [MnE worship]

weorðung f. *worship* ds weorðunge 22/22

weoruld see **woruld**

weoruldhāde see **woruldhād**

wēpan VII *weep* inf. 10(a)/30, 15/38; pret. 3s wēop 14/55

wer m. *man, husband* ns 4/280, 11(a)/1, 16/64; as 18(d)/3172; gs weres 2/35, 18(b)/1352; ds were 2/14, 21/33; np weras 11(b)/1, 11(j)/3, 11(j)/12, 11(o)/6, 19/6, 20/71, 20/142, 20/163, 20/241; ap 4/157, 20/249; gp wera 3/166, 11(c)/3, 13/26, 17/21; dp werum 11(f)/1 [MnE were(wolf)]

wēr f. *covenant, pledge* dp wērum 17/110

werede see **werian**

wergas, weargas see **wearh**

werian 1 *defend, protect* pret. 3s werede 6/14; 1p weredon 18(b)/1327; 3p 12/82, 12/283

wēriġ adj. *weary, exhausted* nsm 17/29, nsn 16/15; asm wērigne 16/57; npm wērige 12/303

wēriġferhð adj. *weary-hearted* npm wērigferhðe 20/290; apm 20/249

wēriġmōd adj. *disconsolate* nsm 15/49, 18(a)/844

werod n. *troop, company* ns 12/64, 12/97; as 12/102; ds werode 4/164, 12/51, weorode 14/152; is werode 6/10, 14/69, werede 14/124; gp weruda 14/51, weroda 20/342

werþēod f. *people* gp werþēoda 13/9

weruda see **werod**

wesan anom. *be* inf. 14/110, 14/117, 15/42, 18(b)/1328. See **bēon**

west adv. *west* 12/97

wēste adj. *deserted* nsm 16/74

wēsten n. *desert, wasteland* ds wēstene 4/82

wēstenstaþol m. *deserted place* ap wēstenstaþolas 13/27

Westseaxe m. pl. (§46) *West Saxons* gp Westsexena 4/155, Westseaxna 6/1, 7/63

wīċ n. *abode* ns 15/32; ap 11(d)/2, 15/52, 18(a)/821

wiċċa m. *warlock, sorcerer* npm wiccan 22/149 [MnE witch]

wiċċecræft m. *witchcraft* as 1/12

wicg n. *horse* ns wycg 11(j)/5, ds wicge 11(j)/14, 12/240

wīcian 2 *dwell* infl. inf. (tō)wīcianne 3/198

wīcing m. *Viking* as 12/139; ap wīcingas 12/322; gp wīcinga 7/11, 12/26, 12/73, 12/97; dp wīcingum 12/116

wīd adj. *broad* apm wīdan 13/39; apm wīde 18(a)/877; compar. wīdre asn 18(a)/763; *enduring* dsn wīdan 20/347 (see ealdor n.)

wīddor see **wīde**

wīde adv. *far, far and wide* 4/148, 4/322, 4/329, 11(d)/5, 11(f)/1, 13/25, 14/81, 15/46, etc.; swā wīde swā *as far as* 7/57; *widely, commonly* 22/75; compar. wīddor 11(k)/10; superl. wīdost *farthest, most widely* 17/57 [MnE wide]

widewe f. *widow* ns 4/267; np wydewan 22/35; dp widewum 4/144

wīdl n. *defilement* ds wīdle 20/59

wīdlāst m. *far wandering* dp wīdlāstum 19/9

ġewīdost adv. superl. *as far apart as possible* 15/13

ġewidre n. *weather, storm* ap gewidru 18(b)/1375

wīdwegas m. pl. *distant regions* ap 18(a)/840

ġewielt see **ġewealdan**

wierþst see **weorðan**

wīf n. *woman, wife* ns 2/4, 2/11, 2/18, 2/24, 11(m)/5, 20/148; as 3/148; gs wīfes 1/29, 2/36, 6/17; ds wife 2/2, 2/8, 2/31, 4/19, 17/45; np wīf 11(o)/6, 20/163; ap 4/16, 4/32, 4/157; gp wīfa 4/20, 14/94; dp wīfum 4/183, 11(a)/1

wīfcȳþþu f. *company or intimacy with a woman* ds wīfcȳþþe 6/10

Wīferþ pers. n. *Wiferth* ns 6/25

wīfian 2 *take a wife, marry* inf. 4/21

wīġ n. *war, battle* ns 16/80, 18/23; gs wīges 12/73, 12/130, 18(a)/886; ds wīge 5/9, 12/10, 12/128, 12/193, 12/235, 12/252, 18(b)/1337; is 10(b)/22

wiġa m. *warrior* ns 11(j)/1, 11(l)/6, 11(m)/1, 12/210, 16/67; as wigan 12/75, 12/235; np 12/79, 12/126, 12/302; gp wigena 12/135, 20/49

wīġbed n. *altar* ap wīgbedo 8/47, wīgbed 8/54, 8/75

Wīgelin pers. n. *Wigelin* gs Wīgelines 12/300

wīġend m. *warrior* as wīggend 20/258; np wīgend 12/302, wīggend 20/69, 20/141, 20/312; dp wīggendum 20/283

wigeð see **wegan**

wīġfruma m. *war-chief* ds wīgfruman 18(c)/2261

wiggend see **wīġend**

wīġhaga m. *battle-wall, wall of shields* as wīhagan 12/102

wīgheard adj. *hard in war, fierce* asm wīgheardne 12/75

wīghyrst f. *war trappings* dp wīghyrstum 13/34

wīgplega m. *battle-play, fighting* ds wīgplegan 12/268, 12/316

wīgsteal n. *place of war, place of idols* (?) np 13/27

wīhagan see wīghaga

wiht see wihte

wiht f. and n. *creature, being* ns 11(b)/1, 11(g)/6, 11(h)/2; as 11(g)/1; ap wuhte 11(l)/1 [archaic MnE wight]

wihte adv. *at all* 11(c)/6, wiht 18(a)/862, 20/274 [MnE whit]

wiites see wīte

wilde adj. *wild* as noun *the wild one* ns 21/18

wilddēor n. *wild beast* np 3/63; ap 3/49, 3/50; gp wilddēora 3/43; dp wilddēorum 2/29

wile see willan

wilġehlēþ m. *familiar companion, comrade* ap wilgehlēþan 11(j)/5

wilġesīþ m. *retainer, dear companion* np wilgesīþas 18/23

willa m. *will, desire, pleasure, delight* ns 14/129, 18(a)/824; as willan 4/115; ds 20/295; gp wilna 18(b)/1344

willan anom. *wish, desire, will* pres. 1s wile 3/146, wille 12/247, wylle 12/216, etc.; 2s wilt 3/95, 3/119, 3/144, wylt 4/167; 3s wile 12/52, wyle 4/22, etc.; 1p willað 12/35, 12/40; 3p 12/46, 19/2, 19/7; subj. 1s wille 12/221; 2s 5/21, 12/37; 3s 4/10, 5/62, 16/14, 16/72, 17/43, 17/97, 17/99, 17/113; pret. 2s woldest 2/65; 3s wolde 1/12, 2/43, 2/58, 2/61, etc.; 3p woldon 4/107, 4/255, 4/275, 4/305, 7/50, 9/85, 12/207, 14/68; subj. 3s wolde 16/28; 3p woldan 8/5. With negative: nyllan *be unwilling, will not* pres. 1s nyle 3/125, 3/129, nelle 4/118, 4/186, 11(h)/15, 12/246; 3s nyle 3/215, nille 17/99, nele 4/125; 3p nyllaþ 3/166, nellað 4/32, 4/310; pret. 2s noldest 2/72; 3s nolde 4/140, 6/20, 7/74, 12/6, etc.; 1p noldon 5/38; 3p 12/81, 12/185, 12/201

wille f. *fountain* ds willan 8/5; ap wellan 11(g)/3 [MnE well]

wilnian 2 w.g. *desire, petition for* pret. 3p wilnedon 10(b)/35

ġewilnian 2 w.g. *desire, wish* pres. 1s gewilnige 4/181

wilnung f. *desire* ds wilnunga 5/45

wilsumnes f. *devotion* ds wilsumnesse 9/119

wilt see willan

Wiltūnscīr f. *Wiltshire* ds Wiltūnscīre 7/73

wīn n. *wine* as 3/141; ds wīne 11(a)/1, 11(j)/17, 20/29; is 20/67

ġewin see ġewinn

wind m. *wind* ns 18(b)/1374; as 20/347; ds winde 11(j)/14, 11(o)/1, 16/76, 21/41

windan III *fly* inf. 12/322; *wave, brandish* pret. 3s wand 12/43, *roll* 20/110; *circle (in the air)* pret. 3p wundon 12/106 [MnE wind]

ġewindan III *go, turn* inf. wīdre gewindan *reach a more remote place by flight* 18(a)/763

windiġ adj. *windy* apm windige 18(b)/1358

wine m. *friend, lord* ns 12/250, 15/49, 15/50; as 17/115; ap winas 12/228

winedryhten m. *beloved lord* as 12/248, 12/263, 18(d)/3175, 20/274, winedrihten 18(a)/862; gs winedryhtnes 16/37

winelēas adj. *friendless* ns 15/10, 16/45

winemæg m. *beloved kinsman* ap winemagas 12/306; gp winemæga 16/7; dp winemagum 17/16

wīngāl adj. *flushed with wine* nsm 13/34, 17/29

wīnġedrinc n. *wine-drinking* ds wīngedrince 20/16

wīnhāte f. *invitation to wine* as wīnhātan 20/8

ġewinn n. *war, battle, strife* as gewinn 12/214, 21/55, gewin 10(a)/1, 11(h)/2, 18(a)/798, 18(a)/877; ds gewinne 12/248, 12/302, 14/65 (*agony*)

winnan III *suffer, struggle, fight* infl. inf. (tō) winnenne 4/205; pres. ptc. nsm winnende 11(l)/6; pret. 1s wonn 15/5; 3p wunnon 18(a)/777 [MnE win]

ġewinnan III *conquer, win* inf. 12/125, 22/162; p. ptc. gewunnen 10(b)/17, 10(b)/28; dsm gewunnenum 4/153

winnende see winnan

wīnreced n. *wine hall* as 18(a)/714

wīnsæd adj. *sated with wine* npm wīnsade 20/71 [MnE sad]

wīnsæl n. *hall* np wīnsalo 16/78

wīnsele m. *hall* ns 18(a)/771

Wintanċeaster f. *Winchester* as Wintanceastre 6/41

winter m. *winter, year* ns 3/10; as 3/154, 8/34, 17/15; gs wintres 8/32, 16/103; ds wintra 3/121, 8/33; gp wintra 6/7, 6/41, 10(b)/29, 16/65; ip wintrum 12/210

wintercearig adj. *desolate as winter* nsm 16/24

wintersetl n. *winter quarters* as 4/164; ap wintersetle 7/62

wintertīd f. *wintertime* ds wintertīde 8/28 [MnE wintertide]

wioldon see wealdan

wiotan see wita

wiotonne see witan
wīr m. *wire, metal rod* dp wīrum 13/20
wīrboga m. *twisted ornamental wire* ip wīrbogum 11(j)/3
wircean see wyrcan
wīs adj. *wise* nsm wisa 3/186, 10(b)/51, 12/
219, 16/64; asm wīsne 3/183, wīsan 18(b)/
1318; dsm wīsan 4/58; apm wīse 5/52
ġewis adj. *aware* nsm 9/124; *trustworthy,
unfailing* asn 17/110
wīscan I *wish, desire* pret. 3p wīscton 4/326
ġewīscan I w.g. *wish, desire* pres. 1s gewīsce
4/181
wīsdōm m. *wisdom* ns 4/58; as 5/12, 5/23,
etc.; ds wīsdōme 5/9
wīse f. *way, manner, wise* as wīsan 2/57,
2/60, 4/102, 4/104 (*idiom*), 9/58 (*task,
assignment*), 9/85, 22/28, 22/63; ap 3/109;
dp wīsum 17/110
wīse adv. *wisely, prudently* 16/88
wīsian 2 *guide* pret. 3s wīsode 12/141
wīslic adj. *wise* nsm 8/21
ġewislīcost see ġewisslīce
wisse see witan
wissian 2 *guide, instruct* inf. 4/42; p. ptc.
gewissod 3/184
ġewissian 2 *guide, direct* pret. 3s gewissode
4/144
ġewisslīce adv. *certainly* 3/184; superl.
gewislīcost 18(b)/1350
wissung f. *guidance* ds wissunge 4/235
wist f. *feasting* ds wiste 16/36
Wīstān pers. n. *Wistan* ns 12/297
wiste see witan
wistfyllo f. *fill of feasting* gs wistfylle 18(a)/
734
wit dual pron. *we two* n 11(e)/7, 15/13, 15/
21; a unc 11(e)/2, 11(e)/7, 14/48, 15/12,
15/22; d unc (refl.) 2/51; g uncer 15/25,
19/19
wita m. *wise man, counsellor,* pl. *the witan* ns
8/24, 16/65; np witan 7/27, 7/59, 18(a)/
778, wiotan 5/3, 6/2; ap 10(b)/66; gp
wiotena 5/41; dp wytum 8/4, witum 8/8,
10(a)/15
witan pret.-pres. *know* inf. 4/33, 22/72
(*show*); infl. inf. (tō) witanne 4/106, (tō)
wiotonne 5/55, 22/76; pres. ptc np
witende 2/11; pres. 1s wāt 8/19, 16/11,
18(b)/1331; 3s 2/9, 4/185, 4/310, 12/
94, 16/29, 16/37, etc.; 1p witan 22/17,
22/83, etc.; subj. wite 18(b)/1367; pret. 1s
wiste 4/13; 3s 8/67, 12/24, 18(a)/764,
18(a)/821, wisse 18(a)/715, 18(b)/1309;
3p wiston 5/32, 9/106 (see note), wiston
20/207, etc.; subj. 3s wisse 16/27 (see
note). With negative: pret. 3s nyste (*did not
know*) 4/17, 20/68

ġewitan pret.-pres. *know, ascertain* inf.
18(b)/1350
ġewītan I *depart* inf. 17/52; pres. 3s gewīteð
18(b)/1360; subj. 3s gewīte 8/31; pret. 1s
gewāt 9/30, 15/9; 3s 12/72, 12/150, 14/
71, 15/6, 16/95, 20/61, 20/145; 3p gewitan 13/9, gewiton 14/133, 18(a)/853,
(w. refl. d.) gewitan 20/290; p. ptc. npm
gewitene 17/80, 17/86
wīte n. *punishment, torment* as 11(h)/6,
15/5; ds wīte 14/61; gs wiites 9/78; np
wītu 5/24; gp wīta 14/87; dp wītum
20/115
wītega m. *prophet* ds wītegan 4/286
ġewitenes f. *departure, death* gs gewitenesse
9/87
ġewitloca m. *mind* ds gewitlocan 20/69
witod adj. *appointed, decreed, ordained* nsm
11(e)/7
witodlīce adv. *certainly, verily* 4/189
wiþ prep. w.a.d. *against, in return for, from,
with* 3/144, 3/146, 4/78, uuiþ 6/7, 7/53,
7/74, etc.; w.g. *to, toward* 12/8, 12/131,
20/162, 22/58; wið þon (þām) þe *provided
that* 4/175, 7/60, 7/65; wið . . . weard
toward 20/99
wiðerlēan n. *requital* ns 12/116
wiðertrod n. *way back* as 20/312
wiðfōn VII *lay hold on* pret. 3s wiðfēng
18(a)/760
wiðhabban 3 w.d. *withstand, hold out against*
pret. 3s wiðhæfde 18(a)/772
wiðmetenes f. *comparison* ds tō wiðmetenesse w.g. *in comparison with* 8/27
wiðsacan VI w.d. or a. *renounce, forsake*
inf. 4/215, 8/51; pret. subj. 3p wiðsōcen
4/325
wiðstondan VI w.d. *withstand* inf. 16/15,
wiðstandan 4/167
wlanc adj. *proud, splendid* nsm wlonc 11(j)/1,
13/34, 17/29, wlanc 18(b)/1332, 21/27;
asm wlancne 12/139, wloncne 11(m)/10;
dsn wlancan 12/240; nsf wlonc 16/80, 20/
325; npm wlance 12/205, 20/16, wlonce
11(o)/6; apm wlonce 11(j)/17
wlætta m. *nauseating substance* ds wlættan
3/165
wlenco f. *prosperity, riches* gp wlencea
10(b)/76
wlītan I *look, see* inf. 20/49; pret. 3s wlāt
12/172
wlitiġ adj. *beautiful* nsm 11(j)/12; nsn 2/12;
gsf wlitegan 20/137; dsn 20/255
wlitiġian 2 *brighten, make beautiful* pres. 3p
wlitigiað 17/49
wlonc see wlanc
wōd see wadan
wōdlīce adv. *furiously* 4/211

wōdon see **wadan**

wōg n. *error* ds wōge 4/123; ap wōh 4/125

wōh see **wōg**

wōh adj. *curved, bent, twisted* ipm wōum 11(j)/3

wōhdōm m. *unjust sentence* ap wōhdōmas 22/165

wōhġestrēon n. *ill-gotten gains* gp wōhgestrēona 22/164

wolcen m. or n. *cloud, sky* np wolcnu 21/13; gp wolcna 11(d)/5, 20/67; dp wolcnum 10(b)/76, 14/53, 14/55, 18/8, 18(a)/714, 18(b)/1374 [archaic MnE welkin]

wōldæg m. *day of pestilence* np wōldagas 13/25

wolde see **willan**

wōma m. *tumult* ns 16/103

womb f. *womb, belly* as wombe 11(b)/5

womfull adj. *foul* nsm 20/77

womm m. *sin, iniquity, defilement* ds womme 20/59; dp wommum 14/14

won see **wann**

wong m. *ground* as 13/31; ap wongas 17/49 (*fields, meadows*)

wonn see **winnan**

wōp m. *weeping, lamentation* as 18(a)/785

word n. *word* as 12/168, 14/35, 20/82, etc.; ds worde 14/111; ap word 4/287, 8/1, 8/41, 9/35, 9/46, 9/56, 11(c)/1, etc.; gp worda 10(b)/81; dp wordum 4/75, 4/188, 5/1, 8/24, etc., wordon 12/306; adverbial g: wordes and dæde *by word and by deed* 22/60, 22/117–18

wordġyd n. *lay, elegy* as 18(d)/3172

ġeworhte see **ġewyrċan**

worhton see **wyrċan**

wōrian 2 *decay, moulder* pres. 3s wōrað 13/12; 3 p wōriað 16/78

worn m. *large number* as 16/91, 18(a)/870; dp wornum 20/163

woroldār f. *worldly honor* as woroldāre 18/17

woroldscamu f. *public humiliation* gs woroldscame 22/107; ds 22/110 [MnE world, shame]

woroldstrūdere m. *despoiler* npm woroldstrūderas 22/150

woruld· f. *world* ns 1/24, 17/49, worold 22/1; as 16/58, weoruld 16/107, 17/87, woruld 20/156, 21/41; gs worulde 4/18, 9/8, 15/46, 16/74, 21/55, worolde 18(b)/1387; ds worulde 4/112, 4/298, 5/25, 9/94, 12/174, 14/133, etc., weorulde 10(b)/51, worolde 22/5

woruldbūend m. *world-dweller, person* gp woruldbūendra 20/82

woruldcræft m. *secular occupation* ns 3/191

woruldcund adj. *secular* gpm woruldcundra 5/4

woruldcyning m. *earthly king* gp wyruldcyninga 18(d)/3180

woruldġesæliġ adj. *prosperous, happy* nsm 12/219

woruldhād m. *secular life* as 9/62; ds weoruldhāde 9/18

woruldrīċe n. *kingdom of the world, the whole world* ds 15/13, 16/65

woruldsælþa f. pl. *worldly prosperity* dp woruldsælþum 10(a)/28

woruldþēaw m. *worldly custom* dp woruldþēawum 10(a)/13

woruldþing n. *worldly affair* gp woruldðinga 5/22

wōum see **wōh**

wrāh see **wrēon**

wrāð adj. *hostile, cruel, angry* dsm wrāþum 18(a)/708; gp wrāðra 14/51, 16/7; dpm wrāþum 11(j)/17 [MnE wroth]

wrāðe adv. *cruelly, fiercely* 10(a)/9, 15/32

wræc see **wrecan**

wræcca m. *wanderer, exile* ns 15/10; gs wræccan 17/15

wræclāst m. *path of exile* ns 16/32; ap wræclāstas 16/5, 17/57, 18(b)/1352

wræcsīð m. *misery* ap wræcsīðas 15/38; gp wræcsīða 15/5

wrætliċ adj. *wondrous, strange, splendid* nsm 11(h)/2, 13/1; nsn 21/3 asm wrætlicne 18(a)/891; asn wrætlic 11(n)/3; nsf wrætlicu 11(c)/2; apf wrætlice 11(l)/1

wrecan V *utter* inf. 17/1, 18(a)/873, 18(d)/3172; pres. 1s wrece 15/1

wrecan V *avenge* inf. 12/248, 12/258, 18(b)/1339; pres. subj. 3s wrece 18(b)/1385; pret. 3s wræc 6/5, 18(b)/1333, wrec 12/279; subj. 3s wræce 12/257 [MnE wreak]

ġewrecan V *avenge* inf. 12/208, 12/263; imp. s. gewrec 20/92

wreccan 1 *arouse, awaken* pret. 3p wrehton 20/228, 20/243

wrēgan 1 *accuse* pres. 3p wrēgað 4/74

wrehton see **wreccan**

wrēon I *cover, wrap* pres. 3s wrīð 11(m)/5; pret. 3s wrāh 11(k)/5

wreotan see **wrītan**

ġewrit n. *writing, writ* as 5/61, 5/65; gs gewrites 9/74; ds gewrite 4/310

wrītan I *write* 1p wrītað 4/45; pres. subj. 3s wrīte 5/81; pret. 3p wreoton 9/70

wrītere m. *writer* ds 4/99

wrīð see **wrēon**

wrixendlīċe adv. *in turn* 9/107

wrixlan 1 w.d. *change, exchange, vary* inf. 18(a)/874

*ġe*wrohtan see *ġe*wyrċan

wudu m. *wood, forest, tree* ns 2/55, 11(n)/16, 14/27, 18(b)/1364, 21/33; as 2/52, 2/58, 12/193; ds wuda 3/122, 4/232, 4/237, 4/247, 19/17; dp wudum 3/64; gp wuda 15/27

wudutrēow n. *forest tree* as 11(n)/3

wuhte see wiht

wuldor n. *glory* ns 4/330, 20/155, 20/347; as 20/342 (*thanks*); gs wuldres 4/264, 14/14, 14/90, 14/97, 14/133, 17/123, 18/17; ds wuldre 11(o)/2, 14/135, 14/143, 14/155, 20/344

wuldorblæd m. *glorious success* ns 20/156

Wuldorfæder m. *Father of Glory, God* gs 9/38

wulf m. *wolf* ns 4/156, 4/234, 4/241, 16/82, 20/206; gs wulfes 4/244; np wulfas 3/25; dp wulfum 20/295

Wulf pers. n. *Wulf* nsm 19/4, 19/13, 19/17; gs Wulfes 19/9

Wulfgār pers. n. *Wulfgar* ns 7/19

wulfheafedtrēo n. *gallows, cross* as 11(n)/12

wulfhliþ n. *wolf-slope, retreat of wolves* ap wulfhleoþu 18(b)/1358

Wulfmær pers. n. *Wulfmær* ns 12/113, 12/155; as Wulmær 12/183

Wulfstān pers. n. *Wulfstan* ns 12/75; gs Wulfstānes 12/155; ds Wulfstāne 12/79

ġewuna m. *custom* ns 4/149; ds gewunan 22/133 (*situation, pass*)

wund f. *wound* as wunde 12/139, 12/271; np wunda 4/260; dp wundum 12/293, 12/303

wund adj. *wounded* nsm 12/113, 12/144

wunden adj. *twisted* nsn 16/32; asn 11(n)/3; dsn wundnum 18(b)/1382 [MnE wound]

wundenlocc adj. *with braided hair* nsf 20/77, 20/103, 20/325

ġewundian 2 *wound* pret. 3s gewundode 6/15; p. ptc. gewundad 6/22, 6/40, gewundod 12/135

wundon see windan

wundor n. *wonder, miracle* ns 4/234, 4/257, 18(a)/771; as 11(c)/2, 18(a)/840; np wundru 4/254, 4/327; ap 4/325, 4/329; gp wundra 4/245, 4/309, 4/322, 9/38; dp wundrum *wondrous thing* 20/8; as adv. *astonishingly, wonderfully* 11(m)/1, 13/20, 16/98, *exceedingly* 21/13

wundorliċ adj. *remarkable, wonderful* nsf 1/17; dsm wunderlicum 4/81

wundorlīċe adv. *wondrously* 4/280

wundrian 2 *wonder, marvel at* pret. 1s wundrade 5/40; 3s wundrode 9/95; 3p wundrodon 4/282

wundru see wundor

wundrum see wundor

ġewuneliċ adj. *customary* nsn 4/184, 4/237

wunian 2 *dwell, subsist, occupy* inf. 3/154, 14/121, 14/143, 15/27, 20/119, 21/18 (*stay*); pres. 1s wunige 11(e)/6, 3s wunað 21/66; 3p wuniaþ 3/64, 14/135, 17/87; pret. 1s wunade 17/15; 3s wunode 6/3, wunade 6/4; 3p wunedon 14/3, 14/155 [MnE won(t)]

ġewunian 2 *remain, be accustomed to* inf. 21/42, gewunigen 10(b)/37 *stand by, support* pres, subj. pi. gewunigen 18/22; pret. 3s gewunade (*was accustomed to*) 9/2; p. ptc. gewunod 10(a)/28

wuniġe see wunian

ġewunnenum see ġewinnan

wuolde (= wolde) see willan

wurde see weorðan

wurdon see weorðan

wurpon see weorpan

wurðan see weorðan

wurðful see weorðful

wurþige see weorðian

wurðlīċe see weorðlīċe

wurðmynde see weorðmynd

wurðode see weorðian

wuton see uton

wycg see wicg

wydewan see widewe

wyle see willan

wylm m. *surge* ds wylme 13/39

wylt see willan

wyn see wynn

wynlēas adj. *joyless* apn 18(a)/821

wynliċ adj. *delightful* compar. apn wynlicran 15/52

wynn f. *benefit, joy* ns wyn 15/46, 16/36, 17/45, 18(c)/2262; as wyn 17/27; gp wynna 12/174, 15/32; dp wynnum 14/15 (as adv. *beautifully*), 16/29; *pleasure* ns wyn 19/12

wynsum adj. *delightful* npm wynsumu 9/69 [MnE winsome]

wyrċan 1 *make, form, produce* inf. 9/3, 9/11, etc., wircean 4/69, wyrcean 20/8, (w.g.) 21/21 (*achieve*); pres. ptc. wircende 7/58; pres. 1s wyrce 3/152, 3/203; 2s wyrcst 3/150; 3s wyrcð 4/329; 3p wyrcað 4/322; subj. 3s wyrce 18(b)/1387; pret. 3s worhte 4/56; 1p worhtan 22/57; 3p worhton 2/16, 4/253, worhtan 7/23, wrohton 7/54; subj. 1s worhte (w.g.) 4/184; *perpetrate* pret. 3p worhtan 22/117; p. ptc. npm geworhte 22/127; pres. 3 wyrcð him tō þrǣle *turns him into a slave* 22/106 [MnE work, wrought] ġewyrċan 1 *make, form, perform* inf. 12/81, 12/264; pres. 3p gewyrcað 22/183; pres. subj. 3s gewyrce 17/74 (*accomplish*); pret. 3s geworhte 1/35, 2/2, 4/53, 9/80; 3p geworhton 14/31, 18(d)/3156, gewrohtan 7/41; p. ptc. asn geworht 9/7; asm geworhtne 17/115 (his geworhtne wine *the friend he has made*); npn geworhte 4/327

wyrd f. *fate, event* ns 10(b)/29, 11(c)/2, 13/24, 14/74, 16/5, 16/100, 17/115, 18(a)/734, 21/5; ds wyrde 16/15; np wyrde 13/1; gp wyrda 14/51, 16/107 [MnE weird]

wyrdan 1 *injure, destroy* pret. 3s wyrde 18(b)/1337

ġewyrht n. *deed* dp gewyrhtum 22/90

wyrhta m. *workman* np wyrhtan 3/206; dp wyrhtum 3/210 [MnE wright]

wyruldcyninga see woruldcyning

wyrm m. *worm, serpent, dragon* ns 11(c)/3, 18(a)/897; as 18(a)/886, 18(a)/891; dp wyrmum 20/115

wyrman 1 *warm* p. ptc. gewyrmed 8/29

wyrmlīċ n. *serpent shape, serpentine pattern* dp wyrmlīcum 16/98

wyrmsele m. *hall of serpents, hell* ds 20/119

wyrnan 1 w.g. *withhold* pret. 3s wyrnde 12/118

wyrp f. *change (for the better)* as wyrpe 18(b)/1315

wyrs adv. (compar. of yfele) *worse* þȳ wyrs (*by so much*) *the worse* 10(b)/76, wyrse 22/3

wyrsa adj. (compar. of yfel) *worse* apf wyrsan 22/170

wyrsian 2 *get worse, deteriorate* pret. 3p wyrsedan 22/33

wyrt f. *herb, plant, vegetable, root* ap wyrta 2/40, 3/170; gp 3/162; dp wyrtum 18(b)/1364 [MnE wort]

wyrtġemang n. *mixture of herbs and spices, unguent* as 3/141

wyrð see weorðan

ġewyrð see ġeweorðan

wyrðe see weorð, -e

wytum see wita

ȳcan 1 *increase, add,* inf. 11(o)/9, 20/183 [MnE eke (out)]

yfel adj. *evil* as yfele 21/50; dsm yfelum 4/303, yfelan 22/133; dsn 22/140; asf yfelan 1/35; npm yfele 4/306

yfel n. *evil, harm* ns 10(b)/55; as 2/11, 4/125, 7/41, etc., yfel after ōðrum *one evil after the other* 22/10; gs yfeles 12/133; ap 7/58, 10(a)/14; dp yflum 10(a)/10

yfele adv. *ill, badly* 10(a)/9

yfelian 2 *deteriorate, grow worse* inf. 22/4

ylcan see ilca

yldan 1 *delay* inf. 18(a)/739

yldestan see eald

yldra see eald

yldrena see ieldran

yldu f. *age, old age* ns yldo 17/70, 17/91; as yldo 21/50; gs ylde 9/19; ds ældo 13/6

yldum see ælde

ylfetu f. (*wild*) *swan* gs ylfete 17/19

ymb prep. w.a. *about, concerning, with regard to, after* 3/65, 5/10, 6/7, 6/36, embe 4/259, 4/290, 12/249, 12/271, etc., ymbe 22/9

ymbclyppan 1 *embrace* pret. 3s ymbclypte 14/42

ymbsettan 1 *surround* p. ptc. npm ymbsette 8/55

ymbsittend m. *neighbouring people* gp ymbsittendra 9

yrgan 1 *demoralize* p. ptc. npm geyrigde 22/99

yrhðo f. *cowardice, slackness* as 12/6, yrhðe 22/166

ġeyrigde see yrgan

Yrmenlāf pers. n. *Yrmenlaf* gs Yrmenlāfes 18(b)/1324

yrmþu f. *hardship* gp yrmþa 15/3; *misdeed, crime* ns yrmþ 22/82; as yrmþe (drēogað þā yrmþe *commit the crime*) 22/76; gs 22/106; *misery* ap 22/15

yrnan see irnan

yrre n. *anger* ns 22/88; as 18(a)/711, 22/42, 22/95, etc.; ds 22/115

yrre adj. *angry* nsm 12/44, 12/253; npm 4/211, 18(a)/769, 20/225

yrremōd adj. *angry* nsm 18(a)/726

ys (= is) see bēon

ȳtmæst adj. *last* ap ȳtmæstan 9/122 [MnE utmost]

ȳþ f. *wave* as ȳþe 11(l)/5, 11(p)/4, gp ȳþa 15/7, 17/6, 17/46, 18(a)/848; dp ȳðum 21/23

ȳþan 1 *lay waste, destroy* pret. 3s ȳþde 16/85

ȳþġeblond n. *commingling of the waves, surge* ns 18(b)/1373

ȳwe see īewan

Indexes to Part One

INDEX OF SUBJECTS

The references are to the numbered sections. The abbreviations n. and fn. stand for 'note' and 'footnote' respectively.

You may find it useful to remember that §§252–268 comprise the Bibliography, and to note the entries 'sound-changes', 'spelling variations', and 'technical terms explained'.

This Index does not give references to what are merely passing mentions of persons, poems or prose texts, places, or things.

A Guide to Old English, Eighth Edition. Bruce Mitchell and Fred C. Robinson.
© 2012 Bruce Mitchell and Fred C. Robinson. Published 2012 by Blackwell Publishing Ltd.

INDEX OF WORDS

The references are to the numbered sections.
The letters LV mean that the word in question will be found in 'Learning the Vocabulary' in the section 'How to Use this Guide'.
The abbreviations n. and fn. stand for 'note' and 'footnote' respectively.

æ follows *a*, *þ* follows *t*.
ċ is to be found under *c*, *ġ* under *g*, and *ð* under *þ*.
ġe- is ignored, so that *ġemunan* appears under *m*.

Nouns, adjectives, and pronouns will be found under the nominative singular, and verbs under the infinitive. Verbs discussed in Appendices A and B only are excluded.

You may find it useful to remember that lists of conjunctions used in adverb clauses are given in §168 (non-prepositional) and §171 (prepositional).

A Guide to Old English, Eighth Edition. Bruce Mitchell and Fred C. Robinson.
© 2012 Bruce Mitchell and Fred C. Robinson. Published 2012 by Blackwell Publishing Ltd.